INDIA INFRASTRUCTURE REPORT 2010

Infrastructure Development in a Low Carbon Economy

List of Contributors

Name of Author	Affiliation	Place	Email Ids
Patricia Clarke Annez	Brookings Institution	Washington DC	pannez@brookings.edu
Kaushik Ranjan Bandyopadhyay	Asian Institute of Transport Development	New Delhi	kaushik.banerjee@gmail.com
Anoma Basu	Indian Institute of Forest Management, Bhopal	Bhopal	anomabasu.fri@gmail.com
Jim Berry	University of Ulster	UK	jn.berry@ulster.ac.uk
Pinaki Bhattacharyya	IDFC Private Equity	Mumbai	pinaki.bhattacharyya@idfc.com
Simon Bishop	Consultant	UK	ssabhishop@hotmail.com
Sweta Byahut	University of Cincinnati	Ohio	byahutsa@mail.uc.edu
Rohit Chadha	Hindustan Petroleum Corporation Ltd.	Bhopal	rohitchadha@hpcl.co.in
Papia Chakraborty	CTRAN Consulting Pvt. Ltd. (A BASIX Group Company)	Bhubaneswar	papiachakraborty@ctranconsulting.com
S. Davenport	NSW Industry and Investment (I&I NSW)	Australia	scott.davenport@industry.nsw.gov.au
Pramod Deo	Central Electricity Regulatory Commission (CERC)	New Delhi	chairman@cercind.gov.in
Abhijeet Deshpande	Independent Consultant	New Delhi	abhijeet48@yahoo.com
Vijay M. Deshpande	Central Electricity Regulatory Commission (CERC)	New Delhi	vijay.vmd@gmail.com
Sreenath Dixit	Central Research Institute for Dryland Agriculture (CRIDA)	Hyderabad	sdixit@crida.ernet.in
Ashish Garg	Indian Institute of Technology Kanpur	Kanpur	ashishg@iitk.ac.in
Joshi Gauravkumar	Adani Institute of Infrastructure Management	Ahmedabad	joshigaurav11@gmail.com
Akshima T. Ghate	The Energy and Resources Institute (TERI)	New Delhi	akshima@teri.res.in
Dilip Kumar Ghosh	Government of West Bengal	Kolkata	dkghosh03@rediffmail.com
Malti Goel	Centre for Studies in Science Policy	New Delhi	maltigoel@mail.jnu.ac.in
Jyoti Gujral	Infrastructure Development Finance Company Ltd.	New Delhi	jyoti.gujral@idfc.com
Manisha Gulati	Infrastructure Development Finance Company Ltd.	Mumbai	manisha.gulati@idfc.com
Chandrashekar Iyer	Meghraj Capital Advisors Pvt Ltd	Mumbai	iyerc@hotmail.com
S. Jayasuriya	La Trobe University	Australia	S.Jayasuriya@latrobe.edu.au
Anuj Singh Katiyar	Indian Institute of Forest Management, Bhopal	Bhopal	anujkatiyar21@gmail.com
Ronnie Khanna	PricewaterhouseCoopers Pvt. Ltd.	Gurgaon	ronnie.khanna@in.pwc.com
Yenneti Komalirani	The Energy and Resources Institute (TERI)	Bangalore	komalirani.y@gmail.com
Akil V. Laxman	PricewaterhouseCoopers Pvt. Ltd.	Bhopal	akil.laxman@gmail.com
Vijay Mahajan	BASIX	Hyderabad	vijaymahajan@basixindia.com
Shishir Maheshwari	IDFC Private Equity	Mumbai	shishir.maheshwari@idfc.com
Suvra Majumdar	CTRAN Consulting Pvt. Ltd. (A BASIX Group Company)	Bhubaneswar	suvra.majumdar@ctranconsulting.com
Stanley McGreal	University of Ulster	UK	ws.mcgreal@ulster.ac.uk
Dinesh Mohan	Indian Institute of Technology Delhi	New Delhi	dmohan@cbme.iitd.ernet.in
Partha Mukhopadhyay	Centre For Policy Research	New Delhi	partha@cprindia.org
Tirthankar Nag	International Management Institute, Kolkata	Kolkata	tirthankar.nag@gmail.com
Ramakrishna Nallathiga	Centre for Good Governance	Hyderabad	ramanallathiga@yahoo.co.uk
Vijay P. Ojha	Institute of Mangement Technology	Ghaziabad	vpojha@gmail.com
J.V.N.S. Prasad	Central Research Institute for Dryland Agriculture (CRIDA)	Hyderabad	jasti@crida.ernet.in
Rita Pandey	National Institute of Public Finance and Policy	New Delhi	rita_pandey@yahoo.com
Dhruba Purkayastha	The World Bank	New Delhi	dpurkayastha@worldbank.org
B.M.K. Raju	Central Research Institute for Dryland Agriculture (CRIDA)	Hyderabad	bmkraju@crida.ernet.in
Sanjiv N. Sahai	DIMTS Ltd.	New Delhi	sanjiv.sahai@idfc.com
Manpreet Sethi	Centre for Air Power Studies	New Delhi	manpreet.sethi@csh-delhi.com
Rajneesh Sharma	PricewaterhouseCoopers Pvt. Ltd.	Bhopal	rishu202@gmail.com
Anoop Singh	Indian Institute of Technology Kanpur	Kanpur	anoops@iitk.ac.in
Ashok Kumar Singha	CTRAN Consulting Pvt. Ltd. (A BASIX Group Company)	Bhubaneswar	ashoksingha@ctranconsulting.com
Shaleen Singhal	University of Ulster	UK	s.singhal@ulster.ac.uk
Bhaskar Sinha	Indian Institute of Forest Management, Bhopal	Bhopal	bsinha@iifm.ac.in
Kala Seetharam Sridhar	Public Affairs Centre	Bangalore	kala@pacindia.org
Lenora Suki	Smart Cities Advisors	New York	lenorasuki@smartcitiesadvisors.com
Sunder Subramanian	ICRA Management Consulting Services Limited	New Delhi	Sunder.Subramanian@imacs.in
Sanjivi Sundar	The Energy and Resources Institute (TERI)	New Delhi	ssundar@teri.res.in
Nachiketa Tiwari	Indian Institute of Technology Kanpur	Kanpur	ntiwari@iitk.ac.in
Videh Upadhyay	Government Counsel and Legal Consultant	New Delhi	videhup@gmail.com
B. Venkateswarlu	Central Research Institute for Dryland Agriculture (CRIDA)	Hyderabad	director@crida.ernet.in
Thomas Zuelgaray	French Ministry of Ecology, Energy and Sustainable Development (M.E.E.D.D.M)	France	thomas.zuelgaray@gmail.com

The views expressed in the report are those of the individual authors and not the institutions they are affiliated to—the IFDC, the 3iNetwork, or the Publishers.

INDIA INFRASTRUCTURE REPORT 2010

Infrastructure Development in a Low Carbon Economy

3iNetwork
Infrastructure Development Finance Company

OXFORD
UNIVERSITY PRESS

OXFORD
UNIVERSITY PRESS
YMCA Library Building, Jai Singh Road, New Delhi 110001

Oxford University Press is a department of the University of Oxford. It furthers the University's objective of excellence in research, scholarship, and education by publishing worldwide in

Oxford New York
Auckland Cape Town Dar es Salaam Hong Kong Karachi Kuala Lumpur Madrid Melbourne Mexico City Nairobi New Delhi Shanghai Taipei Toronto

With offices in
Argentina Austria Brazil Chile Czech Republic France Greece Guatemala Hungary Italy Japan Poland Portugal Singapore South Korea Switzerland Thailand Turkey Ukraine Vietnam

Oxford is a registered trademark of Oxford University Press in the UK and in certain other countries

Published in India
by Oxford University Press, New Delhi

First published 2010

ISBN-13: 978-0-19-807145-7
ISBN-10: 0-19-807145-0

Typeset in 11/13 in Adobe Garamond Pro
by Excellent Laser Typesetters, Pitampura, Delhi 110 034
Printed in India at Rakmo Press Pvt. Ltd., New Delhi 110 020
Published by Oxford University Press
YMCA Library Building, Jai Singh Road, New Delhi 110 001

Contents

SECTION III

Energy Infrastructure

SECTION IV

Transport Infrastructure

SECTION V

Urban Infrastructure

SECTION VI

Rural Infrastructure

SECTION VII

Infrastructure Review

Tables, Figures, Boxes, and Maps

Tables

Figures

Boxes

Maps

Foreword

Building infrastructure has traditionally been carbon intensive—in particular, urban development, power generation, and the transport sector have deep carbon footprints. Against the background of an ongoing global dialogue to reduce carbon emissions, India has taken a voluntary, though non-binding decision to reduce its emission intensity. India is, thus, faced with the daunting task of developing its infrastructure in a low carbon way while staying aligned with its growth ambition, energy security, and poverty alleviation objectives.

While setting emission targets is important, defining a low carbon path is extremely challenging. Since infrastructure investments made today will decide whether India will ride the low carbon path, it is critical that we make appropriate interventions and choices in developing our infrastructure.

India is still at an early stage of infrastructure development, which provides a unique opportunity to achieve a low carbon growth path as we go forward. Given the enormous needs of basic infrastructure service provision—more than 400 million people have no access to electricity; urbanization is nascent; ownership and use of private vehicles is still low—the potential carbon savings could be huge if we get the development strategy right. We have an advantage compared to other countries that are locked into 'high carbon lifestyles' and we can learn from their experiences rather than replicating their models. For example, as is being globally debated, planning for urbanization needs to be rooted in integrated land-use and mobility planning which tries to reduce commuting for work and other needs, incorporates multi-modal transport connectivity, and enables greater walkability.

India Infrastructure Report 2010 (*IIR 2010*) therefore focuses on issues associated with 'Infrastructure Development in a Low Carbon Economy'. The Report covers cross-cutting legal, regulatory, institutional, and financing issues that are needed to facilitate the development and deployment of low carbon technologies. At the same time, it looks at the key drivers for low carbon growth in the major infrastructure sectors and makes recommendations for addressing the challenges associated with such growth.

What is special about this report is the attention it gives to indigenous solutions and interventions at the local level, besides large scale centralized initiatives. Small projects and initiatives at the grassroot level are often left out of mainstream discussions. Given that carbon funds and credit institutions have a bias towards large projects, the *IIR 2010* explores options for aggregating emission reduction credits through microfinance institutions. There is also a potential for creating carbon offsets in agriculture, that is, compensating for carbon emissions in other activities by engaging in low cost mitigation and/or sequestering activities in agriculture.

I hope the report stimulates further debate on strategies and policy issues and is a useful input to policymakers. I would like to thank all those who contributed to the production of this timely report.

September 2010

Rajiv B. Lall

Acknowledgements

When we embarked on the task of choosing the theme in 2009 for *India Infrastructure Report 2010* (*IIR 2010*), we wanted to focus on a contemporary theme which would contribute to shaping the future development of infrastructure in India. While the world was preparing for the United Nations Climate Change Conference in Denmark and India was bracing itself to participate in the global dialogue, our logical choice was to focus on India's infrastructure development in a low carbon way staying aligned with the imperatives of high economic growth, energy security, and poverty alleviation. We are grateful to Ritu Anand for proposing this theme, besides extending her support and guidance throughout the preparation of this report.

Our biggest challenge was to differentiate this report from the plethora of other publications and studies on climate change and developments that were being released around this time. Maintaining the focus on infrastructure for low carbon growth was another daunting task. The framework of the report evolved at the Brainstorming Workshop held in New Delhi on 31 October 2009. It was decided at the workshop that the report should focus on the issues underlying 'How' to achieve a low carbon infrastructure development since most of the other studies and reports focused on estimates and projections of low carbon trajectories. We would like to express our deep gratitude to all the participants of the workshop. Those who have provided valuable insights, even though not contributing to the final report, include Alok Kumar, Anjali Garg, Avinash Agarwal, Chetan Vaidya, Rajiv Shekhar, Ramprasad Sengupta, Sameer Khandekar, Sanjay Banerjee, Sanjeev Tamhane, Satish Koria, Suman Bery, Surojit Bose, V. Balaji, Vineet Sahu, Ashok Emani, Cherian Thomas, Nasra Roy, Piyush Tiwari, Shishir Mathur, Kunal Katara, Veena Vadini, and Subir Paul.

The lively and immensely valuable deliberations at the Writers' Workshop held in New Delhi on 6 and 7 February 2010 helped shape the final report. Our gratitude to all the participants. Those who deserve special mention are Sindhu Subramaniam, Praveen Kulshreshtha, Hippu Salk Kristle Nathan, Nitya Nanda, Souvik Bhattacharya, Gaurang Meher Diljun, K.K. Pandey, and Madhulika Gupta.

This report would not have been possible but for various authors, who made major contributions and despite their busy schedules, cooperated with us throughout. Their patience, when dealing with our repeated editorial requests and reminders, is deeply appreciated. While we acknowledge their contributions, it is needless to say that we, as editors, own up to the errors or omissions arising in the course of editing or finalizing the report.

We thank Rajiv B. Lall, Managing Director and CEO, IDFC Ltd, for his unstinted encouragement and support for the publication of *IIR 2010* and to the 3iNetwork. We also acknowledge the unwavering support provided to 3iNetwork by Samir Barua and S.G. Dhande, Directors of IIM Ahmedabad and IIT Kanpur respectively. We express our deep appreciation for the encouragement received from Prem Kalra and G. Raghuram. We would like to specially thank Geeta Gouri, Ajit Kapadia, Melissa Brown, Anupam Srivastava and Raghuveer Sharma for their very useful suggestions during the preparation of the report. We are thankful to Shekhar Choudhury, Director IIM Calcutta, for his support. We gratefully acknowledge the professional services rendered by Shreemoyee Patra of Lucid Solutions, the editorial consultancy firm.

In bringing out the *IIR 2010*, efforts and support have come from many more. Policy Group in IDFC provided the much needed organizational support. Our thanks to Bharati Sawant, who, tirelessly and with precision, coordinated with the authors and Oxford University Press, New Delhi on a variety of issues and undertook a host of tasks for ensuring smooth progress of the project. The suggestions and editorial support received from Manisha Gulati are deeply appreciated. We would also like to thank Babu Nambiar and Renu Mehtani from IDFC, Delhi, for helping us organize the workshops.

The editorial team of Oxford University Press has, as always, been consistently maintaining quality while accommodating sometimes exacting demands made on them.

Finally, we would to thank all our colleagues at IDFC, IIT Kanpur, and IIM Ahmedabad, who provided us academic and practitioner perspectives on diverse issues related to this report.

Sambit Basu
Runa Sarkar
Ajay Pandey

Abbreviations

ACP	Alternative Compliance Payment
ADB	Asian Development Bank
ADP	Asian Development Plan
AEEI	Autonomous Energy Efficiency Improvement
AERA	Airports Economic Regulatory Authority
AMC	Ahmedabad Municipal Corporation
AMCER	Aggregated Micro-certified Emission Reduction
APPC	Average Power Purchase Cost
ARAI	Automotive Research Association of India
AVERT	Aggregated Voluntary Emission Reduction Transaction
BAU	Business-as-usual
BEE	Bureau of Energy Efficiency
BOQ	Bill of Quantities
BOT	Build-Operate-Transfer
BP	Buyout Price
BRT	Bus Rapid Transit
C&T	Cap-and-trade
CAFÉ	Corporate Average Fuel Economy
CAGR	Compound Annual Growth Rate
CBM	Coal Bed Methane
CBD	Central Business Districts
CCP	Cities for Climate Protection
CCS	Carbon Capture and Storage
CDA	Continuous Descent Approach
CDM	Clean Development Mechanism
CEA	Central Electricity Authority
CER	Certified Emission Reduction
CERC	Central Electricity Regulatory Commission
CFBC	Circulating Fluidized Bed Combustion
CFI	Commercial Financial Institutions
CGE	Computable General Equilibrium
CIC	Central Information Commission
CMM	Coal Mine Methane
CNG	Compressed Natural Gas
CPCB	Central Pollution Control Board
CPP	Captive Power Plants

CSR	Corporate Social Responsibility
DDG	Decentralized Distribution Generation
EAC	Expert Appraisal Committee
ECS	Electrical and Control System
EE	Energy Efficiency
EEI	Energy Efficiency Improvement
EIA	Environmental Impact Assessment
EMC	Energy Management Companies
EMP	Environmental Management Plan
EPCEAS	Equal Per Capita Emissions Allocation Scheme
EPPA	Emissions Predictions and Policy Analysis
ESCOs	Energy Service Companies
EVs	Electric Vehicles
FDI	Foreign Direct Investment
FiT	Feed-in-Tariff
GBI	Generation-based Incentive
GCN	Global Climate Network
GEA	Grandfathered Emissions Allocation
GEF	Global Environment Facility
GHG	Greenhouse Gas
GIFI	Green Infrastructure Financial Institutions
GO	Guarantee of Obligation
GUS	Gram Unnayan Samiti
HAWT	Horizontal Axis Wind Turbines
IATA	International Air Traffic Association
ICLEI	International Council of Local Environmental Initiatives
IPCC	Intergovernmental Panel on Climate Change
IPP	Independent Power Producers
IRC	Indian Roads Congress
IREDA	Indian Renewable Energy Development Agency
ITER	International Thermonuclear Experimental Reactor
ITS	Intelligent Transport System
JNNSM	Jawaharlal Nehru National Solar Mission
JNNURM	Jawaharlal Nehru National Urban Renewal Mission
LCI	Low Carbon Infrastructure
LCOE	Levellized Cost of Energy
LDVs	Light Duty Vehicles
LMIC	Low- and Middle-income Countries
M&V	Monitoring and Verification
MHD	Magneto-hydro-dynamic
MNRE	Ministry of New and Renewable Energy
MoEF	Ministry of Environment and Forests
MoPNG	Ministry of Petroleum and Natural Gas
MoRTH	Ministry of Road Transport and Highways
MoUD	Ministry of Urban Development
MSE	Madras School of Economics
MSW	Municipal Solid Waste
NAAQS	National Ambient Air Quality Standards
NAIP	National Agricultural Innovation Project
NAMA	Nationally Appropriate Mitigation Action Plan

NAPCC	National Action Plan on Climate Change
NEP	National Electricity Policy
NHAI	National Highway Authority of India
NHDP	National Highways Development Project
NMEEE	National Mission on Enhanced Energy Efficiency
NMT	Non-motorized Transport
NPCIL	Nuclear Power Corporation of India Ltd
OA	Open Access
OREDA	Orissa Renewable Development Agency
PBN	Performance-based Navigation
PCB	Pollution Control Board
PCRA	Petroleum Conservation Research Association
PE	Private Equity
PFBC	Pressurized Fluidized Bed Combustion
PHWR	Pressurized Heavy Water Reactors
PIPE	Private Investment in Public Equities
PLF	Plant Load Factor
PPP	Purchasing Power Parity
PXs	Power Exchanges
PSC	Production Sharing Contract
PWD	Public Works Department
RE	Renewable Energy
REC	Renewable Energy Certificates/Credits
REDA	Renewable Energy Development Authority
REGO	Renewable Energy Guarantee and Origin
RES	Renewable Energy Sources
RET	Renewable Energy Technologies
ROC	Renewable Obligation Certificates
ROM	Run-of mine
RPO	Renewable Portfolio Obligation
SEA	Strategic Environmental Assessment
SEZs	Special Economic Zones
SEAC	State or Union Territory Expert Appraisal Committee
SERC	State Electricity Regulatory Commission
SHP	Small Hydro Power
SPCB	State Pollution Control Board
SPVs	Special Purpose Vehicles
TERI	Tata Energy Research Institute
TFC	Tax for Fuel Conservation
TGC	Tradable Green Certificates
TNHC	Third National Highway Contract
UCG	Underground Coal Gasification
ULBs	Urban Local Bodies
WTE	Waste to Energy
VAWT	Vertical Axis Wind Turbines
VC	Venture Capital
VMT	Vehicular Miles Travelled

Introduction

Infrastructure Lock-in and a Low Carbon Growth Path for India

Partha Mukhopadhyay

Infrastructure and Lock-In

The infrastructure investments that are made today will play a critical role in determining whether India will be able to travel on a low carbon growth path tomorrow. This is because today's investments make it costlier to take one set of decisions as compared to another, tomorrow. As a nation, our choices in infrastructure lock us into other choices. Table 1 illustrates such consequences for three Organisation for Economic Co-operation and Development (OECD) countries.

United States' choice of a low density road-centric urban form is partly the reason why its transport sector emissions are almost three times as much as the UK and France, and partly the reason why it is the highest emitter of carbon dioxide, around 20 tonnes per capita, while its European OECD counterparts emit less than half that amount, even though they enjoy a similar standard of living. France's total emissions per capita, of only 6.2 tonnes of CO_2, are comparable to the emissions by the transport sector alone in the US. Further, because France meets around three-fourths of its electricity needs from nuclear energy, it emits less carbon per capita than the UK, even though its electricity consumption of 7,814 kWh per capita far exceeds 6,216 kWh per capita in the UK, which was dependent on coal initially and now on a mix of coal and gas. Indeed, the difference between the per capita emissions of UK and France are almost entirely explained by the difference in the emissions attributable to electricity and heat. Table 1 again shows that there is no mandatory one-to-one relationship between emissions and development, and alternative growth paths have very different carbon consequences.

It is important to bear this in mind, as we in India have yet to make the decisions that will lock in our choices, as is evident from Table 1. Having made those decisions, it

Table 1 Consequences of Infrastructure Lock-in

	GDP per capita (constant 2005 USD PPP)	*Total emissions*	*Transport*	*Electricity and heat*	*Electricity use (kWh per capita)*
		(CO_2 tons per capita)			
United States (US)	42,591	19.5	6.1	9.1	13,582
United Kingdom (UK)	33,408	9.1	2.2	4.0	6,216
France	30,227	6.4	2.2	1.1	7,814
India	2,416	1.2	0.1	0.7	511

Source: Emissions data is from Climate Analysis Indicators Tool (CAIT) and other data is from World Development Indicators. All data refer to 2006.

is now difficult for the US to reorganize its cities so as to achieve European levels of transport emissions. It was a little easier, though still quite difficult, for the UK to move away from coal as its primary source of electricity, to gas, which emits less carbon; which it has done now to a considerable extent. However, a move to nuclear power, like France, is considerably more difficult for the UK, for both technical reasons and those related to public opinion, which is an equally valid consideration in democratic societies. In India too, as the chapter by Manpreet Sethi 'The Nuclear Energy Imperative: Addressing Energy Poverty, Energy Security, and Climate Change in India', notes, the public's concerns will have to be addressed before a substantial increase in the share of nuclear power can be achieved.

Different Kinds of Lock-in

These choices also illustrate two different kinds of lock-in. In the case of energy infrastructure, if India continues to grow at 8 per cent plus per annum, the capacity needed will roughly double every decade (assuming an energy elasticity of slightly less than one). If so, the current installed capacity will constitute only a quarter of the capacity in twenty years time (less if one accounts for retirements and obsolescence). As such, the energy mix can change substantially over this time frame, if incremental investments vary significantly from the installed base. The UK experience is an example of such a transformation. Technological lock-in is thus related to the life of the equipment and the rate of new investment, though the companies that benefit from incumbent technologies may actively try to prevent the emergence of new technologies in the market either through market action or through influencing the policy process. The success of such actions depends on the political economy milieu, which is discussed later in this chapter.

In the case of urban form, the lock-in can be much more severe. For one, the infrastructure shaping these decisions is much more long-lived. The road infrastructure laid down by Robert Moses in the 1930s and 1950s in and around New York City still survives and has defined, and will continue to define the settlement pattern in the future too. Second, these large infrastructure investments then shape a variety of numerous individual and local preferences, like decisions about where to buy a home, where to send your children to school, and indeed which localities will be chosen to establish schools. Such disparate decisions are much more difficult to alter precisely because they are disparate and also because they tend to build on past choices and therefore develop an internal logic of their own, like agglomeration economies. For example, in the US, once a certain school district is recognized as good, there is a tendency for people to move into that area. As such, bringing populations back to live in dense cities, as in Europe, may require city school systems in the US be improved substantially and more importantly, to ensure that this improvement is perceived by numerous individual parents who will make these decisions. This is a much higher order of difficulty than the choice of technology for the next power plant to be built and it is precisely such characteristics that make the lock-in of a much higher order of magnitude.

Different types of changes are thus needed to undo the distinct lock-in effects of inappropriate infrastructure investments; first, technological and the second and more difficult, changes in preferences. It is therefore, incumbent on us to examine the extent of technological lock-in and the effect on preferences that may result from the infrastructure investments that we are making today.

There is also a third kind of lock-in, which emanates from the imperatives of political economy and indeed, technological lock-in and preference lock-in are often mediated through this. Such political economy lock-ins, referred to earlier, are critical to a transition to a low carbon growth path but often neglected. As a result of such lock-in, even where solutions are available, there may be burdens to adoption, based on the differential ability of the affected parties to influence the policy process.

Against this background of different types of lock-in, it is useful to examine the various types of interventions that attempt to move to a lower carbon growth path. These can broadly be classified into three types, namely, (a) Cut carbon—initiatives that reduce the amount of carbon emitted, for example, increasing vehicle fuel efficiency, share of public transport, and the energy efficiency of industrial processes; (b) Capture carbon—initiatives like carbon capture and storage (CCS) from coal-fired plants and afforestation; (c) Change away from carbon—initiatives such as a switch to nuclear power or hydrogen powered vehicles.

A Framework for Organization

Each of these interventions can then generate possible lock-ins, for instance, in the adoption of technology. Investment in CCS could lock investment into large coal-based power plants at specific locations (suitable for carbon capture), which could then act as a barrier to the adoption of a decentralized generation system supported by a smart grid. Likewise, in a switch to solar power, solar photovoltaic has very different grid characteristics vis-à-vis solar thermal technologies and the choice of technologies could therefore lock-in very different structures of transmission grids. A large amount of infirm renewable energy in the grid would also need investments in balancing quick response generation, like gas-based power (a fossil fuel source) as well as regulatory changes.[1]

Similarly, urban planning interventions to decongest cities are often based on the development of satellite cities, with specified minimum plot sizes and investment in road infrastructure to connect relatively isolated communities. In the US, albeit for different reasons, the development of scattered communities has meant that a significant part of the population lives in large suburban houses, relatively far from markets. Their energy consumption in storage of food and air-conditioning of living space is likely to be high, as evidenced by the much higher electricity and heating emissions per capita in Table 1, as is water consumption in watering lawns, etc., as compared to those living in apartments in dense cities in close proximity to amenities. Long years of living in suburbia could generate preferences for a suburban lifestyle and an aversion to the hustle and bustle of the city. The imposition of carbon taxes would affect people with these set of preferences more acutely than others.

Investments in technology and construction of preferences would make sets of actors reluctant to either change their technology (which involves incurring financial cost) or their preferences (emotionally costly and possibly financially too, for example if the value of the suburban property declines after a carbon tax). These actors then try to avoid these costs by influencing the process of policy formulation (see, for example, Kotkin 2010), that is, leading to a political economy lock-in. An Indian example is the extent to which the recommendations of the Expert Committee on Pricing of Sensitive Petroleum Products were implemented by the Government of India (see Box 1). Such an environment is a hurdle in the path of solutions, such as those advanced in the chapter by Rita Pandey 'Pollution-Energy-Carbon Intensity of Urban Transport in India: Dynamics of Government Policy Intervention'.

In this respect, one could argue that the political economy lock-in is derived from either a preference lock-in or a technological one. However, since political positions often exhibit hysteresis, as for example the aversion to

Box 1
Interaction of Technology and Political Economy Lock-in

The case of fuel pricing in India is instructive. Recently, the Government of India decided to allow pricing freedom for the price of petrol.[2] However, the price of diesel is still under the oversight of the government and the taxation on diesel is considerably less than that of petrol, leading to a lower price for diesel at the pump, in contrast to most other countries (see http://www.aip.com.au/pricing/internationalprices.htm).

Consequently, diesel passenger car owners save on operating costs as compared to petrol car owners. Realizing this, the car manufacturers charge a higher price for diesel cars as compared to petrol cars, even though the costs of production for the two types of cars are comparable. Most of the benefit of the subsidized diesel prices thus accrues to the manufacturers of diesel cars in the form of higher margins.[3] The Expert Committee on Pricing of Sensitive Petroleum Products (popularly known as the Kirit Parikh Committee) recognized the political economy problems of freeing up the price of the major transport fuel in a situation of volatile prices. However, to prevent percolations of this subsidy to passenger car manufacturers, it suggested levying a compensatory surcharge on diesel passenger cars linked to the capitalized saving emanating from the differential pricing of petrol and diesel. Based on the existing sales pattern, such a tax could yield upwards of Rs 5,000 crore or well over a billion dollars. However, adoption of such a measure would hurt car manufacturers who specialize in diesel cars since their production capacity and technology is locked into diesel vehicles. To forestall a reduction in their margins, they would lobby for the non-imposition of such a surcharge. Till date, there is neither the surcharge nor much public discussion about the efficacy of such a measure. One can interpret this as an instance of the technology lock-in of car manufacturers being translated into a political economy lock-in of indirect tax policy.

[1] India is relatively liberal in this respect. As chapter 2 by Pramod Deo and Vijay M. Deshpande, 'Low Carbon Path for Meeting the Electricity Needs of the People: Role of Regulatory Commissions' notes, under the new Grid Code of the CERC (Central Electricity Regulatory Commission), the financial burden of all the fluctuations from schedule in case of new solar energy plants and fluctuations within ±30 per cent of schedule in case of new wind energy plants will be shared by all the users of the inter-state grid, removing the financial disadvantage of infirmness from renewable energy. Some would consider this overgenerous.

[2] This is a freedom which has ostensibly been available to oil marketing companies since the demise of the Administered Pricing Mechanism in March 2002 (see http://petroleum.nic.in/webfiles/gazette.pdf), which has never been formally resurrected. This illustrates the distinction between formal and informal structures of control.

[3] This assumes a degree of market power or else this rent would be competed away.

taxation among US legislators, they may turn out to have an independent life of their own, even when the underlying conditions that gave rise to the gridlock may have altered. Besides, the need to use the policy process in order for both technological and preference lock-ins to be effective means that it may be important to look at it independently and separately. A possible framework to view the set of options available is therefore as follows:

Lock-in Potential of Interventions

Table 2 illustrates some of the interlinkages between types of intervention and potential for lock-in. Most of the contributions in this volume, with a few exceptions, refer to initiatives that cut the amount of carbon emissions. Beyond afforestation, whose role in carbon capture can be significant, as noted in the chapter by Bhaskar Sinha, Anoma Basu, and Anuj Singh Katiyar 'Towards A Carbon-Neutral Rural India: Carbon Sequestration Options in Forestry', technologies to capture carbon are still in development. The largest current potential to change away from carbon is in renewable and nuclear energy. The scope for renewable and decentralized options is examined in the chapter by Ashish Garg, Manisha Gulati, and Nachiketa Tiwari 'Moving Towards Low Carbon Economy: The Need for Renewable Energy Solutions: Renewable Energy in India: Capability, Challenges, and Prospects', who also discuss the institutional prerequisites for wider adoption of such technologies in some detail and Chandrashekar Iyer, Rajneesh Sharma, Ronnie Khanna, and Akil V. Laxman in 'Decentralized Distributed Generation for an Inclusive and Low Carbon Economy for India'. In both the chapters, while there is a significant role for change-away technologies like wind and solar, there is also considerable attention paid to biomass, where carbon management needs to be over the life cycle and therefore needs to be supported by strong institutions. However, this can cut both ways. As the chapter by Anoop Singh 'Economics, Regulation, and Implementation Strategy for Renewable Energy Certificates in India', and Pramod Deo and Vijay M. Deshpande, (Chapter 2 of this report) note, support for renewable energy may become excessive in some circumstances, and it is possible that it may lock-in inappropriate technologies, as also inappropriate policies. Lock-in can be present even in areas like afforestation, where the choice of plant species can change local ecosystems in significant ways. Nuclear power, of course, has significant lock-in implications emanating in no small part from the need to decommission the plant at some stage.

There are a number of strategies to cut carbon emissions. A large number of them are about increasing the efficiency of processes, such as using less energy in production, less electricity and heat in air-conditioning, improved fuel efficiency of vehicles, etc. All these involve various technological choices, each of which is subject to lock-in. Evaluating these investments from a technological lock-in potential would require, for instance, examination of the ratio of capital investment to operating expenditure. The higher this ratio, the greater the lock-in potential, since a decision to switch away from such technology will involve the comparison of low operating expenditure with investment that needs to be made in the replacement technology.

Strategies to cut carbon can also involve change in the composition of consumption. The most common example is a switch from personal to public transport. However, even within public transport systems, there are varying degrees of lock-in like vehicle technologies. Fixed infrastructure systems like Delhi's rail-based mass transit, have a higher degree of lock-in than flexible infrastructure systems like an intelligently networked bus system or a bus rapid transit intervention. One has to consider these effects in making a decision about the choice of intervention.

1. Initiatives to cut carbon can also mould preferences. In rural India, as D'Sa and Murthy (2004) suggest, 90 per cent of rural households still depend on traditional form of biomass, composed of firewood (64 per cent), crop residues (13 per cent), and cow dung (13 per cent) for cooking. This is in principle renewable, but firewood collection is not always sustainable. In this context, recent efforts to move rural areas to fuels like LPG, rather than

Table 2 Illustrative Types of Intervention and Potential for Lock-in

Interventions/ Lock-in	*Cut carbon*	*Capture carbon*	*Change away from carbon*
Technology	Efficiency initiatives; choice of public transport technology	Carbon capture and storage, choice of plant species	Renewable energy options; nuclear power
Preferences	Promoting LPG in rural areas; urban building envelopes	Creating demand for national parks	Change in food habits
Political economy	Access policy for captive power	Afforestation policy	Renewable energy policy

options like biogas (which has the additional co-benefit of methane capture as noted in Chapter 11 of this report) and solar cookers (as suggested, for example, in Chapter 10 Part 1) illustrates the possibility that, in the process of moving households away from existing practices, they may be locked-in to an unsustainable fossil fuel, both technologically and through preferences.

Finally, the various policies now being enunciated to either cut carbon capture carbon, or shift away from carbon can themselves become locked-in, driven by the various interest groups that would emerge from the implementation of such policies. This can prevent the growth or even the introduction of superior alternatives in the future, as more investment is directed globally to respond to the challenge of climate change.

Actors and the Policy Process

The contributions in this volume address a number of these challenges and suggest a number of very useful interventions. However, it is important to ask, whether the key actors, who are supposed to intervene in the process of transition to a low carbon economy, have both the financial and institutional ability, and willingness to do so. Both the ability and willingness of the actors may be constrained by different types of lock-in referred to earlier. We consider some of the key actors in the discussion below.

Organized Private Actors

In the case of organized private actors, for example organized industry, it is reasonable to assume that they either have or can acquire the ability to undertake the necessary interventions, such as in improving energy efficiency. In such cases, the interventions need to be focused on increasing their willingness. This can perhaps be realized with appropriate price signals, such as changes in electricity prices, increasing fuel/carbon taxes, etc. Faced with these price signals, these actors should undertake actions to reduce their carbon consumption, for example, by improving energy efficiency. Organized private actors are however, going to resist making changes unless their financial costs are addressed. In many instances, as indicated in the chapter by Dhruba Purkayastha, Manisha Gulati, and Sunder Subramanian 'Financing Low Carbon Infrastructure in India', such actions can be self-financing and the required public intervention may be in ensuring the availability of finance and increasing the awareness of such opportunities. The rapidly growing, though still small, Energy Service Company (ESCO) industry in India points to the potential of such opportunities. Delio et al. (2009) estimated ESCO industry revenue in 2007 to be around USD 17 million, with over 95 per cent of this coming from industry (62 per cent), government (24 per cent), and commercial buildings (9 per cent). This revenue is almost doubling every year.

As the price of energy services and/or electricity rises, such efficiency initiatives become more financially sensible. However, organized private actors can also resist initiatives for such efficiency if they perceive the rise in prices as not due to market forces, such as the rise in the price of crude, which they believe they cannot influence, but due to taxes, such as carbon taxes, which they think they can affect. In such cases, these actors may become unwilling to adapt and expend effort in neutralizing or reversing the intervention. It is here that political economy considerations would become relevant in determining whether such taxes would be levied and collected.

Government Actors

The client mix of the ESCOs in India also point to the challenges in extending such interventions beyond organized private industry. The unorganized private sector, even if it had the willingness (the benefits from energy efficiency may be much larger, given that the energy efficiency of capital is likely to be lower in the sector) lacks the resources and the access to credit required to undertake such actions. The public sector in India, for the most part, on the other hand, lacks both the ability and the willingness to engage in such initiatives. Indeed, the chapter by Patricia Clarke Annez and Thomas Zuelgaray 'High Cost Carbon and Local Government Finance' points out that the current structure of taxing authority in most federal systems would mean that local governments would be at a severe fiscal disadvantage in the event of a rise in carbon prices. As such, overcoming the resistance from such entities would involve modifications to the current federal tax sharing structure, not an issue that is on the minds of most who work on climate change.

In the US, however, the government sector provides much of the demand for services of ESCOs. As noted in Goldman et al. (2002), prior to 1996, 67 per cent of ESCO projects were in the government sector which rose to 75 per cent between 1996 and 2002. The largest segment of this was educational institutions, both local schools (33 per cent) and universities (8 per cent). One can surmise that the funding of local schools directly from local property taxes (it is one of the most visible uses of tax payments by people) may have played a role in their wanting to reduce costs by utilizing the benefits of ESCOs. The manner in which government institutions are structured may therefore play a significant role in determining their willingness and ability to undertake mitigation.

Individual Actors

A third group of actors are individuals/individual households. In this case, those who have the willingness, that is households that spend a relatively larger share of their budget on direct or indirect energy consumption, may not have the ability to modify their behaviour (for example, move from burning firewood for fuel), while those that have the ability may not be as willing, since the relatively lower share of their budget on direct or indirect energy consumption makes them reluctant to modify behaviour beyond a point (for example, switch to public transport or reduce consumption of air conditioning). For most of Indian households, however, the scope for lifestyle changes is limited, since they are already quite low carbon. In 2004–5, only 26 per cent of urban and 8 per cent of rural households owned motorized two-wheelers and just 5 per cent of urban Indians and less than 1 per cent or rural Indians owned cars. The average annual electricity consumption (for electrified households in 2004–5) was only about 630 kWh for rural areas and 1200 kWh for urban areas.[4] The immediate opportunities are not in the household segment, with the particular exception of the top quintile in metropolitan cities. For example, in a large metropolis like Delhi, over half the households in the top 20 per cent consumption bracket own cars, while over 40 per cent of the households in the top 40 per cent consumption bracket own motorized two-wheelers.[5]

These richer households can prove to be a bottleneck in the transition to low carbon growth. They rely on private transport and are increasingly moving to locate in self-contained private housing developments on the outskirts of cities (where it is easier for developers to aggregate land), where they self-provide continuous supply of electricity, using diesel generating sets, and obtain water by pumping groundwater. These households are thus similar to suburban households in the US, with high energy consumption for both living and transportation. Their lifestyles are based on even more private goods than in the US, like private healthcare and education. If they are able to mobilize politically, they would agitate against the kind of compact city forms envisaged by many of the authors in this report such as Dinesh Mohan in 'Urban Transport and Climate Change: Issues and Concerns in the Indian Context'; Ramakrishna Nallathiga in 'Low Carbon Intensity Urban Planning Strategies for India: The Growing Cities of India: Towards Sustainability and Emission Reduction'; Sweta Byahut in 'Low Carbon Intensity Urban Planning Strategies for India: Climate Change and Urban Planning Strategies for India'; Shaleen Singhal, Jim Berry, and Stanley McGreal in 'Linking Regeneration and Business with Competitiveness for Low Carbon Cities: Lessons for India'.

Along with compact cities, issues relating to urban transport, brought out lucidly by Kaushik Ranjan Bandyopadhyay in his chapter 'Reconciling Economic Growth with Low Carbon Mobility in India: Addressing the Challenges' could become a battleground. Already, as Akshima T. Ghate and Sanjivi Sundar in the chapter 'Putting Urban Transport Sector on a Low Energy and Low Carbon Path: A Focus on the Passenger Transport Sector in Million-Plus Cities' bring out, there is significant growth in emissions from passenger transport in India. To counter this trend, Sanjiv N. Sahai and Simon Bishop in their chapter 'Multi Modal Transport in a Low Carbon Future' propose a seamless multi-modal urban transport network with rail, bus rapid transit, and a novel bus concession system that relies on gross cost contracts, on performance-based, management-based on intelligent transport systems, and information integration. However, this kind of scenario becomes a challenge, not so much because it is technologically difficult to design[6] or because existing investments in infrastructure will become stranded, but because it will be politically difficult to execute. While Chapter 20 by Dinesh Mohan (in this report) recognizes this, the trade-off is largely posited as one between personal and private transport. However, there is a further twist to this tale.

Even between different public transport modes, like rail-based and road-based transport, the choice is unlikely to be technical. Both Sanjiv N. Sahai and Simon Bishop

[4] In urban Delhi, which was the highest among all states, it was 2,000 kWh per year per household. This is based on the National Sample Survey (61st Round) conducted in 2004–5. This refers to residential consumption and is not comparable to the figure given in Table 1, which divides the total electricity consumption (including non-residential consumption) by the total population.

[5] Chakravarty et al. (2005) argue that the richer among such households in countries such as India have a relatively high carbon consumption pattern and construct a scheme to allocate carbon allocations by incorporating the income distribution of different countries, to address the criticism of national averages, that rich households in poor countries get a free pass, riding on the poverty of their fellow citizens.

[6] There is also a significant technological challenge. In order to be attractive to the urban resident in India, the public transport system must replicate the benefits of door-to-door travel offered by private transport as closely as possible, at the operating cost of a two-wheeler, which is less than 2 cents or Re 1 per km.

(in Chapter 19 of this report) and Dinesh Mohan (in Chapter 20 of this report) seem to favour road-based solutions as being more amenable for India. However, it is also a fact that rail-based solutions entail much larger expenditure and contract values. If the political and bureaucratic establishments were to intrinsically prefer such solutions because it makes their 'empire' larger or because it offers more opportunities for illegal gratification, then the more expensive solution could be locked-in for political economy reasons, even it were less appropriate.

Adaptation

Much of our discussion thus far has been on the mitigation, consistent with the theme of a low carbon growth path. However, it must be recognized that the existing levels of CO_2 and most plausible scenarios require that we pay attention to scenarios where adaptation to climate change becomes a necessity. These may be along the lines depicted in part by Kala Seetharam Sridhar in her chapter 'Carbon Emissions, Climate Change, and Impacts in India's Cities', focusing on localized effects, but it also involves the recognition that some resources like water may become scarce in a broader sense. This is especially so in India, where scenarios developed by Revi (2008) show that drought and water stress are very possible.

In this context, one infrastructure sector that finds mention by several authors in this report is water. The use of water by humans in urban areas in India consumes considerable amounts of energy. Some of this is expended in pumping the water out of the ground for purposes of irrigation or for transportation from remote sources to large urban areas and for pumping them into large overhead storage tanks by municipal governments. Some more energy is consumed in treating the raw water to make it fit for human consumption. Another significant percentage is used to transport the wastewater to various treatment plants and then treat this water to bring it to a level fit to be discharged into water bodies. In the US, for example, this comprises about 4 per cent of the country's electricity consumption. Viewed from an energy conservation point, the effort is to make these processes more efficient. Climate change requires consideration of additional perspectives; for example, re-examining the processes, such as reducing the need to transport sewage by replacing centralized with decentralized treatment of wastewater and recognizing that water sources may become much more scarce, necessitating more expensive treatment for reuse and supplementation with energy intensive sources such as desalination.[7]

India offers many opportunities to save energy in water use. To begin with, the provision of 24×7 water supply at reasonable pressure would take away the need for millions of households to pump water into their individual overhead storage tanks. Similarly, as noted by Sreenath Dixit, J.V.N.S. Prasad, B.M.K. Raju, and B. Venkateswarlu in the chapter 'Towards A Carbon-Neutral Rural India: Challenges and Opportunities in Agriculture', and Jyoti Gujral, S. Davenport, and S. Jayasuriya in the chapter 'Is There a Role for Agricultural Offsets in Sustainable Infrastructure Development?: A Preliminary Assessment', the adoption of water-saving irrigation practices in crops such as rice (in addition to the increase in energy efficiency of pumps) would reduce the need to pump water. In new urban areas, the prevalence of housing colonies that aggregate multiple households make it institutionally easier to implement decentralized water treatment and reuse. Concomitantly, the rapid growth in new construction makes the installation of dual piping for such reuse more feasible. However, all of these involve substantial institutional interventions in areas like municipal governance and agricultural extension.

Concomitantly, it must also be recognized that much of the water transportation in rural areas currently involves human energy, whether in pulling water out of a well, pumping it using a hand pump or transporting it in pitchers carried by women. There is also little energy used in treatment of water or wastewater. All this is latent demand, which will likely overwhelm savings opportunities referred to above. This however does not detract from the need to undertake these actions, for it would still constitute a considerable reduction from the counterfactual.

More broadly, adaptation and its supporting infrastructure can take various forms. The building of houses in cities for those currently living in informal housing (to enable them to prevent storm damage, flooding, etc.) can be construed as adaptation infrastructure, as would construction of village water ponds, to adapt to water stress. Of course, it is also infrastructure for poverty alleviation. This dual-use property of adaptation infrastructure could be an issue, were there to be a climate deal that provided funding from developed countries to countries like India to defray the costs of investment in adaptation and

[7] In the United States, energy consumption for water treatment and supply is around 0.4 to 0.5 kWh per kilolitre and an additional 0.3 to 0.5 kWh per kilolitre for treatment, based on the nature of treatment technology. In comparison, desalination uses about 5 kWh per kilolitre.

mitigation infrastructure in response to climate change. In addition to any development benefits it may have, mitigation infrastructure has a clear co-benefit in terms of carbon reduction or capture, but the same is not true of adaptation infrastructure, which is designed as a precaution against effects of climate change. Ex post, just like an insurance premium, the more efforts to combat global warming succeed, the more infructuous investments in adaptation will appear, thus affecting their political support.

Way Forward

In the immediate future in India though, there is enough low-hanging fruit, feasible reductions in carbon emissions with limited lock-in. As brought out in many of the chapters in this report, such as by Lenora Suki in 'Drivers of Energy Efficiency Industries: Indian and International Experience in Infrastructure', many interventions have short payback periods from reductions in energy cost. At the grid level, as Pramod Deo and Vijay M. Deshpande notes (in this report), regulators are trying to reduce the electricity tariffs by compelling improvements in generation, transmission, and distribution efficiency, which also result in reducing CO_2 emissions. Many other non-disruptive opportunities also exist in traditional sectors like coal where, even without CCS, as Malti Goel shows in the chapter 'Implementing Clean Coal Technology in India: Barriers and Prospects', there are opportunities for reducing the carbon impact of coal-based energy. Malti Goel also shows how research may be locked into particular technologies like Integrated Gasification Combined Cycle (IGCC), which has received more attention than technologies such as Circulating Fluidised Bed Combustion (CFBC), despite the possibly greater suitability of the latter for the quality of coal available in India.

These opportunities exist not only in the realm of industry but also equally in the realm of services, as Yenneti Komalirani and Joshi Gauravkumar bring out in 'Carbon Dioxide Emission Reduction Potential from Civil Aviation Sector: A Case Study of Delhi–Mumbai Air Route' on increasing the carbon efficiency of operating practices in the airline industry. Exploiting these may however require aggressive outreach about opportunities, which organizations like Bureau of Energy Efficiency (BEE) are engaged in. This will also lead to a culture of carbon-awareness and carbon-efficiency in industry. Indeed, the BEE is going far beyond just awareness-building. It has already begun monitoring large energy users, and using its expansive powers, may mandate energy efficiency interventions in the future. Less visible opportunities, such as interventions in rural cooking and the possible lock-in risks, have already been mentioned earlier. Furthermore, in addition to the direct payback from reductions in energy cost, there may also be additional financial benefits available in the CDM (clean development mechanism) market.[8]

However, going beyond large users still has significant institutional problems, as well as difficulties with accessing CDM benefits. Programmatic CDM was an approach that was supposed to address this problem, but has had limited success. Ashok Singha, Papia Chakraborty, Suvra Majumdar, and Vijay Mahajan in 'Towards India Evergreen: The Role of Micro-Finance Institutions' advocate a complementary approach based, inter alia, on aggregated voluntary emission reduction transactions (AVERT) which avoids the problems that remain even with initiatives such as programmatic CDM. To the extent that it is possible to build the kinds of frameworks envisaged in such mechanisms, one can even envisage the benefits of efficiency being reaped by smaller actors. Such a large but a still relatively limited set of such small actors (compared to interventions in rural cooking) are the numerous captive power plants below 1 MW, which as Tirthankar Nag in 'Captive Generation in India: The Dilemma of Dualism' notes, constitute an aggregate capacity comparable to the larger (above 1 MW) captive plants. Developing an institutional structure to enable these disparate, but numerous actors to access carbon finance is one of the challenges for the future.

For the two actors that seem to have the ability to act, namely, the organized private sector and the richer households, a simple way of increasing their willingness would appear to be to raise the price of carbon. Doing this directly through a formal carbon tax appears difficult, given our current knowledge about the carbon content of various products.

However, a robust intermediate intervention is possible in the form of taxes on universal intermediate items whose carbon content is well-known, such as fuel and electricity. The revenues from such taxes can then be dedicated to supporting efficiency improvements in actors that have the willingness but not the ability, such as the informal manufacturing sector, where the potential for efficiency benefits is high. In this context, there is a vigorous debate (see Box 2) on the effectiveness of cap-and-trade (C&T)

[8] Though the paperwork involved in CDM projects is substantial, there is now growing expertise in Indian consultants to handhold potential beneficiaries through this complex process.

vis-à-vis carbon taxes (CT).[9] In India too, there are plans to introduce tradable renewable energy certificates as an indirect way to develop a carbon market. Theoretically, C&T can attain the required reduction in emission at the lowest possible cost. However, quantification of both baseline and current emissions remains a challenge and, as noted in Box 2, it is limited to points of obligation. In addition, the impermanence of reduction and leakage into non obligated entities could weaken the effectiveness of the C&T regime. A CT regime, or its surrogate, on the other hand, has the potential to increase the price of carbon across the board and provide incentives to all actors, big and small, to reduce carbon consumption.

Like other interventions to reduce carbon emissions, both CT and C&T will need progressive new legislation before they can be put into effect. However, legislation is just a necessary first step. India has some of the most stringent legislation to protect the environment, but its implementation is quite distant.[10] It is thus necessary to consider the machinery that will implement legislation to bring down carbon emissions. Like C&T, the incidence of CT too may be limited to a small number of actors, due to lacunae in implementation and the informality of economic activity that could limit coverage for both options. Of the two, C&T requires the administrative machinery to ensure that every individual point of obligation does not exceed its permitted emissions. In India (and possibly in many other countries), the experience of our state pollution control boards (SPCBs) does not inspire confidence in our ability to monitor individual emitters.

CT, on the other hand, relies on the tax collection machinery. Over the years, this aspect of the Indian

Box 2
Cap-and-trade vis-à-vis Carbon Taxes

Under a CT, each tonne of CO_2 emitted or tonne of carbon contained in fossil fuels would attract an additional specified tax. Entities would cut their emissions, if it were less costly than paying the tax. At a point in time, the tax would be an upper limit on the cost of reducing emissions, but the total amount of CO_2 emitted in a given year would be unpredictable. Since the tax can be levied on most consumption using current administrative mechanisms, beginning with surrogates and making it more precise as better data becomes available on carbon content, it can potentially move the entire economy to a low carbon path.

A C&T scheme limits total CO_2 emissions and mandates points of obligation[11] to possess allowances in order to emit. The initial allowances are allocated based on a proportion of past emissions or through an auction (in which case the government can raise revenue similar to a tax), and are tradable amongst the entities. Entities emitting less than their allowance can sell to those who would be exceeding the allowances they currently posses. They would be willing to pay a price based on the profits they would forego by reducing production. This price then becomes the cost of reducing emissions. A C&T programme would place an upper limit on the amount of emissions but the cost of reduction would vary. *However, this only applies to points of obligation. Emissions from other entities outside the scheme, such as households, would not be directly affected by the scheme.* Instead, since the price of goods and services (for example, transportation or electricity) with higher carbon content would rise as higher costs are passed to consumers, this can then be expected to induce them to move to a lower carbon consumption path.

The European Union's Emissions Trading Scheme (a C&T system to limit CO_2 emissions) has been in operation since 2005. In June 2009, the US House of Representatives passed the American Clean Energy and Security Act of 2009 (ACES) with a narrow margin (219 to 212) and it is now under consideration of the Senate. Popularly known as the Waxman Markey Bill, it establishes a C&T system to limit US CO_2 emissions. It thus appears that C&T is becoming the instrument of choice for limiting emissions. In the US, its adoption is driven partly by its perceived success with SO_2 emissions (Acid Rain Programme), which covers about 700 power plants, where it is thought to have reduced SO_2 emissions at lower than expected cost. But is it really a better choice than a carbon tax? The Congressional Budget Office, in its evaluation (see CBO (2008)), came out in favour of CT vis-à-vis C&T as a more efficient method of reducing emissions largely on the grounds of more widespread incentives; administrative simplicity; and higher predictability of cost, permitting firms to plan ahead and greater possibility of international co-ordination.

So, is the support emanating from the belief that while C&T is not necessarily better, it is clearly more politically feasible, since CT is a political no-no, given the US legislator's aversion to taxes? As Nobel winning economist Paul Krugman puts it '[The US has] a real chance of getting a serious cap and trade program in place within a year or two [and] no chance of getting a carbon tax for the foreseeable future'. Is it political economy lock-in that is driving this policy?

[9] See Chapters 9 and 25 of this report, where C&T trade is discussed in some detail.

[10] See, for example, the various reports of the *Supreme Court Monitoring Committee on Hazardous Wastes*, available at http://www.toxicslink.org/art-view.php?id=64

[11] A person or organization (such as a business) that has a legal responsibility to monitor and report emissions and, at the end of each reporting period, to hold and surrender a quantity of 'emission units' equal to their emissions.

government has improved substantially, especially in collection from larger units, both in terms of direct and indirect taxes and is likely to improve further with the implementation of the Goods and Services Tax (GST). At this point, therefore, it would appear that our ability to implement CT is substantially better than C&T. Our mix of instruments should be informed by such evaluations. In the final analysis, the choice will depend on relative coverage of the extent of carbon emissions. In terms of the two options, it may well turn out that both kinds of regimes may be needed, a C&T that focuses on large emitters and a CT regime that tries to bring the smaller actors into the net.

Once there is effective implementation of regulations that impact carbon emissions, there will be a demand for technologies that can meet this need. This demand will drive the innovation and development of more such technologies and, more importantly, the growth of institutions and firms that will deploy and diffuse them. As Pinaki Bhattacharyya and Shishir Maheshwari in 'Private Equity Financing for CleanTech Infrastructure' argue, India has all the desirable conditions for providing scale opportunities for private equity investments in clean technologies.

Conclusion

The significance of the informal sector and the need for interventions in rural cooking and captive power plants illustrate the singular context for developing a low carbon growth path in India. None of these areas constitute a significant opportunity in developed countries. In addition, in India a critical actor is its independent institutions like electricity regulators, who are taking a proactive stance on energy efficiency and promotion of renewable energy, through feed-in tariffs, demand side management, etc., as seen in the chapter by Pramod Deo and Vijay M. Deshpande. In this, they are following earlier precedents set by courts in the environmental arena, as noted in Chapter 1 'Infrastructure Regulation for Low Carbon Economy: Survey of Key Issues and Concerns' by Videh Upadhyay. In contrast to such proactive efforts from regulators, the chapter by Dilip Kumar Ghosh 'Local Dynamics in the Adoption and Implementation of Low Carbon Technologies: The Case of West Bengal' points to the limited engagement with rural local government, who remain unfamiliar with climate change. Yet, changing the thinking of such leaders is critical to drive 'action that may seem unconventional to the local populace'. This is especially the case in agriculture, given the considerable reduction in emissions possible, with limited lock-in fears, as detailed in chapters 24 Part 1 and 25 of this report. It is thus clear that India may have only limited benefit from foreign models, and would need to develop its own playbook. This is both an opportunity and a challenge.

The disparate and numerous emissions sources in India also mean that traditional CDM or even programmatic CDM can only be of limited benefit. This is especially true for adaptation infrastructure, due to its dual use nature, as noted earlier. India will have to go beyond CDM in financing its adaptation and mitigation efforts and a domestic carbon tax and/or auctioning of C&T permits may be a source of such resources.

These features of the Indian environment indicate that the chances of being locked into inappropriate infrastructure may be high. The National Action Plan on Climate Change (NAPCC) has reinforced a sense of urgency. However there is a danger in pushing too hard. Since the off-the-shelf solutions currently available are not customized for Indian conditions, an unthinking transplantation of technology in the hurry to be energy efficient may lock us into inappropriate technology. A good example of this is the LEED Green Building Standards, which relies on input characteristics rather than output metrics like kWh per square metre, such as BEE. Thus, where part–time, part-space cooling may be more appropriate, and efficient, but full-time, full-space solution for air conditioning may well end up using more energy (see Jiang (2009)).[12] Similarly, in the attempt to tailor solutions to the demands of the CDM market, we may lock ourselves into inappropriate technologies or policies or focus on sectors where the mitigation potential may be smaller, but the applicability of CDM more evident, and neglect sectors that have large mitigation potential but limited applicability of CDM. Concomitantly, positive interventions do exist. It is also possible to lock ourselves into a low carbon path, for example, by investing in seamless facilities for our cities, that makes public transport more convenient and comfortable, with journey times comparable to personal transport, while it stays affordable. This could build preferences for public transport, replacing today's status premium on private transport. Lock-in could thus help as well as harm.

[12] For the US, while Newsham et al. (2009) find that the average LEED building consumes less energy than non-LEED buildings and over 30 per cent of LEED buildings consume more energy than similar non-LEED buildings, Scofield (2009) finds that LEED buildings are statistically equivalent to non-LEED buildings.

Haste is necessary when Earth's survival is at stake, but it is also important to ensure that the infrastructure we build as we hurry does not make matters worse. Ensuring that it needs foresight and wisdom and lots of common sense, all rare qualities today.

References

Climate Analysis Indicators Tool (CAIT) Version 7.0 (2010). World Resources Institute, Washington DC.

Chakravarty, Shoibal, Ananth Chikkatur, Heleen de Coninck, Stephen Pacala, Robert Socolow, and Massimo Tavoni (2009). 'Sharing Global CO_2 Emission Reductions among One Billion High Emitters', *Proceedings of the National Academy of Science USA*. 106(29), pp. 11884–8, 21 July, last accessed August 2010, available at http://www.pnas.org/content/early/2009/07/02/0905232106.full.pdf+html

Congressional Budget Office (CBO) (2008). 'Policy Options for Reducing CO_2 Emissions', A CBO Study, Congress of the United States, February, last accessed August 2010, available at http://www.cbo.gov/ftpdocs/89xx/doc8934/02-12-Carbon.pdf

D'Sa, Antonette and K.V. Narasimha Murthy (2004). *Report on the Use of LPG as a Domestic Cooking Fuel Option in India*, International Energy Initiative, Bangalore, June, last accessed August 2010, available at http://www.bioenergylists.org/stovesdoc/Iei/IEIBLR-LPG-IndianhomesReport.pdf

Delio, Ella Aglipay, Saurabh Lall, and Chandan Singh (2009). 'Powering Up: The Investment Potential of Energy Service Companies in India', World Resources Institute, last accessed August 2010, available at http://www.wri.org/publication/powering-up

Goldman, Charles A., Julie G. Osborn, Nicole C. Hopper, and Terry E. Singer (2002). 'Market Trends in the U.S. ESCO Industry: Results from the NAESCO Database', Energy Analysis Department, Ernest Orlando Lawrence Berkeley National Laboratory. University of California, Berkeley, May, last accessed August 2010, available at http://eetd.lbl.gov/ea/ems/reports/49601.pdf

Jiang, Yi (2009). 'Harmonious with Nature: The Chinese Approach to Building Energy Reduction', in Mark Kelly (ed.) *Public #5: A Human Thing*, last accessed August 2010, available at http://www.woodsbagot.com/en/Documents/Public_5_papers/Harmonious_with_nature.pdf

Kotkin, Joel (2010). 'The War against Suburbia', last accessed August 2010, available at http://www.american.com/archive/2010/january/the-war-against-suburbia

Krugman, Paul (2009). 'Unhelpful Hansen', *New York Times*, 7 December 2009, last accessed August 2010, available at http://krugman.blogs.nytimes.com/2009/12/07/unhelpful-hansen/

Newsham, G.R., S. Mancini, and B.J. Birt (2009). 'Do LEED-certified Buildings Save Energy? Yes, but…', *Energy and Buildings*, 41(8), pp. 897–905, last accessed August 2010, available at http://www.nrc-cnrc.gc.ca/obj/irc/doc/pubs/nrcc51142.pdf

Revi, Aromar (2008). 'Climate Change Risk: An Adaptation and Mitigation Agenda for Indian Cities', *Environment and Urbanization*, 20(1), pp. 207–29, April. last accessed August 2010, available at http://www.iied.org/pubs/pdfs/G02275.pdf

Scofield, J.H. (2009). 'Do LEED-certified Buildings Save Energy? Not really'. *Energy and Buildings*, 41(12), pp. 1386–90, December, last accessed August 2010, available at http://www.oberlin.edu/physics/Scofield/pdf_files/eb-09.pdf

Section I

Legal and Regulatory Issues

1 Infrastructure Regulation for Low Carbon Economy

Survey of Key Issues and Concerns

Videh Upadhyay

Introduction

Infrastructure projects today are the touchstone for realizing India's high growth and development ambitions. However, large infrastructure projects require substantial resources to deliver the big impact in terms of high growth and development. Endeavours such as the ultra mega power projects, dams, highways, airports, and big construction projects typically have long lead times, high costs, and diverse users. Notwithstanding the contentious negative externalities associated with big infrastructure projects, the positive contribution that infrastructure can make to the inclusive growth and sustainable development objectives cannot be understated. Well-designed infrastructure development programmes could play a key role in achieving the Millennium Development Goals (MDG), in particular working towards reducing poverty and ensuring environmental sustainability.[1]

A sound and well-planned infrastructure project can meet a variety of economic, social, cultural, and environmental needs.[2] Thus, from the standpoint of defining a sustainable low carbon trajectory of economic development, it is important not to see large infrastructure projects restrictively as something to be 'contained' for the benefit of the environment and the society. A judicious mix of choices would need to be exercised to maintain the delicate balance of pursing economic growth and ensuring a low carbon sustainable development. It is important to also recognize the limitations in the existing approaches that would need to be overcome.

A Policy Consultation Forum of the United Nations Economic and Social Commission for Asia and the Pacific, after an intensive brainstorming on the subject of 'Promoting Sustainable Infrastructure Development' in a meeting held in Seoul, South Korea, in September 2006, concluded that, 'so far, discussions on infrastructure development have been focused mainly on financing issues and engineering aspects in the region. Mainstreaming environmental aspects and incorporating the eco-efficiency concept into various stages of infrastructure development have not been considered as much as they should have been.' Amongst other insightful conclusions of the Forum, the four that seem most relevant in the Indian context are:

- In many cases, decisions for development of infrastructure are dependent on political decisions, which

[1] The unmet demand for social and physical infrastructure to support the delivery of housing, transportation, energy, water services, and food limits economic opportunity and is, therefore, a major barrier to the achievement of MDG. See the *Report of the First Policy Consultation Forum of the Seoul Initiative on Green Growth* on 'Promoting Sustainable Infrastructure Development' under the aegis of the United Nations Economic and Social Commission for Asia and the Pacific, September 2006.

[2] A 'sustainability' perspective only demands that the economic role and significance of infrastructure should be seen together with the social, cultural, and environmental aspects.

sometimes are not scientifically and environmentally sound.

- The technical expertise of the private sector in development of infrastructure will definitely be beneficial. However, private participation does not automatically guarantee the promotion of sustainable infrastructure. Private participation in infrastructure development needs to be carefully evaluated and scrutinized.
- Strategic Environmental Assessment (SEA) and life cycle assessment, taking into account the long-term impact of infrastructure use, have not been widely applied in infrastructure development in the region.
- There is lack of comprehensive statistical data and valuable information to understand the eco-efficiency levels of existing infrastructure (including long-term environmental impact of usage and life cycle of the infrastructure) and future development plans.

The points raised by the United Nations Commission show that there is a lot to be done as we attempt to align infrastructure projects with the goal of a low carbon economy.

Legal and regulatory reforms are significant drivers for sustainable infrastructure development in India and good governance holds the key to ensuring responsible behaviour. Considering that infrastructure projects are 'all too apparently a process organized through law and legal techniques,'[3] it may be prudent to revisit the prevailing legal provisions and the regulatory mechanisms to provide an enabling framework for low carbon infrastructure development in India. Given that in countries such as India, some of the largest cuts in emissions can come from full adherence to basic efficiency and management parameters; the role of regulation in ensuring compliance becomes important. Effective compliance of legal, policy, and regulatory provisions across sectors can help make projects environmentally sound and ensure substantial development along the low carbon trajectory.

This chapter presents a national cross-sectoral review of the prevailing legal and regulatory initiatives for aligning infrastructure projects with the low carbon economy goal. Through a brief discussion of the role of Courts and litigation, focus is on the challenges in effective administration within the present legal framework, and in this context, discusses how regulation by contract is increasingly becoming important. In this regard, some ways to strengthen project contracts and bid documents are suggested so that appropriate environmental mitigation and enhancement measures are effectively incorporated. The chapter concludes by highlighting major gaps in the legal and regulatory framework for achieving a low carbon objective and proposes reforms needed to overcome deficiencies.

National Policy and Legal Initiatives for Low Carbon Infrastructure Projects

Given the many laws, regulations, and policies that exist historically or have come into existence in more recent years, India should be well on her way to a low carbon future. Some of the key legal initiatives and national policies in this regard are briefly discussed below:

NAPCC, Energy-Efficiency Mission, and the Energy Conservation Act, 2001

The National Action Plan on Climate Change (NAPCC) and the Nationally Appropriate Mitigation Action Plan (NAMA) under it are useful starting points to appreciate the emerging regulatory regime for low carbon energy infrastructure in the country. According to NAPCC, India's vision is 'to create a prosperous economy that is self-sustaining in terms of its ability to unleash the creative energies of the people and is mindful of responsibilities to both present and future generations.' NAPCC lays emphasis upon the development and use of new technologies in order to ensure optimal benefits in terms of climate change mitigation and adaptation, energy efficiency, and natural resource conservation. It embodies eight missions, which pertain to *solar energy, energy efficiency, sustainable habitat, water, sustaining the Himalayan ecosystem, Green India, sustainable agriculture, and strategic knowledge for climate change.* The NAPCC is likely to have decisive impacts on businesses through institutional mechanisms such as subsidy restructuring, lucrative opportunities in clean technologies and renewable energy, energy-efficiency benchmarks and certificates, cap-and-trade schemes, etc. India's Nationally Appropriate Mitigation Action Plan (NAMA) has specified three major missions—energy-efficiency mission, solar mission, and the water mission. In the context of NAMA, the following intervention made by India's Environment Minister in November 2009 deserves notice:[4]

India has several nationally appropriate mitigation actions (NAMAs) which it is considering to convert to nationally

[3] Silbey (1997).

[4] Intervention made by India's Environment Minister at the Pre-COP meeting at Copenhagen on 16 November 2009 and available at http://moef.nic.in/downloads/public-information/Intervention_copehagen.pdf

accountable mitigation outcomes (NAMOs) by indicating specific performance targets in industry, energy, transport, agriculture, buildings, and forestry for the year 2020 and 2030. These NAMOs could be institutionalised through either legislative or executive action and are derived from the National Action Plan on Climate Change and the 11th Five Year Plan document... India will make low carbon sustainable growth a central element of its 12th Plan growth strategy. This will mean taking on commitments to reduce energy to GDP intensity and corresponding emission reduction outcomes for the year 2020.

The above statement should not mean that all the action for energy conservation is to happen in future. Out of three major missions under NAMAs pointed out above, the Energy Efficiency Mission has already made significant progress. A legal catalyst for energy conservation came through in 2001 with the passing of the Energy Conservation Act, 2001 that can play a crucial role in promoting sustainable energy projects. The Act was enacted to provide for efficient use of energy and its conservation.The Act establishes the Bureau of Energy Efficiency (BEE), which holds the power to recommend to the central government the norms for processes and energy consumption standards that are required to be notified.[5] The BEE has created a panel of certified energy auditors and identified nine designated sectors where energy audits are made mandatory. In 2006, India launched a comprehensive *energy labelling programme* for appliances under the framework of the Energy Conservation Act of 2001.[6] Another specific initiative and mechanism aimed at energy savings is the Energy Conservation Building Code. The programme is based on actual performance of commercial buildings in optimizing energy demand based on their locations under five climatic zones.[7] Compliance of the provisions of the Energy Conservation Building Code would invariably result in voluminous energy savings. The Bureau of Energy Efficiency has instituted a panel of experts as well as professionals with a view to build technical capacity for implementation of the code. Other policies and publicly funded programmes on energy conservation and deployment of renewable energy technologies are presented in Box 1.1.

Regulation and Facilitation of Renewable Energy Infrastructure

There are a range of policies and policy instruments at the state level that has been passed in recent years with the mandate to promote renewable energy projects and initiatives. However, when it comes to the legal framework it is the Electricity Act, 2003 and more specifically, the New Tariff Policy (2006) under the Act—which states that a minimum percentage of energy, as specified by the Regulatory Commission, is to be purchased from renewable energy sources—that alone contains a legally binding obligation requiring the creation, transmission, and deployment of renewable energy to address the country's energy and environmental insecurity.

There are specific provisions pertaining to non-conventional energy sources under the Electricity Act, 2003.[8] The Act provides that co-generation and generation of electricity from non-conventional sources would be promoted by the State Electricity Regulatory Commissions (SERCs) by providing suitable measures for connectivity with grids and sale of electricity to any person and also by specifying, for purchase of electricity from such sources, a percentage of the total consumption of electricity in the area of a distribution licensee. Such percentage for purchase of power from non-conventional sources should be made applicable for the tariffs to be determined by the SERCs at the earliest.[9] Progressively, the share of electricity from non-conventional sources would need to be increased as prescribed by SERCs. Considering the fact that it will be some time before non-conventional technologies compete, in terms of cost, with conventional sources, the SERCs may determine appropriate the differential in prices to promote these technologies. Regulatory Commissions, while specifying the terms and conditions for the determination of tariff, shall be guided by the National Electricity Policy (NEP), the Tariff Policy, and

[5] It also has the power to recommend to the central government the particulars required to be displayed on equipment labels or on appliances and the manner of their display.

[6] The programme covers refrigerators, fluorescent tube lamps, air-conditioners, and distribution transformers. The programme follows a five-point rating scale, with one star implying low energy efficiency while a five-star rating represent highest energy efficiency transformers.

[7] The climatic zones being warm and humid, composite, hot and dry, moderate, and cold.

[8] Sections 3, 4, 61, and 86 (1) of the Electricity Act, 2003.

[9] Section 6.4 of the Tariff Policy (non-conventional sources of energy generation including co-generation: Pursuant to provisions of section 86 (1)(e) of the Electricity Act, the Appropriate Commission shall fix a minimum percentage for purchase of energy from such sources taking into account availability of such resources in the region and its impact on retail tariffs. Such percentage for purchase of energy should be made applicable for the tariffs to be determined by the SERCs latest by 1 April 2006.

Box 1.1
Regulatory Efforts in India at Clean Energy and Energy Conservation: An Overview

Over several decades, India has pursued policies and publicly funded programmes that focused on energy conservation and deployment of renewable energy technologies. This has been backed by legislation, regulation, and tariffs arrangements. Some of these are:

1. Reforming Energy Markets (Electricity Act, 2005, Tariff Policy, 2003, Petroleum and Natural Gas Regulatory Board Act, 2006, etc.) involving:
   - removal of entry barriers in exploration, extraction, conversion, transmission, and distribution of primary and secondary energy;
   - institution of price reforms and tax reforms to promote optimal fuel choices;
   - provision of feed in tariffs for renewable energy such as solar, wind, and biomass; and
   - strengthening or introduction of independent regulation.
2. New and Renewable Energy Policy, 2005: The policy promotes adoption of sustainable and renewable energy sources. It also facilitates speedy deployment of renewable technology through indigenous design, development, and manufacturing.
3. Rural Electrification Policy, 2006: The policy promotes renewable energy technologies where grid connectivity is not possible or cost-effective.
4. Bidiesel Purchase Policy: It mandates bio-diesel procurement by petroleum companies.
5. Ethanol Blending of Gasoline*:* The regulation mandates five per cent blending of ethanol with gasoline from 1 January 2003 in nine states and four union territories.
6. Energy Conservation Act, 2001*:* The legislation aims to reduce specific energy consumption in different sectors. It set up the specialized BEE in this regard.
7. Energy Conservation Building Code, 2006: This regulatory code is designed to ensure energy efficiency in all buildings with above 500 kVA connected load or air-conditioned floor area over 1,000 square metres.
8. Bachat Lamp Yojana (Efficient Lamps Programme): It is a country-wide programme for replacement of incandescent lamps by CFLs, and using clean development mechanism (CDM) credits to equate the respective purchase prices.
9. 50,000 MW Hydroelectric Initiative, 2003: One hundred and sixty-two new hydro-electricity projects with 50,000 MW potential have been identified.
10. Other Programmes*:* These include the promotion of solar thermal water heaters, solar PVs, wind power generation, biomass gasifiers, biogas and manure management, fuel cells, and energy recovery from urban wastes and many similar energy saving activities. In addition, the Government of India adopted an Integrated Energy Policy as an overarching framework in 2008.

Source: Ghosh (2009).

promotion of co-generation and generation of electricity from renewable energy sources.[10] Preferential pricing for non-conventional energy resources, therefore, has got a legal mandate.

Regulation by Environment Impact Assessments (EIAs)

One legal instrument that is directly aimed at making projects—especially larger infrastructure projects—environmentally sustainable is the Environment Impact Assessment (EIA) Notification, 2006 passed under the Environment Act of 1986. The EIA, dated 14 September 2006, issued by the Ministry of Environment and Forests, Government of India (GoI), divides all infrastructure projects or activities requiring prior environmental clearance into two categories, 'A' and 'B'.[11] The projects or activities falling under category 'A' require approval from the central government's Ministry of Environment and Forests (MoEF) based on recommendations submitted by an Expert Appraisal Committee (EAC). Projects or activities falling under category 'B' require prior approval of the State Environment Impact Assessment Authority (SEIAA), based on recommendations of a state or union territory level Expert Appraisal Committee (SEAC) before commencing any work on the land except for its acquisitions, which does require prior approval. Pursuant

[10] The Act makes it mandatory to have NEP and the tariff policy based on optimal utilization of resources such as coal, natural gas, nuclear substances or material, hydro, and renewable sources of energy. The Electricity Act also mandates a national policy, permitting stand-alone systems including those based on renewable sources of energy and other non-conventional sources of energy for rural areas.

[11] The projects are categorized into 'A' and 'B' on the basis of the potential impact the projects will have spatially on 'human health and natural and man-made resources'.

to applications for environmental clearance for new projects, the EAC and the SEAC at central and state levels respectively, carry out the four stages of *Screening, Scoping, Public Consultation,* and *Appraisal* prior to environmental clearance of the project.

Some examples of regulation by EIA in different sectors may be seen in Box 1.2 below to appreciate the mechanism of EIA in these sectors in a big way.

The Air Act, 1981—Regulating Emissions

The Air (Prevention and Control of Pollution) Act, 1981 is a comprehensive legislation for prevention, control, and abatement of air pollution especially from 'industrial plants' and for this purpose, it creates and empowers a Central Pollution Control Board (CPCB) and the State Pollution Control Boards (SPCBs). Under the Act, no person shall without the previous consent ('Consent to Establish' and 'Consent to Operate') of the SPCBs, establish and operate an industrial plant in the designated air pollution control areas. Under the aegis of the Act, The National Ambient Air Quality Programme, initiated by the CPCB in 1984, is operated mainly through the SPCBs. The National Ambient Air Quality Standards (NAAQs) are provided for the three pollutants—sulphur dioxide (SO_2), oxides of nitrogen (NO_X), and suspended particulate matter (SPM)—that are regularly monitored.[13] A country-wide network of 290 monitoring stations has been established for NAAQs. It may, however, be noted that in most of the states, not all the sanctioned stations are operational.[14] Some of the implementation issues relating to the capacity and management of the CPCBs and the SPCBs are discussed in sections below. Further, it may be

Box 1.2

Regulation by EIAs in Different Sectors: Some Examples

While a booming construction industry, large power projects (including UMPPs) and intensive oil exploration to monetize the hydrocarbon opportunity may be in the socio-economic interest of our nation, they cannot come at an irreversible ecological loss. Here is how 'Prior Environment Clearance' is mandated for these projects under the EIA Notification, 2006 passed under the Environment Act, 1986:

Environmental Impact Assessment and the Civil Construction Industry: Prior environment clearance from the MoEF is mandatory for 'Building and Construction Projects' and 'All Townships and Area Development Projects' that require large civil construction works if they are above threshold limits under the EIA Notification of 2006.[12] When it comes to cement plants, all cement plants with over 1.0 million tonnes per annum production capacity, being 'Category A' projects, require clearance at the central level whereas plants with less than that capacity are Category 'B' projects with environment clearance required at the state level.

EIA and River Valley Projects and of Thermal Power Plants: All river valley projects which have a capacity of over 50 MW hydro-electric power generation and have over 10,000 ha. of culturable command area need to get clearance from the MoEF at the central level, being Category 'A' projects, whereas those having a capacity of over 25MW hydroelectric power generation are Category 'B' projects requiring clearance from the state level. When it comes to thermal power projects having a capacity of over 500 MW (in case of coal/lignite/naphtha, and gas-based projects) and over 50 MW (in case of pet coke, diesel, and all other fuels) are category 'A' projects, while projects with lesser thresholds are Category 'B' projects.

EIA and Offshore and Onshore Oil and Gas Exploration: Offshore and onshore oil and gas exploration, development, and production require clearance from the MoEF. However, exploration surveys (not involving drilling) are exempted from seeking clearance. Further, all oil and gas transportation pipeline (crude and refinery/petrochemical products), passing through national parks/sanctuaries/coral reefs/ecologically sensitive areas including LNG Terminal require clearance from the MoEF. The same applies to petroleum refining industry and petrochemical complexes (industries based on processing of petroleum fractions and natural gas and/or reforming to aromatics).

Source: EIA Notification, 2006.

[12] The projects at the state level requiring an EIA Report are termed Category 'B1' projects under the EIA Notification, 2006 and `All Townships and Area Development Projects' covering an area of 50 ha or more and or built up area of 1,50,000 sq. metres or more are termed as 'B1' projects.

[13] The previously existing NAAQS were notified for seven air pollutants, that is, suspended particulate matter (SPM), respirable particulate matter (RPM), sulphur dioxide (SO_2), oxides of nitrogen (NOx), carbon monoxide (CO), ammonia (NH_3), and lead (Pb).

[14] A Planning Commission Evaluation of 25 SPCBs across the country found out that only in four states—Rajasthan, Orissa, Assam, and Goa—all the NAAQS stations sanctioned by the MoEF are operating. The status of Karnataka and Haryana is extremely poor in this respect. The position of Bihar, Maharashtra, Uttar Pradesh, West Bengal, and Punjab is also not worth the mention. Not one of the stations in any of the north-eastern states is functional where each state is sanctioned with two NAAQs stations. Among other things, the fund constraint of the CPCB in financing the SPCBs to establish and operate the sanctioned stations also accounts for the difference between the number of sanctioned and operating stations.

noted that NAAQS specified under the Air Act, 1981 were introduced to address the local air pollution issues and the associated local negative externalities. Under the 1981 Act, it may be useful to declare other main greenhouse gases such as carbon dioxide and methane as pollutants so as to bring them under their ambit. This may not be that far-fetched if it is realized that ozone, which has global warming implications, is already known to be a part of the revised NAAQS.[15]

The National Green Tribunal Act 2010 and Some other recent initiatives of the Government of India

The National Green Tribunal Act 2010 that came into being as a law in June 2010 creates a National Green Tribunal for 'effective and expeditious disposal of cases relating to environmental protection and conservation of forests and other natural resources including enforcement of any legal rights relating to environment'. According to the Act 'the Tribunal shall have the jurisdiction over all civil cases where a substantial question relating to environment (including enforcement of any legal right relating to environment) is involved' besides the questions which arise 'out of the implementation' of the specified enactments (Section 14). The law can have far reaching consequences especially as for the first time a national legislation has vested the power in a Tribunal to provide for 'relief and compensation to the victims of pollution and other environmental damage', 'for restitution of property damaged' and 'restitution of environment' (Section 15). Interestingly, the CPCB will also have the power to approach the National Green Tribunal on behalf of the affected persons for grant of relief, compensation or settlement of disputes. How exactly the judicial machinery unfolds under the law would be seen in the coming years but the Tribunal is expected to usher in a new era of responsible and environmentally sound development projects apart from providing for speedier resolution of disputes where 'substantial question relating to environment' gets involved in infrastructure projects.

Before closing this section three of the more important recent initiatives taken by the central government this year specifically for low carbon development in India deserve a quick notice. Firstly, Government of India has set up an *Expert Group on Low Carbon Strategy for Inclusive Growth* with a specific mandate of developing a roadmap for India for low carbon development. The Group has been asked to recommend prioritized actions in sectors such as Electricity, Transport, Industry, Oil and Gas, Buildings, and Forestry. The Ministry of Environment and Forest, Government of India has made clear that the Group's recommendations will become a central part of India's Twelfth Five Year Plan which will come into effect in 2012.[16] Given the Group's categorical mandate and the role that it can play in shaping the Twelfth Five Year Plan, its recommendations across sectors is likely to evince large scale interest. Second, following the Budget Speech of the Union Finance Minister this year when the idea was mooted for the first time, a clean energy cess on coal, at the rate of Rs 50 per tonne has been announced, which will apply to both domestically produced and imported coal. This money will go into a *National Clean Energy Fund* that will be used for funding research, innovative projects in clean energy technologies, and environmental remedial programmes. The expected earnings from this cess is around USD 500 million for the financial year 2010–11. Finally, India's cabinet also approved the *National Mission on Enhanced Energy Efficiency (NMEEE)* on 24 June, 2010. The Mission includes several new initiatives—the most important being the *Perform, Achieve and Trade (PAT) Mechanism*, which while seeking to cover facilities that account for more than 50 per cent of the nationally used fossil fuels, and helping reduce CO_2 emissions by 25 million tonnes per year by 2014–15, mandates that 700 of the most energy intensive industrial units and power stations in India would reduce their energy consumption by a specified percentage.[17] All of these ambitious initiatives and results expected from them over the next few years can be critical to realizing the roadmap for low carbon development.

Role of Courts and Litigation: Some Issues and Aspects

It is also useful to briefly see the impact of litigation in the Supreme Court and the High Courts on making infrastructure projects environmentally sound. For some of the leading cases in the Supreme Court, see Box 1.3.

[15] It may be noted that the MoEF has recently announced the notification of the Revised NAAQS, 2009. In this, other new parameters such as ozone, arsenic, nickel, benzene, and benzo (a) Pyrene (BaP) have been included for the first time under NAAQS, based on CPCB/IIT research, World Health Organization guidelines, and EU limits and practices.

[16] A note of Ministry of Environment and Forests, Government of India titled *India: Taking on Climate Change-Post Copenhagen Domestic Actions*, 30 June 2010 and available at www.moef.nic.in

[17] Ibid.

Box 1.3
Supreme Court of India Handles Environmentally Hazardous Projects: Some Leading Cases

- In *M.C. Mehta* v. *Union of India,*[18] the Apex Court directed shifting/relocation of 168 industries identified as hazardous and large industries operating in Delhi to other towns of NCR as per the master plan of 2001.
- In *M.C. Mehta* v. *Union of India,*[19] the Court passed several directions for preventing air pollution in Delhi. While reaffirming the need for the public transport system to run on CNG, it directed the phasing out of diesel buses in a time-bound manner.
- In *M.C. Mehta* v. *Union of India,*[20] the Hon'ble Court took note of the environmental pollution due to stone-crushing activities in and around Delhi, Faridabad, and Ballabhgarh complexes and directed for relocating of such units within six months.
- In *Vineet Kumar Mathur* v. *Union of India,*[21] intervention of the Court was sought to prevent pollution of river Gomti in UP due to discharge of effluents from the distillery of Mohan Meakins Ltd. The Court directed the removal of deficiencies in the effluent treatment plant as well as imposed a fine of Rs 5 lakh on the company.
- In *S. Jagannath* v. *Union of India,*[22] the Court held that the shrimp industry is to be permitted only after passing a strict environment test.
- In *Vellore Citizens' Welfare Forum* v. *Union of India,* the Court dealt with the problem of pollution being caused by enormous discharge of untreated effluents by tanneries in the state of Tamil Nadu and also imposed a fine of Rs 10,000 on the polluting industries.
- In *Indian Council for Enviro Legal Action* v. *Union of India,*[23] the Court directed closure of industries in Bichhari village in Udaipur (Rajasthan), discharging highly toxic effluents leading to soil and water pollution and also directed for the removal of the sludge, etc. The Court observed that 'Enactment of law but tolerating its infringement is worse than not enacting the law at all.'
- In *M.C. Mehta* v. *Union of India,*[24] (*Calcutta Tanners Case*) the Court directed for the shifting/relocating the tanneries in question causing pollution.

The Efficacy of Litigation as a Mechanism for Controlling Pollution from Projects

Notwithstanding some major verdicts and interventions by the higher courts in leading pollution cases, a Planning Commission Study evaluating SPCBs in 2002 found out that there was a growing disillusionment among these boards with the efficacy of litigation as a control mechanism. The study observed as follows:

Non-installation of abatement mechanisms by the polluting units is a direct consequence of the absence of any effective punitive and deterrent mechanism in case of non-compliance. First, the SPCBs do not have the power to impose on-the spot-fines on persistently non-complying units. In the absence of such power, the State Boards will have to either hope for the non-complying unit to abide by their directions or file a case with the Court of Justice against the said unit and wait for the court verdict. The Court is entitled to impose stringent punishments ranging from imprisonment of 18 months to 6 years plus fine. Courts are generally busy with day-day criminal and civil cases and may keep environmental cases pending for years together. '... The growing disillusionment with the efficacy of litigation as a control mechanism felt by some of the State Boards, especially those of Madhya Pradesh, Tamil Nadu, Punjab, Orissa and Gujarat is evidenced by the negligible number of environmental cases filed by them... it is clear that the cumulative number of cases filed by the State Boards like those of Assam, Punjab, Maharashtra, Gujarat, Kerala, Karnataka and Tamil Nadu was far less than the number of non-complying industrial units. Some State Boards complain that when the cases are finally decided, the verdicts often go against them, for the Courts are said to be reluctant to award 18 months of imprisonment to the recalcitrant units.

It is here that the National Green Tribunal can play a major role in the years ahead. The Tribunal can help decongest the already burdened regular courts. This congestion has been the principal reason for the disillusionment with the Pollution Control Boards (PCBs). Besides, there is a clear lesson in the above that the SPCBs need to be empowered to impose environmental civil penalties (discussed in some detail in the last section below) so that the resort to criminal prosecution—and hence regular criminal cases—declines in future.

[18] Reported in Supreme Court Cases and available at (1996) 4 SCC 750.
[19] Reported in Supreme Court Cases and available at (2002) 4 SCC 356.
[20] Reported in Supreme Court Cases and available at (1992) 3 SCC 256.
[21] Reported in Supreme Court Cases and available at (1996) 7 SCC 714.
[22] Reported in Supreme Court Cases and available at (1997) 2 SCC 87.
[23] Reported in Supreme Court Cases and available at (1996) 3 SCC 212.
[24] Reported in Supreme Court Cases and available at (1997) 2 SCC 411.

Limited Judicial Review on Large Infrastructure Projects

The impact of intervention of the Supreme Court of India and the High Courts on large infrastructure projects can be seen with reference to cases on river valley projects, thermal power plants, mining projects, railway projects, tourism infrastructure, and roads and highways. Over the last two decades, a large number of public interest petitions got filed to challenge large infrastructure projects primarily including dams, power, and mining projects. The grounds for challenge included adverse environmental impacts,[25] safety aspects,[26] inadequate Environment Impact Assessment and Environment Management Plan,[27] extraneous considerations,[28] forced displacement[29] and inadequate resettlement, and rehabilitation measures[30] arising therefrom.[31]

In their litigation against large infrastructure projects, the Courts have generally not ordered the scrapping of any project or any significant restructuring of a project in the face of such challenges.[32] Courts have tended to take the view that considerations of environmental impacts of a project or economic and financial considerations raised technical issues and policy matters, which are best left with the expert authorities of the executive. [33] For example, in the well-known *Sardar Sarovar Project Case,* the Court made it clear as follows:

> There are three stages with regard to the undertaking of an infrastructural project. One is conception or planning, second is decision to undertake the project and the third is the execution of the project. The conception and the decision to undertake a project is to be regarded as a policy decision. While there is always a need for such projects not being unduly delayed, it is at the same time expected that as thorough a study as is possible will be undertaken before a decision is taken to start a project. Once such a considered decision is taken, the proper execution of the same should be taken expeditiously. It is for the Government to decide how to do its job. When it has put a system in place for the execution of a project and such a system cannot be said to be arbitrary, then the only role which a Court may have to play is to see that the system works in the manner it was envisaged.[34]

It will not be out of place to mention here that in practice, the vast majority of issues in the context of infrastructure projects is handled through non-judicial legal means. Although projects are initiated in multiple sectors and in large numbers, litigation has only been pursued in a handful of situations. Environmental and other rights issues are more often resolved by contracts and legislative or executive action. We have looked at some of the key legislative or executive action on infrastructure regulation for low carbon economy in the section above. Let's cast a close eye on regulation by contract in the section below.

Regulation by Contract for a Low Carbon Future

The centrality of contracts in infrastructure projects should not come as a surprise because 'contracts form the framework for project viability and control the allocation of risks.'[35] Project companies responsible for carrying out projects 'are founded upon a series of contracts, which unites various parties in a vertical chain from input supplier to output purchaser.'[36] Even though contracts play an enormous role in carrying out projects, its use and application for aligning projects with the goals of a low carbon economy has been limited for various reasons discussed below.

[25] The Society for Protection of Silent Valley v. Union of India (Unreported).

[26] *Tehri Bandh Virodhi Sangharsh Samiti* v. *State of UP*, 1992 SUPP (1) SCC 44.

[27] *The Goa Foundation and Anr.* v. *The Konkan Railway Corporation and Others*, AIR 1992 BOM 471.

[28] *Centre for Public Interest Litigation* v. *Union of India*, 78(1999) DLT 389.

[29] See for instance *Tehri Bandh Virodhi Sangharsh Samiti* v. *State of UP*, 1992 SUPP (1) SCC 44.

[30] See for instance *Karajan Jalasay Yojana Assargrasth Shakhar Ane Sangharsh Samiti* v. *Gujarat* AIR 1987 SC 532.

[31] Most of the challenges to such projects have been mainly because all such projects require acquisition of substantial areas of land and consequential displacement of a large number of people. This also entails substantial impact on the environment and ecology of the regions. This is because large infrastructure projects will invariably have large impacts and due to the scale of grievances, these cases merit special attention.

[32] *Tehri Bandh Virodhi Sangharsh Samiti* v. *State of UP* (1992) Supp. (1) SCC 44; *Narmada Bachao Andolan* v. *Union of India* AIR 2000 SC 3751.

[33] Upadhyay (2007).

[34] *Narmada Bachao Andolan* v. *Union of India* AIR 2000 SC 3751 at Para 223.

[35] Hoffman (2001).

[36] Esty (2004).

A review of the World Bank-aided projects of the National Highway Authority of India (NHAI) and Public Works Department (PWD) found out that:

Contractors do not integrate environment management into each of their activities. During the field visits undertaken under this review, there was also no convincing evidence that the environment provisions included in the Indian Roads Congress (IRC) guidelines and the Ministry of Road Transport and Highways (MoRTH) specifications are being followed. Some initiatives such as the specific environmental management plan (EMP) mitigation measures are taken because of contract requirements. There is almost no voluntary adoption of good environmental management practices among contractors. Thus, the obligations under Contract become the main tool and the only way to ensure that good practices are implemented on the ground.[37]

As said above, since the obligations under Contract become the main tool and the only way to ensure that good practices are implemented on the ground, it is instructive to see the nature of obligations that typically exists in infrastructure contracts today. A typical Concession Contract for any project says that the Concessionaire shall '*comply with all Applicable Permits and Applicable Laws in the performance of the Concessionaire's obligations* under the Agreement including those being performed by any of the Contractors'. Further, 'The Concessionaire shall, at all times, afford access to the Site to the authorized governmental agency having jurisdiction over the project, including those concerned with safety, security or environmental protection to inspect and to investigate any matter within their authority…' On the other hand, the *Agency/ Owner of the project shall 'assist the Concessionaire to get necessary statutory clearances as regards environmental and other clearances* from various government departments.' Take another random example. In the Oil and Gas sector, there is the 'Production Sharing Contract' (PSC) wherein both the government and the contractor recognize that petroleum operations will cause some impact on the environment in the Contract Area. Accordingly, a typical PSC also stipulates that '*in performance of the Contract, the Contractor shall conduct its petroleum operations with due regard to concerns with respect to protection of the environment and conservation of natural resources*'. Likewise, in a FIDIC- (that is, an acronym for the International Institute for Consulting Engineers) based construction contract for a large dam, there is the provision that the '*Contractor shall take all reasonable steps to protect the environment on and off the Site and to avoid damage or nuisance to persons or to property of the public or others resulting from pollution, noise or other causes arising as a consequence of his methods of operation.*'

Making Contract Clauses More Specific, More Important, and More Integral

If environmental issues are to be woven more closely in the Contracts, they would need to be made *more specific, more important,* and *more integral.* Some suggestions on these lines are outlined below:

- The nature of contract clauses typically shows that there are overall references to applicable laws as a standard practice. The EMP as a whole, but more significantly the mitigation measures and monitoring requirements' tables could be specifically incorporated say, under the Conditions of Particular Application (COPA) in a FIDIC-based contract. Cross-references from the EMP cost table to the Bill of Quantities (BoQ) could also be made and similar cross-references from the EMP could be provided in the Drawings Volume of the bid documents, if the drawings are included in the EMP. In this manner, the EMP could be integrated with the Contract, the Technical Specifications, the Bill of Quantities, and the Drawings that together form the bid documents for a project.
- The tremendous pressure on the contractors to meet deadlines of the project together with the fact that enforcement of legal requirements or guidelines is weak, leaves little room for adoption of good management practices. In this context, a World Bank review team felt that linking the contractor's environmental performance with their payments is possibly the only solution. It also noted that some implementing agencies have tried this approach [for example, the Third National Highway Project (THNP), Package IV D] with a creditable degree of success. Given the above, linking contractors' payments with environmental performance could be formalized and implemented across projects and sectors.[38]
- The incorporation in Contract and Bid documents of some of the good practices being adopted today for similar projects is also one approach that could be taken forward. For example, bidders for India's

[37] Sandhu et al. (2006).

[38] The World Bank review team, however, felt that 'this should only be done in extreme cases and should not be misused by the client. The triggers for holding back or delaying payments to contractors due to non-performance on environment and social issues have to be clearly laid out.' See Sandhu et al. (2006).

Ultra Mega Power-generation Projects (UMPPs), which are evaluated on the basis of tariff, have opted for super critical boilers with commercial finance. This could be made mandatory for all thermal power projects in future.

- To the best knowledge of the author, there are no major examples from projects across sectors where an evaluation of anticipated/unanticipated environmental impacts, an evaluation of the EMP or its implementation in the execution and completion of the project has been carried out. This needs to be made mandatory under the Contract and Bid documents if environmental considerations are to be mainstreamed in the entire project cycle.
- Finally, 'Project Financing' can also serve as a driver for ensuring responsible industrial behaviour for low carbon economy. Lenders can specifically mandate adherence to best practices and norms on socially inclusive and environmentally sound practices as conditions precedent to financial closure and can tie up these at various stages with the 'pre- and post-loan triggers'. They may make sure that through such conditions, adherence to such best practices and norms is diligently observed by the project proponent for the project's entire life-cycle. The standards and guidelines of the multilateral donor institutions such as the World Bank and the Asian Development Bank (ADB) on project financing for infrastructure projects may also provide useful guidance to the lenders in this regard.

Sub-optimal Framework Pointing to Legal and Regulatory Reforms for a Low Carbon Future

The policies and regulations produced by governments for a low carbon future in the context of infrastructure projects are only as good as the government that issues them. It is thus critical to look beyond the policy statements and legal commitments as to how they translate into practice. From the discussion in the preceding sections above, it is evident that there are gaps in the legal and regulatory framework as well as challenges in implementation and compliance of the provisions. Legal and regulatory reforms are imperative for providing the desired framework for achieving low carbon infrastructure development, as well as ensuring effective compliance and implementation of the environmental protection mechanisms.

The sections above present the laws, policies, and regulations put in place for promoting energy conservation and renewable energy. However, *the lack of single window clearance for Renewable Energy (RE) projects* is a major problem. There is a multitude of clearances that may be needed both at the central and state level and the developer loses valuable time and resources obtaining all the clearances. The costs involved in this make some of the smaller projects unviable. This is partly due to the fact that while India has a dedicated Union Ministry for renewable energy, most states have different policies regarding RE projects. It is also that the *states are in varying stages of preparedness* in terms of developing robust law, policy, and institutional mechanisms to promote renewable energy. Notwithstanding the set of various policies, the RE sector is also constrained by *implementation capacity of the nodal agencies*. It is necessary to enhance the capability of states, especially in the implementation of renewable energy programmes. In addition to all of the above, there is a felt need for hard data on effective harnessing of the potential of renewable energy from all possible sources. For example, in the case of hydro-energy, there are hardly any databanks available on water flow from small streams and rivulets. This implies a huge risk for the project to be borne by the project developer alone.

One final point in regard to the regulatory framework for renewable energy projects may be made here. Today, with the exception of the Electricity Act, 2003 and more specifically, the New Tariff Policy, 2006 under the Act, which states that a minimum percentage of energy, as specified by the Regulatory Commission, is to be purchased from RE sources, there is no legally binding obligation facilitating the creation, transmission, and deployment of renewable energy to address the country's energy and environmental insecurity. India still does not have a Renewable Energy policy or a national law on the subject. However, there has been a draft policy statement on new and renewable energy in circulation since 2005 under which an exclusive and comprehensive policy on renewable energy has been proposed, aimed at raising renewable energy capacity to 100,000 MW by 2050, but so far the policy is far from inplementation.[39] In this context, the World Institute for Sustainable Energy, located in Pune, also rightly points out that 'although the power of appropriate legislation to bring about change is amply demonstrated by the Electricity Act, 2003—thus setting in motion a process of reform in the power sector—the Act addresses issues related to renewable power only marginally...

[39] The Draft Policy Statement is available at www.newenergyindia.org

Although the government is committed to promoting the use of renewable energy sources, the commitment is not backed by legislation; and it has remained confined to articulation of policy.'[40] It is also pertinent to note here that unlike the Electricity Act of 2003 that confines itself to generation, transition, and distribution of electricity, a new renewable energy law would necessarily address energy production from renewables in a holistic manner. The need for a national law is also there given that states in India are differently placed in terms of evolving legal and regulatory frameworks for renewable energy. An agreed national binding framework shall thus help encounter the problems due to existence of several state-level policies. The absence of a National Renewable Energy Policy or a National Law on the subject is especially glaring in the context of the fact that legislation for renewable energy has turned out to be a successful instrument in changing the process towards sustainable development in countries such as China, Taiwan, Australia, and Germany.[41]

The *efficacy and state of implementation* of some of the laws and regulations has been open to question. For example, under the Environment Impact Assessment Notification, 2006, the handing over of the responsibility of granting clearance to a large number of projects to the state governments without checks and counter-checks is questioned on the ground that in many instances, the state government is directly involved in seeking investments for the projects and this may potentially conflict with the need for independent environmental assessment of these projects. Exemption of a large number of projects falling under the specified thresholds from EIA has also been seriously questioned in the recent past. The EIA process also fails to differentiate high impact projects from others. Its 2006 Notification continues to be in a state of flux.[42] In order to tighten and monitor the environmental clearance conditions laid down for companies, the MoEF recently constituted a special supervising committee, which 'will adopt a holistic approach to critically examine the issues pertaining to monitoring of environmental clearance issued under the Environment Impact Assessment (EIA) Notification, 2006.'[43]

When it comes to implementation of legislations such as the Air Act of 1981, discussed above, there are again some deep-seated problems. Most SPCBs in the country will find it difficult to produce even a handful of cases where the violators of the standards under the Act have been successfully prosecuted. A Planning Commission evaluation of the 25 SPCBs in the country in 2002 found out that the State Boards are generally dominated by non-technical members. Availability of staff for monitoring a certain number of polluting industrial units is variable. The field formations of State Pollution Control Boards (SPCBs) are not commensurate with the task at hand.[44] The study also found that non-installation of abatement mechanisms by the polluting units is a direct consequence of the absence of any effective punitive and deterrent mechanism in case of non-compliance. SPCBs, being understaffed, is thus a big part of the problem, but a larger legal problem is that the Air Act, 1981 and in fact all the environmental legislations and regulations in India are currently underpinned only by the use or threat of criminal sanctions. Yet, *criminal prosecution is too rigid an approach* to be used for all but the most serious offences. It focuses on achieving punishment rather than prevention, and requires more stringent procedural safeguards, which undermine regulatory efficiency. The problems in pursuing criminal prosecution of environmental offenders also give rise to reluctance on the part of regulatory agencies to pursue more difficult cases.

There is increasing recognition of the benefits of *employing civil penalties* as part of an effective system of regulation. In other countries, environmental regulatory agencies have the power to impose civil penalties for breaches of environmental regulation, as an additional tool to criminal enforcement, which can then be reserved for intentional non-compliance with the law. Civil

[40] The Institute adds: 'The barriers to the development of renewable energy run across a wide spectrum. Comprehensive legislation aimed at removing these barriers and accelerating the development of renewable energy technologies is thus necessary.' See http://www.wisein.org

[41] Another forceful approach is to include renewable energy in sectoral laws like in building codes. For example, UK's building regulations concentrate on energy conservation. In other countries, such as Greece or Israel, there are requirements that new housing should have solar collectors for water heating. See for some such examples, Godfrey (ed.) 2004.

[42] In a proposed set of controversial amendments to the 2006 EIA notification, the centre was considering doing away with the need to seek additional clearance for expansion and modernization, whereby a project authority would be given a 'self-certification option'.

[43] *Committee to Monitor Environmental Clearance for Companies*, 28 December 2009, *Indian Express*.

[44] Planning Commission (2002). This study was taken up at the instance of Planning Commission, with a primary objective of understanding the functioning of the SPCBs and their efficacy in controlling water and air pollution, finding out the efficacy of functional tools employed by them in carrying out their objectives and identifying the constraints to their effective functioning.

penalties can be imposed at the discretion of a regulatory agency for an amount which reflects the circumstances of the regulatory breach, including any financial profits gained from such a breach. They can be used as an alternative rather than a replacement for criminal prosecution, but without the same degree of moral condemnation or administrative burden as the latter. The legal basis for such an approach as the 'Polluter Pays Principle' has been repeatedly held by the Supreme Court of India as part of the law of the land. It is important that amendments be introduced in the pollution legislation, including the 1981 Air Act, to provide for specific legal provisions for imposition of environmental damages/environmental civil liability.

It is also noteworthy that while there are environmental, pollution prevention, and forest conservation laws for two–three decades now in India, the regulatory framework has little support, specifically for low carbon projects. Thus, for example, Compensatory Afforestation is only for diversion of forest land for a project under the Forest (Conservation) Act, 1980 but there is no mandate for such compensatory afforestation even when large-scale diversion of revenue land is involved for mega projects. Another example is that there are no incentives for installation of Common Effluent Treatment Plants (CETPs), and in most high profile projects where CETPs have come through, they have come only under Court Orders. Besides, there are growing reports of legal and foreign exchange bottlenecks that prevent full realization of registered CDM projects suggesting revisiting of Taxation and Foreign Exchange Rules to strategically facilitate such projects.

Finally, economic instruments such as *economic taxes* on energy inefficient/polluting vehicles, tax credits for energy-efficient buildings, differential taxation for appliances, and creation of markets for energy-saving certificates among large firms can all help in achieving energy efficiency gains. Notably, the MoEF had recently requested the Madras School of Economics (MSE) to recommend proposals for eco-taxes on polluting inputs and outputs. One of the main recommendations of the report that followed was that there was no legal obstacle to levying eco-taxes and that they can be part of the budget.[45] The MSE also made it clear that the tax departments have the information base and capability to levy such eco-taxes. Both from the standpoint of legal validity and administrative viability, eco-tax could be explored and introduced. Policies and regulations need to reflect and support such approaches more before time runs out.

References

Chelliah, R.J., P.P. Appasamy, U. Sankar, and R. Pandey (2007). *Ecotaxes on Polluting Inputs and Outputs*, Academic Foundation, New Delhi.

'Committee to Monitor Environmental Clearance for Companies', *Indian Express*, 28 December 2009, Mumbai.

Esty, B. (2004). *Modern Project Finance: A Casebook*, John Wiley and Sons, Inc., New Jersey.

Ghosh, Pradipto (2009). *Climate Change: Perspectives from India*, UNDP, India. Report of the First Policy Consultation Forum of the Seoul Initiative on Green Growth on 'Promoting Sustainable Infrastructure Development' (2006). United Nations Economic and Social Commission for Asia and the Pacific, Bangkok, Thailand.

Godfrey, Boyle (ed.) (2004). *Renewable Energy*, Oxford University Press, USA.

Hoffman, S.L. (2001). *Law and Business of International Project Finance: A Resource for Governments, Sponsors, Lenders, Lawyers, and Project Participants*, Kluwer Law International, The Netherlands.

Ministry of Environment and Forests (2010). *India: Taking on Climate Change-Post Copenhagen Domestic Actions*, 30 June 2010, Government of India, New Delhi.

'National Green Tribunal Soon,' 25 January 2010, *Hindustan Times*, New Delhi.

Planning Commission, (2002). *Evaluation Study of the Functioning of the State Pollution Control Boards,* Government of India Publications, New Delhi.

Sandhu, S.C., Mridual Singh, Tapas Paul, S.Vaideeswaran, and R. Vishwanathan (2006). *Management of Environmental and Social Issues in Highway Projects in India*, World Bank, Washington DC.

Silbey, S.S. (1997). 1996 Presidential Address: 'Let Them Eat Cake: Globalization, Postmodern Colonialism, and the Possibilities of Justice', *Law and Society Review*, 31(2), pp. 207 and 209.

Upadhyay. Videh (2007). *Public Interest Litigation in India: Concepts, Cases, Concerns*, Lexis Nexis Butterworths, India, New Delhi.

[45] Chelliah et al. (2007) and Silbey (1997).

List of Court Cases Referred

Centre for Public Interest Litigation v. *Union of India,* 78(1999) DLT 389.

Indian Council for Enviro Legal Action v. *Union of India,* (1996) 3 SCC 212.

Karajan Jalasay Yojana Assargrasth Shakhar Ane Sangharsh Samiti v. *Gujarat,* AIR 1987 SC 532.

M.C. Mehta v. *Union of India,* (1996) 4 SCC 750.

M.C. Mehta v. *Union of India,* (2002) 4 SCC 356.

M.C. Mehta v. *Union of India,*(1992) 3 SCC 256.

M.C. Mehta v. *Union of India,* (1997) 2 SCC 411.

Narmada Bachao Andolan v. *Union of India,* AIR 2000 SC 3751.

S. Jagannath v. *Union of India,* (1997) 2 SCC 87.

The Society for Protection of Silent Valley v. *Union of India* (Unreported).

Tehri Bandh Virodhi Sangharsh Samiti v. *State of UP* 1992 SUPP (1) SCC 44.

The Goa Foundation and Anr. v. *The Konkan Railway Corporation and Others,* AIR 1992 BOM 471.

Vellore Citizens' Welfare Forum v. *Union of India,* (1997) 2 SCC 87.

Vineet Kumar Mathur v. *Union of India,* (1996) 7 SCC 714.

2 Low Carbon Path for Meeting the Electricity Needs of the People

Role of Regulatory Commissions

Pramod Deo and Vijay M. Deshpande

Introduction

Even though India has been listed as the fourth largest emitter of carbon dioxide (CO_2) in the world in 2007, with approximately 1.324 billion tonnes of CO_2 emissions,[1] its per capita emission, at 1.18 tonnes, stood well below the world average of 4.38 tonnes per capita. Further, India's CO_2 intensity of 0.33 kg per unit of gross domestic product (GDP) in terms of purchasing power parity (PPP) was below the world average of 0.47 kg per unit of GDP (US$ 2000).[2] Studies[3] have shown that, even if GDP were to grow at an aggressive rate over the next two decades, and even if developed countries were to achieve emission reduction by 25–40 per cent, India's per capita emission will be well below the average of the developed countries. So, in absolute terms, India's emission in 2031 would be comparable with the 2007 emission levels of countries such as China and the United States of America.

Recognizing its vulnerability to the consequences of climate change, India has voluntarily decided to reduce its emission intensity (emissions per unit of GDP) by 20–5 per cent of the 2005 level by the year 2020. This proactive step of an unbinding commitment to reduce emissions' intensity helps strengthen India's position as a responsible country. Besides, such a voluntary target helps in successfully defining goal-oriented initiatives for a sustained reduction in emissions' intensity.

Power Sector: Major Contributor of CO_2 Emissions

Approximately 80 to 82 per cent of electricity production in India comes from fossil fuels (Table 2.1). Of these, coal is the dominant fuel, followed by gas. This means that power generation is a major source of CO_2 emissions. Using Central Electricity Authority's (CEA's) weighted average emission factor[4] of 0.82 kg of CO_2 emission per kWh (unit) of electricity generation in India, the level of CO_2 emission from electricity generation is estimated to stand at 585–90 million tonnes per year.

Figure 2.1 shows levels of greenhouse gas (GHG) emissions from the power sector, as compared to the total emissions in India in 2007 without land use, land-

[1] Emissions referred to here denote CO_2 emissions from fuel combustion, International Energy Agency (2009: 52). The recent publication, Ministry of Environment and Forests (2010) puts the estimate at 1.728 billion tonnes of CO_2 emissions in 2007, and per capita emission is estimated at 1.5 tonnes per annum.

[2] Figures quoted here are from International Energy Agency (2009: 47–57). The GDP figures are in constant US$ terms with 2000 as the base year.

[3] Ministry of Environment and Forests (2009).

[4] The emission factor is defined as average CO_2 emitted per unit of electricity generated in the grid. The latest value comes from the CEA (2009a).

TABLE 2.1 Share of Different Fossil Fuels in Total Electricity Generation in India

Type of Generation	*Generation in Million kWh for 2009–10*	*Generation in Million kWh for 2008–9*	*Generation in Million kWh for 2007–8*
Coal	514757	480365	453014
Lignite	24769	22134	23713
Multi-Fuel	457	10029	10036
Gas Turbine/Combined Cycle Gas Turbine	96651	72865	68931
Diesel	4243	4709	3297
Total Fossil Fuel	640877	590101	558990
Total Generation**	766193	717895	699191
Fossil Fuel Generation as % of Total Generation	83.64	82.20	79.90

Notes: ** Domestic generation only, excludes imports from Bhutan.
Source: CEA (2009b and 2010) (Figures have been rounded off).

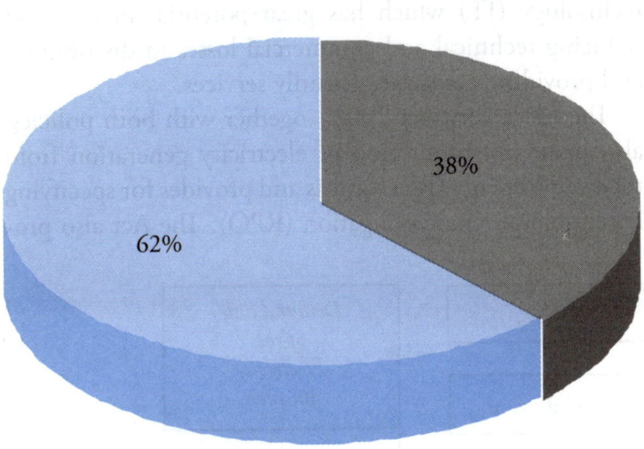

FIGURE 2.1 India: GHG Emissions in Million tonnes of CO_2 Equivalent in 2007

Source: Ministry of Environment and Forest (2010: Table ES1).

use change, and forestry (LULUCF).[5] It is seen that, in percentage terms, GHG emissions from the power sector constituted about 37.8 per cent of India's overall GHG emissions without LULUCF. Thus, any CO_2 emission mitigation strategy in India must pay special heed to the power sector.

Poverty Alleviation and Meeting Minimum Electricity Needs: Implications for CO_2 Emissions

The Indian economy needs to maintain a steady growth rate of eight to nine per cent per annum over the next 20 to 23 years, if it is to liberate the 450 million people currently having incomes less than Rs 60 per day from extreme poverty. Further, electricity being a vital component of infrastructure and a necessity of modern life, its availability will also have to be increased concomitantly with economic growth. As of today, there are approximately 400 million people in India with little or no access to electricity.

The Integrated Energy Policy Report (IEPR) of the Planning Commission estimates that to support and sustain eight to nine per cent economic growth rate over the next 20 to 23 years and to meet the minimum electricity needs of its populace, India's electricity generation capacity will have to increase by five to six times—from about 725 billion units and 166,000 MW in 2009 to 3600 billion units and 800,000 MW in 2031–2, respectively. Given India's energy resource endowment, however, most of the additional capacity generation will have to come from fossil fuels, mainly coal, which in turn would lead to increased levels of CO_2 emissions. At today's weighted average emission factor, this could translate into about 2.952 billion tonnes of CO_2 emissions due to power generation activity in 2031–2.

Measures to Reduce CO_2 Emissions from the Power Sector

The main stages in an electricity cycle[6] are depicted in Figure 2.2, along with a stage-wise depiction of a broad set of initiatives that are either being undertaken or could be undertaken to reduce carbon emissions from power generation and use. While initiatives under 'D'

[5] Ministry of Environment and Forest (2010).
[6] Although system operations form an important part of the overall electricity business, in the present context, this has not been included in the figure.

to 'H' can bring about reduction in generation or in the rate of growth of generation,[7] initiatives under 'B' and 'C' reduce the share of fossil fuels in electricity generation. Initiatives under 'A' result in improving the conversion efficiency of fossil fuel-based electricity generating plants. Thus, although the manner in which they achieve emission reduction differs, all initiatives have the potential to reduce emissions from electricity generation and its use.

Reduction of CO_2 Emissions from the Power Sector: Role of Regulatory Commissions

The Electricity Act, 2003 (EA, 2003) together with the National Electricity Policy (NEP), and the Tariff Policy (TP), provide the necessary regulatory and legal framework for implementation of almost all sets of initiatives mentioned in Figure 2.2. The 2003 Act mandates formulation of both the policies mentioned above for development of a power system based on optimal utilization of energy resources. It also envisages tariff interventions to encourage competition, efficiency, economical use of resources, good performance, and optimum investments. All this, together with the mandate for the regulators to provide for a multi-year tariff regime with emphasis on performance-based regulation of supply side, is proving to be instrumental in enhancing supply efficiency. The National Electricity Policy envisions that efficient technologies such as super critical technology, Integrated Gasification Combined Cycle (IGCC), and large-size units would be gradually introduced for electricity generation for their efficiency and cost-effectiveness. Further, it provides that cost-effective technologies need to be developed for high voltage power flows over long distances to minimize transmission losses. The National Electricity Policy also provides for greater application of information technology (IT) which has great potential in terms of reducing technical and commercial losses in distribution and providing consumer-friendly services.

The Electricity Act 2003, together with both policies, also mandates promotion of electricity generation from renewable energy (RE) sources and provides for specifying renewable purchase obligation (RPO). The Act also pro-

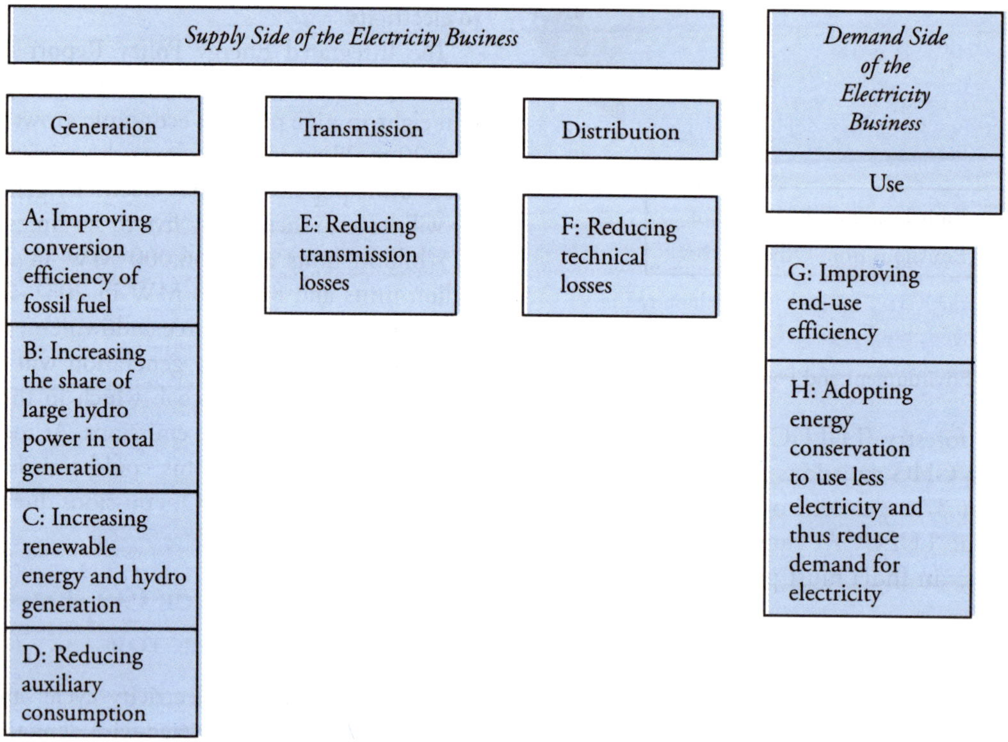

Figure 2.2 Typical Electricity Cycle

Source: Authors' own notes.

[7] Normally, where there are no power cuts, initiatives under 'D' to 'H' will lead to reduction in generation to meet a given load. However, in India, because there are shortages, initiative from 'D' to 'H', depending on when or where they operate, will either reduce generation or the rate of growth of generation.

vides for development of the power market and increase in competition, which in turn would improve efficiency on the supply side. On the demand side, though the Act does not directly mandate energy efficiency (EE) and energy conservation (EC), the NEP and the TP do emphasize upon efficiency in the use of electricity by consumers.

While the Electricity Act 2003 and the policies mentioned above provide the framework for the stakeholders to reduce CO_2 emission, enforcement of regulatory provisions and implementation of initiatives are the key to bringing about reduction in CO_2 emissions and their intensity in the power sector. It is the CERC and the SERCs which, by virtue of their regulatory jurisdiction, are and will remain the main drivers of India's efforts towards a low carbon-intensive power sector.

On the demand side, experiences of several countries in the world suggest that, at the ground level, it is the distribution entities which have been more successful in planning and implementing initiatives for reduction of CO_2 emissions such as 'G' and 'H' mentioned earlier. Thus, once again, the regulatory commissions, more particularly the SERCs, emerge in the role of real drivers in terms of efforts to reduce carbon intensity. An overview of the existing and planned future regulatory efforts for reducing the carbon intensity is given below.

Improving Generation Efficiency

Improving efficiency of fossil fuel-based power generation is an important way to reduce emissions from power generation. The type and quality of coal used as well as operating parameters such as excess air, make-up water consumption, condenser vacuum, secondary fuel consumption, fuel gases' temperature, steam parameters, plant load factor, and others affect the station heat rate (SHR, that is, efficiency of operation) of the thermal power plant. Whether the plant is being operated as a base load or a peaking plant also has a bearing on the operating efficiency of thermal power plants. Operating at consistently higher loads, more near the maximum continuous rating, results in the most efficient operation of the plant.

Scope for Further Improvement in Efficiency of Electricity Generation from Existing Thermal Power Plants

A Central Electricity Authority[8] review of performance of thermal power stations in India for 2007–8 shows that the pan-India weighted average operating SHR is 13.76 per cent higher than the weighted average design SHR. Similarly, an International Energy Agency (IEA) information study of July 2008[9] shows that the average efficiency of coal plants in India for 2001–5 was 27 per cent, among the lowest in the world (world average is 34 per cent). These studies demonstrate that ample scope exists for improvement in the efficiency of electricity generation from thermal power plants in India, and in the heat rate in particular.

Control and Monitoring of Efficiency in Existing Thermal Power Plants

The Central Electricity Regulatory Commission (CERC) and the SERCs have prescribed norms for SHR and secondary fuel consumption for fossil fuel-based thermal power plants under their respective regulatory jurisdictions. The tariffs payable to the generating units are fixed by the regulators after taking into consideration the prescribed norms. The profitability of the generating entities is thus linked to the achievement of the specified norms. Generating stations are prescribed a gradual, improving trajectory through progressively tighter norms every year. Usually, such trajectories are prescribed over the multi-year tariff horizon of five years. Table 2.2 shows the norms prescribed by CERC in 2009 as compared to its 2004 Regulation.

Table 2.2 Norms for Gross SHR Values in CERC (Terms and Conditions of Tariff) Regulations, 2004 and 2009

Description	*Unit Size*	*Gross Station Heat Rate: 2004 Regulation (kcal/kWh)*	*Gross Station Heat Rate: 2009 Regulation (kcal/kWh)*
Existing Thermal Power Plants	200/210/250 MW	2550	2500
Existing Power Plants	500 MW sub-critical technology	2450	2425
Badarpur Thermal Power Plant	–	2925	2825
Talcher Thermal Power Plant	–	3100	2950
Tanda Thermal Power Plant	–	3000	2825

Source: CERC (2004; 2009a).

[8] CEA (2008).
[9] IEA (2008).

In the case of secondary fuel consumption, the Central Electricity Regulatory Commission has slashed the norms from two millilitre (ml) per unit in its (Terms and Conditions of Tariff) Regulations, 2004 to one ml per unit in the (Terms and Conditions of Tariff) Regulations, 2009 (CERC 2009 Regulations). Similar trends are generally seen in respect of heat rate and secondary fuel consumption norms prescribed by the various SERCs.

Efficiency of New Plants

As mentioned above, given the projection for increase in India's energy requirements over the next 20 to 23 years and its energy-resource endowment, most of the increase in energy generation capacity will be coal-based. It, therefore, makes immense sense to ensure that the new capacity coming on stream is inherently efficient. In this context, the CEA has recommended a choice of more efficient super-critical technology with design heat rates in the region of 2079 to 2176 kcal/kWh.[10] It is envisaged that super-critical technology would result in 60 per cent and 90 per cent of the total capacity addition during the Twelfth Plan (2012–17) and Thirteenth Plan (2017–22) periods respectively. Presently, 31 super-critical units of 660–800 MW size are under construction, including all ultra mega power projects with all units based on the efficient super-critical technology.

Recognizing the importance of ensuring that new plants coming on stream are inherently efficient, CERC has provided stringent norms for design SHR for new plants in its 2009 Regulation (Table 2.3).

Reducing Auxiliary Consumption

Auxiliary[11] consumption values in Indian power plants are in the range of eight to 13 per cent for coal and lignite-based plants, zero to one per cent for hydrostations and one to three per cent for gas-based stations. Reduction in auxiliary consumption would mean increase in electricity supply for consumers, and thus reduced levels of emission on a given consumer load. The CERC and SERCs, in consultation with the CEA, have prescribed norms for auxiliary consumption for generating units (see Table 2.4). These norms are used in tariff determination by regulators and are thus linked to the profitability of the generating entities.

Harnessing Full Development of Hydro Potential

Hydroelectricity is a clean and renewable source of energy. The National Electricity Policy emphasizes the need for the development of full hydro potential in the country, which is about 148,700 MW, and out of which approximately 33,000 MW (22 per cent) has been developed. During the Eleventh Plan (2007–12), about 6874 MW of hydro-capacity is expected to be commissioned, of which 3431 MW has been commissioned by the end of 2009. Additionally, benefits from about 6447 MW hydropower capacity are expected to be realized during the period 2012–17.

A 50,000 MW hydropower initiative has been launched under which pre-feasibility reports (PFRs) for

Table 2.3 CERC Design Heat Rates for Coal-based Generating Stations for Commercial Operations after April 2009

Type of Boiler Feed Pump Drive	*Pressure Rating Kg/cm²*	*Superheat/Reheat Temperature in°C (SHT/RHT)*	*Maximum Design Unit Heat Rate (kcal/kWh)*	
			Indian Sub-Bituminious Coal	*Bituminious Imported Coal*
Electrical-driven	150	535/535	2300	2197
Turbine-driven	170	537/537	2294	2191
Turbine-driven	170	537/565	2276	2174
Turbine-driven	247	537/565	2235	2135
Turbine-driven	247	565/593	2176	2079

Source: CERC (2009a).

[10] As compared to this, the weighted average design SHR of existing thermal power plants in 2007–8 was approximately 2,376 kcal/kWh.

[11] CERC (2009a) defines auxiliary energy consumption as 'in relation to a period in case of a generating station means the quantum of energy consumed by auxiliary equipment of the generating station, and transformer losses within the generating station, expressed as a percentage of the sum of gross energy generated at the generator terminals of all the units of the generating station.'

Table 2.4 Norms for Auxiliary Consumption Values in CERC (Terms and Conditions of Tariff) Regulations, 2004 and 2009

Description	*Unit Size*	*Auxiliary Consumption: 2004 Regulation (%)*	*Auxiliary consumption: 2009 Regulation (%)*
Existing Thermal Power Plants	200/210/250 MW	9.0	8.5
Existing Power Plants: 500 MW	Electrical-driven boiler feed pump	9.0	8.5
Existing Power Plants: 500 MW	Steam-driven boiler feed pump	7.5	6.0
Talcher Thermal Power Plant		11.0	10.5
Neyveli Lignite TPS-I		12.0	12.0
Neyveli Lignite TPS-II		10.0	10.0

Source: CERC (2004; 2009a).

162 projects of about 48,000 MW capacities have been prepared in 2004. The PFRs have been made available to the developers. As a follow-up to the PFRs, 78 schemes of 34,000 MW capacities have been identified as low tariff schemes, of which 77 schemes of about 33,950 MW have been taken up for preparation of detailed project reports/implementation.

The CERC has been facilitating the development of hydro projects in view of the huge potential and environmental benefits of hydropower. These projects involve larger capital investment, have long gestation periods, and are subject to uncertainties about availability of water. The CERC has developed a tariff structure to mitigate concerns regarding cash flow for project developers. A cost-plus approach has been adopted, with provisions ensuring recovery of their capacity cost, based on their availability for three hours in a day over the initial 10 years, thus insulating against hydrological risks. The Commission has also set up a task force on peak and off-peak tariffs for generating stations to assess whether there is merit in a higher tariff for supply during peak periods when the value of electricity is the highest. A positive recommendation from the task force will pave the way for providing an incentive to hydro power generation, as storage-type hydro generation essentially caters to peak demand. On the other hand, the GoI has formulated the New Hydro Policy of 2008, wherein the private sector has been exempted from tariff-based bidding up to January 2011. Also, merchant sale up to 40 per cent of saleable energy has been allowed. One per cent additional free power from the project for local area development has been allowed to be accounted for in tariff determination.

Transmission Distribution and Loss Reduction

Transmission Loss Reduction

Overall, technical losses in the transmission system are generally low and varying across states in the range of four to five per cent. At the national level, inter-regional connectivity has been planned with hybrid systems, consisting of High Voltage Direct Current (HVDC), ultra high voltage AC (765 kV), and extra high voltage AC (400 kV) lines. The ultra high voltage systems, which enable significant reduction in transmission losses, can be built to cater to pre-fixed loads of large size. This always leaves a possibility of a certain part of the line capacity remaining unutilized for some time as transmission systems of high capacity need to be planned and executed in advance and the load growth follows. To facilitate construction of such high voltage corridors, CERC has decided to fund the capital servicing of unutilized capacity from the amount available in the Unscheduled Interchange Pool Account.

Distribution Loss Reduction

The lower the distribution losses[12] the higher the proportion of generated electricity available for meeting consumers' demand, thus making it possible to meet their demands with lower CO_2 emissions. The total distribution losses of Distribution Companies (DISCOMs) comprise both technical losses and commercial losses. The technical losses are associated with thermal energy loss, and commercial losses include all other components of financial losses broadly comprising electricity thefts and metering errors.

[12] As explained subsequently, it is actually the technical loss part of the distribution losses that is more important from the CO_2 emissions perspective.

The all-India average Aggregate Technical and Commercial (ATC) loss is about 29 per cent, which includes billing and collection inefficiencies. Since losses have a significant bearing on the financial health of DISCOMs, SERCs set loss reduction trajectories for them to monitor the actual loss against the set target. They also determine tariffs chargeable by DISCOMs, taking cognizance of the regulator-specified loss trajectory (see Table 2.5). Thus, the profitability of DISCOMs is linked to achievement of the loss reduction targets. Incentives are also provided for exceeding the set targets in this regard.

Significance of Technical Losses from the Perspective of CO_2 Emissions

Reduction in carbon dioxide emissions happens when reduction of technical losses results in reduction in electricity generation requirement. Although reduction in commercial losses too can reduce electricity demand, it is not commensurate and cannot be estimated.[13] Although SERCs are rigorously pursuing reduction in distribution losses, only a few DISCOMs such as those in Mumbai have estimated technical losses, and these are evidence

Table 2.5 Approved Loss Targets for DISCOMS (2007–8 to 2009–10)

DISCOM	*Parameter*	*2007–8*	*2008–9*	*2009–10*
Andhra Pradesh				
APCPDCL	Distribution	18.90	16.90	15.90
APEPDCL	Distribution	17.10	15.80	15.10
APNPDCL	Distribution	19.90	18.00	17.10
APSPDCL	Distribution	17.30	15.90	14.90
Delhi				
BRPL	AT&C	31.10	26.69	23.46
BYPL	AT&C	39.95	34.77	30.52
NDPL	AT&C	31.10	22.03	20.35
Gujarat				
DGVCL	Distribution	19.90	15.59	14.45
MGVCL	Distribution	21.60	21.09	15.00
PGVCL	Distribution	36.50	30.22	30.00
UGVCL	Distribution	25.10	16.95	16.00
Haryana				
UHBVNL	Distribution	30.50	28.50	26.00
DHBVNL	Distribution	30.50	28.50	26.00
Himachal Pradesh	T&D	18.50	17.50	15.75
Karnataka				
BESCOM	Distribution	20.50	21.35	20.40
CESC	Distribution	22.00	24.10	23.10
GESCOM	Distribution	27.05	31.00	30.50
HESCOM	Distribution	25.00	25.00	24.00
MESCOM	Distribution	15.00	16.15	16.05

(contd.)

[13] As regards commercial losses, it is important to note that electricity is being consumed but is not billed and paid for either because it is stolen or the meter is faulty. In such situations, when a commercial loss reduction initiative is launched, it does not eliminate the consumption that was happening before. At best, it reduces the consumption as it now has to be paid for.

Table 2.5 (*contd.*)

DISCOM	*Parameter*	*2007–8*	*2008–9*	*2009–10*
Kerala	T&D	20.45	19.55	17.92
Madhya Pradesh				
MPPKVVC (East)	T&D	34.50	32.50	29.50
MPPaKVVC (West)	T&D	30.00	28.50	27.00
MPMKVVC (Central)	T&D	43.00	40.00	37.00
Maharashtra				
MSEDCL	T&D	34.97	31.70	22.50
TPC	T&D	2.93	2.93	2.93
R Infra	T&D	11.52	11.50	10.75
BEST	T&D	11.50	11.00	10.50
Punjab	T&D	20.75	19.50	19.50
Rajasthan				
Ajmer	T&D	34.08	35.00	32.00
Jaipur	T&D	29.51	28.50	23.90
Jodhpur	T&D	31.29	33.00	30.00
Uttar Pradesh				
Agra	T&D	29.10	29.10	29.10
Lucknow	T&D	22.40	22.40	22.40
Meerut	T&D	29.10	29.10	29.10
Varanasi	T&D	26.70	26.70	26.70
Uttarakhand	AT&C	30.17	24.32	22.32
West Bengal				
CESC Limited	Distribution	15.75	15.36	15.11
DPL	Distribution	6.50	6.50	6.10
DPSC Limited	Distribution	5.74	5.60	5.54
WBSEDCL	Distribution	23.00	19.53	18.75

Source: Forum of Regulators (2009).

enough for the extent of reduction in electricity generation that is possible through technical loss reduction. From the CO_2 emissions perspective, therefore, it is clear that SERCs must order the DISCOMs under their jurisdiction to initiate steps to estimate technical losses and, based on these estimates, draw up a technical loss reduction trajectory.

Emission Reduction via Efficiency Improvement through Distribution Franchisees

The EA, 2003 introduced 'franchisee' as a person authorized by a distribution licensee to distribute electricity on its behalf in a particular area within his area of supply without a separate licence from the concerned SERC. Wherever such franchise arrangements are in operation, there has been remarkable improvement in distribution efficiency. Under this scheme, the distribution licensee supplies electricity to the franchisee on payment of a power supply charge committed in the franchise agreement. The committed input rate reflects the franchisee's commitment to improve distribution efficiency, including reduction in ATC losses in the franchise area. The revenue from the sale of electricity in the franchised area is retained by the franchisee, which serves as a source of payment to the distribution licensee as well as for carrying out business in the franchise area. The franchisee is able to improve efficiency, resulting in higher availability of electricity to consumers from the same input energy, thus demonstrating the potential to significantly reduce carbon emissions by supplying the required electricity to consumers out of a much lower level of input energy.

The franchisee model is in operation in few franchise areas in the country and has been particularly successful in Bhiwandi in Maharashtra, where in the first two years of franchise, the franchisee has been able to reduce the ATC losses from 63 per cent in 2006–7 to 19 per cent in 2008–9. This is a real success story.

Considering its potential for increasing distribution efficiency and concomitantly reduction of carbon emissions, the Forum of Regulators (FoR) has in May 2010, commissioned a study for preparing a 'standard model for the distribution franchisee'.

Increasing Renewable Energy-based Generation

Renewable energy sources reduce the share of fossil fuel-based generation and thus contribute directly to the reduction of carbon emissions. During the year 2008–9, RE-based generation was about 3.5 per cent of the total generation in the country—generated from grid-connected RE capacity of about 13,242 MW. In line with the provisions of the 2003 Act, and the directions contained in the TP and the NEP, CERC and SERCs have been promoting the use of renewable sources for grid-connected electricity generation. There are also instances of regulators promoting the use of renewable energy to substitute for grid-connected electricity in some uses. For example, the Karnataka Electricity Regulatory Commission (KERC), through its tariff orders, has incentivized the use of solar

Box 2.1
Promotion of RE-based Generation: Relevant Provisions from Electricity Act 2003 and Tariff Policy

- The preamble of the EA, 2003 states that one of its important objects is promotion of *efficient* and *environmentally benign* policies relating to generation, transmission, distribution, trading, and use of electricity
- Section 86 (1) of the Electricity Act 2003 states that the State Commission shall discharge the following functions, namely:
  - *(e) promote co-generation and generation of electricity from renewable sources of energy by providing suitable measures for connectivity with the grid and sale of electricity to any person, and also specify, for purchase of electricity from such sources, a percentage of the total consumption of electricity in the area of a distribution licensee;*
- Section 61 of the EA, 2003 states that the appropriate Commission shall, subject to the provisions of this Act, specify the terms and conditions for the determination of tariff, and in doing so, shall be guided by the following, namely:
  - *(h) the promotion of cogeneration and generation of electricity from renewable sources of energy;*
- Section 3(1) of the EA, 2003 states: 'The Central Government shall, from time to time, prepare the NEP and Tariff Policy, in consultation with the state governments and the authority for development of the power system based on optimal utilization of resources such as coal, natural gas, nuclear substances or materials, hydro, and renewable sources of energy.' *(emphasis added)*
- Section 4 of the EA, 2003, regarding policy for stand-alone systems, states that:
  - 'The Central Government shall, after consultation with the state governments, prepare and notify a national policy, permitting stand-alone systems (including those based on renewable sources of energy and non-conventional sources of energy) for rural areas.'
- Section 6.4 of the Tariff Policy recognizes that it will take some time before non-conventional technologies can compete with conventional sources in terms of cost of electricity, and therefore, states that the procurement of electricity from non-conventional energy sources by distribution companies shall be done at preferential tariffs determined by the Appropriate Commission. The section further states that:
  - Pursuant to provisions of section 86(1)(e) of the Act, the Appropriate Commission shall fix a minimum percentage for purchase of energy from such sources, taking into account availability of such resources in the region and its impact on retail tariffs. Such percentage for purchase of energy should be made applicable for the tariffs to be determined by the SERCs at the latest by 1 April 2006.
  - Such procurement by distribution licensees for future requirements shall be done, as far as possible, through a competitive bidding process under Section 63 of the Act, within suppliers offering energy from same type of non-conventional sources. In the long term, these technologies would need to compete with other sources in terms of full costs.
  - The Central Commission should lay down guidelines within three months for pricing non-firm power, especially from non-conventional sources, to be followed in cases where such procurement is not through competitive bidding.

water heaters by providing a monthly rebate of Rs 50 to 80 in the electricity bills of all domestic consumers using solar water heaters on a regular basis.

Electricity Act, 2003 and Promotion of Renewable Energy-based Power Generation

The real impetus to renewable energy for power generation was provided by the 2003 Act. Prior to the Act, RE-based power generation was mainly being developed through private investments by prescribing fixed tariffs for renewable energy (along with annual escalation rates) and allowing banking and wheeling of power thus generated. These attempts, however, achieved mixed results, as prior to the Act, no specific legal provisions existed to make purchase of renewable energy mandatory. The Act explicitly provides for the development and promotion of RE-based power generation (see Box 2.2 for details). The regulations, formulated by SERCs under the provisions of the Act, have helped to overcome barriers being faced by stakeholders. The promoters and investors in RE-based generating plants are now assured that their plants will be connected to the grid, and the electricity thus generated will be bought by the DISCOMs at a preferential tariff determined by the respective SERCs over the life of the plant. Similarly, bankers and financiers have better assurance that there is a ready market for the electricity generated by their clients. Also, the preferential tariffs with long-term validity have enabled promoters, investors, bankers, and financiers to estimate future cash flows and profits from the RE projects with greater certainty. On the other hand, this has also provided assurance to DISCOMs that power purchase cost from RE sources, which is more expensive than conventional power, will be allowed as a strategic pass-through in the annual revenue requirement of the DISCOMs.

Preferential Renewable Energy Tariffs

Following the provisions of the EA, 2003 and the Tariff Policy, several SERCs have come up with preferential tariffs (see Table 2.6), while SERCs in Orissa, Jammu and Kashmir, and Arunachal Pradesh are yet to specify preferential tariffs from RE sources.

Renewable Purchase Obligation (RPO)

Following the provisions of the Electricity Act, 2003 and the Tariff Policy, each DISCOM or the state as a whole is given, through Renewable Purchase Obligation (RPO), a mandate to ensure that a certain percentage of energy consumed comes from RE-based generation. Such targets are being issued by different SERCs, either as consolidated targets or as separate targets for each RE source such as biomass, wind, and small hydro power. The RPO targets

TABLE 2.6 Preferential Tariffs in Various States

(Rs per kWh)

State	*Wind*	*SHP**	*Biomass*	*Bagasse*	*Solar PV***	*Solar Thermal***
Andhra Pradesh	3.37	2.6	4.15	3.29	7	7
Gujarat	3.37	–	3.08	3	–	–
Himachal Pradesh	–	2.87	–	–	–	–
Haryana	4.08	3.67	4	3.74	15.96	
Karnataka	3.40	2.8	3.1	3.06	15.4	3.4+12
Madhya Pradesh	3.97	–	3.40	2.82		
Maharashtra	3.5	3	3.04	3.05	3+12	15
Rajasthan	3.65	–	4.48	–	15.7	
Tamil Nadu	3.39	–	4.5	4.38	3.15	3.15
West Bengal	4	3.6	4	2.55	11	11
Punjab	4.04	3.81	4.04	3.81	–	–
Uttarakhand	–	3.25	–	2.33	–	–
Bihar	–	–	3.33	3.51	–	–
Chhattisgarh	–	–	3.05	–	–	–
Kerala	3.14	2.44	–	2.8	15.8	–

Notes: *Small hydro power; ** generation-based incentive, wherever applicable.
Source: Various tariff orders of SERCs.

have also been mandatory for open-access consumers as well as for captive consumers. Several states have come up with RPO targets for various RE sources (see Table 2.7). However, SERCs from Jharkhand and the north-eastern states are yet to issue RPO orders.

Renewable Energy-based Power Generation Capacity and Potential

India today has approximately 17,593 MW (on 30 June 2010) of RE-based generation capacity (Table 2.8). The national share of renewable energy in total installed generation capacity is approximately nine to 10 per cent and the share of RE generation in total generation is approximately 3.5 per cent. Almost 75 per cent of this capacity has come on stream in the past five to six years, thereby indicating the boost that has been provided to RE by the facilitative provisions of the 2003 Act and the subsequent policies and regulations. Although recent years have witnessed accelerated RE-based generation capacity addition, the current RE-based installed capacity is only eight per cent of the total RE potential (Table 2.8), which at the current commercially exploitable levels, is of the order of 183000 MW. Thus, there exists huge untapped potential to reduce the share of fossil fuels.

Emerging Challenges and Recent CERC and Forum of Regulators (FoR) Initiatives to Further Accelerate the Pace of RE Generation and Future Actions

The regulatory framework for the promotion and development of RE-based generation has been in place for the past five to six years and has thrown up the need for regulatory refinements to address challenges that have cropped up. The Forum of Regulators (FoR)[14] had set up a Working Group on renewable energy to provide guidelines, methodologies, and framework for its development. The working group[15] addressed issues pertaining to RPO percentage specification, pricing of renewable

Table 2.7 RPO as Specified by Tariff Orders of SERCs (as percentage of total sale of electricity)

State	*Source/Utility/DISCOM*	*RPO for the Year*					
		2006–7	*2007–8*	*2008–9*	*2009–10*	*2010–11*	*2011–12*
Andhra Pradesh		5	5	5			
Chhattisgarh	Biomass	–	–	5	5	5	
	Small hydro power	–	–	3	3	3	
	Others	–	–	2	2	2	
Delhi			1	1	1		
Gujarat		1	2	–	–	–	–
Haryana			3	5	10	10	10
Karnataka		10	10	10	–	–	–
Kerala		5	5	5	–	—	–
Madhya Pradesh				10	10	10	10
Maharashtra		3	4	5	6	–	–
Punjab			1	1	2	3	4
Rajasthan		2.5	4.88	6.25	7.45	8.5	9.5
Tamil Nadu		10	10	10			
Uttar Pradesh		7.5	7.5	7.5	7.5	7.5	
Uttarakhand			5	5	8	9	10
West Bengal	WBSEB			4.8	6.8	8.3	10
	CESC Limited			4	6	8	10
	DPL			2.5	4	7	10

Source: Various tariff orders.

[14] FoR is a statutory body constituted under Section 166 (2) of the EA, 2003 for harmonization, coordination, and ensuring uniformity of approach amongst regulatory commissions (CERC and SERCs) across the country.

[15] Forum of Regulators (2008).

Table 2.8 Installed RE-based Generation Capacity till 31 October 2009 and RE-based Generation Potential

Type of Generation	*Source*	*Achievement till (31.6.2010) (MW)*	*Overall Potential (MW)*
Grid Connected Power Generation	Bio-power	901	16881
	Wind power	12010	45195
	Small hydro power	2767	15000
	Cogeneration (bagasse)	1412	5000
	Waste to energy	72	7000
Sub-Total Grid Connected Capacity		17,162	133,000*
Distributed Generation	Solar power	12	50000
	Biomass	238	
	Biomass gassifier	125	
	Waste to energy	53	
	Solar PV power plants + street lights	3	
	Aero-generators/hybrid systems	1	
Sub-Total Distributed Generation Capacity	432	50000	
Total RE Based Generation Capacity	17593	183,000	

Note: * When additional potential of about 45,000 MW is considered from fuel wood plantations on 20 million hectares of wasteland, yielding woody biomass with calorific value of 4000 kcal/kg, and efficiency of 30 per cent and plant load factor of 75 per cent for biomass.

Source: Planning Commission, Eleventh Plan document and MNRE major achievements (available on MNRE web site: www.mnre.gov.in)

energy, incentives, and grid connectivity for RE-based generating units.

Variation in Preferential Tariffs across Different States

The preferential tariffs issued by various State Electricity Regulatory Commissions (SERCs) differ widely, as can be seen in Table 2.6. Such varying tariffs can create doubts in the minds of investors and financiers about returns from investing in RE-based generating plants. On 16 September 2009, drawing upon the provisions of Section 61 (a)[16] of the EA, 2003, the CERC issued a comprehensive regulation for tariff determination from RE sources (Renewable Tariff Regulation). This Regulation, besides defining norms, also provides guidance on the methodology for tariff determination with respect to RE-based generation from wind, solar, small hydropower, biomass, and non-fossil fuel-based co-generation for uniformity in preferential tariff computation process across different states.

The Central Electricity Regulatory Commission followed up its Regulation with a *suo moto* Order on 3 December 2009, which provides generic tariffs for RE technologies (see Table 2.9) determined in accordance with the norms and methodology clearly specified in the Renewable Tariff Regulation.

These tariffs are expected to serve as benchmarks and reference tariffs for various stakeholders at the state level, including SERCs. This Regulation also provides for CERC to determine the generic tariff on the basis of the *suo moto* petition at least six months in advance at the beginning of each year of the control period for RE technologies, thus allowing the Commission to capture advances in technology and its effects on generic tariffs, if any, for future projects only.[17]

Non-compliance with RPO Targets

In some states, DISCOMs have failed complying with or have been finding it difficult to meet the RPO targets. For example, as against an RPO[18] target of 10 per cent,

[16] Section 61(a) of the EA, 2003, which provides that the SERCs in determining tariffs for generating and transmission companies shall be guided by the principles and methodologies specified by the CERC.

[17] Tariff determined each year will have a validity period. Any RE-based generation coming on stream during the validity period will have the same levelized tariff, as is applicable for the period, throughout its life.

[18] Per cent of total energy consumed/sold in the state or by the DISCOM has to come from RE-based generation.

Table 2.9 Generic Tariffs for RE Technologies as Contained in CERC Order of 3 December 2009

RE Technology	*Zone/Region*	*Levelized Tariff (Rs/kWh) without tax incentives**	*Levelized Tariff (Rs/kWh) with tax incentives**
Wind	Wind Zone 1, Capacity utilization (CU) of 20%	5.63	5.26
	Wind Zone 2, CU of 23 %	4.90	4.58
	Wind Zone 3, CU of 27%	4.17	3.89
	Wind Zone 4, CU of 30%	3.75	3.50
Small Hydro Power	Himachal Pradesh, Uttarakhand, and North-eastern states (Below 5 MW)	3.90	3.67
	Himachal Pradesh, Uttarakhand, and North-eastern states (5 MW to 25 MW)	3.35	3.14
	Other states (below 5 MW)	4.62	4.35
	Other states (5–25 MW)	4.00	3.75
Solar PV	All India	18.44	17.14
Solar Thermal	All India	13.45	12.54
Biomass Power Plants	Andhra Pradesh	4.25	4.05
	Haryana	5.52	5.42
	Madhya Pradesh	3.93	3.83
	Maharashtra	4.76	4.66
	Punjab	5.49	5.39
	Rajasthan	4.73	4.63
	Tamil Nadu	5.08	4.98
	Uttar Pradesh	4.47	4.37
	Others	4.88	4.78
Non-Fossil Fuel- based Co-generation	Andhra Pradesh	4.93	4.78
	Haryana	5.78	5.65
	Madhya Pradesh	4.80	4.68
	Maharashtra	4.29	4.16
	Punjab	5.75	5.62
	Tamil Nadu	5.10	4.98
	Uttar Pradesh	5.21	5.06
	Others	5.17	5.04

Note: *Such as accelerated depreciation.
Source: CERC (2009).

in Madhya Pradesh and Chhattisgarh, the achievement is 0.11 per cent and 3.7 per cent respectively. In Maharashtra, the achievement is 3.17 per cent against the target of five per cent. Similarly, the achievement in Uttar Pradesh is 2.44 per cent against the target of 7.5 per cent. In Rajasthan, against a target of 9.5 per cent, the achievement is approximately 7.5 per cent. On the other side, there are also instances where the targets have been achieved or over-achieved. Tamil Nadu, Karnataka, and Punjab are some of the states which have either achieved the RPO targets or have exceeded them.

The inability of DISCOMs to meet the targets under RPO is often attributed to the fact that these targets are either too stiff to start with or are being ramped up over the years for it to be practically achievable. In some instances, these targets have not been in line with the potential and infrastructure available in the state.

The absence of disincentives for not meeting these targets is also one of the reasons for complacency.[19] In order to resolve the issue of the appropriate level of RPO targets for various states, FoR has commissioned a comprehensive study to estimate the RE generation potential

[19] CERC (2010).

(technology-wise) in various states. The study further assesses the impact of recommended RPO targets on the cost of power and tariffs in various states, provide guidance to SERCs, and will lead to setting up of realistic and achievable targets.

Incremental RE Capacity Additions Reaching a Plateau in the Past Two or Three Years

Having witnessed the initial burst in incremental capacity additions after the EA, 2003 was notified, incremental renewable energy power generation capacity seems to have reached a plateau. Thus, 430 MW of incremental RE capacity came up in 2002–3, 849 MW in 2003–4, 1366 MW in 2004–5, 2011 MW in 2005–6, and 2138 MW in 2006–7. Since then, however, the yearly incremental capacity has remained in the region of 2000–2200 MW. One reason cited for incremental renewable energy capacity reaching a plateau is that states who were aggressively promoting RE generation have achieved RPO targets (for example, Karnataka and Tamil Nadu) and in spite of exploitable renewable energy potential still left, neither the state governments nor the DISCOMs have enough incentive to continue purchasing costly RE power, as that increases the overall power cost, and consequently, the consumer tariffs. Table 2.10 shows average cost of power procurement for DISCOMs in various states. Although the average cost of power in one or two DISCOMs is comparable

TABLE 2.10 Average Cost of Power Procurement for Distribution Companies for 2005–6 to 2007–8

(Rs/kWh)

State	*DISCOM/Procurement Entity*	*2005–6*	*2006–7*	*2007–8*
Andhra Pradesh	APCPDCL	1.94	2.04	2.21
	APEPDCL	2.12	2.21	2.43
	APNPDCL	1.96	2.11	2.35
	APSPDCL	2.04	2.08	2.38
Assam	ASEB	1.84	2.04	1.84
	CAEDCL	1.74	1.93	3.04
	LAEDCL	2.21	2.37	3.42
	UAEDCL	2.42	2.64	3.14
Bihar	BSEB	1.79	1.82	2.01
Chhattisgarh	CSEB	0.72	0.78	0.99
Delhi	BRPL	2.17	2.31	2.83
	BYPL	1.71	1.88	2.62
	NDPL	2.11	2.19	2.70
Gujarat	DGVCL	3.02	3.18	3.22
	MGVCL	2.46	2.70	2.80
	PGVCL	1.59	1.95	2.17
	UGVCL	1.83	2.09	2.25
	GUVNL	2.11	2.36	2.60
Haryana	DHBVNL	2.05	2.37	2.92
	HPGCL	1.23	1.32	1.54
	UHBVNL	2.08	2.33	2.83
Himachal Pradesh	HSEB	1.73	1.95	2.13
Karnataka	BESCOM	2.14	2.47	2.65
	GESCOM	1.84	1.76	2.10
	HESCOM	1.90	1.81	1.97
	MESCON	2.06	2.41	2.42
	CESC	1.89	1.91	1.89

(contd.)

Table 2.10 (*contd.*)

State	*DISCOM/Procurement Entity*	*2005–6*	*2006–7*	*2007–8*
Kerala	KSEB	1.08	1.03	1.26
Maharashtra	MSEDCL	2.04	2.16	2.16
Madhya Pradesh	MPMKVVCL	1.74	1.92	1.91
	MPPaKVVCL	1.69	1.85	2.14
	MPPKVVCL	1.88	2.06	2.11
Orissa	CESCO	1.25	1.41	1.42
	GRIDCO	1.41	1.17	1.20
	NESCO	1.22	1.17	1.47
	SESCO	1.16	1.10	0.88
	WESCO	1.44	1.30	1.76
Punjab	PSEB	0.71	1.19	1.47
Rajasthan	AVVNL	2.09	2.17	2.68
	JDVVNL	2.15	2.18	2.61
	JVVNL	2.13	2.19	2.67
Tamil Nadu	TNEB	1.48	1.63	1.90
Uttar Pradesh	DVVNL	2.34	2.41	2.36
	MVVNL	2.08	2.41	2.55
	Paschim VVNL	2.34	2.41	2.55
	Poorvi VVNL	3.83	2.41	2.55
	UPPCL	2.09	2.12	2.22
	KESCO	2.33	2.40	2.55
West Bengal	WSEB/WSEDCL	1.86	1.85	2.22

Source: Extracted from Power Finance Corportion (2009).

to the generic tariffs of renewable energy power, the overall average cost of power in states are generally lower than generic RE tariffs.

Realizing that higher cost of renewable energy generation is the key impediment to further harnessing its large potential in states which have fulfilled their RPO targets despite it still remaining unexploited, both CERC and FoR initiated efforts to develop a mechanism that would combine the merits of instruments such as the RECs with the RPO to enable sharing of the economic burden of higher RE costs of electricity consumers in India, and not just consumers from the states who have this substantial potential. The efforts culminated in framing of CERCs REC Regulations, 2010 (see Box 2.2). This Regulation provides a mechanism whereby states having a relatively poor endowment of renewable energy resources, for example, Delhi, can meet their RPO targets by acquiring requisite levels or numbers of RECs from the market. In practice, the Regulation allows only the RE generators to own the RECs, whose level or number depends on the amount of renewable energy (in MWH terms) generated and injected. The DISCOMS from states such as Delhi, who want to fulfil their RPO targets, will have to acquire the RECs from the RE generators. The REC mechanism is such that the DISCOM actually absorbing this generation will not have to pay more than its liability to meet its own RPO target, even though it may be absorbing renewable energy power over and above its RPO target. The state or DISCOM is thus cost-neutral to the amount of generation taking place and being absorbed in the state by the DISCOMS. It is this aspect of the mechanism that is expected to provide the much needed boost to successfully harnessing the true RE potential in any state.

In a sense, therefore, the Renewable Energy Certificate (REC) mechanism entails transfer of the economic burden of higher RE generation costs from states having achieved their RPO targets to states yet to do so, although the actual production of RE-based electricity may still take place in states that have already fulfilled their targets. Further, besides providing the necessary thrust to better exploiting the RE potential in the country, this mechanism would provide a platform for open-access, captive, individual, and corporate consumers of electricity to meet their targets (when such targets are prescribed); and also provide them a platform to express in a big way their 'green intents' or 'green credentials'.

Promotion of Solar Energy-Based Power Generation

The launch of the Jawaharlal Nehru National Solar Mission (JNNSM) has provided a major thrust to India's virtually unexploited (see Table 2.8) solar electricity generation potential of 50,000 MW. Under the Mission, 20,000 MW of solar power generation capacity is expected to be created by 2022. In Phase 1 lasting up to 2013, the JNNSM targets 1000 MW of capacity creation and another 3000 MW capacity is envisaged to be created in Phase 2 by 2017.[20]

The Mission envisages the use of the regulatory framework of RPOs and RECs as the key driver for promotion of solar power generation in the first two phases. It, however, envisages creation of solar-specific RPOs and RECs to provide exclusive priority to the development of solar power. The Mission also proposes to start with an RPO target of 0.25 per cent for Phase 1 and to reach a level of three per cent by 2022—strategically envisages generation from small solar PV located on roof-tops and small solar plants connected to low tension (LT) or 11 KV grid.

Accommodating the provisions of the Mission, the CERC, in its REC regulation, has provided for creation and transfer of solar-based RECs. Further, to facilitate the interconnection of small and roof-top solar PV systems with LT and/or 11 KV grid, CERC, FoR, and the CEA are already working on initiatives such as: (i) development of appropriate interconnection standards; (ii) development

Box 2.2
Salient Features of REC Framework

- Cost of electricity generation from RE sources is classified as cost of generation equivalent to conventional energy sources and cost for environmental attributes.
- RE generators will have two options: (i) either sell the renewable energy at preferential tariff or (ii) sell electricity generation and environmental attributes associated with RE generations separately.
- The environmental attributes can be exchanged in the form of REC.
- REC will be issued to the RE generators for 1 MWh of electricity injected into the grid from RE sources.
- REC would be issued to RE generators only.
- REC could be purchased by the obligated entities to meet their RPO target under Section 86 (1) (e) of the Act. Purchase of REC would be deemed as purchase of RE for RPO compliance.
- Grid-connected RE technologies with minimum capacity of 250 KW and approved by the Ministry of New and Renewable Energy (MNRE), Government of India,would be eligible under this scheme.
- RE generations with existing power purchase agreements (PPAs) are not eligible for REC mechanism.
- SERC to recognize REC as valid instrument for RPO compliance.
- SERC would define open access consumers, captive consumers as obligated entities along with distribution companies.
- SERC to designate state agency for accreditation for RPO compliance and REC mechanism at the state level.
- CERC to designate central agency for registration, repository, and other functions for implementation of REC framework at national level. (The National Load Dispatch Centre has been designated as a central agency)
- Only accredited projects can register for REC at the central agency.
- Central agency would issue REC to renewable energy generators for specified quantity of electricity injected into the grid.
- REC would be exchanged only in the CERC-approved power exchanges.
- Price of electricity component of RE generation would be equivalent to average power purchase cost of the DISCOM including short-term power purchase but excluding renewable power purchase.
- REC would be exchanged within the forbearance price and floor price. The forbearance and floor price would be determined by CERC in consultation with the central agency and FoR from time to time.
- In case of default, SERC may direct the obligated entity to deposit into a separate fund to purchase the shortfall of REC at forbearance price.
- However, in case of genuine difficulty in complying with the renewable purchase obligation because of non-availability of certificates, the obligated entity can approach the Commission for 'carry-forward' of the compliance requirement to the next year.

Source: CERC (2010).

[20] The discussion is mostly based on the JNNSM document available on the MNRE website *www.mnre.gov.in*

of specifications for equipments that could be used for generating roof-top or small solar PV power; (iii) metering arrangements required for accounting of electricity generated from such small systems (net metering protocols); and (iv) development of model power purchase agreements between roof-top and small solar PV generators and the distribution companies with a view to converting each of the initiatives into model guidelines/regulations at a later date.

Together, the efforts to promote renewable energy generation are expected to increase its quantum and also its share in total electricity generation in the country, thereby contributing to the reduction of CO_2 emissions and rate of growth of emissions.

Conservation and Efficient Utilization of Electricity

Conservation and utilization of electricity in end uses such as lighting, heating, cooling, and pumping is one of the most economical ways to bring about low carbon-intensive economic growth and development. Conservation and efficiency either reduce the demand for electricity or reduce the rate at which this demand rises, leading to reduction in growth rate or demand for electricity generation. In the Indian context, one unit of electricity saved at the point of use translates into reduction in generation requirement by 1.26 units.[21] Considering that the weighted average emission factor per unit of electricity generation in India is 0.82 kg of CO_2, one unit of electricity saved through conservation or by improving the efficiency of use of electricity translates into saving of about 1.03 kg of carbon emissions.

Immense potential exists to save electricity in every sector of the Indian economy. The Integrated Energy Policy Report (IEPR) of the Planning Commission[22] estimates that the cost-effective saving potential through conservation and energy efficiency is at least 15 per cent of the total generation. Considering that the total national generation in 2008–09 was approximately 725 billion units, it can be estimated that conservation and efficiency have the potential to realize large reduction in carbon emissions, by about 112 million tonnes per year, if all the available existing saving potential is realized and strategically taken into consideration.

Energy efficiency also assumes importance in the wake of the huge demand-supply gap in India, high transmission and distribution (T&D) losses, fuel constraints, and environmental concerns that the power sector faces today. Capacity addition involves long gestation periods and is beset with several constraints. The demand-side management and energy efficiency can provide, although partly, an alternative to capacity addition.

Energy Conservation Act, 2001 (ECA), Bureau of Energy Efficiency (BEE), and National Mission on Enhanced Energy Efficiency (NMEEE)

While the Energy Conservation Act (ECA), 2001 provides an overall strategic framework for energy efficiency improvement, the BEE and the State Designated Agencies (SDAs), which are institutions created under the 2001 Act, are entrusted with the strategic roles of capturing the available energy efficiency and energy conservation potential in the country.

The Bureau of Energy Efficiency (BEE), over the past three to four years, has initiated a number of programmes to capture EE potential in various sectors. Three main instruments as laid down in the ECA, 2001, which are EE labelling, energy conservation building codes, and energy efficiency in 'designated' and notified industries under the ECA have been operationalized. The EE programmes have also been launched in agricultural pumping, government buildings, and municipal and local bodies. Capacity building and strengthening of the SDAs has also been initiated. A large pool of BEE-certified energy managers and energy auditors has been created under its national certification programme and this pool of professionals will be supplemented by a cadre of certified EE measurement and verification professionals. In addition, under the NMEEE, which is one out of the eight missions planned under the National Action Plan on Climate Change (NAPCC), it is envisaged that the ongoing efforts of BEE will be provided further depth and breadth through the development of market-tradable instruments such as energy efficiency certificates (EECs) under the proposed Perform, Achieve, and Trade (PAT) programme. Support will also be provided through initiatives such as the market-transformation initiative, power sector technology-strategy initiative, EE-financing initiative, and the setting up of Energy Service Companies (ESCO) to strengthen the delivery function of EE/EC. Although the norms for designated industries under the PAT are being designed by BEE, CERC is finalizing the strategic norms for thermal power plants.

[21] The figure is arrived at, assuming average auxiliary consumption of seven per cent, transmission losses of five per cent, and distribution system technical losses of approximately 10 per cent.

[22] Planning Commission (2006a).

Separate Independent but Coordinated Efforts and Role of DISCOMs and Power Sector Regulators in Demand Side Management

Notwithstanding the efforts of the Bureau of Energy Efficiency (BEE) and the initiatives proposed under the NMEEE, it is recognized that these efforts need to be supplemented by several independent, but coordinated initiatives, if wide coverage and penetration of EE and EC practices are to be achieved. The fact that a well-functioning EE market[23] does not exist in India further strengthens the need for independent but co-ordinated supplementary efforts in the area of energy efficiency.

In many parts of the world, such independent efforts in the area of energy efficiency have come from power sector utilities. American, European, Australian, and even some Asian power utilities have been involved in EE and EC activities since the 1970s with a view to bringing about desired changes in consumer demand. In the 1980s, this broad set of EE activities, undertaken by power utilities to bring about a desired change in consumer demand, came to be known as demand side management (DSM) in the US (see Box 2.3 and 2.4 for DSM components and nature and type of DSM initiatives). Utilities in the US and other countries continue to be engaged in these activities and have mainstreamed DSM in their organizational structure.

The importance of demand side management in the functioning of utilities in the US can be gauged from the fact that power utilities there now spend as much as two per cent to over 3.3 per cent of their annual revenues on these activities.[24]

Similar to power utilities in the US and other countries, there is nothing in the EA, 2003 to stop the DISCOMs in India, which are closest to the consumers, from launching independent supplementary initiatives in the DSM area under the supervision of the Electricity Regulatory Commissions (ERCs). Although there is no specific provision in the 2003 Act that directly mandates DISCOMs and/or regulatory commissions to encourage DSM/EE in various end-uses, the National Electricity Policy put emphasis on DSM, EE, and EC. Section 61 of the EA, 2003, inter alia, mandates the Regulatory Commissions to determine tariff after considering factors that would encourage efficiency, economical use of resources, and optimum investments. Section 42(1) of the 2003 Act provides that the distribution licensee should develop and maintain an efficient, co-ordinated, and economical distribution system in his area of supply.

While these sections in the 2003 Act can be considered to be pointing towards efficient and economical use of electricity, it cannot be considered to be pointing exclusively towards DSM. A more direct reference to DSM can be found in Section 86 (4) of the Act, which states that the SERCs shall be guided by the National Electricity Policy (NEP) and the National Electricity Plan. The NEP, notified by GoI in February 2005, explicitly provides for energy conservation, wherein the Policy stipulates that ERCs should ensure adherence to energy-efficiency standards by utilities (see Clause 5.9.6 of the NEP). In Maharashtra, where DSM activities in a planned manner are being implemented since 2004–05, the SERC has been actively promoting efficient utilization of electricity, its conservation, and DSM as a power shortage mitigation strategy by exercising its power vested under Section 23 of the EA, 2003 to regulate supply, distribution, consumption, or use of electricity in times of exigencies. It is, however, evident that in India so far the ERCs' initiatives in the EE and EC space have been motivated to do so more by the existing situation of energy shortage rather than by environmental concerns.

Status of Implementation of DSM

The peak load management part of the demand side management is being addressed by using the instrument of time-of-the-day (TOD) tariffs. However, given that India has demand as well as energy shortages and hydro generation is often used for peaking purposes, not much by way of reduction in emissions is being achieved by TOD tariffs, as the tariffs while helping in shifting the consumption of electricity, are not helping in reducing consumption. Also, it is not as if non-peak power generation is non-fossil fuel-based.

The energy efficiency, the fuel substitution part or the demand response part of the DSM, however, is not

[23] A well-functioning EE market is characterized by a market that has a large number of manufacturers willing and interested in producing energy-efficient products, goods, and services; adequate supply of efficient products, appliances, and goods; large number of consumers who are willing, interested, and motivated to buy/adopt EE goods, services, and practices; large number of financiers and bankers who are willing, interested, and motivated to finance these goods, services, and practices; and large number of EE delivery entities to provide these services.

[24] CAMPUT, 2006. *Demand Side Management: Determining Appropriate Spending Levels and Cost-Effectiveness Testing*, A Report prepared by Summit Blue Consulting LLC and The Regulatory Assistance Project (RAP). The Report has been prepared for the Canadian Association of Members of Public Utility Tribunals (CAMPUT), 30 June 2006.

Box 2.3
DSM Components

Demand side management (DSM) consists of three components: energy efficiency, load management (LM), and fuel substitution (FS) where another source of energy is used in lieu of electricity. FS would lead to reduction in electricity demand; at the same time it would also lead to increased use of another energy source (for example, natural gas). Consequently, analysis of this resource would need to consider non-electricity sector issues also.

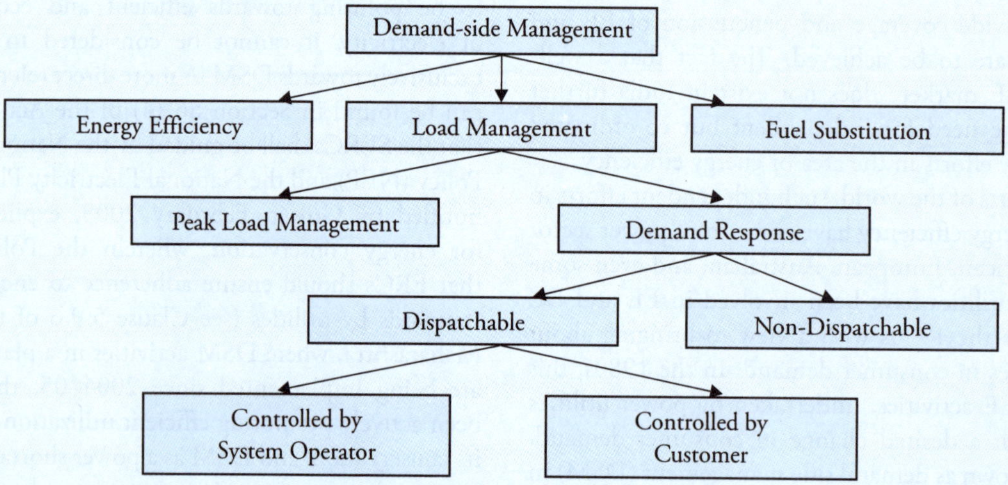

Energy Efficiency is designed to reduce electricity consumption during all hours of the year, attempting to permanently reduce the demand for energy in intervals ranging from seasons to years and concentrates on end-use energy solutions.

Load Management is designed to change demand for energy in intervals from minutes to hours and associated timing of electric demand (that is, lowering during peak periods) through appropriate pricing, load control signals, or other incentives to reflect existing production, and all delivery costs.

Load Management resources can be further classified in two types —peak-load management (PLM) and demand response (DR). PLM attempts to 'shift load permanently from the peak period to off-peak period'. A simple example of the PLM programme is the time-of-day (TOD) tariff. In contrast, DR attempts to either 'shift or 'forego electricity usage only during specific events (for example, system emergencies). In some years, there may be many DR events while in others there may be no DR events. Examples of DR include direct load control (DLC) and interruptible tariffs, critical peak-pricing programmes (CPPs).

Source: Based on personal communication with Ranjit Bharvirkar of Lawrence Berkeley National Laboratory (LBNL) in December 2007/January 2008, and MERC Background Paper: Draft Cost-Effectiveness Assessment Guidelines for DSM Measures and Programmes, January 2009.

being practised on a large scale, except by DISCOMs in Maharashtra (see Box 2.5), Delhi and, to an extent, in Karnataka and Haryana. In Maharashtra, under the directions and guidance of the Maharashtra Electricity Regulatory Commission (MERC), DISCOMs have been running DSM programmes since 2005. To give impetus to DSM, its programme cost-effectiveness assessment and implementation framework regulations have been prepared by MERC in April 2010. The SERCs of Gujarat, West Bengal, Haryana, Rajasthan, Himachal Pradesh, and Chhattisgarh are discussing introduction of DSM in DISCOMs coming under their respective jurisdictions.

Experiences in Maharashtra and Delhi have shown that the SERCs can play an important role in inducting the DISCOMs in supplementing the efforts of BEE and NMEEE to bring about widespread and accelerated adoption of EE and EC practices. DISCOMs, hitherto, have only been involved in the supply side of the business and have responded to their consumers' rising electricity demand or to the rising demand-supply deficit through supply side options such as purchasing electricity from outside sources and reducing transmission and distribution losses. They have thus not been involved in harnessing the potential of demand side resources through DSM programmes. Keeping this in mind, the Forum of Regulators (FoR) constituted a Working Group (WG) on DSM and EE in July 2008, which has since brought out a strategy report. As per its recommendations, a major initiative is being undertaken by FoR to introduce DSM

Box 2.4
Nature and Type of DSM Initiatives

Demand side management (DSM) programmes, as practised the world over, have varied in their character from being simple 'information only' programmes that inform the users about the generic options available for conservation of electricity and its efficient utilization, to DSM 'resource acquisition' programmes that reduce electricity consumption and load, including peak load, through appropriately formulated DSM initiatives by consumers, energy service companies (ESCOs), equipment manufacturers/ suppliers or others, with payments made to them by the utility in return for the resulting energy and load reductions. Thus, DSM programmes include:

- information programmes that inform the target consumers about the possibilities for energy efficiency and conservation in specific end-use and specific technology;
- technical assistance that provide energy audit services for consumers to identify where the energy conservation or demand reduction potential exists, what is its quantum and what its cost-benefit analysis is;
- financial assistance programmes that help consumers pay for DSM. These programmes could include providing initial capital, hire-purchase schemes, leasing, low-interest loans, rebates/discounts, etc.;
- direct installation programmes that provide comprehensive design, financial and installation services to the consumers to physically install equipment or put in place energy conservation/energy efficiency measures at the consumers' end, either by the utility's own staff or through utility hired contractors;
- alternative tariff programmes that include time-of-day (TOD) tariffs and tariffs that foster conservation and efficient utilization of electricity in target consumer segment and/or target end-use; and
- market transformation programmes that promote accelerated and wide-scale penetration of a particular type of energy efficient service, practice, or technology without the need for any continuous intervention by the utility.

Source: From 'Demand-side management from a sustainable development perspective: experiences from Quebec (Canada) and India', by Quebec Agence de l'efficacite energetique, Econolar International, IREDA and TERI, 2003.

in all states on a uniform basis, which includes training of personnel from the SERCs and distribution utilities[25] and also preparing guiding documents such as:

- Report on institutionalizing DSM;
- DSM regulations;
- Manual on cost-benefit analysis of DSM programmes;
- Manual on development of standard processes for design, development, and implementation of DSM programmes;
- Report on tariff restructuring and impact assessment; and
- Manual on monitoring and verification protocol for DSM programmes.

With these efforts, it is envisaged that target-based DSM programmes, which capture the available EE/EC potential, could be introduced in almost all states in 2010–11.

Funding for DSM

World-wide experience has shown that the funding for demand side management activities essentially comes from the consumers of utilities. Once the DSM targets are set, its related programmes to meet these targets are identified and the funds required for implementing these programmes determined. The required funds are collected from the consumers of the utility by:

- a rate surcharge, such as the 'system benefit charge' or 'societal benefit charge (SBC)' or public goods charge (California): these surcharges are typically mandated by legislation and are charged as a percentage of utility revenue and are collected from consumers either as a percentage of their bills or as per unit charge; and/or
- the utility's overall rates: the DSM funds requirement and budget is included in the utility's ARR.

The State Electricity Regulating Commissions (SERCs) of Maharashtra and Delhi have adopted the second approach. Thus, these two SERCs have allowed DISCOMs in the states to recover all costs incurred by them in any DSM-related activity by adding these costs to their ARR to enable their funding through tariff rates.

From studies in North America, it is generally seen that the present energy efficiency funding level for a number of

[25] FoR has signed an MoU with the Lawrence Berkeley National Laboratory (LBNL), for providing advice and capacity building. NABL has already conducted training programmes of SERC and DISCOM personnel in March, June, and August 2009.

Box 2.5
DSM Initiatives in Maharashtra

In Maharashtra, under the leadership of the then Chairperson of the Maharashtra Electricity Regulatory Commission (MERC), Pramod Deo, DSM was introduced in 2005. As a result of MERC's directives, the first ever serious effort was made by the DISCOMs in the state to implement DSM and EE programmes. Recognizing that mere directions to the utilities to capture the available DSM and EE and EC potential would not suffice, MERC took the following complementary measures:

Recovery of DSM and energy efficiency-related costs

Recognizing that the DISCOMs would need regulatory approval to recover costs associated with undertaking EE/DSM programmes, MERC allowed DISCOMs in the state to recover all costs incurred in any DSM and EE related activity, including planning, designing, implementing, monitoring, and evaluating DSM, EE, and EC programmes through aggregate revenue requirement.

Capacity Building

The Commission enhanced its internal capacity by creating a dedicated DSM cell within the organization in early 2006, in order to ensure compliance with the Commission's directions and to facilitate the regulatory process in EE and DSM activities. Further, recognizing that the DISCOMs in the state have limited experience and knowledge in the establishment of a self-sustaining, market-based cycle of DSM and EE programme development, financing and implementation, the Commission provided support and guidance to the DISCOMs in DSM and EE programmes. Further, the Commission entered into a Memorandum of Understanding (MoU) with the California Energy Commission (CEC), California Public Utilities Commission (CPUC), and Lawrence Berkeley National Laboratory (LBNL) of the US, to develop its own capacity and also that of the utilities in the areas of EE, DSM, load research, integrated resource planning, and demand response, etc.

Load Research

Recognizing that DISCOMs in the state had virtually no category-wise demand and consumption data beyond the system level demand (that is, no data on contribution of sector or segment or end-use or technology to the total demand, both in terms of quantum or timing) which is so vital in strategizing and planning EE or DSM programmes, the MERC through its multi-year tariff (MYT) orders of April/May 2007, directed all the DISCOMs in the state to undertake systematic load research and to make this research an integral part of their day-to-day operations.

In addition, the Commission, through its orders on load management penalties and incentives, was able to create a fund of Rs 700 million, which the MERC allowed the DISCOMs to use in the initial years for DSM pilot projects such as promotion of both CFLs and efficient fluorescent lamps; energy saving in high rise building pumping; promotion of efficient street lights; promotion of LED-based traffic signals; of DSM resource acquisition through DSM bidding mechanism; a combined energy conservation awareness campaign by Mumbai DISCOMs; agricultural pumps capacitor installation project; and training programmes for DISCOM personnel in DSM.

Source: Author's own.

major utilities and jurisdictions varies between two per cent to slightly above 3.3 per cent of their respective revenues. The studies also indicate that even after spending as much as 3.3 per cent of the annual revenues on yearly DSM activities, many of the jurisdictions in North America could not fully exploit all the cost-effective DSM potential available in their jurisdictions. In India, back-of-the-envelope calculations show that spending three per cent of the annual revenue of the distribution utilities on DSM would in all likelihood put a burden of approximately Rs 0.09–0.10 per kWh[26] on consumers, if the burden is shared across the entire consumer base of the DISCOMs, including below poverty line (BPL) and agricultural consumers. If these categories of consumers are excluded, then the burden on the rest of the consumers, assuming consumption in the BPL and agricultural category to be 25 per cent of the total consumption, could be anywhere between Rs 0.13 to Rs 0.15 per kWh. Since this may be unsustainable, a modest spending of approximately 0.5 to one per cent of the annual revenue on DSM could be an acceptable level of spending. However, looking at the North American experience, this level of funding may not be able to exploit all the available DSM potential. The funding from ARR will, therefore, have to be supplemented by funding from the states in the nature of budgetary support. It is here that the additional funding

[26] Data for the year 2007–8 from the Power Finance Corporation report on performance of power utilities shows that DISCOMs covered in the report had revenue of approximately Rs 150 billion and the corresponding sale was 456 billion units.

to the states, under the centre–state mechanism, in the form of incentives for meeting the pre-specified DSM targets could be considered to exploit the available DSM potential.

Summary and Future Work

There are enormous opportunities to make the power sector less carbon-intensive and reduce the rate of growth of emissions at every stage of the electricity cycle. While some of the ongoing initiatives such as improving generation efficiency, reducing auxiliary consumption, or reducing the transmission and distribution losses, etc. do result in reducing the CO_2 emissions, they are being emphasized by the regulators more for the impact they have on reducing the cost of electricity generation or on reducing the cost of electricity to the consumers rather than for reducing the CO_2 emissions. On the other hand, regulatory emphasis on promotion of RE-based generation and electricity conservation and its efficient use are two areas which are being emphasized by the regulators for their direct bearing on the reduction of CO_2 emissions from the power sector. Both these areas have very high potential in reducing carbon intensity and carbon emissions from the power sector. From the IEPR of the Planning Commission, it is seen that by 2031–32, reduction in CO_2 emissions from the power sector, because of DSM and RE-based power generation (see Scenario 11 in the Report) as compared to the scenario where these two options are not considered (Scenario 5) will be about 600–700 million tonnes—about 400 million tonnes from DSM and the balance from RE-based generation. If India is to succeed in bringing about a meaningful and sustained reduction in its carbon intensity and carbon footprint, it is these two areas which will provide the key.

Direction of Future Efforts to Promote RE-based Generation

While the preferential tariffs and renewable purchase obligations (RPO) targets coupled with market–tradable RECs are expected to lead to accelerated creation of RE-based generation capacity, regulatory attention will also need to focus on the issues arising out of the in-firm nature of RE power. Power output from RE-based generation, especially from wind, small hydropower, and solar-based power generation, is in-firm, that is, it varies by the minute, by the time of the day, and also seasonally. To facilitate implementation of the National Action Plan on Climate Change, which calls for significantly increasing the share of electricity generated from renewable energy, CERC in April 2010, notified the new Grid Code, to facilitate larger integration of renewable energy sources with the grid. As per the new Grid Code, the financial burden of all the fluctuations from schedule in case of new solar energy plants and the fluctuations within ±30 per cent of schedule in case of new wind energy plants will be borne by all the users of the inter-state grid.

Thus project developers and the host states will not be at a disadvantage from such fluctuations. New wind energy generators will be able to fine-tune their schedules (based on forecasting) as close as three hours before actual generation.

The absorption of renewable energy-based in-firm generation in the grid can be also increased by inducting the Smart Grid technology, which is a platform for integrating renewable energy generation (such as solar and wind), smart meters, demand response, and many more technologies into the DISCOM's distribution system. In recognition of the importance of Smart Grid, the US Energy Secretary, Steven Chu, has placed the Smart Grid at the top of the US Department of Energy's priorities. China has also recognized the importance of the Smart Grid technology. Considering the importance of this technology, regulatory steps are being contemplated to induct it to facilitate absorption of larger amounts of in-firm RE-based power into the grid (Box 2.6 provides a brief description of the Smart Grid concept).

Direction of Future Efforts to Promote DSM

It is evident that both energy efficiency and conservation have a large potential to reduce the growth of carbon emissions. Besides, they also have the potential to obviate the need for new capacity additions as well as to mitigate the power shortages in the country. The EA, 2003 and NEP provide the necessary legal framework for its implementation through DISCOMs under regulatory supervision. Besides the ongoing initiatives of the Forum of Regulators, the following actions are needed to strategically operationalize DSM faster:

DSM Capacity Building

Today, there is a dearth of qualified demand side management experts in India. Training and capacity building, especially in finance and marketing, which are the essence of the DSM programme, are vital for the success of the programme's initiatives. Hence, efforts to strengthen planning, designing, and implementation of DSM by creating a cadre of DSM professionals are being contemplated. FoR is expected to play a lead role in this effort, for which it has entered into a Memorandum of Understanding (MoU) with the regulatory and research entities, namely, the California Public Utilities Commission (CPUC), California Energy Commission (CEC), and Lawrence

Box 2.6
Smart Grids

Smart Grid means a grid which increases the robustness, efficiency, and flexibility of the power system. It is also sometimes called a 'self-healing grid.'

A power system or grid operator would like to have in place a system where the grid either solves its problems itself or the operator is informed in advance of an impending grid disturbance so that remedial action can be taken to prevent the disturbance. From the point of view of consumers, they would like to have optimum utilization of the power system, that is, network optimally loaded at all times, so as to minimize the cost. Consumers would also like to have minimum interruption of supply. It is desirable to reduce the effects of carbon emissions on the environment and, at the same time, get power supply in a reliable manner. The grid operator would not like the unpredictable nature of wind and solar energy to give him nightmares due to inadequate predictability of these sources. The Smart Grid achieves all these and more.

The US Department of Energy lists seven objectives of a Smart Grid:

- enabling informed participation by customers;
- accommodating all generation and storage options;
- enabling new products, services, and markets;
- providing the power quality for the range of needs in the twenty-first century economy;
- optimizing asset utilization and operating efficiently; addressing disturbances through automated prevention, containment, and restoration; and
- operating resiliently against all hazards.

Source: V.S. Verma, CERC (2010).

Berkeley National Laboratory (LBNL). Entities from California have been chosen as partners of the MoU in view of the significant achievements of the State of California in the US. The state has managed to maintain its consumption per capita at about the same level for more than 30 years since 1975. CEC and CPUC have played a lead role in limiting energy and load growth during both the short- and long-term periods by directing and facilitating the California Utilities to plan and implement target-based DSM programmes. The CPUC, in September 2009, approved EE programmes for 2010–12 with a total budget of \$3.1 billion for California utilities—Southern California Edison, Pacific Gas and Electric Company, San Diego Gas and Electric Company, and Southern California Gas Company. This is the largest commitment ever made by a state to energy efficiency. These programmes are expected to create energy savings of almost 7,000 gigawatt hours: the equivalent of three 500 MW power plants and will avoid three million tonnes of greenhouse gas emissions. In addition, the EE programmes are expected to result in creation of about 15,000–18,000 skilled green jobs. Already, under the MoU, experts from LBNL, CPUC, and CEC have conducted three training programmes for the SERCs and DISCOMs.

Database Development

There is also a need under the Forum of Regulators' (FoR) umbrella to initiate efforts to create a DSM database. It is envisaged that the database will develop information on deemed savings possible due to EE and EC (kWh/kW/KVA), cost of measures, life (how long savings are available), timing (when savings are available—daily, morning, afternoon, evening, night, seasonally), avoided-costs of power procurement and capacity addition, and tariffs.

Load Research

As has been done in Maharashtra, there is a need for the SERCs in other states to direct the DISCOMs under their jurisdictions to undertake load research and consumer survey exercise on a continuous basis and make these activities an integral part of the DISCOMs' day-to-day operations. Load research is the starting point of any DSM planning and programme design exercise, and unless the required inputs are available from load research and consumer survey studies, very little progress can be made towards capturing the available EE and EC savings through DSM programmes on a sustained basis. To facilitate introduction of load research and consumer surveys, necessary efforts under the FoR umbrella need to be initiated.

Incentives to DISCOMS

In the cost plus regulatory regime under which DISCOMs operate in India, they neither stand to lose nor gain by running DSM programmes, provided they are allowed to recover the costs they incur to run these programmes. In a strict sense, therefore, DISCOMs have no motivation to run these programmes, except as fulfilment of a regulatory requirement. To motivate DISCOMs to take up DSM activities voluntarily, they would need to be incentivized. The September 2008 Report of the Forum on DSM provides a broad outline of the possible ways to incentivize DISCOMs to undertake DSM, including:

- allowing them to earn additional return on equity for undertaking DSM in place of supply side resources. Such an incentive could be in the form of additional return on equity (say, one per cent incremental return on equity) for DSM/EE programmes in subsidized consumer categories.
- higher incremental return on equity (say two per cent) to be provided to utility for investments in DSM programmes in subsidizing categories such as commercial and industrial sectors. This will encourage utilities to undertake DSM even in subsidized categories.

Also, since demand side management in the long run would obviate or defer the need for augmentation of the distribution capacity, it would also obviate or defer the need for capital/equity infusion. However, since DISCOM profitability is linked to return on equity, DSM in the long run might affect this profitability. To overcome this, it has been suggested that DISCOMs be incentivized to take up DSM by developing a mechanism to treat part or whole of the expenses incurred on DSM similar to any capital expenditure, with its attendant return on investment benefits.

Thus, in view of the recommendations of the Report, the Forum will formulate suitable incentive mechanisms for implementing DSM.

Ensuring Subsidy Payments by State Governments

There is a need for State Electricity Regulatory Commissions to ensure that consumers, who are being provided subsidy by the state governments, are billed by the DISCOMs at the SERC-determined unsubsidized tariff, if the state governments fail to pay the subsidy on time in accordance with Section 65 of the EA, 2003. It has been observed that although the state governments fail to pay the subsidy, the DISCOMS continue to bill the consumers who are being provided subsidy at the subsidized rates rather than at the unsubsidized rates. This action by DISCOMs perpetuates wasteful use of electricity as the consumers being provided subsidy either pay nothing or pay very nominal charges for electricity they consume, and hence have no motivation to economize electricity use. SERCs' insistence on following the provisions of Section 65 of EA, 2003 will induce state governments to reduce the subsidy being provided or will make the DISCOMs financially better and prevent wasteful use of electricity.

Other Areas Requiring Regulatory Attention

Ensuring Compliance of Regulatory Directives

From the rendition provided above, it is clear that India has a good deal of ongoing regulatory initiatives to address, directly or indirectly, the CO_2 emissions issue in the power sector. But having in place good regulations is only half the work done. What is perhaps more important is that regulatory directions and intentions are translated into intended results for which acting on the regulatory instruments available for enforcing compliance in line with regulatory directions is very important. It is in this respect that power sector regulators, especially the regulators in the states (the SERCs) need gearing up on an urgent basis.

Under the cost-plus-regulatory regime, the utilities in India should not be making losses if they meet the norms prescribed by regulators for various operating parameters, provided the subsidy claimed/booked by the utilities is paid to them by the state governments. In reality, however, DISCOMs directly supplying electricity to consumers suffer heavy cash losses, as depicted in Table 2.11.

TABLE 2.11 Aggregate Cash Loss of DISCOMs

(Figures in Rs Million)

Description	*Formula*	*Year 2005–6*	*Year 2006–7*	*Year 2007–8*
Cash Profit Loss on subsidy received basis (+)	A	(-)32680	(-)83110	(-)109630
Subsidy booked	B	122330	135900	193790
Subsidy received from government	C	109380	128360	163030
Subsidy shortfall	D= B-C	12950	7540	30760
Cash Profit considering all the booked subsidy was received	E= A+D	(-)19730	(-)75570	(-)78870

Note: Minus sign (-) indicates loss; (+) = Cash Profit = (Profit after tax + depreciation + miscellaneous expenses written off + deferred tax)

Source: Extract from Power Finance Corporation (2009: Annexure 1.2.1, 1.2.2, 1.2.3, and 1.4.1).

Under the cost-plus-regime, explanation for the major portion of such losses could be non-adherence to the operating performance norms prescribed by the regulators. The sustained level of cash losses are not only critically affecting viability of the power sector, but also point to the fact that the operating performance norms prescribed by the regulators are not being met. Thus, any regulatory intent to bring about a reduction in CO_2 emissions through adherence to the prescribed norms may not materialize unless regulatory compliance is strictly enforced. The regulators are, of course, seized of the problem and recognize the need to make compliance monitoring more effective. In fact, in the recent (1 February 2010) meeting of the Forum, it was agreed that the mechanisms ensuring compliance of various regulatory directives need to be institutionalized. As an important step in this direction, it has been agreed by the Forum that a draft regulation for compliance audit by the Regulatory Commissions would be prepared. Such a regulation would, it is envisaged, help in effective monitoring of the compliance and not just remain an issue to be discussed on the sidelines at the stage of annual tariff determination.

Tracking and Monitoring Technical Losses in the Distribution Systems

Reduction in distribution losses also has the potential to bring about reduction in the growth rate of emissions. However, there is a need to formulate specific targets for technical loss reduction. Since no data exists on the level of technical losses, such estimation studies will have to be taken up and SERCs will have to direct the DISCOMS under their jurisdiction to take up technical loss estimation studies as well as making the necessary resources available for them.

References

Canadian Association of Members of Public Utility Tribunals (2006). 'Demand Side Management: Determining Appropriate Spending levels and Cost-Effectiveness Testing', Summit Blue Consulting LLC and the Regulatory Assistance Project, 30 June.

Central Electricity Authority (2008). *Review of Performance of Thermal Power Stations: 2007–08*, Government of India, Ministry of Power, New Delhi, September.

——— (2009a). *CO_2 Baseline data for Indian Power Sector: User Guide version 5.0*, Government of India, Ministry of Power, New Delhi, November.

——— (2009b). *Monthly Generation Report*, Government of India, Ministry of Power, New Delhi.

Central Electricity Regulatory Commission (2004) *Central Electricity Regulatory Commission (Terms and Conditions of Tariff) Regulations, 2004*, New Delhi. .

——— (2009a). *Central Electricity Regulatory Commission (Terms and Conditions of Tariff) Regulations, 2009*, New Delhi,

——— (2009b). *Central Electricity Regulatory Commission (Terms and Conditions for Tariff Determination from Renewable Energy Sources) Regulations, 2009*, New Delhi.

——— (2009c). *Central Electricity Regulatory Commission Order: Determination of Generic Levelized Generation Tariff Under Regulation 8 of the Central Electricity Regulatory Commission (Terms and Conditions for Tariff Determination from Renewable Energy Sources) Regulations, 2009. Petition No.284/2009 (Suo Moto)*, New Delhi.

——— (2010). *Central Electricity Regulatory Commission (Terms and Conditions for Recognition and Issuance of Renewable Energy Certificate for Renewable Energy Generation) Regulations, 2010*, New Delhi.

Forum of Regulators (2009). *Draft Report on Analysis of Tariffs*, New Delhi.

——— (2008). *Report of the Working Group on DSM and Energy Efficiency*, New Delhi.

——— (2008). *Report on Renewables*, New Delhi.

Government of India (GoI) (2001) *The Energy Conservation Act, 2001, Act 52 of 2001*, Government of India, New Delhi.

——— (2003). *The Electricity Act, 2003, Act 36 of 2003*, Government of India, New Delhi.

International Energy Agency (IEA) (2008). *Efficiency Indicators for Public Electricity Production from Fossil Fuels*, IEA Information Paper, IEA, Paris.

——— (2009). *Key World Energy Statistics—2009*, IEA, Paris.

Maharashtra Electricity Regulatory Commission (2009). *Background Paper: Draft Cost Effectiveness Assessment Guidelines for DSM Measures and Programmes*, MERC, Mumbai.

Ministry of Environment and Forest (2010). *India: Green House Gas Emissions 2007*, Government of India, Ministry of Environment and Forest, New Delhi.

——— (2009). *India's GHG Emissions Profile: Results of Five Climate Modeling Studies*, Climate Modelling Forum, Ministry of Environment and Forests, Government of India.

Ministry of Power (2005). *The National Electricity Policy*, Government of India, Ministry of Power, New Delhi.

——— (2006). *The Tariff Policy*, Government of India, Ministry of Power, New Delhi.

Planning Commission (2006). *Eleventh Five Year Plan Document, 3*, Government of India, Planning Commission, New Delhi.

——— (2006a). *Integrated Energy Policy—Report of the Expert Committee*, Government of India, New Delhi.

Power Finance Corporation (2009). *Report on Performance of Power Utilities for the year 2005–06 to 2007–08*, Government of India, Ministry of Power, New Delhi.

Prayas (2009). *Review of the Distribution Franchisee Model implemented by MSEDCL in the Bhiwandi Circle*, Prayas (Energy Group), Pune.

Web Links

Jawaharlal Nehru National Solar Mission, Mission Document. Available on Ministry of New and Renewable Energy website: http://www.mnre.gov.in

Renewable Energy, 'Major Achievements'. available on Ministry of New and Renewable Energy website: http://www.mnre.gov.in

National Action Plan on Climate Change. Available on http://pmindia.nic.in/climate_change.htm

National Mission on Enhanced Energy Efficiency. Available on http://www.energymanagertraining.com

3 Economics, Regulation, and Implementation Strategy for Renewable Energy Certificates in India

Anoop Singh

Introduction

Renewable energy sources (RES) have been promoted through a number of policies including subsidies and fiscal incentives, as well as regulatory provisions. Attractive fiscal policies like higher depreciation and the Renewable Portfolio Obligation (RPO) with Feed-in-Tariff (FiT) have provided significant impetus to growth of renewable energy in the electricity sector in India.[1] Economic efficiency of renewable energy promotional policies like RPO with FiT has been questioned as these do not provide incentive for cost reduction and exploitation of cost-effective resources with appropriate technology (Singh 2009). Tradable Renewable Energy Certificates (RECs) are identified as market-based instruments that can help promote RES in a cost-effective manner (Nielsen and Jeppesen 2003; Morthorst 2000; Voogt et al. 2000).

Renewable Energy Credits or RECs are used as a disclosure, marketing and compliance mechanisms in a number of countries. These are called Renewable Obligation Certificates (ROCs) in the UK and 'green tags' or Tradable Green Certificates (TGCs) across many countries in the Europe, Guarantee of Origin (GO) or Renewable Energy Guarantee of Origin (REGO) is often used in the European Union (EU) as a disclosure mechanism. At least 21 REC schemes were under operation in a number of jurisdictions including the UK, Italy, the Netherlands, Sweden, Australia, and numerous states in the US (Mendonca et al. 2010; Bertoldi and Huld 2006). In the Indian context, Singh (2006 and 2009) discusses the advantages of RECs and proposes its implementation to bring in economic efficiency in promotion of RES. The Central Electricity Regulatory Commission (CERC) has recently issued regulations[2] for introducing a market for RECs in the country (CERC 2010a).

This chapter critically examines the above regulations and identifies areas for improvement. We discuss the impact of market segmentation into solar and non solar RECs, and propose a multiplier scheme. The chapter demonstrates that the high level of floor and forbearance prices translate to a windfall gain and represent a higher implicit price of carbon, and need to be revisited. While presenting a mechanism for price discovery of RECs, it also highlights the importance of a buyout price. The chapter proposes a linkage between the FiT and REC mechanisms. It begins by highlighting the role of RECs

[1] Section 85 (e) of the Electricity Act 2003 empowers the State Electricity Regulatory Commissions (SERCs) to specify a percentage of the total consumption of electricity in the area of a distribution licensee to be procured from RES (RPO). The Act also empowers the SERCs to determine tariffs for the promotion of co-generation and generation of electricity from renewable sources of energy.

[2] Hereinafter, referred to as the REC Regulations.

in promoting RES in an economically efficient manner. We also present a framework for developing a market for RECs, and discuss institutional mechanisms and role of various stakeholders.

Traditional Policy Framework and its Impact on Renewable Energy Development

The Government of India (GoI) has outlined eight missions under the NAPCC as mitigation and adaptation strategies to address climate change. The NAPCC augurs to promote development of renewable energy sources in the country. It sets a target of 5 per cent renewable energy purchase for 2009–10 and which will increase by one percentage point for the next 10 years (GoI 2009a). During the year 2008–9, while renewable energy sources contributed 7.78 per cent of generation capacity its energy contribution was merely 3.49 per cent (estimated from CEA 2009a). This can be attributed to a faulty policy approach that provided tax incentives for investment in capacity addition rather than generation of electricity. This has been addressed to some extent through feed-in-tariff approach and generation-based incentives.

Due to disparity of resource endowments, and the policy and regulatory environment, the development of renewable energy sources varies across states in the country (Figure 3.1). Renewable energy sources, especially wind resources, have been extensively exploited in some of the states in the southern and western regions of the country. Biomass-based plants have made significant contribution in some of the states in the northern and the western regions. States in the eastern region have generally lagged behind in the exploitation of RES. Given the resource disparity and variations in the policy and regulatory environment across states, some states may be able to set and achieve higher RPO targets while others may lag behind. With an increasing share of renewable energy, the cost of power procurement and hence the impact on consumer tariff cannot remain insignificant. Given the existing pressure to reduce costs and the inability to increase tariffs, obligated entities (especially the distribution companies) may find

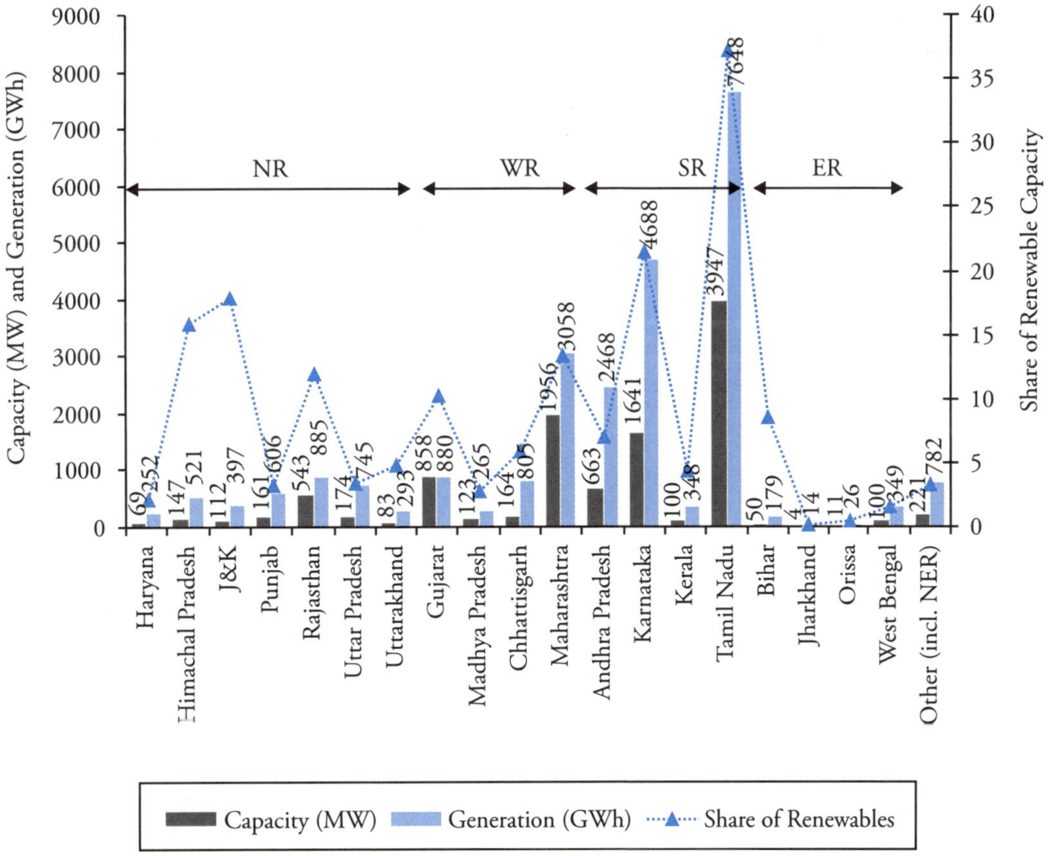

Figure 3.1 Capacity and Electricity Generation from Renewable Energy Sources (2008–9)

Source: CEA (2009a).

it difficult to meet increasing levels of RPO in future. Role of market mechanisms, like the one discussed below, with an appropriate institutional structure could help achieve a higher share of renewable energy in a cost-effective manner.

The RPO targets differ significantly across states. While some SERCs have specified separate RPOs for different RES, others have chosen to specify a common RPO target. RPO targets for all the obligated entities within a state are the same, with the exception of the states like Karnataka and West Bengal. The choice of a level of RPO seems to be influenced by, among other factors, resource endowments, existing capacity as well as policy and regulatory environment. The experience with the implementation of RPO across different states presents some interesting insights (Table 3.1).

Distribution utilities in Tamil Nadu and Karnataka, which have rich wind energy resources, have been able to meet rather ambitious RPO targets. A modest RPO target in Gujarat was achieved but it remained unaccomplished in Punjab. Ambitious targets set up for Chattisgarh, Haryana, Madhya Pradesh, Rajasthan, Uttar Pradesh, and Uttaranchal did not materialize. The obligated entities in most of the other states also fell short of the RPO targets.

Table **3.1** RPO and its Compliance across States

(in percentage)

States	*RES*	*RPO Targets*					*RPO Performance*		
		2007–8	*2008–9*	*2009–10*	*2010–11*	*2011–12*	*2007–8*	*2008–9*	*2009–10*
Andhra Pradesh[#$]		5	5	5	5	5	*4.41*	*3.95*	*4.06*
Bihar[@]				4	5	6	0.82	0.57	NA
Chhattisgarh	Wind		2	2	2		0	0	0
	Biomass		5	5	5		4.02	NA	3.60
	Small Hydro		3	3	3		0.34	NA	0.26
	Total		10	10	10		4.36	NA	3.62
Delhi		1	1	1	1		NA	NA	NA
Gujarat		1	2	2			2.07	NA	2.55
Haryana		3	5	10	10	10	NA	*0.01*	*0.01*
Himachal Pradesh	Small Hydro	20	20	20			NA	NA	NA
Karnataka		7–10	7–10	7–10			*9.30*	*10.80*	*11.04*
Kerala		5	5	5			0.01	0.09	0.51
Madhya Pradesh	Wind		5	6	6	6	0.08	0.07	0.06
	Biomass		2	2	2	2	0	0	0
	Co-generation		3	2	2	2	0	0	0
	Total		10	10	10	10	0.08	0.07	0.06
Maharashtra[$]		4	5	6			3.35	3.36	4.25
Orissa		3	3	4			0	0	1.59
Punjab		1	1	2	3	4	*0.69*	*0.74*	*1.49*
Rajasthan[$]	Wind	4	5	6	6.75	7.50	2.18	3.42	2.74
	Biomass	0.88	1.25	1.45	1.75	2	0.39	1.48	0.49
	Total	4.88	6.25	7.45	8.50	9.50	2.57	4.90	3.23
Tamil Nadu		10	10	13			11.65	12.08	*13.79*
Uttarakhand		5	5	8	9	10	1.4	1.7	*2.18*
Uttar Pradesh		7.5	7.5	7.5			1.25	2.44	2.97
West Bengal		0.95–3.8	2–4.8	4–6.8	7–8.3	10	NA	0–0.37	0-0.34

Note: [#] RPO target of 5 per cent for 2012–13 and 2013–14; [@] RPO target of 7 per cent for 2012–13; [$] The RPO target also applicable to captive and open access consumers; Numbers in italics are projections filed with regulators by the distribution utilities.

Sources: GoI (2009b), Singh (2009), FoR (2008), Bloomberg New Energy Finance (2010), and relevant regulations of SERCs.

This could be attributed to, among others, ambitious RPO targets, slower growth in renewable capacity addition in comparison with conventional fuels, operational constraints due to uncertainty associated with natural resources and the absence of an effective deterrence. The regulatory vacuum to address some of these issues limits the scope for setting up an 'appropriate' RPO target, and provide an effective mechanism and institution to achieve this in a cost-effective manner.

In states like Karnataka and Tamil Nadu, where obligated entities have surpassed RPO targets, there would be additional increase in consumer tariffs as high cost power procurement from renewable energy sources was compulsorily absorbed beyond the RPO targets. A mechanism to 'sell' the additional renewable energy procurement to 'obligated entities' who are falling short of the RPO target would not only lower the burden on consumer tariffs (in Karnataka and Tamil Nadu, in this case) but would also improve compliance with RPO regulations elsewhere in the country. Further, absence of 'banking' in the prevailing RE policies would not permit the two states to take credit of the 'excess' purchase of RE in a year and utilize the same to meet the RPO target for subsequent years.

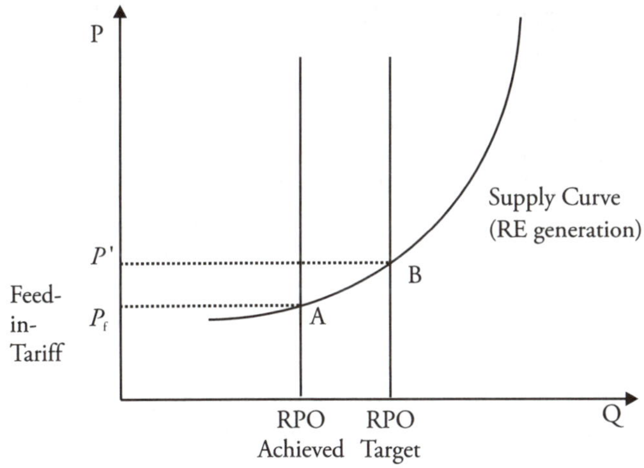

Figure 3.2 Feed-in-Tariff and Shortfall in RPO Compliance

Source: Author.

The RPO targets are not economically related to the prescribed level of FiT in most states, leading to a demand-supply mismatch for electricity generated from RES. This is reflected in the failure of RPO compliance across many states (Figure 3.2). The prevailing RPO regulations across various states specify procurement of electricity generated from RES at a separately specified FiT. Since supply curve is unobservable to the regulators, FiT may not ensure sufficient supply of RE to ensure RPO compliance. Limited RES endowments and absence of a conducive investment climate also withhold growth in supply of RES. Apart from this, variation in natural conditions bring in added uncertainty in generation of electricity from RES. Further, the RPO target is expressed as an inelastic demand curve, thereby providing no economic flexibility to the obligated entities. The National Tariff Policy, issued under the Electricity Act 2003, enables utilities to invite competitive bids for supply of electricity including that from RES. However, such a mechanism has found limited acceptability as attractive FiT tariffs are in place in most states and obligated entities continue to fall short of targets. If the utilities are allowed to procure RE from outside the state, the access to low-cost resources elsewhere in the country would help lower the cost of RPO compliance. However, the benefit of low-cost RES at far off locations would be lost by the cascading transmission charges. Also the challenge in scheduling this power and the concern for transmission constraints may also prevail over the perceived cost advantages.

Need for Effective Regulations and Role of RECs

The traditional approach to regulate and promote RES across most states has proved to be ineffective in meeting the regulatory objectives. The failure in RPO compliance and limited access to electricity generated from RES presents the following challenges to regulators and policymakers:

- How to address underachievement of RPO Target?
- How to address limited endowment of RES in a state (for example, Delhi)?
- How to improve access to 'green electricity' to consumers who want higher share of RES in their energy basket?

Apart from the above, the rigidity of existing RE regulations across the states is also resulting in higher cost of RPO compliance to the extent it is being met in some states. These rigidities, among others, include non-credit for purchase of electricity generated from RES outside the state and the absence of banking. This limits the potential of economically harnessing and trading of 'surplus' renewable electricity across the country. Apart from additional costs due to transmission charges, physical transmission of renewable electricity faces challenges like scheduling and transmission congestion. Alternatively, the economic benefits from trade of renewable electricity can be harnessed by separating 'green attributes' of renewable electricity as 'renewable electricity certificates' (RECs). The RECs can be used towards RPO compliance and can also be traded among the eligible entities. Singh (2009) suggested that a national market for RECs in India would promote RES in an economically efficient manner and would assist cost-effective compliance of RPO targets. It is expected to address the challenges identified above. The main advantages of a REC mechanism are highlighted below.

- **Flexibility in RPO compliance (Compliance market)**

One of the key characteristics of RECs is to help identify the source of electricity as a renewable one. This is primarily used to assist in compliance monitoring by regulatory institutions. This is often referred to as the compliance market. Apart from this, it also provides a flexibility mechanism wherein obligated entities, instead of procuring electricity generated from RE sources, can meet their RPO targets through purchase of RECs. From the regulators' point of view, RECs assist in accounting towards RPOs. As discussed later in the chapter, the existing REC regulations do not credit RECs for purchases made by the obligated entities under their RPO obligations under a feed in-tariff (FiT) scheme. Providing for this would not only help establish a better compliance mechanism but also encourage participation of such obligated entities in the RECs market and, hence, enhance liquidity for the same.

- **Voluntary purchase of 'Green Electricity' (Voluntary market)**

While the primary goal of the RECs is to address the needs of the compliance market, it can also serve as a useful tool for meeting the 'green electricity' needs of the voluntary market. Such applications include participation by corporate as a part of their Corporate Social Responsibility (CSR) and by philanthropic organizations as well as individuals (Singh 2009). In 2004, voluntary market in the USA was estimated to account for about 3 million MWh of green electricity with an estimated market value of \$ 15–45 million. This is projected to go up to 20 million MWh of green electricity with an estimated market value of \$ 100–300 million by 2010 (Holt and Bird 2005). RECs for voluntary market are often purchased by the electricity retailers to re-bundle this with 'grey electricity' for sale of 'green electricity' to the retail consumers. Apart from this, large consumers also buy RECs directly to green their electricity consumption.

The increase in voluntary demand for RE by residential and commercial consumers in the US is driven by green products offered by utilities and competitive electricity suppliers, and RECs (Table 3.2). While the compliance market may remain the primary driver for the RECs in India in the initial stage, the scope for voluntary market purchases would remain promising in future.

Table 3.2 Voluntary Purchase of Renewable Energy by Customer Type in the USA

S.No.	*Year*	*2005*	*2006*	*2007*	*2008*
1	Residential (GWh)	3,000	3,200	4,500	5,500
2	Commercial (GWh)	5,500	8,700	13,600	18,800
3	Total (GWh)	8,500	11,900	18,100	24,300
4	Share of Commercial (in per cent)	65	73	75	77

Source: Cook and Karelas (2009).

- **Marketing 'Green Electricity' to final consumers**

Growing consumer awareness for green energy options has led to an increase in demand for such products by electricity consumers across the world. While consumers do have an option to invest in renewable energy facilities like roof-top solar PV or solar thermal systems, their willingness to pay a premium for 'green power' is opening up new opportunities for RECs. The way green attributes are separated and sold as RECs, these can later be recombined with 'grey' electricity and be marketed as 'green electricity' to final consumers (see Figure 3.3). Such a marketing strategy not only helps to expand the market for 'green electricity' beyond utility purchases, but also improves access to the same to utilities in locations not endowed well with RES.

- **Efficiency in investment and choice of appropriate technology**

Unless held by artificial constraints, investment is expected to flow to the opportunity of maximum returns. Under the prevailing FiT scheme, alternate technologies and resources do not compete in a common framework to gain from economic efficiency.[3] Further, depending on the returns perceived by the investors in a state, the respective states may either fall short of the RPO or may overshoot the target (as noted earlier). Given a technology and resource independent single market price of RECs, the incentives would be to develop the cost-effective resources and hence, avoid economically inefficient investment.

[3] This is evident from the fact that states endowed with unfavorable resource endowments generally have higher tariffs for electricity generated from wind energy. For example per unit tariff for wind energy-based electricity generation for the states of Tamil Nadu, Maharashtra, and Madhya Pradesh were Rs 2.75, Rs 3.5, and Rs 3.97 respectively.

- **Incentives for cost reduction and benchmarks for innovation**

Cost of service or rate of return regulation does not provide efficiency for cost reduction. The FiTs are determined as a cost plus tariff on the basis of normative parameters for various cost parameters like capital structure, cost of financing, fuel cost (where applicable), O&M costs, etc. Inability of regulators to overcome the information asymmetry in determining these normative parameters gets translated into lack of incentives of cost reduction, if such norms are lax. A graduate 'sunset clause' (discussed later in the chapter) provides a benchmark for researchers as well as manufacturers to strive for efficiency improvement and cost reductions.

- **Avoiding transmission of electricity**

Being a credit mechanism, a national level RECs scheme does not require transmission of electricity from renewable energy sources, thereby avoiding transmission costs, potential transmission congestion, and operational issues with Load Despatch Centres. Given the challenges faced in operationalizing open access across various states, RECs would help expand the market for electricity generated from renewable energy sources. Due to scheduling constraints with RE-based electricity generating plants, a greater share of RE would bring in additional challenges for the system operator. However, with improved weather monitoring and forecasting tools, some of these concerns are expected to be partially addressed.

- **Efficient implementation of promotional policies by the government**

Under a REC scheme, government support to renewable energy can be transferred through the REC market. By purchasing and extinguishing RECs from the market, the government can help prop up the market price of RECs. The investors' concern for uncertainty in prices of RECs can be addressed by the government by ensuring market intervention if RECs prices fall below a pre-determined level. This would limit the government's role to reducing market uncertainty rather than transfer of resources.

The economics of off-grid RE-based rural and remote electrification projects is often unfavourable and need to be supported through public funding. Such projects can get a shot in the arm through the REC mechanism if these are made eligible to participate in the scheme. Additional revenue from sale of RECs would help support the operation and maintenance cost of such projects, thereby reducing the cost to be borne by beneficiaries of such projects. Certification and verification mechanism for such projects can be managed through local administrative authorities to reduce the associated transaction costs.

A Framework for Implementing RECs in India

The process of implementing and operationalizing a REC framework in India requires new institutions and new role for existing institutions to undertake the following responsibilities: registration of eligible RE plants, verification of the electricity produced, tracking the RECs as their ownership changes till these RECs are ultimately surrendered and extinguished towards RPO compliance (Figure 3.3). Given that India would have a national REC market, there is a greater role of central agencies like the National Load Despatch Centre (NLDC), who could work with state agencies in setting up the certification and the verification process. As trading of RECs would take place only on Power Exchanges (PXs), the national REC registry needs to follow changes in ownership and ensure that there are no duplications of RECs issued RE plant during a period. The REC regulations propose registration of RE generators for the REC scheme only. The registration process should be open to 'non-REC' generators as well. Since a RE plant can potentially shift between a FiT and a REC scheme, it would be prudent to keep track of all RE plants and their performance. The basic information to be sought from 'non-REC' RE plants at the time of registration could include location, capacity, ownership, technology, and fuel/resource. Apart from this, an annual reporting requirement can seek information on changes in capacity, generation, and sale of electricity under the FiT scheme. This would facilitate easy migration of the RE generators between the REC and the FiT mechanism, and would help validation of the plants performance irrespective of its revenue scheme. Availability of such information at a national level would reduce information asymmetry for the regulators and assist in improving policy and regulatory environment for development of RES.

The successful implementation of an REC scheme not only depends on efficient and effective regulation but also on the quality of the institutions managing various stages in the REC process. The REC implementation framework presented in Figure 3.3 also incorporates some of the suggestions presented elsewhere in the chapter. While the primary goal of the REC mechanism is to support the compliance market, a regulatory environment should facilitate the development of a voluntary market as well. The voluntary market includes direct purchase of RECs as well as purchase of 'green electricity'. The RECs can be bundled with 'grey electricity' to market and sell 'green electricity'. A 'green electricity' certification process would

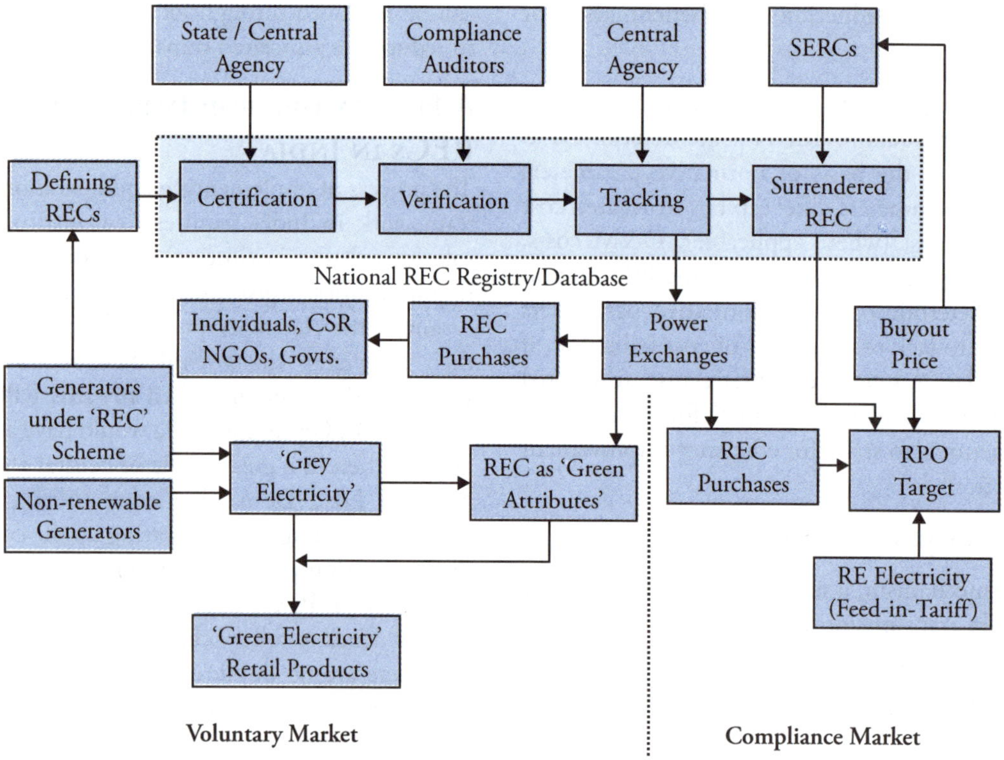

Figure 3.3 A Framework for Implementing Renewable Energy Certificates in India

Source: Author.

be required to establish authenticity of 'green electricity' to be marketed by distribution licensees and electricity retailers in future.

It is understood from the REC regulations that the REC mechanism would involve existing institutions from state as well as from the central level. Given that the institutional practices and the quality of governance vary across states, it would be advisable that CERC develops a common template for agencies to take up various responsibilities at the state level. These templates should include standardized processes for accreditation, de-accreditation, and registration of RE generators, issuance of certificates in dematerialized forms, selection of verification auditors, etc. Standarization of processes would be desirable from the market design perspective since RECs would be traded nationally at power exchanges (PXs). Further, to ensure ease of monitoring and transparency, a common national-level IT platform should be developed to manage the National REC Database. This should include information on registration of RE generators, issuance of RECs in each compliance year, RECs surrendered, and cancellation of RECs due to verification failure, etc. A system of coding the certificate should be inclusive and future-ready so as to include certain additional information, which may not even be deemed important at the moment. A suggested coding scheme may include information on the following: identity of the RE plant, location (by postcode), technology, fuel/resource, installed capacity, vintage, registering agency, verification agency, year of credit, period of credit, date of issue of certificate, status on receipt of public support, if any, and unique certificate number, etc.

CERC's Framework for Introducing RECs in India

On 14 January 2010, the CERC issued[4] final regulations for introducing RECs, called the Central Electricity Regulatory Commission (Terms and Conditions for recognition and issuance of Renewable Energy Certificates for Renewable Energy Generation) Regulations, 2010. The main features of the same are as follows:

- RECs, along with pooled purchase price of electricity, offer a revenue alternative to the feed-in-tariff regime and would operate concurrently with the later.

[4] Under the provisions of sub-section (1) of Section 178 and Section 66 read with clause (y) of sub-section (2) of Section 178 of the Electricity Act, 2003.

- There will be a central level agency to be designated by the Central Commission for registration of the RE generators participating in the scheme and for the issue of REC to RE generators.
- The scheme provides RE generators with two options—either to sell the renewable energy at preferential tariff (FiT) fixed by the concerned Electricity Regulatory Commission or to sell the electricity generated and the environmental attributes associated with RE generation separately.
- On choosing the second option, the environmental attributes can be exchanged in the form of REC, one REC being equivalent to 1 MWh of electricity generated from RES. Compensation of electricity sold to a distribution company would be equivalent to weighted average power purchase cost of the distribution company including short-term power purchase but excluding renewable power purchase cost.
- The regulations propose to issue separate RECs for solar and non-solar RES.
- The REC can be traded only in the Power Exchanges approved by CERC within the band of a floor price and a forbearance (ceiling) price to be determined by CERC from time to time.
- The distribution companies, Open Access consumers, and Captive Power Plants (CPPs) will have the option of purchasing the REC to meet their RPO.

While they are introduced with noble intentions, these regulations have room for improvement. Some of the key aspects of these regulations are critically examined in the following sub-sections, where suggestions for improvement are also outlined.[5]

Eligibility for REC: Scope for Off-grid RE Projects

The eligibility for crediting REC is limited only to electricity generated from grid-connected renewable energy sources and fed into the grid. The REC regulations also stipulate that such generators should not be a part of a prevailing FiT regime in the respective state. This undermines the role of stand-alone RE generation plant supporting remote/rural electrification schemes. Due to geographical disadvantage and lower scale of operations, such projects are often characterized by cost disadvantages, and hence any additional potential support like from revenue from RECs, would have been a shot in the arm for such initiatives in the country. Such examples include the hybrid system operational in the Sundarbans, solar PV-based plants supplying electricity to remote villages in the Durbuk region of Ladakh, etc. The Electricity Act 2003 has enabled licence-free generation and distribution by off-grid projects and the Jawaharlal Nehru National Solar Mission (JNNSM) envisions a significant role for solar energy-based schemes to provide electricity access to remote and rural areas in the country. With the existing form of REC regulations, such stand-alone generators have missed the opportunity to benefit from the same. It should also be highlighted here that, in principle, the CDM process does not exclude stand-alone projects of such nature.

Any operational issue with reference to information asymmetry can be resolved as provided elsewhere in the REC regulations itself. The regulations allow participation of RE generators not covered under scheduling and dispatch procedures. In such cases RECs are to be granted on the basis of 'written communication' of distribution licensee to the concerned State Load Dispatch Centre. A similar approach can be followed to record the number of RECs generated by recognizing written communication from an appropriate local administrative authority or energy agency. In the initial phase, stand-alone RE projects developed by NGOs/government agencies/local bodies, and those registered under the CDM process should be included to benefit from REC credits. This would also ensure effective implementation of government policies to support stand-alone projects. The amount of support available from such agencies may be linked to the RECs generated by such projects.

Category of Certificates: Avoid Market Segmentation

The REC Regulations define two categories of RECs—(i) Solar Certificates and (ii) Non-solar Certificates. There are pros and cons of separate categorization of the RECs depending on the source of energy or the geographical jurisdiction. Solar-specific RPOs are prevalent in 12 states in the US including New Jersey, New York, and Washington DC (Wiser and Barbose 2008). Solar-specific RECs are traded in New Jersey. Given the significant cost difference across the two categories, such a categorization may help in defining and seeking compliance of source-specific RPO, solar RPO in this case. However, this would reduce liquidity and trade in the two separate markets as

[5] A part of the discussion presented herein is based on the submission made by the author to the CERC during a hearing on the subject.

compared to a common market for RECs. As discussed later in the chapter, a unified market for RECs would also bring in more elasticity on the supply side, thereby reducing REC price volatility. While some of the SERCs in India have specified source-specific RPOs (Table 3.1), solar-specific RPOs have recently been introduced in some states. Nevertheless, the objective of providing greater support to solar energy can be achieved through little modification in the proposed regulations by using a multiplier for different sources as described in Singh (2009). A multiplier scheme essentially allows participation of all RES in a common REC market by using a multiplier to define the equivalent number of RECs (as suggested in Table 3.3 below).

A common scheme for multipliers can be set by CERC under the REC regulations in accordance with the resource endowments and the economic viability of various RES.[6] The multipliers can be worked out on the basis of an average benchmarked cost of electricity produced from various RESs.

A multiplier-based mechanism to combine RECs for different energy sources under a single certificate scheme has been adopted in Italy (IEA 2010) and in the UK (Ofgem 2010). Adoption of a scheme of multipliers, which allows for the credit of multiple RECs per unit of electricity generated from different RES towards overall RPO of an obligated entity, may necessitate an amendment in the Electricity Act 2003. Given the benefits of a unified REC market, this initiative merits attention as a market for RECs is yet to roll out in the country. The experience with the existing categorization would also help in taking such a call in future.

Sunset Clause for Technologies Achieving Grid-parity

A sunset clause essentially aims to reduce support for technologies that gradually become economically viable or in other words achieve grid parity in terms of costs. In future, the REC multiplier for maturing technologies can be gradually reduced in line with their cost competitiveness. This would be able to target support only to the technologies with significant cost disadvantage, as the numbers of credits to accrue to such technologies would remain higher as compared to maturing technologies. In fact, a pre-specified schedule of declining multipliers would provide a benchmark for cost reductions to be achieved to remain viable in the changing environment for RECs for the particular technology.

Denomination of Certificates and Expansion of Voluntary Markets

The REC regulations define the denomination of each REC to represent 1 MWh of electricity generated from a renewable energy source and injected into the grid. A higher denomination has the following implications:

i. Exclusion of small RE generators
ii. Limited participation of smaller buyers
iii. Adjustment for quantity less than 1 MWh[7]

By allowing accumulation of electricity generated in quantity less than one MWh in phases, the issues (i) and (iii) have only been partly addressed in the recently issued REC regulations. The voluntary markets can only be exploited by utilities willing to re-bundle RECs with 'grey electricity' for sale of 'green electricity'. Due to higher

Table 3.3 Tariff for Renewable Energy Source and an Illustration of the REC Multiplier

Renewable Energy Source	*Tariff (Rs/kWh)*	*REC Multiplier (xREC)*
Wind (Tamil Nadu)	2.75 and 2.90	1
Biomass (Tamil Nadu)	3.15	1.1
Solar	SERC's FiT + 15 (MNRE)	4–5
Solar PV (Gujarat)	13 (12 yrs.), 3 (next 13 yrs.)	
Solar Thermal (Gujarat)	10 (12 yrs.), 3 (next 13 yrs.)	~3

Source: RE Tariff orders of respective SERCs.

[6] Since the economic viability of various RESs would depend on the resource endowment and state-specific characteristics, separate REC multipliers can also be defined by the respective SERCs under a common framework to be developed by the CERC.

[7] The REC regulations propose this to be included with the credits for RECs for the next period. While this allows for inclusion of parts of one MWh, the credit for the same is delayed by at least a fortnight.

denomination, individual voluntary participation would remain limited.

In order to enhance market participation and to improve liquidity in the market for RECs, the denomination of a single REC should be smaller than 1 MWh. It can perhaps be set in 'units' of 100 kWh. Higher denominations for RECs would be unfavourable to small RE facilities. A smaller denomination (such as the 100 kWh equivalent) would facilitate participation of small buyers as well as small projects across the country.[8]

This would expand the scope of voluntary markets[9] and facilitate the reach of the market to individuals and smaller organizations. Smaller denomination for RECs would be a boon for small solar projects as envisioned under the JNNSM. Roof-top solar PV facilities with net metering can also be credited with RECs in a manner similar to that proposed for larger projects thereby making it a more attractive option for investment.

Absence of Banking of RECs

The REC regulations specify the validity of a REC to be 365 days from crediting. The performance of renewable energy-based electricity generating plants is significantly dependent on the natural conditions like wind speed, solar insolation, rainfall, etc. Even in the case of biomass plants, availability of biomass often influences the operating performance of RE generators. This makes it challenging to dispatch electricity generated from RES. In this context, it would be difficult to project the number of RECs that could be earned and transferred by a generator to the obligated entities. Given such uncertainty, flexible mechanisms such as extended validity to facilitate banking of certificates, and partial rollover of RPO are crucial components of efficient regulatory practices. With banking provisions, obligated entities can procure additional RECs in a given year over and above their current year RPO target[10] and seek credit for the same in a future period. The validity of tradable RECs extends up to two years and five years after the issuance in Italy and Belgium (Flanders) respectively. In the case of UK, Poland, Denmark, and the Netherlands, certificates have unlimited validity. As discussed in a later section, banking of certificates would be an economic solution to reduce volatility in the price of RECs.

Choice of Regulatory Deterrent: Setting a Buyout Price

In the absence of an effective deterrent to failure in meeting the RPO targets, obligated entities do not have enough motivation to pursue such targets diligently. A penalty for failure to meet the RPO, though applicable in Maharashtra and Rajasthan,[11] is yet to test the grounds. In economic terms, the penalty should be higher than P', the minimum price which would ensure long-term investment in RES to assist RPO compliance (see Figure 3.2). Ideally, obligated entities would avoid a 'penalty' and, hence, procure electricity from RES or buy RECs to ensure RPO compliance. Lack of investment in RES in a state is often used to justify shortfall in meeting the RPO targets. With emergence of a market for RECs, this issue would cease to exist under an appropriate regulatory environment.

There are economic as well as legal aspects to a penalty-based deterrence mechanisms.[12] As an alternative to a penalty, regulators can specify a buyout price (BP) or alternative compliance payment (ACP) for RECs. The regulatory body could essentially 'print' and 'sell', to the 'obligated entities', the number of RECs required to make up for the RPO shortfall at a pre-determined buyout price. Hence, the argument for lack of supply would not hold. While delivering the same outcome, this mechanism may avoid the legal complications of implementing a 'penalty'. The uncertainty associated with the market price of RECs may dissuade investors from putting faith in the REC scheme. In economic terms, buyout price should essentially be equal to the marginal social benefit of electricity sourced from RE sources over that from non-renewable sources. In other words, it is the value of the environmental attributes of 'green electricity'. The SERCs

[8] While participation of small buyers would not impose significant transaction costs, smaller buyers may face higher transaction costs unless alternate registration and verification schemes are designed in line with small-scale projects under the Clean Development Mechanism (CDM).

[9] Utility/retailer-based voluntary markets involving sale of re-bundled 'green electricity' would not be influenced by higher denominations due to the scale of operation of such activities in future.

[10] Especially, when REC prices are low.

[11] In Maharashtra, the applicable penalty for 2009–10 is Rs 7 per kWh. In the case of Rajasthan, the penalty was fixed at Rs 3.59 per kWh for 2007–8 (Singh 2009).

[12] Enforcement of a penalty mechanism is often subjected to legal disputes wherein the 'affected' party may need to establish the loss incurred. This time-consuming process often defeats the very purpose of instituting a regulatory penalty.

could specify state-specific buyout price that would represent the value of absence of green attributes of a unit of electricity in the given state. This would also be guided by the resource endowments of the state, the existing and upcoming investment, and the RPO target and historical compliance thereof. A buyout price would essentially function as a forbearance price for the RECs as prescribed under Section 9 of the REC regulations (discussed further in a later section). The prescribed level of BP or ACP in some of the jurisdictions in Europe and the US are given in Table 3.4 below. The ACP that undergo automatic cost recovery in the US states of Maine, Massachusetts, New Hampshire, New Jersey, and Rhode Islands works like a buyout price.

Table 3.4 Buyout Price for RPO Shortfall

Country	*Per 1 MWh equivalent REC*
Belgium (Flanders)	Euro 125 (from April 2005)
Poland	Euro 60 (2005–06)
UK	£30 (2002–03) £37.19 (2009–10)
Australia	Aus $ 40
Maine (USA)	$ 57.12 (2008)
Massachusetts (USA)	$ 58.58 (2008)

Sources: RECs (2005), Ofgem (2010), Rossiter and Singh (2006), and Wiser and Barbose (2008).

A buyout mechanism would also ensure that the payments by obligated entities would go into building a buyout fund rather than paying steep REC prices. This buyout fund could be utilized to support RES in the state, and to increase consumer awareness about RECs and 'green electricity'. Failure to pay buyout price due to insolvency or other reasons can be addressed through a mutualization mechanism as in the case of the UK.[13] In the case of insolvency of an obligated entity to pay the buyout price thus leading to a shortfall in buyout fund, all other entities who have met their obligations make good the shortfall, up to a prescribed limit. While disallowance of the payment towards buyout price in the utilities revenue requirement may seem to be a more effective deterrent, it would work against the interest of the consumers. The utilities would effectively be willing to pay a higher price for RECs, which would be a pass-through, than making buyout payments.

Linking FiT and REC Mechanisms

A standard REC scheme implemented across most of the countries is a standard 'cap-and-trade' mechanism, wherein utilities are required to meet their respective RPOs. Any shortfall can either be covered by purchasing the RECs from other utilities in the market or by paying the buyout price. India is perhaps the only country to have two alternate revenue schemes for investors in RE plants—(i) FiT Scheme and (ii) Renewable Energy Certificate Scheme.

While concurrence of the two schemes poses some challenges for implementation, it also opens new opportunities to derive synergies between the two schemes for, (i) Certifying Guarantee of origin under the FiT Scheme and (ii) Augmentation of REC supply from the FiT Scheme. The 'guarantee of origin' for the existing FiT Scheme across states is based only on the disclosures made by the obligated entities. The registration and verification mechanism built into the REC framework can be effectively extended to perform the above task for the FiT mechanism as well. Since obligated entities include numerous captive and open access consumers, which are expected to grow in numbers in future, the existing self-certification scheme could be strengthened through the registration process built into the REC mechanism. Towards this end, RECs can initially be credited to all electricity generated from RES including those under the FiT scheme. The RECs issued to projects under the FiT scheme needs to be compulsorily surrendered towards RPO compliance. The obligated entities can then be allowed to compulsorily bank and sell excess[14] RECs over and above the RPO target on a power exchange in a subsequent compliance year. If shortfall in RPO targets can be made good through purchase of RECs, the same philosophy should theoretically hold true for excess RECs as well. This would give incentive to the obligated entities to procure RE even in excess of their respective RPO and also lower the financial burden of excess RE procurement as in the case of Karnataka and Tamil Nadu. Such a proposal can be operationalized only if RECs are issued to all RE projects under the FiT scheme. Alternatively, excess RECs can be bought by the buyout fund at a pre-determined floor price, once sufficient funds are accumulated into the same. Most of RECs to be issued under the FiT scheme are expected to be surrendered and extinguished towards RPO compliance. Since the obligated entities in most states fall

[13] See Ofgem (2010) for details.

[14] Note that obligated entities in some of the states like Karnataka and Tamil Nadu excess their RPO targets (Table 3.1).

short of their RPO targets, the supply of excess RECs from the FiT mechanism would help arrest the REC prices in a market expected to witness shortages in the initial stage.

Price Discovery in the Market for RECs

Before discussing the conditions for price discovery, we identify potential stakeholders on the demand as well as supply side in a market for RECs. The demand side would include, (i) Obligated entities with a shortfall in RPO target, (ii) RE generators under REC scheme who are not able to ensure a contractual supply of RECs, (iii) Voluntary demand for RECs (either direct purchases or through re-bundled 'green electricity'), and (iv) Potential government support to REC market. The obligated entities may generally include the distribution licensees, open access (OA) consumers and captive consumers. Given that it is only the distribution licensees who have traditional 'access' to electricity generated from RES, the market for RECs would provide an alternate platform for RPO compliance for the OA and captive consumers. Due to a specified minimum RPO, demand for RECs would be relatively inelastic[15] (Figure 3.4). The demand curve would shift to the right as RPO targets are gradually increased and growth in supplies under the FiT scheme is not able to fill this gap.

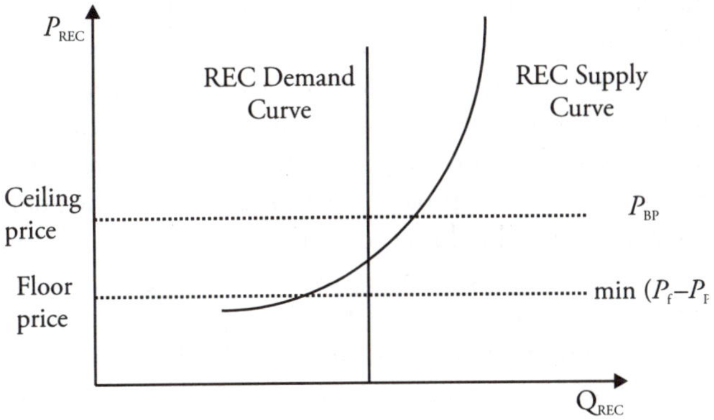

Figure 3.4 Price Discovery for the RECs

Source: Author.

On the supply side, the potential suppliers for RECs include, (i) RE generators under the REC scheme, (ii) Obligated entities with excess RECs, (iii) Banked RECs from projects under the FiT or REC scheme, and (iv) Small RE generators under JNNSM or other such schemes, if made eligible. The supply side of RECs would also be relatively inelastic as marginal cost for most of RES (for example, solar and wind) are very low. The variation on the supply side would be driven by investments as well as seasonal variations. The inelastic nature of the demand and supply side would bring in higher volatility in REC prices. The demand as well as the supply side of RECs could become more elastic through appropriate regulatory interventions.

Introduction of banking of RECs would make the demand more elastic. During the periods of oversupply (and lower prices), obligated entities can make excess purchases and use them later in periods of lower supply. Similarly, RE generators can withhold RECs in a period of oversupply (and lower prices), and sell them in periods of lower supply (and higher prices). A mix of technology would make the supply more elastic than a single technology (as in the case of solar RECs). Further, a cap (forbearance) and a floor price for the RECs can also help in arresting volatility within the two bounds (Figure 3.4). These are discussed in the next section.

The REC regulations allow for price discovery at power exchanges (PXs). However, multiplicity of PXs may be a cause for concern for the liquidity in the market, at least in the initial phase.[16] In the initial stage, the demand for RECs would come primarily from the obligated entities failing to achieve their RPO targets. The captive and open access consumers have relatively lower RE requirements and face higher transaction costs to meet their RPO targets under the FiT scheme. Given reasonable REC prices, such entities may participate actively in the market for RECs.

In the absence of a buyout price for making good the shortfall in RPO target, credible demand for certificates may not materialize in the near future. Due to potential windfall gains, new RE projects in Rajasthan, Tamil Nadu, and Maharashtra would primarily come under the REC scheme. Obligated entities, who overshoot their RPO targets could be a potential net supplier for RECs in the initial stage, if permitted. There is a case for the regulatory changes to enhance the participation of such entities in the market and to offload excess RE procurement through the REC mechanism.

Setting Floor and Forbearance Price for RECs

Under appropriate regulatory environment, the forbearance and the floor price would emerge from the system

[15] In discussing a market for RECs here, we ignore the presence of a FiT mechanism for simplicity.

[16] This concern may not arise in case obligated entities are credited RECs under the FiT scheme and if such entities participate in trading on in RECs.

itself and there would not be a need to specify these separately. The price of RECs would be capped from below by the difference between prevailing FiT P_f and the Average Power Purchase Cost (APPC) P_p. Since both of these differ across states, the minimum level of the difference $(P_f - P_p)$ across the states would act as the underlying floor price for the national market[17] (Figure 3.4). This difference is essentially a hedonic price[18] for the 'green attributes' of electricity generated from RES. If the price of REC falls below this level, RE generators are better off selling their output under the FiT scheme, and vice versa. The REC price would be capped from the above by the minimum specified buyout price (P_{BP}) across states.[19] The obligated entities in a state with a minimum buyout price would be the first one to opt to pay buyout price than paying for a REC price higher than this level.

The CERC has recently specified forbearance and floor price for solar and non-solar RECs (Table 3.5). The CERC (2010b) estimated the difference between feed-in-tariff and APPC $(P_f - P_p)$ across the states and chooses the maximum level as forbearance price (Rs 3.9 per kWh for non-solar case). Further, a floor price is set to ensure economic viability of RE projects. Due to paucity of space, we do not discuss the relative advantage or disadvantages of the approach to fix the two price limits as proposed in this chapter and that adopted by the CERC. As discussed below, the CERC approach has led to higher floor as well as forbearance prices.

TABLE 3.5 CERC's Forbearance and Floor Price for RECs

	Non solar REC (Rs/MWh)	*Solar REC (Rs/MWh)*
Forbearance Price	3,900	17,000
Floor Price	1,500	12,000

Source: CERC (2010b).

The choice of maximum difference not only encourages inefficiency in choice of resource and technology but also provides potential windfall gain to technologies which have significant cost advantage. This is also not consistent with the Electricity Act 2003, Section 61(c), which states that determination of tariff by the appropriate commission should be guided by 'the factors which would encourage competition, efficiency, economical use of the resources, good performance and optimum investments'. Further, the National Tariff Policy also states that the 'new capacity addition should deliver electricity at most efficient rates to protect the interests of consumers'. While preferential tariffs and promotion of RES is desirable and should continue, no room should be left to breed inefficiency in investment and operation in the sector.

Tariffs are the most appropriate instruments to ensure efficient choices by producers in choice of technology and appropriate renewable energy source. A higher floor price for REC would not provide incentive for cost reductions and improvement in technology. The prescribed levels of floor and forbearance price provide a room for windfall gain for investors in RES in some states. Table 3.6 illustrates this for non-solar RECs. The effective peak and floor tariff for non-solar technologies in the minimum and the maximum level of revenue investors would make per unit of electricity supplied form RE projects in the respective states. The effective floor tariff works out to be higher than the prevailing FiT in some states. This would clearly increase the cost of RPO compliance and pass on excess burden to consumers in such states. This is in contract the philosophy of the RECs, which are expected to bring down the cost of compliance.

We can note from Table 3.6 that the wind energy projects in Tamil Nadu, Rajasthan, and Maharashtra would find the REC market more lucrative than selling the electricity under the applicable FiT in the respective states, and make windfall gains as compared to the latest FiT. In the case of biomass and co-generation projects in Maharashtra and biomass projects in Tamil Nadu, the FiT scheme would remain the more attractive alternative. Even within the CERC approach, the forbearance and the floor price for RECs should be set at the respective minimum levels observed across the states. This would encourage efficiency and remove room for windfall gain for certain technologies in a few states. Accordingly, these two price limits should not be higher than the equivalent of Rs 1.66 per kWh and Rs 0.29 per kWh, respectively (based on data presented in CERC 2010b).

The electricity generated from RES embodies green attributes that offset carbon emissions on account of use of fossil fuels in electricity generation. Given the floor and the forbearance price of REC fixed by the CERC,

[17] Theoretically speaking, only when the supply of RECs from the state with this minimum difference is exhausted, the floor price would automatically move to the second lowest difference and so on.

[18] Hedonic price is generally used to estimate the economic value of environmental attributes that influence market prices. This is often applied to value local environmental attributes embedded in housing prices.

[19] Theoretically speaking, only when the demand of RECs from obligated entities in the state with the minimum buyout price is exhausted, the forbearance price would automatically move to the second lowest buyout price and so on.

TABLE 3.6 Forbearance and Floor Price for RECs: Encouraging Inefficiency and Windfall Gains

State (1)	*RES* (2)	*Tariff as per RE Tariff Regulation* (3)	*APPC for 2009–10* (4)	*Difference between RE tariff and APPC* (5) = (3)–(4)	*Effective Peak Tariff for non-solar* (6) = (4) + P_{FB}	*Effective Floor Tariff for non-solar* (7) = (4) + P_{FL}	*Prevailing Feed-in-Tariff*[@] (8)	*Windfall Gain*[#] (9) = (7)–(8) to (6)–(8)
Rajasthan	Wind	5.63	2.57	3.06	6.47	4.07	3.83	0.24–2.64
Tamil Nadu	Wind	4.17	2.51	1.66	6.41	4.01	3.39	0.62–3.02
Maharashtra	Wind	5.63	2.51	3.12	6.41	4.01	2.86–4.29	0–3.55
Maharashtra	SHP	4.31	2.51	1.8	6.41	4.01	3.14	0.87–3.27
Maharashtra	Biomass	4.76	2.51	2.25	6.41	4.01	4.98	0–1.43
Maharashtra	Co-gen.	4.8	2.51	2.29	6.41	4.01	4.79	0–1.62
Tamil Nadu	Biomass	5.08	2.51	2.57	6.41	4.01	4.66	0–1.75

Notes: All figures are in Rs/kWh. Apart from columns 6–9, the rest of the data is from CERC (2010 b); P_{FB}—Forbearance price for non solar RECs (from Table 3.5); P_{FL}—Floor price for non-solar RECs (from Table 3.5); APPC - Average Power Purchase Cost; @—The prevailing feed-in-tariffs are from latest available tariff orders of respective SERCs. #—Minimum (maximum) level of windfall gain corresponds to the floor (forbearance) price.

one can infer the implicit carbon value embedded in the RECs. Table 3.7 gives an illustration of the same for solar as well as non-solar RECs. It is based on the assumption that environmental attributes of RECs represent only the carbon displacement from conventional electricity generation. This is achieved by applying the baseline data for the Indian power sector worked out by the CEA (2009b). We use both simple operating as well as combined margins to illustrate our approach.

One can note that the floor and the forbearance price set by the CERC translate to a carbon price of about Euro 25 (Euro 198) and Euro 64 (Euro 281) respectively. In contrast to this, the CERC future price on the European Climate Exchange ranged between Euro 10.88 and Euro 14.45 in 2010. It touched a low of Euro 7.39 in February 2009 and a peak of Euro 23.88 in July 2008. Clearly, the floor and forbearance price of RECs have been set higher and do not conform to the carbon value witnessed in the environmentally conscious regions like the European Union. Additionally, RE generators may also be able to sell CDM credits separately. There is clearly a need for corrective action.

TABLE 3.7 Floor and Forbearance Price: Implicit Price of Carbon[20]

	Units	*Non-Solar*		*Solar*	
		For Simple Operating Margin (excl. Imports)	*For Combined Margin (excl. Imports)*	*For Simple Operating Margin (excl. Imports)*	*For Combined Margin (excl. Imports)*
Operating/Combined Margin	tCO_2/MWh	1.009	0.859	1.009	0.859
REC floor Price	Rs/MWh	1500	1500	12000	12000
Implicit floor price of carbon	Rs/tCO_2	1486.02	1746.01	11888.20	13968.07
Implicit floor price of carbon	Euro/tCO_2	24.77	29.10	198.14	232.80
REC forbearance price	Rs/MWh	3900	3900	17000	17000
Implicit forbearance price of carbon	Rs/tCO_2	3863.66	4539.62	16841.61	19788.10
Implicit forbearance price of carbon	Euro/tCO_2	64.39	75.66	280.69	329.80

Note: 1 Euro = Rs 60.
Source: Author.

[20] The implicit price of carbon is calculated as the REC floor price divided by the emission factor (obtained from simple operating or combined margin).

Conclusions

The basic principles of market design often flow from economic theory and are then 'tuned' to address market imperfections. Introduction of renewable energy certificates in India brings new opportunities and challenges for various stakeholders. The traditional policy and regulatory framework for promotion of renewable energy sources is based on specification of an RPO for the obligated entities, who need to compensate the RE generators as per the prevailing feed-in-tariff, which varies across states. The demand-supply mismatch is manifested in the shortfall in meeting RPO targets across most of the states in India. The prevailing conditions disregard economic efficiency wherein the most economically viable resources should be utilized first using the appropriate technologies. The variations in resource endowments and RPO targets further complicate the situation. Apart from setting more realistic RPO targets based on techno-economic studies, a market-based mechanism for RECs, seems to offer promise to partly address the prevailing economic anomalies and bring greater participation in the promotion of RES.

The CERC's regulation for developing a market for RECs in the country is a welcome step in this direction. However, the framework for developing a market for RECs brings in new imperfections and does not provide enough incentive for efficient investment and operation. There is clearly a scope for improvement. The chapter highlights many such issues and supports them with economic arguments. The vision for developing a thriving market for RECs needs to imbibe greater economic efficiency and expand the scope for participation. This would help encourage the obligated entities to meet their RPO targets in a cost-effective manner. The existing levels of floor and forbearance price do not encourage efficiency and seemingly provide windfall gain to RE investors in some states. This exercise may be revisited in the line of arguments presented in the chapter. Absence of banking and a buyout price also remain key hurdles to developing an efficient market for RECs. These can be specified at the state level by individual SERCs. The institutional set-up to register and track the RECs would serve a meaningful role in providing similar services for projects under the FiT scheme as well. The chapter also suggests a mechanism for trading excess RE procured by the obligated entities over and above the applicable RPO targets, through the REC mechanism. This opportunity should also be utilized to enhance support to small but socially desirable applications like stand-alone rural electrification schemes and development of a voluntary market.

Adoption of market-based instruments like RECs should be based on principles which encourages choice of cost-effective RES and promotes efficient investment and operation of RE plants across the country. By setting a higher forbearance and floor price for RECs, we seem to have missed this opportunity to effectively use a new market institution to meet the above objectives and to strengthen the ethos established under the Electricity Act 2003 and the National Tariff Policy. The REC regulations leave a room for improvement and the proposed suggestions merit regulatory attention.

References

Berry, D. (2002). 'The Market for Tradable Renewable Energy Credits', *Ecological Economics*, 42, pp. 369–79.

Bertoldi, P. and T. Huld (2006). 'Tradable Certificates for Renewable Electricity and Energy Savings', *Energy Policy*, 34, pp. 212–22.

Bloomberg New Energy Finance (2010). Personal Communication through email, July 2010.

Central Electricity Authority (CEA) (2009a). *All India Electricity Statistics—General Review 2009*, Central Electricity, New Delhi.

——— (2009b) *Baseline Carbon Dioxide Emissions from Power Sector*, Central Electricity Authority, Ministry of Power, Government of India. New Delhi, accessed in July 2010 from http://www.cea.nic.in/planning/c%20and%20e/Government%20of%20India%20website.htm

Central Electricity Regulatory Commission (CERC) (2010a). *Terms and Conditions for Recognition and Issuance of Renewable Energy Certificate for Renewable Energy Generation Regulations, 2010*, Central Electricity Regulatory Commission, New Delhi.

——— (2010b). *Determination of Forbearance and Floor Price for the REC Framework, 2010*, Central Electricity Regulatory Commission, New Delhi.

Cook, O. and A. Karelas (2009). *Insights into the Renewable Energy Market: A Brief Overview of Procurement Trends, Drivers, and Impacts of Voluntary Commercial Purchasers*, Center for Resource Solutions. Francisco, California.

FoR (2008). *Policies on Renewables: Report*, Forum of Regulation, Central Electricity Regulatory Authority, New Delhi.

Government of India (GoI) (2010). *Jawaharlal Nehru National Solar Mission*. Ministry of New and Renewable Energy, Government of India, New Delhi.

——— (2009a). *National Action Plan of Climate Change (NAPCC)*, Government of India, New Delhi.

——— (2009b). *Report on Development of Conceptual Framework for Renewable Energy Certificate Mechanism for India*, Ministry of New and Renewable Energy, New Delhi.

Gillenwater, M. (2008). 'Redefining RECs—Part 1: Untangling Attributes and Offsets', *Energy Policy*, 36, pp. 2109–19.

Holt, Ed and Lori Bird (2005). *Emerging Markets for Renewable Energy Certificates: Opportunities and Challenges*, Technical Report, NREL/TP-620-37388, National Renewable Energy Laboratory, Colorado.

International Energy Agency (IEA) (2010). Renewable Database, http://www.iea.org/textbase/pm/?mode=re&id=4107&action=detail

Mendonca, M., J. David Jr., B. Sovacool (2010). *Powering the Green Economy: The Feed-in Tariff Handbook*, Earthscan Publications, London.

Morthorst, P.E. (2000). 'The Development of a Green Certificate Market', *Energy Policy*, 28, pp. 1085–94.

Nielsen, L.T. Jeppesen (2003). 'Tradable Green Certificates in Selected European Countries—Overview and Assessment', *Energy Policy*, 31(1), pp. 3–14

Office of the Gas and Electricity Markets (Ofgem) (2010). 'The Renewables Obligation Buy-out Price and Mutualisation Ceiling 2010–11', Ofgem, London, accessed in March 2010 from http://www.ofgem.gov.uk/Media/PressRel/Documents1/RO%20Buy-Out%20price%202010%2011%20FINAL%20FINAL.pdf

Renewable Energy Certificates or Credits (RECs) (2005). *The Use of the Guarantee of Origin*, RECS International, Utrecht.

REN21 (2009). *Renewables Global Status Report 2009 Update*, REN21 Secretariat, Paris.

Rossiter, D. and A. Singh (2006). *Australia's Renewable Energy Certificate System*, Office of the Renewable Energy Regulator, Canberra, Australia.

Singh, Anoop (2009). 'A Market for Renewable Energy Credits in the Indian Power Sector', *Renewable and Sustainable Energy Reviews*, 13, pp. 643–52.

——— (2006). 'Nationally Tradable Renewable Energy Credits for Renewable Portfolio Obligation in the Indian Power Sector', SEE Conference Proceedings, Bangkok, 21–23 November 2006.

Voogt, M., M.G. Boots, G.J. Schaeffer, J.W. Martens (2000). 'Renewable Electricity in a Liberalized Market—The Concept of Green Certificates', *Energy and Environment* 11, pp. 65–79. (as cited in Nielsen and Jeppesen 2003)

Wiser, R. and Galen Barbose (2008). 'Renewables Portfolio Standards in the United States—A Status Report with Data through 2007', LBNL 154E, Lawrence Berkeley National Laboratory, Berkeley, California.

Section II

Financing Infrastructure Development along Low Carbon Trajectory

4 Financing Low Carbon Infrastructure in India

Dhruba Purkayastha, Manisha Gulati, and Sunder Subramanian

Introduction

Growth on a low carbon economy trajectory has the potential to yield multiple benefits for India. These include, enhanced energy security from efficient energy usage (both supply and demand sides) and renewable energy projects; human health benefits from non-polluting transport; and environmental benefits through improved forestry and natural resource management, waste reduction programmes, and reduced emissions of local pollutants from energy facilities. As such, reducing carbon intensity of growth is an imperative. A shift to low carbon infrastructure (LCI)[1] growth would necessarily have to be progressive and will need a mix of enabling factors—spanning the right policy environment, tec nology and process innovation, human and institutional capacity, markets and regulatory frameworks, and more importantly, access to dedicated finance directed towards low carbon growth initiatives.

But how much financing will be required? Various estimates are available at the global level (see Table 4.1) but as far as India is concerned, no readymade estimates are available. Such an estimation requires a great deal of information about physical impacts of LCI; the mitigation and adaptation needs of the country; the expected economic growth, population growth, demand for infrastructure, use of clean technologies, and finally, the funding requirements of such needs. Nevertheless, it would suffice to say that the funding requirement is huge and could easily run into billions of dollars. A study by McKinsey & Company[2] corroborates this. According to this study, a projected increase in emissions to 5–6.5 billion MT of carbon dioxide equivalent in India could be lowered by 30 per cent to 50 per cent by 2030 by investing in energy-efficient technologies in road transport, power, buildings, and appliances. The report suggests that incremental capital of about 600–750 billion euro ($874 billion to $1.1 trillion) would be needed between 2010 and 2030, even after accounting for steep declines in the cost of emerging technologies such as solar power.

The estimates are staggering—and there is no clear understanding of how these financing requirements will be met. Against this backdrop, this chapter examines the options for financing LCI in India. The main questions addressed here are:

- What is the role of the public and private financial sectors in supporting the implementation of a low carbon development strategy?
- How can international and domestic financing mechanisms facilitate new public and private sector investment to facilitate low carbon growth, build carbon market access, accelerate technological innovation, and support adaptation to the impacts of climate change?
- How can the country generate new and additional funds to finance such infrastructure development?
- What should be the role of commercial banks and financial institutions in facilitating such infrastructure development?

[1] Low Carbon Infrastructure is a broad-based term encompassing all possible measures to reduce carbon footprint in basic infrastructure services such as green/energy-efficient transport, renewable power, reduced carbon emissions in coal-based power, etc.

[2] McKinsey & Company (2009).

TABLE 4.1 Estimated Costs of Addressing Climate Change at the Global Level

Study	*Adaptation costs*	*Mitigation costs*	*Total costs*
OECD Environmental Outlook to 2030		0.5 per cent of global GDP in 2030 and 2.5 per cent of global GDP in 2050	
IPCC Fourth Assessment Report: Climate Change 2007		0.6 per cent of global GDP in 2030 and about 1.3 per cent of global GDP in 2050	
UNDP Human Development Report 2007–8	$ 86 billion by 2015	1.6 per cent of global GDP between 2007 and 2030	
UNFCCC Dialogue on long-term cooperative action to address climate change by enhancing implementation of the Convention, 2007	Indicatively at least $ 44–166 billion	approx. $ 200–210 billion	approx. $ 248–381 billion from private and public sources in the year 2030 to return global GHG emissions to the level of 2004
Stern Review: The Economics of Climate Change, 2006			1 per cent of global GDP by 2050
Copenhagen Accord, 2009			$ 30 billion during 2010–12 and $ 100 billion a year till 2020

Source: Authors' own.

- How should public finance directed for low carbon be intermediated/distributed?

Barriers to Financing Low Carbon Infrastructure

Before exploring financing options for LCI, it is necessary to get a sense of the current barriers to financing such infrastructure. The barriers for financing would differ from project to project but can generally be classified under the following three categories:

Divergence between social and private costs

The first and perhaps the most important barrier to the financing of LCI projects is the existence of 'externalities'. Negative externalities arise when an entity's actions impose costs on others for which the entity does not pay. Similarly, positive externalities arise when the entity's actions generate benefits for others for which the entity has to incur costs. Externalities can be internalized if those who benefit or bear costs are made to pay in the latter case or are compensated in the former. The social benefits from avoided carbon-inflicted damages are much larger than the private benefits to carbon emitters and are often much greater than the social costs of the investment required to cut emissions. Put more simply, the investments in low carbon infrastructure usually do not generate adequate returns on investment given the potential for generating revenue from LCI. The theoretical solution would be to price the damage done and force the polluters to pay for it, thus internalizing the externality. However, this solution cannot be adopted without public intervention. The absence of such intervention leads to a huge divergence between the social and private costs, and therefore provides little incentive for investments in LCI. In addition there are inadequate incentives for research, development, and commercialization of lower carbon technologies[3] (LCT). There are of course other discontinuities that sit alongside, but are often not included, in the traditional economic analysis. For example, traditional power infrastructure is often supported by extensive implicit subsidies, which is not available to smaller scale distributed forms of renewable power.

Credit market failure

Many of the barriers to LCI and related technology development or transfer are the same as the barriers to growth and investment, that is, a poor investment climate, due to a variety of factors—political, regulatory, administrative complexity, etc. Financial intermediation for LCI through banks or through markets for financial instruments is hindered by:

- lack of familiarity in the lending community with LCT and consequently, LCI leading to the inability to assess risk appropriately;

[3] LCT refers to the development of low carbon technology such as specific solar technology or bio-fuels which could then be applied for LCI.

- high transaction costs relative to conventional project financing. This is due to lack of maturity of various clean technologies with higher initial capital outlay and long payback periods, increasing the risks leading to higher interest rates being charged;
- absence of long-term funds and hence financing instruments;
- tendency of the lenders to frequently consider asking for recourse, that is, looking at the borrower's assets along with the project's ability to finance itself due to the risks associated with LCT; and
- inadequacy/unsuitability of bank regulations and investment policies for LCI, since such regulations and policies are often geared for larger conventional projects.

Intergenerational barriers

In simple terms, this barrier deals with the classic question of why should the existing generation bear the cost of investing in clean technologies, while the benefits would arguably accrue to future generations? The question can, of course, be asked differently by asking why the cost of pollution caused by the existing generation be borne by the future generations.

Towards an LCI Financing Framework

Given the context outlined in the section above, we now take a look at the broad contours of an LCT/LCI financing framework. The LCT/LCI financing needs can be divided into two broad phases, with Phase I dealing with LCT development and Phase II dealing with the roll-out of commercialized clean technologies. Phase I can be further split into three sub-phases (see Figure 4.1).

> Phase I: This phase covers the stages from technology innovation and development to scale-up, when the technology can be deployed commercially, but has not yet achieved the volumes and cost reductions necessary for it to be fully competitive with conventional technologies. This phase ends with the achievement of full commercialization.
>
> Phase II: This phase refers to the post commercialization stage when the technology is being rolled out at a commercial level to produce goods and services. At this stage, attention would also have to be paid to the needs of businesses that produce, distribute, and sell such goods and services.

The financing strategy for each phase would have to be geared to the financing needs of that phase. Therefore, in suggesting the financing options for these phases, we first identify the gaps in financing in respective stages, and then suggest an appropriate strategy to address this gap: mechanisms for enabling directed funding and options for meeting the incremental finance requirement. Of course, this does not take into account the significant allocation of R&D spending which takes place in a corporate context rather than on a project basis—in the case of the power sector, examples would include GE, Suzlon,

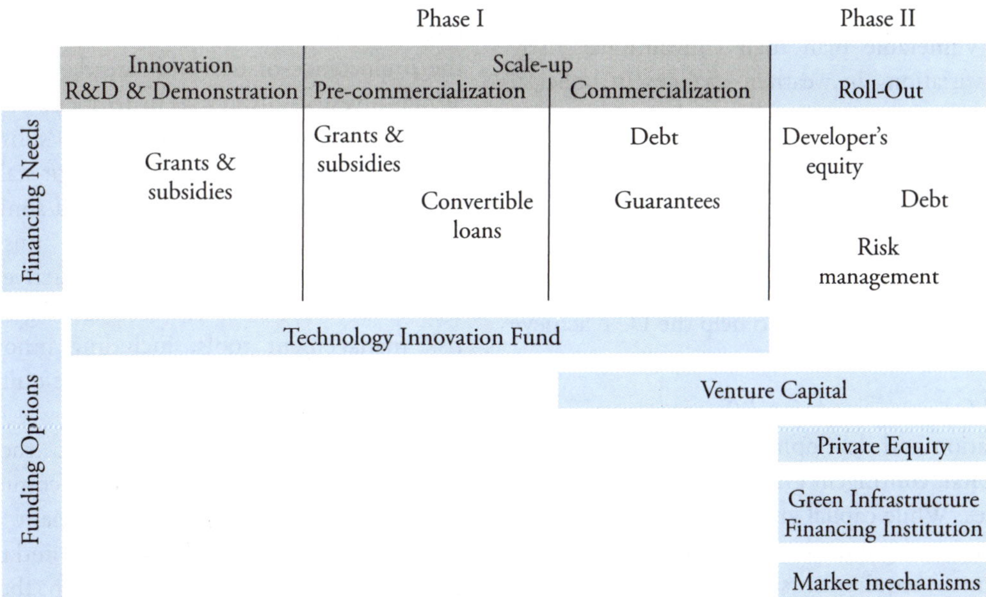

Figure 4.1 LCI/LCT Finance Continuum—Financing Needs and Some Possible Options

Source: Adapted from UNEP SEFI's Sustainable Energy Finance Continuum.

Siemens, the global energy companies, and existing power companies. Also, capital will flow in the face of significant barriers when there is great potential for marketplace change (through new price signals) or great potential for technological innovation. In the markets that we most commonly refer to when making this type of argument, for example, telecom and pharma, venture capital has often flowed quickly as a result of new technology and regulatory opportunities.

Enabling Directed Funding of LCI

Phase I: Innovation to scale-up

This phase can be divided into two broad parts (i) research, design, and development, and (ii) pre-commercialization and commercialization. In the first part, a general lack of funds for basic innovation and development and a funding gap when technologies move beyond the research stage, (popularly referred to as the 'valley of death') inhibits progress from getting to and through the demonstration stage. Some technologies or projects may be too far along to get funding from traditional sources that fund research; at the same time, they are unable to attract investors, because they are perceived as being 'too early' in the stage of technology development. This is because there is scarcity of risk capital focused towards this stage for three reasons:

- Technologies are subject to extensive timing uncertainty in this stage, thereby increasing strategic and financial risk.
- In demonstration and deployment, LCTs are more financially vulnerable than their conventional alternatives to variations in weather, changes in political support, and operational failure due to system complexity.
- Business risks are also significant because of capital intensity, high costs of production and consequently, low market demand. This increases the physical, political, and operational risks associated with them. This results in lack of availability of funds to help the LCT achieve full commercialization.

The typical financing needs for different stages of technology innovation and development (see Figure 4.1) include seed capital, contingent grants, debt financing, and debt guarantees. While capital grants are self-explanatory, contingent grants are grants that are 'loaned' without interest or repayment requirements until the technology and intellectual property (IP) have been successfully exploited. Such grants can serve to cover some of the costs during the highest risk development stages, and in some cases they increase investor confidence, which helps to leverage highly needed risk capital. These grants can be particularly effective during high risk demonstration phases when the technology start-up has little or no access to capital. The advantage of contingent grants over conventional grants is that they steer the technology developer and entrepreneur towards private and commercial financing.

To a smaller extent, debt financing, in the form of soft and convertible loans, can help bring technologies through to revenue generation and commercialization. However, local commercial financial institutions (CFIs) that is, banks, non-banking financial companies (NBFCs), and micro-finance institutions are reluctant to invest at this stage due to the high risks involved. The high-risk nature of new technology makes typical credit instruments such as loans difficult to access, particularly when the technology incubator has a weak history of investment, collateral or revenue flows for debt-servicing. Therefore, availability of debt guarantee mechanisms is useful as it can offset some of the risk of the CFIs.

Strategy to Enable Directed Financing in Phase I

Innovation Funds and Venture Capital

Given the risks associated with funding LCT in Phase I and the longer timeframe over which these risks are experienced, there is limited willingness by the private sector in India to invest at this stage. Therefore support for development and commercialization of LCTs needs to be significantly augmented by targeted public sector financing interventions, directly by the Government of India (GoI), through its agencies or indirectly through universities or research institutes. It may also be useful to acknowledge the importance of demand-side regulatory drivers here. While investors always seem to focus on explicit incentives, for example, feed-in-tariffs and subsidized funding, history often shows that a limited, but stable set of policy initiatives is often as important. In a similar vein, policy uncertainty—including politically unsustainable tax incentives—can often be value destructive. Also note that where risk is a barrier to securing long dated financing, risk management tools, including innovative FX and credit insurance schemes, can also be quite powerful and less expensive/intrusive.

Public sector funding would reduce the risks of investing in LCTs and demonstrate their commercial viability so as to create scaled-up, commercially viable business activity. This in turn would stimulate and mobilize private finance and investment to scale-up their deployment over time. *It is therefore important that* the GoI creates a Technology Innovation Fund (TIF), which would address a variety of financing needs required for technology innovation and diffusion through targeted interventions such as technology incubation, field trials, capacity building, and seed capital (see Table 4.2).

Setting up the TIF is also in line with the announcements made by the GoI in its budget for FY 2010–11, wherein it has proposed deployment of a National Clean Energy Fund (NCEF) for funding research and innovative projects in clean energy technologies. It is not yet clear whether the NCEF will take up equity in clean energy projects or undertake debt financing of such projects or it would only support early stage low carbon innovation. However, this fund is limited to the area of clean energy and would not support LCT in other areas/sectors. A TIF focused entirely on LCT would better serve the need of the hour and would also serve to overcome the usual criticism levied at the GoI for introducing overlapping funding schemes, making the public sector funding landscape difficult to navigate for companies constrained by limited time resources besides creating bureaucratic hurdles.

Initially, the TIF in India may have to be capitalized by the GoI. It could also seek or leverage contributions from international financial institutions (IFIs) such as multilateral and bilateral development banks and international financial institutions which are seeking to cost-effectively deploy funds in the area of technology innovation and development in India. Subsequently, when sufficient momentum has built up and some progress has been made, the fund can play an important role in leveraging private financing sources such as venture capital (VC) into the LCT area by securitizing debt and equity investments at a sufficient level to draw in a matching level of venture capital investment. It could invite contributions from corporate leaders interested in investing in the development of LCTs. In fact, private sector investors may accept lower returns while co-investing alongside the GoI, multilateral and bilateral development banks and IFIs. Else, technology incubators and innovators could leverage support from the fund for obtaining assistance from commercial financing vehicles such as Venture Capital (VC) at the later stages in the technology development cycle.

Several examples of such innovation funds exist across the world. The UK Carbon Trust (see Box 4.1), the China Environment Fund, the Canadian Technology Early Action Measures (TEAM) fund, the Massachusetts Sustainable Energy Economic Development Fund, and Massachusetts Pre-Development Financing Initiative are along the lines of the proposed fund. Initiatives similar to the UK Carbon Trust have been deployed in Australia in the form of a Low Emission Technology Fund that provides finance for large-scale demonstration of industry-led low emission technology projects, to reduce the costs of developing such technologies. Many companies that have been funded by these sources have subsequently received further private and public financing or have commercially replicated their technology in the marketplace.

Although early international experiences indicate that VC has not been a very successful route for raising finances for Phase I and several VC firms have in fact had bitter experiences with their investments in this phase, such a situation has arisen mainly because these firms did not have strong business plans, technologies were embryonic, and markets were completely dependent on regulation. More recently, however, the experience with VC funding has been relatively positive and successful examples of VC investment in LCI in developing countries can be found in both Phases I and II. One example (while specifically tailored to unserved or under-served low-income communities) is that of E+Co, which has offices in eight international locations and has seed-financed over 200 clean energy companies located in developing countries in

Table 4.2 Role of the Suggested TIF in India: Types of Interventions and Gaps Addressed

Intervention by Technology Innovation Fund	*Gaps addressed*
Grants and subsidies for applied research and development of prioritized technologies	Inadequate funding support for relevant applied research for technologies where private funding is minimal due to classic innovation barriers
Funding to evaluate technology performance	Uncertainty and scepticism about in-situ costs and performance, and lack of end-user awareness
Business incubation and enterprise creation assistance	Lack of seed funding and business skills within research/technology start-ups—the 'cultural gap' between research and private sectors
Early stage funding for low carbon ventures	Co-investments, loans, or risk guarantees to help viable businesses in early stages attract private sector funding
Deployment of existing energy-efficiency technologies	Encourage uptake of cost-competitive LCTs

Source: Authors' own.

Box 4.1
The UK Carbon Trust

The Carbon Trust was set up in 2001 by the UK government as an independent company to accelerate UK's move to a low carbon economy. The Trust uses a range of targeted interventions to develop commercially viable low carbon technologies, including:

- Technology acceleration projects in wave and tidal-stream power, micro-combined heat and power, advanced metering, low carbon buildings, biomass and offshore wind, which address specific shared technical and market barriers faced by industry participants. For example, the Marine Energy Challenge, focused on wave and tidal-stream power, was completed in 2006 and achieved a significant technology cost reduction, developing a route to cost-competitiveness for wave and tidal-stream energy devices.
- Business incubation services providing targeted advice on intellectual property protection, intellectual property licensing, fund-raising and business planning to low carbon start-ups.
- Enterprise development where the Carbon Trust has built six new businesses, including Partnerships for Renewables which secured over £100m of private sector funding from £10m public sector investment, accelerating the deployment of wind farms on UK public sector land.
- Early stage venture capital support for low carbon companies (which face a funding gap).
- Deployment of existing energy-efficiency technologies through advice and resources to help businesses and the public sector identify and cut carbon emissions, working with over 50 per cent of the FTSE 100 companies, conducting over 3,500 site surveys annually and providing over £18m in interest-free loans annually.

The fund has also helped shape up the policy landscape for low carbon growth in the UK by providing policy and market insights and by demonstrating the viability and business case of low carbon technology opportunities. To date, the Carbon Trust has made 11 investments totalling over £9m, which have leveraged £91m of private investment into low carbon companies.

Source: The Carbon Trust.

the past ten years, in part through an investment fund mandate from the IFC. It makes debt and equity clean energy investments ranging between $ 25,000 to $ 1,000,000. Besides capital, it also provides tools and business know-how to make clean energy businesses successful. India can aim to target much of such funding by improving the overall environment for investment in the country. It may be useful to highlight that there has been positive activity in VC funding targeted towards LCI in India in recent years in Phase I as well as Phase II (see Table 4.3).

But such financing has its share of drawbacks. For example, VC can be costly for the technology developer, because the investors receive both equity shares in the start up as well as a role in the management and technical developments of the company. While private VC financing is desirable it may be useful to think of a combined Public-Private Model which could then work well for both the financial risk-taker and the innovator.

Foreign Direct Investment

Capital flows from foreign sources can meet part of the huge investment requirement for the transition to LCI. *Therefore, besides the creation of a technology innovation fund, there is a need to consciously tap greater Foreign Direct Investment (FDI) in Phase I as a means of strengthening the technological prowess for low carbon development.* FDI, with its potential benefits of technology and knowledge transfer, can contribute not just in monetary terms but also fulfil many technology related needs of the country. In fact, by setting environmental requirements (such as a comprehensive suite of policies intended to encourage energy efficiency or by altering price signals to large/inefficient users and technologies), India can use its purchasing power to transfer environmentally sound technologies into the country or it can encourage the diffusion of technologies, thus making them accessible to local industry. This is important because the transfer of technologies cannot be accomplished by way of trading of goods and services or through investment of financial resources.

Many Indian companies either do not have the required R&D base or are not willing to spend their limited resources on modern technologies that can reduce the carbon footprint. Moreover, activities focused on improving the society at large and Corporate Social Responsibility (CSR) are not something which the indigenous companies focus on and that, too, in such a scale so as make a significant difference, although it cannot be denied that this is a thrust area for many indigenous companies. Therefore, FDI can only help improve the scenario in terms of environmental sustainability.

Phase II: Roll out

LCI projects generally operate with the same financing structures as applied to conventional infrastructure projects and businesses. At the same time ventures involved in low carbon goods and/or services also need to be given due attention, while making clear distinctions between projects, products, and services. These are linked but have different investment propositions with differentiated risk/reward profiles. Funding strategies are not uniform (many projects will be funded 3:1 by debt while a start-up LCT company making an innovative project will often be funded through two or three rounds by venture capital). Examples of ventures could include energy service companies undertaking energy-efficiency (EE) improvement projects or ventures producing and selling solar power based applications such as solar lighting systems, solar water heating systems, or alternative fuel-based systems. Such ventures often need financing support at all stages commencing with start-up capital to raising funds for operation and expansion.

The main forms of capital involved in Phase II (see Figure 4.1) include equity investment from the owners of the project, loans from banks, insurance to cover some of the risks, and possibly other forms of financing, depending on the specific project needs. The financing characteristics for different projects may vary from renewable energy projects to low carbon transport options such as hybrid or electric vehicles, but the fundamental capital needs generally remain the same. Guarantee programmes may also be crucial for certain types of projects to ensure access to affordable debt financing.

Traditionally, financing for this stage has been provided by CFIs and international financial institutions (IFIs), with the latter having played a significant role through a variety of interventions (see Box 4.2). Most of these interventions involve provision of concessional or grants funding to a local CFI, which then provides structured adapted financing for LCI development. The role of CFIs in funding LCI has been limited. However, CFIs do fund LCI in forms other than project finance. For example, EE projects are often funded under loans for procurement of new machinery (which is more energy efficient). Several CFIs in the country have now started dedicated programmes or offerings by way of structured products to meet the specific needs of LCI. One example here is the lending programmes for EE developed by CFIs such as the State Bank of India, Canara Bank, the Bank of India, Union Bank, and the Bank of Baroda the Small Industries Development Bank of India's (SIDBI's) funding of such projects in the small and medium enterprises segment is another example. However, public sector CFIs are still the largest credit providers to LCI given the fact that they have traditionally served social and other non-economic objectives of the government.

While at the role of CFIs, it is necessary to highlight the role of the Indian Renewable Energy Development Agency Limited (IREDA) in financing renewable energy

Box 4.2
Role of International Financial Institutions in Financing LCI Projects

International financial institutions can take many forms. These include assistance from multilateral and regional development banks, bilateral development institutions, and international financial agencies that provide support for country-level low carbon growth efforts, including the adoption of LCTs, through the combination of conventional lending, concessional funding, carbon finance, and guarantees, which in turn can leverage traditional commercial lending. The range of assistance provided by them covers the following:

- Credit lines to designated local financial institutions (DFI) or local CFI that in turn provide structured adapted financing to the projects
- Guarantees to mobilize domestic lending for LCI projects and companies by sharing with local CFIs the credit risk of project loans they make with their own resources
- Debt financing of projects by entities other than DFIs and CFIs
- Private equity funds investing risk capital in companies and projects
- Venture capital funds investing risk capital in technology innovations
- Carbon finance facilities that monetize the advanced sale of emissions reductions to finance project investment costs
- Grants to share project development costs
- Loan softening programmes to mobilize domestic sources of capital
- Technical assistance to build the capacity of all actors along the financing chain

Examples of IFI assistance in India include the loans to the IREDA by the World Bank, ADB, and KfW Germany, USAID funding of EE through ICICI Bank which lends 50 per cent of project cost at 9 per cent interest rate and Yes Bank credit guarantee, and many more.

Source: Authors' own.

and EE projects. The GoI, realizing the barriers associated with financing these projects, under its strategy to develop a sustainable path of energy development created IREDA in 1987. IREDA's resources have come mostly from international assistance and domestic borrowings in the form of borrowings from other banks and issuance of long term bonds. IREDA has sanctioned loans of about Rs 10,355 crore since its inception. However, other areas of LCI have not been equally fortunate.

Going forward, given the huge investment requirements to enable a strategic shift towards LCI, it is clear that these cannot be met only by local CFIs, which find several more profitable projects competing for their funds and IFIs who must provide similar assistance across several developing countries. Even IREDA with its limited mandate and funding sources would not be able to make the desired impact. Therefore, there is a need to broaden the sources of funds for financing LCI as well as the manner in which these funds are intermediated. On the equity side, there is a need to encourage new financing sources which can help LCI projects as well as business involved in the LCI space meet the equity requirements.

Strategy to Enable Directed Financing in Phase II

Debt finance

A new Green Infrastructure Financial Institution

Effective long-term availability of funds for facilitating the shift to LCI would necessitate large-scale, well constructed involvement of local CFIs. However, given the barriers to investment described earlier in this chapter, the extent of funding undertaken by CFIs would be limited. *There is therefore a need to have a dedicated financial institution with specific focus on driving the transformation to LCI. It is suggested that the GoI restructure and empower IREDA as a Green Infrastructure Financial Institution (GIFI) towards this end. IREDA already has substantial sector-specific expertise in some areas of LCI and can easily fit into the shoes of a GIFI. However, IREDA would have to be significantly strengthened to be made capable of responding to, and in many areas anticipating, the needs and complexities of the low carbon transition and thereby designing new and efficient financial instruments to meet these needs.*

The concept of a 'sector specific structured financial institution' such as a GIFI is not new to India. IREDA itself is a case in point. Other similar institutions in the country include the National Bank for Agricultural and Rural Development, Power Finance Corporation, Rural Electrification Corporation, Industrial Development Bank of India, Small Industries Development Bank of India (SIDBI), and more recently India Infrastructure Finance Company Limited. These institutions were created with the objective of channelizing investment in the sectors under their mandate and most have done commendable work to this end.

The proposed GIFI can be visualized to carry out the following functions:

- Facilitating, financing, and syndicating the delivery of low carbon investment programmes
- Acting as a supervisory body to ensure that government funds or grants are effectively utilized for LCI
- Providing guarantee facilities on behalf of the GoI through allocation of a Statutory Government Guarantee or GIFI Guarantee Scheme
- Filling the debt gap for LCI through provision of direct loans as well as syndicated loans (loans supplemented by loans from other CFIs) to LCI and provision of credit lines to identified partner CFIs
- Facilitating a transparent communication of government policy
- Promoting skills/capacity building on LCI by designing and running training programmes
- Acting as an intermediary of local cap and trade mechanisms as well as green/renewable energy certificates and making such instruments liquid.

The creation of a GIFI would however require a large pool of technically qualified talent. The government would therefore have to undertake a huge capacity building exercise across relevant institutions in the country to create such a pool of talent. A start has already been made under the National Solar Mission which aims to train at least 100,000 specialized personnel across the skill spectrum for employment in the solar industry. But greater attention has to be paid to the creation of skills across the broad set of LCI.

Role of Commercial Financial Institutions

Even with the creation of a Green Investment Bank, CFIs would continue to play an important role as an intermediary between investors, and companies/organizations operating green projects. *CFIs, both in the public and private domain, must consider developing financial product modifications to match the characteristics of different types of low carbon or green infrastructure projects. This would help expand the market for such loans and could increase uptake of financially viable, yet unimplemented projects.* The task would perhaps be simpler if CFIs look at such products or servicing such needs as a way to expand and strengthen their position in a specific market or business line.

CFIs can also consider strengthening the environmental risk management system by better evaluating and addressing carbon risks in the financing and construction of infrastructure. Signing up to the Equator Principles (EP) or the UN's Principles for Responsible Investment are perhaps the easiest way to do that.

There have been several arguments against Indian CFIs signing up to the EP. While a debate on this issue is beyond the scope of this chapter, the point remains that CFIs can take several steps to ensure that infrastructure projects funded by them are benign to the environment. The development of 'carbon principles' jointly by Citi, JPMorgan Chase, and Morgan Stanley (see Box 4.3) could be a guiding force in this regard.

The GoI has taken several steps to facilitate greater funding of specific LCI by CFIs especially banks. For instance, under the National Mission on Enhanced Energy Efficiency (NMEEE) it has created a Partial Risk Guarantee Fund, which will be a risk-sharing mechanism that will provide commercial banks with partial coverage of risk exposure against loans made for energy-efficiency projects. This will reduce the risk perception of the banks towards lending for new technologies and new business models associated with EE projects. While this is a welcome initiative, it would not be wrong to say that instead of creating separate financing machineries for different LCI, initiatives such as these can all be combined under one roof through the GIFI.

In addition, the GoI should consider declaring defined LCI such as renewable energy, EE, and clean transportation projects as a priority sector.[4] The inclusion in priority sectors will enhance credit availability at lower rates, lead to greater participation by CFIs in such projects, and eventually make available more funds for such projects.

Box 4.3
Carbon Principles Formulated and Adopted by Citi, JP Morgan Chase, and Morgan Stanley

Citi, JPMorgan Chase, and Morgan Stanley formed a consortium and consulted with power companies and environmental groups in the US to develop a process for understanding carbon risk around power sector investments needed to meet future economic growth and the needs of consumers for reliable and affordable energy. The outcome of this initiative has been the development of an Enhanced Diligence framework to help lenders better understand and evaluate the potential carbon risks associated with coal plant investments. The carbon principles and associated Enhanced Diligence represent an important step by these banks in contributing to the efforts to address growing greenhouse gas emissions. These principles are as follows:

- *Energy efficiency*: 'An effective way to limit carbon dioxide emissions is to not produce them. The adopting financial institutions will encourage clients to invest in cost-effective demand reduction, taking into consideration the value of avoided carbon dioxide emissions. We will also encourage regulatory and legislative changes that increase efficiency in electricity consumption including the removal of barriers to investment in cost-effective demand reduction. The institutions will consider demand reduction caused by increased energy efficiency (or other means) as part of the Enhanced Diligence Process and assess its impact on proposed financings of certain new fossil fuel generation.'
- *Renewable and low carbon distributed energy technologies*: 'Renewable energy and low carbon distributed energy technologies hold considerable promise for meeting the electricity needs of the US while also leveraging American technology and creating jobs. We will encourage clients to invest in cost-effective renewables and distributed technologies, taking into consideration the value of avoided carbon dioxide emissions. We will also encourage legislative and regulatory changes that remove barriers to, and promote such investments (including related investments in infrastructure and equipment needed to support the connection of renewable sources to the system). We will consider production increases from renewable and low carbon generation as part of the Enhanced Diligence process and assess their impact on proposed financings of certain new fossil fuel generation.'
- *Conventional and advanced generation*: 'In addition to cost effective energy efficiency, renewables and low carbon distributed generation, investments in conventional or advanced generating facilities will be needed to supply reliable electric power to the US market. This may include power from natural gas, coal and nuclear technologies. Due to evolving climate policy, investing in carbon dioxide-emitting fossil fuel generation entails uncertain financial, regulatory and certain environmental liability risks. It is the purpose of the Enhanced Diligence process to assess and reflect these risks in the financing considerations for certain fossil fuel generation. We will encourage regulatory and legislative changes that facilitate carbon capture and storage to further reduce carbon dioxide emissions from the electric sector.'

Source: Morgan (2008).

[4] At present the priority sector broadly comprises agriculture, small-scale industries and other activities/borrowers such as small business, retail trade, small transport operators, professional and self-employed persons, housing, education loans, microcredit, etc.

The GoI can also draw inspiration from the Dutch Green Funds Scheme to develop innovative schemes that encourage the funding of green projects by local CFIs (see Box 4.4).

While on the subject of the role of CFIs, it may be useful to highlight that besides direct financing of projects, CFIs can also play an enormous role in creating a retail market for products and services that in turn promote low carbon infrastructure growth. An example here would be renewable energy applications such as solar home lighting systems and solar water heaters. If consumer durable loans are available for such products on easy terms and conditions, it would help create a market akin to that for consumer goods and would incentivize people to integrate renewable energy applications into their home, thereby avoiding fossil fuel based generation. Similarly, cheaper home loans for home owners/buyers installing roof-top photo voltaic (PV) systems would encourage the uptake of such homes and provide an indirect incentive to real estate developers to integrate roof-top photo voltaic in buildings.

An example of such an initiative can be found in the Standard Chartered Bank, which, as part of its efforts to expand financing for green development, has developed a 'green product innovations guide', a tool to help generate ideas for environment-oriented products and services in the countries where it operates. Under this guide, the Bank rolled out a 'Go Green' campaign in Malaysia where it donated RM3 to the Malaysian Nature Society Tree Planting Programme for every customer who activated their online banking before a pre-specified date. This campaign was then replicated it in countries such as Pakistan, the UAE, and South Korea. One may argue that initiatives such as this one are more in the nature of fulfilling a bank's CSR and can hardly be qualified as active interventions. But initiatives such as these help create awareness which could be effective in raising funds through other methods such as green bonds.

Box 4.4
Funding Green Projects through Commercial Financial Institutions—The Dutch Experience

The Netherlands has adopted a unique method of funding green projects. This method, called the Green Funds Scheme, was launched in 1995 by the Dutch government and comprises the Green Projects Scheme (which establishes the conditions governing the projects), the Green Institutions Scheme (which regulates the role played by the financial institutions) and finally the tax incentive for individual investors (which gets the flow of funds under way).

Under the Green Funds Scheme, a tax incentive scheme has been provided to encourage individual investors to put money into green projects that benefit nature and the environment. Individuals who invest in a green fund or save money with financial institutions practising 'green banking' receive a rate lower than the market interest rate but the tax incentive compensates for this. In their turn, the banks charge green projects a low interest rate. Generally in the Netherlands, an individual investor would normally pay 1.2 per cent capital gains tax on the amount invested. But green capital is exempt up to a maximum of Euro 53,421 per person (as in 2007). Green investors also pay less income tax on their green capital. Their reduction is 1.3 per cent, so the total tax advantage is 2.5 per cent. This means they can accept a lower interest rate or dividend on their investment.

The Green Projects Scheme designates projects that are eligible for green project status. There are a few technical and financial conditions, but the main requirement is that these are new projects providing a significant and immediate environmental benefit. Projects are divided into categories such as renewable energy, construction infrastructure, voluntary soil decontamination, organic farming, etc.

The Green Institutions Scheme involves the creation of a 'green fund' or a 'green bank' in participating commercial banks and financial institutions. The banks issue bonds with a fixed value, term and interest rate, or shares in a green investment fund. Usually, the interest rate or dividend paid by the bank is lower than the market rate, which means that the bank can in turn invest the funds in green projects at a lower interest rate. The banks then use the capital in the green fund to offer soft green loans to finance green projects. The banks are obliged to put at least 70 per cent of that money into certified green projects. They may invest the remaining 30 per cent elsewhere to spread the risk and to compensate for financing barely profitable projects. The Dutch central bank and the tax authorities supervise the process.

The implementation of this scheme has yielded many benefits. First, following the implementation of this scheme, the green capital available under the green institutions scheme rose to Euro 5 billion in 2005. Of this, roughly 85 per cent has actually been invested in green projects. In fact, now the CFIs ask developers to consider sustainable energy financing, rather than the other way round. Second, the scheme has also had an impact on the way in which people think about their responsibility for the environment. The scheme enjoys broad public support in the Netherlands and has encouraged the banking sector to offer a wide range of sustainable investment products, enhancing its contribution to corporate social responsibility. And together with other tax incentives and grants, the scheme has increased environmental investment among entrepreneurs.

Source: SenterNovem, http://www.senternovem.nl/mmfiles/GreenFunds%20scheme_tcm24-223487.pdf

Equity finance

Given that equity represents the owner's contribution, there is no doubt that the equity finance needs would have to be mobilized. But for this moblization, LCI must be made attractive by way of risk mitigation measures and adequate institutional mechanisms to enable debt financing. The creation of TIF and GIFI will serve the precise purpose of providing the institutional mechanism that would make LCI attractive for equity investments.

The main sources of finance that can be tapped for LCI are venture capitalists, private equity (PE) funds, pension funds (mostly international), and hedge funds who invest in companies or directly in projects or portfolios of assets. These funds blend public, private, and philanthropic sources of financing and engage in investments depending on the type of business, the stage of development of the technology, and degree of risk associated therein. The characteristics of some of these equity funds are provided in Table 4.3.

It is heartening to note that LCI in India is rapidly emerging as a new asset class for many of these funds. Recent estimates indicate that capital raised by international PE and VC funds focused on India grew by 67 per cent between 2007 and 2008 with a quantum increase in investment going towards clean technology (see Table 4.4). Another exciting development is that there has been a dramatic growth in PE funds within the country (see Figure 4.2) and many of these have shown a clear intent of investing in LCI.

Examples of domestic PE funds include Jacob Ballas Capital India, Chrys Capital, Actis, ICICI Ventures, IDFC Private Equity, IL&FS, and Baring India. Many of these such as IDFC Private Equity have consciously built a green infrastructure portfolio, with an estimated investment of over Rs 1,000 crore ($ 200 million) either invested in, or already committed, to such infrastructure. Similarly, VC firms are setting up exclusive carbon funds for clean infrastructure projects which have the potential to generate carbon credits. The IFCI Venture Capital Fund (see Box 4.5) is one such example. The GoI too has announced the creation of a Venture Capital Fund for Energy Efficiency (VCFEE) under the NMEEE, which would be implemented from 1 April 2010. It is expected that the VCFEE will ease a significant barrier from the viewpoint of risk capital availability to energy service companies and other companies who invest in the supply of energy efficient-goods and services.

While VC and PE funds are becoming active investors in this space and have the potential to fill the equity gap, there is little scope to tap the domestic pension funds for financing LCI in the short to medium term. There are two main reasons for this. The first is the absence of a comprehensive old age income security system in the country. With the organized workforce accounting for only about 10 per cent of the total workforce, the coverage by government provident funds or private pension schemes is rather low. The second is that the regulations applicable to such funds have historically been based solely on investment

Table 4.3 Characteristics of Different Types of Equity Funds

	Venture Capital Funds	*Private Equity Funds*	*Pension Funds*
Sources of finance	Sources with high-risk appetite such as insurance companies, pension funds, mutual funds, high net worth individuals	Sources with medium-risk appetite such as institutional investors and high net worth individuals	Organized sector workforce, companies in the organized sector by way of their contribution towards the benefit of employees, labour unions, and the government
Investment areas	New technology, start-up companies	Companies and projects with more mature technology including those preparing to raise capital on public stock exchanges (pre-IPO stage), demonstrator companies, or under-performing public companies	Public equity (via stock markets), corporate and government bonds, real estate, inflation-linked assets (such as commodities, inflation linked bonds), specialized Private Equity or Venture Capital funds
Investment horizon	4–7 years	3–5 years	'cash yielding' investments, that is those that generate a stream of cash year on year
Return requirement	Many multiples of original investment (50–500% IRR)	Higher return requirement (typically 25% IRR)	Low-risk appetite, stable returns at around the 15% level

Source: UNEP Sustainable Energy Finance Initiative, Bloomberg New Energy Finance, and the Royal Institute of International Affairs (2010).

TABLE 4.4 PE and VC Funds Focused on India: by Sector and Stage

Sector	*2008 closes ($ million)*	*No. of Funds*	*2007 closes ($ million)*	*No. of Funds*
General	4963	23	3230	16
Agribusiness	85	1	NA	NA
Clean Technology	100	1	NA	NA
Technology	583	5	625	3
Industrials/Mfg	200	1	214	1
Infrastructure	1632	5	500	1
Consumer	147	1	NA	NA
Total	7710	37	4569	21
Stage				
Buyout	1340	1	1750	2
Growth/Expansion	3860	18	1615	15
Venture Capital	1110	16	804	4
Multi-stage	1400	2	NA	NA
Total	7710	37	4569	21

Source: Emerging Markets Private Equity Association (2009).

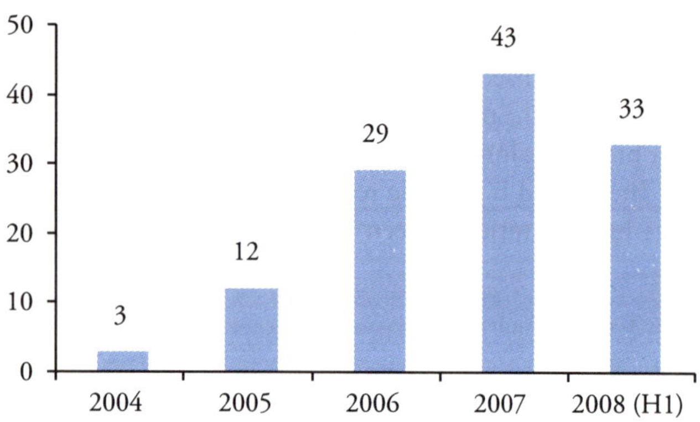

FIGURE 4.2 Number of PE Funds Launched in India during 2004–8

Source: IFC (2009).

in government-run saving plans and fixed income instruments. It is only in the last year or two that the government has been prepared to introduce a small degree of flexibility in terms of asset allocation, and even this has not yet been fully rolled out. Therefore, it is unlikely that this segment can be tapped.

However, there is hope from international pension funds, which have started looking at increasing their exposure to India. Examples of such funds include the two Dutch pension funds, Algemene Pensioen Groep N.V. (APG) and The Stitching Pensioenfonds voor de Gezondheid, Geestelijke en Maatschappelijke Belangen (PGGM). The strategy of both these funds appears to be to invest directly in these assets classes in India, rather than invest as limited partners in a third-party private equity or infrastructure funds. Although the trend of investments by pension funds is at an early stage, providing a favourable investment environment to such funds would help raise finance.

While there is no doubt that the growing PE and VC market would be an important source of funds for equity financing, these funds come with their pros and cons. For example, PE business models rely on high returns. Therefore, business would need to carefully evaluate the benefits and costs of obtaining such funding. In order to encourage greater funding of LCI by equity funds, an array of policy measures need to be adopted to tackle the range of market failures involved and to facilitate the necessary private finance flows. Possible policy measures include tightening building codes and fuel efficiency standards, implementation of renewable portfolio obligations for power distribution utilities, and urban planning utilizing the latest technologies.

RAISING INCREMENTAL FUNDS

The huge funding requirement for LCT/LCI has already been discussed. Given the limited availability of funds from the usual sources like budgetary support by the GoI, IFI assistance and the retail deposit base of banks, it is imperative that additional instruments/sources be explored to raise funds. Three options can be considered

Box 4.5
The IFCI Green India Venture Fund

The IFCI Venture Capital Fund, which was set up as a subsidiary of IFCI Ltd in 1975 with the objective of providing the much needed risk capital at the start up stage for green field projects, has floated the Green India Venture Fund with a corpus of Rs 330 crore ($66 million). The life of the fund will be seven years with three prolongation options of one year each. IFCI has made a 10 per cent sponsor contribution towards corpus of the fund and the remaining corpus will be raised from other financial institutions/banks/companies/multilateral agencies and foreign investors. The fund will invest in the following areas:

- Energy-efficiency equipments, industrial process, lighting, and building material
- Renewable energy such as wind, solar, and biomass
- Energy storage technology, process, equipment such as fuel cells, advance batteries, hybrid systems
- Waste management including waste recycling, waste usage
- Water treatment and water conservation
- Pollution control projects/processes and technologies
- Transportation: Vehicles, logistics, structures, fuels, etc., aimed at improving efficiency and/or reducing negative environmental impact
- Materials with clean and environment friendly applications
- Afforestation and reforestation activities
- Manufacturing/Industrial process aimed at reducing negative ecological impact

The investment criteria for the fund are as follows:

- Investments to be made generally by way of equity and equity linked investment instruments in companies operating to achieve aims indicated in the investment objective of the fund.
- At least 50 per cent of investment to be made in companies engaged in energy/power related activities/ projects
- Maximum investment per portfolio company not to exceed 10 per cent of the Fund Corpus
- Appropriate mix of investments in various companies engaged in, amongst others, CDM projects and other projects engaged in reducing negative ecological impact, efficient usage of resources such as energy, power, etc., and other related sectors.
- Investment to be made in generally early stage investment or expansion capital stage

Source: IFCI Venture Capital Funds Ltd.

for this purpose. These are issuance of green bonds, a carbon cess, and domestic carbon market mechanisms.

- Green bonds

Green bonds are typically tax-exempt bonds, which are issued by federally qualified organizations and target institutional and retail investors. Therefore, they help raise additional funds from consumers and the private sector rather than general taxation. Green bonds could be related to specific technologies or projects to ensure that the money raised is invested in a particular set of projects. On the other hand, bonds could be generic in nature as far as the technology or project is concerned and the proceeds could be used to finance any LCI project that meets predefined criteria.

The willingness of investors to buy such bonds will be determined by their risk-return characteristics and competitiveness vis-à-vis 'normal' bonds. Therefore, within the category of green bonds, different products could be developed to cater to different risk. However, large institutional investors may also be concerned about how bond proceeds are used. They would therefore expect credible evidence that tangible benefits will be delivered.

Several examples of green bonds can be found globally. For example, the World Bank Green Bond issued through the International Bank for Reconstruction and Development raises funds from fixed income investors for World Bank projects that seek to mitigate climate change or help affected people adapt to it. The bonds garnered funds from socially responsible institutional investors, high-net-worth individuals as well as retail investors. Four such bond issues have been floated by the World Bank till date. A special 'green account' has been used for proceeds from green bonds. At the end of every quarter, funds are deducted from this account and added to the World Bank's lending pool for 'green' disbursements to support eligible projects. The experience with these bonds has shown that investors are interested in products that offer both appropriate risk-adjusted returns and contribute to the climate.

However, green bonds are not free from problems. Since these bonds are tax free and are government backed finance, they would compete for finite financial resources of the GoI—either from public debt or taxation—and such approaches could create a moral hazard in that the government could be asked to fund sub-optimal projects on the understanding that it bears the risk of commercial failure. Anyhow, green bonds can only be a temporary measure, designed to bridge a market gap because in the long term, the policy and regulatory framework must provide a clear market signal for the shift to LCI.

- Carbon Cess/Levy

Another option that can be explored to raise funds is that of a carbon cess/levy. Such a cess/levy can take many forms. It can be a direct levy on airline travel and shipping, conventional power/fossil fuel generation, private transport, diesel, fuel oil and kerosene products; a cess on certain categories of electricity consumers; heavier customs duty on energy equipment for fossil fuels; a levy on energy-intensive materials or on energy-intensive industries. The proceeds of the suggested cess can go towards a fund established specifically for this purpose. This suggestion is already being explored by the GoI, albeit in a small manner. It has announced the levy of a clean energy cess on coal @ Rs 50 per tonne in its budget for FY 2010–11. This cess will be applicable to the coal produced within the country as well as on imported coal. The proceeds of the cess will go into the NCEF.

Such a fund as proposed here—possibly called as low carbon development fund—should be ring-fenced under a legislative framework so as to ensure that the proceeds of the fund are utilized for funding green infrastructure and technologies. It can be modelled on the Central Road Fund, which is a dedicated fund created from the levy of a cess on petrol and diesel (Rs 2 per litre on petrol and High Speed Diesel). The fund is distributed for development and maintenance of national highways, state roads, rural roads, and for provision of road overbridges/underbridges and other safety features at unmanned railway crossings under the Central Road Fund Act 2000.

It is suggested that the low carbon development fund be utilized by the GoI in two ways. First, part of the fund could be placed under the GIFI which would use it to provide debt financing for projects and part of it could be utilized by GoI and its agencies towards lowering the capital cost of LCI projects by way of viability gap funding that is a grant to meet a portion of the capital cost of the project with the objective of improving the commercial viability of the project.

A global example of a similar cess is the Thai Energy Conservation Promotion Fund (ECON Fund) which was launched as part of the Thai Energy Conservation Act in 1992 to provide financial support for projects ranging from EE, demonstration and dissemination of renewable energy technologies, R&D projects, projects on market enhancement for renewable energy technology equipment, and training and promotional campaigns. The fund receives revenue from a small tax on benzene, diesel, fuel oil, and kerosene products sold and used in Thailand. In India, the states of Maharashtra and Karnataka have levied a cess on the consumption of electricity. The proceeds from the cess are used to fund certain categories of LCI (see Box 4.6).

- Domestic Market Mechanisms

Besides the above options that serve to directly raise funds, there is a need to strengthen domestic market mechanisms that could provide for indirect funds for LCI. This is all the more pressing because of the uncertainty surrounding the Clean Development Mechanism (CDM) post 2012 (see box 4.7). The first option that can be explored in

Box 4.6
Green Cess on Electricity Consumption in Maharashtra and Karnataka

In Maharashtra, the state government jointly with a private sector financial institution—the Infrastructure Leasing & Financial Services (IL&FS)—has promoted the Urjankur Nidhi Trust Fund to promote non-conventional energy projects in the state. The fund would initially promote bagasse-based co-generation power projects which have a significant potential in Maharashtra. The fund would provide financial support in the form of equity with maximum support per project of up to 20 per cent of the project cost or 20 per cent of the corpus, whichever is lower. The fund will also provide crucial support functions during project development, project management, and distribution of resulting power.

The fund has a corpus of Rs 418 crores of which Rs 218 crores would be contributed by the government of Maharashtra. This fund would be replenished through the imposition of a green cess of 4 paisa per unit on industrial and commercial power consumers in Maharashtra. The other 200 crores would be contributed by private institutional investors.

In Karnataka too, the state government has levied a cess called Green Energy Cess at 5 paisa per unit on commercial and industrial consumers. It is expected that the cess would generate Rs 55 crore annually. A part of the proceeds raised through this cess will be set aside for the Energy Conservation Fund. The remaining proceeds would be utilized for financing renewable energy projects in the state, strengthening the evacuation system for such projects and for an integrated information and communication programme in the state.

Source: Maharashtra Energy Development Agency (2010); Karnataka Renewable Energy Development Limited (2010).

Box 4.7
Carbon Finance under the Clean Development Mechanism

The Clean Development Mechanism (CDM) is an arrangement under the Kyoto Protocol that allows industrialized countries with a GHG reduction commitment (called Annex 1 countries) to invest in ventures that reduce GHG emissions in developing countries where costs are lower than in industrialized countries. The benefits of these reductions are monetized through the issuance of Certified Emissions Reductions (CERs). A price on these CERs enables the monetisation of future cash flows from the advanced sale of CERs. This is popularly known as carbon finance. A total of 373,747,027 CERs have been issued till date under this framework and over 1,730,000,000 CERs are expected until the end of 2012.

Though India does not have any emission reduction target, it is able to sell CERs pursuant to the CDM, to large emitters covered by the EU ETS, countries that have emission reduction targets under the Kyoto Protocol, or any other entity that wishes to purchase such CERs for compliance purposes. India ranks second by number of projects registered by the CDM Executive Board at 491 and second by volume of issued CERs at 77,296,186 as of 10 March 2010.

Though CDM is an important financing mechanism for incremental costs, it has been well short of the scale required. This is because the carbon market has not provided investors with the strong, long-term price signals that are necessary to support large investments in low-carbon solutions. The primary reason for this lies in the uncertainty regarding the future international climate regime on account of the long-term framework for the post-2012 period. Second, the short-term, compliance-driven buying interests in industrialized countries have not supported large, cleaner investments in infrastructure that have long-term emission reduction potential. Third, the project-by-project approach under the Kyoto Protocol involves high transaction costs for developers of LCI and has therefore been unsuccessful in generating a large-scale transformation to LCI.

Source: Authors' own.

this regard is the cap and trade system. Cap and trade is basically an environmental policy tool that delivers results with a mandatory cap on emissions while providing sources flexibility in how they comply. Under such a system, a company is given a limit or cap on its carbon emissions. If its emissions come under the cap, it can use the difference as a credit that can then be sold to another company. If a company goes over its cap, it must buy carbon credits to make up the difference. These carbon credits can be traded on an open market like a stock exchange. Alternatively, the government can auction the emissions permits to the companies required to reduce their emissions. This would create a large and dependable revenue stream. These financial resources could be used to finance LCI.

Other market mechanisms that have recently been created in the country and need to be made operational at the earliest are RECs or energy-efficiency certificates (EECs). The idea of RECs is to create two different markets with RE, one for physical electricity produced and the other for the environmental attributes of such electricity. With such a system, RE is fed into the electricity grid and sold at market prices, but the RE producer also receives a certificate that is sold on the market created for certificates and improves the competitiveness of the renewable production. The market for RECs has recently been created through regulations to that effect by the Central Electricity Regulatory Commission (CERC). Two categories of RECs have been created therein—solar RECs and non-solar RECs (RECs issued to renewable energy other than solar). This is in keeping with the country's target for increasing the installed capacity of solar power to 20,000 MW by 2022 under the GoI's National Solar Mission. Each REC issued would represent one Megawatt hour of electricity generated from an RE source and injected into the grid. Further, only generators of RE not selling electricity to distribution utilities through power purchase agreements at preferential tariffs will qualify for RECs. Renewable energy certificates will be transacted only through a power exchange, which will also facilitate their price discovery.

EECs or Energy Savings Certificates (ESCerts) are certificates issued as a result of achievement of certain pre-defined energy savings as a consequence of energy efficiency improvement measures. In Europe, several countries have already implemented a white certificate scheme. These include France, Italy, and the UK. Like RECs, White Certificates too, facilitate the financing of EE projects. ESCerts have been introduced by the GoI under the NMEEE. Specific Energy Consumption (SEC) norms would be set for 714 units in 9 energy intensive sectors and ESCerts would be issued to those who exceed their target SEC reduction. It is envisaged that trading of ESCerts would be carried out bilaterally between any two designated consumers (within or across the designated sectors), or on the power exchanges.

Conclusion

The key ingredient in successfully addressing a low carbon growth path in India is a massive amount of new investment in LCT and consequently LCI. This leaves us with the question: how can the country facilitate more of this kind of investment? The solution to this question involves the development of a coherent financing strategy. This chapter has proposed such a strategy by answering two important questions, that is, the institutional mechanism for enabling credit, thereby making it attractive for equity investors to invest in this space and the channels to raise extra funds for such investment. Needless to say, fostering the growth of clean technology companies and projects would also require an appropriate regulatory environment and would also be defined by commercial realities.

In conclusion, the overall financing strategy has three broad components: (i) create a technology innovation fund to finance LCT innovation and diffusion; (ii) create or adapt existing financial institutions into a dedicated financial institution with a mandate and comprehensive strategy for providing debt financing to LCI; and (iii) establish/strengthen the domestic carbon trading market. The institutional mechanisms proposed here will provide the *terra firma* for leveraging private financing sources. Some part of the incremental financing requirement can be met through issuance of green bonds and levy of a carbon cess.

References

Climate Change Capital (2009). *Accelerating Green Infrastructure Financing: Outline proposals for UK green bonds and infrastructure bank*, Briefing Note1, March 2009, available at http://www.climatechangecapital.com/media/2153/Accelerating%20Green%20Infrastructure%20Financing%20Final%2021-05-09.pdf

Emerging Markets Private Equity Association (2009). *Fundraising and Investment Review 2008*, April 2009.

Forum for the Future (2010), *Clean Capital: Financing clean technology firms in the UK*, United Kingdom, available at http://www.forumforthefuture.org/files/Cleancapital.pdf, last date of access 15 February 2010.

Grantham Institute for Climate Change and the Environment (2009). *Meeting the Climate Challenge: Using Public Funds to Leverage Private Investment in Developing Countries*, London School of Economics, September 2009, available at http://www2.lse.ac.uk/GranthamInstitute/publications/OtherPub/Leveragedfunds/Meeting%20the%20Climate%20Challenge.aspx

International Finance Corporation (2009). *IFC Sustainable Investment Country Reports: Sustainable Investment in India 2009*, May 2009, available at http://www.ifc.org/ifcext/sustainability.nsf/AttachmentsByTitle/p_Sustainable_investment_in_India2009FINAL/$FILE/Sustainable_investment_in_India2009FINAL.pdf

IFCI Venture Capital Funds Ltd. (2010). Available at http://www.ifciventure.com/, last date of access 20 January 2010.

Karnataka Renewable Energy Development Limited (2010). Available at http://kredl.kar.nic.in/Renewable%20Energy%20Policy%202009.doc, last date of access 15 February 2010.

Maharashtra Energy Development Agency (2010). Available at *http://www.mahaurja.com/pdf/urjankur.pdf*, last date of access, November 25, 2010.

McKinsey & Company (2009). *Environmental and Energy Sustainability: An Approach for India*, August 2009.

Morgan, J.P. (2008). *Leading Wall Street Banks Establish the Carbon Principles*, February 2010. *http://www.jpmorgan.com/pages/jpmorgan/news/carbonprinciples*, last date of access 15 January 2010.

Nazworth, Napp (2009). *Cap-and-Trade Versus Carbon Tax: Two Ways to Reduce Carbon Emissions*, April 2009, available at http://pollution-control.suite101.com/article.cfm/capandtrade_versus_carbon_tax#ixzz0h0iYowsc

Senter, Novem (2007). *The Green Funds Scheme*, SenterNovem publication, 3GB0701, November 2007, available at http://www.senternovem.nl/mmfiles/GreenFunds%20scheme_tcm24-223487.pdf, last date of access 20 January 2010.

The Carbon Trust, UK, http://www.carbontrust.co.uk/

The Cleantech Group (2008). *Cleantech Venture Capital and Private Equity Investments in India*, 2008

The World Bank (2008). *Scaling Up Carbon Finance In India; Background Paper—India: Strategies for Low Carbon Growth*, 2008, available at http://moef.nic.in/downloads/public-information/LCGCarbonJune2008.pdf, last date of access 15 February 2010.

UNEP and Partners (2009). *Catalysing Low-carbon Growth in Developing Economies: Public Finance Mechanisms to Scale up Private Sector Investment in Climate Solutions*, 2009.

UNEP Sustainable Energy Finance Initiative (2005). *Public Finance Mechanisms to Catalyze Sustainable Energy Sector Growth*, 2005, available at http://www.energy-base.org/fileadmin/media/base/downloads/SEFI_Public_Finance_Report.pdf, last date of access 3 January 2010.

UNEP Sustainable Energy Finance Initiative, Bloomberg New Energy Finance, and The Royal Institute of International Affairs (2010). *Private Financing of Renewable Energy—A Guide for Policymakers*, UK.

United Nations Framework Convention on Climate Change (2010). *Clean Development Mechanism*, http://cdm.unfccc.int/Statistics/index.html, last date of access 20 February 2010.

5 Private Equity Financing for CleanTech Infrastructure

Pinaki Bhattacharyya and Shishir Maheshwari

Introduction

With the intensive use of natural resources in general and fossil fuels in particular, humanity is faced with its adverse impact on the environment. Without lowering the emission of carbon in the environment, there is a greater consensus today among scientists and researchers that the adverse climate change will become imminent. It has become, therefore, imperative that cleaner technologies, in terms of higher efficiency, using renewable resources, and lower carbon footprints, are adopted to continue economic development without impacting the environment adversely. *The environmental imperative has been supported by fundamental macroeconomic drivers, energy security, and increasing economic viability of cleaner technologies.* The CleanTech[1] sector worldwide has attracted an increasing share of investment. Equity investment globally has been growing at a 36 per cent compound annual growth rate (CAGR) and reached a level of about $ 19 billion in 2009 (see Figure 5.1).

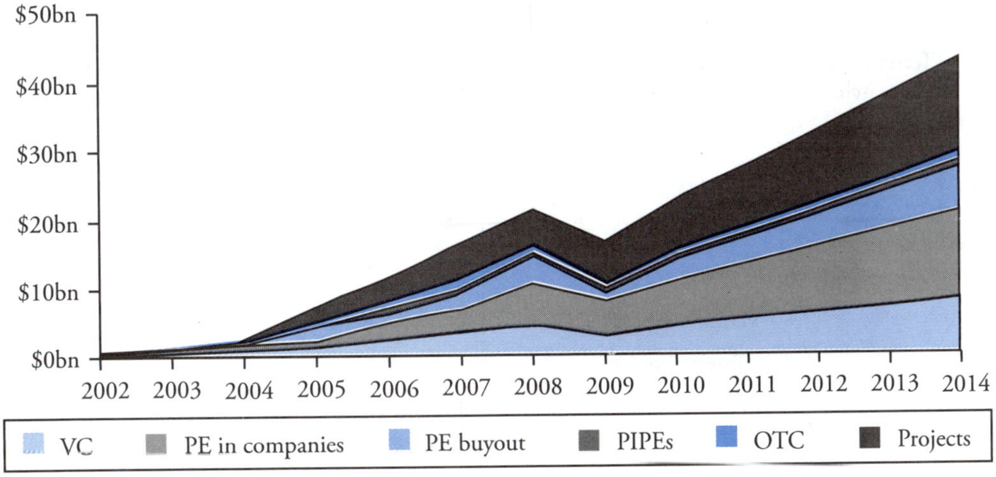

Figure 5.1 Global Growth in CleanTech Infrastructure Private Equity Investments[2]

Source: Bloomberg New Energy Finance.[3]

[1] CleanTech is a term used to describe technologies that address the resource limits in energy, water, and materials. In this chapter, the term has been used to primarily mean renewable energy.

[2] PIPE: Private Investment in Public Equities.

[3] Bloomberg New Energy Finance publication titled, *Cleaning up 2009* in April 2009.

It is noteworthy that almost 80 per cent of the investment has been pumped into deployment of CleanTech Infrastructure, that is, into projects and value chain enablers. This trend has accelerated as many of the technologies are now in the deployment phase which is very capital intensive. In the Indian context, which is the focus of this paper, *deployment of CleanTech infrastructure is of paramount importance* to address India's current energy supply and security issues that can decelerate the buoyant growth.

The deployment of CleanTech is very capital intensive. The sources of equity capital as shown below in Figure 5.2 to fund the deployment involving manufacturing scale-up and asset finance include private equity (PE), public equity, and corporate finance. CleanTech entrepreneurs tend to be small and tapping the public equity markets need more scale. Hence PE plays an important role in the deployment phase by investing in growth equity as the entrepreneurs scale up their operations.

Hence it is important to understand what drives the private equity investment. Thus this chapter examines the fundamental drivers in the Indian context, the types of opportunities that have attracted PE investments in the CleanTech infrastructure space (with a focus on renewable energy infrastructure which is a subset of the CleanTech infrastructure space), so far, and factors that could be further worked upon to accelerate this trend.

Investments in CleanTech in India

We are at the beginning of a transition phase in the power sector wherein a significant portion of the energy mix will switch to renewables by the end of the century. The supportive policies, technological progress, and macro drivers have so far created a congenial climate for investment. This has channelized a lot of investment in the space, but mostly towards asset deployment.

The Role of Market Drivers in CleanTech Investments

The global energy market has been driven by five key drivers—energy prices and volatility, energy security, climate change, policy and technological innovation (see Figure 5.3). These drivers are not only applicable in the Indian context but are also much more pronounced due to the baseline resource/energy shortage, the high growth rate and huge energy imports. The solution is available in the form of huge renewable resources waiting to be tapped. The prospects are bright as only about 14 per cent of the overall renewable energy[4] potential in the country has been tapped so far. These several strong and sustainable drivers have established India as one of the most attractive CleanTech infrastructure investment destinations in the world. India has a leading position in several segments

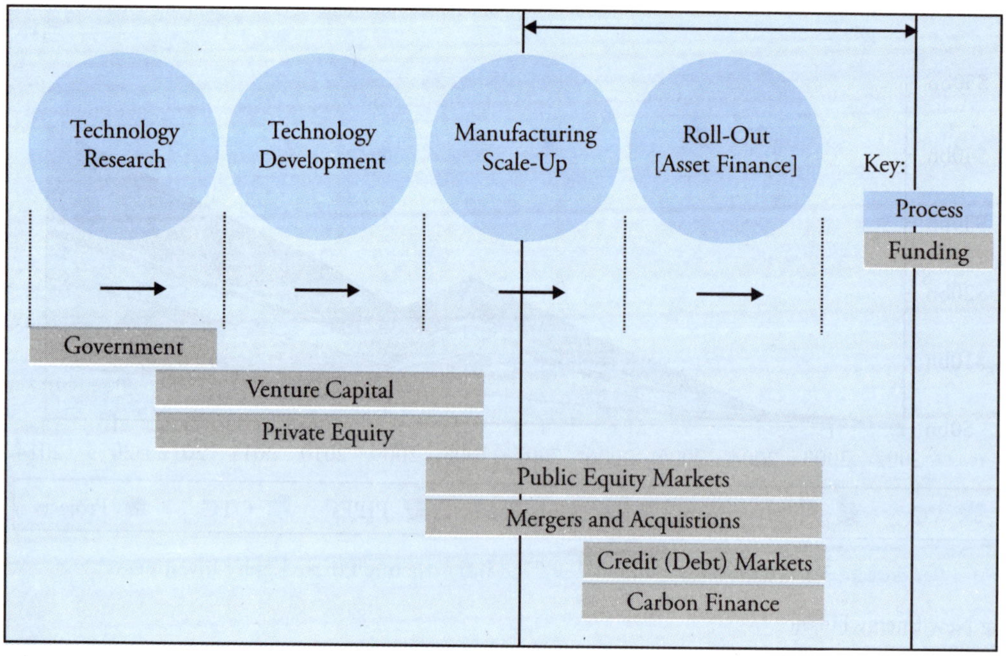

FIGURE 5.2 Role of Private Equity in the Investment Spectrum

Source: Authors' own.

[4] Ministry of New and Renewable Energy.

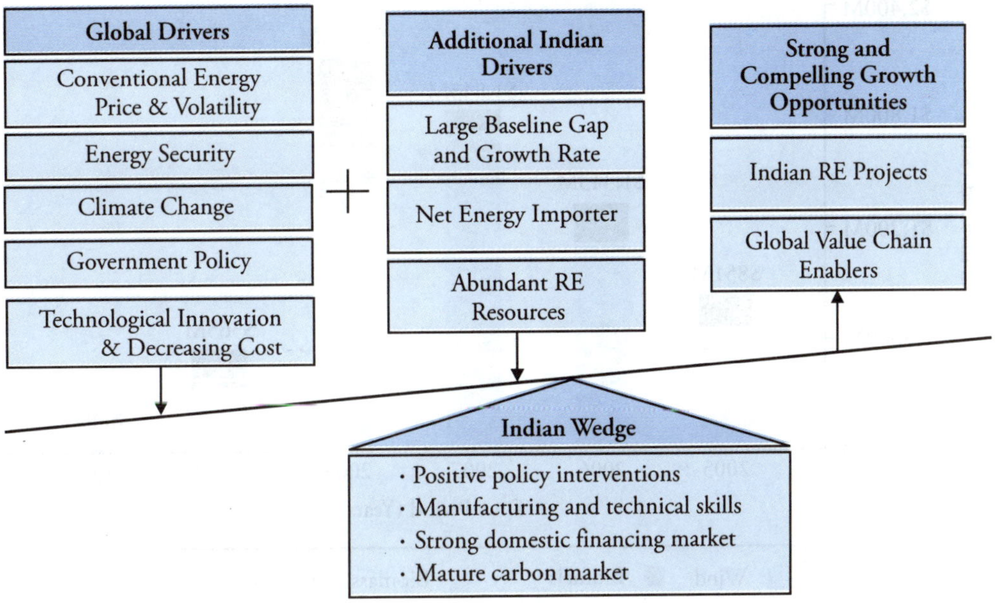

FIGURE 5.3 India has the Macro Drivers and Wedge in Place to be a Key Market

Source: Authors' own.

including a fifth global rank in wind.[5] Further, a positive policy direction, inherent strengths in manufacturing, large domestic financing market, and a mature carbon credit market presents compelling growth opportunities for CleanTech in India in the form of project-based opportunities and global value chain enablers.

Buoyed by the factors discussed above, the PE investments in this sector[6] in India started in 2004, when Citigroup Venture Capital (CVC) invested $ 22.5 million in Suzlon Energy Ltd. The investment in the sector has been growing at a CAGR of about 25 per cent since 2005. The decline in 2009 was triggered by the global financial crisis; however the growth has picked up again this year. the Indian investment landscape has been dominated by investment in projects/assets especially in the wind and small hydro sectors. However, the capital flow has been quite small compared to the global investment in the sector.

The Challenge of Grid Parity

Private equity investors also want to see attractive business models based on fundamental cost competitiveness without incentives, as the risks then would be much lower. Hence the 'heart of the matter' is the race to grid parity. As most of the technologies for electricity generation based on renewable energy sources are currently costlier than the conventional sources, there is an inbuilt reluctance and economic disadvantage associated with their use. If the costs of the electricity generated by the renewable sources of energy and delivered to the grid could be brought close to or lower than the costs associated with conventional sources, the adoption of these technologies will be embraced without any special incentives or interventions. This is where India occupies a strategic position on two counts: (1) India has a large domestic market that can provide scale and reduce cost by being a testing ground for technologies at the inflection point of commercialization and (2) The inherent strengths of technical competence with cost leadership make companies supplying to the global market very attractive. So India is in an advantageous position for accelerating the race towards grid parity. For instance, in India wind farm costs are almost half of that in Europe and the United Staes. The levellized cost of energy (LCOE) analysis below (see Figure 5.5) illustrates this point.

One of the key observations from the above figure is that there is a very wide range of renewable energy costs ranging from INR 17 per unit in case of solar Photo Voltaic (PV) to as low as INR 2.20 per unit in case of small hydro projects. However, except solar, the LCOE for all renewable energy technologies/options is comparable

[5] Bloomberg New Energy Finance.

[6] In this article, the word 'sector' primarily refers to renewable energy which is a subset of the CleanTech Infrastructure sector.

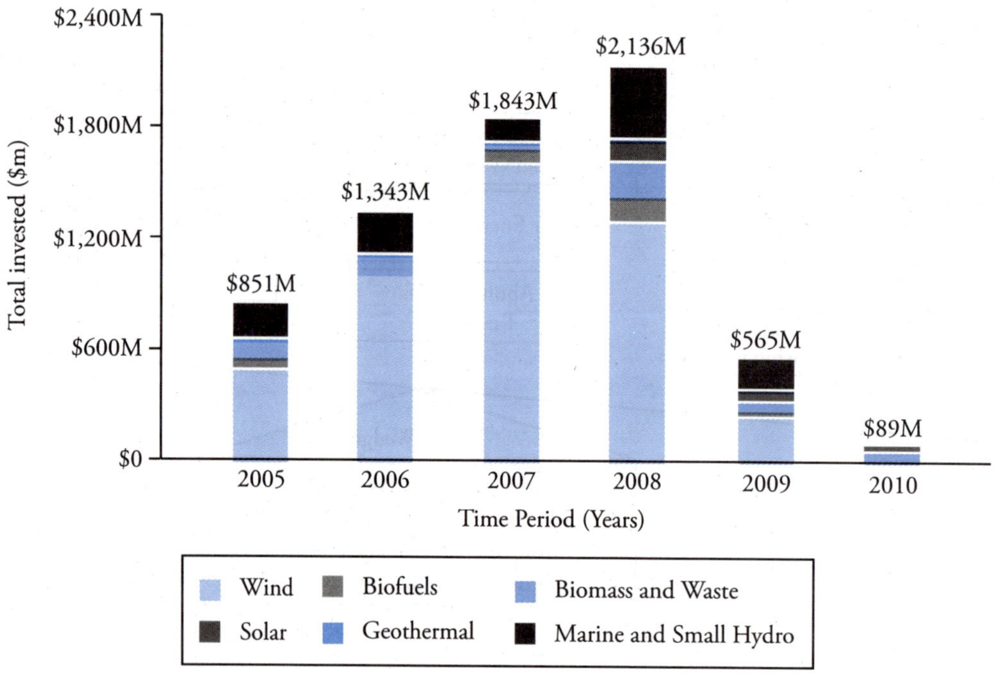

FIGURE 5.4 CleanTech Infrastructure (Energy) Investments in India

Source: Bloomberg New Energy Finance database.

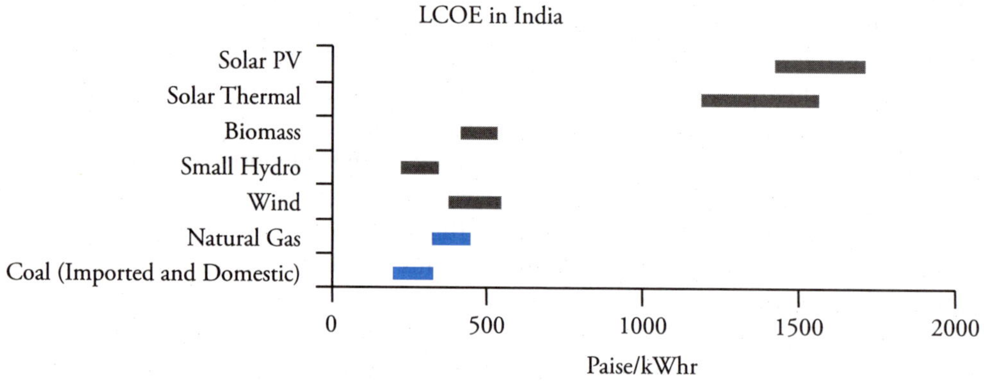

FIGURE 5.5 Increasing Competitiveness of Renewable Energy Based on Indicative LCOE

Source: IDFC Private Equity research.

to conventional power costs. It is found that under Case I of the competitive bidding for procurement of electricity, where the fuel source and location is not specified for medium- to long-term power purchase agreements, the revealed prices for fossil fuel based electricity have ranged between Rs 3–4 per unit. For the short-term merchant power from fossil fuel sources, the price realized is between Rs 4–8 per kWh.

PE Investment Opportunities in India

The Private Equity Investment opportunities in India have been in different segments or parts of the value chain, and there have been different responses in each segment by the investors. In this section, we identify the underlying segments and the activity levels, attractiveness, and challenges in each of these segments.

Project-based Investment Opportunities

Investment Activity so far

Given the regulatory framework prevalent in the country, most of the investment in the renewable energy sector started through balance sheet financing of medium- and large-sized corporations, where these entities took advantage of the depreciation tax shield to reduce their tax liability. However, with the emergence of Independent Power Producers (IPPs) in the renewable energy space over the last four years, the Indian financial institutions have evolved from balance sheet financing to project financing. In 2006, about 50 per cent of the amount invested in the renewable energy sector was balance sheet funding which reduced to 30 per cent in the year 2008. A number of these IPPs have received backing by PE funds (see Table 5.1).

Segment Attractiveness

The project deployment segment has become increasingly attractive as more technologies have improved in terms of the risk-return combination. India is very attractive for this segment on account of several reasons as shown in Figure 5.6 and the key reason is that the deployment cost is amongst the lowest in the world. For instance, even in the mature wind segment, it is half the cost when compared to the US or Europe. Further, policy and regulatory directions, with the announcement of generation-based incentives, national solar mission, renewable energy tariffs, and proposed renewable energy certificates combined with the availability of project debt financing, have positioned IPPs as an attractive investment opportunity.

Preferred Business Models

The key attributes that PE investors look for in these IPPs is a focus on renewables, strong management teams with technology, development, financing and regulatory expertise, and asset diversification with a significant component of operating assets. Rather than small single project developers, the IPP model has been attracting much more investments as it provides economies of scale to boost project returns and create an entity that can be listed based on multiples valuation or a valuation that provides value to the asset pipeline to amplify the overall returns. Some PE companies have taken the initiative to create innovative business models and then invest in those; the setting up of Green Infra Limited being a case in point (See Box 5.1).

Potentially Competitive Global Suppliers

From 2004–5 onwards when the global CleanTech market took off, some sectors such as wind and solar grew so rapidly that the supply-chain was unable to keep pace. By 2008, the supply chain moved into balance as the credit crisis hit the world, leading to an over-capacity situation that put severe pressure on prices. Since 2009–10

Table 5.1 IPPs in Renewable Energy Segment Received Support of PE Funds

Company	*Set-up*	*Investor*	*Operational Capacity (MW)*
Green Infra Ltd.	2009	IDFC PE Fund II and Fund III	124 MW (Wind)
Orient Green Power	2007	Olympus Capital, Bessemer Ventures, Shriram EPC	175 MW (Biomass—40MW, Wind – 135MW)
Greenko	2006	Global Environment Fund, Aloe Environment Fund, TPG Growth	120 MW (Hydro—78MW, Biomass -42MW)
Auro Mira Energy	2005	Baring PE	17.5 MW (Biomass)
Shallvahana Green Energy	1980s	Axis PE, IL&FS Financial Services	35 MW (Biomass)

Source: IDFC Private Equity research.

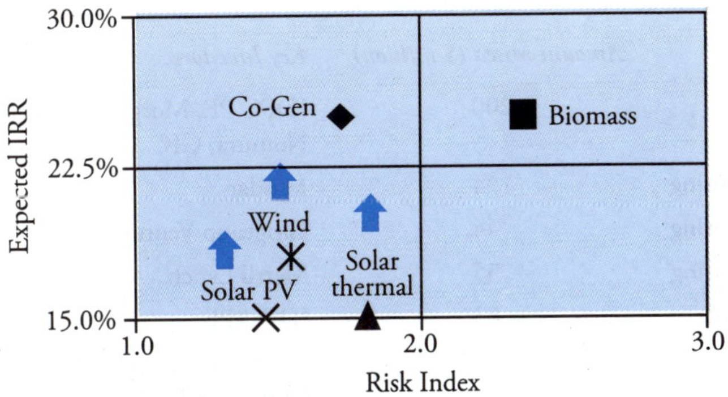

- Huge untapped potential
- Progressive government policy
- Strong domestic project finance market
- Low deployment cost
- Lack of large RE focused IPPs

Figure 5.6 Renewable Energy Project Segment—Risks, Indicative Returns, and Attractiveness of India

Source: Internal IDFC Private Equity research.

Box 5.1
Green Infra Limited: An Innovative Business Model

Introduction

Green Infra Ltd. ('GI' or 'Company') was set up by funds managed by IDFCPE to build a platform with aggregation and development capabilities in the renewable energy sector. GI is an IPP and develops/operates renewable power generation projects across the wind, solar, biomass, waste-to-energy, small hydro, and energy efficiency verticals. At present, the Company has 124 MW of operating assets in India and aims to reach 1GW of total capacity in the next 2–3 years.

Business model

GI generates power utilizing renewable sources of energy and sells it to a variety of customers. The Company follows both organic and inorganic routes to develop generation capacity across verticals. Through the acquisition-led route, the Company seeks to acquire attractive operational assets to provide an immediate boost to its generation capacity. It also provides a plug-and-play platform for smaller entrepreneurs in the sector. For the organic route, the Company works with leading project advisors/technology providers to identify and develop greenfield project opportunities in the above mentioned sectors. The Company has a diversified customer base, including public sector utilities and some of the leading corporations in India, including the Tata Group. The strategy enables GI to maximize the returns at a listing event while realizing synergies and economies of scale across the projects.

Journey so far

Within 18 months since inception, GI has become one of the largest renewable energy IPPs in the country (one that is not a subsidiary or arm of a large corporate group) and today has 124 MW of high-quality operational wind assets. It has successfully pioneered the sale of wind power on a group captive basis. In July 2009, the Company acquired a 100 MW portfolio of operating wind farms from BP, one of the largest recent transactions in India's renewable energy sector. This year, it is evolving as the first renewable IPPs in India to have a presence across each technology vertical. The Company has a pipeline in excess of 500 MW across different verticals.

Source: Authors' own.

onwards, some key markets such as Germany and Spain announced cut backs in the incentives being given to CleanTech segments. These trends at different points in time underlined the importance of cost advantage as the key criteria to define market survival and leadership. In this period, since 2003 onwards, the local Indian market started opening up for renewable energy projects and thus became a good testing ground for technologies developed in the west that were at an inflection point of commercialization. As far as the suppliers are concerned, the local market also became a hedge to the volatility of the global markets. These trends created a very strong investment case for enablers supplying to the global market. There has been an evolution of a complete ecosystem including a strong manufacturing base for the alternative energy sector. Given India's strength in cost-efficient manufacturing, the companies involved in manufacturing/production of wind turbines and, solar cells have drawn strong PE interest. Some of the transactions in the CleanTech value chain in the last five years are highlighted in Table 5.2 below:

Table 5.2 Select PE Transactions in Enablers along the Renewable Energy Supply Chain in India

Company Name	*Sector*	*Amount raised ($ million)*	*Key Investors*
Moser Baer Photo Voltaic	Solar	200	IDFC PE, Morgan Stanley, CS, Nomura, GIC, CDC
Winwind	Wind turbine manufacturing	174	Masdar
Suzlon Energy Limited	Wind turbine manufacturing	44	Citigroup Venture Capital, Chrys Capital
Vestas RRB India	Wind turbine manufacturing	55	Merril Lynch
Seforge Limited	Wind turbine components	83	IDFC-PE
Shriram EPC	EPC-biomass and wind turbine manufacturing	39.5	Bessemer Venture Partners, ChrysCap, UTI ventures, Argonaut
Emergent Ventures India	Carbon advisory	10	IDFC-PE

Source: Internal IDFC Private Equity research.

Investment Opportunities in Value Chain Enablers

The key attributes of an enabler along the renewable energy supply chain that a PE investor would be looking at would include sales diversification in terms of geographies and a mix of short-term and longer-term orders with an anchor customer, sustainable cost advantage, access to technology, and a strong cohesive team. Some of the segments along the supply chain in the CleanTech space that PE investors may find attractive and the attributes or business models that underscore their attractiveness are discussed below.

Solar Energy Segment

The global solar segment has been a hotbed for innovation as it is destined to be the long-term market leader. It has been going through a down cycle following the global economic crisis of 2008–9 that is leading to a shakeout. After the crisis we are in an oversupply market that is going to last. As a result, the market price has dropped sharply by 40–50 per cent. It is a survival of the fittest situation and a winner would need staying power plus scale, cost advantage, ability to keep pace with changing technology, sales diversification, and a strong domestic market. India is a good market to create successful enablers targeting the world market as the National Solar Mission has opened up a strong domestic market in addition to the other reasons as shown in Figure 5.7 below.

For example, IDFC PE invested in Moser Baer PV in 2007–8 that straddled multiple technologies while developing a customer base in Europe and leveraging its experience in lowering the manufacturing cost. The opening of the Indian market would provide a good hedge to the downturn in the European markets.

Wind Energy Segment

Recovery from the oversupply situation in the global wind segment is in sight. Again, to be successful in this segment one needs staying power in addition to customer diversification, scale, and cost advantage (See Figure 5.8). The key reason why India is a germane market for this is the very large and mature wind market in India.

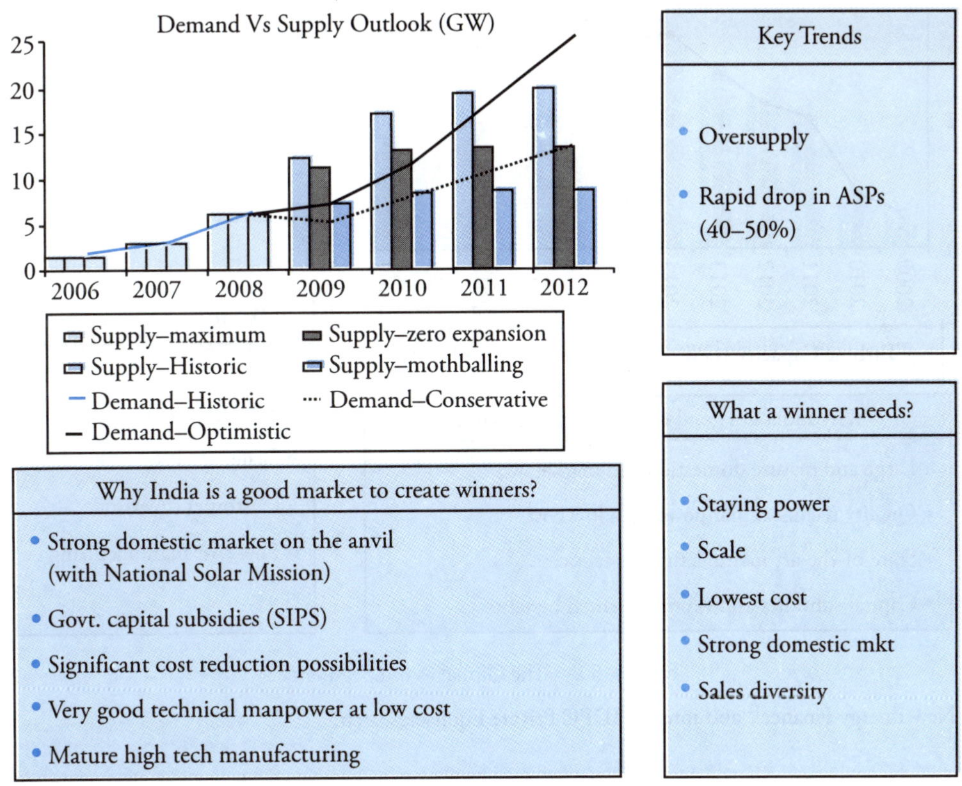

FIGURE 5.7 The Global Solar Enabler Segment

Source: Bloomberg New Energy Finance[7] and internal IDFC Private Equity research.

7 Bloomberg New Energy Finance presentation dated 5 November 2009 in London by Michael Liebriech in E2DS conference.

Two types of business models are attractive to investors in this segment. The first model is to manufacture wind turbines by getting access to superior technology and which can be combined with the local manufacturing advantage. But the challenge is to penetrate an overcrowded market. The large local market, alliances with farm developers outside India and the ability to provide attractive pricing can mitigate the risk. One such example is Masdar Cleantech Fund's[8] investment in WinWind.[9] Further, it may be also attractive to manufacture components of wind turbine generators that can supply to the global wind market and is not dependent on the sales of one turbine supplier. An example of such an investment is IDFC Private Equity's investment in SE Forge.[10] The challenge in this model is to develop the components and develop a large diversified customer base. The challenge could be mitigated by an anchor customer concept followed by customer diversification by supplying to other wind turbine manufacturers as well as non-wind segments such as power and heavy engineering.

Carbon Mitigation Services Segment

The global carbon market has been at the crossroads with a failure to reach a global consensus post-Kyoto Protocol. The way that the climate policy negotiations are evolving, it is envisaged that the post-Kyoto period, that is the post-2012 phase, will be marked by the emergence of several local markets for carbon trading. A successful service provider to the carbon market needs a high local supply base to get to scale, access to low cost quality manpower and access to the global buyer market. India is a good place for creating winners as the local carbon mitigation market is huge.

An example of an innovative model in the carbon segment is Emergent Ventures India (EVI). In 2008, IDFC PE invested in EVI and it has emerged as one of the top

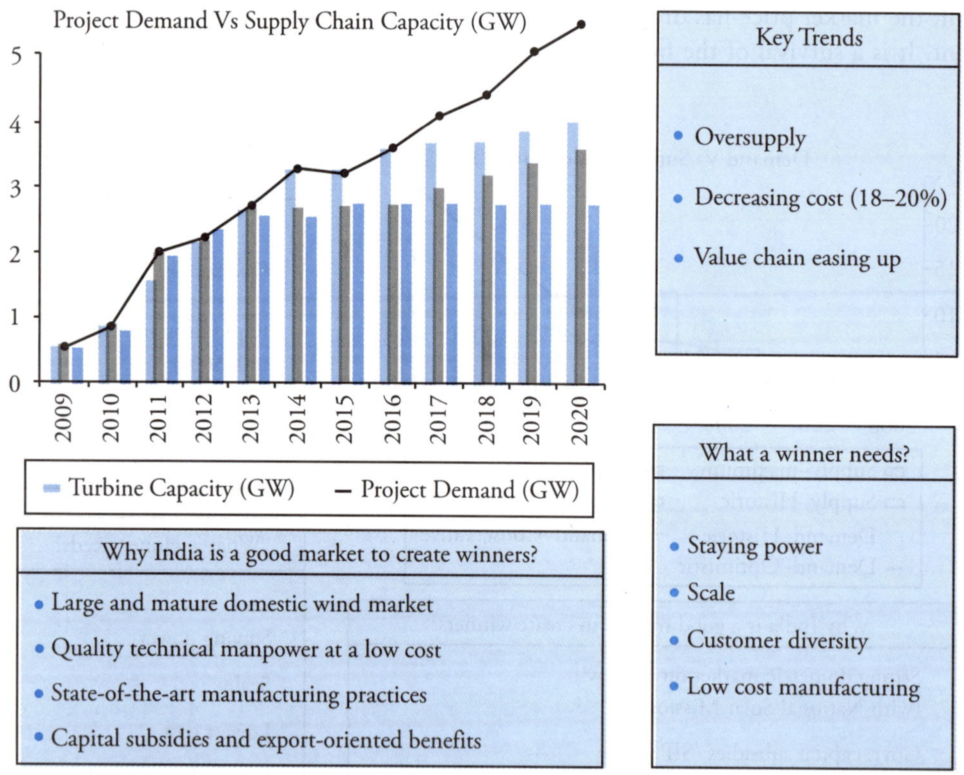

Figure 5.8 The Global Wind Segment

Source: Bloomberg New Energy Finance[11] and internal IDFC Private Equity research.

[8] Masdar Cleantech Fund is a leading fund based in United Arab Emirates.

[9] WinWind is a recent entrant in the wind market with turbines based on technology developed in Finland and manufacturing facilities in India.

[10] SE Forge is a subsidiary of Suzlon Energy Limited. It has one of the largest state-of-the-art forging and foundry facilities in India. It supplies large castings and forgings to the Indian and global wind turbine manufacturers.

[11] Bloomberg New Energy Finance presentation dated 5 November 2009 in London by Michael Liebriech in E2DS conference.

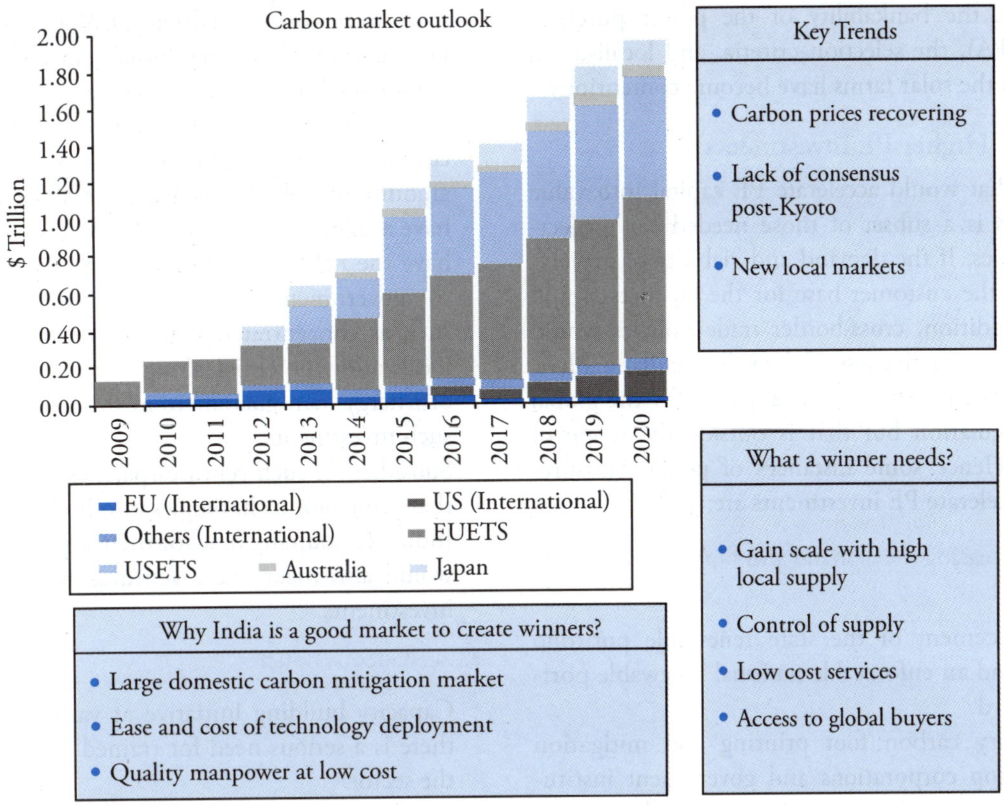

FIGURE 5.9 Global Carbon Enablers

Source: Bloomberg New Energy Finance[12] and internal IDFC Private Equity research.

carbon service providers in India. The uniqueness of the business model of EVI was that it has evolved iteratively over time. It started with a carbon advisory business that expanded around the world in buyer and supplier countries. Then it developed the carbon procurement business by proactively developing renewable energy projects and is evolving as a master contractor for such projects. As a third step it developed a carbon value advisory business by providing climate change consulting services to corporations. Each business vertical is complementary and has served as a hedge to the other business vertical in order to mitigate the post-Kyoto risk.

Role of the Policy

Policy Evolution

Policy is the key to leverage the flow of PE capital into the CleanTech Infrastructure sector. The overall policy direction in India has been positive in terms of increasing the attractiveness of the sector for the flow of PE capital. However long-term policy stability is important as the nature of the underlying cash flows justifying these investments is long term. The key drivers for PE capital have been the renewable portfolio standards, generation-based incentives, capital subsidies, opening up of power trading, and more recently the National Solar Mission and the REC policy. It is important that the policy interventions are made at the right point to increase the flow of PE capital. For instance, the GBI not only incentivized the maximization of the utilization of the wind resources but also made the segment more attractive for IPPs and not just driven by tax breaks.

Policy Implementation

But the real challenge so far has been in the implementation of the policies, which needs to be improved to convert the huge interest generated by policy announcements into real investments. For instance, a huge interest resulted from the announcement of the National Solar Mission. However the implementation could be delayed as several

[12] Bloomberg New Energy Finance presentation dated 5 November 2009 in London by Michael Liebriech in E2DS conference.

issues such as the bankability of the power purchase agreement (PPA), the selection criteria, and localization component in the solar farms have become contentious.

Measures for Higher PE Investments

The policies that would accelerate PE capital into value chain enablers is a subset of those needed for project-based companies. If the demand and viability of projects improve then the customer base for the enablers would increase. In addition, cross-border trade policies would also impact the attractiveness of the value chain enablers. The value chain enablers are also impacted by the global policy and regulation but that is outside the scope of this chapter. Hence some instances of policy measures that would accelerate PE investments are:

Policies for increasing the demand and supply of renewable energy projects:

- Strict enforcement of the state renewable portfolio standards and an enforceable national renewable portfolio standard.
- A mandatory carbon foot printing and mitigation policy for top corporations and government institutions can increase the demand for renewable energy and other carbon offset projects.
- Make it mandatory for independent power producers and state/central utilities to have a certain percentage of renewable energy generation base.

Policies for improving the economics of renewable energy projects

- Policies to enable tax benefit driven and cash returns driven investors to come together in the same wind project so as to bring down the weighted average cost of equity as the tax driven investor has a lower cash return appetite. Joint participation by both sets of investors had been a very strong driver of equity investments in the US wind market.
- Dedicated long-term lending for the sector wherein the banks need to allocate a certain percentage of the loan book to the sector.

Policies for accelerating the cross-border partnerships to transfer, deploy, and localize clean technologies

- There are several technologies that have gone through the long research and development phase and are now ready to be commercialized. Deploying such technologies in India can meet India's current energy needs, commercialize the technology, and bring down their cost by localization. However to make such projects commercially viable for equity investors, a significant amount of debt is needed. But since these projects have a significant technology risk, the lenders may not have the risk appetite. A loan guarantee scheme from the government for projects using new technologies, such as concentrated solar power, that have a strong localization potential along the lines of Department of Energy loan guarantees in the US would accelerate such investments.
- Subsidies for such ventures/partnerships/joint ventures that bring new technologies into India and also develop India as a sourcing base for their deployment elsewhere would also make these ventures attractive for equity investments.

Miscellaneous policies

- Capacity building initiative at various institutions as there is a serious need for trained human resources in the sector.

Conclusion

Overall, based on the experiences and learning so far, there are clear messages emerging for the key stakeholders in the sector namely; the PE investors, the entrepreneurs, and the policymakers. For the PE investor in the sector, it is clearly an attractive opportunity with a potential of strong secular growth based on robust drivers. Though, some operational challenges continue to exist but with clearer government support towards the sector, the issues should be resolved in the near term. That drives the message for the regulators and policymakers, who need to focus on policy stability, quick implementation, and a stronger interface with the industry players to provide the impetus at the right place and time. The entrepreneurs, on the other hand, have several innovative business models to build a renewable energy platform. However, the key to attracting PE capital is to focus on sustainable copetitive advantage that can be achieved through cost leadership, being ahead on the technology curve, development expertise, and development of diversified customer base.

6 High Cost Carbon and Local Government Finance

Patricia Clarke Annez and Thomas Zuelgaray*

Introduction

Global climate change has certain unique features in terms of optimal policy. Some of these have been discussed already at the global level and some at the national level. This chapter contends that these features will also have implications for fiscal federalism and this area has yet to be given the consideration it deserves. Cities, in particular, need to consider the following points:

- Climate change is a global externality. Accordingly, any reduction in carbon emissions[1] has equal value for mitigating climate change—no matter where the reduction takes place;
- This implies that the optimal Pigovian tax for reducing carbon emissions is the same world-wide, and *a fortiori*, nation-wide. In this way, the cost of reducing global emissions will be minimized because all potential emitters face the same incentive to reduce emissions and will thus face price signals to reduce emissions at least cost first;[2]
- Partitioning the world into different groups who must reduce emissions looking only at their opportunity set rather than the world-wide set of opportunities for least cost emission reductions will increase the world-wide cost of mitigation. Thus, any policy for mitigation should seek to adhere as closely as possible to the principle of a uniform carbon price. Otherwise, the efficiency cost of a major reduction of a critical input economy-wise will be increased, and this is neither desirable nor necessary;
- This does not imply that all emitters should bear equally all the economic and financial costs of reducing emissions. An equitable policy response requires separating these two aspects of policy formulation. It is quite likely to be the case that considerable negotiations will be needed to create a credible system for burden sharing that will compensate poor countries for the costs they must bear to address a problem that is not of their making. This is because their contributions to the existing GHG stocks are minimal. Even future emissions will not materially change this calculus when considered on a per capita basis;
- Nonetheless, long-term strategy should move at a suitable pace towards uniform pricing of the marginal greenhouse gas emission. This implies that the costs of energy will have to increase in developing countries;

* The authors would like to thank the participants in the World Bank Urban Research Symposium for the comments received on the paper and the National Institute of Urban Affairs in India for hosting us to do this research. This article is based on a paper originally presented at the Fifth World Bank Urban Research Symposium in Marseille France 26–30 June 2009.

[1] Following common practice, we refer to all GHG emissions as carbon. This is merely a shorthand for purposes of simplicity. Optimal policies will have to distinguish between GHGs based on their different forcing factors (effect on climate). Abstracting from certain scientific uncertainties, these are relatively easily reduced to broadly accepted carbon equivalence factors.

[2] For purposes of simplicity, we ignore questions of phasing here. It may well be politically impossible to raise carbon prices equally worldwide in the immediate or even medium term.

- Whether or not carbon taxes or cap-and-trade systems (C&T) are used to drive up the cost of carbon and reduce emissions, this principle still holds. There are important differences between cap-and-trade and carbon tax systems, but for the purposes mentioned in this chapter, the only one that matters is fiscal. A carbon tax, by definition, gives rise to government revenues. C&T systems need not. For our purposes, we will assume that governments would sell emissions permits to obtain an equivalent quantity reduction, so the C&T and carbon tax would have the same revenue implications. Therefore, for simplicity, we discuss carbon taxes here, and leave any assessment of the desirability of a tax versus C&T outside our discussion; and
- This chapter explores a third element of necessary policies—fiscal burden sharing, that is, possible intergovernmental imbalances that would arise because different levels of government will be exposed to different combinations of higher costs and higher revenues. Discussions have already started regarding the international implications of burden sharing. This chapter also delves into the question of intergovernmental burden sharing between sub-national governments, including municipal and national governments, and to a lesser extent, the question of how to manage the interpersonal burden sharing within the national economy.

So what is the impact of high cost carbon on local government finance?

High cost carbon affects municipal finances from the expenditure side. How significant an effect this will be depends on the functional responsibilities of the local government. Interestingly, some of the most basic functions are also some of the most carbon-intensive. For example, garbage collection/disposal, street lighting, water delivery, transit, operating schools, and other municipal buildings are energy-intensive responsibilities of the local government.

Higher cost carbon could also affect the revenue side for municipalities. However, it is quite likely to be the case that the revenues of municipalities are much less sensitive to energy costs than are their expenditures. Moreover, local government revenue sources are often not well-structured to capture higher energy prices. For example, water charges in many places in India are charged as a fixed cess (fee) on top of property taxes, and would thus not have any ready mechanism for responding to higher energy costs. In contrast, solid waste collection fees, frequently charged out as a fixed percentage of the electricity bill, might fare better. Likewise, municipalities that receive a share of gasoline taxes, such as in Spain, could fare better than most of those in South Asia where taxation of energy has been kept at the federal level.

To make an assessment of the initial impact of higher carbon taxes on municipalities, the carbon content of their revenues and expenditures needs to be measured, along with the price sensitivity of both flows. A more general equilibrium assessment would look at the impact once higher carbon prices had worked their way through the price system to understand both the medium and long-term impacts. It is probable that unintended fiscal imbalances could be provoked at the sub-national, especially municipal, level due to higher carbon taxation, if there are no compensating measures designed into the tax system.

This chapter uses municipal revenue and spending data to develop a simple model of the financial impacts of higher energy costs in various scenarios. The purpose here is to illustrate the direction of impacts and interactions that may occur in different municipal finance contexts. This rough modelling exercise is intended to sensitize local, central, and provincial governments to the likely implications of higher energy prices so that appropriate compensatory measures are considered as part of an overall package of policies for mitigating greenhouse gas emissions. Without such measures, there are likely to be unintended consequences that could include a rapid run-up of municipal indebtedness or cutbacks of services—all of which might be avoided by properly redistributing tax revenues across levels of government.

Review of Literature

A large body of literature already exists on the establishment of an environmental tax and its impact on the economy. However, this literature rarely takes into account the case of developing countries. Moreover, if literature on the relation between government tax and sub-national government tax exists, in the case of environmental tax, this analysis is almost always posed in the context of a unitary government. All this literature seeks to evaluate is the optimal environmental tax. Major contributions in that direction have been made by Bovenberg, Goulder, Parry, and many co-authors in the mid-1990s, using a general equilibrium framework.

The relations between national government taxation and sub-national government tax can be found in the work of Besley and Rosen (1998) on the vertical externalities in tax setting with the cases of taxes imposed on gasoline and cigarettes. Estimating the magnitude of the responses to federal tax when the federal government increases its taxes, they find that there is a significant positive response to state taxes. However, they suggest more research to estimate how analyses of efficiency consequences of federal excise taxes would change when effects upon state tax rates are taken into account. They also warn us that if a positive interdependence between federal and state tax rates exists, then there is a risk that non-co-operative tax setting between federal and state governments results in excessive taxation of common tax bases. Fredriksson and Fredriksson and Mamun (2008) also studied the vertical externalities in cigarette taxation. They suggested that an increase in the federal cigarette tax may reduce the average state cigarette tax rate. They concluded that a federal tax hike may reduce state tax revenues through changes in both the tax rate and the base.

Not much research exists in this area on experiences of developing countries. However, we can quote the work of Chelliah et al. (2007) on the question of environmental tax. On matters of sub-national government finance and intergovernmental transfers, we can quote the work of Anwar Shah (2006) with his guide to intergovernmental fiscal transfers. Then, another work of interest and relevance is Ahmad and Stern (2009) on effective carbon taxes and public policy options. This chapter, based on the Indian case, evaluates which level of government might be responsible for the administration of this kind of tax. Their conclusion is that such a tax has to be a central excise tax and that it is not desirable to introduce differentiation into state-level value added taxes (VATs), at least for the Indian case. Their conclusion corresponds to our starting point for this chapter, which is a tax administered at a central level and harmonized across all countries.

Structure of Municipal Finances

To examine the questions described above regarding the impact of higher energy costs on municipalities, we considered two different groups of municipalities, those in Maharashtra, India, and those in Spain. We examined two concrete examples of city finances for specificity. However, this should not be construed in any sense as a projection of likely effects for a representative set of cities internationally. The finances of local governments around the world are sufficiently diverse to render such an exercise meaningless. Cities concerned with this issue will need to conduct such exercises themselves. This simulation instead is meant to be illustrative of the direction and order of the magnitude of effects one might expect, given the structural characteristics of municipal finances in the two countries. The most important structural characteristics that most cities around the world share are: (i) a cost base that is relatively energy-intensive and (ii) a revenue base that is not sensitive to energy prices. It is these features that drive the structural imbalances that we wish to explore in this chapter. Any variation across cities in terms of energy efficiency or energy savings programmes will of course affect the specific impact of higher energy prices in individual cities, and no illustrative model can seek to include such a degree of detail.

We have compared Spanish municipalities with Indian municipalities (for example, Maharashtra) because they differ in important ways. Spanish municipalities share some revenue sources that are tied to energy spending. Indian municipalities do not. Spanish municipalities have a wide array of complex functions such as primary education delegated to them. Indian municipalities focus on key basic services such as solid waste management and street lighting. The comparison of the two is again merely illustrative of how these differences in structural characteristics affect the financial impact of higher energy prices. They are not meant to encompass all possible scenarios for differential impacts in different municipalities.

For both sets of municipalities, we have reasonably detailed data on the structure of expenditures and revenues. The data for Spain are at the national level, thus covering all municipalities. For India, no such data exists, so we validated this data by comparing it with somewhat more aggregated data from Kundu (2002) for the city of Ahmedabad, and from Mohanty et al. (2007) for the 35 metropolitan cities in India. The structure of expenditures and the types of revenue sources in both these alternate data sources, while more aggregated than our Maharashtra data, appear reasonably similar, which gives us some confidence that the more detailed data from Maharashtra is representative.

These two examples of Spain and India represent systems that differ in important aspects, that is, sources of revenues, the structure of functions devolved, and hence spending among others. Thorough knowledge of the structure of municipal expenditure is essential to understand how their finances will be affected by a fluctuation of energy prices. Since there appears to be no direct measure of energy consumption for municipalities in either country, we approximate energy consumption by separating into different categories, the different types of expenditures by intensity of energy consumption. We have also reviewed the structure of revenue flows, to understand which of these may be sensitive to energy prices.

Revenue

India and Spain have both decentralized many functions to sub-national government: states for India and provinces for Spain. However, there is considerable difference in how the municipalities are financed in India and Spain. Spain is examined as a whole because most

Spanish municipalities have similar revenue structures (except for the Basque province). For India, we chose to study Maharashtra, because the State Finance Commission of this state made a great effort to collect data on municipalities' finances—only a few Indian states have undertaken this exercise with such accuracy.

For the Spanish municipal finances, we relied on the interesting work of DEXIA[3] which presents data on finance-related functions of sub-national governments in the European Union.

Spanish Municipalities

In Spain in 2005, 23 per cent of the total sub-national government revenues—to the tune of 43 EUR billion, or four per cent of GDP—went to municipalities. The revenue was sourced fairly equally from taxes (33 per cent), grants (36 per cent) and other sources such as fees and asset sales (31 per cent), as shown in Table 6.1.

Table 6.1 Sources of Revenue for Spanish Municipalities

Spanish Municipalities revenue in 2005	*€ MM*[4]	*per cent of total revenue*
Tax revenue	14,201	33.1
of which own-source tax	(13,482)	(31.4)
of which shared tax	(719)	(1.7)
Grants	15,540	36.2
of which general grants	(7,085)	(16.5)
of which earmarked grants	(8,455)	(19.7)
Other	13,132	30.6
of which asset sales	(106)	(0.2)
of which fees	(8,094)	(18.9)
Total	42,873	99.9

Source: DEXIA (2008).

Tax Revenue Spanish municipalities have own taxes' revenue and revenue from shared taxes. Their own taxes represent 95 per cent of municipal tax revenue. Municipalities raise several local taxes; the most important are shown in Table 6.2, below:

Municipalities with more than 75,000 inhabitants and capitals of provinces receive shared tax receipts. A summary of these shared tax revenues are shown in Table 6.3.

There are several pathways through which energy price increases could affect this municipal revenue base. For own-source revenues, however, all of these would be second-order effects, since none of the revenues are directly tied to energy prices. These second-order effects could be significant if, for example, the relative price of housing and motor vehicles, were to decline in the face of higher energy prices. A Computable General Equilibrium model would be an excellent tool for exploring these impacts. In this simplified model, municipal own-source revenue is assumed to be unaffected by fluctuations in the price of energy. However, in the case of Spain, we consider that the shared excise taxes fluctuate with fluctuation of the price of energy because this tax includes a hydrocarbon tax. Currently, this excise is a per unit charge, and would thus not fluctuate with energy prices. However, a carbon

Table 6.2 Own-Source Tax Revenue for Spanish Municipalities

Own-source tax revenue	*€ MM*	*Municipalities*	
		per cent of tax revenue	*per cent of total municipal revenue*
Tax on property	6,800	48	16
Tax on construction, installations, and works	2,200	15	5
Tax on motor vehicles	2,000	14	5
Tax on economic activities	1,300	9	3
Tax on capital gains in urban areas	1,200	9	3
Total	13,500	95	32

Source: DEXIA (2008).

[3] DEXIA, Collective work under the direction of Dominique Hoorens, (2008): Sub-national government in the European Union. DEXIA Editions, July 2008.

[4] MM = Million.

TABLE 6.3 Shared Tax Revenue for Spanish Municipalities

Shared tax revenue	*Municipalities*		
	€ MM	*per cent of tax revenue*	*per cent of total municipal revenue*
1.7 per cent of the Personal Income Tax	370	2.6	0.9
1.8 per cent of the VAT	250	1.8	0.6
2.0 per cent of the excise taxes	99	0.7	0.2
Total	719	5.1	1.7

Source: DEXIA (2008).

tax that is *ad valorem*, could at least be shared following the current sharing principle.

Grants Municipalities receive an unconditional grant from the central government: the municipal share of the state tax (criteria are population, fiscal effort, and the inverse of fiscal capacity). It represents 17 per cent of total revenues.

They also receive grants earmarked for specific investment projects such as transport infrastructure and represent 20 per cent of total revenues.

Other Revenue User charges on services or administrative functions supplied to all citizens, fees, and asset sales are the other sources of financing made available to Spanish municipalities.

Indian Municipalities (Maharashtra)

The state of Maharashtra has two forms of urban local bodies (ULBs): municipal corporations and class municipal councils. The Municipal Corporations include megacities such as Mumbai, which are interesting in their own right, but quite different from the smaller cities and towns covered in the municipal councils. In Maharashtra, there are three types of municipal councils: 'A', 'B', and 'C' representing in this order, the most populous cities to the least.[5] We strategically cumulated the incomes and expenditures of the three types of municipal councils.

The structure of revenues in Maharashtra is distinct from the Spanish municipalities. Grants from the state government represent two-thirds (that is, 64 per cent) of the total revenue for municipalities in the state, whereas own-source tax revenue represents just 17 per cent of the total. This is partly a consequence of the logistic difficulties faced in collecting taxes for the municipalities. Moreover, the absence of a system of shared taxes explains why grants are so important in municipal revenues. The general revenue structure and a breakdown of the state's own-source tax revenues are shown in Table 6.4 and Table 6.5 respectively.

TABLE 6.4 Sources of Revenue for Maharashtra Municipalities

Municipalities revenue in 2000	*Rs. MM*	*per cent of total revenue*
Tax revenue	1,875	16.6 per cent
Grants	7,272	64.2 per cent
Other	2,178	19.2 per cent
Total	11,326	100.0 per cent

Source: *Maharashtra Human Development Report* (2002).

Tax Revenue

Indian municipalities have their own taxes revenue but no revenue from shared taxation. Municipalities raise several local taxes, and the most important are the following:

Grants Grants from the states represent 64 per cent of the total municipal revenue. Municipalities are financed by about 30 state grants. Most of these grants are for specific purposes, although incentive grants are provided to encourage better performance in collecting water charges and property taxes. The most important grants are: Dearness Allowance Grant, Grant for reimbursement of salary and leave salary of Chief Officers, Land revenue and non-agricultural assessment grant, Entertainment Grant, Stamp Duty Grant, Pilgrim Tax, Minor Mineral Grant, Profession Tax Grant, Road Grant, Octroi Compensation Grant (Octrois have been abolished in 2000),

[5] The budgets for Spanish municipalities taken from DEXIA include capital budget items. However, for the Indian municipalities, the capital budget items were insignificant and fluctuated greatly across municipalities and over time. Since we were concerned with the reliability of this data, we did not include capital budget items on either the cost or revenue side for the Maharashtra municipalities.

TABLE 6.5 Own-Source Tax Revenue for Maharashtra Municipalities

Own-source tax revenue		*Municipalities*	
	Rs. MM	*per cent of tax revenue*	*per cent of total municipal revenue*
Property Tax	1,038	55	9.2
Water Charges	578	31	5.1
Conservancy and Sanitation	21	1	0.2
Street Lights	0,1	0	0.0
License Fees and Entertainment	67	4	0.6
Building Rents	171	9	1.5
Total	1,875	100	16.6

Source: *Maharashtra Human Development Report* (2002).

Primary Education Grant, Slum Improvement, and Incentive Grant.

Many of these grants compensate municipalities for local taxing powers that were repealed, most notably octroi. The principles upon which they are distributed are not uniform, and are often *ad hoc*. This lack of predictability affects planning of expenditure strategies for municipalities.

Other Revenue

Other revenue sources represents 19 per cent of municipal revenue. These sources include parking fees, permit fees, service fees and user charges, rent from commercial complexes, development fees for granting permission to construct buildings on vacant plots, and other fees and charges.

Expenditures

Here focus is on the comparison of expenditures for Spanish and Indian municipalities. The structure of expenditure of both the municipalities is very different. While Spanish municipalities spend 30 per cent of their revenue in capital expenditure, almost all the revenue of Indian municipalities is spent in current expenditure, most of which is dedicated to staff cost.

Functions assumed by municipalities also differ, even if there are some common responsibilities such as water supply and garbage collection. These common expenditures, however, do not account for the same percentage of the total expenditure in the two countries. In the following analysis here, we will detail these expenditures from the point of view of energy consumption.

In 2005, the Spanish municipal expenditures reached 43.5 EUR billion, which represents 13 per cent of total public expenditure in Spain, and 4.5 per cent of GDP. These ratios are among the highest in the European Union. Seventy per cent of municipal expenditure is current expenditure, of which 45 per cent (representing 30.6 per cent of total expenditures) is staff cost. The remaining 30 per cent is capital expenditure.

In contrast, the municipal expenditures in Maharashtra reached INR 11,121 million. This expenditure is almost entirely current expenditure, as the reported capital expenditure is minimal.

Municipal expenditures for India and Spain have been itemized by function and are shown in Table 6.6 and Table 6.7, respectively. It should be noted that for India, obligatory functions such as water supply, fire brigades, and street lighting are distinguished from discretionary functions such as urban poverty alleviation and controlling stray/dangerous animals. For both Spain and India, it is expected that different municipal functions will require energy inputs at varying degrees of intensity.

Unfortunately, there is little published data on the actual use of energy in different municipal functions. This is because separate activities are often not ring-fenced and actual energy usage is not tracked. Therefore, we imputed energy intensities to different activities based on the likely profile of energy use. So we created three different categories of spending, based on energy intensity of total spending, made reasonable assumptions about the extent of energy use in each, which we then varied later in sensitivity testing. This followed categorizing the different functions according to percentage of costs incurred for the energy: insignificant (0 per cent), significant (20 per cent), and intense (90 per cent). These imputed intensities reflect fairly conservative assumptions on intensity of energy use by category.

We used the same coefficients for the municipalities in Spain and India for simplicity, since there is little data

Table 6.6 Energy Intensity of Municipal Expenditures in Maharashtra, India

Energy consumption	*Sector*	*per cent of total expenditure*	*Budget (Rs MM)*
Insignificant	General administration, salaries, pension & pensionary benefits etc.	28.7 per cent	3,389
	Administration of Shops & Establishment Act 1948, & Markets (D)	0.3 per cent	35
	Total	29 per cent	3,423
Significant	Fire brigade (O)	0.3 per cent	32
	Slaughter houses (D)	0.0 per cent	4
	Education, libraries, free reading halls etc. (D)	9.3 per cent	1,099
	Museums, art galleries, recreation centres, playgrounds, Gardens etc. (D)	0.7 per cent	87
	Epidemics & public health (O)	1.4 per cent	169
	Other expenditure	32.8 per cent	3,873
	Total	45 per cent	5,263
Intense	Roads (O)	8.1 per cent	953
	Street lighting (O)	3.3 per cent	386
	Sanitation, solid waste management & drains, Mechanical & electrical etc. (O)	5.6 per cent	664
	Water supply (O)	9.6 per cent	1,133
	Total	27 per cent	3,137
Total		100 per cent	11,822

Source: Authors' own.

Table 6.7 Energy Intensity of Municipal Expenditures in Spain

Energy consumption	*Sector*	*per cent of total expenditure*	*Budget (€ MM)*
1. Insignificant	General public services	33	16,432
	Social protection	8	4,068
	Total	42	20,500
2. Significant	Education	5	2,200
	Health	1	622
	Recreation, culture and religion	11	5,351
	Public order and safety	8	3,882
	Total	25	12,055
3. Intense	Housing and community amenities	10	4,693
	Economic affairs	14	6,998
	Environment protection	10	4,993
	Total	34	16,684
Total		100	49,239

Source: Authors' own.

available to determine whether these differ. Thus, what drives the differences between the two is the distribution of spending by function. Of course, with better data, such estimates can be refined.

In comparison to Spanish municipalities, we observe that the share of functions not using energy is more important in the Spanish case than the Indian. This is somewhat surprising given that a large share of Indian municipality spending is for payrolls. Actually the difference is the share of spending for services that use little energy. Spanish municipalities have programmes of social protection, which represent almost 10 per cent of their expenditure. In Indian municipalities, the amounts spent on such programmes is much smaller.

By contrast, a larger share of spending in Indian municipalities is on activities consuming significant amounts of energy. For example, a large number of public buildings require energy for heating and cooling and public transport, which appears in the category 'other expenditure'.[6] Since public transport and environment are important items in this category, we chose to categorize this spending as one with 'significant' energy content, that is, 20 per cent.

Municipal functions with greater intensity of energy consumption are more significant in Spain with large spends on public transport infrastructure, industry, communication and construction, and upkeep of social housing. Energy-intensive functions of Indian municipalities are essentially water supply, garbage collection, street lighting, and sewage, thus representing 27 per cent of the total expenditure incurred.

Despite differences in the basic structure of functions and expenditures, it turns out that in both sets of municipalities (Spanish and Indian), roughly one-third of the spending is energy-intensive and thus sensitive to energy prices.

Economic Model

We now present the model used to simulate the impacts of higher energy prices on municipal finances with a view to understanding the effects of policies that increase the price of traditional energy. For these simulations, we will establish three different scenarios. In the first one, we allow municipalities to increase their deficit in the face of higher energy costs. This implicitly assumes that higher deficits can be financed—which may or may not be true. However, this scenario gives some sense of the financing requirement. In the second and third scenarios, we assume no additional financing is possible, so the initial deficit is held constant, and municipalities take decisions on expenditure cuts.

To simplify, we will consider only two prices. First, it is the average unit price of energy P_E (whatever the source of energy) in municipal expenditures. The other price, P_{NE}, is the average unit price of all the municipal expenditures except energy goods.

With these prices are associated quantities: Q_E is the quantity spending on energy and Q_{NE} the quantity of spending that do not consume energy.

Notations:
P_E: Unit price of energy
P_{NE}: Unit price of municipal expenditures not linked to energy
Q_E: Quantity of spending on energy
Q_{NE}: Quantity of spending that do not consume energy

R: Municipalities revenue:
R_E: Revenues linked to energy prices
R_{NE}: Revenues not affected by energy prices

E: Municipalities expenditure:
E_E: Expenditures only linked to energy prices
E_{NE}: Expenditures not affected by energy prices
X: Municipalities deficit

Equations:
$E_i = P_i . Q_i$ (Equation of expenditure)
$R + X = E$ (Budgetary equation)

Scenario 1: Deficit Endogenous

Here we consider the deficit as an endogenous variable. Q_E is also a endogenous variable which depends on the fluctuation of the energy price with an elasticity ε. P_E', the new energy price, is the exogenous variable. All the rest is constant. The aim is to highlight the impact of fluctuation in energy price on municipal deficits. The full derivation of the following equations has been omitted, but can be obtained by contacting the authors.

The budgetary equation is: $P_E . Q_E + P_{NE} . Q_{NE} = R + X = E$

We shock the price of energy: $P_E . Q_E + \Delta(P_E . Q_E) + P_{NE} . Q_{NE} = R + X + \Delta(R + X) = E + \Delta E$

The new budgetary equation is: $P_E' . Q_E' + P_{NE} . Q_{NE} = E'$

With:

- $P_E' = P_E + \eta$
- $Q_E' = \left[\varepsilon . \left(\frac{P_E'}{P_E} - 1 \right) + 1 \right] . Q_E$
- $E' = R' + X'$

[6] Unfortunately, the expenditure accounts of Indian municipalities include a large item (other expenditures) greater than 30 per cent of total, which includes a large number of disparate items. Further, decomposition of those items would be needed to get a better sense of how energy-intensive spends are.

Then we have two different cases due to structural differences between Spanish and Indian municipalities' sources of income.

Indian Case:

The incomes of Indian municipalities are not sensitive to the price of energy. Thus energy prices only affect the cost base and spending: $R' + R$ and $X' = E' - R$,

We have, therefore, the new deficit:

$$X' = P_E'.\left[\varepsilon.\left(\frac{P_E'}{P_E}-1\right)+1\right].Q_E + P_{NE}.Q_{NE} - R$$

Spanish Case:

This is more complex because some of the municipal incomes came from shared tax, which is linked to the hydrocarbon price. Municipal incomes are, therefore, composed of a part which is not linked with energy price, and another which fluctuates with the price of energy (with an elasticity ε_R):

$$R = R_E + R_{NE};$$

with elasticity: $\varepsilon_R = \dfrac{\frac{\Delta R_E}{R_E}}{\frac{\Delta P_E}{P_E}}$

After several intermediate steps, the form of the new incomes is given by: $R' = R_{NE} + R_{NE}'$

with: $R' = R + \Delta R_E'$ and $R_E' = R_E\left(1+\varepsilon_R..\left(\frac{P_E'}{P_E}-1\right)\right)$

For the simulation, we will take: $\varepsilon_R = 1$. This merely assumes that any increase in energy prices and tax revenues will be passed through fully in the taxes shared with the municipalities. As municipal revenues increase, they must decide how to spread income between the two types of spending, that is, energy-sensitive and non-energy-sensitive. We assumed to share this increase in income between energy and non-energy expenditures according to their share in total spending after the price shock.

a is the percentage of new energy expenditure in total new expenditure:

$$a = \frac{P_E'.Q_E'}{E'}$$

and *b* is the percentage of non-energy expenditure in total new expenditure:

$$b = \frac{P_{NE}.Q_{NE}}{E'}$$

Finally :

$$E_E' = P_E'.Q_E' - a.\Delta R$$
$$E_{NE}' = P_{NE}'.Q_{NE} - b.\Delta R$$

and

$$X' = E_E' + E_{NE}' - R$$

Scenario 2: Non-energy Expenditures Endogenous

In this scenario, we consider the municipal deficit as a constant—a municipality cannot increase its deficit. With this consideration, the quantity Q_{NE} becomes an endogenous variable of the model. However, the elasticity of Q_{NE} face to P_E is considered to be zero. Q_E remains an endogenous variable and P_E an exogenous one. All the rest is constant.

Equations and development are the same than for the scenario 1, except that Q_{NE} has became the endogenous variable instead of *E*. Therefore, we obtain: $P_E'.Q_E' + P_{NE}.Q_{NE}' = E$

With:

- $P_E' = P_E + \eta$
- $Q_E' = \left[\varepsilon.\left(\frac{P_E'}{P_E}-1\right)+1\right].Q_E$
- $Q_{NE}' = \dfrac{E - P_E'.Q_E'}{P_{NE}}$

***Indian Case*:**

In this case, this is the final equation.

***Spanish Case*:**

Here we still have the incomes which are endogenous.

Then:

$$P_E'.Q_E'' = P_E'.Q_E' - a.\Delta R$$
$$P_{NE}.Q_{NE}' = P_{NE}'.Q_{NE} - b.\Delta R$$

With *a* and *b* as the percentages of non-energy expenditure in total expenditure if the total expenditure was endogenous variable,

we finally obtain: $Q_{NE}' = \dfrac{E - P_E'.\left(Q_E' - a\frac{\Delta R}{P_E'}\right)}{P_{NE}}$

Scenario 3: Non-energy Spending Endogenous, Redistribution of Expenditure Shares

This scenario is similar to scenario 2 because deficit is a constant and Q_{NE} an endogenous variable. Difference is that we consider that the cost of this fluctuation in energy price on quantity of goods and services supply by municipalities will be redistributed between quantities spending on energy and non-energy. In this case, the local government chooses to keep the part of each energy and non-energy expenditures in total expenditure after the shock of the energy price constant.

$$P_E'.Q_E' + P_{NE}.Q_{NE} = E'$$

With:

- $P_E' = P_E + \eta$
- $Q_E' = \left[\varepsilon.\left(\frac{P_E'}{P_E} - 1\right) + 1\right].Q_E$

α is the percentage of energy expenditure in new total expenditure, and β the one of non-energy expenditure :

$$\alpha = \frac{P_E'.Q_E'}{E'} \qquad \beta = \frac{P_{NE}.Q_{NE}}{E'}$$

The final equation is given as:

$$Q_{NE}' = \frac{E - P_E'.\left(Q_E' - \alpha\frac{\Delta E}{P_E'}\right)}{P_{NE}}$$

With:

- $P_E' = P_E + \eta$
- $Q_E' = \left[\varepsilon.\left(\frac{P_E'}{P_E} - 1\right) + 1\right].Q_E$

ΔE the variation of total expenditure if E would be an endogenous variable

Indian Case:
In the Indian case, this is the final equation.

Spanish Case:
Here we still have the incomes which are endogenous. So, we finally obtain on the same structure than the equation founded in scenario 2:

$$Q_{NE}' = \frac{E - P_E'.\left(Q_E' - \alpha\frac{\Delta E}{P_E'} - a\frac{\Delta R}{P_E'}\right)}{P_{NE}}$$

Simulations and Results

Using the preceding economic model, we simulated the three scenarios with different parameters to evaluate the impact of an increase of the energy prices on municipal finances. In this part, we will discuss and interpret the results including an analysis of the sensitivity of the results to different parameters used in the model.

Initial Conditions

First of all, we input the initial conditions for the two different types of municipalities of our model.

Initially, the unit prices of energy and non-energy goods are input to value 1. That clearly explains the equality between quantities and expenditures in these charts.

The types of municipalities in India and Spain are too different to compare the sums that appear in these charts. We can, however, compare the distribution of the finances. The shares of *Ee*[7] and *Ene*[8] in total expenditure are almost the same for India and Spain as we saw earlier. By contrast, the ratio of the deficit to total expenditure *X/E* is much higher in the Spanish case. As a consequence, the increase in the deficit in scenario 1 is much less than in the case of India.

The elasticity of the municipal energy consumption with respect to quantity of energy goods face to its prices an important parameter. In the literature, we found estimated elasticities around -0.4 and -0.2. (-0.2 short-term provided by INSEE[9] and the RAND[10]) for individuals.

We expect a municipality to have lower short-term price elasticity for energy spending, since reducing energy expenditures could involve reductions of critical public services such as street lighting and garbage collection. Soft options such as using public transport rather than a car are

[7] Expenditure on energy.

[8] Spends on goods not using energy.

[9] INSEE : Institue National de la Statistique et des Etudes Economiques. French national institute for statistic and economic studies. Danielle Besson, Insee (2008) : Consommation d'énergie: autant de dépenses en carburants qu'en énergie domestique. Insee Première N°1176, février 2008.

[10] The RAND Corporation is a non-profit research organization providing objective analysis and effective solutions that address the challenges facing the public and private sectors around the world. Toman et al. (2008).

TABLE 6.8 Initial Conditions for Economic Model of Maharashtra Municipalities

India	R (Incomes)	113,259	Part of energy consumption:	Insignificant : 0 per cent
(Rs Lakhs)	E (Expenditures)	118,221		Significant : 20 per cent
				Intense : 90 per cent
	X (Deficit)	4,962		
	Ee (Energy expenditure)	38,754	Qe (Quantity of energy consumed)	38,754
	Ene (Non-energy expenditure)	79,467	Qne (Quantity of non-energy goods consumed)	79,467

Source: Authors' own.

TABLE 6.9 Initial Conditions for Economic Model of Spanish Municipalities

Spain	R (Incomes)	42,873	Part of energy consumption :	Insignificant : 0 per cent
(€ MM)	E (Expenditures)	49,239		Significant : 20 per cent
				Intense : 90 per cent
	X (Deficit)	6,366		
	Ee (Energy expenditure)	17,427	Qe (Quantity of energy consumed)	17,427
	Ene (Non-energy expenditure)	31,812	Qne (Quantity of non-energy goods consumed)	31,812

Source: Authors' own.

not possible for these public services. But with time and technological progress, this elasticity will become higher in absolute terms. That is why we will separate short-term price elasticity from the long-term. Short-term price will be assigned an elasticity of -0.1 and long-term -0.4, which represent extreme values.

Simulations and Results—Scenario 1

In scenario 1, the deficit is endogenous. This means that municipalities are able to borrow to finance an increase in their deficit, which bears the brunt of the increase in the price of energy. Municipalities need not reduce spending on goods not using energy, and the reduction of their spending on energy is just influenced by their response to a higher price.

Results:

Short Term: Elasticity = -0.1

As would be expected, deficit expands substantially with the increase in the price of energy. The first observation is that for a 20 per cent increase in energy prices, deficits in India (Maharashtra) rose by 140 per cent and by 50 per cent in the Spanish case (see Figure 6.1). It is, therefore, easily understandable that a municipality cannot sustain such a rapid increase of deficit finance. An increase of five per cent leads to an increase of 50 per cent of the deficits in India. Expenditures are too sensitive to energy prices for municipalities to tackle an increase of even five per cent in energy prices without serious fiscal difficulties. The intuition behind this result is essentially that in municipalities with limited resources, functions, and financial capacity, their deficit is relatively small in relation to their energy-related spending. A significant increase in the price of energy could put them in financial distress.

The percentage impact on the deficit in Spain is much less significant for the same increase in the energy price, even though the percentage of spending sensitive to energy prices is relatively similar. This is because the baseline deficit in relation to total spending is much higher in Spanish municipalities, indicating significantly more access to deficit finance than in the Indian case. Hence, the increase of deficit is lower for a given energy price increase.

If we examine the quantity of energy consumed (see Figure 6.2), we first note that both groups reduce energy use substantially even though energy spending increases. Because of the relatively low elasticity with respect to price, the price increase outpaces the capacity to cut back on the quantity of energy consumed, at a rate of 10 to 1 for an elasticity of 0.1.

To summarize scenario 1, in the short-term, a small increase of energy price has the desired effect of reducing the quantity of energy consumed, although it is quite

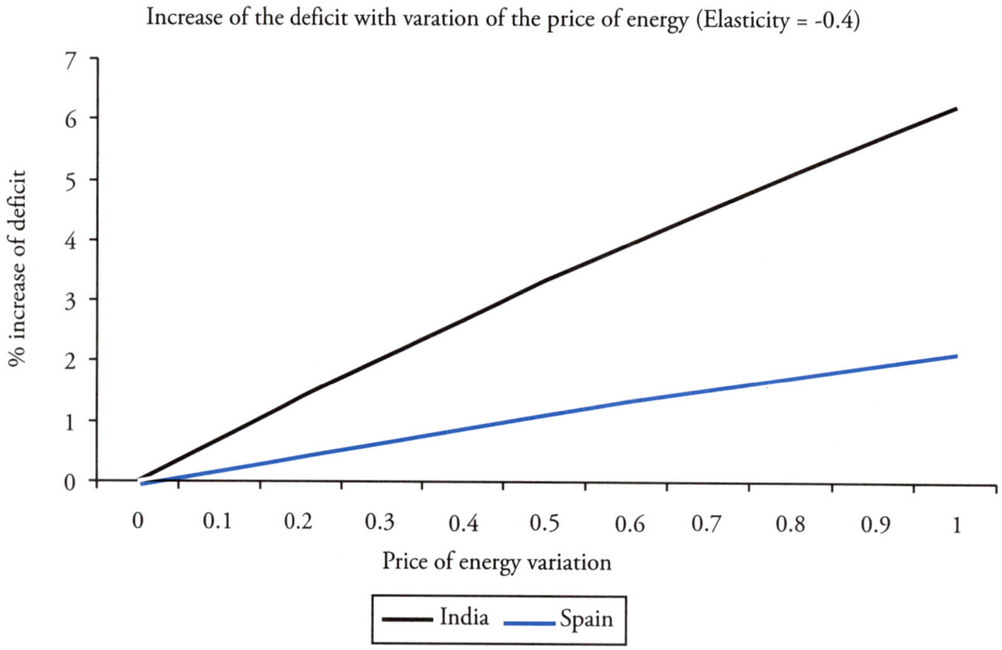

Figure 6.1 Short-Term Impact of Energy Price Variation on Municipal Deficit

Source: Authors' own.

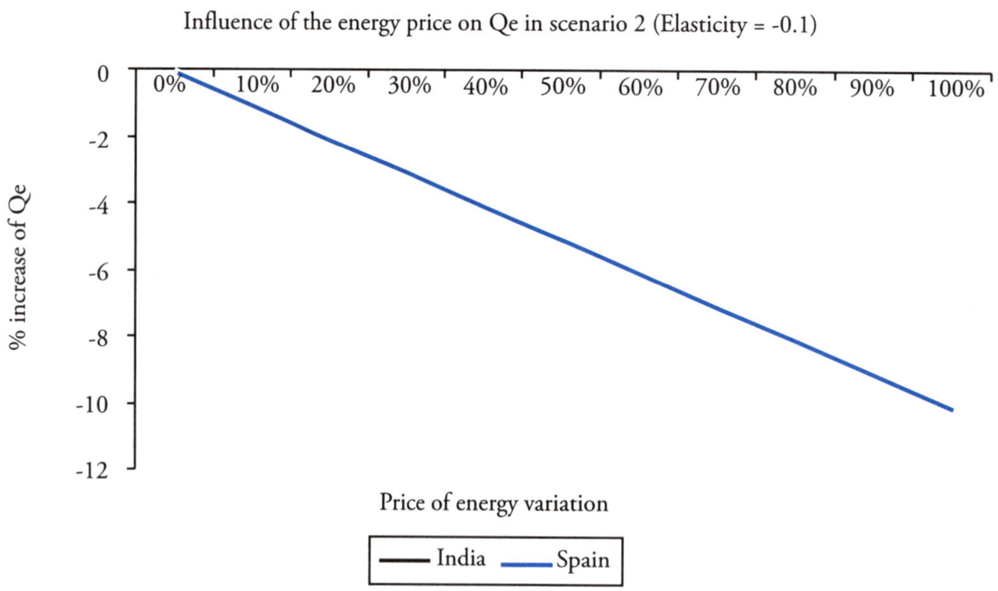

Figure 6.2 Short-Term Impact of Energy Price Variation on Quantity of Energy Expenditures

Source: Authors' own.

limited. This comes at the cost of an increase in the deficit for both sets of municipalities, which is a very dramatic one in the Indian model. The impact of the shared tax on energy is limited in Spain because it is very small in relation to the increase in spending. If the impact of this shared tax in Spain is only a one per cent reduction in the deficit, then energy prices increase by 70 per cent.

Long-Term: Elasticity = -0.4

Over the long-term, with technical progress and investments in new technologies, municipalities are better able to reduce consumption in the face of higher energy prices. We represent this long-term scenario by increasing the price elasticity to -0.4. The results are shown in Figure 6.3 below.

Before discussing the results, it is worth noting that there is nothing automatic about moving from the short- to the long-term scenario. As we saw above, municipalities will face chronic deficits as a result of energy price increases, and will thus have no fiscal space for investment in energy-efficient technologies. Their creditworthiness ratios will all be deteriorating as spending increases, yet they will need to borrow to finance current spending. Without some concessional finance or grants, it is hard to imagine moving to this long-term scenario.

In the long-term, with an elasticity of -0.4, we see that the impact of an increase of energy price on deficit is, as expected, much less than in the previous case. This time with a 20 per cent increase in energy prices, deficits in India rose by 80 per cent and by 30 per cent in the Spanish case (see Figure 6.4), as opposed to 140 per cent and 50 per cent in the previous case. The quantity of energy consumed declined much more than in the earlier case (see Figure 6.9). This scenario that contrasts impacts of energy price increases under long- and short-term elasticities illustrates that the long-term impact on municipalities' deficit could be much less serious, although still substantial. However, the increase in elasticity of energy consumption over the long-term assumes that there is capacity, financial and otherwise, in municipal governments to invest in energy-saving technologies. The observed low level of investment spending in the Indian municipalities suggests that this capacity does not exist today.

Simulations and Results—Scenario 2: Fixed Fiscal Deficit

Here we assume that municipalities are not able to expand borrowing to absorb the impacts of an energy price increase. The deficit remains fixed at its initial value and spending must be restructured to cope with higher energy costs. In this scenario, we assume that spending on energy-based goods responds as seen in scenario 1, is based on elasticity with respect to price. All other spending is reduced to meet the fixed deficit target.

Results:

Short-Term: Elasticity = -0.1

In this scenario, the impact of an increase of energy price on the quantity spending on energy is the same as before. We still have a decrease of one per cent of quantity for a 10 per cent increase of energy price. Now it is the quantity spending on activities that do not use energy (*Qne*) that must be reduced to meet the deficit target. As discussed above, this would cover items such as social welfare spending, salaries, including teachers in the case of Spain, and general administration. The intuition behind this formulation is that the energy spending is related to basic services that must be maintained. If fiscal restraint is needed, the salary bill, social safety nets, and administration costs are more likely candidates for spending cuts.

This set of assumptions results in fairly dramatic cuts in non-energy spending. *Qne* decreases by close to

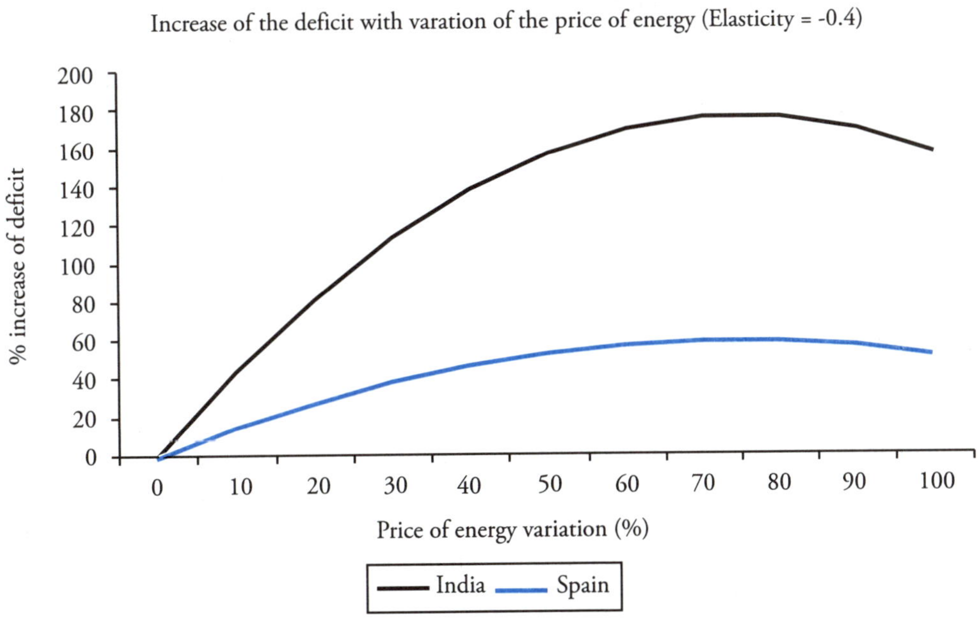

FIGURE 6.3 Long-Term Impact of Energy Price Variation on Municipal Deficit

Source: Authors' own.

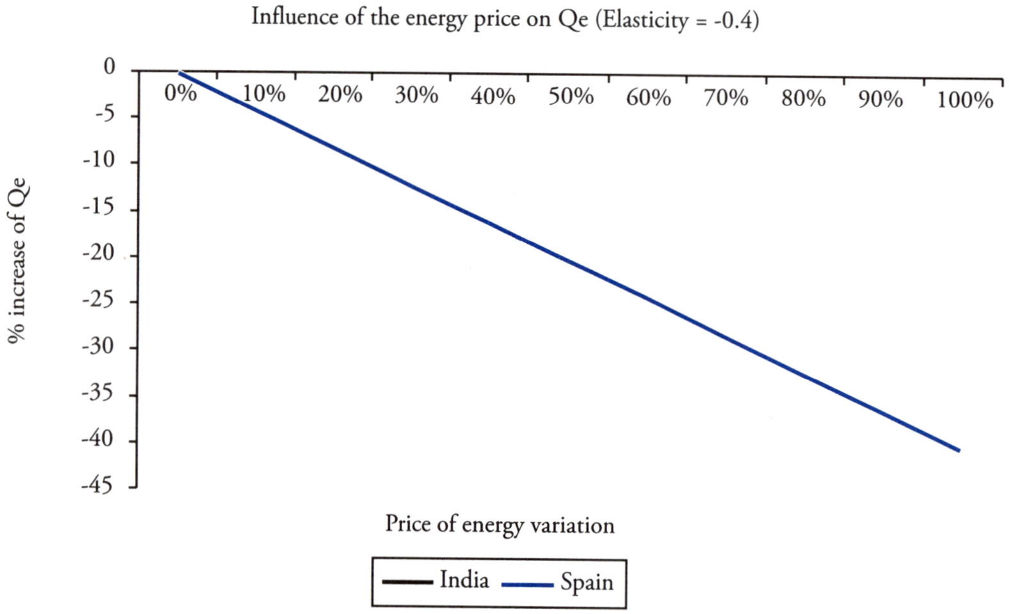

Figure 6.4 Long-Term Impact of Energy Price Variation on Quantity of Energy Expenditures

Source: Authors' own.

20 per cent when the energy price rises by 50 per cent. Such a 20 per cent across the board cut in non-energy spending seems hardly conceivable for any municipality, even those most committed to belt tightening.

Figures 6.5 and 6.6 show the quantities of goods and services provided by local governments in response to higher energy prices in a fixed-deficit scenario. The first line *Qe* plus *Qne* shows the total impact of the higher prices on ability to spend. The two others show how it is divided between energy and non-energy goods, if one seeks to protect energy-intensive public services and absorb the shock through cuts in discretionary spending. It seems highly unlikely, however, that such dramatic cuts would actually be sustained. Hence, it is more likely that spending in both areas would have to be cut in a scenario of strong fiscal restraint. This has been well examined below in scenario 3.

Simulations and Results—Scenario 3

This scenario is similar to scenario 2 in that the municipalities' deficit is constant. The difference is that in this scenario, the burden of an increase of energy price will be shared between the quantity spending on goods that are non-energy using (*Qne*) and quantity spending on energy (*Qe*). Now municipalities will choose to cut their spending on energy to protect some spends on energy non-intensive goods, for instance, payrolls and wages. How do they choose to share the burden? It is assumed that municipalities reduce pro rata all expenditure categories by the same percentage to reach the new level of spending. The result is that *Qe* will decrease more significantly than scenario 2, and *Qne* will reduce less than in the previous scenario.

Results:

Short-Term: Elasticity = -0.1

As in scenario 2, we follow the evolution of *Qne*. As expected, the reduction of *Qne* is less important than seen in scenario 2 (compare Figure 6.7 and Figure 6.8 with Figure 6.5 and Figure 6.6). For example, for a 50 per cent increase of energy price, *Qne* decreases by 12 per cent in scenario 3 whereas *Qne* decrease by 22 per cent in scenario 2. The results are similar for both India and Spain. The wedge between the two scenarios increases as the energy price increases. Nonetheless, even with this more even-handed sharing of the pain of higher price increases, the burden on public services, social safety nets, and required reductions in salary bills is dramatic and hardly likely to be sustainably benefitting.

Of course, *Qne* is preserved because *Qe* decreases more rapidly than in scenario 2. If we take a look at the evolution of the total quantity (*Qe* + *Qne*), it decreases more rapidly than in scenario 2 for both Spanish and Indian municipalities. Overall, this shows there is no escaping the costs of higher energy prices. While scenario 3 is a more balanced strategy, if deficits cannot be accommodated, public services tend to suffer considerably as energy becomes more expensive.

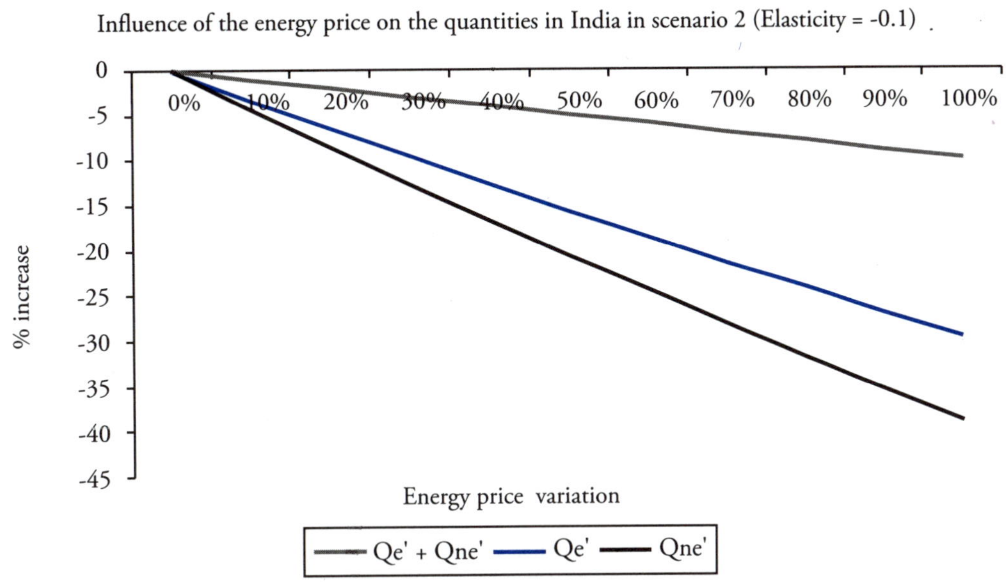

Figure 6.5 Short-Term Impact of Energy Price Variation on Municipal Expenditures in Maharashtra, India (Scenario 2)

Source: Authors' own.

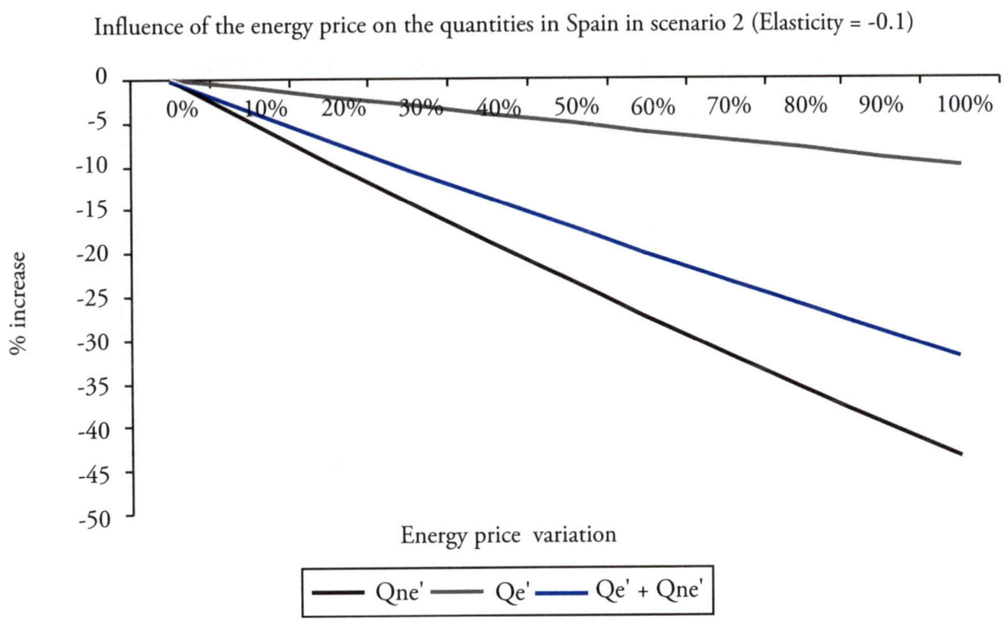

Figure 6.6 Short-Term Impact of Energy Price Variation on Municipal Expenditures in Spain (Scenario 2)

Source: Authors' own.

Sensitivity to the Elasticity Parameter

One of the most important parameters of the model is the elasticity of expenditure on energy with respect to the price of energy. To evaluate its influence on the model, we will see its impact on the deficit (scenario 1) for an increase of energy price by 50 per cent (see Figure 6.9). As we see, elasticity has a strong influence on the increase of deficit. That is why we examined different elasticity values (-0.1 short-term and -0.4 long-term) to evaluate the impact on deficit. The longer the period of adjustment, the higher one would expect the elasticity to be. This sensitivity thus illustrates that this problem is not necessarily permanent, but more of a transitional phase, albeit over a period of decades, provided assistance is offered to facilitate

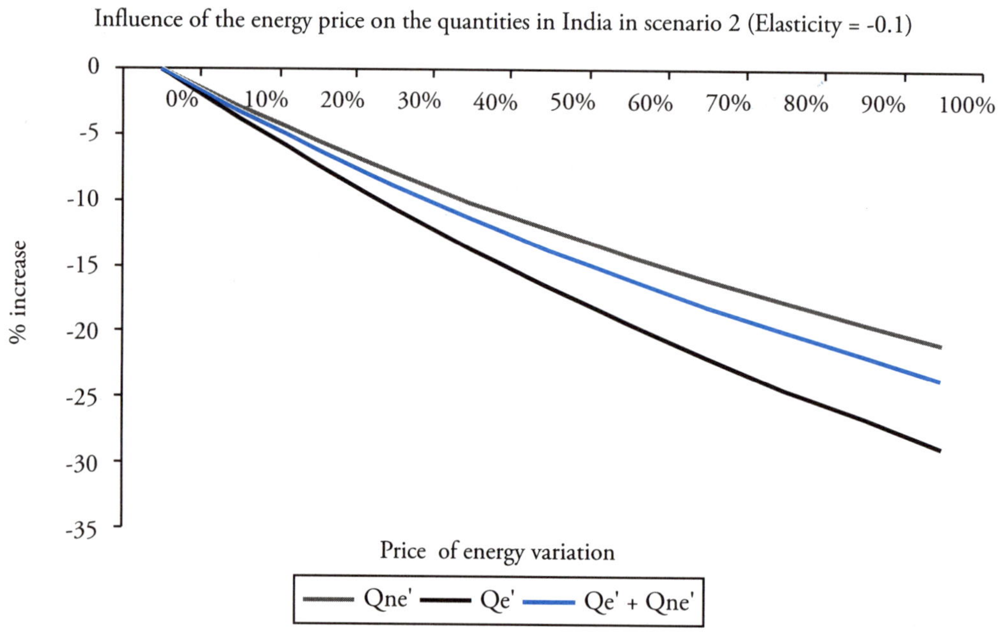

Figure 6.7 Short-Term Impact of Energy Price Variation on Municipal Expenditures in India (Scenario 3)

Source: Authors' own.

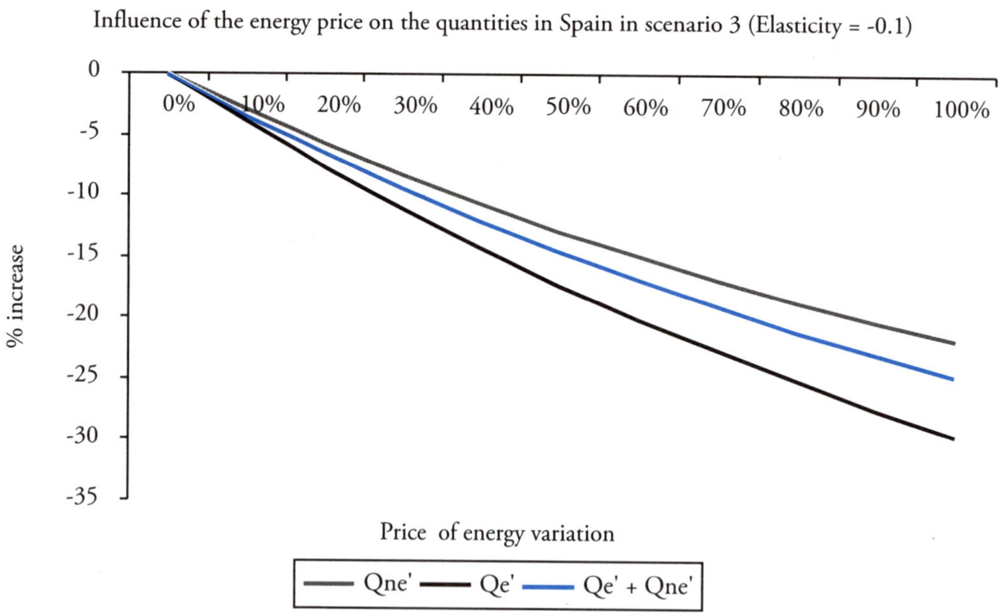

Figure 6.8 Short-Term Impact of Energy Price Variation on Municipal Expenditure in Spain (Scenario 3)

Source: Authors' own.

adoption of improved technologies, which will in turn allow reduced energy consumption with the same level of service. This graph indicates that, at very high elasticities, that is, in the very long term, responding effectively to higher energy prices can lower the overall energy bill for municipalities, and thus reduce a significant element in their cost base.

Local Government Management of Carbon Costs and Emission

This study sought to examine the fiscal impact on local governments of a climate change policy that raises energy prices. One of the most efficient policies for reducing GHG emissions is the imposition of higher energy prices

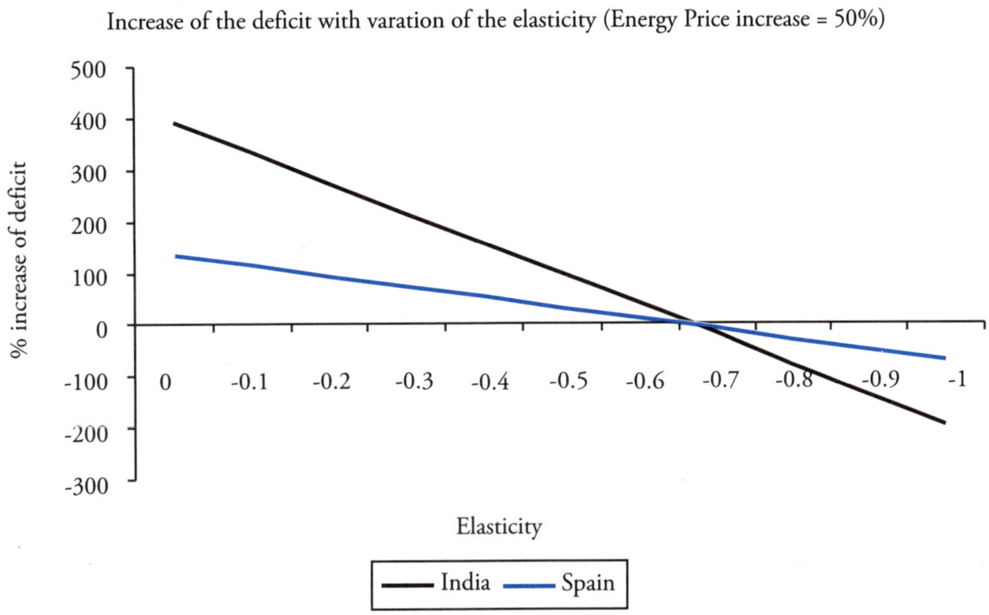

FIGURE 6.9 Sensitivity of Deficit to Elasticity of Expenditures

Source: Authors' own.

throughout the global economy to elicit reductions in GHG-intensive energy use. These price changes are necessary to provide incentives to invest in energy-saving technologies, to improve management practices, etc. If designed correctly, such green taxes can act as a fiscal boon to the government in general, because taxes (or their equivalent in auctioned permits) can bring substantial revenues to the government.

This study also looks beyond the unitary government to examine the consequences for different levels of government with different taxation powers and spending profiles. We used data on the spending and revenue profiles of two sets of local governments, that of Maharashtra, India, and Spain. In both cases, we found stylized facts that are quite representative of local governments worldwide. Local government revenues are not highly sensitive to the price of energy. Therefore, there will be no fiscal gain for local governments if energy prices increase, as they must.Even in the case of Spain, energy spending is much more substantial than their small share in the national energy taxes.

On the other hand, many public services that local governments provide are energy-intensive. The ability to substitute away from energy in providing these services is quite limited in the short-term, even more limited than for individual consumers. For example, garbage cannot be hauled in public transport, but must instead rely upon conventional trucks until alternate technologies are available. The demand for these basic services is not likely to go down in response to the higher energy costs needed to deliver them, because these services are not priced directly, and because political resistance to rapid tax or tariff hikes would be substantial. Oftentimes, municipalities have little information on their own energy consumption, given that charges for energy are typically intergovernmental dues and not always handled very transparently. For these reasons, municipalities will have difficulty in reducing their energy bills in the short-term.

As a result, raising energy prices will create quite an adverse fiscal shock for local governments. Our analysis illustrates just how adverse this shock could be, and how the structure of spending affects the magnitude of the fiscal shock. Smaller, less diversified governments currently operating at a low level of service provisioning and with a very small operating deficit will be harder hit, precisely because the most basic services tend to be energy-intensive, and their energy bill is high in relation to their current deficit financing envelope. However, all municipalities would be faced with serious consequences. Whether the shock is absorbed in deficit spending or in fiscal restraint, there will be a substantial shock. The pain results from the difficulty of reducing energy spending quickly in the short-term.

The policy implications are clear, and they consist in reconsidering fiscal federalism in light of the climate change challenge. The level of government taxing energy will be running large surpluses corresponding to these dramatic fiscal crises provoked at the local level in the scenarios we have examined. Compensation for local governments hard hit by high energy bills makes sense both to protect the financial integrity of local governments and ensure reasonable service delivery. It makes a great deal more sense to compensate these local governments plunged into a crisis that is not of their own making, using the extra funds generated at higher levels of government from energy taxation.

This also makes more sense than the alternatives. Asking municipalities to cover these energy-induced deficits by hiking their own taxes or charges would just involve burdening consumers already hit by higher energy prices for their own consumption, and this could quite likely lead to a tax-payer rebellion. Asking them to reduce critical public services like solid waste management to meet a local budget constraint when surpluses are swelling at higher levels is counter-productive. It would also lead to an unintended increase in government saving that throws the overall government fiscal stance out of balance. This notion of compensation of local governments is similar to that which has occasionally been proposed for private consumers hit by carbon taxes (or the impacts of a cap-and-trade system). There it has been argued that the carbon tax proceeds could be redistributed to the general public through a reduction in something such as the payroll tax. The key is to find a reasonable compensation system that is not tied directly to energy spending, which would blunt incentives to conserve. Something like a poll credit (as opposed to a poll tax) might have the desirable properties.

Insights for Managing Energy Consumption at the Municipal Level

Generating more and Better Information on Energy Consumption

One key insight from this study is that information on energy consumption at the municipal level is very scarce indeed—too scarce for effective management of energy consumption. Far too many municipalities receive their electricity bills late and with too little detail because these are essentially intergovernmental dues. Costs for providing essential services such as street lighting and solid waste management are not ring-fenced. Accordingly, it is hard to know how much of the energy bill is dedicated to different services in a municipality. This makes it difficult to understand where to look for efficiency improvements and to measure progress when steps are taken to make energy use more efficient.

Introducing pricing of various services that reflect the costs of supply, including increased energy prices

A stylized feature of local government services around the world is the difficulty in charging directly for services provided, many of which are public or semi-public in nature. It is impossible to charge for park maintenance and street lighting through user charges. General benefit taxes such as the property tax are used for this purpose, and these are very ill-suited to reflect the impact of energy costs of supplying many services. Indian municipalities tend to rely less than most local governments on general cesses for key services, tacked on to property taxes that are highly politicized and where valuation is less frequent than it needs to be. Continuing this practice will blunt the capacity of local governments to pass through energy costs to service users, and accordingly, manage their derived demand for energy from providing key services. Ideally, a separate user charge for these services, based on costs, should be introduced. However, that may not be possible in the immediate term. A simple, if somewhat blunt tool for achieving this goal is to piggy-back charges for energy-intensive services such as water and solid waste management to electricity bills rather than property taxes. If charged as a percentage of the electricity bill (rather than a fixed rupee amount), these fees will tend to rise with higher energy costs, provided of course that power companies also raise their rates. It may also be legally and administratively possible to introduce energy surcharges on property taxes. It would be useful to explore these options. If legal hurdles can be surmounted, an essential element in introducing energy surcharges or in passing through energy costs in direct user charges for water and solid waste is credible information documenting the impact of higher energy costs on service delivery (see point 1 above).

Obtaining alternate sources of finance to manage the overall tax payer's burden when higher energy costs are passed through to the consumer

The goal of increasing energy prices in the economy is to shift consumption away from carbon-based energy sources—not to raise government revenues. In the short-term, since the elasticity of energy demands are low, government revenues are likely to increase with higher energy taxation. Without compensation, the overall burden on tax-payers will increase, creating a difficult environment for local governments seeking to pass through higher energy costs for providing basic services. National governments should consider compensation that alleviates the tax-payer's burden in two forms: (i) reduction of other federal taxes that have no link to energy consumption and (ii) sharing the revenue windfall with lower levels of government who must pass energy costs through to consumers. These measures would create an environment more conducive to taking necessary pricing measures in local government services.

Providing investment funding sources tied to energy improvement

The simulations in this study show that the impacts of higher energy costs could be quite dramatic, particularly for those local governments whose activities are concentrated in very basic service delivery, usually those least able to weather such a storm. Such governments will face increasing revenue deficits, and will find their capacity to borrow to invest in energy-saving technologies eroded, just when they need it most. Rather than cracking down on the apparent fiscal indiscipline of these local governments, higher level governments should consider providing dedicated funds, with appropriate conditions, that will assist local governments in making the necessary transition. Such funds need not offer a pure subsidy. Provided other measures are taken to lighten the fiscal burden of higher energy prices, this will not necessarily be needed. However, it is likely that some assistance directed to investments in reducing the carbon footprint of basic municipal services will help overcome some of the rigidities and difficulties typically encountered in shifting to new technologies and systems.

References

Ahmad, Ehtisham and Nicholas Stern (2009). 'Effective Carbon Taxes and Public Policy Options', London School of Economics, Asia Research Centre Working Paper 28, London, February.

Besley, Timothy J. and S. Harvey Rosen (1998). 'Vertical Externalities in Tax Setting: Evidence from Gasoline and Cigarettes', *Journal of Public Economics,* 70 , pp. 383–98.

Besson Danielle, Insee (2008). 'Consommation d'énergie : autant de dépenses en carburants qu'en énergie domestique', Insee Première No. 1176, février.

Bovenberg, Lans and H. Lawrence Goulder (1996). 'Optimal Environmental Taxation in the Presence of Other Taxes: General- Equilibrium Analyses', *The American Economic Review,* 86(4), pp. 985–1000, Pittsburgh, American Economic Association, September.

Bovenberg, Lans, and A. de Mooij Ruud (1997). 'Environmental Tax Reform and Endogenous Growth', *Journal of Public Economics*, 63(2), pp. 207–37, January.

Chelliah, R.J., P.P. Appasamy, R. Pandey, and R.J. Sankar (2007). 'Eco-taxes on Polluting Inputs and Outputs', Academic Foundation, New Delhi.

DEXIA (2008). Collective work under the direction of Dominique Hoorens. Sub-national government in the European Union, La defense (France), DEXIA Editions, July.

Fredriksson, G. Per and A. Khawaja Mamun (2008). 'Vertical Externalities in Cigarette Taxation: Do Tax Revenues Go up in Smoke?', *Journal of Urban Economics*, 64, pp. 35–48.

Goodstein, Eban (2003). 'The Death of the Pigovian Tax? Policy Implications from the Double-Dividend Debate', *Land Economics*, 79(3), Place, University of Wisconsin Press, pp. 402–14, August.

Government of Maharashtra (2002). *12th State Finance Commission*, Maharashtra.

Howarth, Richard B. (2005). 'The Present Value Criterion and Environmental Taxation: The Suboptimality of First-Best Decision Rules', *Land Economics*, 81(3), University of Wisconsin Press, Madison, Wisconsin, USA, pp. 321–36.

Kundu, Debolina (2002). 'Provision of Infrastructure and Basic Amenities: Analysing Institutional Vulnerability', in Amitabh Kundu and Mahadevia Darshini (eds), *Poverty and Vulnerability in a Globalizing Metropolis*, Manak Publications, Ahmedabad, pp. 132–70.

Mohanty, P.K., B.M. Misra, Rajan Goyal, and P.D. Jerome (2007). 'Municipal Finance in India: An Assessment', Development Research Group Study No. 26. Reserve Bank of India, Department of Economic Analysis and Policy, Mumbai.

Planning Commission, Government of India, (2005). *Draft Report of the Expert Committee on Integrated Energy Policy*, Government of India, New Delhi. Text available at http://planningcommission.nic.in/reports/genrep/intengpol.pdf (August 2010).

Shah, Anwar (2006). *A Practitioner's Guide to Intergovernmental Fiscal Transfers*, World Bank Institute Washington DC: World Bank.

The Maharashtra Human Development Report (2002), prepared by the State with the help of the Minister for Finance and Planning. Report available (in April 2009) at planning commission.nic.in/popup/shdr/maharashtrahdr.pdf

Toman Michael, James Griffin, and Robert J. Lempert (2008). 'Impacts on U.S. Energy Expenditures and Greenhouse-Gas Emissions of Increasing Renewable-Energy Use', Santa Monica, RAND Corporation, USA.

7 Towards India Evergreen

The Role of Micro-Finance Institutions

Ashok Singha, Papia Chakraborty, Suvra Majumdar, and Vijay Mahajan*

Introduction

India is a land of contradictions where plenty and poverty, wisdom and ignorance, and voice and deprivation exist side by side. Much the same way, at one end of the spectrum, demand for energy by industries and services touches unprecedented levels as India marches on the inexorable growth path, while on the other end 76 million homes in India have no access to electricity. This chapter deals with this fundamental dilemma—how to enable millions of poor people to enhance their livelihoods and quality of life, and yet do it in a manner that is not GHG emission-intensive; in essence enabling equitable development along a low carbon path.

This chapter outlines the obstacles in promoting and financing any over-arching strategy to support new practices in agriculture, improve the efficiency of local power generation capabilities using renewable sources, and reduce the energy intensity of small enterprises. Financing options for adopting mitigation measures—from government outlay to long-term loans to microfinance—are discussed and reasons for market failure explored. The chapter strategically highlights why the CDM is not very effective for promoting grassroot measures towards a low carbon path. A proposal for two new instruments to be administered by micro-finance institutions, aggregated micro-certified emission reductions (AMCERs) and aggregated voluntary emission reduction transactions (AVERTs), for harvesting carbon credits to improve the viability of micro-level initiatives is being discussed here. The argument here holds that the concerted application of all these steps will firmly put India on the low carbon path, creating a prospect of 'India Evergreen'.

The Low Carbon Pathway: India Evergreen

India's quest for growth is a rational choice and is seen as the ticket to freeing the people from hunger, livelihood insecurity, breaking intergenerational transmission of poverty, and ensuring universal access to basic education and health care. Growth translates to increases in energy demand, which is presently being met by oil, coal, and gas, all of which are finite in terms of supply. Despite knowing that these resources are depleting fast and in a 'not so distant' future, they will run out, the human tendency is to live in a state of denial, rather than exercising caution and restraint in the use of these resources. Acts of wanton energy wastage are ubiquitous, seen not just in industry and the government, in choice of policy, technology, and transport, but also in daily choices and practices within homes.

* The authors are associated with CTRAN, a BASIX group company engaged in Energy, Environment, Climate Change, and CDM.

Meaningful action can only be catalyzed through attitudinal transformation at the individual level, community level, and policy and institutional transformation at the macro-level with heightened awareness about the potential dangers of climate change.

Such a transformational outcome cannot be brought about without direct involvement of stakeholders at the grassroot level, changes in the institutional framework for financing, and creating appropriate incentives for adoption of cleaner and greener technologies and practices. Any such strategy would have to target reductions in energy intensity through:

- Improvements in agricultural and non-agricultural practices in rural areas.
- Development of local power generation capacities based on renewable resources to service unserved areas and reduce pressure on the grid.
- Improvements in practices in urban manufacturing, construction, and services.

Reducing Energy Intensity in Agriculture

Agriculture accounts for little less than one-fifth of the total GHG emission of India. Appropriate agricultural practices and sustainable use of water are both critical to India, which is predominantly an agrarian economy in terms of percentage of the population dependent on the sector for livelihoods.

The mitigation options in the agricultural sector have been discussed further in this chapter.

Small-Capacity Power Generation Locally Using Renewable Resources

The development needs of the rural areas are inherently linked with energy security. A low carbon framework would require lesser dependency on fossil fuel. The potential power that small capacity hydroelectric units (25 MW capacity) set up in remote hilly regions of India can generate is estimated to be about 15 GW. Unfortunately, only ten per cent of this capacity has been installed. An attractive alternative to this lies in biomass power generation, which can serve as excellent technology for electrifying rural areas. Aggregate biomass[1] combustion-based co-generation of power possible in process industries such as sugar, rice, and paper mills is very high, as discussed in Table 7.1.

Although distributed generation and small renewable products have also seen corporate investments, as is evident in the case of Lanco Infrastructure, Suzlon Green, Enercon, and ITC, this has been so far a part of their corporate social responsibility measures rather than a business strategy. Most of the investments are in the small wind firms.[2]

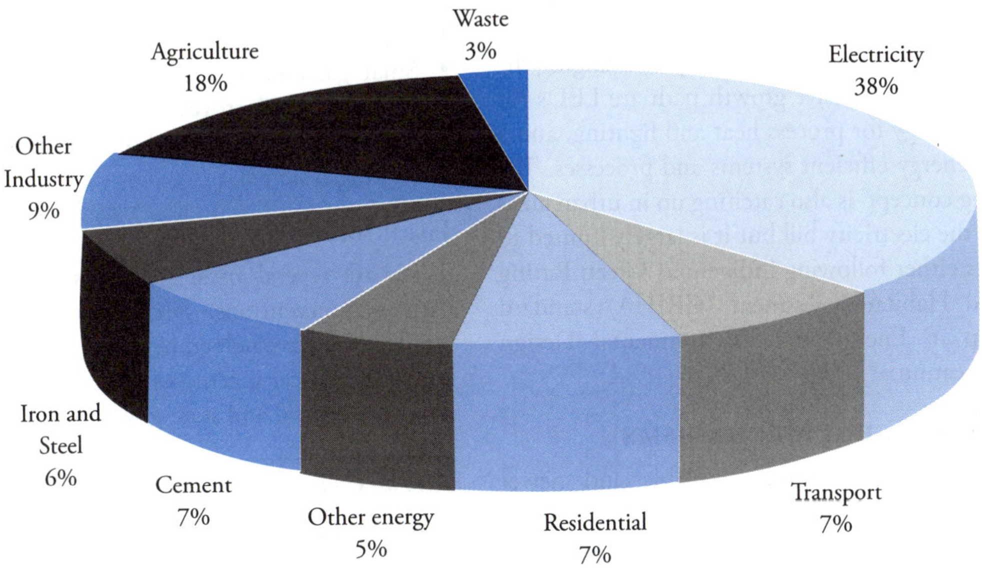

Figure 7.1 Emission Profile of India 2007

Source: http://www. moef.nic.in/downloads/public-information/Report_INCCA.pdf.

[1] Fuel wood, crop residues, and animal dung.
[2] Mukhopadhaya and Chakraborty (2005).

TABLE 7.1 Biomass-based Generation in India

Biomass-based generation	*Potential in MW*	*Achievement as on July 2009 in MW*
Bio-power (agro residues and plantations)	16881	773.3
Bagasse co-generation	5000	1155
Biomass/co-generation (non-bagasse)		175.78
Biomass gasifier		107.02
Total biomass-based generation	21881	2211.1

Source: MNRE (2009).

Reducing Energy Intensity in Manufacturing, Construction, and Services

The manufacturing sector is the largest consumer of commercial energy compared to the other industrial sectors in India (GoI 2007). In producing about a fifth of the country's gross domestic product (GDP), this sector consumes about half the commercial energy consumed for industrial use. Energy use intensity in some designated industries such as textile, paper, and steel is higher (though comparable to energy efficiency parameters world-wide), because of the manufacturing processes involved despite the companies having invested in latest equipment and processes (Mukhopadhyaya and Chakraborty (2005). Therefore, further reduction of energy intensity in large industries is not only cumbersome and industry associations feel that it could make them non-competitive. The energy intensity is higher in micro, small, and medium industries and it has got the maximum potential to become energy efficient.

Some of the technologies that can help in changing the conventional energy-intensive growth path are LEDs for lighting, solar energy for process heat and lighting, and a wide array of energy-efficient systems and processes. The 'green building concept' is also catching up in urban areas due to rise in the electricity bill but it is largely limited to big developers either following indigenous Green Rating for Integrated Habitat Assessment (GRIHA) standard or Leadership in Energy and Environmental Design (LEED) certification.

Existing Financing Mechanisms

Several technologies are already available and newer ones are emerging from heightened consciousness for low carbon economic development. However, there are several concerns due to which actual investments in the several available and new clean technologies have not reached their potential. Financing for such projects can be primarily through (i) equity and debt financing by the financial institutions and market, (ii) fiscal incentives and subsidies, and (iii) carbon finance.

Investment in Green Projects

Conventional investments in green projects include investments in projects such as wind and hydro power. In the last five years, banks have also financed co-generation projects in sugarcane, rice mills, flour mills, solvent extraction units, etc. Many of these projects receive easy finances from banks, if backed by large industrial groups (as stated earlier) such as Lanco infrastructure, Suzlon Green, Sree Renuka Sugar, ITC, etc.

Although investment options exist for several other projects that are attractive, they do not get attention because of their scale and being perceived by the bankers as too risky. Few such projects are:

- Projects with improved jute retting processes.
- Farmers seeking loan for paddy production using the SRI process.
- Fuel switch projects from coal to biomass.
- Vermicomposting and organic farming.
- Agro-forestry projects.
- Pico-hydel projects.
- Small gassifiers/biogas.
- Improved cook stoves.
- Solar installations (solar home lighting systems or water heating systems).

Fiscal Incentives

There are several fiscal mechanisms to incentivize low carbon interventions. For example, the incentives for wind power have helped in steady growth of this sector in India. The fiscal incentives available for the wind power from the central and state governments are:

From the Central Government	*From the State Government*
Income tax holiday	Energy buy-back
Accelerated depreciation	Power wheeling and banking facilities
Concessional custom duty/ Duty-free import of machinery	Sales tax concession benefits
Capital/interest subsidy	Electricity duty exemption
100% FDI under automatic approval route	Capital subsidy

Similarly, government support, both fiscal and financial, is extended for promoting solar energy:

- *Issue of Concessional Customs Duty Certificate* (CCDC) on items imported for solar thermal and photovoltaic power generation projects.
- *Exemption from excise duty.*
- *Generation-based incentive*[3] (GBI) scheme announced by the Ministry of New and Renewable Energy (MNRE), GoI, for the developers to support a total capacity of 50 MWp from 2007 to 2012.
- *Rebate on Electricity Tariff*: Rajasthan (15 paise/unit), Karnataka (50 paise/unit), West Bengal (40 paise to a maximum of Rs 80), Assam (Rs 40), Haryana (Rs 100/100 lpd up to 300 lpd), and Uttaranchal (Rs 75 per sq. m.). Other state regulators are also considering such proposals which were deliberated in the Forum of Regulators.
- *Subsidy Programme,* both capital subsidy and interest subsidy (refer to the section on 'Energy' in this volume).
- *Rebate on Property Tax:* Thane, Amravati, Nagpur, and Durgapur Urban Local Bodies are providing 6 to 10 per cent rebates on the property tax for the usage of solar energy— both PV and solar water heaters.

The MNRE is also promoting biomass gasifier-based power plants for producing electricity, using locally available biomass resources in rural areas where surplus biomass such as small wood chips, rice husk, *arhar* (lentil) stalks, cotton stalks, and other agro-residues are available to meet the unmet demand of electricity for lighting, water pumping, and micro-enterprises, including telecom towers, etc. For these systems, the central financial assistance ranges from Rs 10,000–15,000 per kw. In general, these fiscal incentives have been effective for promoting relatively large investments by the corporate sector but have not been able to promote the appropriate investments and practices at the grassroots level in rural areas.

Carbon Funds

There are several funds available internationally which hold relevance to rural India, such as the Bio-Carbon Fund, Community Development Carbon Fund, German Climate Protection Fund, etc. However, the most attractive options in India so far has been the CDM with a global market size of USD 126,345 million, of which India holds a four per cent share (World Bank 2009). India has 1406 CDM projects in the pipeline as of May 2010, based on UNEP data.

The CDM, proposed in the Kyoto Protocol offers developing countries access to both finance and technology for mitigation measures by allowing Annex-I countries (developed countries who are signatories to the Kyoto Protocol) to offset their emissions through investment in emissions reduction in non-Annex-I countries. Simply put, a project activity in a developing country that reduces green house gases, expressed in the multiple of tonnes of CO_2 equivalent reduction termed as Certified Emission Reduction (CER) unit, is used as an offset in a developed country against the mandated reduction. CDM is considered a fair compensation for equity in carbon space. The reasons why developing countries or poorer countries fail to invest in clean technologies are embedded in growth aspirations, energy efficiencies, political imperatives, and high technology costs. CDM provides one way of reducing (see Figure 7.2) that cost. The typical CDM project cycle is given below:

All the CDM projects are not born equal and carry different kinds of risk. This risk determines the appetite of the carbon funds to invest in such projects. Figure 7.2 demonstrates that point. Traditionally, carbon funds have preferred large projects offering them a large quantity of CER from a single project, and as far as possible, from a single industrial facility with strong process control ensuring easy monitoring and verification by independent verifiers (termed as Designated Operational Entities).

All these analyses show a clear disconnect: the needier segment is largely out of the purview of the green financing and policy in India, which is largely in favour of potential developers of wind, solar, and large hydroelectric projects. The bankers, financial institutions (FIs), and carbon funds are hesitant to lend to smaller units with a higher risk profile. As evident in Figure 7.3, most micro-finance institutions (MFIs) and rural financing institutions aiming to make a difference in green financing stay in the first quadrant.

Therefore, it is important to understand this market failure before we come up with a strategy to make the process more inclusive and 'India Evergreen'.

Challenges and Market Failures

Markets have traditionally favoured the big *vis-à-vis* the small. At the macro-level, major emitters such as the

[3] The high cost of solar PV equipment results in a higher cost of generation, which restricts the growth of power generation. The GBI scheme guarantees an overall tariff of Rs 15 per kWh for solar PV, which consists of GBI and the preferential tariff offered by the state utility. So, GBI is equivalent to (Rs 15—rate fixed by the State Electricity Regulatory Commission) per unit of solar energy.

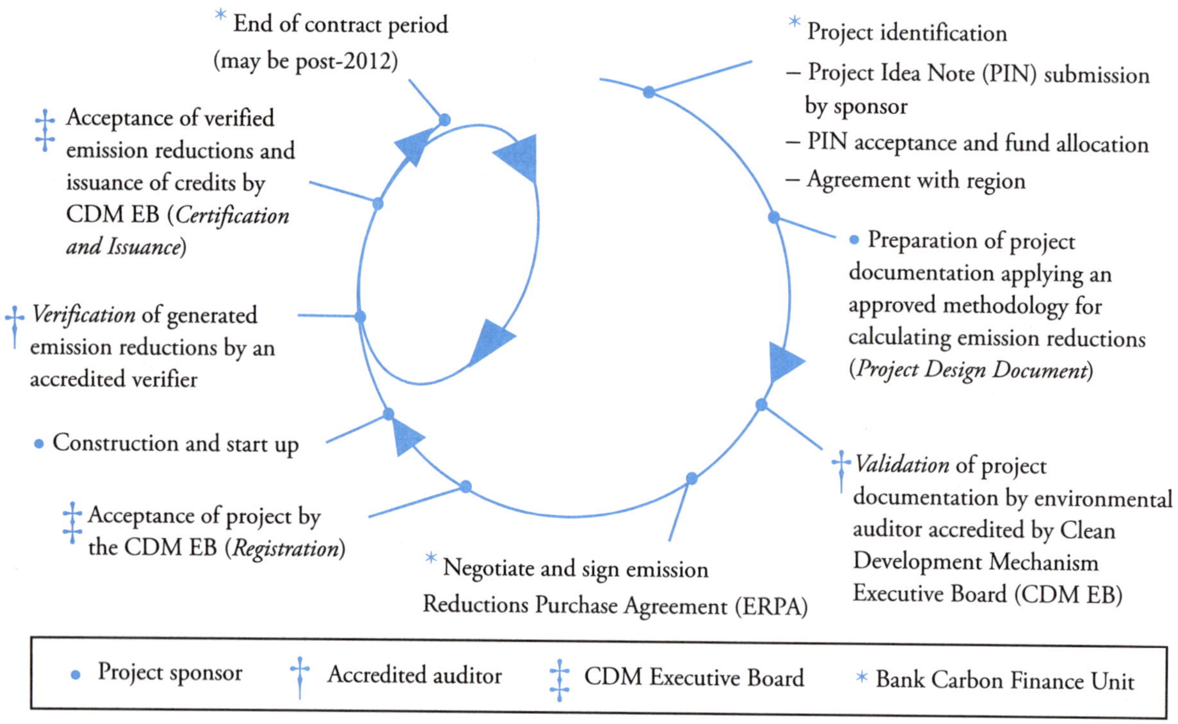

FIGURE 7.2 Clean Development Mechanism Project Cycle

Source: UNFCCC.

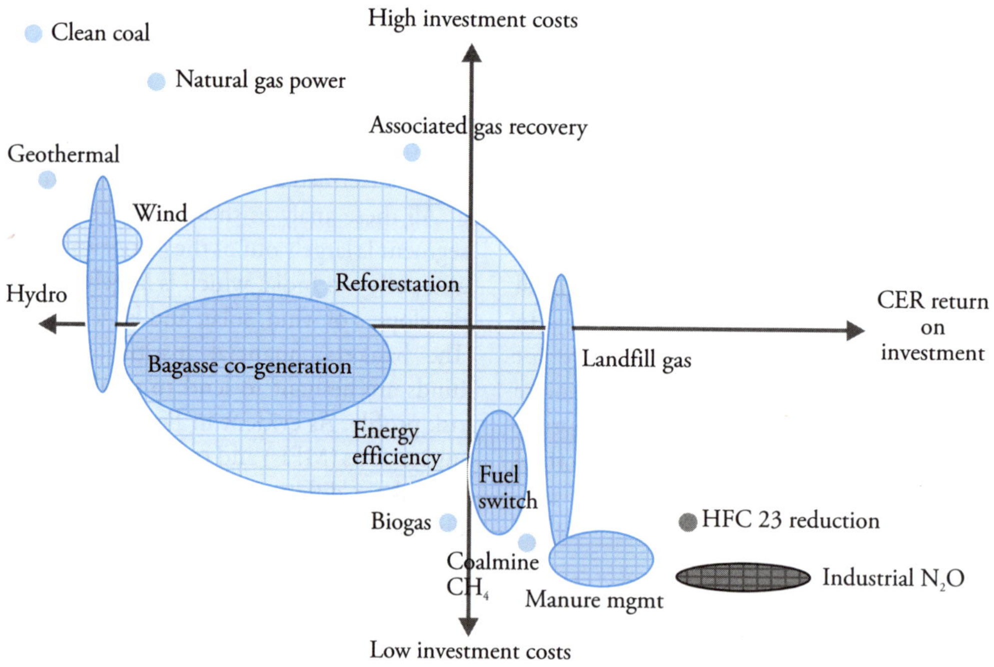

FIGURE 7.3 Investment Pattern in CDM Projects

Source: UNDP (2008).

US are free of any binding targets to reduce emission. UNFCCC, as an institution, has not been able to help in the smooth flow of funds and technology to needy nations. At the micro-level, all major financial institutions are comfortable when backed by guarantee by large corporate groups for clean projects. It becomes difficult to convince bankers to fund clean technologies in rice mill clusters, textile clusters, or household bio-digester financing.

The reasons are not difficult to fathom. Big and small institutions behave differently both with and without incentives. Externalities involved in green financing for small players include the range of capacity building for compliance to green norms, CDM standards, ability of the firms to work together, and the cost of organizing them to achieve the scale for financing. These are reflected in transaction costs and elements of risk and are the major considerations deterring such financing for smaller CDM projects.

Credit Policy

Considering that India now has a NAPCC that gives an over-arching framework, it is important to link it to credit policy of the country. Countries such as China and many European Nations have already established that link. Our financial sector has been late in responding to this trend, but it is likely to emerge as an important driver across all sectors of the economy. A clear example is the Equator Principles, a voluntary set of principles for environmental and social risk management in project finance, adopted by an increasing number of leading banks operating in developing countries. One of the reasons why there has been low credit off-take from formal banking for water conservation, manure management, and household bio-digester projects is because there is no over-arching guidance from the top management or awareness at the branch level.

Carbon Market Failures

The first failure is at the macro-level. With no legally binding agreement to reduce emissions, the Business As Usual (BAU) scenario with the continuation of current energy consumption patterns can only precipitate disaster. The Copenhagen Conference of Parties (CoP) attempted unsuccessfully to develop a global consensus for limiting emissions. The negotiations, which will be carried forward in Mexico, should ideally translate to a set of regulatory policies and instruments that ensures that the cost of emission is higher than the cost of mitigation. Only then can it be ensured that market response is aligned with the outcomes envisaged in the Kyoto Protocol.

The second market failure stems from the structure of global carbon markets, which impose a high transaction cost on the process of applying for mitigation and adaptation financing. Once a country applies for financing of a project under CDM, the Executive Board (EB) of UNFCCC usually takes an extremely conservative stance in approving methodologies. Designated Operational Entities (DOEs) take their time over validating them in different ways. Pressure groups from the industry as well as non-governmental organizations (NGOs) with opposing views introduce differing degrees of doubt about any methodology, making project formulation and verification even more expensive. The buyers in the Annex-I countries tend not to buy smaller lot emission reduction units and forestry credits.

To top it all, the UNFCCC-EB stipulates that, for a project to be eligible for financing under CDM, it must be a voluntary activity and not one undertaken under regulatory duress. Schneider (2007) and Hepburn (2007) suggests that due to this, CDM can in fact create a perverse incentive for governments in developing countries to avoid enacting or implementing policies that result in emission reducing activities. Doing so might reduce opportunities to garner CER[4] revenues. For example, the conversion of buses to compressed natural gas (CNG) in Delhi did not qualify under CDM as it was done under Court direction. A remedy has come in form of the proposed policy-based or programme-based CDM. However, Schneider points out that a policy-based CDM approach raises concerns regarding the assessment of additionality, as there are several motivations for the adoption of policies, and GHG mitigation may only be one of them. He further suggests that policies and measures could be credited indirectly through sectoral approaches. This has been discussed later in the chapter.

To sum up, following are the key barriers to a faster transition towards a low carbon economy:

- Lack of constructive dialogue among major emitters and a huge trust gap.
- Few DOEs to assure the quality of the projects under CDM.
- Hard position of developed countries to transfer technology and finance to developing countries and subtle attempts to link it to trade and competitiveness.
- Lack of co-ordinated action at the national and state level to ensure that the economy moves to a low carbon path.
- Lack of fundamental changes in consumer behaviour, supply chain structure and management, and business models of enterprises.
- Lack of capable institutions to take on climate resilient action at the grassroots level.

[4] Certified Emission Reduction: one tonne equivalent of CO_2 emission reduction.

Strategic Direction for 'India Evergreen'

A green economy requires significant innovation, enterprise and policy backing, and right institutions with right tools to reach to the bottom of the pyramid. Promotion of clean renewable energy in rural areas harnessing the resources available in the immediate neighbourhood, reducing the carbon footprint of enterprises in the entire supply chain,[5] improving the energy efficiency of existing MSMEs, involving innovative instruments and methods to aggregate micro-CERs from households, small holders, and sustained involvement of MFIs and NGOs who provide last mile access to the rural communities are important elements of the 'India Evergreen' strategy.

Promoting Renewable Energy

India has focused largely on solar energy under the NAPCC. Many countries have a cogent blend of policy and regulation to improve investments in renewable energy. Some of the regulatory and promotional interventions that try to promote renewable energy have been listed below (Table 7.2) to address the issue of market failure in a limited way.

Despite the thrust given earlier to harnessing wind and now solar energy, decentralized generation has not received the attention it deserves. Many banks and financial institutions are still jittery in supporting it as they are not convinced about the small-scale decentralized generation projects in rural areas. Surplus availability of biomass mainly from agro-waste and forest waste for the IPPs and their competitive use would be a critical factor for driving sustainability (both in terms of market and pricing), but it would require substantial policy support. To illustrate, oil mills can offer much higher price and can have higher value realization by installing mini-co-generation power plants and export a small quantity of power to the local grid. This would provide the highest value realization from biomass but would require community and industry partnership.

Greening the Industry

The Compensatory Afforestation Fund, created through the contribution of industries, helps to promote plantation in degraded areas and poor people can participate in this through Joint Forest Management Committees. There is significant potential for ecosystem payments by industries to fund mitigation activities involving land use such as mid-season drying of irrigated rice, and land-use change practices pertaining to conservation agriculture and conversion of low-productivity crop land to pasture or agriculture and, in some cases, to forests. Some industries have started doing this as part of their corporate social responsibility initiative.

Efficiency Improvements

Small industries have a substantial scope to make their processes efficient. Many of them do not take action as they are often unaware about the long-term benefit and cost. To address this, the Government of India recently

Table 7.2 Policies Promoting Renewable to Address Some Aspect of Market Failure

Country	*RPS/RPO*	*GEC/REC*	*Feed-in Tariff*	*Production Tax Credit*	*Investment Tax Credit*	*Generation Based Incentive*	*Financial Assistance*	*Tax Holiday*	*Legislative Support*
US	☑	☑	☑	☑	☑	☑	☑	☑	☑
UK	☑	☑	☑			☑		☑	
Germany			☑		☑	☑	☑	☑	☑
Denmark		☑	☑				☑	☑	
India	☑	CERC Regulation notified	☑	☑	☑	☑	☑	☑	
China			☑		☑	☑	☑	☑	☑

Note: RPS: Renewable Portfolio Standard; RPO: Renewable Portfolio Obligation; GEC: Green Energy Certificates; REC: Renewable Energy Certificate.
Source: Compiled from UNEP, CEU assessment of policy instruments for GHG reduction from the building sector, and IREC Webinar (23 June 2009).

[5] A recent McKinsey study shows that 40–60 per cent of companies' total carbon footprints reside upstream in their supply chains, suggesting the scale of the opportunity.

formed the Bureau of Energy Efficiency (BEE), which would play a key role in the mission of enhanced energy efficiency and intends to finance energy efficiency through ESCOs. These companies operate in a shared saving business model. Another important instrument is the trading of the energy efficiency certificates, also referred to as white certificates or E-CERT, which is discussed to a great extent here.

Bank-rolling Green Investments

The initial lukewarm response of banks to finance renewable projects has changed of late. Large mainstream banks are prioritizing their clean technology portfolio. SIDBI, State Bank of India (SBI), IDBI, Syndicate Bank, and ICICI Bank are in the forefront of such financing schemes. The SBI has introduced its 'Green Homes' scheme, whereby it has decided to assist environment-friendly residential projects by offering concessions such as reduced margin (20 to 15 per cent), softer interest rate (25 basis point lower than the card rate), and zero processing fee on home loans. But still there are issues with recognizing the revenue streams from CDM, and investment in both green field and brown field small-scale projects.

Reaching the Unreached: Micro-finance for Household Level Financing

Micro-finance Institutions address the credit market failure in general. Advancing the same argument, the MFIs can address the unreached people at the bottom of the pyramid to commit to the low carbon path. They can support both social and environmental goals by incorporating environmental education and empowerment into their lending programmes. Several micro-finance institutions such as SEWA and *Grameen Shakti* have taken the lead in developing energy-financing products in the space of lighting (solar PVs). Others such as BASIX and SKS have started offering support for the marketing of renewable energy products, both through financing as well as through the use of their distribution channels for deepening the usage of environment-friendly products among their customers. BASIX offers agricultural and business development services to promote SRI, vermi-composting and also one of the leading micro-finance institutions in offering weather insurance. Its group company, CTRAN, aggregates the carbon credit from small holders and passes on the benefit to its customers, thus enhancing the value. MFIs can offer newer products in rural areas for solar drying of food products, solar chargers, and energy efficient and labelled equipments to their customers to help the low carbon economy, reduce energy poverty, and create green collar jobs in rural areas.

There are certain green products that have distribution synergy in the MFI channel, such as crop loans for low carbon agriculture, such as the system of rice intensification (discussed in the agenda pertaining to the rural section in this chapter), low carbon energy such as solar photovoltaic, solar water heater, bio-gasifier, manure management, such as vermicompost and the NADEP method of composting.[6]

The distribution synergies can be found in the following manner:

- Rural communities need energy solutions at the local level, many are off-grid, and the MFIs are embedded with the communities and work in such areas where access to credit and other infrastructures are low.
- MFI representatives touch households in regular intervals and provide required capacity building support, as these are taken to be solutions to small decentralized projects and help in removing barriers for CDM.
- Many MFIs have technological solutions, better governance and interface with the community, serve as an ideal aggregator and provide a shared infrastructure for monitoring and verification (a stand-alone monitoring process for CDM is transaction cost-intensive). For example, a customer service agent/loan officer is expected to touch a client at least once in 30 days. The same person can provide crucial support in helping the customer in collecting the requisite data. The MIS system of the MFI can be modified to be used as a platform to be the repository of such data so that the transaction cost for verification could be reduced. Many MFIs extensively use mobile-based technology to reduce the transaction cost and the same platform can be shared for tracking and aggregating small CERs. (CTRAN is helping bar-coding energy-efficient devices to track usage, penetration, and aggregation)
- However, while technology and human interface are most suited to reduce transaction cost if the green projects are structured through MFIs, the problem is there in product structuring for green financing. Most MFIs have loans with very short repayment period (almost weekly), while the revenue from CDM

[6] Various methods of composting have been researched both under aerobic and anaerobic conditions. The NADEP method of composting developed by N.D. Pandhari Pande from Maharashtra is one such process facilitating aerobic decomposition of organic matter. This method takes care of all the disadvantages of heaping of farm residues and cattle shed wastes, etc. in the open.

projects come after a long gestation period (anywhere after 18–24 months) after its inception. This requires significant innovation in structuring both the product and transaction model.

Making small-BIG: Programmatic CDM

Programmatic-CDM (P-CDM), a new instrument under the Kyoto Protocol for small low carbon projects, gives a unique opportunity to achieve scale through aggregating CERs from several smaller units and even permitting combination of technologies and methodologies. The institutional framework demands voluntary co-ordinated action by a private or public entity which co-ordinates and implements any policy/measure or stated goal (that is, incentive schemes and voluntary programmes), which leads to GHG emission reductions that are additional to any that would occur in the absence of the Programme of Activities (PoA) as per the UNFCCC guidelines. This particular provision provides additional flexibility and does not distinguish between sectoral and policy-based CDM.

The key characteristics of programmatic CDM include:

- It occurs as the result of a deliberate programme, which may be a mandatory or voluntary government policy (BLY in Box 7.1 above is a voluntary programme) or a voluntary private initiative.
- It results in multiple dispersed actions, not necessarily occurring at the same time. The type, size, and timing may not be known at the outset, and each type of Emission Reduction (ER) action will need to use appropriate baseline and monitoring methodology.

There is one acting agent, and that is the BEE.

The key issues and processes involved in operationalizing programmatic CDM so as to act as a financing mechanism for low carbon infrastructure development is best explained in Figure 7.4, that is, the key processes related to aggregation of emission reductions.

The blue ovals (U1–Un) are small-holders or households who want to use certain green solutions (for example, vermicomposting). The first challenge (listed in the green bars) is to mobilize them to explain to them the benefit of choosing that action, the cost involved, and measure their willingness to take up that activity and scaling up through peer groups, demonstration, etc. The second challenge is to impute a technology which meets the prevailing conditions in the grassroots level (need to have biomass, livestock loans, etc.). The third challenge is to see the prevailing practice and tweak it to meet the CDM methods and monitoring and verification (M&V) protocol (pit arrangement and social noting of compost loads, etc.). The last and the most important aspect is to find an institution that stays engaged to ensure the continuity of the project, support the verifiability, and long-run sustainability of the co-ordinated action, which is largely voluntary. The orange oval to aggregate the micro-CERs and assist in the verification represents a public institution such as the Orissa Renewable Development Agency (OREDA) in bio-gas or BEE in BLY, and BASIX[7] or Chhattisgarh Tribal Development Society for vermicompost). The

Box 7.1
Bachat Lamp Yojna: P-CDM

The Bachat Lamp Yojana (BLY) promotes replacement of inefficient bulbs with Compact Fluorescent Lamps (CFLs) by leveraging the sale of CERs under the CDM. The scheme provides a unique platform for a robust public-private partnership between the Government of India, private sector CFL suppliers, and state-level Electricity Distribution Companies (DISCOMs). It provides a framework to distribute high-quality CFLs at about Rs 15 per piece to the households of the country. Under the scheme, only 60 Watt and 100 Watt incandescent lamps have to be replaced with 11 to 15 Watt and 20–25 Watt CFLs respectively. The BEE will undertake monitoring of each project area as required under an approved methodology of CDM.

Given the high transaction cost of preparation and registration of CDM projects and the fact that the public sector in India does not possess adequate capacities to undertake them, BEE has developed a PoA which would serve as an umbrella CDM project, once registered with the CDM Executive Board. The individual projects, designed to be in conformance with the umbrella project, would be added to the latter as and when they are prepared. The development of the PoA is a voluntary action on the part of the BEE and it would not seek any commercial revenues from the PoA.

Source: BEE Press Release (2010).

[7] The Agricultural and Business Development Service Team of BASIX helps in identifying customers interested in vermicomposting. They follow up with them in different kinds of loan products and advisory services to see that the pits are compliant to procedures required for AMCERs. CTRAN provides the detailed protocol for its aggregation, documentation, transaction, and verification for issuance. It assists in product and transaction structuring.

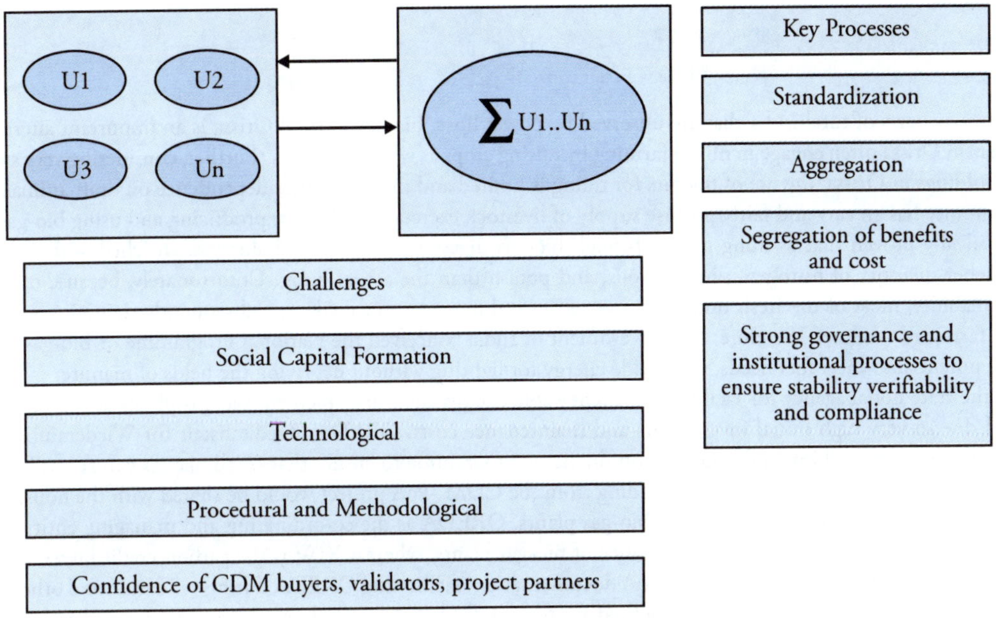

Figure 7.4 Key Processes Relating to Aggregation of Emission Reductions

Source: CTRAN.

violet bars show the key processes which are involved in the total process of aggregation.

Unlike the normal CDM project, where one has to produce only one project design document (PDD), in the programmatic CDM, one has to have a design document (DD) for the whole programme of activity that will outline some probable number of smaller projects (called CDM project activity or CPA), and this is called PoA DD. This document will provide the overall approach including the institutional arrangement, M&V framework, and the hypothetical number of CPAs that are likely to be covered under the programme. Subsequently, a generic CPA design document is prepared (this template would be used for all future projects) entering this PoA, followed by preparing a real project design document.

Consider the example of the Orissa Bio-gas Programme, launched by OREDA (see Box 7.2). Under the programme, some of the households obtain finance for their bio-digesters. OREDA makes an estimate of coverage to put a projection of the CPAs. Subsequently, a real client is picked up for the preparation of the CPA design document. The validator has to validate all the three documents.

The problem is that the DoEs[8] do not take risks on the monitoring of the CPAs, as the UNFCCC has a liability clause on them (if the CPAs are duplicated, the DoE has to have a compensation mechanism for CERs). The DoEs require strong agency, strong and robust M&V protocol, and also charge heavily for the validation of PoAs. While the P-CDM is a win-win situation for the kind of market failure to make the market inclusive through MFIs, it has not taken off.

Therefore, there is no mechanism by which mitigation actions at the micro-level, from households, agriculturists, livestock grazers, forest dwellers, and micro-enterprises can be taken to the carbon market. It is in this context that Mahajan and Singha (2007) have proposed two new instruments—AMCERs and AVERTs. It is only when these instruments are widely available and traded, can the dominance of large industries be reduced in the carbon market.

Innovative Alternatives—AMCERs and AVERTs[9]

The 282 CDM projects from India registered by the CDM Executive Board have already resulted in over 28 million tonnes of certified CO_2 emissions reductions (CII 2009). More than three-fourth of the CERs issued have been from large industries. Aggregation of Micro-Certified Emission Reduction (AMCERs) Units is difficult and challenging

[8] Accredited Entities with UNFCCC tasked to validate CDM projects and their verification.

[9] Mahajan and Singha (2007) first introduced these terms, AMCERS and AVERTs.

Box 7.2
Bio-gas Programmatic CDM in Rural Orissa

As is true for many parts of rural India that are unserved by power lines, bio-gas in rural Orissa is an important alternate source of energy. Farmers in Orissa often engage in mixed farming by raising crops as well as livestock. Further, considering very small and fragmented landholdings in Orissa, the use of tractors for tilling is limited and there is greater dependence on draft animals. Hence, the farming community has an easy and fairly profuse supply of livestock excreta to utilize for producing and using bio-gas efficiently.

It is scientifically proven that as dung passes through bio-gas digesters, the resultant slurry is enriched with nutrients, which can yield a higher quantity of nitrogen, phosphorous, and potash than the actual dung. Unfortunately, because of the decline in fuel wood availability, most of the fresh dung is converted into dung cakes for cooking, subsequently depriving agricultural land of traditional farmyard manure. Therefore, the Government of India conceived the National Programme of Bio-gas Development, which has the potential to meet fuel needs, to provide energy for lighting without depriving the fields of manure.

OREDA, the state nodal agency for facilitation of renewable energy, tried to implement bio-gas plants at the state level but this attempt failed due to very high initial investments and maintenance costs. OREDA, Kreditanstalt für Wiederaufbau (KfW), and BASIX's CTRAN have entered into a unique carbon financing programme to ensure that small players can access funds under the programmatic CDM. The benefits from carbon trading from the CDM -PoA project would be shared with the households who are meeting their cooking energy requirements from bio-gas plants. OREDA as the co-ordinating and managing entity of CDM-PoA would be responsible for monitoring and maintenance of bio-gas plants, whereas KfW is the carbon credit buyer, and CTRAN is responsible for conducting baseline study, CDM-PoA documentation, facilitating OREDA during validation and other due diligence for CDM. Hence, the bio-gas owner will be benefited from the CDM-PoA by availing of maintenance and repair service of the bio-gas plant free of cost for 10 years of operation.

The programme will have several CDM project activity (CPA) lots with each CPA of 7000 units and each unit bearing a unique number and a size of about 1–3 m^3. Total accumulated thermal capacity of the digesters in a CPA would be below 45 MW. The carbon credit from the programme will be around Rs 1000 per digester annually. Participating households will reduce firewood consumption of 1.7 tonnes and 1.3 tCO_2e on an annual basis at individual household level.

Source: Orissa Renewable Development Agency.

because of the high transaction cost, lengthy CDM project cycle as well as low interest evinced by validating agencies, and carbon market buyers and consultants. So when rice mills switch from coal to husk, food-processing units recover methane from waste water, brick units and ceramic units attempt fuel switch and other small-holders in small industry, agriculture and forestry use DSM measures, attempt methane management and carbon sequestration in sinks—these remain excluded from the purview of CDM financing.

CTRAN has attempted to use the bundling and Programmatic Clean Development Mechanism (P-CDM) route to bring special focus on aggregating the small lots of CERs through specialized agencies, fine-tuning processes and technologies so that the carbon market is deepened and linked to the bottom of the pyramid. This, however, requires extensive grassroots presence, familiarity with social processes, institutional development, familiarity in de-scaled technology, seamless and cost-effective verification processes, and strong knowledge of various carbon market operations (both regulated and voluntary). Since the AMCER and AVERT mechanisms are tailored for each micro-low carbon infrastructure project, it is difficult to discuss generalized key processes related to developing AMCERs and AVERTs. Instead, the experience of CTRAN, an organization involved in developing AMCERS, with respect to putting together a solar water heater CDM project has been discussed in Box 7.3.

Many small devices reducing emissions such as solar lantern, bio-gas units, and small hydel units generate small lots of CERs. Similar to the financial services sector where large banks do not show enough interest for small customers, in the carbon market too, large compliance buyers (those who have carbon tax or emission reduction quota on them) do not show much interest in these small CER lots. They concentrate more on low hanging fruits like large industrial process plants with large volumes of emission reduction potential.

To attract the interest of players in the carbon market, both the schemes, that is, AMCERs and AVERTs aggregate micro-emission reductions into larger tradable units. Where a rigorous verification is possible, one tonne of carbon dioxide emission in a year is termed as one CER and can be traded in the European Carbon Exchange. Where the verification is not as rigorous, the emission reductions can still be sold, but at a lower price, in exchanges such as the Chicago Climate Exchange.

The aggregated micro-certified emission reductions (AMCERs) provides a mechanism by which these small volumes can be aggregated and presented in a lot

Box 7.3
Steps taken by CTRAN to Develop a Solar Water Heater CDM Project

- The project initiated with preliminary discussion with aggregator, an MNRE Approved Solar Water Heater Manufacturer in a cluster, with the basic idea to enhance the market penetration of solar water heaters in the country. In spite of the huge cost saving potential the product has neither been commercialized nor widely acceptable in spite of long and tiring efforts by the government.
- Our first work was to understand the market imperfection and factors/barriers preventing its propagation and factors preventing its commercialization. A baseline survey was carried out across five states (Maharashtra, Madhya Pradesh, Gujarat, Karnataka, Orissa) to understand the factors preventing the propagation of the technology or the devices commonly used in different sectors to address the requirement of hot water.
- The survey portrayed few of the major lacunae in the sector that has prevented its propagation of which the lack of awareness among the end users on the cost economics, higher capital and recurring expenditure, and lack of availability of the product and knowledge among the supplier, dealers and installers on the product portfolio are mostly cited.
- After understanding the existing scenario the next step was to aggregate other manufacturers and dealers in the domain to come under a single umbrella to mitigate the existing barrier through CDM Revenue.
- It was planned that the CDM Revenue to be obtained against each installation which is less than 1tCO_2 per annum will be provided to the customer by reimbursing their annual operation and maintenance expenditure.
- Although the plan was widely accepted, the uncertainty in CDM revenue and the required expenditure was a major bottle-neck for the investors to invest.
- In order to have the initial funding to take up the project under CDM bilateral and multilateral funding, agencies were approached for funding.
- A German-based power generating company agreed to support the project as a part of meeting the compliance.
- With support from international agencies the first step was to carry out stakeholders' consultation workshops in five states to create awareness among the users and how CDM revenue can benefit them in enhancing the financial viability.
- As a statutory part of the CDM process, the following steps were adopted:
  - Installation of SWH at client premise.
  - Maintenance of the database.
  - The client signing an agreement whereby the CER right is being transferred to the project management entity.
  - The project management entity on other hand signed a separate agreement with the international agency whereby they transfer the carbon credit right to the agency. As a part of the agreement the buyer will transfer money to the project management entity against the total verified CER each year.
  - The third contract under the project is signed between the project management entity whereby the entity is liable to transfer the CDM revenue to the individual manufacturer/dealer/distributor to take care of the operation and maintenance of the project proponent and the individual manufacturer/distributor/dealer is liable to undertake the O&M and as a discount to the end user. This will make the product attractive and better market penetration and win-win for participating MFIs also.
- The project was planned with 40 manufacturers and around 30,000 end users. As all the end users couldn't be accepted under a single project therefore the second phase of the project was planned on First in First Out (FIFO) basis.

Source: CTRAN.

commensurate to the buyers' needs. It is not easy to make suitable institutional arrangements, to demonstrate fulfilment of the additionality criteria, and meet monitoring requirements at a transaction cost that makes the project viable. If AMCERS succeed, they will have the effect of making carbon markets inclusive and deep. Micro-finance institutions are natural channels for AMCERs, as they can in the first place provide finance for the adoption of measures, which can reduce emissions—whether it is solar lighting, bio-gas plants, or evergreen agriculture. AVERTs are aggregated verified tradable lots. These are aggregated from projects which do not conform to the CDM route but possible to structure through a variety of voluntary market mechanisms and widens the choice for the small holders. In many cases, this is attempted where defending the CDM additionality is considered risky.

In this case, the transaction is structured from the supply side. Many of these offsets are used by corporats for their CSR obligation but not as a compliance product. The entity decides that it is going to support plantation activity among tribals and calculates the sequestered carbon for being carbon neutral. CTRAN is working with agencies to have carbon neutrality pilots. In this case, the carbon foot printing of the host and the project determines the transaction model and financing. A lot of capacity building is required for these kinds of projects and these are structures where this is part of a long-term engagement than a stand-alone action.

Efficient mobile technology with wider reach and suitable structuring and blending with MFIs channels, can further render the AVERTs and AMCERs as efficient market solutions for an evergreen India. Small lots of emission reduction units can be generated from the distribution of solar lanterns, energy-efficient devices such as CFL, LED lights, and other green consumables with an individual loan. Group loans can be extended to self-help groups (SHGs) using renewable energy for food processing, vermin-composting, etc. Groups can even take loans for bio-biomass-based distributed generation, solar power, etc. and distribute them to other households. The same can also generate AMCERs. MFIs would play the role of an aggregator and some may even consider the AMCER-traded revenue as collateral.

- The project has completed the CDM cycle now and waiting Executive Board Approval for the registration.

Conclusion

India has the potential right to grow without inducing inequity and exclusion. The poor have the right to access carbon markets and can participate meaningfully. Considering this, the debate centres on who will pay for them to do so.

We need to deconstruct our dialogue, need strong institutions (both technical and financial) which can support and sustain this green-tech movement. We need collective action from emitters. There has to be a greater disclosure both from the banks as also non-banking financial intermediaries, and industry on direct action for greening their portfolios. We also need policies that incentivize households to reduce their carbon footprint.

Traditional policy-based and market-based incentives are skewed in favour of large industries. This must change as the scope of further reduction is less and welfare cost is high. AMCERs and AVERTs are proposed as tools which conform to the existing market mechanism and can address the core barriers in programmatic CDM, which was mooted to address the core issue of scale, bundling, and transaction costs. The strategy presented in this chapter will attract carbon market players, banks, MFIs, and communities into a meaningful partnership. This will help India to stay evergreen and grow—that is, India Evergreen!

References

Atmanand, Amit K. Gupta, and Rishabh Raman (2009). 'Energy and Sustainable Development–An Indian Perspective, World Academy of Science, Engineering and Technology' 54, 2009.

BEE Press Release (2010). *Press Trust of India*, 3 May 2010.

Bhalla S. (2009). India: Need for Change in Climate in www.oxusinvestments.com

CII (2009). *Building a Low Carbon Economy*, CII discussion paper.

Government of India, Planning Commission (2009) Integrated Energy Policy 2008.

Gujja, Biksham, N. Loganandhan, V. Vinod Goud, N. Loganandhan, and V.V. Goud (eds). (2009). *System of Rice Intensification Experiences of Farmers in India.* ICRISAT–WWF Project.

Hepburn, Cameron (2007). Carbon Trading: A Review of the Kysto Mechanisms. Annual Review of Environment and Resources, 32, November 2007.

Mahajan, Vijay and Ashok Singha (2007). 'Deepening the Carbon Market For the Poor', Mimeo.

Ministry of New and Renewable Energy Sources (MNRE) Government of India, available at www. mnes.nic.in

Ministry of New and Renewable Energy (2009). *Akshay Urja* 3(1).

Mukhopadhyaya, Kakali and D. Chakraborty. (2005). 'Energy intensity in India during pre-reform and reform period' An Input-Output Analysis Paper submitted for the Fifteenth International Input-Output Conference to be held at the Renmin University in Beijing, China, 27 June–1 July, 2005.

NATCOM (2007). *Report on India's GHG Emissions 2007*, Ministry of Environment and Forest, Government of India, available at http://www.moef.nic.in/downloads/public-information/Report_INCCA.pdf

Painuly J.P. (2000). 'Kyoto Protocol and Voluntary Commitments: What are the Risks to Developing Countries' Invited Paper, International Symposium on Development Policies for the New Millennium in Honour of Professor Kirit S. Parikh, IGIDR, 12–14 July 2000.

Roy, Joyashree and Ranjana Mukhopadhyay (2005). 'Energy and Infrastructure Needs In India: An Input-Output Analysis.'

Sahu, Santosh and K. Narayanan (2009). 'Determinants of Energy Intensity: A Preliminary Investigation of Indian

Manufacturing', MPRA Paper No. 16606, posted 4 August 2009/15:50.

Schneider, Gia (2007). Credit Suisse in 2007 Market Perspective IETA/IEA/EPRI, 7th Annual Workshop on Greenhouse Gas Emission Trading, October 2007.

Schneider and Hepburn (2007). Available at www.cozoffsetresearch.org/policy/-CDM.html

Smith P., D. Martino, Z. Cai, D. Gwary, H. Janzen, P. Kumar, B. McCarl, S. Ogle, F. O'Mara, C. Rice, B. Scholes, and O. Sirotenk (2007). 'Agriculture. In: Climate Change 2007: Mitigation.' Contribution of Working Group III to the Fourth Assessment Report of the Intergovernmental Panel on Climate Change in B. Metz, O.R. Davidson, P.R. Bosch, R. Dave, L.A. Meyer (eds), Cambridge University Press. Cambrdige, UK and New York.

Thakur, A.K., Norman Uphoff, and Edna Antony (2009). 'An assessment of physiological effects of system of rice intensification (SRI) practices compared with recommended rice cultivation practices in India'. *Expl Agric.* (2010), 46(1), pp. 77–98, Cambridge University Press 2009 doi:10.1017/S0014479709990548

United Nations Development Programme (UNDP) (2008). 'CDM Projects Finance Perspective', A presentation by Robert Kelly (UNDP), 27 March 2008.

World Bank (2009). *State and Trends of the Carbon Market 2009*, Washington DC.

Section III

Energy Infrastructure

8 Drivers of Energy Efficiency Industries

Indian and International Experience in Infrastructure

Lenora Suki

India is rapidly embracing energy efficiency as the key to mitigating the impact of climate change, increasing energy security, and improving economic productivity and competitiveness. Rising and volatile energy prices, concerns about global energy supply, and budgetary pressures to liberalize energy subsidies are penetrating the country's collective consciousness. Globalization is creating new demands for trade and investment competitiveness. Electricity demand is exploding with rapid economic growth, and haphazard urbanization is putting more cars out onto the roads and more pollution in the air. Energy shortages and unreliable power are persistent challenges, especially in agriculture. Not surprisingly, then, every segment of the Indian economy is increasingly aware of the need for energy efficiency.

Although efficiency is probably India's cheapest energy source, the opportunity is not yet fully visible. Technology advances and becomes more cost-effective, but energy efficiency investments face economic constraints, political barriers, technical challenges, and institutional shortcomings. Invisibility is a constraint in itself. Albeit quantifiable in lower electricity bills, efficiency matters mostly if your bill reflects the cost of providing the power. For many Indians, more often than not, it doesn't, and hence, a certain inertia and high discount rates for efficiency investments. Lower GHG emissions, reduced pollution, better quality power—all are desirable but difficult to pin to energy efficiency. Despite quick payoffs on many investments, moving to energy efficient air-conditioners, lighting, motors, drives, cars, and buildings will cost consumers and businesses, and the incentives are fragmented and asymmetric.

That said, India is making great strides to put proper economic rationales and incentives in place. The government recognizes energy efficiency as necessary to transition to the low carbon economy. International models are arriving via overseas development assistance, consulting firms, equipment manufacturers and others, while Indian realities are shaping domestic adaptations and innovations. Strategic decisions are being taken as to which approaches, such as (ESCOs), are promoted. Yet modernization to the next generation of technology will be unevenly distributed as India's impressive technical capacity is dampened by human and financial resource gaps. As resources are mobilized towards these goals, albeit in inadequate fits and starts, India has great potential to build a diverse energy efficiency industry with concerted, persistent, and widespread effort.

This article outlines India's potential for and barriers to energy efficiency in infrastructure. It considers the role of technology as a driver and a challenge to a rapidly growing developing country.[1] It explores the diverse roles of government and a burgeoning institutional landscape, concluding with the analysis of prototype financing

[1] Transportation and agriculture do not receive extensive treatment here despite ample scope for energy efficiency.

transactions. Indian experience is compared and contrasted with international examples, illustrating how markets for energy efficiency grow and prosper.

The Energy Efficiency Opportunity in India in Context

An energy efficiency market or industry 'constitute[s] unique means of providing energy services while lowering energy consumption and reducing our environmental impact.'[2]

Energy efficiency must play a key role in mitigating the rise of GHG emissions from the exploding pace of worldwide energy demand. McKinsey and Company's recent analysis of energy efficiency insists it could be 'a vast, low cost energy resource' but only with 'a comprehensive and innovative approach to unlock it'.[3] Already efficiency measures introduced between 1974 and 2006 in 11 IEA member countries dramatically reduced energy consumption; without them, total consumption would have been 58 per cent higher. In the US alone, energy efficiency potential is 23 per cent by 2020.[4] For upfront investments of $520 billion, a fourfold increase in current energy efficiency investment, the payoff in savings would be $1.2 trillion.[5] The European Union has a similar energy savings potential of 20 per cent by 2020 at a direct cost of more than EUR100 million annually by 2020.[6] Nonetheless, with returns on energy efficiency averaging 17–20 per cent,[7] these savings could deliver 60 per cent of all cost-effective emission reductions in a scenario aiming for a 60–80 per cent cut in emissions by 2050.[8] However promising, not only have achieved savings fallen short but also the pace of implementation of energy efficiency measures has slowed in the past two decades. As a result, energy efficiency gains halved from 1.9 per cent per year on average from 1974 to 1990 to only one per cent.[9]

Against that backdrop, developing economies are expected to generate about three-quarters of the coming decade's global increase in energy demand and about two-thirds of the energy-related CO_2 emissions growth with efficiency measures expected to yield 45 per cent of the reduction in CO_2 emissions from 2005 through 2030.[10] In the IEA's current reference scenario, China and India alone account for 43 per cent of the increase in energy demand through 2030 and, in a high growth scenario, it could be as high as 54 per cent.[11] Looking at infrastructure, this is particularly significant as more than two-thirds of that increase is from road transport alone (freight and passenger), whereas industry still dominates final energy use (28 per cent in India, 42 per cent in China, and 32 per cent for the world average).[12]

India has a structural need for energy efficiency as a net energy importer and a heavy coal user with marginal gas resources. Even if the per capita commercial energy consumption is only 20 per cent of the world average, 4 per cent that of the US, and 28 per cent that of China, the 400 million people currently without basic electricity services arguably represents the largest pent-up consumer demand for electricity services in the world for an already stressed power sector (Table 8.1).[13] Outside of growth in energy usage from population demands, inefficient energy use cuts across the whole economy. Energy intensity per unit of GDP[14] is 3.7 times Japan's and 1.5 times the US's—far higher than US, Europe, and Japan in key sectors like steel and ammonia.[15]

[2] Ehrhardt-Martinez and Laitner (2008).

[3] McKinsey & Company (2009).

[4] McKinsey & Company (2009) refers solely to end use efficiency, that is savings of energy consumed in business, residential, agricultural, and industrial settings, as opposed to energy efficiency from source through transformation to distribution.

[5] These are present value calculations based on a 7 per cent discount rate and McKinsey & Company's modelling of 675 energy saving measures with equipment replacement when NPV positive and no carbon price, which would increase returns (McKinsey & Company 2009).

[6] Commission of the European Communities (2006).

[7] Estimates can vary widely about the return on investment to energy efficiency measures because the analysis depends on which measures are considered, the time horizon of analysis, discount rates, energy price assumptions, etc. Most estimates, however, settle in this range. Ehrhardt-Martinez and Laitner (2008) describes the risk-return as being similar to investing in a US small company index with the return range above with standard deviation approximating US Treasury bonds (approximately 5 per cent).

[8] IEA (2007).

[9] IEA (2010).

[10] IEA (2007).

[11] Ibid.

[12] Ibid.

[13] IEA (2010).

[14] India Renewable Energy Development Authority (IREDA) and Bureau of Energy Efficiency (BEE).

[15] IEA (2007).

TABLE 8.1 Power Sector Challenges and Benefits of Energy Efficiency

(in percentage)

Transmission and distribution losses from 20 per cent in the south to 43 per cent in the northeast
Lack of credit to ESCOs and EMCs
Power supply deficits of 4.5 per cent in the eastern region to 13.7 per cent in the western region
Peak deficits of 7 per cent in the eastern region to almost 18 per cent in the west and Northeastern Regions
High dependence on imported energy for 60 per cent of total consumption
High ash content of coal resources

Source: Salman (2002).

TABLE 8.2 Substantial Energy Savings Potential in Infrastructure

Intervention	*Sector*	*Potential energy savings (in percent)*
Various (motors, drives, capacitors, etc.)*	Cross-cutting	10–20
Buildings	Urban	50–60
Goods from road to rail	Transport	80
Urban transit	Transport	67
Lighting	Commercial/industrial/ institutional	75
Efficient pumpsets	Agriculture	30

Note: *Industries cited include steel, cement, aluminum, glass, ceramics, textiles, and others.
Sources: BEE and IREDA.

India's national low carbon growth strategies recognize the relief offered by more efficiency. The Ministry of Power foresees the potential to create 25,000 MW of capacity in the electricity sector with 23 per cent energy savings potential in industry and agriculture alone. Even with massive investments in renewables, hydropower, and natural gas,[16] the Energy Conservation Act of 2001 includes 10,000 MW of avoided capacity investment and a 20 per cent increase in energy efficiency by 2016 through supply and demand rationalization.

Ambitious as it sounds, the Indian economy's mix of old, sub-standard plant, equipment, and infrastructure with modern, highly efficient installed capacity makes for variable savings potential, disparate implementation, and unique challenges depending on the sector.[17] Although industry has received the most attention, transport, lighting, buildings, power, and agriculture have dramatic savings potential (Table 8.2).

As a final contextual perspective, energy efficiency in India means more than just climate change mitigation. These savings also increase energy security and independence. Competitiveness improves with reduced demands on and for infrastructure, as well as development of domestic manufacturing and service capacity. Jobs come from energy efficiency investments; in the US, most recent estimates suggest 1.3 million to 3.7 million potential jobs.[18] Decelerating India's reliance on coal improves air quality in cities and benefits public health. Finally, where energy efficiency markets prosper, energy end users often get increased power choice and quality with their shrinking carbon footprint.

Yet, these positive prospects belie hurdles, which may delay and dampen the final impact of energy savings measures, the most significant of which are as follows:

- Cross-subsidized electricity prices leading to wastage in residential and agricultural sectors.
- Limited information about the benefit of energy efficiency investments and technologies.
- Lack of enforcement of standards, codes, and labelling.
- Mistrust of counterparties in the context of weak contract enforcement.[19]
- Bias against the counterintuitive disposal of existing plant and equipment.
- Difficulty of measuring 'negawatts' (or efficiency savings) in the context of project cash flows.[20]

[16] These government plans include the XIth Plan, National Energy Policy, and the framework issued by the Prime Minister's Council on Climate Change in June 2008.

[17] Although analysis of the steel and cement industries lies outside the scope of this article, the embodied energy in the production and transport of these materials, as well as other interior and building finishes, contributes substantially to infrastructure's carbon footprint.

[18] Ehrhardt-Martinez and Laitner (2008).

[19] Counterparties can include financial institutions, manufacturers, and service providers (for example, auditors, energy service companies, energy management companies).

[20] 'Negawatts' are an informal term for energy efficiency savings, a wordplay on the production of negative megawatts. Measurement can be especially challenging in the context of scant baseline measurements or inconsistent benchmark methodologies. Also, when efficiency improvements are spread across multiple larger investments, disaggregating the efficiency component from complex projects and re-aggregating the contribution from efficiency across projects can be complicated.

- Asymmetric risk/reward distributions (mostly in the building sector for owner/investors versus tenants).
- Competing objectives in complex planning situations involving new investments and development.
- Inadequate investment in supportive institutional mechanisms and human resources.
- High transaction costs from legal, technical, and transactional complexities, like non-standardized deal structures and substantial technical content of project appraisal, development, and monitoring.

All of the above make potential energy savings difficult to realize, especially in a high growth economy where the default pose assumes growth and technological advancement as primary goals and energy efficiency as a passive by-product or not an issue at all. Agents—from borrowers to bankers to consumers—are more risk averse and, therefore, discount rates and opportunity costs high relative to comparable economic activity.

The Promise and Challenge of Energy Efficiency Technologies

The growth of an energy efficiency industry relies on the diffusion of existing technologies and technological innovation (see Table 8.3). Technology can drive policy, institutional and financing responses, and vice versa, regulation, economics, and design norms can shape technology.[21] Although low tech, zero cost, and low cost improvements can yield surprising savings,[22] these low hanging fruit, once picked, must yield to scaled-up and more advanced EE investment and EE initiatives. In buildings, for example, the commissioning process central to energy management strategies emphasizes both low cost adjustments and more time and capital-intensive investments over time.

Cost-benefit analyses of energy efficiency technologies tend to project solid returns and short payoff periods (Table 8.4). In the US, the average cost of energy savings has been priced at \$0.02–\$0.03 per kWh, the lowest cost versus all other technologies but biomass, which prices at the low end of energy efficiency.[23] Even in India, with its price distortions, the returns from energy efficiency are sufficiently high in commerce and industry to incentivize investing in energy savings measures. Energy price

Table 8.3 Priority Areas of Energy Efficiency Investment in Infrastructure

Technology	*Sector*
Lighting technologies (e.g. LED, CFLs)	Municipalities/ buildings
Variable frequency drives	Buildings/ cross-sectoral
Air handling units	Buildings
EE HVAC systems	Buildings
Control technology for HVAC systems	Buildings
Motion and daylight sensors	Buildings
Energy monitoring software and management systems	Cross-sectoral
Building automation systems	Buildings
CFC Free EE chillers	Buildings/ cross-sectoral
District heating systems	Municipalities/ buildings
Commercial and industrial boilers	Cross-sectoral/ buildings
Combined Heat and Power (CHP)	Power
Supercritical steam generators	Power
Smart grid innovations (e.g. intelligent meters)	Power
Electric energy storage	Power
Pumping/irrigation	Agriculture
Building materials (fly ash, low energy compounds, local/regional production, recycled materials, etc.)	Buildings

Note: HVAC: Heating Ventilation and Air Conditioning.
Source: Author's own.

subsidies do lengthen payback periods in households, but not for lack of technologies. Payback periods can be brought down and returns boosted by lifting subsidies in tandem with efficiency initiatives.

Regardless of how worthwhile the investment and available the technology, the decision equation has behavioural components. Discomfort with replacing a plant with remaining useful life and undepreciated capital costs, higher first costs than more accessible substitutes, unavailability of certain technologies and widely varying savings estimates can all raise risk perceptions and can

[21] See Sathaye et al. (2006) for a comprehensive discussion of technology's impacts on the economics of energy efficiency with specific references to India.

[22] Information and practical guidance are already being disseminated by public, private, and civil society bodies in India. See the BEE/ICFI manuals on achieving energy efficiency in hotels, schools, and hospitals (http://www.bee-india.nic.in/), as well as the Indian Green Building Council (www.igbc.in) and the Confederation of Indian Industry-Green Business Centre (www.greenbusinesscentre.org).

[23] Cooper (2009).

TABLE 8.4 Profitability of Selected Home Energy Upgrades in the United States

Energy Efficiency Upgrade	*Price*	*Annual Savings*	*Simple Payback (yrs)*	*Rate of Return (in per cent)*
Fluorescent Lamps and Fixtures	$200	$80	2.5	41
Duct sealing	$250	$95	2.6	41
ENERGY STAR Clothes-washer	$194	$66	2.9	37
ENERGY STAR Refrigerator	$97	$23	4.2	27
ENERGY STAR Dishwasher	$29	$5	5.5	18

Source: Lawrence Berkeley National Laboratory, Home Energy Saver (online) http://hes.lbl.gov/consumer/profitable.

stymie good projects.[24] Planning, monitoring, feedback, and adjustment to energy savings measures can be time-consuming. Modifying processes and resource utilization can entail follow-on costs, some of which are intangible and easily misunderstood. Worker training can cause delays and frustration. Disputes over savings measurements can lead to legal disputes.

Clearly then, higher direct and indirect costs of problematic or complex projects may not be fully accounted for and downside risks may be higher than calculated, lowering returns, and lengthening payoff periods. Technology may not match up well with behaviour and institutions, as illustrated below:

- Lighting can be mass produced and easily replaced. CFL bulbs cost more than incandescent bulbs but pay off in less than two years. Yet, getting low and moderate income people to buy them requires investment in information and financing mechanisms (see Box 8.1).
- Variable speed drives in motor control applications (in washing machines, chillers, HVACs, etc.) can pay off in 1–5 years, but they have to be maintained correctly to achieve savings.
- IT-enabled solutions, like building automation systems, aid in maintenance, data collection, benchmarking, and metering, among other information and management functions. Taking advantage of their functionality requires substantial manager training.
- A substantial part of buildings' energy efficiency can come from better design and planning, using building orientation, daylighting, shading, and natural ventilation, along with insulation, more efficient chillers and better air-conditioners. Yet, common practice in project management may preclude such foresight, except in large or high-end projects.
- One cause of client mistrust of ESCOs is their espousal of certain technology solutions, partly because many represent controls or equipment companies, whereas clients would prefer insight that better links efficiency investments with their business realities.[25]
- Fuel cells' payoff of more than 50 years effectively isolates them to demonstration use despite the need for such technologies in urban transport, for instance.

Table 8.5 summarizes technology-related gaps for energy efficient infrastructure but certain conclusions can be distilled about the role of technology:

- Ample technical capacity exists in India to foster national competitiveness in energy efficiency, but increased investment in training and institution-building is necessary at all levels.[26, 27]
- Information asymmetries, especially given rapid technology change, must be addressed with better data, public information and improved benchmarking.
- Legal insufficiencies in intellectual property, code, and contract law enforcement must be rectified.

[24] Interviews with real estate development and green building professionals in India suggest large cost differentials or difficulties sourcing EE investments for certain equipment: thermal storage, under-floor space conditioning, geothermal systems, LED lighting, methane-fuelled cooling systems, insulating media, and exterior building facades. Interviewees' estimate of the cost differential for higher technology green building elements ranges from 5–8 per cent all the way to 30 per cent although different levels of experience and market awareness probably accounts for some of the large discrepancy (Author's interviews).

[25] World Resources Institute (2009).

[26] Developing countries like India, Brazil, and China are starting to complement imported technologies with those of domestic design and production. The World Resources Institute's New Ventures India programme (www.newventures.org) has already supported and has incubated companies producing EE technologies, such as HMX Systems, an environmentally friendly HVAC producer.

[27] These goals are already mainstreamed into the global dialogue on climate change. See GEF (www.gefweb.org), Intergovernmental Panel on Climate Change (http://www.ipcc.ch), and the United Nations Framework on Climate Change (www.unfccc.int).

TABLE 8.5 Technology Related Gaps for Energy Efficient Infrastructure

Sector	*Role of Energy Efficiency Related Technology and Technology Transfer*
General	• Improved indicators and data collection about availability, quality, and flows of EE technologies
	• Technology performance benchmarks and sound indicators for technological improvements
	• Better information systems, links with international/regional networks, development of information clearing houses and firms, trade publications, electronic media, and civil society
Buildings	• Promotion of demand-side management, as for EE lighting, appliances, and equipment
	• R&D and product development for climate appropriate space conditioning, thermal systems, building controls, lighting, building envelope, etc.
Transport	• Improved design and maintenance of transport modes, alternative/improved fuels, vehicle use changes, and modal shifts
	• Management systems for transport demand reduction
	• Advanced urban planning and transport demand planning tools
Power/energy	• Demand response systems, electrical energy storage
	• Energy information systems, communication technologies for demand side management
Agriculture	• R&D and information databases for improved practice, such as irrigation systems and biogas recovery systems, and support to credit and savings schemes
	• Energy efficient pump sets

Governments and Energy Efficiency Industries: From Market Failure to Market Success

Governments' varied roles in the energy efficiency challenge highlight the extent of market failure. Although barriers to energy efficiency need to be lowered, sustainable change cannot be based on regulatory compliance alone. Policy, law, regulation, target-setting, compliance and enforcement, plus supportive programmes and incentives, must be in place to build competitive energy efficiency markets. As just one perspective on the role of government in building these markets, a survey of US investors in CleanTech emphasizes that energy prices, environmental public policy, and public awareness drive their investments, all of which are within the mandate of governments to address (Table 8.6).

TABLE 8.6 US CleanTech Investors' Perspectives on Governments and Sector Investment Drivers

(in per cent)

Proportion of investor respondents agreeing with the statements below	
Proactive environmental public policy can drive new CleanTech business to a state or region.	84
Current federal policies w.r.t. CleanTech affect the likelihood of investing in CleanTech companies.	72
High energy prices are an important influence on investment decisions.	
Investors who rate this factor critical.	45
Investors who rate this factor important.	41
Public awareness of climate change is second largest critical/important influence on investment.	79

Source: Stack (2007).

India's government initiatives are stimulating innovation by bringing in international models, adapting them to domestic conditions and promoting homegrown responses. From the Energy Conservation Act of 2001 to the National Action Plan on Climate Change and the National Mission on Enhanced Energy Efficiency (NMEEE), agencies and regulators have been established, codes and standards defined, and additional institutional support extended to public, private, and civil society participants in energy efficiency. Most government initiatives seem to be stimulating competition and increasing penetration across sectors, as illustrated by these key examples:

- The NMEEE plan aims to stimulate ESCOs, utilities, municipalities, and financial institutions with fiscal instruments, a programme to trade energy savings certificates, a partial risk guarantee fund to support commercial bank lending, a venture capital fund to capitalize ESCOs, establishment of a state-owned ESCO and project facilitator (Energy Efficiency Services Limited—EESL), a resource centre for public information, and voluntary passenger car fuel economy labelling.
- BEE has mandated energy audits, created building, and appliance rating systems (for example the Energy Conservation Building Code or ECBC) and generated public information and sectoral guidance on energy

efficiency. As part of this, new government buildings are being built according to green and energy efficient standards, and pilots of retrofits of existing government buildings and schools are under way. A CFL replacement programme is also being run nationwide (see Box 8.1 below).

Box 8.1

Monetizing India's Compact Fluorescent Lamp Replacement Initiative[28]

India's countrywide compact fluorescent lamp (CFL) bulb replacement programme, the Bachat Lamp Yojana (BLY), has won UN approval to make it the world's largest carbon credit project under the Clean Development Mechanism (CDM) of the Kyoto Protocol. With at least 1.4 million CFL bulbs already distributed and most Indian states, except in the northeast, developing their own programmes, the BEE is taking aim at India's 400 million incandescent light bulbs.

Converting to CFLs could reduce over 6,000 MW in electricity demand and 40 million tonnes (MT) of carbon dioxide per year (one tonne per lamp replaced) by exchanging 60W and 100W incandescent bulbs for 11–25W and 20–25W CFLs respectively. Despite a positive pilot experience by BESCOM in Bangalore,[29] the high price of CFLs versus incandescent bulbs (8–10 times) still drives a wedge in sales[30] (Graph 8.1 below) as do poor-quality bulbs, shortcomings in standards and labelling, and embryonic customer awareness. As a result, India's household CFL penetration remains under 10 per cent.

CFL vs. Incandescent Bulbs Market Volume (2007)

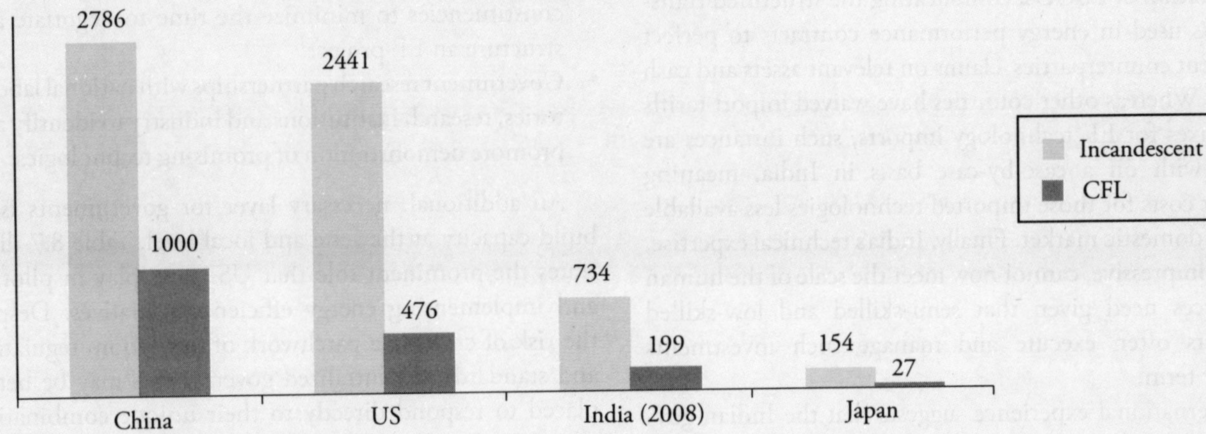

Sources: Sasi (2010) and IEA (2010).

The programme is meant to attract both domestic manufacturers and carbon credit investors. While suppliers sell to households at subsidized prices (Rs 15 per CFL bulb versus Rs 130 otherwise), sales are aggregated as CDM projects to generate carbon credits for reducing CO_2 emissions. Investors earn these credits by financing the gap, and aggregation eliminates due diligence on each transaction, facilitating CDM investors' capacity to generate returns on investment. Limited data suggest that domestic CFL production has experienced a compound average growth rate of 52 per cent with 58 per cent average annual growth of total consumption from 2005–8, so uptake should be promising with appropriate incentives and information.[31]

Despite its potential, the challenges faced by such projects elsewhere include public awareness, education, and distribution, especially in rural areas. Subsidy-setting (average: 40 per cent–60 per cent), other incentives (for example, for marketing) and private sector partnerships (as with retailers, distributors, suppliers, and utilities) are all key success factors.[32] Labelling and testing also need to mitigate the problem of low-quality bulbs undermining confidence.[33] Potential supply chain bottlenecks and their impact on price also must be monitored. Finally, even though CFLs diminish demand for polluting electric power and bring down the production of greenhouse gases and other pollutants, the mercury content of CFL bulbs poses environmental threats from uncontrolled disposal in large quantities. Given the size of India's programme, credible recycling efforts must be put in place.[34]

[28] Except where noted otherwise, information about the BLY program is cited from Sasi (2010) and Ghosh (2010).

[29] The BESCOM Efficient Lighting Programme indicated peak demand savings of up to 13 MW, as well as insights about information, marketing, and market distribution mechanisms.

[30] International Energy Agency (2010b) provides comparative sales volume data for 2007.

[31] Author's calculations and USAID–ASIA (2009).

[32] USAID–ASIA (2009).

[33] Most similar programmes (92 per cent) experienced less than 5 per cent quality failure rates. USAID-ASIA (2009).

[34] CFLs contain only small amounts of mercury (1.4–2.5 mg/bulb). Energy Star, the US agency in charge of standards and labelling for energy efficiency, estimates that if all 290 million CFL bulbs sold in 2007 went to a landfill instead of recycling, they would add 0.16 metric

- The IREDA's energy efficiency lending cushions early business development costs and buffers non-performance risk. It also aims to propagate models across sectors and passes them on to financial institutions to commercialize.
- TERI's GRIHA standards and the BEE's ECBC-adapted US and the European green building codes to Indian conditions, addressing energy resources, end uses, intermediaries, user types, and climate variation.

Despite India's comprehensive approach, certain structural challenges under government purview may act as brakes on progress towards energy efficiency goals.The power cross subsidy for agriculture undermines this mission, wasting power and water while delivering poor service. India's weak legal system also limits the market penetration of ESCOs, complicating the structured transactions used in energy performance contracts to perfect different counterparties' claims on relevant assets and cash flows. Whereas other countries have waived import tariffs and taxes for EE technology imports, such instances are dealt with on a case-by-case basis in India, meaning higher costs for those imported technologies less available in the domestic market. Finally, India's technical expertise, albeit impressive, cannot now meet the scale of the human resources need given that semi-skilled and low-skilled workers often execute and manage such investments longer term.

International experience suggests that the Indian government at all levels can further influence price signals, lower risk perception, disseminate information, stimulate knowledge creation, and develop human resources. The following observations derived from international experience (with examples in Table 8.8) illustrate the range of government roles in promoting efficiency:

- Restructuring electricity markets toward real-time and time-of-use pricing.
- Deploying IT-enabled measurement and management tools (for example, smart meters, building automation).
- Rebates, subsidies, and tax credits for residential and commercial EE investment, such as subsidized loans for purchase of CFLs.
- Grants for knowledge creation and training resources, both online[35] and on-the-ground.[36]
- Tax credits for process improvements such as combined heat and power generation.
- Procurement reform, such as lists of environmentally preferable services, suppliers, and goods.
- Legislation to promote performance contracting by sub-national entities.[37]
- Centralized information resources providing standardized contract terms for specific types of projects and constituencies to minimize the time to negotiate and structure an EE project.
- Government research partnerships with national laboratories, research institutions and industry to identify and promote demonstration of promising technologies.

An additional, necessary layer for governments is to build capacity at the state and local level. Table 8.7 illustrates the prominent role that US states play in piloting and implementing energy efficiency initiatives. Despite the risk of creating a patchwork of legislation, regulation and standards, decentralized governments may be better placed to respond directly to their unique combination of geographic, economic, social, and political conditions helping to develop best practice and share lessons from experience for other states and local governments.

Finally, moving beyond codes, compliance and enforcement are a universal challenge to governments in developed and developing countries alike, one that combines soft (for example, training, awareness) and hard (for example, permits, inspections) elements.[38] Recent legislative events in the US may be instructive for India given the latitude

tonnes or 0.16 per cent to existing mercury emissions, which come largely from coal-fired electric power. That said, the environmental consequences are not negligible; incineration, an oft-used means of managing garbage, is strongly discouraged, and disposal of broken bulbs requires extreme care.

[35] Finland has even sponsored a computer game that tests players' ability to transport themselves across the country through multiple modes of transport with the lowest carbon footprint (IEA Energy Efficiency Policy Database (www.iea.org/textbase/pm/index_effi.asp).

[36] A recent example is the US' Green Jobs Act of 2007, which includes funding to establish job training programs; to collect, analyse, and provide data about green jobs and skills; to link R&D in CleanTech industries to job standards and educational curricula; and create 'pathways out of poverty' through occupational training, support services for workers in training, especially veterans, displaced workers, and at-risk young people.

[37] Goldman et al. (2005) suggests allowing multi-year financial commitments, contracting based on 'best value' and life-cycle assessments, social investment hurdles, and maximum payback times.

[38] In light of the varied activities, only some of which can be matched with revenues, funding comes from a range of sources in most countries, including permit and inspection fees, government grants, energy efficiency funds, and new governmental and non-governmental groups.

TABLE 8.7 US Financial Incentives for Energy Efficiency

	Personal Tax	*Corporate Tax*	*Sales Tax*	*Property Tax*	*Rebates*	*Grants*	*Loans*	*Bonds*	*Green Building*
Federal	2	4	0	0	0	2	4	0	0
State	13	8	9	6	936	56	205	3	18
Totals	15	12	9	6	936	58	209	3	18

Rules, Regulations, and Policies for Energy Efficiency

	Appliance/Equipment Standards	*Energy Standards for Public Buildings*	*Building Energy Codes*	*Public Benefits Funds*
Federal	1	1	0	0
State	13	50	53	23
Totals	14	51	53	23

Source: Database of State Incentives for Renewables and Efficiency. http://www.dsireusa.org

that Indian states have in developing policy. In this case, state governors accepted funding for energy efficiency activities through the economic stimulus in return for commitment to adopt residential and commercial building codes consistent with or exceeding internationally agreed codes, as well as to develop and implement a plan with training and enforcement provisions to achieve 90 per cent compliance with codes by 2017. Yet, progress and compliance at the highest decision-making levels appears to be falling short.[39]

Even with policy implementation shortcomings at the highest levels, the working level insights from US municipalities and counties can surely be adapted across other sectors. Agencies in charge of implementing building code plans have found that non-compliance has come from lack of training about efficiency standards, confusion about specific implementation requirements, skepticism about the business case for energy efficiency, and failure to keep up with code changes. Indeed, the best way to simplify enforcement and minimize the high cost of enforcement action is to emphasize compliance through intensive training, communication, outreach, regular inspections, and ongoing evaluation.[40]

For India, the process has only just begun, and the current phase is more targeted towards ensuring the participation of stakeholders across industry, public sector, professional services providers, and others. The emphasis in the NMEEE is on transforming markets, building manpower, mandating norms, training energy auditors and managers, and strengthening state-designated agencies. Current enforcement, in the building sector, for instance, is meant to be by local code and implementation and certification by independent accreditation agencies. No doubt a long road lies ahead.

THE ENERGY EFFICIENCY INSTITUTIONAL LANDSCAPE: SPURRING INNOVATION THROUGH DIVERSITY

Where large-scale energy efficiency efforts, government enabling, and appropriate economic signals converge, new markets are evolving. Business opportunities are spinning out of policy, technology, finance and economic development, yielding improved efficiency, lower costs for end users, attractive returns on investment, and climate change adaptation. Sector specialization is already visible across utilities, materials, and capital goods manufacturers, controls and technology companies, service providers, and others. Bolstering ties between these market agents—across disciplines—is necessary to help the institutional ecosystem

[39] In fact, 14 major stakeholders in building energy efficiency in the US have expressed their concern that very few US states have moved forward to live up to their commitment (Alliance to Save Energy 2009). Indeed, one interviewee in the United States insisted 'building glass boxes is illegal in New York, but somehow they keep building these buildings with expensive and energy intensive glass curtain walls'.

[40] The City of Seattle's Department of Planning and Development has an intensive design screening process and dialogue with the design team to match its aim of 20 per cent energy savings above current ASHRAE standards. Staff and inspectors receive regular training and offer training sessions to the building community to cover specific aspects of the code and code changes. They also produce memos and handouts, as well as manning a technical hotline. In Dakota County, Minnesota, the permitting and inspection teams regularly evaluate major projects to communicate widely the business case for energy efficiency, as well as conducting independent reviews and regular periodic post-occupancy evaluations. (REEEP, ASE, and ACORE 2010).

Table 8.8 Governments' Varied Roles in Building Energy Efficiency Industries

Intervention	*Objectives*	*Examples*
Legislation–Regulatory Framework–Institutions	• Vision/strategy, mandates, and goal setting for public buildings, facilities management, energy use, and procurement • Commitment setting for GHG reductions • Authority to agencies, states, and municipalities to carry out and implement EE and resource conservation initiatives • Power sector deregulation, electricity pricing rationalization, requirements for utility demand side management (DSM), metering, and reporting • Development of energy savings performance contracts • Protection of and legal reform for intellectual property rights • Judicial reform for transparency, regulatory review, and enforcement • Financial reform for FDI, structured finance, investment funds, etc.	Germany National Energy Efficiency Action Plan CA Global Warming Solutions Act *New York Appliance and Equipment Energy Efficiency Standards Act
Standards definition	• Government building, facilities management and energy use, renovation and new commercial and residential building standards • Appliance, equipment and materials rating, and labelling • Efficiency and emissions standards in transportation	Washington DC—all new development to be LEED and Energy Star
Fiscal Policy	• Taxes on carbon, VAT, energy use, etc. • Import tariff exemptions for EE and clean energy technologies • Tax credits, accelerated depreciation for EE investments	EU energy/electricity tax minimums Multiple countries—Accelerated EE investment depreciation Belgium residential EE tax credits Australia rail transport tax credits Indonesia import duties and VAT holiday, loss carry forwards
Financial Incentives	• Grants and loans for energy savings efforts • Support to venture capital, commercial credit, and environmental finance markets (subsidized and market) • Low interest credit for export of EE technologies and services (developed countries) • Subsidies for green commercial and residential mortgages • Public benefits funding (via user taxes/surcharges) for DSM, research centres, technology/R&D programmes, and international partnership programmes • Rebates for energy efficient behaviour or distributed generation	CA Public Utilities Commission's Self-Generation Incentive Programme Japan New Energy and Industrial Technology Development Organization (NEDO) CA state pension funds Green Wave investment initiative Alberta Canada residential rebates Mexico subsidies and low interest loans for CFL purchases
Information	• Energy usage, EE technologies, co-investment opportunities • Institutional networks and linkages with public, private, and civil society entities	France ADEME Espace Info-Energie Germany Initiative Energie Effizienz
Other	• Skills and leadership development programmes (training, recognition, etc.) • Institutional networks and linkages with public, private, and civil society entities, both domestic and international • Streamlined permitting, approval and procurement processes	US Green Jobs Act 2007

Notes: CA = California. ADEME = Agence de l'Environnement et de la Maitrise de l'Energie (www.ademe.fr). *New York's Appliance and Equipment Energy Efficiency Standards Act of 2005 is unusual in setting energy efficiency standards that will have a substantial impact on residential buildings' energy use by addressing vampire electricity demand and appliances not included in federal regulations.

Source: IEA Energy Efficiency Database (http://www.iea.org/textbase/pm/index_effi.asp), Stark et al. (2007).

evolve (Figure 8.1).[41] Sector-specific convening platforms, consensus-building, policy consultation, training/education and research opportunities are all well tested.

The Indian government is targeting specific institutions (for example, utilities) and building stronger links between them and groups of end users, attempting to stimulate infrastructure providers to innovate with ESCOs, commercial banks, and specialized funds. Institutional ties across other actors, like legal services and manufacturing companies, are growing via hands-on project engagement. Other segments that play to India's core strengths can be nurtured, among which IT-enabled energy efficiency products and services (for example, building controls and smart grid technologies) and sustainable building materials from India's consumer, industrial and agricultural waste stream.[42] Likewise, human capital and technical capacity has to be built at the state and municipal levels, in civil society, in academia, and in the semi-skilled and low-skilled workforce to ensure that energy efficiency penetrates past elite decision-makers.

Real business opportunities are necessary to draw the range of service industries—law, finance, consulting, investments, media, and information providers—into market responses for infrastructure. Legitimizing energy management as a profession and discipline will be helped by increased compliance and code enforcement mechanisms, for instance. The following brief tour of the institutional landscape first touches on the positive role ESCOs can play but also suggests additional institutional routes to promote energy efficiency beyond them.

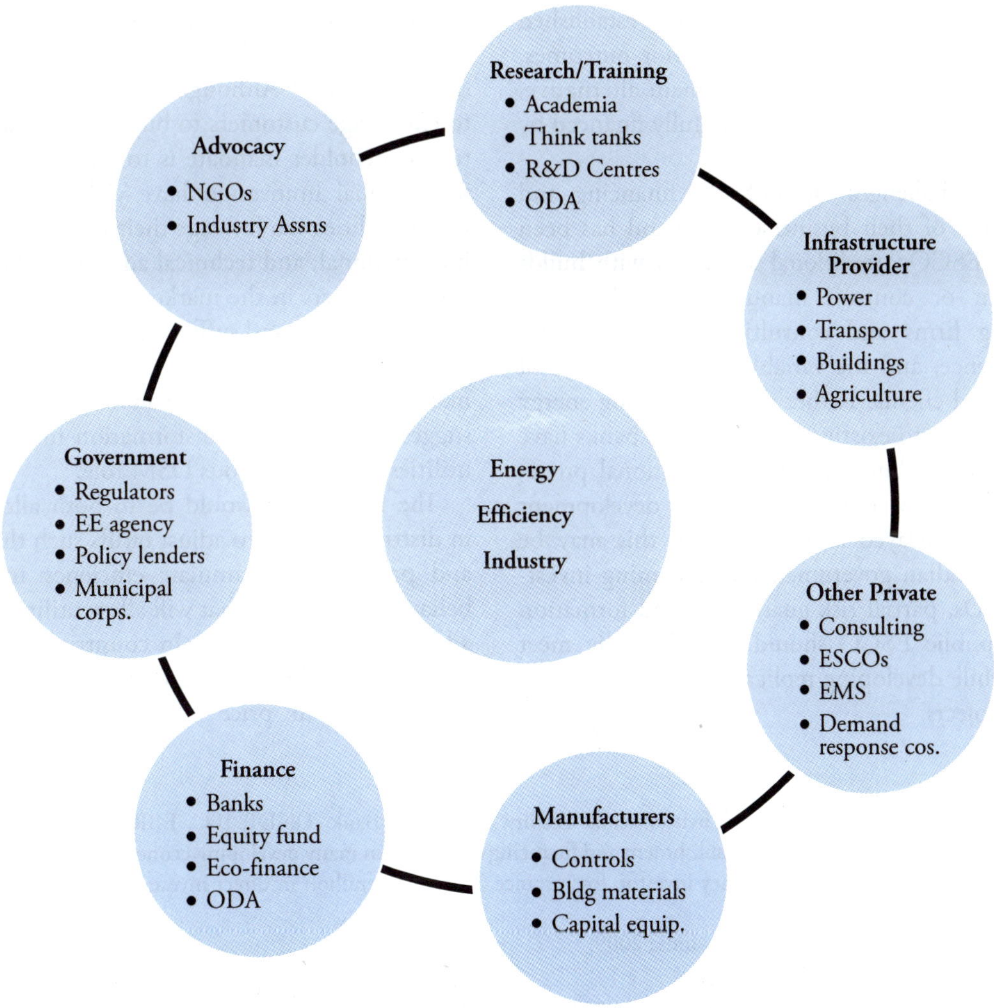

FIGURE 8.1 The Institutional Ecosystem of the Energy Efficiency Industry

[41] In fact, Taylor et al. (2008) suggests that advancing EE is primarily a question of institution building.

[42] As an example, the Confederation of Indian Industry's Green Business Centre showcases environmentally responsible domestic (and foreign) products and services, such as high fly ash content bricks or bagasse office furniture.

Energy Service Companies (ESCOs)

Pioneers of energy performance contracting, ESCOs are a policy darling because of their prevalence and success in varied markets.[43] Their competitive advantages rest on three characteristics—specialization in energy management, ability to aggregate projects, and expertise in delivering complete turnkey projects of technical advisory plus financing. ESCOs' significance in infrastructure has focused primarily on buildings and lighting so far, 36 per cent of their business in India,[44] and well-managed ESCO-led projects have had short payoff times (as short as 1–2 years), solid IRRs, and low risk profiles.[45] In a shared savings model, a well-capitalized ESCO eliminates up-front project costs for the client by putting up its own capital or a loan arranged by the ESCO. The ESCO then shares energy savings with the client according to performance, absorbing shortfalls below established benchmarks as well as surpluses for superior outcomes. A guaranteed savings model, the other main alternative, is fee-based and performance driven but fully financed by the client.[46]

ESCOs face challenges on both the financing and the demand side of their businesses. Demand has been dampened by ESCOs' traditional affiliation with building equipment or controls manufacturers, the entry of engineering firms and consulting companies with limited experience, and the variable creditworthiness of both ESCOs and clients. Rather than integrating energy efficiency lending into existing business lines, banks have hesitated to develop lines of credit, institutional procedures, and staffing for ESCO deals. State development funds have been delayed as well, though this may be changing. The Indian government's forthcoming investments in ESCOs, partial risk guarantees, and formation of a captive public ESCO should hypothetically meet these needs while developing replicable models for more challenging projects.

Among the drawbacks, ESCOs' limits are being tested in ways that may preclude their widespread use and penetration into smaller projects. Lack of trained personnel, difficult transactions, and a challenging contracting environment can be addressed through other institutional avenues while the ESCO sector develops. Disputes over energy savings measurement suggest information problems and needed capacity building to conduct due diligence, monitoring, and loss control. Standardizing and streamlining ESCO deals would make a welcome contribution, but so too would consideration of how to best leverage existing institutional infrastructure like utilities for demand side management, academia and NGOs for training and monitoring, and other models for new ventures.

Utilities

Demand side management (DSM) and active load management present both competitive hurdles and opportunities for utilities.[47] Although it may appear counterintuitive to encourage customers to buy less electricity while utilities' shareholder mandate is to sell more, incentives and institutional innovation have yielded success stories in which utilities can leverage their financial, organizational, informational, and technical advantages better than most existing players in the market. These successes assume an organized sector and sufficient generating capacity whereas in India, the continued neglect of the power sector in many states, ongoing power shortages, and load shedding suggest that market transformation must occur prior to utilities playing a serious DSM role.

The ideal route would be to both allow open access in distribution and to adjust tariffs such that competition and price signals stimulate efficiency investments and behavioural changes that will allow utilities to offer value-added efficiency services. In countries adopting time-of-use or real-time pricing, as well as distributed generation, the increase in price volatility and the lower price

[43] Programmes financed by the Global Environmental Facility, the World Bank, UNDP, IFC, EBRD, IADB, and other overseas development agencies have supported the establishment and financing of ESCOs in many developing economies. The Global Environment Facility (GEF) is the primary energy efficiency investor, for instance, with $850 million in direct investment in 90 countries and nearly $6 billion in co-financing (GEF 2009).

[44] World Resources Institute, New Ventures India 2009.

[45] Ibid.

[46] Types of performance-based contractual agreements include guaranteed savings, shared savings, pay-from-savings, and asset ownership/chauffage. Non-performance-based approaches include design/build, fee-for-service, and fixed price contracts. For detailed descriptions of these contract types, refer to Goldman et al. (2005).

[47] Demand side management is a cooperative efforts between utility and consumers to conserve energy and/or to optimize electricity demand to manage around utilities' peak loads. Active load management practices allow the utility to shift precisely quantified loads for relatively specific periods of time to accommodate explicit needs. The first is generally in the customer's control, while the second is more utility controlled.

transparency have raised demand for efficiency services. In India, by contrast, the persistent cross-subsidy to households and agriculture precludes adjustment, leading to wasteful water and electricity use. Limited metering and measurement also diminishes this potential.

With adjustment in tariffs and competition, DSM programmes may have more potential, but they must nonetheless be low cost, offer high savings potential, ensure revenue neutrality to utilities, and be market viable. For instance, the level of rebates must adequately reflect the present value of the savings, and subsidies on items like CFLs have to encourage sufficiently high participation. Without much experience and little information about costs of DSM programmes in India, pilots will be necessary to benchmark programme costs.

Even without adjustments, the commonly used means of incentivizing utilities' participation work is by decoupling electricity sales revenues from efficiency goals, allowing recovery of lost revenues through other charges. In India's case, the bottleneck is so intense that utilities scarcely face a competitive threat as any power saved is immediately consumed by another underserved consumer. Still, performance incentives specifically for utilities can be mandated by government. Utilities can be offered financial incentives for reaching savings targets and performance targets, a share of benefits derived from joint efficiency initiatives with consumers or higher rates of return on efficiency investments (for example, smart metering or CHP). Discounts and rebates can also be offered with funding from public benefits charges, but the potential impact of this practice may be dampened by only making utilities indifferent to efficiency.

In a more competitive environment, utilities can also sell new DSM business lines like equipment, advanced information tools (for example, smart meters), weatherization, and energy audits. Demand response incentives can be funded by rebate programmes, which utilities may also earn revenue to administer.[48] Despite the potential, incumbent utilities in the US and Europe have bumped awkwardly towards a more competitive environment. Increased savings, consumer choice, and value-added services have been small comfort to utilities slow to adjust.[49]

Demand Response Companies

These companies offer smart grid-like benefits to business and residential customers. The energy savings are realized through IT-enabled monitoring tools that remotely manage, guarantee, and compensate for service reductions in peak demand conditions. The customers get new information about their energy use, and the demand response company optimizes their draw on the grid. While the US's positive experience came partly from economic stimulus measures, the promotion of smart grids and meters fuelled a burst of investment in home energy management companies. Even if widespread distribution of home energy management systems are unlikely in India, promoting the capacity to remotely curtail demand and give users greater control over their consumption would be desirable to optimize electricity usage during peak load times while giving consumers choice.

Energy Management Companies (EMCs)

EMCs roll the ESCO concept into a range of services like procurement, logistics, price risk management, data and information services, demand response management, carbon management, and site development—essentially a one-stop energy management solutions provider driven by information technology tools. Unlike ESCOs, financing is a less common activity. EMCs can lower risk and costs for of energy users by negotiating among utilities, optimizing natural gas transportation, buying bulk energy, analysing energy use and new or existing infrastructure projects. EMCs have also proven successful in linking water, wastewater, and effluent management to energy management services. Of course, a key observation is that uncertainty, volatility, and heightened competition in deregulated and rationalized energy markets drives the business opportunity.

Niche Financial Intermediators

Specialized environmental finance institutions in many countries, not unlike IREDA in India or other development finance institutions, have become more diverse, offering debt, equity, and project aggregation through funds. As energy efficiency projects with highly specific project parameters require creative structuring backed up by either long experience or standardized process and documentation, firms focusing on environmental markets have begun to create a niche. As aggregators, they can specialize in carbon credits or affordable housing, for instance, lengthening financing tenors and securing lower rates for projects. They can also administer funds and programmes, as for green mortgages and home weatherizing, on behalf of municipalities and public agencies.

[48] Galbraith (2010).

[49] In France, for example, a dispute between Electricite de France (EDF) and Voltalis, an upstart demand management company, caused EDF to demand compensation from Voltalis for revenues lost to energy efficiency.

Non-governmental Organizations

NGOs work successfully with government, utilities, financial institutions, and energy companies to propagate energy efficient practices on the ground, fill information gaps, and reduce risk perception of new technologies. They can act as the missing link between utilities and successful DSM programmes, lessening the conflict of interest for utilities. By penetrating economic segments not reached by ESCOs and EMCs, NGOs can boost the adoption of zero cost and low-cost energy saving measures and administer funds targeting marginalized groups like farmers or low-income city dwellers. NGOs also help fill education and training gaps. At the other end of the spectrum, industry and trade associations, like the Confederation of Indian Industry and the Federation of Indian Chambers of Commerce and Industry (FICCI), provide services (for example, audits, training), data and information, policy advocacy, and certification programmes. A third type of NGO supports municipalities in ESCO-like projects, training and supporting local government partners, advising on equipment, coordinating audits, assisting with documentation and other roles, the result of which is a better trained municipal work force, more credibly implemented projects, and easier project replication.[50]

Financing Vehicles: Matching Form and Structure to Market Gaps

Financing for energy efficiency projects in developing economies has improved over recent years as models are integrated from developed countries and adapted to local realities. These financing structures essentially attempt to diminish the emphasis on first costs in evaluating investments that result in energy savings. The most easily accessible means of financing energy efficiency projects—internal balance sheet financing, plain vanilla commercial credit, and vendor finance—are all available in India to the creditworthy entities who can easily internalize the entire risk and return of an energy efficiency project.[51] Not so for entities with capital constraints.

This leaves out the majority of energy efficiency projects due to their small size and institutional complexity. Commercial banks are a major source of finance for energy efficiency projects in developed markets, along with ESCOs and other niche financial intermediators. By contrast, Indian commercial banks have shied away due to the transaction intensive process. Further, only the largest ESCOs are sufficiently capitalized to kick start the market with shared savings contracts. The government's answer includes partial risk guarantees for banks, equity for ESCOs, and formation of a captive public ESCO.

Despite being more complex, structured finance (see Figure 8.2) has promoted access to energy efficiency finance for projects not suited to the plain vanilla finance options. These models rely on the ability to ring-fence cash flows from the project, as opposed to the borrower, matching and directing those cash flows to debt service. Customized structures can accommodate varied sizes, terms, and sponsorship. They can be implemented by non-bank financial and non-financial institutions, in addition to ESCOs, vendors, and commercial banks. Aggregation of smaller projects can also make them investible. Importantly, varied vehicles can be used to create legal claims on the relevant assets for counterparties. Ultimately, credit is enhanced by removing exposure to the balance sheet of the end user, sometimes with features like partial credit guarantees and reserve funds.

Whether these innovations lower borrowing costs and improve project terms is debatable. Progress in India has been slow despite government efforts in the policy, regulatory, and institutional spheres. Interest rates remain high and transaction costs steep. Structuring is time consuming and complex despite experimentation with creative financial structures.[52] Disputes over project results and savings measurement run afoul of the inadequate contracting environment. These challenges and those that follow can hamper financing and the willingness to invest in the energy efficiency business:[53]

- Limited recourse finance from commercial lenders is constrained, and project finance aimed at reducing operational cash flows is unusual.
- Matching operational cash flow reductions with debt service relies on the service provider's expertise in energy

[50] Alliance to Save Energy (http://www.watergy.net) is an international NGO with a programme called WATERGY in six developing countries that focuses on the nexus between energy and water use efficiency.

[51] Large hotels, for instance, have taken up energy efficiency projects readily, financing them on their own balance sheets or with plain vanilla commercial lending. The economics for hotels may improve by aggregating services and procurement over more hotels, or they may gain additional competitiveness by internalizing learning from implementation.

[52] Kehew et al. (2005) discusses IREDA's innovative financing structures, as well as those of the state of Tamil Nadu.

[53] The experiences of ICICI, SBI, and Canara Banks have been little documented, but the constraints they faced in attempting to build EE financing businesses include complex loan structures, legal hurdles, and lack of institutional capacity (Selman 2002).

Box 8.2
Structured Finance and Risks in Energy Efficiency Finance

Key Elements of Structured Finance for Energy Efficiency Projects

- Appraisal, definition of savings measures, and baseline measurement
- Integrity of the valuation of assets
- Isolation of cash flows
- Clear identification and distribution of risks
- Credit enhancement features
- Matching of cash flows to debt service
- Ongoing measurement, monitoring, and verification
- Performance payments (if included)

Best Case: Finance providers get paid 'automatically' via project cash flows.

Worst Case: Finance providers get paid via claims on assets.

Selected Risks in Energy Efficiency Finance

Legal	Intricate structuring of claims on cash flows and assets Systematic monitoring Incentives and guarantees
Technical	Definition of energy savings measures Consistent calculation of life-cycle costs versus first costs Technology choice and appropriateness Credible and mutually agreed measurement and verification protocols Standardized savings benchmarks and measurements
Human	Technological expertise of service provider Multi-stakeholder planning and implementation Motivation and training of employees
Financial	Valuation of equipment, anticipated energy savings, and credit enhancement Counterparty default and personal guarantees of sponsors
Institutional	ESCO experience consistency with project complexity Bank structuring and loan monitoring capacity, integration with other business Guarantee facility levels, leverage, and administration

Source: Author's own.

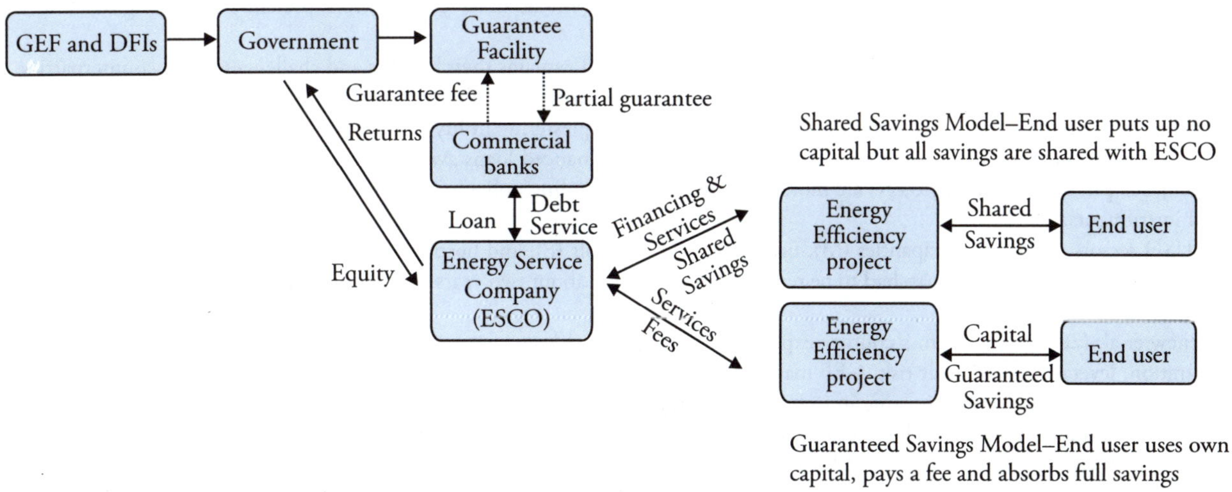

FIGURE 8.2 Promoting ESCOs to Deliver Energy Efficiency Services

Sources: Selman (2002); Kehew et al. (2005); Eckel (2008); Taylor et al. (2008); and Hamilton (2009).

savings projection and measurement.[54] The challenge of measuring savings calls for clear definition of project elements, savings expectations, financing terms, and measurement and monitoring arrangements, all of which difficult for non-technical staff to monitor.

- Standardized documentation and structuring templates do not yet exist.[55] Finance providers must exercise creativity in structuring obligations, project risk, and claims on assets and cash flows.[56] Project collateral may also not be normally separable and saleable in case of failure or default.
- The small size of many projects may not attract institutional interest, especially relative to the complexity of the financing. They also compare poorly with rapid growth and high returns in more straightforward sectors of bank credit portfolios.[57]
- Lengthy planning in the lead-up to financing and implementation are common in sectors with complex budgeting or bureaucratic decision-making.[58]
- End users can be reluctant to offer the credit enhancements demanded by commercial banks (for example, personal guarantees, real property collateral).
- Large, experienced, and well-recognized equipment and controls companies may extend full recourse vendor finance to their most creditworthy clients, limiting the penetration of energy efficiency improvements and potentially covering a single or very narrow set of energy efficiency investments.
- Tradeoffs in the quality of the equipment or the vendor based on cost can amplify project risks due to technical inexperience or lack of understanding of the end user's business.
- Partial risk guarantees may not incentivize sufficient due diligence and monitoring due to the level of guarantees set or lack the technical expertise within the implementing authority. Guarantee facilities can take on too much leverage and amplify default probabilities.[59]

The diagram above (Figure 8.2) illustrates the basic elements of structured finance for energy efficiency with ESCOs as the delivery mechanism. Key elements of this plan include:

- The ESCO's role as a specialized entity using energy performance contracts to define energy efficiency projects, to achieve energy savings for clients, and to 'pool' projects within its portfolio;
- Two delivery models, shared savings and guaranteed savings, differing by (1) the end user's commitment of capital and (2) the formula by which savings are shared and the end user avoids or delays upfront capital expenditures and capital budgeting decisions;[60]
- Commercial banks as a source of debt capital to ESCOs, either lending to the end user, to the ESCO for multiple projects, or to the project, in which case debt service would be matched to savings, with a claim on the residual value of the equipment or plant in case of default;[61]
- The availability of a funded by GEF or another development finance institution partial risk guarantee, for which the bank pays a fee and receives security in knowing that some percentage of the portfolio is covered; and
- Government capitalization of the ESCO with equity for which the ESCO will pay shareholder returns.

[54] In fact, these measurement functions rely on not just ESCOs but also energy auditors. Although there are training and accreditation programmes in India, concerns about energy auditors' competency and the accuracy of their work present a stumbling block to ESCO development and energy efficiency projects in general (WRI 2009).

[55] Maclean (2008) thoroughly models several financing structures and explains their benefits and challenges for all counterparties.

[56] More senior claims on assets, such as with buildings, make structuring difficult. Cities are now promoting energy efficiency in the residential sector by establishing a first lien through property taxes or sequestering utility payments.

[57] Projects mentioned in WRI (2009) start at $12,000 while GEF-financed loans average $6.5 million, substantially larger than most ESCO projects, primarily because projects are more comprehensive, including policy/regulatory frameworks, standards and labelling, and financial instruments.

[58] MUSH sectors include municipalities (M), universities (U), schools (S), and hospitals (H). Selman (2002) for instance, discusses a project with IREDA in which the loan had to be rescheduled twice over about two years because of difficulties defining the project and its component elements.

[59] Kehew et al. (2005) discuss cross country experiences with partial risk guarantee facilities and how guarantee levels can affect their administration, leverage, and default risk. GEF manages the risk of sub-optimal guarantee facility administration by taking the first loss position in the capital stack while investing in technical assistance and institution building (GEF 2009).

[60] The most common projects of this profile have been in the MUSH sector (municipalities, universities, schools, and hospitals) and among SMEs. In a guaranteed savings model, the ESCO carries the entire risk of the project success in return for fees. The guarantee is rarely for the entire amount of the estimated savings to ensure that the end user is likewise invested in a positive outcome. Different formulae for sharing savings can tilt the ESCO's reward to later years.

[61] Debt can still be partial or full recourse requiring other guarantees, such as personal or bank guarantees or other real collateral. If lending to the ESCO, the ESCO's credit will be evaluated rather than the project.

Box 8.3
A Tradable Energy Efficiency Certificates Market

India's soon-to-be-launched market for tradable energy efficiency certificates is another market-oriented innovation to mitigate India's output of GHGs and pollution and avoid new installed capacity. The potential size of the BEE's new Perform, Achieve and Trade (PAT) proposal is pegged at Rs 740 billion ($16 billion) in five years.[62] The envisaged savings of 10,000 MW per year is enough to power Delhi and Mumbai combined, reducing energy use by 7 to 8 per cent—10 million tonnes of oil equivalent and avoided capacity addition of 5,623 MW.[63] The exchange traded system may help India meet its target of cutting carbon intensity by as much as 25 per cent from 2005 levels by 2020.[64] Although power plants and railways are the only infrastructure sectors included in this first stage of the programme, improvements across other energy-intensive inputs, such as cement, iron, and steel, will diminish the embedded energy in large-scale infrastructure.

The basic plan mimics carbon trading. Efficiency targets will be derived from sector consumption and efficiency measurements, standards and targets.[65] Companies reducing their energy consumption within three years earn 'white certificates' and can sell their credits to those missing their targets. The BEE is advancing the enabling amendments to the 2001 Energy Conservation Act to develop the market for tradable energy certificates.

Similar programmes have had mixed success, albeit with different structures. A 2008 study of European schemes found that trading energy efficiency was effective only in Italy.[66] Otherwise, companies were more interested in their own energy efficiency competitiveness and disincentivized by the potential of competitors benefiting from their austerity or innovation. Likewise, focusing on energy supply vs. distribution and involving a monopoly supplier had less impact than hoped.

In India's case, diversification across industries may mitigate these effects. Most importantly, as with carbon caps, the most pressing incentives for change come from strict caps to cut energy use.

The advantage of structured finance is the ability to accommodate varied credit relationships, aggregation, and enhancement features. End users can be private or public. The ESCO could hypothetically be any institution performing specialized energy management services. The commercial bank's involvement can depend on comfort and creditworthiness. The first charge on cash flows in case of default may come from a reserve fund capitalized through varied means, including a public benefit charge, utility bills, property tax collections or grant funds—or a personal guarantee.

A final word on the following particularly innovative international experiences in energy efficiency project finance would emphasize the importance of matching institutional form and financial structure to market realities:

- *Pooling bonds and funds* for infrastructure and energy efficiency helped states and municipalities to aggregate smaller residential, commercial, lighting, and other urban efficiency projects into larger loans or bonds with credit enhancements such as first liens on properties and utility payments.[67, 68] Municipal lighting ESCO projects funded by the Tamil Nadu Urban Development Fund (TNUDF) helped the state tap domestic capital markets. Later with this kick start, urban local bodies were able to refinance these credits through commercial means.[69]
- *Energy saving insurance (ESI)* has evolved to respond to disputes over baseline measurements and subsequent realized energy savings in ESCO projects.[70] ESI has been found to yield high quality projects with careful, independent monitoring at a lower cost than a guaranteed savings model. Insurers' intense scrutiny to avoid underperformance and litigation is seen by the insured as reducing the perceived complexity of the projects. ESI may help smaller ESCOs become more

[62] Pearson (2010).

[63] *The Hindu Business Line* (2010)

[64] Pearson (2010).

[65] Sasi (2010).

[66] Mackenzie (2010).

[67] The basic model below is being adapted and adjusted in several municipalities and counties in the US, Berkeley, California among them. This structure has allowed municipalities to deliver financing to residents and businesses for approved EE building improvements.

[68] MacLean (2009) discusses several experiences that apply this model, referring specifically to the retrofit of low cost housing blocks in Eastern Europe, with extensive reference to the particular complexities of financing multi-family housing projects.

[69] The TNUDF Scheme created a hard credit culture but also had sufficient credit enhancement for investors due to a conservatively capitalized reserve fund and revenue offset capacity vis-à-vis government transfers in case of non-payments (Kehew et al. 2005)

[70] Energy savings insurance has received little research attention despite its apparent value in certain circumstances. Although insurance companies indicate that ESI is a product in their environmental and energy business lines, Mills (2003) is one of the only analyses.

competitive even with sub-optimal access to finance. Downside protection may encourage deeper efficiency initiatives beyond the 'low hanging fruit'. While ESI may not suit the Indian market in the same form as in the US and Canada, loss control, reinsurance and independent external project monitoring would be welcome in India. DFIs or policy banks could mimic certain ESI features with independent safeguards, quality assurance measures, additional staff training or other project modules to protect investments in ESCOs, and shore up client perception.

- *Tax-exempt municipal leasing* in the US is a common tool to facilitate cities' access to finance for energy efficiency projects as the tax exemption on municipal interest income lowers the investment hurdle rate and broadens the pool of potential investors. Cities can also bypass the capital budgeting process, absorbing energy savings that are structured to exceed lease payments.
- *Revolving loan funds for small-scale energy efficiency projects* provide low cost loans for energy efficiency from zero interest capital on-lent by the government to commercial banks or other counterparties. Those entities in turn take the default, marketing and business risk. Thailand's government experienced no defaults on four funds, losing only the time value of money vs. the loans' average payback periods of 2.4 years. The Municipal Network for Energy Efficiency's revolving funds in Armenia leveraged seed funds of no more than $1000 into small interest free loans of $500–600 with six month repayment. Low income families weatherized and insulated exteriors and fixed plumbing, reporting greater physical comfort, lower energy bills, and health and social benefits.[71]
- *Energy efficient or green mortgages* in the US carry lower interest rates to reflect energy efficiency improvements in new home construction, allowing home-buyers to pay for energy efficient elements over time. These mortgages also build recognition in residential markets of energy efficient labelling.

The takeaway is that transparent, well designed, and effectively implemented energy efficiency projects can be incubated with disciplined performance expectations but credit enhancement and later submitted to market hurdle rates and agents when institutions fill specific market gaps—the need for better M&V, risk management, industry specialization, or deal aggregation.

Box 8.4

State Energy Conservation Funds and Partial Risk Guarantee Funds

The Energy Conservation Act of 2001 requires states to identify State Designated Agencies (SDAs) to develop and implement the Energy Conservation Action Plan (ECAP). One key element of the ECAP is that states must also establish State Energy Conservation Funds (SECF) to finance energy efficiency programmes and programme management costs.[72] States will have to chip in for these funds in order to receive support from the BEE, which has pledged a total of Rs 70 crore for the initiative.

These agencies and facilities, of which Kerala's EMC and recently formed Kerala SECF (KSECF), are likely to grow in future with increased state level buy-in and capacity, regulatory evolution, donor or commercial bank funds, carbon credits, and electricity surcharges.[73] The KSECF's activities, for instance, will include underwriting financing mechanisms like subsidies for energy audits and partial risk guarantees to stimulate commercial funding of conservation projects. SECFs will also play a visible role in encouraging ESCOs, training energy users and managers, and increasing awareness of energy efficiency.

State Energy Conservation Funds' Energy Savings

Programme year	*Savings (MW)*	*Target Avoided Capacity (MW)*
2007–8	126.78	126.78
2008–9	660.43	500

Sources: India BEE.

The BEE's programme includes implementing a partial risk guarantee fund to compensate for the financial sector's reluctance to underwrite energy efficiency. The level of government guarantee is critical. Too low a rate discourages the financial sector's participation and fails to cover the business start-up costs. Too high a guarantee rate discourages due diligence and monitoring.

[71] MUNEE (2006).
[72] BEE (2009).
[73] Limaye (2008).

Final Observations

India is poised to enjoy the potential of energy efficiency as its cheapest route to energy security, a vehicle for transitioning to a low carbon economy, a way of improving health and livelihoods, and an engine of growth and competitiveness. Models from abroad are already being shaped to Indian realities in technology, government, institution building, and financing. Specialization, diversification, and replication are creating a burgeoning market.

Barriers on both the supply and demand sides have to be removed. The government must commit to sustained effort to encourage uptake of efficiency measures through policy, regulation, and demonstration. India's access to energy efficient technology should be advanced much as the country's domestic capacity to innovate and compete as a solution provider. Fostering collaboration and competition among service providers and investment delivery mechanisms is also a key to increasing choice and access to energy users. The institutional ecosystem is already populated by organizations whose networks and infrastructure can be leveraged to nurture energy efficiency agents of all sizes. Communication, information, recognition, training, and technical assistance are all tools for stimulating both 'push' and 'pull'.

The following areas stand out for special attention:

- The limited supply of and poor quality of data and information on energy efficiency in India undermines efforts to make the economic case for efficiency.
- Investment opportunities must be nurtured in the energy efficiency industry. While government and external resources can be used to develop and demonstrate innovative projects, the financial support and credit enhancement must be applied with market discipline and hard budget constraint to transition these energy efficiency investments to fully market-driven investment vehicles.
- Government should remove barriers and relieve price distortions while maintaining a neutral view on institutions, recognizing that a diverse institutional environment may distribute the needed efficiencies more evenly.
- The opportunity to test the edge of the policy and regulatory envelope should be embraced. The government has to lead in setting standards, enforcing codes, educating for energy efficiency at all levels, building and procuring, and communicating with the public.

References

Alliance to Save Energy (ASE) (2010). 'Renewable Energy and Energy Efficiency Partnership (REEEP) and American Council on Renewable Energy (ACORE) (2010)', *Compendium of Best Practices: Sharing Local and State Successes in Energy Efficiency and Renewable Energy from the United States*, Washington DC.

——— (2009). 'Nation's Leading Building Energy Efficiency Experts Clarify ARRA Funding Ties to State Energy Code Adoption And Enforcement', Washington DC.

Bertoldi, P. and S. Rezessy (2005). *Energy Service Companies In Europe: Status Report 2005*, European Commission DG Joint Research Center, Ispra, Italy.

Bureau of Energy Efficiency (2009). Briefing Note on the *National Mission on Enhanced Energy Efficiency*, Ministry of Power, Government of India, New Delhi.

——— (2009). 'The Action Plan for Energy Efficiency', available at http://www.bee-india.nic.in/useful downloads.php

Broido-Johnson, Claire (2009). 'Municipal Energy Financing', Conference on the American Recovery and Reinvestment Act (ARRA) of 2009: Innovative Energy Efficiency Financing Approaches, Department of Energy, Energy Efficiency and Renewable Energy Program, Washington, DC, June.

Chadha, Mridul (2010). 'India launches energy conservation fund, aims at saving 25,000 MW', *CleanTechnica.com*, 20 March. http://cleantechnica.com/2010/03/20/india-launches-energy-conservation-fund-aims-at-saving-25000-mw/

Commission of the European Communities (2006). 'Action Plan for Energy Efficiency: Realizing the Potential', European Commission, Brussels.

Cooper, Mark (2009). 'A Consumer Analysis of Energy Efficiency and Renewable Energy Standards: The Cornerstone of Consumer-Friendly Energy/Environmental Policy,' Consumer Federation of America, Washington DC.

Du Pont, Peter (2007). 'International Survey of CFL Program Experience', USAID-ASIA, presented at the regional workshop: *Confidence in quality: eliminating shoddy CFL products within ASEAN countries*, October. http://www.efficientlighting.net/doc/20071114(10).pdf

Eckel, Jeffrey (2008). 'Innovative Financing Structures and Business Models', 2nd Annual Energy Efficiency Finance Forum, Arlington, VA, April 2008.

Ehrhardt-Martinez, Karen and John A. Laitner (2008). 'The Size of the U.S. Energy Efficiency Market: Generating a More Complete Picture', American Council for an Energy-Efficient Economy (ACEEE).

Environmental Fiscal Reform for Poverty Reduction, Organisation for Economic Co-operation and Development, Paris, 2005.

EnergyManagerTraining.com, (2010). 'CFL lighting scheme—Bachat Lamp Yojana', http://www.energymanagertraining.com/CDM/cdm_main.htm

Energy Sector Management Assistance Program (2009). 'Large Scale Residential Energy Efficiency Programs Based on CFLs'. http://www.esmap.org/esmap/sites/esmap.org/files/216201021421CFL Toolkit Web Version 021610 REVISED.pdf

Enigin.com (2010). 'India Launches Initiatives Promoting Energy Efficiency' *32* March. http://www.enigin.com/about/enigin-plc/news/-/enigin-news-india-launches-initiatives-promoting-energy-efficiency

Galbraith, Katie (2010). 'Why is a Utility Paying its Customers?' *New York Times,* 23 January.

Ghosh, Padmaparna (2010). 'CFL gamble pays off, UN okays project', LiveMint.com, 2 May. http://www.livemint.com/2010/05/02203913/CFL-gamble-pays-off-UN-okays.html

——— (2007). 'Govt's CFL power saver plan trips over ownership of subsidy', *LiveMint.com,* 2 August 2007. http://www.livemint.com/2007/08/02235951/Govt8217s-CFL-power-saver-p.html

Global Environment Facility (2009). *Investing In Energy Efficiency: The GEF Experience.*

Goldman, C., N.C. Hopper, and J.G. Osborn (2005). 'Review of US ESCO Industry Market Trends: An Empirical Analysis of Project Data,' *Energy Policy*, 33, pp. 387–405.

Goldman, C. (2003). 'Overview of US ESCO Industry: Recent Trends and Historic Performance,' *International Workshop On Energy Efficiency Services Industries*, Shanghai, China, 8 September, pp. 1–33.

Hamilton, Kirsty (2009). *Energy Efficiency and the Finance Sector*, UNEP Finance Initiative Climate Change Working Group.

International Energy Agency (IEA) (2007). *World Energy Outlook 2006*, Paris.

——— (2008). *World Energy Outlook 2007*, Paris.

——— (2010a). *World Energy Outlook 2009*, Paris.

——— (2010b). *Phase out of Incandescent Lamps*, Paris.

Intergovernmental Panel on Climate Change (2000). *Methodological and Technological Issues in Technology Transfer: A Special Report of IPCC Working Group III.*

Kehew, Robert, Tomoko Matsukawa, and John Petersen (2005). *Local Financing for Sub-Sovereign Infrastructure in Developing Countries: Case Studies of Innovative Domestic Credit Enhancement Entities and Techniques*, World Bank Infrastructure, Economics and Finance Department, Washington, DC.

Limaye, Dilip R. (2008). *Establishment of the Kerala State Energy Conservation Fund.* Eco Asia Clean Development and Climate Program, November 2008.

Lawrence Berkeley National Laboratory Environmental Energy Technologies Division (2005), available at http://hes.lbl.gov/consumer/profitable

McKinsey & Company (2009). *Unlocking Energy Efficiency in the U.S. Economy.*

Mackenzie, Kate (2010), 'Why efficiency schemes and markets don't always mix', *The Financial Times*, 15 January. http://blogs.ft.com/energy-source/2010/01/15/why-efficiency-schemes-and-markets-dont-always-mix/

Maclean, John (2008). *Mobilizing Commercial Financial Institutions for Energy Efficiency and Small-Scale Renewable Energy Finance In Developing Countries: Financial Products, Program Designs, and Scale-Up Strategies*, Kfw Financial Sector Development Symposium.

Mills, Evan (2003). 'Risk Transfer via Energy-Savings Insurance,' *Energy Policy*, 31, pp. 273–81.

MUNEE (2006). *Alliance to Save Energy—Armenia, Municipal Network for Energy Efficiency, Yerevan, Armenia.*

Municipal Network For Energy Efficiency (2006). *Building Energy Efficiency Revolving Fund Program in Gumri, Vanadzor and Maralik*, Bureau of Energy Efficiency, available at http://www.bee-india.nic.in.

Padmaparna Ghosh (2010). 'CFL gamble pays off, UN okays project', *LiveMint.com,* 2 May.

Pearson, Natalie (2010). 'India Plans $16 Billion Energy-Saving Credit Market', *Bloomberg.com,* 14 January http://www.bloomberg.com/apps/news?pid=20601130&sid=ajp7FRqhqF4k

Phadke, Amol A., Jayant A. Sathaye, and S. Padmanabhan (2005), *Economic Benefits of Reducing Maharashtra's Electricity Shortage Through End-Use Efficiency Improvement*, Ernest Orlando.

Rand Corporation (2007). *The Public Benefit of California's Investments in Energy Efficiency*, 2000.

Renewable Energy and Energy Efficiency Partnership (REEEP), Alliance to Save Energy (ASE), and the American Council on Renewable Energy (ACORE) 2010. *Compendium of Best Practices: Sharing Local and State Successes in Energy Efficiency and Renewable Energy from the United Sates.*

Salman (2002). *Central Electrical Authority data through March 2010*, Ministry of Power, New Delhi.

Sasi, Anil (2010). 'Carbon Credits to Subsidize Lamp Cost—CFLs to Switch off Incandescent Bulbs Nation-wide', *The Hindu Business Line,* 1 May 2010 http://www.thehindubusinessline.com/2010/05/02/stories/2010050252080101.htm

——— (2000). 'Govt. to Fix Targets for Saving Energy, Issue Tradable White Certificates', *The Hindu Business Line*, 2 May 2010. http://www.blonnet.com/2010/05/03/stories/2010050351900100.htm

Sathaye, Jayant A., Stephane De La Rue Du Can, Satish Kumar, Maithili Iyer, Christie Galitsky, Amol Phadke, Michael Mcneil, Lynn Price, Ranjit Bharvirkar, and

S. Padmanabhan (2006). *Implementing End-use Efficiency Improvements in India: Drawing From Experience in the US and Other Countries*, Ernest Orlando, Lawrence Berkeley National Laboratory Environmental Energy Technologies Division.

Selman, Sanford J. (2002). 'Focus On Commercial Banking Windows', Proceedings of UNF/UNEP/World Bank Project: Developing Financial Intermediation Mechanisms for Energy Efficiency Projects in Brazil, China, and India, Fort Aguada Beach Resort, Goa, India.

Sharma, Rakesh (2007). 'India's CFL Makers Boost Capacity as Demand Soars', *LiveMint.com*, 4 September 2007. http://www.livemint.com/2007/09/04150617/India8217s-CFL-makers-boost.html

Stack, James (2007). *Cleantech Venture Capital: How Public Policy Has Stimulated Private Investment*, Environmental Entrepreneurs, Cleantech Venture Network LLC.

Taylor, R.P., C. Govindarajalu, J. Levin, A.S. Meyer, and W.A. Ward (2008). *Financing Energy Efficiency: Lessons from Brazil, China, India, and Beyond*, World Bank, Washington, DC.

The Hindu Business Line (2010). 'Government to Fix Targets for Saving Energy', 2 May.

USAID–ASIA (2007). 'International Survey of CFL Program Experience: Responses from 26 programs in 14 countries'. http://www.efficientlighting.net/doc/20071114(10).pdf

——— (2009). 'Phasing in quality—harmonization of CFLs to help Asia address climate change'

Vestel, Leora, and Tom Zeller (2009), 'The Future is not so Bright', *LiveMint.com,* 31 March 2009. http://www.livemint.com/2009/03/31212332/The-future-is-not-so-bright.html?h=B

Vine, E. (2005) 'An International Survey of The Energy Service Company (ESCO) Industry', *Energy Policy* 33, pp. 691–704.

Waide, Paul (2010). 'Phase Out of Incandescent Lamps—Implications for International Supply and Demand for Regulatory Compliant Lamps', *International Energy Agency (IEA) Information Paper,* April. http://www.iea.org/publications/free_new_Desc.asp?PUBS_ID=2256

World Resources Institute (2009). *Powering Up: The Investment Potential of Energy Service Companies in India*, Washington DC.

9 International Trading of Emission Rights

Its Implications for Low-Carbon Growth in India

Vijay P. Ojha

Introduction

Developing countries, including India, have been absolved of any responsibility towards reducing emissions in the first commitment period, that is, 2008–12, of the Kyoto Protocol. This is not surprising as India's per capita carbon dioxide (CO_2) emission is very low: only 1.36 tonnes per annum, which is less than one-third of the world average per capita emission of 4.39 tonnes per annum.[1] However, in absolute terms, India is the fifth largest emitter of fossil fuel-derived carbon dioxide, and its total emissions are growing rapidly. India is now under severe international pressure to accept binding commitments for emission reduction in the post–2012 phase of the Protocol, which it has managed to evade for the time being, as evinced at Copenhagen in December 2009. Interestingly, however, realization has deepened among social commentators, activists, and even policymakers that it would be in India's own interest to aspire and plan for a low carbon economic growth in the coming three or four decades. This chapter is inspired by this view, even though it deals with the implications for international trading of emission rights for India.

The Kyoto Protocol includes three mechanisms, namely (i) international emission trading (IET), (ii) Joint Implementation (JI), and (iii) Clean Development Mechanism (CDM) to achieve GHGs emissions reduction most efficiently, that is, in the least cost manner. The latter two are referred to as 'project-based mechanisms' in that they generate emission reductions from projects. The difference between IET and the project-based mechanisms is that the former is contingent upon the setting of a quantitative restriction on emissions, while the latter are predicated on the idea of 'production' of emission reductions (regardless of whether there are emissions reduction targets or not). The JI has been formulated to encourage production of emission reductions in Annex-I (developed) countries,[2] while CDM is meant to promote production of emissions reduction in non-Annex-I (developing) countries. The development and operation of qualified CDM projects produces Certified Emissions Reductions (CERs) for the actual amount of emissions reduction achieved in the host developing country, which can be sold privately (voluntary primary market) or traded internationally in the secondary carbon emissions market.

However, notwithstanding the overlap across the three mechanisms, we are concerned here exclusively with cap-and-trade under IET. As of now, IET is of concern to Annex-I countries only. But it is most unlikely that the situation would remain that way, that is to say, the way

[1] These figures are taken from World Bank (2010).

[2] Annex-I countries refer to the OECD countries, the countries in Central and Eastern Europe, and the Russian Federation, which have agreed to emissions reduction obligations under the Kyoto Protocol. The specific emissions reduction commitments of these countries are listed in Annex-I of the Protocol, hence they are referred to as Annex-I countries.

climate policy stances of the Annex-I and the non-Annex-I countries are evolving, the latter group of countries will not remain mere bystanders for long. Indeed, in all likelihood, the developing countries would have a major role to play in the ongoing negotiations on climate change. As Chander (2004) cogently argues, 'they (developing countries) have a stake in the ongoing negotiations on the form and mechanism of emission trade. The negotiations on climate change should ultimately aim at fixing pollution rights or entitlements for each country according to some agreed upon equity principles, and the Kyoto Protocol can be and may be viewed as a step in this direction.' In other words, once emissions trade among Annex-I countries is institutionalized, the developing countries will be able to better assess the potential gains from such trade, and might be tempted to participate in a global emissions trade in the post-Kyoto phase of climate change negotiations.

If India were to participate in a global regime of tradable emission permits, how would the consequences for its economic and infrastructural growth be affected by the different modes of emission entitlements and what role can internal policy play in maximizing (or minimizing) the resulting gains (or losses)? Informed discussions are already taking place in Indian policy circles around this question. This chapter attempts to further analyse and estimate the *pros* and *cons* of the two main modes of allocation of emission permits, which represent the two opposing extremes of the range of emissions allocation schemes, which would most likely form the subject matter of a negotiation between the developed and developing countries. These two options at the extreme ends of the range of emissions allocation schemes are:

- Grandfathered Emissions Allocation (GEA) Scheme in which emission permits are allocated on the basis of the aggregate emissions level of a predetermined year (that is, the benchmark year), say 2010—which is 1546.44 million tonnes. Hence, under this scheme, the quota for aggregate emissions for each of the years in the period, 2010–40 is 1546.44 million tonnes, and
- Equal Per Capita Emissions Allocation Scheme (EPCEAS) in which the aggregate emissions entitlements for India for all the years are fixed at the level arrived at by multiplying the average global per capita emission (4.39 tonne per capita) with India's population for a benchmark year, say 2010—which is 1175.22 million. Specifically, this implies an aggregate emissions entitlement of 5159.22 million tonnes, that is, 4.39 x 1175.22—of CO_2 emissions for each of the years in the period 2010–40. It may be noted that by taking a *given* average global per capita emission and by applying the 2010 population figure to each of the future years, the aggregate emissions allocated is maintained at an unchanged level over the years. Such a *static* equal per capita emissions allocation scheme would, as argued by Parikh and Parikh (1998), ensure equity between the developed and developing countries, and, simultaneously discourage the latter from allowing unrestrained growth in their populations.

It is well known that the developed countries favour the GEA scheme. However, it is morally perverse (Joshi and Patel 2009), and, as we shall see, economically extremely damaging to the growth and poverty-reduction objectives of the developing countries (for example, India). Naturally then, the developing countries have been vehemently opposed to it.

The developing countries, particularly China and India, are ardent advocates of the EPCEA scheme. The EPCEA is morally principled, and as we shall see, also hugely beneficial to the growth and poverty-reduction objectives of the Indian economy. But it is consistently opposed by the developed countries, which typically have high per capita emission and would, under the EPCEA regime, have to purchase permits from the developing countries, most of whom have low per capita emission. Annex-I countries would thus end up yielding massive financial transfers to the developing countries under such a scheme. In other words, EPCEA, despite being ethically unassailable, may not be politically feasible.

From India's viewpoint, the two emissions allocation schemes, GEA and EPCEA, correspond respectively to the lower and upper bounds on the gains from participation in a global regime of tradable emission permits. Obviously then, a quantitative assessment of the lower and upper bounds of the range of outcomes emanating from India participating in an IET regime would be a valuable policy input.

Moreover, the role of a key internal (domestic) policy, namely, enhancing energy efficiency in the economy, which can run concurrently and complementarily with India's participation in IET, needs to be understood.

This chapter, therefore, analyses the impact of India's participation in IET with GEA and EPCEA on carbon emissions, GDP, infrastructural development, and poverty in the Indian economy for a 'normal' and then an 'enhanced' rate of energy-efficiency improvement (EEI), with the help of a neoclassical type price-driven Computable General Equilibrium (CGE) model capable of endogenously determining poverty, which is a major consideration in India. Additionally, with a view to drawing concrete policy implications, the chapter goes beyond the analysis of the modelling results, and specifically delves into the question of how much untapped potential there is in the Indian economy for the enhanced EEI assumed in select policy scenarios.

The rest of the chapter is organized as follows: an analysis of the results of four relevant policy scenarios with reference to the business-as-usual scenario, all developed through a CGE model of the Indian economy. This is followed by expounding on the issue as to how tangible measures can be undertaken to achieve increases in energy efficiency, and thus a low-carbon growth in India. The chapter concludes with suggestions related to policy implications of the results of the four relevant policy scenarios. The Appendix furnishes the data tables related to the policy scenarios.

Modelling the Policy Scenarios

A detailed description of the 11-sector CGE model used to generate the relevant policy scenarios mentioned here can be found in Ojha (2009).[3] Technical details, such as, equations of the model, parametrization, and data collection for the model, are furnished in Appendices 2 and 3 of Ojha (2005).

The CGE model for this analysis employs the basic data of the Indian economy for the year 1989–90, which have been sourced from the CSO-NAS[4] and the CSO–IOTT.[5] Other parameters and initial values of different variables have been estimated from the data available in various other published sources.[6]

Still other parameters such as the technological and the distribution parameters of the production functions employed in the CGE model are estimated using the method of calibration. The calibration method is a commonly used deterministic approach for calculating selected parameter values from a single-period benchmark 'equilibrium' data set.[7] Through calibration, certain model parameters are estimated in a CGE model on the basis of a single observation. While this is a definite shortcoming of this approach, the overwhelming advantage is that it enables the replication of the benchmark equilibrium data set, which is required for the validation of the CGE model solution (Shoven and Whalley 1992).

A difficulty was encountered in finding a reliable estimate for the rate of EEI in the Indian economy. Energy-saving technological progress is incorporated in our model by making the autonomous energy efficiency improvement (AEEI) assumption used in other carbon emission reduction models, such as General Equilibrium Environmental Model (GREEN); (Burniaux et al. 1992) and Emissions Predictions and Policy Analysis (EPPA); (Babiker et al., 2001).[8] As in the EPPA and GREEN models, we also assume that AEEI occurs in all sectors except the primary energy sectors (coal, crude petroleum, and natural gas) and the refined oil sector. The GREEN model assumes a one per cent annual increase in energy efficiency, while in the EPPA model there is an even higher annual growth rate of energy efficiency, that is, 1.4 per cent initially, though it slows down over time according to a logistic function. However, we followed the GREEN model in assuming one per cent annual increase in energy efficiency, and found the model solution approximating reasonably well the observed data on sectoral and economy-wide energy use.

Finally, a sequence of equilibria based on a time series data of the exogenous variables—two primary ones being the aggregate real investment and the available labour supply—of the model is obtained for the period 1990–2040. From the sequence of equilibria, the growth paths of selected variables of the economy—such as, GDP, aggregate consumption, sectoral outputs, CO_2 emissions, and poverty ratio—with five-year time intervals, are delineated to describe the business-as-usual (BAU)/reference scenario. The policy scenarios are then evaluated with respect to the BAU scenario.

Using our Computable General Equilibrium model, we develop alternate policy scenarios for India's participation in IET under GEA and EPCEA, firstly, with normal (1.0 per cent) and, secondly, with enhanced (1.2 per cent) annual rates of growth in AEEI, for the 30 year

[3] There are five energy (infrastructural) sectors—electricity, coal, refined oil, natural gas, crude petroleum and six non-energy sectors—agriculture, transport, energy-intensive goods, other intermediates, consumer goods, and services.

[4] Central Statistical Organization—National Accounts Statistics (CSO–NAS) of India, various issues from 1989–90 to 1992–3.

[5] Central Statistical Organization (1997: Input-Output Transactions Table 1989–90) (CSO–IOTT).

[6] Full information on the data sources is available in Appendix 3 of the author's SANDEE working paper (Ojha 2005).

[7] Note that the data reported for the Indian economy in the CSO–NAS and CSO–IOTT are assumed to be representing equilibrium flows for the concerned year.

[8] Note GREEN and EPPA are respectively acronyms for General Equilibrium Environmental Model and Emissions Prediction and Policy Analysis.

period, 2010–40. In all, there are four policy scenarios, as mentioned earlier.

For the policy scenarios 1a and 1b, concerned with GEA, the emission quota is fixed for all the years at the (aggregate) emissions level of the year 2010,which is 1546.44 million tonnes at the annual rates of AEEI at 1.0 per cent and 1.2 per cent respectively. For the policy scenarios 2a and 2b, concerned with EPCEA, the emissions are capped for all the years at 4.39 tonnes per capita using the population in the benchmark year 2010, which amounts to an aggregate emissions level of 5159.22 million tonnes again at the annual rates of AEEI at the same per cent figures already mentioned earlier.[9]

The four policy scenarios are summarized in Table 9.1 given below.

It follows that, while the policy scenarios 1a and 2a are instrumental in defining the lower and upper bounds of the outcomes possible from India's participation in IET, the policy scenarios 1b and 2b serve to delineate what we may term as the augmented lower and upper bounds of the same.

Policy Scenario 1a

In this policy scenario, India participates in international emissions trading with GEA. Hence, its emissions quota is fixed at 1546.44 million tonnes—which is the 2010 level of CO_2 emissions in the BAU scenario—for all the years in the period 2010–40. However, there is scope for going beyond this limit through purchase of emission permits in the international market at the prevailing world market price, which would in effect induce a transfer of wealth out of India. In this scenario, India is a net buyer of tradable permits throughout the period, that is, 2010–40, as its CO_2 emissions after 2010 are far in excess of the fixed quota of 1546.44 million tonnes. Expectedly, GDP will decline as compared to the BAU scenario.

The GDP loss in scenario 1a relative to the BAU scenario over the 30 year period is in the range of 2.40 to 3.60 per cent. Taking a (simple) average of 30 years, GDP declines by 2.69 per cent (Table 9A.1). Infrastructural requirements diminish, and, therefore, outputs of the infrastructural sectors—electricity, coal, refined oil, natural gas, crude petroleum, and transport—decline over the 30-year period in the range of 2.5 to 5.5 per cent (Table 9A.2). Poverty increases significantly in scenario 1a. The number of poor people will increase by 3.11 per cent in 2015 and by 7.01 per cent in 2040 (Table 9A.1). For the whole 30-year period, the cumulative emissions will decline by 5.09 per cent (Table 9A.3).

In short, there are high costs imposed on the Indian economy due to losses in GDP, infrastructural outputs, and poverty reduction in case of its participation in IET with GEA based on India's 2010 emissions level.

Table 9.1 The Policy Scenarios

	Annual Rate of Energy Efficiency Improvement (in per cent)	*Policy Instrument*	*CO_2 Emission Restriction*
Policy Scenario 1a (GEA)	1.0	Internationally Tradable Permits	Total CO_2 emissions fixed at the 2010 level of emissions
Policy Scenario 2a (EPCEA)	1.0	Internationally Tradable Permits	4.39 tonnes CO_2 of per capita (*population of benchmark year 2010*)
Policy Scenario 1b (GEA)	1.2	Internationally Tradable Permits	Total CO_2 emissions fixed at the 2010 level of emissions
Policy Scenario 2b (EPCEA)	1.2	Internationally Tradable Permits	4.39 tonnes CO_2 of per capita (*population of benchmark year 2010*)

Note: Carbon emissions are (12/44) times the carbon dioxide emissions.

[9] To capture sensitivity of results to different permit price levels, each of the four scenarios are worked out for two alternate exogenously given permit price levels—(a) US$20 and (b) US$30 per tonne of carbon dioxide emitted, which is Rs 332 and Rs 498 per tonne respectively at the 1989–90 exchange rate of Rs 16.60 per dollar. But the results of the four scenarios—1a, 2a, 1b, 2b—reported here are for the permit price equal to US$20 per tonne of carbon emitted. In reality, the permit price will be determined within a global trading system of permits, which, for example, has been modelled by Ellerman et al. (1998) or by Edmonds et al. (1993) in the Second Generation Model (SGM). However, ours is a country-specific model concerned with how India is poised to gain or lose from an internationally tradable permits regime. Moreover, under the 'small-country' assumption, India's sale or purchase of permits does not affect the latter's world market price. For India, therefore, the world market price of permits can be treated as exogenously given (Fisher-Vanden et al. 1997 and Murthy et al. 2000).

Policy Scenario 2a

In this scenario, India participates in international emissions trading in partnership with EPCEA. Hence, the per capita carbon emission quota is fixed at 4.39 tonnes. This translates into an aggregate emission quota of 5159.22 million tonnes (that is, 4.39 times the 2010 population of 1175.22 million) for each of the 30 years, 2010–40.

The precise procedure followed in this scenario is to fix an upper limit of 5159.22 for total emissions. However, the upper limit on emissions becomes binding only in 2032 in this scenario. Till then, India has surplus emission permits which it sells in the international market. This leads to a transfer of wealth into India, which in turn boosts GDP and poverty reduction. Beyond 2032, the Indian economy turns around from being a seller to a buyer of emission permits in the international market. However, the GDP continues to be higher in comparison to those of the BAU scenario, even after this turnaround. This is mainly due to the higher capital stock with which the economy is endowed as a result of cumulatively larger accretions to this stock over the years in scenario 2a.

The gross domestic product gains in scenario 2a relative to the BAU scenario over the 30-year period are in the range of 5.50 to10.00 per cent. Taking the average for 30 years, GDP increases by 7.44 per cent (Table 9A.1). Infrastructural requirements increase, and, therefore, outputs of all infrastructural sectors rise over the 30-year period in the range of four per cent to 10 per cent (Table 9A.2). Poverty decreases significantly in scenario 2a. The percentage of poor people will decrease by 6.36 per cent in 2015 and by 1.62 per cent in 2040 (Table 9A.1). For the whole 30-year period, the cumulative emissions will increase by 6.18 per cent (Table 9A.3).

Further, India stands to gain substantially in terms of the gross domestic product, infrastructural development, and poverty alleviation, while maintaining its CO_2 emissions below the stipulated maximum till 2032.

Policy Scenario 1b

In this scenario, India participates in international emission trading with GEA, and concomitantly, enhances the energy efficiency in the domestic economy, so that the annual growth rate of energy efficiency increases from 1.0 per cent (which prevailed in the scenario 1a) to 1.2 per cent. Expectedly, GDP and other losses in this simulation will be of lower orders of magnitude, in comparison to policy scenario 1a.

The gross domestic product losses in scenario 1a relative to the BAU scenario over the three decades, 2010–40, are in the range of 2.00–3.00 per cent. Taking the average for 30 years, GDP declines by 2.25 per cent (Table 9A.1). Infrastructural requirements diminish, and, therefore, outputs of all infrastructural sectors—electricity, coal, refined oil, natural gas, crude petroleum, and transport—decline over the 30-year period in the range of 2.25 per cent to 3.50 per cent (Table 9A.2). Poverty increases significantly in this scenario and the number of poor people increases by 3.04 per cent in 2015, and by 5.32 per cent in 2040 (Table 9A.1). For the three decades, the cumulative emissions decline by 24.49 per cent (Table 9A.3).

Policy Scenario 2b

In policy scenario 2b, India participates in international emissions trading with the EPCEA scheme, and simultaneously, boosts its growth rate of AEEI from 1.0 per cent per annum (which prevailed in scenario 2a) to 1.2 per cent per annum. So, in effect, this simulation is nothing but a bolder version of simulation 2a. Significantly, the Indian economy remains a seller of emission permits in the international market all through the three decades, 2010–40, in scenario 2b.

The gross domestic product gains in this scenario relative to the BAU scenario over the three decades is in the range of 7.00–10.00 per cent. Taking the average for 30 years, GDP increases by 8.10 per cent (Table 9A.1). Infrastructural requirements increase, and, therefore, outputs of all infrastructural sectors—electricity, coal, refined oil, natural gas, crude petroleum, and transport—rise over the 30-year period in the range of 5.5 per cent to 10.0 per cent (Table 9A.2). Poverty decreases significantly in this scenario. The percentage of poor people decreases by 6.41 per cent in 2015, and by 3.79 per cent in 2040 (Table 9A.1). For the 30-year period, the cumulative emissions decrease by 15.90 per cent (Table 9A.3).

An Appraisal of Policy Scenarios

From the results of scenarios 1a and 1b, it follows that the lower bound and the augmented lower bound of (average) GDP gains from India's participation in IET are -2.69 per cent and -2.25 per cent respectively. The inference which is unequivocally implied is that India should shun outright any persuasion to partake in international emissions trading based on grandfathered emissions allocation.

Likewise, according to the results of scenarios 2a and 2b, the upper bound and the augmented upper bound of (average) GDP gains from India's participation in IET are 7.44 per cent and 8.10 per cent respectively. Clearly then, India should look forward to join IET with EPCEA.

Apart from the gross domestic product gains involved, another important aspect of the outcomes of the policy scenarios is the decline in carbon emissions achieved. In this regard, scenario 2a fails to a great extent, because the increase in GDP comes with an increase in emissions. Cumulative emissions for the 30-year period increase by 6.18 per cent in scenario 2a. So, scenario 2b is a real winner because not only are the GDP gains higher, but alongside there is a decline in cumulative emissions by 16 per cent. *This is a crucial result of our modelling exercise, because it highlights the paramount importance of the domestic policy of enhancing energy efficiency.* Not only does the latter play a vital role in reducing carbon emissions, but also helps in augmenting GDP gains by prolonging the period for which India remains a net seller of internationally tradable emission permits and allows us a greater bargaining power in any multilateral negotiation.

Energy-Efficient (Low Carbon) Growth in Infrastructure

In our appraisal of policy scenarios above, especially scenarios 2a and 2b, we have noted that EEI translates readily into carbon savings, thus enabling a low carbon economic (*read* infrastructural) growth, and at the same time enhancing GDP gains from its participation in international trading of emission rights with the equal per capita emission entitlements scheme. Motivated by the need to provide energy security to its people, India has already been engaged in efforts towards the promotion of energy efficiency in its economy much before global warming caused by anthropogenic emissions of GHGs became a burning issue. Hence, what is required under the present circumstances, wherein every nation is beckoned to ostensibly contribute to climate change mitigation, is that India intensifies its prevailing efforts towards EEI. It is, therefore, imperative that we make a broad assessment of the latent potential of EEI in the Indian economy, before drawing the relevant policy conclusions from our modelling exercise. To this we now turn.

Most (95 per cent) of the carbon emissions in the Indian economy are energy-related (Garg and Shukla 2002). At the same time, it is well established by now that coal will remain as the mainstay of India's commercial energy basket through the next two or three decades (TERI 2006; Rai and Victor 2009; and Chikkatur and Sagar 2009). This, however, does not bode well for energy security in the Indian economy because: (i) it is being realized that India's coal reserves are limited, which will not suffice for the existing and the prospective needs of thermal power plants over their lifetime, say 50 years,[10] (ii) coal prices in the future will rise due to higher cost of extraction from deeper domestic reserves and/or due to increasing import dependence in the most likely eventuality of increasing international coal prices, and (iii) poor quality of Indian coal (owing to high ash and moisture content and low calorific value), which is getting worse over time, resulting in an increasing amount of coal required to produce a given amount of electricity. In other words, the present technology and efficiency of India's thermal power plants is far below the internationally acceptable standards. This is manifested in the existing sub-critical pulverized coal technology of most Indian thermal power plants. It is obvious then that there exists immense scope for improving the energy efficiency and thereby lowering carbon emissions intensity (that is, carbon emissions per unit of output) in thermal power generation in the Indian economy.

The fly-ash contained in the coal mined in India acts as an insulator in the boiler, and reduces the heat transmitted from the burnt coal to the boiler tubes. All this considerably lowers thermal efficiency of the electricity generating process. Even a simple modification in the technique of thermal electricity production such as the use of clean coal, which is coal obtained after beneficiation—a process which filters out the ash content of the coal—will thus lead to a significant improvement in the thermal efficiency.

The clean coal technologies or the advanced thermal power technologies are deservingly high priority items in the policy agenda for energy-efficiency improvement in the Indian economy. It is heartening to note that the process of adoption of more efficient coal-power technologies such as ultra-super-critical (USC) and integrated gasification combined cycle (IGCC) has already begun. With some international cooperation, which India should not shy away from, this process can easily be intensified (Chikkatur and Sagar 2009).

Besides the power sector, there is scope for reducing coal-based energy in various energy-intensive industries such as steel, ceramics, brick kilns, and cement.

Energy security demands that oil-based energy also be economized in India to reduce the latter's high dependence on oil imports. Oil-based energy is mostly employed in the domestic transport sector and fortunately there is considerable scope for saving oil-based energy in this sector. Increasing the share of public transport and

[10] As per the Integrated Energy Policy (IEP) 2030 scenario of GoI (2006).

rail-driven locomotion, usage of alternative fuels such as CNG and energy-efficiency improvements in vehicles would lead to substantial energy savings translating readily into almost commensurate carbon savings.

In the 'residential and commercial' sector too, there exists huge scope for energy-efficiency improvement. Using efficient motors in space conditioning and replacing light bulbs and tube lights with CFLs will go a long way towards energy savings and consequent carbon savings. While desirable change in this direction is already taking place, the pace of improvement needs to be enhanced, which can be done easily if the government works proactively in the matter.

The above list of technological upgradations and improvements for enhancing energy efficiency is by no means exhaustive, but it does represent the larger part of the feasible set of energy-saving (climate-friendly) technological policy options in India.

A related question in the matter of energy-efficiency improvement is whether energy sector reforms are consistent with the effort directed towards technological upgradation with a view to boosting energy efficiency. The answer to this question is, in our view, in the affirmative.

Oddly, energy efficiency in India is found to be improving even in the pre-reform era—from 1970s to the 1990s—when state monopoly in production and underpricing of electricity was the order of the day. Measured in terms of $PPP, energy intensity in India declined from 0.28 toe/$1000 of GDP in 1980 to 0.19 toe/$1000 of GDP in 2002, a decrease of approximately two per cent per annum, which exceeds the world average reduction in energy intensity of 1.5 per cent during the period 1980–2002. Clearly, energy efficiency in this period was rising despite (and not because of) the bureaucratic control and management of the exclusively government-owned power sector. The decline in energy intensity in the country since 1970–71 (which got accelerated during the 1980s) has been in a large measure due to the increase in the share of commercial energy *vis-à-vis* non-commercial energy in total energy consumption. On an average, commercial energy sources are at least twice as efficient as non-commercial sources in the delivery of energy services. Moreover, the increasing service orientation of the Indian economy has contributed significantly to the decline in energy intensity (Ahluwalia and Goyal 2009).

It follows that if the trend of EEI was an ascending one within an energy sector subjected to all kinds of commands and controls all through the 1980s and 1990s, then with the initiation of reforms with the (new) Electricity Act, 2003 by the Indian Parliament (GoI 2003), the future in India holds in store even greater scope for EEI. It may be mentioned here that many critics of the reforms in the power sector do not tire of pointing out that these reforms do not go far enough to usher in a market-oriented environment in which efficiency is automatically and irreversibly promoted. But this is an extreme view. The fact of the matter is that, in an acutely energy-deficient economy such as India, the power sector cannot be entirely market-driven. Moreover, realistically speaking, the transition from a state-controlled monopolistic and monolithic power sector to a competitive, forward-looking, and dynamic power sector has to be a gradual one. The new liberalized policy regime for the power sector is after all still an evolving one. It has already taken a major stride forward by envisaging open access, by introducing greater transparency, a level playing field for both public and private enterprises, and by rationalizing the pricing policy for power. All these in themselves portend large gains for energy efficiency in the Indian economy. The clock is ticking towards the eventual emergence of a market-based energy sector, which will be the harbinger of even more rapid progress for energy efficiency in India.

Last, but not the least, the National Solar Mission to be launched under India's NAPCC and its forthcoming three-stage nuclear power programme, is bound to result in a major stride towards energy-efficiency improvement.

The host of energy-efficiency improvement measures outlined above, if implemented effectively, can enable India to benefit immensely from international trading of emission rights within a favourable emissions allocation scheme in which India turns out to be a net seller of emission permits for a considerably long period. Conversely, participation in international emissions trading based on such a beneficial emissions allocation scheme will provide the country with the much needed flow of funds from abroad, which in turn would facilitate its energy-efficiency improvement programmes. In other words, there is clearly a bilateral causation at work between international emissions trading and the promotion of energy efficiency in the Indian economy. The two will, in all likelihood, reinforce each other.

Caveats and Policy Guidelines

To the discerning reader, it would have already occurred that the bilateral causation between the pace of energy-efficiency improvement and the inflow of funds generated by the international emissions trading is not captured in our CGE model—the latter treats the rate of energy efficiency improvement as autonomous. In fact, overcoming this limitation of the model is the main motivation for including the extended discussion on the relation between the two earlier.

Moreover, the usual caveat about the results generated from a CGE model based upon restrictive assumptions, which may not hold in the real world, applies. However, the model is useful in giving an overall sense of the co-movement of the related variables in the business of policymaking for a low carbon growth in the Indian economy—that has valuable lessons for the policymakers (Bergman 2005).

In the context of international emissions trading, the first milestone to arrive at in the policy-maker's journey is a consensus on the type of emissions allocation scheme. As we have already seen, the EPCEA scheme, though a favourite of the developing countries, is unacceptable to the developed countries, and the GEA scheme, which the developed countries habitually propose, is doomed to outright rejection by developing countries. So, some thought has to be spared for 'intermediate' arrangements between these two extremes. Interesting suggestions on intermediate emission allocation regimes have been made by many analysts (Joshi and Patel 2009 and Jacoby et al. 2008). However, we have not undertaken a detailed evaluation of the various intermediate options on emissions allocation schemes for IET, with a view to identifying and recommending *the* best possible option for India.[11]

Instead, we will proffer a generic rule of thumb to evaluate the worth of an intermediate option from India's viewpoint. As we have seen above, the GEA for India implies a commitment to restrict total emissions for all years up to 2040 to 1547 million tonnes, the benchmark year being 2010. Similarly, under the EPCEA based on the benchmark population of the year 2010, India is obliged to maintain 4.39 tonnes of per capita carbon emission, which effectively translates into an upper limit on total emissions of 5159 million tonnes for all the years up to 2040. It is thus easy to see that with some effort, all conceivable intermediate emissions allocation regime options can be mapped on a continuum of total emissions commitment, beginning with 1547 million tonnes (GEA) and ending with 5159 million tonnes (EPCEA) for the next three decades for India, if the benchmark year is 2010. Proximity to the latter figure is what should incline Indian policymakers towards a proposed emissions allocation regime—which may not exactly be the equal per capita emissions allocation but something that is nearly the same—in the real-world bargaining.

Conclusion

Internationally pressurized or not, it would be in India's own interest to aspire and plan for a low carbon path of economic growth in the coming three or four decades. Planning for climate change mitigation in India should not rule out but in fact include the possibility of participating in a global regime of tradable emission permits. However, India should move cautiously towards its participation in such a regime, first by ascertaining that the international emissions trading regime is based either on equal per capita emissions allocation, or if that is not possible, on some criterion which comes close to it. Second, to reap the harvest of international emissions trading with equal per capita emissions allocation, India must be able to maintain the status of a net seller of emission permits for a long period of time. To ensure this, a proactive domestic policy drive for enhancing energy efficiency must be pursued concurrently with its participation in an international trading emissions regime. This will protract the period for which India remains a net seller of emission permits and amplify both GDP and poverty reduction gains. Most significantly, it will facilitate low carbon economic growth in the Indian economy, as energy savings transmute eventually into carbon savings. The other way round, participation in international emissions trading would generate an inflow of funds from abroad, which can be used for financing the energy-efficiency improvement programmes of the Indian economy. That is to say, participating in a global trading regime of emission permits and pursuing an energy-efficiency improvement programme at home are mutually supportive for India.

It follows that, by combining participation in an international emissions trading regime with faster energy efficiency improvement, not only will India reap handsome climate policy dividends by enabling low carbon growth in the domestic economy, but also significantly contribute to mitigation of global warming. This is truly a *win-win* policy scenario. If India can work towards a scenario like this, it can actually transform a crisis into an opportunity.

[11] In any case, such an exercise may well turn out to be futile, as the real world of bargaining is known to throw up surprises.

References

Ahluwalia, S.S. and A. Goyal (2009). 'Energy Efficiency and Conservation' in *Asian Development Bank: Energy Infrastructure, Priorities, Constraints, and Strategies for India,* Oxford University Press,New Delhi.

Babiker, M.H., J.M. Reilly, M. Mayer, R.S. Eckaus, I.S. Wing, and R.C. Hyman (2001). 'The MIT Emissions Prediction and Policy Analysis (EPPA) Model: Revisions, Sensitivities and Comparison of Results', Report no. 71, MIT Joint Program on the Science and Policy of Global Change, Cambridge, M.A.

Bergman. L (2005). 'CGE Modeling of Environmental Policy and Resource Management', in K.G. Maler and J.R. Vincent (eds), *Handbook of Environmental Economics,* Chapter 24, Elsevier.

Burniaux, J.M., G. Nicoletti, and J.O. Martins (1992). 'GREEN: A Global Model for Quantifying the Cost of Policies to Curb CO_2 Emissions', *OECD Economic Studies,* 19, Paris.

Chander, Parkash (2004). 'The Kyoto Protocol and Developing Countries: Strategy and Equity Issues', in Michael Toman, Ujjayant Chakravarty, and Shreekant Gupta (eds), *India and Global Climate Change: Perspectives on Economics and Policy from a Developing Country,* pp. 271–82, Oxford University Press, New Delhi.

Chikkatur, A.P. and A.D. Sagar (2009). 'Rethinking India's Coal-Power Technology Trajectory', *Economic and Political Weekly,* 14 November.

CSO–IOTT (1997). *Central Statistical Organization—Input-Output Transactions Table—1989–90,* Government of India, New Delhi.

CSO–NAS (various issues). *Central Statistical Organization—National Accounts Statistics (various issues from 1989–90 to 1999–2000),* Government of India, New Delhi.

Edmonds, J., H.M. Pitcher, D. Barns, R. Baron, and M.A. Wise (1993). 'Modelling Future Greenhouse Gas Emissions: The Second Generation Model Description', in Lawrence R. Klein and Fu-Chen Lo (eds),*Modelling Global Change,* pp. 295–362, United Nations University Press, Tokyo.

Ellerman, A.D., H.D. Jacoby, and A. Decaux (1998). 'The Effects on Developing Countries of the Kyoto Protocol and CO_2 Emissions Trading', Report No. 41, MIT Joint Program on the Science and Policy of Global Change, Cambridge, M.A.

Fisher-Vanden, K.A., P.R. Shukla, J.A. Edmonds, S.H. Kim, and H.M. Pitcher (1997). 'Carbon Taxes and India', *Energy Economics,* 19, pp. 289–325.

Garg, A. and P.R. Shukla (2002). *Emissions Inventory of India,* Tata McGraw Hill Publishing Company, New Delhi.

GoI (2006). 'Integrated Energy Policy: Report of the Expert Committee', New Delhi, Planning Commision, Government of India.

——— (2003). *Main Features of the Electricity Act (2003),* Ministry of Power, Government of India, http://www.powermin.nic.in/acts_notification/electricity_act2003/preliminary.htm

Jacoby, H.D., M.H. Babiker, S. Paltsev, and J.M. Reilly (2008). 'Sharing the Burden of GHG Reductions,' *The Harvard Project on International Climate Agreements, Discussion Paper, 2008–9.*

Joshi, V. and U.R. Patel (2009). 'India and a Carbon Deal,' *Economic and Political Weekly,* 45(31), August.

Murthy, N.S., M. Panda, and K. Parikh (2007). 'CO_2 Emission Reduction Strategies and Economic Development in India', *Margin: The Journal of Applied Economic Research,* 1, pp. 85–119, New Delhi.

Ojha, Vijay P. (2009). 'Carbon Emission Reduction Strategies and Poverty Alleviation in India,' *Environment and Development Economics,* 14(3), pp. 323–48 .

——— (2005). 'The Trade-Off Among Carbon Emissions, Economic Growth and Poverty Reduction in India', *South Asia Network for Development and Environmental Economics (SANDEE) Working Paper 12–05.* Also available on website: http://www.sandeeonline.org/publications/working_papers/wp12/

Parikh, J. and K. Parikh (1998). 'Free Ride through Delay: Risk and Accountability for Climate Change', *Environmental and Development Economics,* 3(3), pp. 295–317.

Rai, V. and D. Victor (2009). 'Climate Change and the Energy Challenge: A Pragmatic Approach for India', *Economic and Political Weekly,* August.

Shoven, J.B. and J.Whalley (1992). *Applying General Equilibrium,* Cambridge University Press, New York.

The Energy Resources Institute (TERI) (2006). *National Energy Map for India,* TERI Press, New Delhi.

World Bank (2010). *World Development Indicators,* The World Bank, Washington DC.

Appendix 9A

Table 9A.1 Policy Scenarios: Selected Macro-variables

	GDP (%age diff. from BAU Sco.)	*Cons. (%age diff. from BAU Sco.)*	*CO_2 Emissions (%age diff. from BAU Sco.)*	*Per Capita Emission based on 2010 popln. (in tonnes per capita)*	*Poverty Ratio (in per cent)*	*No. of Poor (in million)*	*No. of Poor (%age diff. from BAU Sco.)*
			Policy Scenario 1a				
2010	0.00	0.00	0.00	1.32	15.30	179.80	0.00
2015	–2.42	–2.71	–3.49	1.69	7.92	100.04	3.11
2025	–3.17	–3.94	–4.41	2.96	1.48	21.03	4.98
2035	–3.46	–3.82	–6.17	5.05	0.23	3.52	6.13
2040	–3.56	–3.99	–5.98	6.63	0.08	1.33	7.01
30-year average	–2.69	–3.06	–4.29				4.36
			Policy Scenario 2a				
2010	9.84	9.36	9.23	1.44	14.01	164.63	–8.43
2015	8.28	7.19	7.51	1.89	7.19	90.85	–6.36
2025	7.36	6.06	6.68	3.30	1.35	19.07	–4.79
2035	6.55	5.86	5.62	5.68	0.21	3.19	–3.63
2040	5.52	4.30	5.34	7.43	0.08	1.22	–1.62
30-year average	7.44	6.57	6.75				–5.04
			Policy Scenario 1b				
2010	0.00	0.00	0.00	1.32	15.30	179.80	0.00
2015	–2.18	–2.52	–6.06	1.54	7.92	99.97	3.04
2025	–2.78	–3.19	–14.46	2.20	1.47	20.82	3.94
2035	–2.86	–3.13	–28.73	2.93	0.23	3.48	5.12
2040	–2.47	–2.33	–41.85	3.01	0.08	1.31	5.32
30-year average	–2.25	–2.49	–17.46				3.69
			Policy Scenario 2b				
2010	9.84	9.36	9.23	1.44	14.01	164.63	–8.43
2015	8.48	7.31	3.98	1.83	7.19	90.81	–6.41
2025	7.87	7.09	–4.87	2.94	1.33	18.90	–5.66
2035	7.45	6.91	–19.96	4.21	0.21	3.16	–4.56
2040	7.40	6.88	–35.05	4.38	0.07	1.20	–3.79
30-year average	8.10	7.40	–8.37				–5.73

Table 9A.2 Policy Scenarios: Infrastructural Outputs

	GDP	Electricity	Coal	Natural Gas	Refined Oil	Crude Petroleum	Transport	Energy-Intensive industries
Policy Scenario 1a — *percentage difference from the BAU scenario*								
2010	0.00	0.00	0.00	0.00	0.00	0.00	0.00	0.00
2015	–2.42	–2.71	–3.06	–2.78	–3.07	–2.86	–2.94	–3.68
2025	–3.17	–3.54	–3.94	–3.60	–3.83	–3.58	–3.73	–4.41
2035	–3.46	–4.05	–4.59	–3.87	–4.15	–3.96	–4.05	–4.94
2040	–3.56	–4.31	–4.62	–3.84	–3.91	–4.25	–4.03	–5.03
30-year average	–2.69	–3.12	–3.56	–3.05	–3.14	–3.14	–3.12	–3.87
Policy Scenario 2a								
2010	9.84	9.43	8.80	9.55	9.24	9.50	9.15	8.81
2015	8.28	7.94	7.55	7.82	7.77	7.87	7.70	7.23
2025	7.36	6.82	6.35	6.87	6.67	7.05	6.98	6.24
2035	6.55	6.28	5.70	5.97	6.16	6.04	6.23	5.18
2040	5.52	4.98	4.38	5.29	4.89	5.07	5.11	4.04
30-year average	7.44	7.01	6.51	6.99	6.91	7.04	6.91	6.25
Policy Scenario 1b								
2010	0.00	0.00	0.00	0.00	0.00	0.00	0.00	0.00
2015	–2.18	–2.51	–2.57	–2.78	–2.74	–2.59	–2.51	–2.40
2025	–2.78	–3.18	–3.50	–3.29	–3.02	–3.14	–3.17	–3.12
2035	–2.86	–3.41	–3.12	–3.45	–3.14	–3.06	–3.16	–3.23
2040	–2.47	–3.09	–2.69	–2.83	–2.83	–2.87	–2.74	–3.22
30-year average	–2.25	–2.67	–2.60	–2.64	–2.65	–2.59	–2.58	–2.66
Policy Scenario 2b								
2010	9.84	9.51	9.25	9.26	9.18	9.33	9.17	8.19
2015	8.48	8.26	7.43	7.93	8.13	8.09	7.77	7.05
2025	7.87	7.23	6.72	7.41	7.27	7.21	7.60	6.27
2035	7.45	6.92	6.61	6.91	7.13	7.10	7.16	6.09
2040	7.40	6.73	6.47	7.19	6.80	6.88	7.11	5.81
30-year average	8.10	7.55	7.05	7.63	7.55	7.63	7.61	6.60

Table 9A.3 Cumulative CO_2 Emissions for the period 2010–40

(in million tonnes)

BAU Scenario	*29405.89*	*%age diff. from BAU. Sco*
Sco. 1a	27909.57	–5.09
Sco. 2a	31221.95	6.18
Sco. 1b	22203.36	–24.49
Sco. 2b	24730.47	–15.90

10 Moving Towards Low Carbon Economy: The Need for Renewable Energy Solutions

Part 1 Renewable Energy in India: Capability, Challenges, and Prospects

Ashish Garg, Manisha Gulati, and Nachiketa Tiwari

Introduction

In pursuit of its ambition of high growth with sustainable development, India faces the dual problem of securing large energy supplies while containing adverse environmental consequences within acceptable limits. Providing universal access to energy remains a continued challenge as does its evil twin, 'rising greenhouse gas (GHG) emissions'. A recent report by the GoI indicates that the power sector has emerged as the biggest culprit for GHG emissions, accounting for about 38 per cent of the total GHG emissions of the country in 2007. The sector, primarily based on burning fossil fuels has seen an intimidating CAGR of 5.6 per cent in emissions between 1994 and 2007 (see Table 10.1.1).

Table 10.1.1 GHG Emissions in India by Sector between 1994 and 2007 (in million tonnes of CO_2 equivalent)

	1994	*2007*	*CAGR (%)*
Electricity	355.03 (28.4%)	719.30 (37.8%)	5.6
Transport	80.28 (6.4%)	142.04 (7.5%)	4.5
Residential	78.89 (6.3%)	137.84 (7.2%)	4.4
Other Energy	78.93 (6.3%)	100.87 (5.3%)	1.9
Cement	60.87 (4.9%)	129.92 (6.8%)	6.0
Iron and Steel	90.53 (7.2%)	117.32 (6.2%)	2.0
Other Industry	125.41 (10.0%)	165.31 (8.7%)	2.2
Agriculture	344.48 (27.6%)	334.41 (17.6%)	–2.0
Waste	23.23 (1.9%)	57.33 (3.0%)	7.3
Total without LULUCF	1,251.95	1,904.73	3.3
LULUCF	14.29	–177.03	
Total with LULUCF	1,228.54	1,727.71	2.9

Note: Figures in brackets indicate percentage emissions from each sector with respect to total GHG emissions without land use change and forestry in 1994 and 2007 respectively.
Source: Ministry of Environment and Forests (2010).

Renewable Energy (RE) has long been recognized in India for its enormous potential in meeting the energy needs of a growing country in a carbon-smart way. RE solutions may be applied to the issues of rural electrification and sustainable development while creating employment opportunities at all stages of the value chain. Ironically, however, the adoption of RE technologies (RETs) has proceeded at a pace that is far slower than the need of the hour. This paper examines the current status of RE development in India and the major barriers to realizing its true potential. It also analyses technological developments of specific RE resources, to better understand

and resolve technology-related issues in harnessing RE potential. Finally, it discusses the policies and measures for overcoming barriers to large-scale deployment of RE.

Status of RE Development

According to the MNRE, the country has an estimated RE potential of around 85,000 MW from commercially exploitable sources: ~45,000 MW from wind; ~15,000 MW from small hydro; and ~25,000 MW from biomass and wastes. Additionally, there is potential to generate about 50 MW per square km using solar energy. However, RE contributes only ~10 per cent of the total installed power capacity of the country (see Figure 10.1.1). Moreover, wind energy accounts for ~70 per cent of the total existing RE capacity currently as shown in Figure 10.1.2. Interestingly, over 75 per cent of the total RE capacity addition has taken place within the last decade, during the Tenth Five Year Plan (FYP) and the ongoing Eleventh FYP.

Initiatives for Development of RE So Far

India is one of the few developing countries that has focused on harnessing RE. Following the first oil shock in the 1970s, which highlighted the concerns of energy security, India recognized the relevance of RE and took

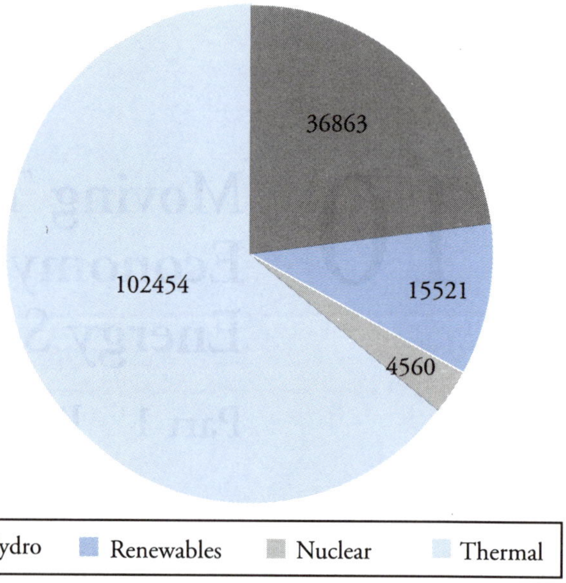

Figure 10.1.1 Role of Renewable Energy in India's Power Generation Capacity as on 31 March 2010* (in MW)

Note: *According to the MNRE, the total RE capacity in the country as on 31 March 2010 was 16,808 MW. The difference in magnitude of RE capacity addition as reported by different agencies in the country arises on account of discrepancies in data reported and the different time frames when such data is reported. The objective here is to indicate the extent of RE capacity existing in the country.

Source: Central Electricity Authority (2010).

Technology-wise RE capacity

RET	Installed Capacity
Small Hydro Power	2,735
Co-generation-bagasse	1,334
Wind Power	11,807
Bio Power	857
Waste to Energy	65
Solar Power	10
Total	16,808

Share of different technologies in total RE capacity

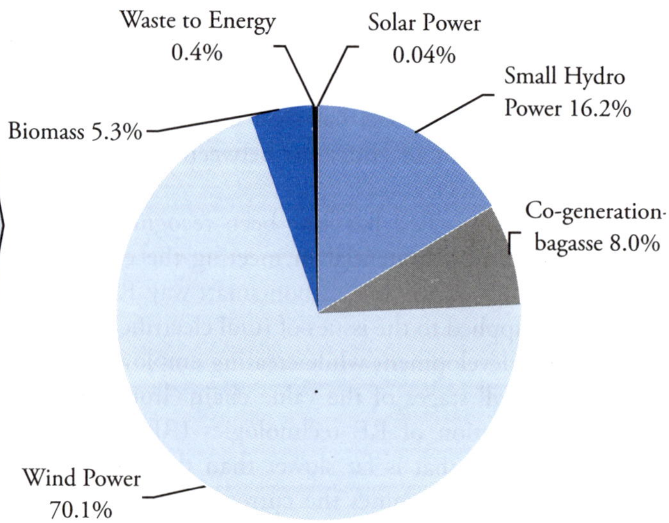

Figure 10.1.2 Grid-interactive Renewable Energy Capacity in India as on 31 March 2010 (in MW)

Source: Ministry of New and Renewable Energy.

various initiatives to promote it. Some major policy initiatives between the 1970s and the early 1990s are outlined below:

- Establishment of the Commission for Additional Sources of Energy in 1981 under the Department of Science & Technology for developing and demonstrating RETs and establishment of the Department of Non-conventional Energy Sources (DNES) in 1982 in the Ministry of Energy.
- Assessment of wind-resources and publication of a data-book in the early 1980s.
- R&D, capacity building, and demonstration programmes in the areas of biogas, cooking stoves, and solar energy in the 1980s.
- Establishment of the IREDA in 1987 to finance RE projects.
- Transformation of the DNES into a full-fledged (MNES; now MNRE) in 1992.
- Recognition of RE for power generation in 1992, by their inclusion in the Eighth Five Year Plan (1992–7).

In 1993, the MNES issued policy guidelines allowing the provision of fixed tariffs for the purchase of power from RE. These guidelines were valid for a period of ten years and prescribed a price of Rs 2.25/kWh with a 5 per cent annual escalation (with 1993 as base year). The ministry also allowed wheeling and banking of energy from RE sources to facilitate private investments in the sector. These guidelines were adopted by utilities in different states with minor variations. Several states even brought out their RE policies, based on MNRE's guidelines; some providing additional incentives for RE investments.

The enactment of the Electricity Act 2003 radically changed the legal and regulatory framework for this sector, making it mandatory for SERCs to promote RE within their jurisdiction. It has specific provisions for determination of RPO, that is, the quantum of RE power to be procured by distribution utilities and FIT for RE sources at the state level. Figure 10.1.3 maps capacity addition in RE capturing milestones events in the period 1993 to 2010.

Overview of Technology Development

Currently, there are many RETs available in the market that can contribute to sustainable development and energy security. In practice, however, many of these technologies are new and rarely used. As far as India is concerned, as also globally, wind technology has reached high levels of techno-economic maturity—wind power forms

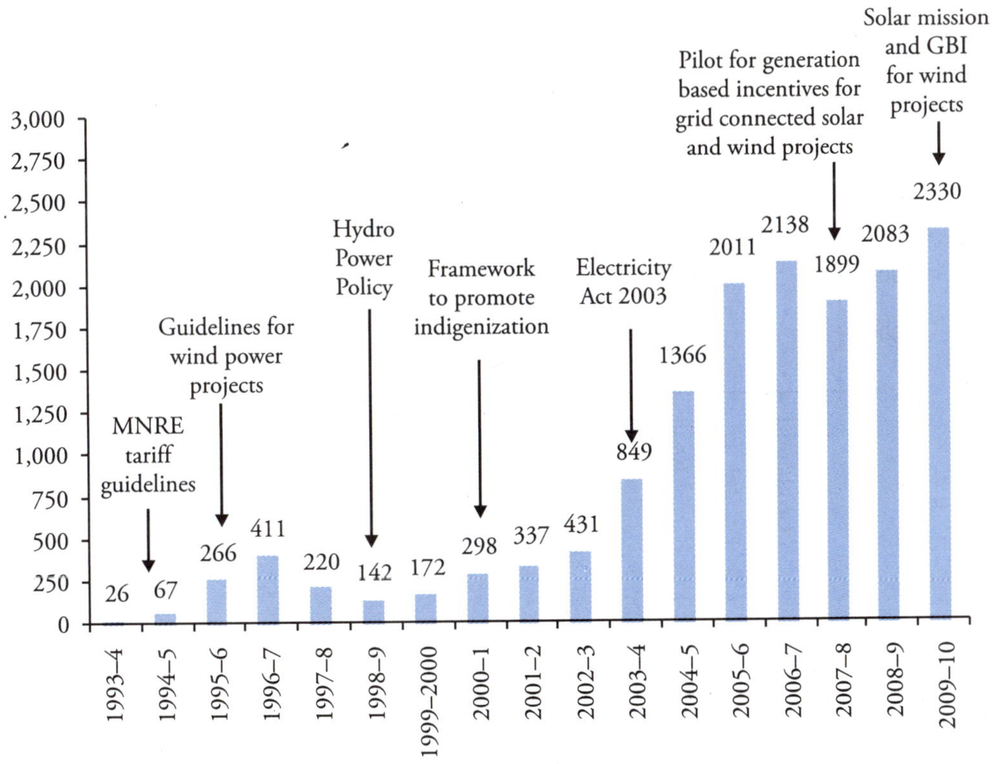

Figure 10.1.3 Major Events Influencing RE Development in India (in MW)

Source: Authors' own.

70 per cent of the total installed RE capacity in the country. On the other hand, solar power, which is available in India in abundance, is yet to make any noticeable contribution to renewable energy generation in the country. This is primarily because the current technologies are yet to reach cost-effective and economically viable platforms (see Figure 10.1.4). With emphasis on promotion, development, and deployment of solar energy technologies in India, GoI has launched the ambitious National Solar Mission (NSM) which targets 20,000 MW of installed solar power capacity, aiming to achieve grid parity for solar power by 2022.

The other non-conventional energy source covered in this paper is Waste to Energy (WTE). Urban India generates between 0.2 kg to 0.6 kg per capita per day of Municipal Solid Waste (MSW) which is expected to reach ~1 kg per capita per day in 2030 according to a report by the World Bank.[1] The fact that the urban population is projected to be ~40 per cent of the total population in 2030 as compared to 28.7 per cent in 2005, the problem of MSW management in our cities will get significantly amplified. The option of simply dumping MSW in the landfills will not be available in a few years time. A TERI publication[2] estimates that the cumulative requirement of land for disposal of MSW, would amount to around 1,400 km^2 by 2047. Increasingly, scarcity of land and resistance from adjoining rural areas to dumping of urban waste in their vicinity will aggravate the problems of waste disposal. Further, GoI has issued the MSW (Management and Handling) Rules 2000 (MSW Rules) that prohibit landfilling of untreated MSW. Given this daunting reality of solid waste that India will produce in future, together with the prevailing problems of waste disposal and related environmental concerns, it is imperative that issues in WTE be well understood and adequately addressed.

In the above context, this paper provides an overview of the current and future wind, WTE, and solar power technologies, their present status in India and potential for India. The paper also highlights the barriers which affect the large-scale implementation of RETs in the country and finally makes certain recommendations which could potentially lead to improved RET implementation and energy production, awareness among the people, and an improved better supply-chain network in India.

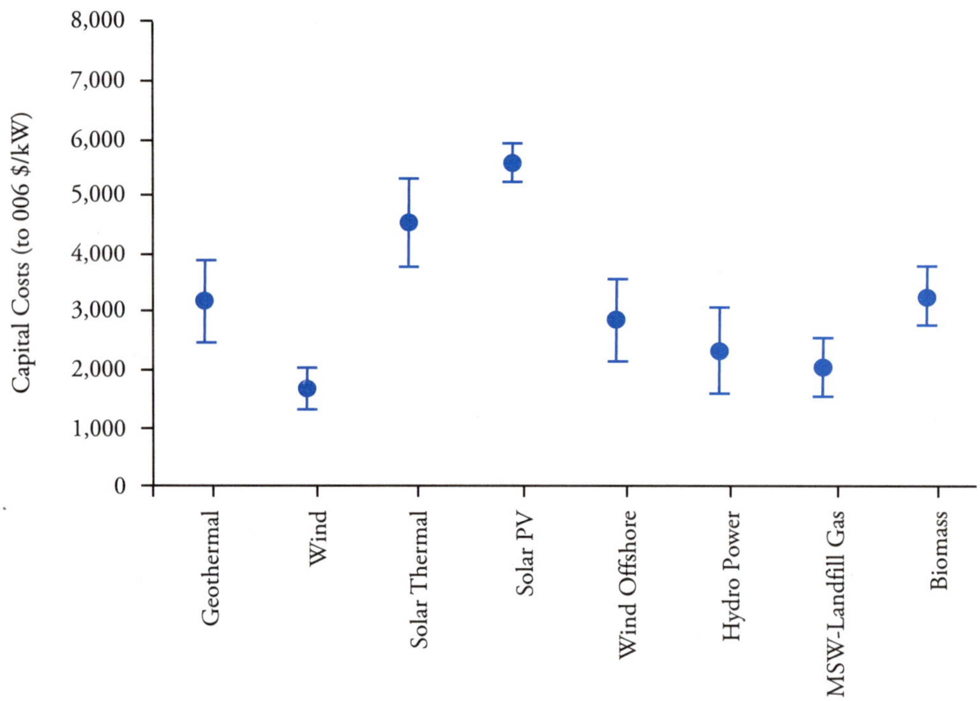

Figure 10.1.4 Capital Cost for Different Renewable Energy Technologies*

Note: * Cost of construction if no interest was incurred during construction.
Source: National Renewable Energy Laboratory.

[1] Hanrahan et al. (2006).
[2] Singhal and Pandey (2001).

Wind Energy Technologies

Basically, all the wind energy technologies such as wind turbines or wind mills or wind pumps convert wind energy into electrical or mechanical energy. Of these, wind turbines grab attention because they can convert wind energy directly into electricity. Simplistically, wind turbines can either rotate about a horizontal shaft or a vertical shaft. Brief descriptions of these two methodologies are provided below:

Horizontal Axis Wind Turbines

Horizontal Axis Wind Turbines (HAWTs) have the main rotor shaft at the top of a tower. They are accompanied by an electrical generator. These turbines are so oriented that they are directed towards incoming wind. In case of small turbines, their direction is controlled by a simple wind vane, while larger turbines are controlled by the combination of a wind sensor and a servo motor. Most turbines also have a gearbox, which converts the slow rotation of a blade into a higher RPM (rotations per minute) which is appropriate for electrical generators.

As blades in a HAWT rotate, they generate turbulence behind them. Thus, the turbine is usually pointed upwind relative to the tower. Further, to ensure that turbine blades do not get pushed into the tower due to pressure from winds, they are made sufficiently stiff, placed sufficiently away from the tower, and also tilted forward into the wind. These machines, when used in wind farms for commercial production of electricity, have three blades, and pointed into the wind with the help of computer controlled motors. Their blades could be as long as 40 meters, and the wind turbine steel tower could be up to 90 meters tall. The blades rotate at an RPM of 10–22, and the speed at the blade tip could be as high as 90 m/s. All turbines have shut-down features to ensure that the turbine does not operate at high wind speeds (above 80 km/hr) to avoid damage.

The advantage with HAWTs is that they have variable blade pitch, which enables these machines to harness maximum amount of energy at a given point of time. Their tall towers allow them to access higher wind speeds. For some locations, it has been estimated that for every 10m increase in elevation, the wind speed and power output increase by 20 per cent and 34 per cent, respectively. Further, since their blades always move perpendicular to wind, the blade receives power through the whole rotation. Finally, the face of a HAWT blade is struck by wind at a consistent angle as the blade rotates. This ensures consistent lateral loading of the blade over the course of a rotation, which in turn reduces vibration-stresses in the turbine and noise generated by it.

However, HAWTs are bulky machines, cumbersome to transport and install. Transportation costs for HAWTs can be as high as 20 per cent of the total equipment cost. Further, given the enormous blades, massive towers are needed to support these blades, gearbox, and the generator, significantly raising project costs. These large machines reflect electromagnetic signals disrupting the performance of radar devices in the neighbourhood. Moreover, HAWTs require large areas for installation, often leading to opposition from local populace.

The downward variant of these turbines, where the turbine faces away from the wind, has blades placed at the rear of the Nacells. This variant experiences significant fatigue caused by the stresses of turbulence as a blade passes through the tower's wind shadow. It is for this reason that most of the HAWTs in use are of the upwind variety.

Another drawback of the HAWT construction is the occurrence of cyclic stresses and vibrations. Given that wind speeds are higher at higher elevations, the blade tip sees maximum wind force when it is at the highest point in its circle. Also, at the lowest point, not only is the wind speed least, but the tower itself also hinders the airflow. These two effects produce a dip in torque and force on the turbine blade. These variations generate cyclic stresses on a large number of HAWT components, thereby increasing the maintenance costs of HAWTs significantly, and also reducing the overall life of the turbine. These effects are more pronounced for designs which have an even number of blades.

Vertical Axis Wind Turbines

The main rotor shaft in vertical axis wind turbines (VAWTs) is arranged vertically. A central advantage of such a configuration is that the turbine does not have to be pointed into the wind direction for effectiveness. This feature of VAWTs is particularly useful in locations where wind direction changes frequently. Another benefit of such a configuration is that the gearbox and generator can be placed closer to the ground and the tower does not have to support it. One key limitation of VAWT configuration is that the torque generated by the panes is pulsating in nature.

VAWTs are difficult to mount on towers, and thus they are installed closer to the base. Given the fact that wind velocity is lower near the ground, such turbines harness less energy vis-à-vis HAWTs. Further, wind flow is usually turbulent at lower altitudes because of the presence of numerous objects. This turbulence is a source of noise, vibrations, and consequent wearing out of the moving parts of the turbine. However, for turbines mounted on rooftops, the building generally redirects wind over the roof, thereby increasing wind speed.

VAWTs do not require structures as massive as the HAWTs for mounting. This not only reduces initial capital requirement, but also makes them easier to maintain because most of the moving parts of the turbine are closer to the ground. Further, VAWTs require lesser start-up wind speeds vis-à-vis HAWTs. Given their configuration, they may be constructed where taller structures like HAWTs are prohibited. Moreover, such structures, when placed on higher elevations such as hilltops, can take the advantage of the higher speeds present at such elevations. VAWTs also have lower noise signatures vis-à-vis HAWTs.

However, the fundamental configuration of VAWTs also lends them to several limitations. The entire weight of the turbine is borne by the bearings located at the bottom. Further, each blade sees cyclic and reversing loads as it completes a full turn. This increases the chances of blade failure by fatigue. Also, given that the lower parts of the turbine bear the entire weight of the structure above, changing parts of lower components becomes very difficult. Finally, given the fact that rotors located closer to ground see winds with lower speeds, a HAWT tends to produce more energy vis-à-vis a VAWT while occupying similar footprints or height.

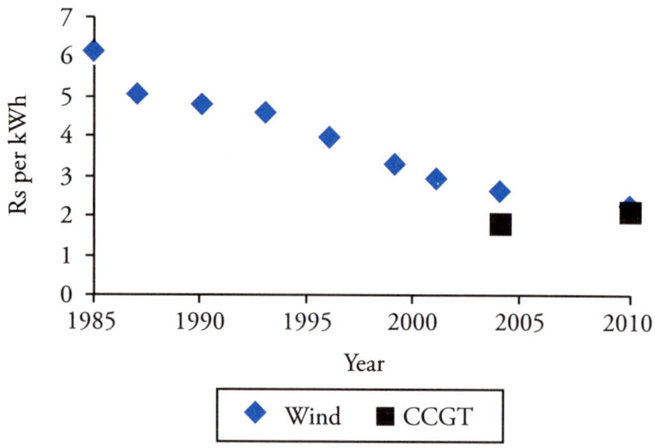

Figure 10.1.5 Unit Cost of Wind Energy

Note: Original data was in per kWh. An GBP-INR exchange rate of 70 has been used for conversion.
Source: Risoe.

Economics of Wind Power

The economics of a wind power plant depends on five key parameters—installation costs, O&M costs, average wind speed and electricity generated, economic life of the equipment, and financing cost. Installation costs include the purchase price of the complete system (including tower, wiring, utility interconnection or battery storage equipment, power conditioning unit, etc.) plus delivery and installation charges. Amongst these, the more important parameters are the investment expenses and electricity produced by the wind turbine. As the amount of energy produced is strongly dependent on the wind conditions, choice of an appropriate site is of paramount importance for an economically viable wind power project. The cost of supply from wind projects has steadily declined over the last two decades, and currently wind turbines operating at appropriate locations are cost competitive vis-à-vis traditional power plants, especially once penalty[3] for carbon emissions is imposed on traditional power plants. This is shown in the Figure 10.1.5.

Wind energy economics differs from conventional energy economics in a crucial way—the cost of wind energy is dominated by capital expenses (capex), while in traditional power plants, fuel costs are most significant contributors to the overall energy cost. A detailed break-up of primary sources of costs for wind energy, and energy from an average CCGT (combined cycle gas turbine) power plant is shown in Figure 10.1.6. In case of wind energy, capex is dominated by the cost of wind turbines itself. Table 10.1.2 shows the cost break-up of a typical mid-sized wind turbine deployed in Germany with capacity in the 850–1,500 MW range. Of the data presented in the Table, figures corresponding to costs attributable to turbine, foundation, electric insulation, are highly relevant to the Indian market as well.

Clearly, as shown in Table 10.1.2, the cost of turbines alone accounts for 74–82 per cent of total capital expenditures incurred while developing a wind power plant. The machinery of a typical wind turbine is composed of six sub-systems; blades, tower, electrical and control system (ECS), nacelle and yaw system (NYS), gearbox, and hub. Figure 10.1.7 provides a break-up the costs of a wind turbine by itself, in terms of the individual costs of these subsystems.

However, wind energy has higher O&M costs as compared to conventional power plants. These costs are attributable to five key parameters; insurance, regular maintenance, repair, spare parts, and administration. Given that most of the wind turbines in operation are barely two to three decades old, limited data are available on these costs.

[3] Carbon emission penalty for 2004 and 2010 was assumed to be Rs 0.28 and 0.42 per kWh, respectively. (*Source*: Risoe)

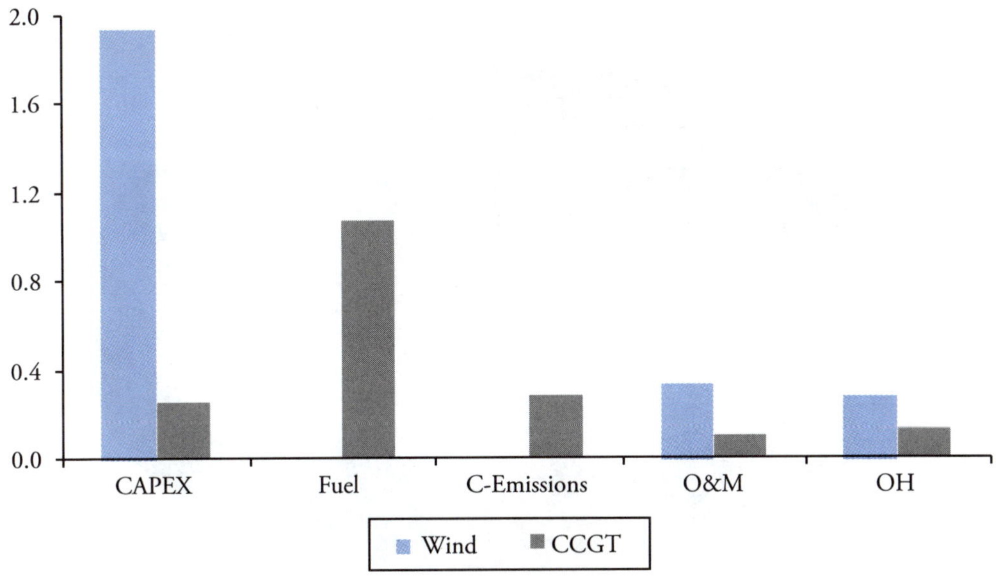

Figure 10.1.6 Break-up Costs for Wind and Conventional Energy

Source: Risoe, BP Power, and BVG Estimates.

Table 10.1.2 Break-up of CAPEX for a Medium-sized Wind Turbine (850 kW–1,500 MW)

	Share of CAPEX (%)
Turbine	74–82
Foundation	1–6
Electric Insulation	1–9
Grid Connection	2–9
Consultancy	1–3
Land	1–3
Financial Costs	1–5
Road Construction	1–5

Source: Wind Energy—The Facts—Costs and Prices.

- Experiences from Denmark, Germany, Spain, and UK have shown that O&M costs are in general at an average[4] level of approximately Rs 0.72 to 0.90 per kWh of wind power produced.
- There is moderate amount of data to show that newer and more powerful wind turbines incur about half the O&M costs of older turbines.
- Data on O&M costs for countries listed above also shows that O&M costs are relatively low in the first few years of turbine's life-cycle. However, after the tenth year, many turbines require major repair and reinvestments. This is particularly true of turbines which produce 55 kW of power.
- Expenses for insurance, administration, and regular service remain fairly constant over a turbine's life-cycle.

Planning for Wind Turbine Technology Development

It has been estimated that CO_2 reductions attributable to wind power industry growth could be anywhere between 62 and 548 million metric tonnes annually.[5] However, a considerable part of India's wind energy potential still remains untapped in the absence of appropriate technologies which meet India's needs effectively. Thus, India's wind turbine technology requires improvements in following direction:

- Indian wind farms have very low capacity utilization factors.[6] Quite often, this poor performance is attributed to the mismatch between Indian wind conditions and turbine technologies deployed in India. In general, the average wind speed in India is less than that in European coasts, it is highly variable within each state over a period of time, and the wind is laden with dust. The turbines being used in India have not been adapted for such uniquely Indian operational conditions. Significant mismatch exists between imported equipment

[4] The average is for the entire lifetime of wind turbine.
[5] Global Wind Energy Council (GWEC) (2009).
[6] Rajsekhar et al. (1999).

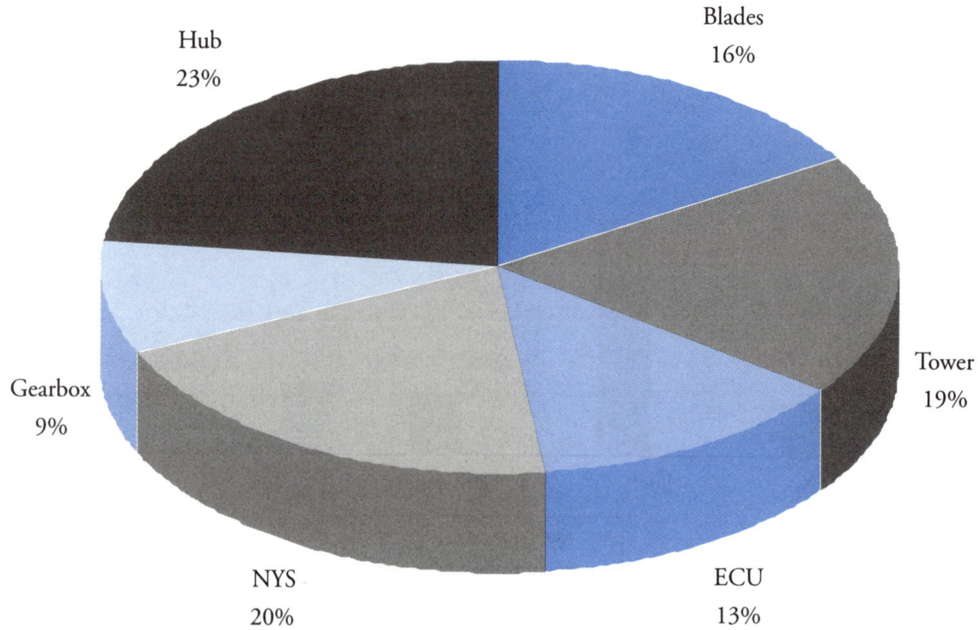

FIGURE 10.1.7 Break-up of Cost of a Wind Turbine

Source: BVG Associates & Berr.

which constitutes over 70 per cent of wind turbine and local parts. This too, leads to reduction in capacity utilization of Indian wind farms. Appropriate policies have to be crafted, which induce the industry to aim at increasing capacity utilization metrics. This is a *low hanging fruit* waiting to be harvested.

- As per DOE estimates,[7] capacity improvements could also be made by inducing technological development in areas of advanced tower concepts, advanced rotors, and better drive-train systems. Improvements in these areas could enhance capacity factors by as much as 11 per cent, 35 per cent, and 8 per cent, respectively.

Policy initiatives to promote indigenous design, development and production of higher capacity turbines in India through robust public-private-partnerships may reap gains in terms of lower land requirement, lower O&M costs, and faster commissioning. In this regard, the experience of companies like Suzlon,[8] could come in very handy.

Waste-to-Energy Technologies

There are various technological options which can be deployed for recovery of energy from MSW. While some of these have already been applied on a large scale both in India and abroad, some others are in advanced stages of development globally. These are summarized in Figure 10.1.8.

Physical

Physical WTE technologies mechanically process waste to produce forms more suitable for use as fuel such as refuse-derived fuel (RDF). It consists largely of organic materials taken from solid waste streams, such as plastics and biodegradable waste. The waste is processed to remove non-combustible and separate glass and metals for recycling. It is then shredded into a smaller, more uniform particle size for burning. The residual material is then burned in boilers on-site or compressed into pellets or bricks for use as solid fuel. This, in fact, is the main difference between RDF and incineration. Unlike incineration where waste is burnt, RDF produces pellets which are burnt to generate energy. This technology has now been deployed in some waste processing plants in the country to produce pellets that are sold to industrial units for use as fuel. RDF plants involve significantly more processing than incineration to remove non-combustible and oversized items as well as moisture. The latter is very important in India as most

[7] International Energy Agency (IEA) (2009).

[8] Suzlon is an Indian company which is fifth largest manufacturer of wind turbines in the world. It has a global footprint in terms of market, and also technological expertise.

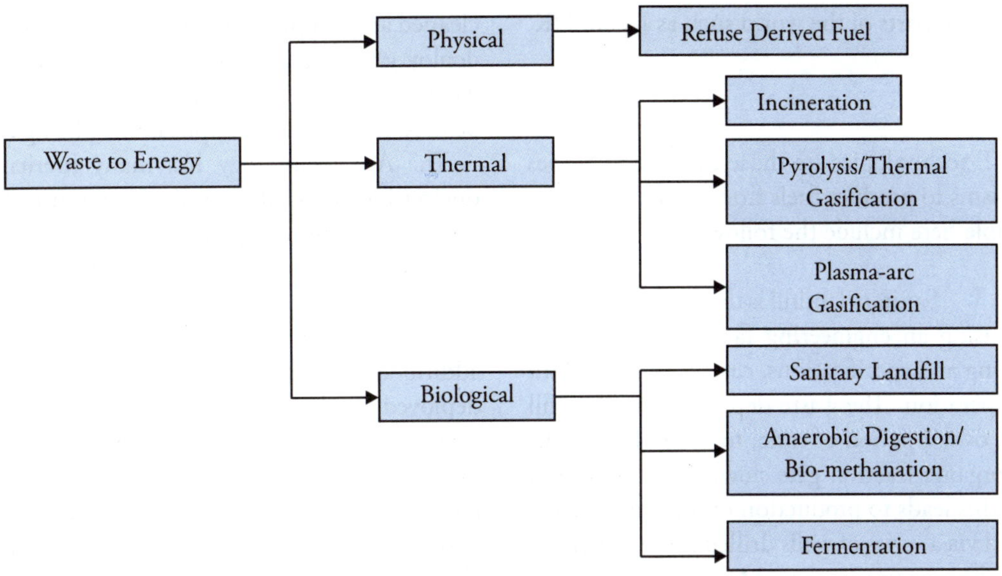

FIGURE 10.1.8 Technology Options for WTE

Source: Authors' own.

India garbage has very high moisture content. The derived fuel, therefore, has greater heat value than unsorted and unprocessed waste.

Thermal

Thermal WTE technologies use heat or combustion to treat wastes and include the following:

Incineration: Incineration or direct combustion is a mature and well-established technology where waste can be directly combusted in incinerators as a fuel with minimal processing or separation, in a process known as mass burn. Heat from the combustion process is used to turn water into steam, which is used to power a steam-turbine generator to produce electricity. All the organic matters, whether putrescible or not, are reduced to ash. The disadvantage, however, is the low heat value of the energy produced and cumbersome handling. Further, though the technology has advanced to incorporate air-pollution control systems in waste incinerators, ash or other pollutants captured in this process must still be disposed of.

Pyrolysis and Thermal Gasification: These are proven methods for processing homogenous organic matter like wood, pulp, etc., and are now being recognized as an attractive option for the treatment of MSW. Pyrolysis is the process of thermal decomposition of organic matter at high temperatures in an inert (oxygen-deficient) atmosphere or vacuum, producing a mixture of combustible and non-combustible gases, pyroligenous liquid, chemicals, and charcoal. On the other hand, gasification involves thermal decomposition of organic matter at high temperatures in the presence of limited amounts of air/oxygen, producing mainly a mixture of combustible and non-combustible gas. The gas generated by either of these processes or the charcoal in case of pyrolysis can be used in boilers to provide heat, or can be cleaned up and used in combustion turbine generators. One of the advantages of these technologies is that handling gas is easier than solid fuel. Moreover, a limited plant area is required as compared to other technologies. However, the sophisticated cooling, handling of cleaning systems, and regular operation and maintenance make these technologies costly.

Plasma-arc Gasification: This is an emerging technology utilizing thermal decomposition of organic wastes for energy/resource recovery. It uses a plasma-arc torch to produce temperatures as high as 13,000°C. This extreme heat breaks down most types of wastes, forming a gaseous mixture of hydrogen and carbon monoxide, called syngas, and a rock-like solid by-product called slag, which can be used in construction or as road asphalt. The syngas can be converted into a variety of marketable fuels—including ethanol, natural gas (methane), and hydrogen—or it can be used to generate electricity directly. The advantage of plasma-arc technology is that it ensures the near complete decomposition of waste and the plasma converters could consume nearly any type of waste, whether biodegradable or not. However, the technology is expensive and remains at early stage, though demonstration plants are operational in some parts of the world such as Japan, UK, and Canada.

Biological

Biological WTE technologies are those that use microbes or other organisms to produce fuels from waste. The technologies available here include the following:

Sanitary Landfill: Sanitary landfill is the scientific dumping of MSW using an engineering facility that requires detailed planning and specifications, careful construction; and efficient operation. The waste deposited in a landfill gets subjected, over a period of time, to anaerobic conditions and its organic fraction gets slowly volatilized and decomposed. This leads to production of methane, which can be captured via a series of wells drilled into the landfill and connected by a piping system. Methane can then be burned in a boiler as a heat-energy source, used in internal-combustion engines after removing water vapour and sulphur dioxide, or used for electricity generation via gas turbines. Typically, production of landfill gas starts within a few months after disposal of the wastes and generally lasts for about ten years or even more depending upon mainly the composition of wastes and availability/distribution of moisture.

The main advantage of sanitary landfill as compared to waste that is simply dumped is the protection of public health and environment. It reduces emission of organic compounds and toxicants into the atmosphere. Land and water contamination due to leachate migration is also minimized. However, landfills imply large dedicated land requirement and generally in the outskirts of cities. This is increasingly becoming a problem since stretches of land in the outskirts of cities are fast vanishing due to rapid urbanization. Moreover, separation of non-biodegradable solid waste such as plastics has to be done before waste is dumped into landfill sites. This technology often faces the highest public opposition because of the general tendency of 'don't dump in my backyard', emission of foul odour, and problems of pests and rodents. These landfills also form breeding grounds for vector-borne diseases.

Anaerobic Digestion (AD) or Bio-methanation: This technology first involves treatment of waste to remove inerts and non-biodegradable materials, upgrade and homogenize the feedstock for digestion- and to promote downstream treatment processes. The organic fraction of wastes is then fed to a closed container (biogas digester) where, under anaerobic conditions, the organic wastes undergo bio-degradation producing methane-rich biogas which can be utilized for cooking/heating applications, or cleaned and supplied as natural gas. Biogas plants can also deploy gas/steam turbines to convert gas into electricity, which can either be fed into the main utility grid or can be used use on-site in applications like lighting.

The AD technology has many merits. Besides producing biogas, it also produces manure. Of course, the quality of manure depends upon the composition of the input waste. However, the technology is a slow process. Non-biodegradable organic fraction cannot be digested and hence, needs to be disposed of without treatment or, additional technology (such as gasification) needs to be deployed for the refractory organics.

Table 10.1.3 provides a comparative analysis of the different technologies. It is obvious that all technologies have some merits and demerits. The choice of technology has to be matched to the quantity, and the physical and chemical properties of waste. The importance of these aspects when choosing the technology to be deployed is evident from the early experience with WTE in India (Box 10.1.1).

Solar Energy

Although solar radiation bestows us with abundant energy which can be harnessed to meet most of our light and heat requirements, only a tiny fraction of this potential is converted using available technologies. While passive or indirect approaches to harnessing solar energy, such as architectural design, are employed for space heating and cooling, more direct or active applications for collecting and converting solar energy into electricity are realized through technologies such as solar photovoltaic panels and solar thermal collectors. Following sections primarily focus on two direct technologies that is solar thermal collectors and solar photovoltaic panels.

Solar Thermal Power Generation Technologies

Solar thermal power systems convert the incident solar radiation into thermal energy by two means: (i) using flat plate collectors and solar cookers, typically low temperature technologies and (ii) using solar concentrators, a high temperature technology.

Solar Flat Plate Collectors and Solar Cookers (Low Temperature Technology): In these two devices, solar radiation falls on a dark flat plate though a glass cover followed by absorption by the plate surface. The absorbed thermal energy is transferred to the adjacent tubes carrying a circulating working fluid such as water. This is normally used for providing hot water or for space heating in the buildings. The typical temperatures produced by these technologies are below 150°C. This technology is relatively

Table 10.1.3 Comparative Analysis of Technological Options for Recovery of Energy from Wastes

		Incineration	*RDF*	*Pyrolysis*	*Gasification*	*Sanitary Landfill Gas*	*Bio-Methanation*
1	Suitability	• Waste with low moisture and high calorific value • Excessive inert content affects net energy recovery	• Waste remaining after removing the recyclable and inert fraction of waste • Suitable for high moisture waste	• Waste with high organic matter • Excessive moisture affects net energy recovery	• Waste with high organic matter • Excessive moisture affects net energy recovery	• Biodegradable solid waste	• Commonly used for domestic sewage and organic wastes treatment • Application for MSW gradually increasing • Unsuitable for wastes containing less organic matter
2	Status of commercialization	• Oldest prevailing technology world-wide; commercially proven	Established technology in many parts of Europe and the world	• Has been proven technically at pilot scale but not at commercial scale • First commercial plant operational in Germany	Has been proven technically at pilot scale but not at a commercial scale	Commercially proven	Commercially proven for treatment of domestic sewage and organic wastes
3	Energy recovery	• Power efficiency: 25%–30% Heat only and CHP: can reach >70%	• Power efficiency: 25%–30% Heat only and CHP: can reach >70%	Approx. 15%	Power efficiency: 25%–30% depending on waste type and plant size	30–40% of the total gas generated; the remaining gas escapes in the atmosphere	Approx. 30%
4	Requirement for segregation	High	Very high	High	High	High	High
5	Direct energy recovery	Yes	No	Yes	Yes	No	No
6	Land requirement	Low; 0.8 hectare*	Low; 0.8 hectare*	Low; 0.8 hectare*	Low; 0.8 hectare*	Very high; 36 hectares**	Low-moderate 2 hectares*
7	Concern for toxicity of products	High; both emissions and solid residues can be toxic	Very high; when burnt some pollutants can be carcinogenic in nature.	High; toxic emissions from syngas burning	High; toxic emissions from syngas burning	Moderate/High	Nil; but can be toxic if incoming waste is not properly segregated
8	Concern for atmospheric pollution	Very high	Very high	High	High	High; problem of foul odour can never be completely eliminated	Low
9	Sustainability of source/waste stream	Moderate	Low	Low	Low	Moderate	Low
10	Reduction in volume of waste	Up to 90%	Up to 60%	Up to 90%	Low	Moderate/High	

Notes: * Based upon typical installations and ** for areas away from coast.
Source: Authors' own.

Box 10.1.1
Experience with Waste to Energy Technologies in India

The experience with WTE in India has been mixed. While there are several success stories in industrial and small decentralized operations, there have been some setbacks as far as energy recovery from MSW is concerned. The commercial MSW-based WTE facilities were set up by private entities who received waste from the urban local bodies and sold the energy generated by the facility to the local power distribution company.

The first such facility was set up in 1987 in Delhi, based on incineration technology to produce 3.5 MW power but soon became inoperative. The fate of the 5 MW project in Lucknow, which started commercial operations in 2003, was similar. Based on an imported biomethanation technology used in over 50 WTE plants worldwide, the plant only reached 1 MW and was closed down within six months. The reasons for failure in both cases were the same—mismatch in quality of waste received and plant design, non-availability of 'acceptable waste' (the waste had high inert content that is less biodegradables), and poor accountability on part of the urban local body for the waste supplied.

The RDF technology-based power plants at Vijayawada and Hyderabad, of 6 MW each, also started commercial operations in 2003. However, to overcome the poor heat value of MSW received, that is, about 1,000 kCal/kg and way below the optimum 2,500 kCal/kg, the plants supplement MSW with agro wastes as auxiliary fuel. These wastes form about 30 per cent of the fuel input and are often procured at Rs 1,000–1,200/MT, thereby adding substantially to operating costs. On the whole, the RDF plants remain grossly underutilized as the desired amount of MSW is not being received.

A casual reading of these experiences would lead to the conclusion that the major WTE technologies, that is, incineration, bio-methanation, and RDF have failed in India. However, deeper analysis makes it clear that the failure of WTE lies in issues in MSW management (starting from the generation of waste by an individual to final disposal by the local government) and problems of adaptation of technology. Lack of proper waste analysis before finalization of technology and size led to technology and waste feedstock mismatch. The variability in quantum and heterogeneity of delivered waste due to poor waste management and governance of urban local bodies affected plant operations.

The failure of the Delhi and Lucknow projects attracted severe criticism of the government's MSW-based WTE programme. Public Interest Litigations challenged GoI for providing subsidies of Rs 10 crore per MW and interest subsidies of 15 crore per MW without undertaking proper cost-benefit analyses. They also criticized the promotion of technologies having a high capital cost despite the availability of cheaper technologies such as composting. The Lucknow project is estimated to have cost Rs 84 crore with cost over-runs, that is, Rs 13–17 crore per MW. As a result, the Supreme Court (SC) gave a stay on GoI grants to such schemes in May 2005 and WTE was almost written off.

However, it got a lifeline when the SC in May 2007 allowed GoI to subsidize five WTE plants on a pilot basis. In 2008, three MSW processing facilities with power plants (two in Delhi and one in Guwahati) were awarded to private players. The projects were developed through special purpose vehicles (SPVs), which undertook the project development activities of waste characterization, technology selection, plant design and engineering, and finalization of contractual agreements. The GoI is providing a subsidy of Rs 10 crore per MW to these projects. The SPVs have been transferred to successful bidders following tariff-based competitive bidding.

simple and straightforward to install and use. As a result, there has been considerable growth in India, especially in the past 10 years, in the installation of solar thermal technology using flat plate collectors, as shown in Figure 10.1.9, making India as one of the major markets of this technology.

Another use of low temperature solar thermal collectors is in solar cooking. As per the report of the Press Bureau of the Government of India, published in 2007, there are over 5,25,000 solar cookers installed in India, making it the second largest country only after China in the use of solar cookers.

Solar Concentrators or Concentrating Solar Collectors (High Temperature Technology): In solar concentrators, solar radiation is concentrated on a receiver tube by specially configured arrays of reflecting devices. The thermal energy from concentrated solar radiation is transferred to a flowing fluid in the tube. The temperatures attained in this technology are typically much higher than simple flat plate collectors and are also referred to as high temperature solar collectors. Solar concentrators can be categorized into three basic types:

- Reflecting parabolic trough systems which yield temperatures of ~400°C and hence produce steam for generating electricity;
- Parabolic dish-shaped reflector systems which yield temperatures of ~1000°C and achieve the highest efficiencies for converting solar energy to electricity; and
- Power tower systems which yield temperatures in the excess of 1000°C. These systems make use of heliostats to track the movement of the sun throughout the day to reflect and concentrate the sunlight onto a central

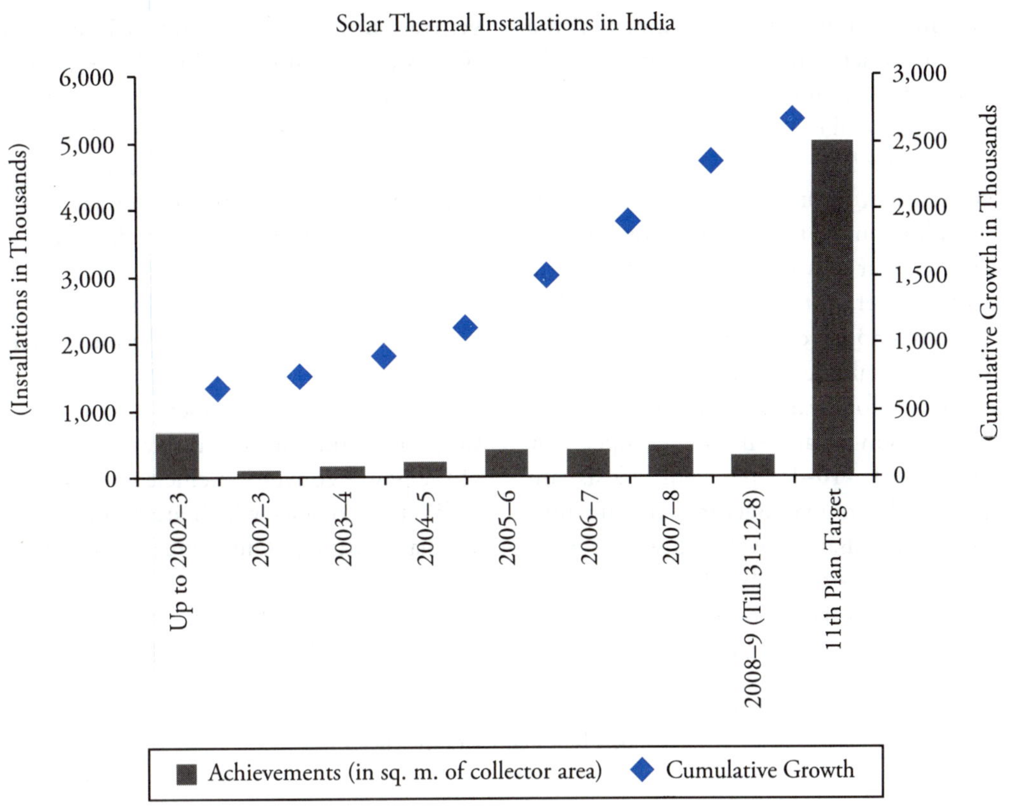

Figure 10.1.9 Growth in Solar Thermal Installations

Source: MNRE.

tower-mounted receiver where the energy is transferred to a heat transfer fluid. This energy from the fluid is then transferred either to the storage or to power-conversion systems.

Present Status of Solar Thermal Technologies: As mentioned above, the use of low temperature solar thermal technologies such as flat plate collectors and solar cookers have found significant progress in India. According to the data available from MNRE,[9] India has more than 140 manufacturers of solar flat plate collectors and evacuated tube collectors. This technology can be further promoted in those areas of India which experience severe or long winters such as hilly regions and north and central India. The payback period for this technology is estimated to be between five to ten years in India because of higher solar insolation and relatively simple design.[10] The costs of simple family-use 100 litre solar water heaters are anywhere between Rs 10k–20k with prices varying from state to state.

As far as high temperature solar concentrator technology is concerned, India does not yet have any working solar thermal power plants. Although, in 1989, MNRE (then MNES) started India's first Solar Thermal Power Plant of 50kW capacity using parabolic trough collector technology or line focusing at Gwalpahari in Gurgaon, the plant was operated for only about a year and was closed down due to lack of spare parts. Subsequently, some studies were made for setting up plants in Rajasthan but any tangible outcomes are yet to be seen. Solar thermal power generation has tremendous promise in a country like India with high solar insolation to meet its soaring electricity demand, as suggested by a techno-economic study made by Beerbaum and Weinrebe.[11]

Solar Photovoltaic Panels

Solar photovoltaic (PV) is a technology which has so far attracted maximum attention primarily because energy from incident solar radiation on to the PV panel is directly converted into electricity. This is caused by the

[9] MNRE, http://mnre.gov.in/ind-menu.htm; http://mnre.gov.in/list/list-fpc-m.htm; http://mnre.gov.in/list/list-etc-m.htm

[10] http://www.teriin.org/opet/reports/solarthermal.pdf

[11] Beerbaum and Weinrebe (2000).

photoelectric effect in which light photons knock off the electrons in the semiconductor junction, known as a P-N junction made from a n-type and a p-type semiconductor of PV panel giving rise to flow of electricity across the junction. Solar PV technologies can be broadly defined into three categories: first, second, and third generation technologies, depending on the time of development.

The first generation solar cells are expensive but provide high-efficiencies of ~24 per cent, closer to the theoretical maximum efficiency of ~33 per cent. These cells are made of highly pure single crystal silicon (which are expensive) and use a single junction for creating electricity.

The second generation solar cells are cheaper but yield lower efficiency of ~10–15 per cent. Costs are lower because these cells are manufactured in thin film form thus minimizing the usage as well as loss of silicon, albeit yielding inferior structural quality. Cost reductions, however, more than compensate for the reduction in efficiency. The most popular materials used for second generation solar cells are copper indium gallium selenide (CIGS), cadmium telluride (CdTe), amorphous silicon (a-Si), and microcrystalline silicon (mc-Si). Though second generation solar cells have been touted as a technology that can potentially outrun fossil fuels in cost effectiveness, this may not occur until 2015 or even later.

Third generation solar cell technologies such as organic solar cells, including polymeric and dye-sensitized solar cells, are under R&D. These devices are expected to be large area and low-cost yielding moderately efficient cells (10–15 per cent).

A comparative plot presented in Figure 10.1.10, shows the performance of various solar cell technologies in terms of the power conversion efficiencies.

PV technologies which are being successfully adopted and have future potential are as follows:

Bulk Technologies: These are typically wafer-based technologies where 150–250-microns-thick device ready

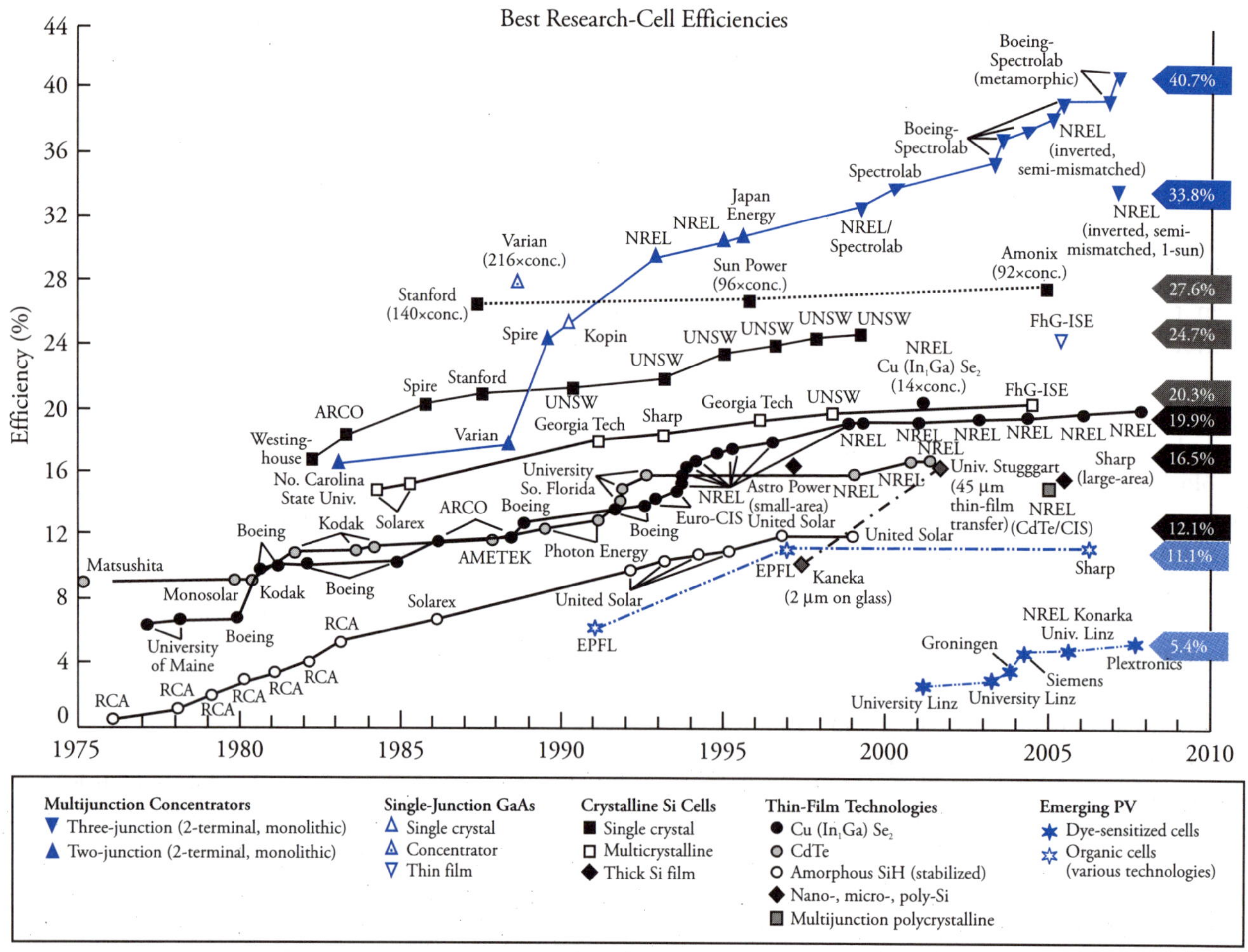

FIGURE 10.1.10 Comparison of the Power Conversion Efficiencies of Various PV Technologies

Source: Kazmerski (2010).

wafers are joined together to form a solar cell module. Commercially, silicon is the only viable material in bulk technologies primarily due to its abundance and low cost as compared to other semiconductors. Bulk silicon can be further classified based on crystallinity and crystal size into ingot, ribbon, or wafer.

- Monocrystalline silicon (c-Si): Single crystals of Si are prepared using processes such as Czochralski or float zone process. However, high processing cost of single crystal wafers results in the expensive cells. The cost is also augmented by sawing loss of Si incurred during formation of square shaped wafers from cylindrical ingots.
- Polycrystalline or multicrystalline silicon (poly-Si or mc-Si): These are processed from cast square ingots, which are large blocks of molten Si that is carefully cooled and solidified. In comparison to the c-Si based cells, poly-Si cells are less expensive but are less efficient.
- Ribbon silicon: This is a variant of poly-Si and is manufactured by drawing flat thick films from molten silicon, resulting in a poly-Si type structure. PV cells based on ribbon Si have lower efficiencies than poly-Si, but are cheaper due to a great reduction in silicon waste as no sawing is needed.

Thin Film Technologies: The impetus to thin film technologies came primarily from the cost of the silicon wafer and the wastage of silicon in bulk silicon wafer manufacturing as a result of sawing. Thin film solar cells are manufactured by growing one or more thin layers of semiconductor materials on a substrate, typically glass, using cost-effective large area thin film fabrication techniques. The primary materials used for this technology were silicon, in amorphous or multicrystalline form, or cadmium telluride (CdTe). Subsequently, thin film solar cells of variety of other materials were developed including copper indium gallium selenide ($CuInGaSe_2$ or CIGS), dye-sensitized solar cells (DSSC), and organic solar cells (OSC), last being mostly at the stage of R&D. Although most thin film technologies show efficiencies lower than bulk Si, multilayer technologies or tandem solar cells combining different semiconductors resulting in better utilization of solar radiation can yield higher efficiencies, albeit cost-effectiveness is yet to be seen.

Present Status of Solar PV: Figure 10.1.11 provides a comparison of various PV technologies present in the market. Clearly c-Si and mc-Si technologies are superior in terms of efficiencies but also higher in terms of material cost. From the cost point of view, a-Si, DSSC, CIGS (or CIS), and CdTe technologies look more favourable, although the commercial viability of technologies such as CIS and DSSC is still questionable. First Solar[12] in USA is promoting CdTe thin film technology and soon expects to roll out commercial products with efficiencies above 10 per cent although long-term success of the product is yet to be assessed. A few companies in USA and East Asia are developing CIGS as solar cells with efficiencies of 15 per cent and above and expect to roll out commercial products in the near future. In India, Moser Baer has started operations to develop thin film silicon solar cells although no cost estimates have been revealed yet.

DSSC solar cell technology is being tested for commercialization and one of the manufacturers, G24i, is expecting its 30 MW DSSC production line to be operational soon.[13] Organic solar cells are not appropriate for comparison yet, primarily due to stability issues as well as relatively higher costs of currently used semiconductor materials, bulk manufacturing operations are yet to take shape. From India's perspective, R&D investment in these futuristic technologies will be fruitful for the country to develop the technologies indigenously, which may again lead to cost reduction in the long term. Polymer solar cell technology is an especially promising technology because of the potential of using cheaper processing methods such as spin coating or solution deposition on large area substrates from a solution containing the semiconducting polymer. Although the costs of organic semiconductor materials are very high at the moment, once the technology is successfully established, costs can be significantly lowered, resulting in lower electricity production costs.

While India has reasonably good manufacturing capability of Si-based solar panels, touching about 1.2 GW,[14] the electricity production using solar PV is miniscule, about 2.12 MW,[15] and is mainly attributed to higher costs, mostly above Rs 15 per kWh. Most applications include off-grid applications such as solar water pumps, solar lanterns, street lighting systems, and home-lighting in rural and off grid areas. Worldwide, technological advances coupled with efficiency gains, have led to significant

[12] http://www.firstsolar.com/en/index.php

[13] http://www.g24i.com

[14] http://www.eetindia.co.in/ART_8800606445_1800007_NT_482d2e5e.HTM

[15] MNRE (2009).

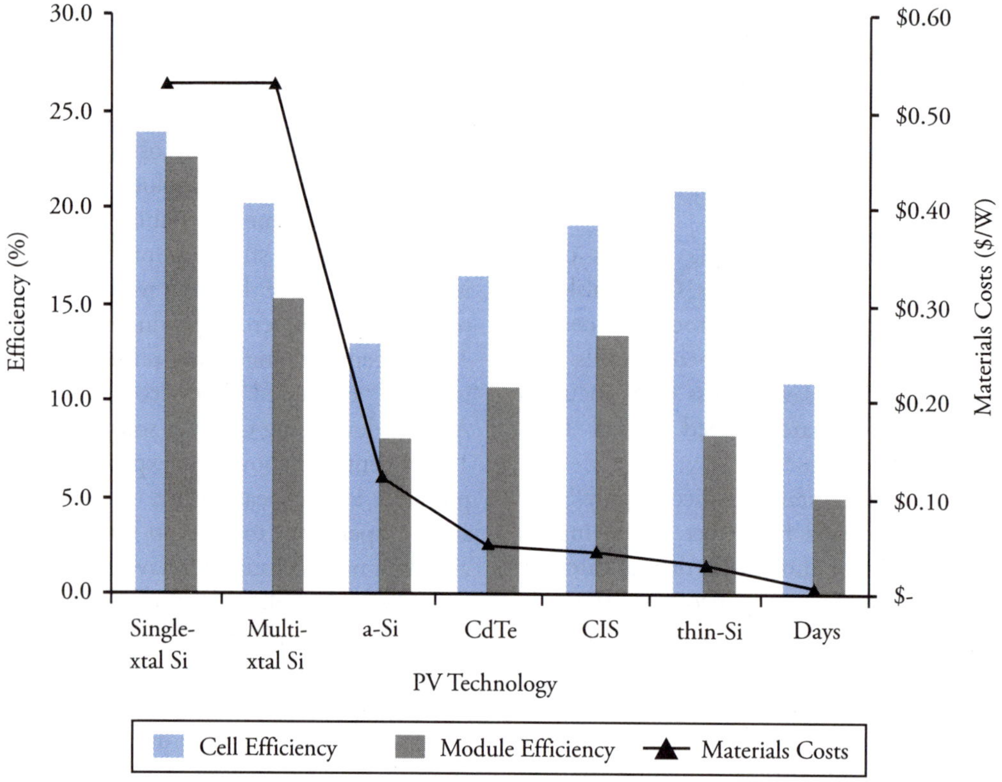

Figure 10.1.11 Cost and Efficiency Comparison of PV Technologies

Source: Baumann et al. (2004).

reduction in the cost of PV capacity from approximately USD 300 per watt module in 1956 to less than USD 5 per watt module in 2009. A popular solar energy website, Solar Buzz, estimates current solar electricity prices at ~34 cents per kWh for residential sector and ~19 cents per kWh for the industrial sector while the module costs are about USD 4.21 per W.[16] The costs in India are estimated to be at around Rs 15 to Rs 30 per unit compared to around Rs 5 to Rs 8 per unit for conventional thermal energy.[17] The aim would be reduce the module costs by 50 per cent and reduce the costs of solar electricity by at least half. The US government's EIA's Annual Energy Outlook 2009 projects that, by 2030, overnight capacity costs for new generating plants using solar photovoltaics will be 37 per cent lower than that in 2009. Another prediction based on 25kW array as per Emcore's Concentrator Photo Voltaic (CPV) presentation is that the cost of solar electricity would go down to as low as 4.30 cents (~Rs 2.50) per kWh in 2019.[18] In addition, the efficiency of PV applications is expected to improve as the technology continues to be developed. It is expected that the share of PV power in global power production would increase to 6–9 per cent by the year 2030.[19]

Barriers to Development of RE

As mentioned earlier in this paper, the GoI through the Ministry of New and Renewable Energy (MNRE) and Ministry of Finance (MoF), and the state governments have used a number of policy instruments to promote RE (see Table 10.1.4). The electricity regulators have also taken progressive measures to promote RE (see Table 10.1.5) in the country. However, despite these initiatives, RE is yet to realize even half of its potential. This is because several barriers, including those in the policy and regulatory framework, continue to hamper its development. Some of these barriers are generic in nature while some are specific to certain technologies. A brief summary of these barriers is discussed below.

[16] http://www.solarbuzz.com/SolarPrices.htm

[17] http://www.renewableenergyworld.com/rea/partner/movya-realty/news/article/2010/03/low-cost-land-cheap-laborbest-electricity-rates-welcome-to-gujarat-india-for-solar-power-generation-project

[18] http://www.unenergy.org/Popup%20pages/kWh%20Costs.html

[19] European Photovoltaic Industry Association (2007).

Policy and Regulatory Barriers

Policy Framework for RE: There is no single comprehensive policy statement for RE in the country. Policies have been issued as and when necessary to facilitate the growth of specific RETs. Further, the plans for development of RE are not consistent with the policies. Table 10.1.6 indicates that the RE capacity addition targeted by MNRE and that planned under the NSM is inadequate to meet the target generation mandated under the NAPCC.

Policies for specific RETs are also lopsided. For example, the GoI, in December 2009, announced GBI for grid-connected wind projects (commissioned after the

TABLE 10.1.4 Policy Instruments for Promotion of RE

Name of Instrument	*Objective*	*Applicability*
Fiscal interventions		
(a) Capital Subsidy	Provide a subsidy to bring down upfront investment costs	– Demonstration small-scale projects in hydro, biomass, and wind power – Solar power applications
(b) Indirect Taxes: Cess, Exemption from VAT/ Sales Tax and Electricity Duty, Exemption from Import/ Excise Duty, Accelerated Depreciation (AD)	Lower the gap between RE-based power and conventional power	– AD only for wind and solar – Technology neutral in case of other interventions
(c) Direct Tax Exemptions/Tax Holidays	Provide direct tax exemptions which incentivize RE-based power generation	Technology neutral
(d) Interest Subsidies	Provide a subsidy on interest to reduce the cost of capital and in turn life-cycle cost of projects	– Demonstration small-scale projects in hydro, biomass, and wind power – Solar power applications
Production Subsidies generation based incentives (GBI)	Provide an incentive for production of power	Solar and wind
RE Funds	Provide low-cost funds to promote investments in RE	Technology neutral
Demonstration Projects and R&D Grants	Showcase technology development	Technology neutral
State RE Policies (including issues such as development of transmission networks to connect RE projects, and wheeling and banking, third party sale)	Provide a policy framework for encouraging RE investment in the state	Technology neutral or technology specific depending on state

Source: Authors' own.

TABLE 10.1.5 Regulatory Framework for Promotion of RE

Type of regulation	*Objective*	*Applicability*
Tariff related		
(a) Feed in Tariffs (FIT)/ Preferential Tariffs	Provide an assured price for RE projects feeding into the grid	Technology neutral
(b) Terms and conditions for determination of tariff	Provide an assured price for RE projects feeding into the grid	Technology neutral
Renewable Purchase Obligations/ Renewable Portfolio Standards	Provide a target of RE share in power generation and distribution to encourage RE generation	Technology neutral or technology specific depending on state
Regulations addressing systemic issues such as open access, development of transmission networks to connect RE projects, and wheeling and banking, third party sale	Facilitate development of RE plants, and allow RE generators flexibility in generation and sale of power	Technology neutral or technology specific depending on state

Source: Authors' own.

announcement of the scheme but on or before 31 March 2012) at Rs 0.50 per unit of electricity fed into the grid for a period not less than four years and a maximum period of 10 years. Developers can avail either GBI or accelerated depreciation (AD) of up to 80 per cent of project cost in the first year under the Income Tax Act. The GBI will be applicable to a maximum capacity of 4000 MW during the remaining period of the Eleventh Plan. However, this GBI will be provided only to wind projects selling power to state utilities as well as captive wind power projects. Projects undertaking third party sale (TPS) by way of merchant power or open access are excluded from the purview of the scheme. This provision clearly needs reconsideration in view of the objective of harnessing RE to the extent possible. Another issue is that though the scheme provides for exclusion of GBI in determination of tariff by State Regulators, CERC's regulations state that the GBI would be considered while determining the tariff. Consistency between the policy and regulatory framework is absolutely necessary.

The policy framework at the state level is no better. In fact, many state policies have only created uncertainty for investments in RE. For example, in Madhya Pradesh, the policy for promotion of RE waives off wheeling charges as well as cross subsidy surcharge for RE. Instead, the state government would provide subsidy to the distribution utilities towards wheeling charges to the tune of 4 per cent of the energy injected at the rate of prevailing energy charges. The policy also exempts wind energy from the payment of electricity duty for a period of five years from CoD provided actual generation is at least 70 per cent of the energy generation declared in the Detailed Project Report (DPR). However, the policy is applicable only for a period of five years. In case of biomass projects, most states don't have defined policies as far as the radius within which such plants can be established. It has been seen that biomass plants have come up in close proximity to each other thereby affecting the availability of fuel to each other. As a result, these plants have been rendered unviable.

Regulatory Framework for RE: Several measures have been taken by regulators to promote RE (as discussed in the Legal and Regulatory Section of this report). However, there are several inadequacies in the regulatory framework. Although the RPO, as provided in the Electricity Act 2003 and mandated by the regulators, is a powerful tool for the promotion of RE, there are several inadequacies. While some states have specified modest levels of RPO despite good resource potential, others have either not allowed the procurement of RE from outside the state or have specified a ceiling on the procurement of RE. The enforcement of RPO is an even bigger issue. Thus far, only a few states such as Rajasthan and Maharashtra have specified penalties mechanism on distribution utilities in case the RPO is not met by them. Even in these two states, only the Maharashtra Electricity Regulatory Commission has penalized the utilities in Maharashtra for not meeting the mandated RPOs.

Besides RPO, FIT also plays a crucial role in the promotion of RE. Analysis of RE capacity addition indicates that almost all biomass and wind capacity has been added in states that specified an FIT. The same is true for small hydro to a large extent. However, FIT determined by SERCs is often based on norms for which inadequate justification is provided. In some cases, these norms are

Table 10.1.6 Mismatch between RE Capacity Envisaged Under Policy and Capacity Addition Targeted

	2009–10	*2010–11*	*2011–12*	*2016–17*
Energy Requirement (in million units or MU)[a]	8,20,920	8,91,203	9,68,659	13,92,066
Share of RE as mandated under NAPCC (in %)[b]	5	6	7	12
Quantum of RE required (in MU)	41,046	53,472	67,806	1,67,048
RE capacity addition targeted by MNRE (in MW)	15,542[c]	20,376	25,211	57,000
Solar capacity targeted under JNNSM (in MW)			1,000	10,000
Quantum of RE available (in MU)[d]	29,952	39,269	50,514	1,29,122
Additional RE required to meet RE share mandated under NAPCC (in MU)	11,094	14,203	17,292	37,926

Notes: [a] As per 17th EPS.
[b] 5 per cent in 2009–10 and 1 per cent increase each year.
[c] As on 31 October 2009.
[d] Assuming a capacity utilization factor of 22 per cent.
Source: Authors' own.

not specified at all while by others, the tariff of other RE sources in the state has been adopted as a reference point. Further, many SERCs have determined FITs for limited periods without indicating the regulatory framework beyond such periods. This gives rise to regulatory uncertainty, affecting bankability of the project.

Institutional Barriers

Lack of coordination and cooperation within and between the central government, state governments, state nodal agencies, and other concerned agencies delays and restricts the progress of RE development. Though several states claim to have adopted a single window for RE project approval and clearance, its effectiveness is questionable. Moreover, delays in obtaining clearances for projects awarded through competitive bidding result in the levy of a penalty on the developer.

Financial Barriers

RE developers in India sometimes face difficulty in financing projects. Many of these are related to the inherent characteristics of these projects. Resource assessments for such projects, in most cases, need to be site-specific and involve estimating 'climactic conditions' over a long period of time. RETs involve large upfront investment cost in generation equipment, resulting in high up-front costs and a heavy initial burden to be financed over the life of the project. Barriers include the enormous paperwork and costs associated with identifying and obtaining access to finance for small and medium-scale RE projects relative to their financing needs; limited understanding of RE in financial institutions; lack of familiarity and awareness of technologies, particularly for those that have recently achieved commercialization. Further, many RE project developers are often small, independent, and newly established, lacking the institutional track record and financial strength needed to secure non-recourse project financing. Lenders often perceive them as high risk and are reluctant to provide non-recourse project finance.

Market-related Barriers

Transmission Network: Non-availability of evacuation infrastructure and grid integration challenges are amongst the biggest problems affecting RE projects development, particularly small hydro power (SHP) projects or wind projects that are located at remote locations with limited or no evacuation infrastructure. Though states are required to provide infrastructure for evacuation of power from RE projects, in practice it is the RE developer who has to provide for such infrastructure, thus affecting the project cost. Even in states providing evacuation infrastructure, such infrastructure is inadequate.

Development of evacuation infrastructure and providing grid connectivity for RE sources is considered the responsibility of the transmission utility. However, the distribution licensees also have a major role to play in the evacuation of RE generation, as many RE sources are often connected at distribution voltages. The Forum of Regulators (FoR) has noted that barring few utilities, such as the Maharashtra State Electricity Transmission Company Ltd., Rajasthan Vidyut Prasaran Nigam, and Himachal Pradesh State Electricity Board, others have not included evacuation infrastructure for RE as part of their overall transmission or distribution capex plans. Even for these utilities, lack of funds is a major issue to give effect to their plans. Also utilities are often not well aware of the transmission requirements for evacuation of RE-based power.

High Equipment Costs: It is perceived that volumes and advancement in technology would drive down capital costs. However, the capital cost of even the commercially deployed technologies has not declined over the years, despite their increasing capacity. On the contrary, it has been observed that developers or equipment providers have been quoting increasing capital costs over the last few years. The CERC has observed that a trend analysis of capital cost for wind projects funded by IREDA for the period from the FY 2004–5 to FY 2008–9 indicates that the average capital cost has gone up from Rs 4.79 Cr/MW to Rs 5.76 Cr/MW. Several reasons have been cited for this, which include huge demand supply gap due to export of equipment, inadequate built-up capacity in the Indian RE equipment industry and cartellization of equipment suppliers. As a result, the cost of power from these RETs remains high.

Absence of a Supply Chain: The large-scale implementation of many RE projects or RE-based applications faces barriers from the absence of the related supply chain in India. For example, in the solar energy segment, there are no manufacturers for silicon crystals and wafers in the country and the limited number of equipment suppliers for cells. There are few commercial enterprises supplying renewable electricity technologies or applications and services. Most technologies are not made within the country but are imported. As a result, spare and replacement parts when required may not necessarily be readily available, especially in more remote locations. The services for installation of equipment and after sale services are not available. Further, the quality of equipment is often inconsistent due to the absence of industry standards in terms of durability, reliability, performance, etc. and the spares are expensive. The lead time for supply of balance of supply materials is very high.

Issues for Biomass Projects: As far as biomass technology goes, unreliable feedstock supply, absence of an organized fuel market, and frequent price fluctuations threaten project viability. The processing, transportation, and storage of biomass is also an issue. It was seen that in early 2000, the cost of biomass was nominal (Rs 300–400 per tonne) in most states. Over the years, the increase in demand of biomass for power generation as well as its alternative uses has resulted in a supply deficit in this sector and hence, spiralling biomass prices touching Rs 3,500 per tonne in some states.

Inadequate Market Prices: Currently, electricity tariffs do not reflect the environmental costs of using fossil fuels in electricity generation, thereby masking the striking environmental advantages of the new and cleaner energy options. Undertaking life-cycle assessment costs of fossil fuel-based power plants and RE-based power plants would make RETs competitive with traditional fossil fuel electricity sources.

Technological Barriers

Technology barriers take three basic forms. The first is access to technology. Many technologies are not available locally, and therefore the local know-how is poor. Second, for new RETs, the implementation risks are high. To illustrate, since solar thermal technology is at a development stage, the risks are not clearly known. Further, even though the technology may have been deployed elsewhere in the world, the expected performance of such technology under Indian conditions is not known. The third barrier is the risk of technology obsolescence. Buyers of power usually enter into long-term price contracts with RE projects. With costs expected to reduce significantly in future for many technologies, new projects based on the same technology may be more competitive and buyers, mostly the utilities, may be hesitant in procuring expensive power from older projects. While this may not be a risk for developers per se as they would be protected under a long-term contract, financiers of RE projects are particularly concerned about such risks of technology obsolescence.

Technology continues to be the Achilles, heel even for commercially deployed RETs. For instance in the case of wind, as also mentioned in the section 'Planning for Wind Turbine Technology Development', capacity utilization factors are typically low in Indian wind farms, partly because of the fact that wind turbine technologies are not designed to match the Indian wind quality and conditions. Moreover, imported technology also contributes to significantly higher costs.

Information Barriers

Despite efforts in recent years, the awareness of RETs—particularly on their applications at the local level—remains very low. Information availability to potential investors, financing institutions as well as local agencies on technology, prices and their effectiveness even for grid-connected RETs remains low. Therefore, it is not surprising that the information and awareness levels on RETs and their applications is even lower as far as households and communities are concerned. This lack of information is compounded by the lack of trained personnel for training, demonstration, and maintenance and operations of RETs. Experience indicates that subsequent to installation of RE projects/applications, no proper follow-up or assistance was available for their maintenance, thereby severely affecting their working.

Recommendations

While some RETs, such as wind, have become competitive with conventional technologies, the same is not true for most other RE options. Many RETs, such as solar technology, are yet to achieve a scale that brings down the costs to a competitive level. Others such as WTE have proven to be successful, but mostly in industrial and small decentralized operations. For these reasons, India has—time and again—been looking at policy mechanisms that would give more support to RE development. These policies aim to stimulate the commercialization of new technologies, expand the use of existing technologies, and ultimately reduce the costs of RE.

Though these policy measures have yielded success in some cases, wind being an example, the country continues to lack a comprehensive policy framework for RE. Although each RET would need a specific policy given its current status of deployment and cost competitiveness, a comprehensive RE policy or action plan that includes both long-term and short-term strategies is critical for the all-round development of RE. The Energy Coordination Committee of GoI has approved the preparation of such an RE law to provide a comprehensive legislative framework for all types of RETs, their usage and promotion. However, GoI has fixed no timeframe for the enactment of such a law. It is proposed that GoI expeditiously enact this much-desired law. States must also be encouraged to remove policy and regulatory uncertainty surrounding RE.

The real need is for localizing technology by developing indigenous manufacturing capacity for RETs and demonstrating their performance. This will allow adaptation of the technology to the Indian operational conditions, enhance technical knowhow locally, and enable reductions in the unit cost of RE equipment. This would also help overcome the post-installation problem faced by the users and strengthen the after-sales service network for RE projects and applications. This requires careful planning that allows for the steady increase of component manufacturing (and the gradual decrease of imported technology) as local expertise is developed. Development of equipment standards and testing programmes will also encourage greater market penetration by increasing the faith in these technologies. The government has been insisting on adherence to IEC/International standards for equipment and civil works for many RETs. However, standards need to be mandated as is now being proposed for solar power projects.

The design and expansion of the transmission system, particularly at the state level, should cover the evacuation and transmission infrastructure requirements of RETs. Grid connectivity to RE projects should be provided by state transmission utilities through their capital expenditure plans that are approved by the SERCs. There is also a much stronger need for co-ordination and consultation between the state transmission utilities and the nodal agency responsible for development of RE at the state level for the development of transmission infrastructure for RE projects under implementation or planned.

As far as the financing of RE projects is concerned, some problems can be addressed by including RE under the priority sectors for lending. At present the priority sector broadly comprises agriculture, small-scale industries, and other activities/borrowers (such as small business, retail trade, small transport operators, professional and self-employed persons, housing, education loans, microcredit, etc.). The inclusion of RE in priority sectors will increase the availability of credit to this sector and lead to larger participation by commercial banks in this sector.

There is also an urgent need to carry out detailed resource assessments for many RETs to fix the baseline for total resource potential, and further identifying what is technically exploitable and economically feasible. This is true even for RETs that have been commercially deployed at a large scale in the country, such as wind. There is a need to develop a far more refined wind map, with strong focus on assessment of off-shore wind energy potential, and influence of land features such as hills, buildings, forests, on wind conditions at specific locations.

Finally, large-scale capacity building to increase the planning skills and understanding of RETs by utilities, regulators, and local and municipal administrations, and improving the general awareness on RETs will go a long way in increasing the acceptability of RETs as well as aiding potential investors and sponsors of such projects. In particular, efforts must be made to enhance awareness and availability of information amongst the public at large.

References

Baumann, A., Y. Bhargava, Zx Liu, G. Nemet, and J. Wilcox (2004). MSE/C226, University of California, Berkeley, 6 December.

Beerbaum, S. and G. Weinrebe (2000). 'Solar Thermal Power Generation in India—A Techno-Economic Analysis', *Renewable Energy*, 21(2), pp. 153–74.

Central Electricity Authority (2010). 'Power Scenario at a Glance', Integrated Resource Planning Division, April.

European Photovoltaic Industry Association (2007). in K. McDonald (ed.). *Solar generation.* European Photovoltaic Industry Association and Greenpeace International.

Fthenakis, V.M. (2004). *Renewable and Sustainable Energy Reviews*, 8, pp. 303–34.

Global Wind Energy Council (2009). *Indian Wind Energy Outlook 2009*, September, p. 23.

Hanrahan David, Sanjay Srivastava, and A. Sita Ramakrishna (2006). *Improving Management of Municipal Solid Waste in India Overview and Challenges*, Environment and Social Development Unit, South Asia Region, May.

Indian Wind Turbine Manufacturers Association (2009). *Indian Wind Energy Outlook 2009*, September, pp. 7.

International Energy Agency (2009). 'Technology Roadmap', *Wind Energy*, pp. 19.

Joseph, Kurian (2007). *Lessons from Municipal Solid Waste Processing Initiatives in India,* paper presented at the 2nd International Symposium MBT 2007, 22–4 May, Hanover, Germany.

Kazmerski, Lawrence (2010). 'NREL Compilation of Best Research Solar Cell Efficiencies', National Renewable Energy Laboratory (NREL).

Ministry of Environment and Forests (2010). *India: Greenhouse Gas Emissions 2007*, Government of India, New Delhi, May.

Ministry of New and Renewable Energy (2010). http://www.mnre.gov.in/Solar-water-heaters/manufacturers.htm, as noted in 2010.

——— (2009). http://www.mnre.gov.in/solar-water-heaters.htm, February.

——— (2006). *Information Booklet on Energy Recovery from Wastes*, Government of India, New Delhi.

Ministry of Urban Development (2005). *Report of the Technology Advisory Group on Solid Waste Management*, constituted by Government of India, May.

Morthorst, Poul Erik (2009). *Wind Energy, The Facts, Costs & Prices*, compiled by Sr. Research Specialist, Riso National Labs, Denmark, March, available at http://www.ewea.org/fileadmin/ewea_documents/documents/publications/WETF/Facts_Volume_2.pdf

National Renewable Energy Laboratory, Energy Technology Cost and Performance Data, available at http://www.nrel.gov/analysis/costs.html

Rajsekhar, B., F. Van Hulle, and J.C. Jansen (1999). 'Indian Wind Energy Programme: Performance and Future Directions', *Energy Policy*, 27, pp. 229–678.

Risoe, PB Power, Est. by BVG. Data from www.investni.com/bruce_valpy.ppt

Singhal Shaleen and Suneel Pandey (2001). 'Solid Waste Management in India: Status and Future Directions', *TERI Information Monitor on Environmental Science*, 6 (1).

Supreme Court of India (1999). *Report of the Committee on Solid Waste Management,* March.

The Central Public Health and Environmental Engineering Organisation (2000). *Manual on Municipal Solid Waste Management,* Ministry of Urban Development, Government of India, New Delhi.

Part 2 Captive Solar: Does it Make Business Sense?

Abhijeet Deshpande and Rohit Chadha

The real solution to India's energy needs to achieve inclusive and sustainable development goals can be found in energy sources that have low-impact on the environment and are easily available. Non-conventional or renewable energy (RE) has the true potential to fulfill these criteria. India recognizes the importance of this and has been focusing on harnessing RE for more than two decades.

Development of RE in India received a major thrust since the enactment of the Electricity Act 2003, and has assumed greater importance as well as direction in the wake of the NAPCC declared by the GoI (2008). Considering the enormous potential of harnessing solar energy as a future source of energy and its advantage of permitting decentralized distribution of energy, the Solar Mission was declared as one of the eight missions under the NAPCC. The Jawaharlal Nehru National Solar Mission under the NAPCC was formally launched on 11 January, 2010, with a target of 22,000 MW of solar capacity by 2022, which includes large PV and solar thermal plants, smaller rooftop PV systems, and off-grid distributed solar plants. However, in this journey of harnessing the RE, and more so solar energy, the key challenge is the economic viability of renewable energy projects and cost-effectiveness of using RE. This paper seeks to examine whether RE can be a commercial and competitive choice for electrification.

With most states in India, reeling under high power supply deficit situation, diesel-based captive power is extensively used by the big residential and commercial establishments to meet their power requirements. Such dependence on diesel-based power generation is not only expensive and susceptible to global price volatility, but is also environmentally extremely polluting. *A typical business-house taking cognizance of this and preparing to comply with evolving and 'more-stringent' environmental norms while retaining competitiveness would ask the question: Does it make business sense to alter the fuel-mix to include renewable energy in captive generation?*

The authors look at a company's business-as-usual scenario (that is generating power using diesel) and the budgetary risks associated with it and then go on to analyse the economics of investing in solar power. To this effect the authors seek to assess the economic viability of using captive solar power by considering the LCoE. This empirical analysis is carried out for a large business park (CyberPark, name changed) operated by real-estate player in Gurgaon, Haryana.

Case Background

Site Profile

CyberPark, being one of the early business parks in the area, is a densely populated business park today. It is strategically located adjacent to the Delhi–Jaipur freeway (NH-8). Spread over 125 acres, it houses more than 10 large buildings. Its proximity to the international and domestic airports makes it one of the most sought-after business destinations in Gurgaon.

The tenants at CyberPark are mostly large multinational companies working on a multi-year lease with the developer. The businesses of these tenants vary widely across media, consulting, chemicals, finance, and information technology. Each building has about 15 floors plus multi-level car parking. Nearly every building has a café, food court, and other recreational amenities of its own. In addition, the developer provides for common facilities like maintenance of roads, street lighting, water, security, etc.

Energy Profile

Though on the outside CyberPark looks like a swanky office complex, on the inside, it is a gas-guzzler with primary reliance on captive diesel-based power generation for its electricity needs. It does not get electricity from the state-owned utility operating in this area.

Every building in the complex has six diesel generators, of 1,500 KVA each for a total power generation capacity of 9,000 KVA per building. The energy requirements for such business areas are understandably, large. There are two distinct sets of generators: (i) to cater to the minimum load required for lighting, computers plus other emergency operations and, (ii) others for running ACs, lifts, or other power applications.

Case Data and Critical Factors

Considering the relatively small footprint of a captive solar power plant, the suitability of solar power is to supply power for a fraction of the first set of load/applications, that is lighting, etc.

A utilities manager from the building's administration team provided the energy consumption data for two buildings that he directly managed and for a period of two weeks, that is 23 February–8 March 2009. Boxes 10.2.1 and 10.2.2 reproduce the sample data for reference. Important things to note here are the critical factors affecting the cost of electricity generation.

First, tenancy rates of various buildings in this business park vary. This is because some of the buildings are newly constructed (for example, building 1 is a relatively new building and tenancy rate is not 100 per cent. Therefore, only four DG sets (I to IV) remain utilized, while two DG sets (V and VI) are not commissioned, whereas building 2 is fully occupied). Therefore, to that extent, the number of diesel generators (per building) in operation will vary. (However, it is expected that under growth-oriented economic conditions, tenancy rates of CyberPark will remain in the range of 80–100 per cent).

The second important factor is the variation in the weather conditions. The sample data provided is for the end of winters in north India which is usually considered a pleasant weather and therefore the load conditions are considered non-peak at this time. The peak conditions are experienced in the summer months of May and June, when space-conditioning (AC) requirement is at its maximum.

Box 10.2.1

CyberPark—Building 1 Data

DG Set#	*Avg Load (KVA) (in per cent)*	*Avg Running Hrs Per Day*	*Fuel Consumption Litres Per Week*	*Units Generated Per Week*	*Fuel Efficiency*
Week 1: 23 February–1 March 2009					
I	61.96	10.17	14,063	53,296	3.78
II	61.38	4.43	6,262	23,242	3.73
III	60.23	8.05	10,647	40,490	3.79
IV	35.66	6.21	8,553	32,500	3.79
V	0.00	0.00	0	0	0.00
VI	0.00	0.00	0	0	0.00
Total	N.A.	N.A.	39525	1,49,528	3.78
Week 2: 2 March–9 March 2009					
I	58.02	10.09	13,945	49,600	3.78
II	55.15	3.19	4,323	15,000	3.73
III	59.40	10.31	14,402	52,295	3.79
IV	51.33	7.88	11,137	40,100	3.79
V	0.00	0.00	0	0	0.00
VI	0.00	0.00	0	0	0.00
Total	N.A.	N.A.	43,807	1,56,995	3.58

Energy Requirement and Cost Assessment

Average Weekly Fuel Consumed (in litres)	41666.00
Average Weekly Units Generated	153261.50
Price of Diesel (Subsidized and in INR/Litre)	29.37
Average Weekly Cost of Diesel	1223730.42
Cost of Electricity Generated (including maintenance and per unit)	9.98

Source: CyberPark Utility Manager.

Box 10.2.2
CyberPark—Building 2 Data

DG Set#	*Avg Load (KVA) (in per cent)*	*Avg Running Hrs Per Day*	*Fuel Consumption Litres Per Week*	*Units Generated Per Week*	*Fuel Efficiency*
Week 1: 23 February–1 March 2009					
I	40.31	7.09	9,005	34,300	3.81
II	53.82	6.32	8,750	33,100	3.78
III	61.16	9.82	13,415	50,800	3.79
IV	52.73	12.81	17,460	66,100	3.79
V	26.16	4.11	5,495	20,900	3.80
VI	51.54	8.83	11,905	45,200	3.80
Total	N.A.	N.A.	66,030	2,50,400	3.79
Week 2: 2 March–9 March 2009					
I	40.94	5.93	8,041	28,000	3.48
II	49.88	12.29	17,090	59,300	3.47
III	57.60	8.31	11,375	40,900	3.60
IV	59.36	14.32	20,200	71,600	3.59
V	32.37	3.84	5,035	18,200	3.62
VI	43.26	11.01	15,350	56,000	3.65
Total	N.A.	N.A.	77,091	2,74,000	3.55

Energy Requirement and Cost Assessment

Average Weekly Fuel Consumed (in litres)	71,560.50
Average Weekly Units Generated	2,62,200.00
Price of Diesel (Subsidized and in INR/Litre)	29.37
Average Weekly Cost of Diesel	21,01,731.89
Cost of Electricity Generated (including maintenance and per unit)	10.02

Source: CyberPark Utility Manager.

Next, at the time (February–March 2009) the data was sampled, the diesel rate experienced by the developer was pegged at Rs 29.37 per litre. However, the developer has also experienced the other extreme price (in recent times) of Rs 45.00 per litre during the year—2008 global oil-shock. These two price-ends become our extreme-points for analysis. (A maintenance margin of 25 per cent is considered for computing the average variable cost of electricity generation in the following boxes).

And finally, two important operational factors that affect the cost of electricity generation are: i. fuel-efficiency and ii. the cost of maintenance of diesel generators. The utilities' manager provided an estimate for this at 20 per cent of the variable cost of electricity generation. This includes the annual maintenance contracts with the generator-manufacturers, cost of labour employed to operate the DG sets, etc.

Scenario Analysis

Though the average load per generator varies in the range of (approximately) 25–60 per cent of its capacity, it would be on the higher side, depending on the occupancy rates and seasonal variation. The average load per generator during peak months (May and June) and near-capacity tenancy rate is expected to be about 80 per cent.

If load conditions can be defined as light (about 50 per cent), medium (between 50–60 per cent), and high (about 80 per cent) and corresponding diesel prices can be defined as low (less than Rs 30.00 per litre), medium (between Rs 30.00 and Rs 37.50), and high (between 37.50 and 45.00), then there are a total of nine possible combinations of price variation for the client depending on load conditions and price of diesel (in Rs per litre). For example, *light load and low fuel price, light load and medium fuel price*, and so on. However, for us to get a sense of the variability of cost of electricity we consider the two extreme scenarios that is, light load and low fuel prices and high load and high fuel prices.

Extreme Point 1: Light Load and Low Fuel Prices

Based on the case data provided earlier in this document, we can deduce that when each DG set is loaded up to 40 per cent, an estimated 40,000 litres of fuel is consumed every week per building (using 6 DG sets). With a price of diesel at Rs 29.37, this is a cost of Rs 1.748 million on a weekly basis.

At this weekly consumption level (litres 40,000) and an average fuel efficiency of 3.6 units per litre (CyberPark utility manager), the total electricity generated comes to about 1,46,800 units (for one building in one week) and therefore, the variable cost of electricity comes approximately to Rs 10.00 per unit.

Extreme Point 2: High Load and High Fuel Prices

It is estimated that under peak conditions, DG sets are loaded up to 80 per cent and an estimated 90,000 litres of fuel is consumed every week per building (using 6 DG sets). Moreover, price of diesel itself is known to fluctuate and touch upwards of Rs 45.00 per litre (as happened in 2008) to give a second (and a higher) estimate of weekly cost of fuel as Rs 4.05 million.

At this weekly consumption (litres 90,000) and an average fuel efficiency of 3.67 (CyberPark utility manager), the total electricity generated comes to about 3,30,300 units (in one week) and therefore variable cost of electricity comes close to about Rs 15.00 per unit.

Average Cost of Electricity

Thus we observe from the above analysis that the client faces an average variable cost of electricity that ranges (approximately) between Rs 10.00 per unit to about Rs 15.00 per unit for Extreme Points 1 and 2 respectively.

Annual Energy Expenses

From the ongoing figures, it is not difficult to see that the annual fuel requirement may range between 2.08 million (=40,000*52 weeks) litres and 4.68 million (=90,000*52 weeks) litres of diesel. This translates to an annual estimated cost of diesel to range between Rs 61.0896 million (=2,080,000*29.37) and Rs 210.6 million (=4,680,000*45) depending upon the prevailing price of diesel (see Box 10.2.3—factors affecting annual fuel expenses). It is important to note here that these annual figures are estimates for one building only.

Although, we don't have sufficient data to provide for an accurate figure of the annual expenses for all 10 buildings in the CyberPark, a linear estimate would put this annual expense approximately between Rs 610.896 million (Extreme Point 1) and Rs 2,106 million (Extreme Point 2).

Macro-Economic Factors

There are at least two more factors that potentially impact the effective annual energy expenses and eventually the effective average cost of electricity for the developer:

- Government spending, that is, subsidies on diesel and
- Fluctuations in foreign currency (used to buy crude oil).

Box 10.2.3

Factors Affecting Annual Fuel Expenses (figures for one building only)

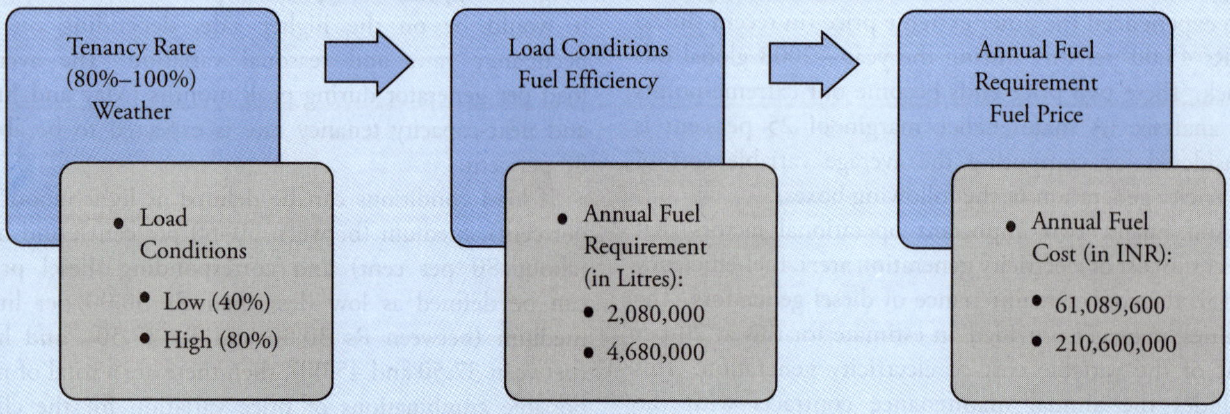

Source: Authors' own (Based on data from CyberPark Utility Manager).

So, the effective average cost of electricity is bound to touch higher figures; for example, assuming a 30 per cent subsidy on diesel, the average variable cost of electricity lies between Rs 13.00 and Rs 19.50. If we also add the fluctuations in foreign currency to our sensitivity analysis, the cost to the consumer will be very different than what is actually experienced.

Solar: Risk Mitigation Option?

In the preceding section, we see that though the developer pays for the 'firm' power, he bears a high financial risk of 'infirm' cost (this is true, even if we do not consider the macro-economic factors). Now what we want to test is, whether the developer could diversify its energy portfolio (by including off-grid solar power) to mitigate the financial risks that it faces from relying on diesel alone?

Technical Viability

Given the location and density of the buildings, a solar photovoltaic (PV)-based power plant complementing diesel-based captive generation appears to be an appropriate solution. However, to start with, we need to know whether the proposed diversification strategy and a hybrid solution (with diesel to power heavy applications like elevators and solar power for lights, PCs, and emergency) is technically viable. We consider two key factors to assess this.

Solar Insolation

Solar insolation in Haryana ranges from 5.5 kWh to 6.5 kWh per square metre of area and has about 320 clear sunny days in a year with six hours of power-grade sunlight per day. This offers good potential for generation of power through solar energy in the state (Haryana Renewable Energy Development Agency—HAREDA).

Area

Typically, an area of 15 sq. meters (or 161.458 sq. ft.) is required per kWp of Solar PV installation.[1] Now, as already mentioned, CyberPark is built over 125 acres with 10 buildings. Each building has a floor area (approximately) of 40–45,000 sq. ft. This implies that each building in the business park allows for a maximum SPV installed capacity of about 250 kWp on its roof-top.

Commercial Viability

The three possible scenarios for raising finance are to:

- Raise finance at market rates; and/or
- Raise finance using various incentives available through the government and international frameworks like the UNFCCC- promoted carbon finance mechanisms;
- Raise finance as a mix of above two scenarios. Raise part finance at market rate and still avail of the incentive.

However, to conduct commercial viability assessment we consider Scenario 1 and Scenario 2. The next two sections look at various incentives (national and international) available and applicable to the developer.

Available Incentives

National

Finding seed capital is the biggest challenge for someone willing to invest in solar power. To this effect, the Government of India has made funding schemes available with the Ministry of New and Renewable Energy (MNRE) and IREDA (see Boxes 10.2.4 and 10.2.5).

International

A captive solar project in India (as envisaged in this document) helps mitigate environmental degradation and to that extent should be eligible to earn CERs (under UNFCCC's Kyoto Protocol mechanisms)—provided the 'additionality' of the project is established. The CERs earned can be traded and sold on a commodity exchange (for example, MCX).

Applicable Incentives

Out of all the available national and international incentives, let us look at the ones applicable for the developer and their respective extents.

MNRE Schemes

CyberPark, being off-grid, can utilize the terrace of the building by leveraging on MNRE's Scheme 2 (as mentioned in Box 10.2.4)—*Solar Roof Top Programme for Abatement of Diesel and other Fuel Oil* with capital subsidy (up to 40 per cent of the capital cost). Please note that for the Eleventh Plan period, this scheme works with a budget of Rs 480,000,000 (Rs 48 crores) and can only be availed of on a first-come-first-served basis (MNRE). Please also note that Scheme 2 imposes a capacity constraint of 100 kWp. Hence, for assessing the commercial viability, we consider a solar pack of 100 kWp against a diesel generator of 125 KVA (that is 100 kW).

[1] CEA (2009) DPR for Grid Interactive Roof Top Solar PV Power Plant at Sewa Bhawan, Central Electricity Authority, December 2009 available at http://www.cea.nic.in/god/dpd/detailedprojectreport.pdf

Box 10.2.4
MNRE's Schemes (Including Capital Subsidy)

Scheme's	*Scheme 1: Solar Cities*	*Scheme 2: Solar Roof-top Programme for Abatement of Diesel and other Fuel Oil*	*Scheme 3: Grid Interactive Solar Power and Solar Thermal Power*
Objective	To promote use of renewable energy in urban areas by providing support to municipal corporations for preparation and implementation of a road map to develop their cities as solar cities.	To promote roof-top SPV systems on building to replace DG sets installed for minimum load requirement (varying between 25 KW to 100 KW) for operation during load shedding. A roof-top SPV system can be with or without grid interaction.	To provide generation-based incentive of a maximum of Rs 12 per kWh to grid interactive SPV plants of a minimum installed capacity of 1 MWp which are commissioned by 31 December 2009.
Physical Target	NA	4.25 MW	NA
Budget	Rs 300 million	Rs 480 million	NA
Financial Provisions	Up to Rs 5 million per city/ town. Financial assistance for installation of various renewable energy devices and systems can be availed as per provisions of various schemes of MNRE.	Central financial assistance in form of capital subsidy of up to 30 per cent to commercial organizations and up to 40 per cent to non-commercial organizations.	The incentive will be released by IREDA to the eligible SPV power project developer on quarterly basis on receipt of certified information the net electricity fed to grid from the SPV power project during the period of the claim.

Source: MNRE (2009).

Box 10.2.5
IREDA's Interest Subsidy Scheme

Features	*Norms*
Eligibility	Individuals, intermediaries, and commercial organizations
Rate of Interest	7 per cent (commerical borrowers who can claim depreciation benefits)
	5 per cent (individuals and other organizations)
	2.5 per cent or 4.5 per cent (intermediaries who borrow funds from IREDA for lending at 5 per cent or 7 per cent rate of interest will be charged an interest rate of respectively by IREDA. Intermediaries will not be able to claim depreciation benefit)
Loan Period	6 years
Moratorium	1 year
Amount of Loan	80 per cent of the cost of the project
Loan's Upper Limit	No limit
Service Charges	1 per cent of loan distributed
Systems Covered	All types of SPV Systems except solar pumps. Systems should conform to the MNRE specification and guidelines for 2001–02 or 2002–03, certificates from Solar Energy Centre (SEC)/other Authorized Test Centres (ATC)

Source: IREDA.

Interest Subsidy Scheme

Under IREDA's interest subsidy scheme, the developer meets the eligibility criteria (for lending at 7 per cent for commercial borrowers) to cover the balance cost of SPV power plant with an assumed capital structure of '80–20' debt-equity ratio. It is also eligible to claim the accelerated depreciation benefit.

Carbon Finance

The proposed SPV power plant will assist the developer to earn CERs (subject to establishing the 'additionality' of the project). As calculated using the tools available from UNFCCC's website (available at http://cdm.unfccc.int/EB/017/eb17repan3.pdf), the project could earn an estimated 138 CERs per annum.

The cash flows arising out of all these applicable incentive schemes are considered while computing the levellized costs of energy for the scenario—'solar with incentives', in the next section.

Decision Criteria

We now compute the LCoE of a SPV Power Plant and DG Power Plant (both of equivalent capacities). The LCoE for the SPV Power Plant at 'CyberPark' is worked out considering two different scenarios—with and without incentives; while the LCoE for the DG power plant has been worked out considering the two extreme points referred earlier. In addition, we also compute the LCoE for a third and 'average point' scenario for diesel. Box 10.2.6 shows various parameter-assumptions in the computation of the LCoE.

- Note for SPV Parameters: As per Scheme 2 by MNRE, central financial assistance does not cover the cost of battery. However, MNRE does recommend a minimal battery back-up of 1 hour. Thus, for computing LCoE for SPV scenarios, we've assumed a battery back-up for 90 minutes with a replacement every 10 years.
- Note for Diesel Parameters: While the technical assumptions (O&M expenses, escalation, etc.) are based on data gathered from the site, the commercial assumptions (capital structure, salvage value, etc.) are normative.

Box 10.2.7 contrasts the LCoE for SPV against that of diesel. First, we plotted the LCoE range of diesel (Rs 7.40/kWh—Rs 15.18/kWh) against fuel prices on the independent axis and then (for ease of comparison) we superimposed the LCoE of solar as horizontal lines for two scenarios (with and without incentives): Rs 8.01/kWh and Rs 10.65/kWh respectively.

Box 10.2.6
Parameter-assumptions Adopted in the Computation of the LCoE

	SPV Power Plant		*DG Power Plant*		
Parameters	*With Incentives*	*Without Incentives*	*Extreme Point 1*	*Average Point*	*Extreme Point 2*
Power Plant Capacity (kW)	100	100	100	100	100
Useful Life (Years)	25	25	10	10	10
Normative Capital Cost (INR)	17,00,000,000	170,000,000	20,000,000	20,000,000	20,000,000
Annual Energy Production (kWh)	175,200	175,200	350,400	525,600	700,800
Capacity Utilization Factor (per cent)	18	18	NA	NA	NA
Annual O&M Charges (per cent)	5	5	20	20	20
Escalation (per cent)	5	5	10	11	12
Debt (per cent)	80	70	70	70	70
Equity (per cent)	20	30	30	30	30
Salvage Value (per cent)	10	10	10	10	10
Loan Tenure (Years)	6	10	10	10	0
Interest Rate (per cent)	7	14.29	14.29	14.29	14.29

Note: Annual O&M Expenses for SPV Power plants is computed as a percentage of capital cost whereas of the DG Power plant it is as a percentage of fuel expense (*Source*: CyberPark Utility Manager)
Source: Authors' own (Based on data from CyberPark Utility Manager).

Box 10.2.7
LCoE Comparison

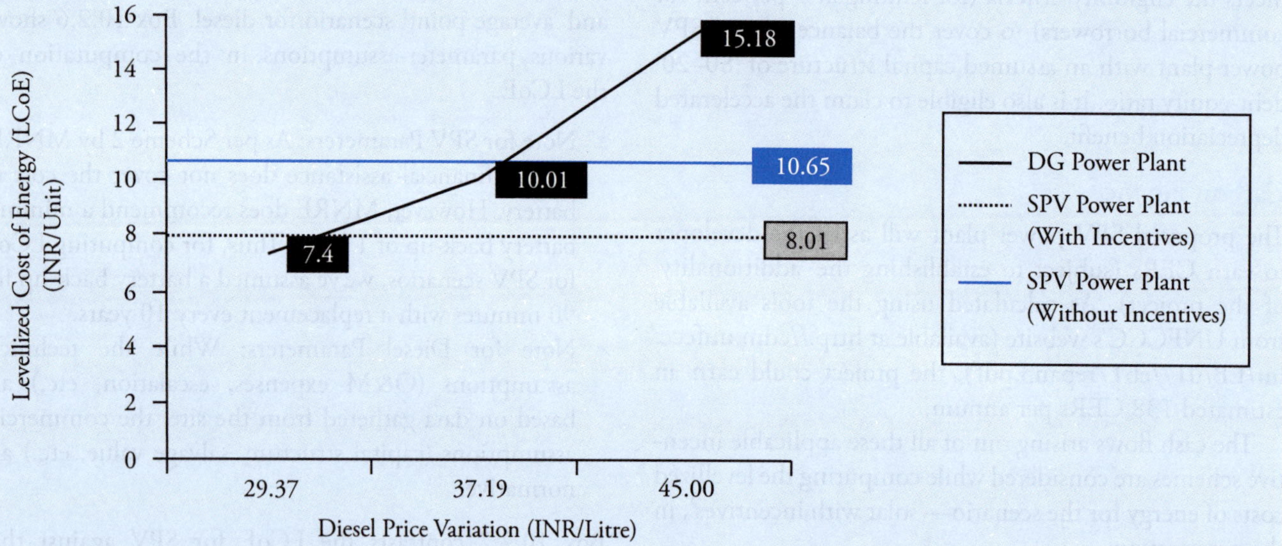

Source: Authors' own.

Observations and Discussion

The LCoE comparison provides interesting results for buildings (like CyberPark) that are not connected to the grid and rely solely on diesel-based power generation.

It is observed that the levellized cost of solar energy for both scenarios (that is, with and without incentives) falls within the range defined by the two extreme points for levellized cost of diesel-based power generation. This indicates that solar power is competitive against diesel and developer retains the choice between 'firm power and infirm costs' (that is, in the case of diesel) versus 'relatively infirm power and firm costs' (for solar). Therefore, solar power may act as a risk mitigation option against variations in diesel-prices and in load conditions (as defined by tenancy rates and weather). This appears true even while the developer raises finance at market rates.

Thus, the answer to the question—whether the developer could diversify its energy portfolio (by including off-grid solar power) to mitigate the budgetary risks that it faces while relying on diesel alone—looks encouraging for the adoption of SPV power plant by business houses.

What this further shows is that developer is not necessarily constrained by the 100 kWp capacity-limit defined by MNRE (to avail central financial assistance); rather, the only constraint is the area available on the terrace. In our case, with an available roof top area of 40,000–45,000 sq. ft. (approximately) per building, this translates to a maximum installed capacity of about 250 kWp per building.

However, the developer would obviously prefer to first install and exhaust the incentivized capacity of 100 kWp and then scale-up progressively to reach the constraint defined by the available area on its roof-top. Therefore, a preferred solar adoption strategy may include a phased installation approach.

Future Trends: Advantage Solar

With reference to the CERC notification dated 8 December 2009, the capital cost of SPV power plant is proposed to be reduced to about Rs 152 million (from the current Rs 170 million) per MW for the year 2010–11. Hence the LCoE for SPV is expected to decrease.

Moreover, removal of diesel subsidy or an upward movement of diesel price will increase the LCoE for diesel-based generation. This will further enhance the competitiveness of SPV power plant against that of DG power plant.

Role of Incentives

Though, LCoE for solar is competitive even without the incentives, the current government financing schemes and *The Kyoto Mechanisms* should continue (and perhaps be enhanced to remove the cap of 100 kWp from MNRE's scheme 2—*Solar Roof-Top Programme for Abatement of Diesel and other Fuel Oils*) to promote off-grid installations in urban services sector. These incentives would motivate commercial establishments to jump-start a sustainable-energy investment strategy.

Adoption Challenges

For an existing site (like CyberPark), the solar investment may appear to be a relatively large upfront investment. However, if we compare and contrast it against the overall cost of developing and maintaining a business park; it'll only be a fraction. Thus, notwithstanding government efforts to facilitate financing options through the National Solar Mission, there remain challenges of raising awareness and investor confidence.

References

Central Electricity Authority (2009). *Detailed Project Report for Grid Interactive Roof Top Solar Photovoltaic Power Plant at Sewa Bhawan,* R.K. Puram, New Delhi, available at http://www.cea.nic.in/god/dpd/detailedprojectreport.pdf

Central Electricity Regulatory Authority (2009). *Terms and Conditions for Tariff Determination from Renewable Energy Sources,* notification No L-7/186(201)/2009-CERC, 16 September.

Government of India (2003). *The Electricity Act, 2003,* Act 36 of 2003, New Delhi, May 2003

IDFC (2009). 'Building Integrated Photovoltaic in Rabi Rashmi Abasan: A "ray" of Hope for Sustainable Energy Solutions', *Policy Group Quarterly,* 6, December.

Ministry of New and Renewable Energy [MNRE] (2009). *National Solar Mission,* Government of India, 18 July.

UNESCAP Theme Study (2008). *Energy Security and Sustainable Development in Asia and the Pacific,* 11 April.

UNFCC approved baseline methodology (2004). '*AM0019—Renewable energy project replacing part of the electricity production of one single fossil-fuel-fired power plant that stands alone or supplies electricity to a grid, excluding biomass projects*', Version 1, 6 December, available at http://cdm.unfccc.int/EB/017/eb17repan3.pdf

11 Decentralized Distributed Generation for an Inclusive and Low Carbon Economy for India

Chandrashekar Iyer, Rajneesh Sharma, Ronnie Khanna, and Akil V. Laxman

Background

Power is essential for the socio-economic development of a country and is being recognized as a basic infrastructural requirement. Rising demand for energy in the developing world has given rise to two main challenges for the power sector—the addition of new generation capacity and expansion of the current transmission and distribution infrastructure. Decentralized generation has the potential to solve both these issues, particularly in remote areas. Access to modern and reliable source of energy is a major driver for rural development and improved livelihoods. Electrification is a significant step towards poverty alleviation, income generation, health, and other developmental objectives. Electrification has a major impact on rural society by bringing in higher productivity through electrical machinery, higher number of productive hours in the day through electric lighting and better access to affordable education, health, and entertainment. It enhances the quality of life of the rural populace and holds out hope for a better future.

According to the 2001 Census, the rural household electrification of India was around 43.52 per cent, which implies that a large section of India's rural population does not have access to electricity, let alone a reliable supply of it. As a result, rural households spend huge amounts of money on expensive and environmentally damaging resources such as charcoal, wood, and kerosene. The low income households spend a considerable amount of their time in collecting wood for their kitchens and are exposed to indoor air pollution on a daily basis which according to World Bank estimates, is responsible for over 1.5 million deaths[1] per year the world over. About 42 per cent[2] of households in India use kerosene as the primary source of lighting and the GoI incurs a subsidy bill of nearly Rs 2,765 crores[3] (2009–10) to provide subsidized kerosene and LPG to the populace. This subsidy bill would come down dramatically if all households used electricity as their primary source of lighting.

Grid Extension (GE) and Decentralized Distributed Generation (DDG) are the two basic means used to electrify rural areas. GE involves laying out distribution infrastructure to reach out to the villages while DDG comprises small, modular, decentralized off-grid energy systems located in or near the place where energy is used.

While grid extension is a costly solution for connecting to remote locations and populations spread over a larger area, it does offer the benefits of being connected to the grid with access to relatively cheaper source of electricity, continuous supply, and access to energy generated by

[1] The World Bank (2007).

[2] National Sample Survey Organization (2008).

[3] Union Budget 2010–11.

generating stations located far away from the consumption point. On the other hand, the maintenance of a large distribution network and high Transmission and Distribution (T&D) losses on such a network are issues that the utilities have to deal with. Grid extension becomes prohibitively expensive in the cases of remote villages which are hard to reach due to their location constraints. Most rural electrification in India is currently implemented through this option.

DDG is the other option for rural electrification that has been implemented successfully across the world in nations such as Cambodia, Nepal, China, and Philippines. DDG can be based on either conventional or renewable sources and is usually implemented in remote villages where connectivity to the grid is not feasible or cost-effective. DDG enables electricity generation at the local level using locally available resources ensuring reduced dependence on external resources. Local distribution networks or micro-grids are set up over a cluster of villages and powered by a local generating plant which may be based on conventional fuels such as diesel, natural gas, fuel oil or on renewable energy such as wind energy, solar energy, hydro power, and biomass. DDG is also promoted by the GoI through the Rajiv Gandhi Grameen Vidyutikaran Yojana (RGGVY) (scheme of Rural Electricity Infrastructure and Household Electrification) which aims at electrifying about 1.15 lakh unelectrified villages and 2.34 crore BPL (Below Poverty Line) households. This scheme includes a capital subsidy of Rs 540 crore for DDG for the Eleventh Five Year Plan.

The high cost of extending electrical grid coverage to remote areas can enhance the viability of renewable energy technologies, such as solar PV. The availability of clean electricity not only helps households avoid the health risks associated with conventional forms of energy, such as kerosene, charcoal, and disposable batteries, but also helps the global environment through avoidance of GHGs and conventional air pollution associated with fossil fuel-based forms of electricity. Table 11.1 shown below shows the CO_2 emissions reduced by the usage of RE DDG units as against conventional sources of electricity.

DDG systems also have a definite positive impact on the rural economy due to introduction of a new revenue generating entity (the DDG unit) into the system and the jobs that are created due to its establishment. Biomass-based DDG units are quite well suited to rural areas as they enable the farmer to reduce electricity expenses by selling the biomass to the DDG unit, in addition to the benefits that come with electrification such as higher productivity and better access to communication, etc.

Table 11.1 Emission Reduction due to Use of RE DDG

Grid Emission Factor (India)[4]	0.80	tCO2/MWh
Estimated monthly household consumption	50	kWh
No. of households in village	50	Households
Annual consumption of a village	30000	kWh
CO_2 emission reduced compared to regular sources	24	tonnes/year/village

Source: Authors' own.

Penetration of DDG

As on 30 April 2010, 16.1 per cent[5] of India's villages were still unelectrified. These villages are expected to be electrified through a mix of GE and DDG. The MNRE has undertaken the remote village electrification programme targeted at electrifying unelectrified remote census villages and remote unelectrified hamlets of electrified census villages where grid connectivity is either not feasible or not cost-effective. A total of 5259 remote villages/hamlets were identified in 2001 for rolling out the project, out of which 3332 villages have already been covered.[6] The plan is to electrify 296 villages through distributed generation technologies of biomass gasification and small hydro.

Barriers to Penetration

Over 158 million households in India[7] have limited access to modern energy sources like electricity and non-traditional cooking fuels like LPG (liquefied petroleum gas). Instead they rely on inefficient and polluting energy sources such as kerosene, wood, dung, and other biomass.

RE based-DDG projects across the world have been successful in areas where demand exists and DDG has been found to be economically viable. However, successes at the local or the micro-level have rarely been scaled up. This is due to a number of institutional, financial, and technical reasons. In this section, we look at the issues that have impeded the development of RE-based DDG projects.

[4] CEA (2008).
[5] Ibid.
[6] MNRE.
[7] Census of India (2001).

Rural Energy Synonymous with Rural Electrification

Over the years, planners have regarded delivery of rural energy services as synonymous with rural electrification. This is reflected by the fact that once a village has been declared electrified, the energy needs of the village are deemed to have been met, regardless of whether electricity is available to that village and whether the village rural electrification infrastructure is operational throughout the year. At the same time, energy needs related to cooking, water extraction, and space heating have not been looked at as an integral component of this energization programme and thus are developed as disjointed and specific programmes catering to a particular end use.

Poor Access to Credit

The rural poor, owing to limited cash flows have limited options for investing in clean energy technologies like solar home lighting systems. In light of this, access to credit becomes crucial for facilitating access to clean energy technologies, especially for relatively capital intensive DDG systems. Owing to the consumptive nature of energy, cumbersome procedures involved in accessing formal credit and the reluctance of formal banking institutions to provide credit to the poor for meeting their household energy needs, especially in the remote areas, the poor have remained outside the mainstream, especially in terms of accessing clean technologies like solar home lighting systems, biogas plants, etc. The poor are unable to provide the required guarantees and hence, financial institutions do not develop packages for decentralized rural energy programmes. In cases, where institutions like SELCO (Solar Electric Light Company) have been able to facilitate access to credit (see Box 11.1), the development of DDG energy technologies have taken place at a much faster pace than in areas where these facilities are not available.

> **Box 11.1**
> **SELCO Model**
>
> The organization has formed a steady relationship with nine regional rural banks, commercial banks, NGOs, and rural farmer cooperatives to develop financial solutions which match the needs of the rural folk after considering the cash flows of the targeted audience. For example, SELCO helped a small handloom weaver community in Doddaullarthi, Karnataka, to finance their lighting needs by arranging for finance from the local village bank with instalments suited to their income levels. It also helped fund the margin money required for the loans with support from Renewable Energy & Energy Efficiency Partnership (REEEP).
>
> *Source*: SELCO with REEEP.

Financial institutions in India, due to lack of adequate knowledge of these technologies, their advantages, and their returns, are not convinced enough to lend for the purchase of these (RETs) especially solar PV technologies. These technology options do not directly result in productive and income generating activities and thus, in absence of enough information, banks and FIs find it hard to justify lending to the rural consumers for these packages.

Lack of Adequate Information/Data for Market Development

Limited data and information exists for rural energy entrepreneurs looking to enter the clean energy DDG market. However, due to the fact that a number of government agencies collect data at the rural level that focus on different aspects of energy, including resource availability, supply potential, and to a limited extent demand assessment, this data is neither shared nor collated into a single database for an informed decision-making system either by the government or private sector.

Implementation of Policy and Regulatory Frameworks

The EA 2003

The Electricity Act 2003 (EA 2003) has been the most important driver of reform in the electricity sector over the last decade. The EA 2003, besides providing for the overall development and management of the Indian electricity sector has included some legislative provisions facilitating and promoting adoption of renewable energy technologies for rural electrification through:

- Section 6—which obligates the state government to supply electricity to all areas, including villages and hamlets.
- Section 13—which exempts the need for a distribution, transmission, and trading licence based on recommendation of the state government for local authority, panchayat institution, co-operative society, or franchisees.
- Section 14—which exempts licence to a person who intends to generate and distribute electricity in a rural area notified by the state government. Furthermore, a person exempted under the 8th Proviso of Section 14 as above would also be free from purview of appropriate commissions in matters pertaining to determination of tariffs.
- The retail tariffs for such exempted persons would be based on mutual agreements between such persons and the consumers.

The legislative provisions do provide for mutually agreed tariffs. However, the tariffs of grid-connected consumers are decided by the respective regulatory commissions and are lower than the average cost of supply for the area in the case of domestic and agricultural consumers. The lower tariffs are a result of the cross-subsidizing effect that the higher tariffs paid by high tension (HT) consumers have on the overall revenue of the distribution companies. In the case of DDG, the tariffs are mutually decided between the generator producing electricity using DDG means and the end consumers. The remote areas electrified by DDG typically do not have any subsidizing consumers, thus resulting in higher tariffs for the domestic consumers.

Rural Electrification Policy

The Rural Electrification Policy declared in 2006, aims at provision of access to electricity for all households, quality and reliable power supply at reasonable rates, and minimum lifeline consumption of one unit per household per day as a merit good by year 2012. It specifies the approach to be used for rural electrification through DDG and GE along with the financing and implementation mechanism required for such projects.

The RGGVY Programme

The Government of India, in February 2005, launched a large-scale electrification effort, called the Rajiv Gandhi Grameen Vidyutikaran Yojana with the objective of speeding up rural electrification under the 'Power for all by 2012' initiative. The RGGVY programme envisaged a major grid extension and reinforcement programme, especially for that of the rural grid. RGGVY also envisaged the use of DDG systems based on conventional and non-conventional sources where grid supply is not feasible or cost-effective.

The RVE Programme

The Government of India also launched the Remote Village Electrification (RVE) programme through the MNRE for supplementing the efforts of the Ministry of Power (MoP). The RVE is responsible for electrifying unelectrified remote census villages (with a population of less than 100 inhabitants) and remote unelectrified hamlets of electrified census villages where the grid connection is either not feasible or not economical (because they are located in forests, hills, deserts, or islands) and where DDG projects are not implemented by the RGGVY of the MoP. The status of RVE is given in Table 11.2.

Table 11.2 Status of Remote Village Electrification

	State	*Total Villages sanctioned since 2001*	*Villages completed up to 2007*	*Ongoing Villages*
1	Madhya Pradesh	199	30	150
2	Gujarat	38	38	–
3	Rajasthan	327	218	85
4	Chhattisgarh	368	325	43
5	Maharashtra	271	120	148
6	Karnataka	20	16	–

Source: MNRE.

The GoI for the last five decades, through its various committees and groups, has tried to address the issues related to provision of rural energy services resulting in programmes related to rural electrification, promotion of RETs improved *chullahs* (cook stoves), biogas development, etc. The impact of such programmes, over the years, though significant has not been to the level expected, on account of the increasing population, limited increase in income levels, attention to supply rather than demand, and use of inefficient institutional mechanisms for delivery of these services that has lead to leakages, higher losses, and low availability.

One of the very strong messages that has come out from a number of failed rural energy programmes has been the fact that delivery of rural energy services has become synonymous with grid extension and that grid extension programmes have their own limitations and have been able to meet the energy requirements only in a limited manner.

The case of DDG programme has been similar. DDG has been dependent on national programmes that have either been technology-centric or end-use-based without any inter-linkages. Owing to a rigid programme-based approach, little or no attention has been given to either the effectiveness of these programmes or the issues that promote human welfare through a measurable approach. Hence, in spite of the existence of these programmes for nearly two decades, their impact on the development scenario in general and the rural energy scenario in particular, has been limited.

Lack of Research and Development (Including Customization) in Technology

In spite of the need, sufficient emphasis has not been laid on technology development in the national level energy programme. In the entire planning mechanism there is no emphasis on the necessity of designing devices as per the needs of the community and this is reflected in the absence of a mechanism that can take and incorporate feedback for assessing R&D requirements from the community in the planning process. For instance, the kerosene devices used in rural areas for lighting purposes are technically archaic in nature. This not only results in higher kerosene consumption, but also in higher emissions of smoke and poor luminosity.

Limited Inter- and Intra-agency Coordination

Currently, DDG programmes are largely being implemented by government agencies, and on a much smaller scale, by non-government organizations. In case of government agencies, there is neither intra- nor inter-agency coordination. An example of lack of intra-agency coordination is the fact that there is no synergy between the improved *chulha* programme and the biogas programme. In some cases, biogas subsidy is extended to the households that are using improved *chulha* and vice versa. This may be justified in certain situations, but it is highly probable that the concerned beneficiary may have only required a biogas plant, rather than an improved *chulha*. This leads to duplication of efforts and of resources that could have been applied productively elsewhere. The cases of lack of inter-agency coordination are far too many. The biogas programme, the improved *chulha* programme, and the marketing of LPG are all directed at meeting the cooking requirements in rural areas, but each programme has its own targets, which are pursued independent of each other.

Lack of Adequate Awareness about RETs in Rural India

The use of RETs and their advantages are still not widely known in rural India. As a result most rural folk are not aware of these technologies and their advantages. Furthermore, the high up-front cost of these technology options make RE-based DDG options out of the reach of the common rural consumer unless backed up with some support and access to financing

Lack of Confidence in RETs in Rural India

Even in areas where the rural consumers are aware of these technologies, that is, in areas where pilot projects or large-scale programmes have been implemented, the limited success of these projects/programmes have resulted in the consumers often being wary of investing in these technologies due to their past failures. The rural poor have a very limited risk-taking capacity and unless completely certain as to the products sustainability and viability, would not take the risk of investing in it.

Risks Associated with Developing a Marketing Enterprise in RE Technologies

Entrepreneurs face issues like competition from highly subsidized yet unsustainable RE products being marketed by the state Renewable Energy Development Authorities (REDA) under the MNRE programmes. These government programmes are often seen as another target to be achieved, and as a result, the product development and customization to local needs, sustenance, after sales services, etc., are poor. Besides, the marketing skills and knowledge of entrepreneurs with regard to RETs are often not very developed. Entrepreneurs face large pre-investment risks associated with the costs of marketing, contracting, and information collection.

One of the key requirements for entrepreneurs includes upfront investment in the supply chain to ensure smooth delivery of services. For instance, the availability of spares in the local market or trained mechanics, who undertake repairs and change installations, can contribute to sustained delivery of services.

Small-scale local entrepreneurs may also need to be made aware of the unexploited market potential in the sector and be provided with initial assistance in market research and development. In order to encourage such innovation and ownership, micro-credit schemes have supported the development of local capacities to plan, execute, maintain, and finance rural infrastructure.

Willingness to Pay

Successful deployment of rural energy interventions is contingent upon widespread willingness to pay amongst rural households and energy users. Willingness to pay in turn is contingent upon the following broad conditions:

- Availability and access to credit.
- Image and brand status of service/product provider.
- Earlier experience with such products.
- Cost comparison with incumbent energy source—break up between up-front costs and variable costs.
- Impact on livelihood.
- Life of the product and daily operability of the product.
- Repair and maintenance of the product and the availability of spare parts and service network.

These, however, are quite likely to be only perceived barriers. It has been seen that electricity consumption has high value for rural households and where access exists, willingness to pay is high, even amongst poorer households.

Consumers are generally willing to pay significantly more for shorter outages and better-quality supply even in grid-connected areas. This is also confirmed by observations that in remote and off-grid areas consumers are willing to pay a premium for electricity connections, either from diesel generators or for non-conventional connections.

An appropriate example of this would be the Gosaba Rural Energy Cooperative Society in West Bengal where consumers have shown a willingness to pay market rates when the choice is between no supply and a basic level of supply with demonstrable benefits despite the area being amongst the poorest in the region (South 24 Paraganas where Gosaba Island is located ranks 14 among 18 districts of West Bengal in declining order of per capita income). The Gosaba Off-grid Cooperative Society is promoted and assisted by West Bengal Renewable Energy Development Agency (WBREDA). The society, which generates electricity using a 500 KWe biomass gasifier plant, currently supplies electricity to about 1,000 households and small businesses through a 11 KV distribution system. An interesting aspect of the Gosaba electricity supply scheme is that initially while the plant started off with just one 100 KW gasifier plant and supplied to only 25 consumers, the plant quickly scaled up to 500 KW to supply electricity to over 900 consumers for 16 hours a day once the local people were convinced of the potential benefits. The domestic consumers pay Rs 5/kWh as compared to Rs 9/kWh being borne by them for diesel-based generation before the start of the Gosaba project. An average household consumption is between 1–3 units/day and is also charged a fixed charge of Rs 75/month. So, a typical household consuming 60 units a month would pay Rs 375/month as electricity charges.

It has been seen that rural communities are able and willing to pay for reliable electricity services, especially where good-quality electricity connections exist and the positive impact on rural incomes can offset the cost of the electricity supply. If electricity generation and supply is directly tied to income generation activity, the community's ability to pay for electricity services are further enhanced.

Financial Viability

Financing is a major issue for DDG systems based on renewable energy. The major components related to cost are capital cost and operation and maintenance cost. The relatively high capital cost results in the overall high cost of generation related to these systems. Owing to the lower income levels, the rural households are generally able to meet the operational costs and some part of the capital cost related to the DDG systems. The relatively high capital expenditure requires the government to provide support in the form of capital subsidy/grant to render the DDG systems financial viability. The involvement of the local community stakes in a way enhances the viability of the project.

The graph (Figure 11.1) comparing costs of a diesel versus a solar system (25 k\KW) is shown below. The sharp spikes in cost of the solar system are caused by the very high cost of battery replacement after every five years. The spike in cost of diesel generator (DG) is caused by the system replacement. In a comparison between 25 KW solar and DG systems, over a 20 year period, the user gains a net positive amount by installing a solar system. The difference between the cost savings (gap between the lines), is greater than the difference in the initial capital investments, making the solar system a viable alternative to diesel generation under the given set of assumptions. (No depreciation benefits have been included in the analysis)

The Alternative Energy Promotion Centre (AEPC) in Nepal has been implementing various mini-grid and off-grid renewable Rural Electrification (RE) projects, where the contribution of the community is as high as 50 per cent of the project cost. This has increased the sustainability of the project as the members of the community set the tariffs, manage the project, ensure O&M, and also undertake other development work in the village from the funds created under the project.

Limited Site Specific Site Options

The DDG-based renewable energy projects are site specific and may face issues related to limited options for technology selection owing to its dependence on the availability of the locally available renewable energy resource and dispersed population. Further, low levels of population density may offer low levels of demand, resulting in short hours of operation of the system thereby impacting the project viability.

Institutional Aspects

The DDG based on renewable energy mainly caters to the remote areas, which face issues related to lack of local technical and management capacity for operation and maintenance. This hinders the successful operation of the DDG-based system and can further increase the cost of running such systems, thereby impacting the financial viability as well.

Owing to the remote location of the renewable energy-based DDG system, usually the distance between the local

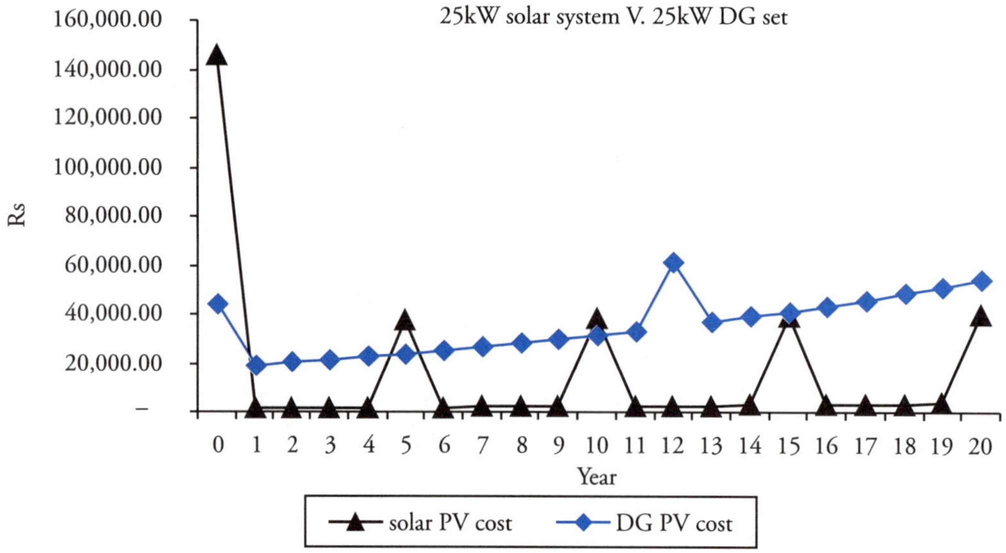

Figure 11.1 25 KW Diesel System v/s 25 KW Solar PV System

Source: Authors' own.

manufacturer/service providers is large. Visits of the local manufacturer/service providers for service and support are therefore expensive and not executed regularly.

Lack of planning to keep sufficient feedstock for the biomass-based DDG systems and mismatch between the needed electricity for use of specific applications and the supplied energy can further impact the performance of the DDG systems.

Programme Effectiveness

The key issues impacting the programme effectiveness are detailed below:

- Lack of participation: To date local institutions, including Panchayat Raj Institutions, community organizations, and NGOs have had little involvement in rural electricity supply through DDG systems. The experience of other sectors, such as rural water supply and natural resource management, demonstrates significant potential benefits from greater participation of local institutions.
- Lack of performance monitoring of the DDG systems and delay in disbursement of grant/subsidy by the government.

Lessons from Successful Experiments in DDG

Need for Well-designed Business Models: Gasification-based Mini Grid, Uganda

A mini grid connected to a 10 KW gasifier unit fuelled by eucalyptus prunings has been installed on a Ugandan farm. The gasification system has been running since August 2006 on a daily basis for six hours in the evenings producing 3 KW on single phase only. The gasifier unit is supplied with eucalyptus prunings from the 100-acre farm and hence is guaranteed fuel supply for operations.

The system highlights the success that gasifier systems can have in ensuring electricity supply in rural areas. Business models have to be carefully designed keeping in mind feedstock supply, conversion technology, and energy allocation. The business models should also provide suitable incentives to both the farmers and the entrepreneurs in order to ensure a mutually benefiting sustainable system. The farmers supplying biomass could be compensated by reduction of their electricity bills to that extent and the entrepreneur could be incentivized by ensuring adequate returns on the investment through fair tariffs. Without reliable business models, investors will not take the risk of investing. Capacity building is essential to develop and promote business opportunities.

Financing Arrangements: Small Hydro-based Off-Grid Electrification, Nepal

Small hydro projects in KW capacity were planned under the Renewable Energy Development Programme (REDP) to electrify remote rural areas. The cost of these plants varies from $ 1500/KW to $ 2000/KW. 243 SHP (Small Hydro Project) projects established so far total 3MW capacity.

This highlights the need for government support for DDG-based renewable projects. Loans from banks funded 50 per cent of the project cost. The Government of Nepal loaned 10 per cent of the project cost to the community through its Local Area Development. IFIs (World Bank, UNEP) contributed to the project through a grant to the tune of 40 per cent of the project cost. Tariff is set by the community and once the repayment of loan is done, the tariff is lowered. The community creates a fund from the revenue collected from consumers and it is used for community development programmes. This kind of financing arrangement ensures a lower tariff burden on the consumers and sustainability of the project.

Capacity Building: Biomass Energy for Rural India Project (BERI), India

This project aims at the promotion of decentralized mode of power generation from biomass fuels to cater to rural demand. It is supported by the state government, central government, UNDP, and Indo-Canada Environment facility and covers 24 villages.

This project recognizes the need for capacity building of stakeholders involved in DDG from biomass in order to ensure sustainability of such projects. It includes long-term training for entrepreneurs, NGOs, managers, and women in planning, management of bio-energy systems and business skills for the success of rural bio-energy development institutions. Potential technicians, preferably from among the targeted community are also trained on the technical operations of the bio-energy systems to ensure the availability of a talent pool to operate and maintain such systems. NGOs, community-based organizations, and entrepreneurs are given training with focus on developing business skills such as marketing, finance, accounting, billing, and project development, and establishing linkages with micro-credit organizations, NGOs, and other village-level groups for enabling cost recovery.

Involvement of Local Population: Desi Power, India

Decentralized Energy Systems India Private Ltd (DESI Power) works on DDG system implementation in the villages of India. DESI Power has set up a 74 KW biomass-based energy power plant in Badarbahari village in Bihar, which it runs through a community-driven model.

DESI Power's business model is based on building and operating biomass gasification-based power plants in direct association with local partners and later on transferring the plant to the partner under mutually agreed terms. The local partner may be an NGO, a panchayat, a co-operative body or an industry, actively involved in these projects right from the beginning. The 'EmPower' Partnership Programmes run by DESI Power help in setting up micro enterprises owned and managed by local village organizations. A number of power plants and the linked micro enterprises in neighbouring villages form a cluster having an intrinsic relationship between them, providing mutual support and markets for survival as well as growth. The project has provided direct employment to 19 locals and has been declared a Winner at the World Bank Global Development Marketplace Competition 2006 in Washington with a prize of USD 200,000.

Willingness to Pay: Sagardweep Rural Energy Development Co-op Society Ltd, India

WBREDA implemented a Solar PV programme benefiting 30 per cent of the 6,000 families in Sagardweep Island. A dozen mini-grids (25–28.5 KWp), each costing about Rs 1 crore supply grid quality power for 4–6 hours in the evening at the rate of Rs 8 per unit to about 100–150 consumers. The mini-grids are operated by local co-operative societies formed by people using the grid. The project was financed through a government subsidy of Rs 6 million and a loan of Rs 4 million from WBREDA at one per cent interest.

The consumption is regulated by MCBs in the consumers' premises and is monitored from a computerized central console, which houses the batteries. Local youths trained for day-to-day management of the system, are paid Rs 900 per month. Billing, collection, and maintenance of discipline is done by the society which remits the collection to WBREDA. The results are so satisfactory that there is a queue of villagers willing to pay Rs 10 per unit for power.

Impact on Environment: Green Power Rural Energy Programme, India

In villages surrounding the Similipal Tiger Reserve, Green Power International is working with WWF Orissa and Gram Swaraj Mayurbhunj to install 15 Rural Energy Units of Biogas. Each unit will reduce demand for timber by about 1500 metric tonnes per unit per year by utilizing biogas technology. This will go a long way in preserving vegetation and sustaining biodiversity, while also providing cheap and reliable source of energy for the villages in which they are installed.

It is estimated that each household biogas plant can save eight tonnes of firewood, 64 litres of kerosene and 1.2 acres of forest each year. About five tonnes of natural bio fertilizer is produced by each biogas plant annually which contains three times more nitrogen than chemical fertilizers. It is estimated that each household provided with a biogas plant will save almost 1,000 hours annually usually spent in firewood collection and cooking. Biogas plants contribute to the reduction of greenhouse effect by converting natural methane into fuel. One kilogram (kg) of methane causes greenhouse effect damage equivalent to 25 kgs of carbon dioxide.[8]

Financing Arrangements: The UNEP PV Loan Support Programme, India

In the year 2003, the United Nations Environment Programme (UNEP) recognizing the need for cheap credit as a necessary primer for kick-starting any DDG project catering to the market segment at the bottom of the pyramid, launched an initiative to bring down the cost of consumer credit for solar PV home lighting systems in India.

The $7.6 million initiative was implemented through two of India's largest banking groups, Syndicate Bank and Canara Bank, and provided low interest loans to 19,533 households to install domestic solar power systems. The interest rates ranged around 5 per cent per annum compared to 11–12 per cent per annum normally charged to consumers. These two banks offered loans also through 'group lending' schemes which enabled the poorest of the poor to participate in the southern states of Kerala and Karnataka. The programme had approved four companies to offer systems under the programme and these were Selco, Tata-BP Solar, Shell Solar, and Kotak Kurja.

Proposed Solution

The promotion of renewable energy-based DDG systems requires initiatives across different fronts. The framework shown below (Figure 11.2) shows a few of the key factors which will impact the degree of success that DDG implementation will have on rural electrification in the country.

- Rural electrification policy:

The current rural electrification policy discusses in detail the means of achieving 100 per cent rural electrification and providing reliable power supply at reasonable rates to all rural households. It also lays out the institutional arrangements necessary to achieve its aim. However, it stops short of appointing a single nodal agency to drive the goal of rural electrification and coordinate all rural electrification efforts.

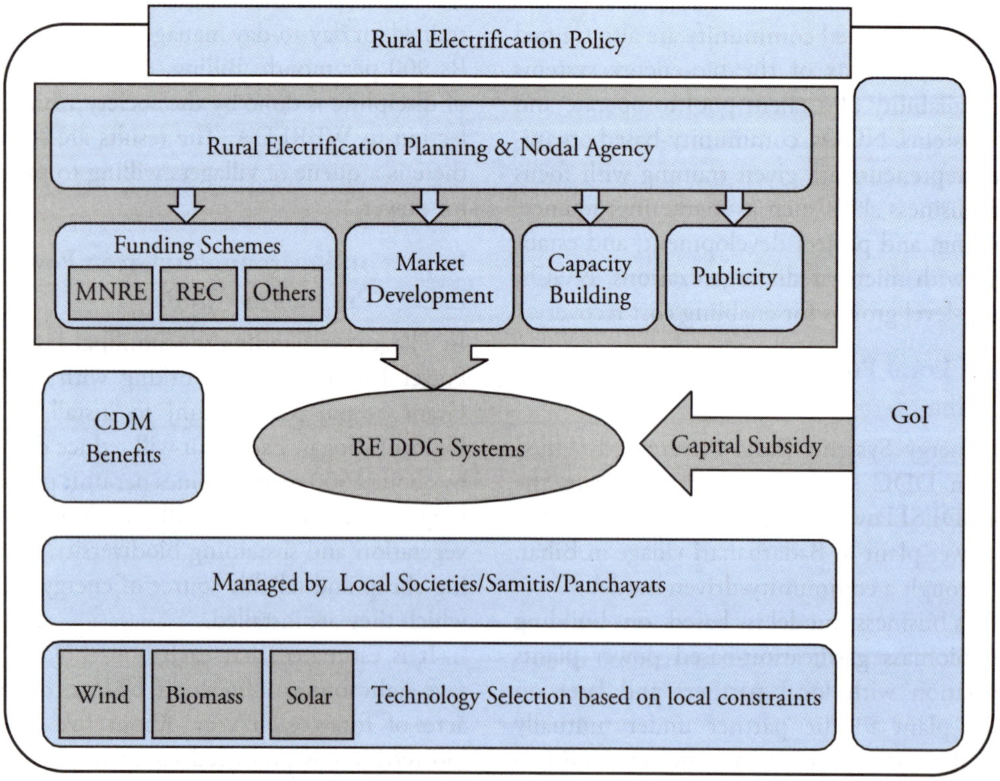

Figure 11.2 Proposed Framework for DDG System Implementation

[8] Green Power India, accessible at http://greenpowerindia.org

- Centralized planning and nodal agency:

A single nodal agency is required to drive rural electrification efforts in order to ensure proper implementation of schemes. This proposed agency would be the central coordinating agency for all rural electrification efforts and would be responsible for planning of future rural electrification schemes in order to avoid overlap of the scope of different schemes. The agency would oversee the channelling of funds for the purpose through various agencies, including the REC and MNRE. The agency would also be responsible for undertaking market development activities in order to develop an active market for DDG systems. This would be done by encouraging private players to enter this field by making available all data required for estimation of market potential and future target areas from a centrally maintained database and help in developing a viable business model for private players in the sector. The agency would also undertake capacity building activities and would train technical staff for the upkeep of the DDG systems among others. Publicity drives highlighting the benefits of DDG systems and assuring the public of their reliability would also form part of the scope of work of the agency.

- Management of DDG systems:

The DDG systems would have to be managed by the local society/panchayat present in the area in order to ensure that the scheme would have public welfare as its main focus, as well as to ensure sustainability of the system.

- Technology selection:

The technology to be used for rural electrification through the renewable DDG route should be selected based on the potential for each technology in the area, availability of feedstock, total demand, and cost of implementation. This requires careful planning based on various drivers, that is feedstock supply, ability to operate, maintain, and service the newly installed systems and potential applications for income generation.

- Capital subsidy from government:

Rural societies are generally able to bear the operational expenses involved in the generation of power through DDG sources. So, considering the relatively high capital expenditure required for DDG systems, the government would have to provide support in the form of capital subsidy/grant in order to ensure financial viability of the DDG systems.

The manner of disbursal of capital subsidy by the government to DDG projects must be based on output-based contracting wherein the focus is on the output produced, and operators are given the flexibility and incentives to innovate and implement based on local constraints. This results in arrangements where contracts are drawn and subsidies/concessions are awarded for a specific time period. The issues of tariff setting, service quality, technology options, bundling of one or more services is spelt out in the contract which guides the functioning of such an arrangement.

- Overcome high cost of electricity purchase through dedicated fund:

A dedicated fund can be formed to overcome the high cost of electricity purchase from DDG based projects. The fund can be established by levying a surcharge on the urban/HT consumers. This can be at par with the cross-subsidization of the domestic consumers by the HT consumers.

- CDM benefits:

All RE DDG systems qualify for CDM benefits but the small organizations managing these facilities might not have the ability to access the concessions and incentives which may be available under CDM schemes. An institutionalized arrangement with the help of the state nodal agency, which could support all these managing bodies and get them these benefits, would lead to improvement in the economics of power generation.

References

Biomass Energy for Rural India Society, available at http://bioenergyindia.kar.nic.in Central Electricity Authority, available at www.cea.nic.in)

Buchholz, T., I. Da Silva, T. Volk, T. Tennigkeit (2007). Economics of a Gasification Based Mini Grid—A Case Study of a 10 kW unit in Uganda. Proceedings of the Industrial and Commercial use of Energy Conference, Cape Town, South Africa, 29–30 May, pp. 125–9.

Central Electricity Authority (2001). *Progress Report of Village Electrification as on 30-04-2010*, May.

Central Electricity Authority (2008). *CO_2 Baseline Database for the Indian Power Sector*, Ministry of Power, Government of India, October.

Census of India (2001). *Data Table- Fuel used for Cooking*, accessible at http://censusindia.gov.in/Census_Data_2001/Census_data_finder/HH_Series/Fuel_used_for_cooking.htm

Decentralized Energy Systems India Private Ltd's, available at www.desipower.com

Ghosh, Debyani, Ambuj Sagar, V.V.N. Kishore (2004). *Scaling up Biomass Gasifier Use: Applications, Barriers and Interventions.*

Green Power India's, available at www.greenpowerindia.org

Intergovernmental Panel on Climate Change, *Fourth Assessment Report*, Ministry of New and Renewable Energy (www.mnre.gov.in).

Ministry of New and Renewable Energy, *Remote Village Lighting Programme*, accessible at http://mnre.gov.in/prog-rvlp.htm

National Sample Survey Organization (2008). *Household Consumer Expenditure in India, 2006-07*, Ministry of Statistics and Programme Implementation, Government of India, October 2008, accessible at http://mospi.nic.in/rept%20_%20pubn/ftest.asp?rept_id=527&type=nsso

SELCO with REEEP. 'Access to Sustainable Energy Services via Innovative Financing', Vienna, Austria. http://www.selco-india.com/pdfs/selco_booklet_web.pdf

The World Bank (2007). *World Development Indicators 2007*, available at http://siteresources.worldbank.org/DATASTATISTICS/Resources/table3_13.pdf

UNDP. *Financing Options for Renewable Energy: Country Experiences*, UNDP Regional Centre in Bangkok, Thailand.

Union Budget 2010–11. Government of India, accessible at http://indiabudget.nic.in/ub2010-11/eb/sbe72.pdf

United Nations Environment Programme, available at www.uneptie.org

12 Captive Generation in India

The Dilemma of Dualism

Tirthankar Nag

The power sector in India is facing significant shortages for both energy and peak to the tune of 10.1 per cent and 12.7 per cent[1] respectively in 2010, and the deficit has been growing over the years as generation capacity addition has been unable to keep pace with the rapidly growing demand. Further, where power is available, the quality of supply has been a major concern for the consumers suffering economic losses. Growth and development needs are expected to further add to the demand for energy, thus exerting stress on existing energy resources. Load shedding or curtailment of power has been widely resorted to by distribution companies to manage the power deficit. Thus, faced with the acute power deficit situation, the paying consumers, primarily industrial and commercial establishments, in their effort to secure their supply have been depending largely on captive power plants.

Captive power plants have been growing at a fairly aggressive pace in India. In 2008, the total installed capacity of captive plants in India, where plants are greater than 1MW in size, was about 25 GW; these constitute around 17 per cent of the total installed capacity in India. Studies have also inferred that it would be beneficial to encourage captive growth in India as this can add the much needed capacity while increasing competition in the power market (Hansen 2008). Thus, by encouraging captive capacity addition so far to overcome the power crisis affecting economic productivity, policymakers have in fact devised a way to add the much needed generating capacity (Joseph 2010) so as not to jeopardize the desired growth momentum. The phenomenal growth of captive power plants over the years has created a dual track in the power sector. It is also a reality that the growth of captive plants, which may have been spurred by specific failures in the state system, is expected to continue (forecast by Crisil Research 2009) and perhaps cannot be reversed easily in the medium term.

India is also faced with the daunting task of balancing its growth and development objectives with the challenge of ameliorating environmental damage and the threat of climate change. The complexity arises from the fact that India's energy use comprises mostly of fossil fuels, making the energy sector one of the greatest contributors to global emissions in the country. The power sector accounts for around 40 per cent of total GHG emissions in India, with coal generating 72 per cent of utility supplied electricity in the country. The choice of fuel for captive generation is no exception. A key concern with this dual track power sector development is that proliferation of spatially distributed fossil fuel-based smaller captive plants is likely to be environmentally more damaging than the well planned and monitored development of large utility power plants. Thus, the dilemma of dualism arises from the low carbon development perspective!

While there are a number of studies which have examined the development of generation utilities (that is non-captive power plants), few studies have explored the issues

[1] CEA (2010).

around growth of captive plants and fewer still on their effect on the environment. This chapter examines the growth of captive power plants in India and tries to assess the environmental implications of such proliferation of captive generation. To this effect, this paper identifies key factors contributing to the adverse emission intensity associated with the prevailing captive generation. The paper further infers and argues that through better capacity utilization, bringing more uniformity in state policies, rationalizing cross subsidies and tariffs, and encouraging use of low carbon fuel, the emission intensity of captive generation could be mitigated considerably.

Growth of Captive Power in India

Historically the growth of captive plants in India has been quite steep. Just after independence in the late 1940s the country had only 544 MW of non-utility plants generating about 1300 GWh. With industrialization in the early 1980s and lesser reliability of state-owned supply, the captive capacity addition received a boost which continues even today (see Figure 12.1). Captive power plants are owned by the industry, primarily for self-consumption. The captive capacity as of March 2007 was 22,335 MW with a total generation of 82 TWh. However, this accounts for only plants in the organized sector having more than 1 MW capacity (see Figure 12.2). This growing captive capacity has been mostly catering to the captive demand of the parent industries and played very little role in catering to the overall system demand. Till recently, surplus power from captive plants, after meeting self-requirements, could not be sold to third parties, a situation which changed with the introduction of the Electricity Act 2003 that provides transmission open access to these plants. Further, India has targeted electricity access to all by 2012. Centralized generation alone is unlikely to meet this target, and in this context captive and distributed generation systems are likely to be important (Banerjee 2006).

A study by Shukla et al. (2004) has shown that the growth of captive plants in India can be broadly attributed to (a) need for backup power arrangement, (b) requirement of better quality supply, (c) the co-generation benefits of steam and electricity from production process of industries, and (d) need to generate electricity at costs lower than the high industrial tariffs set to cross subsidize other categories of consumers.

Though captive capacity in India has been growing, the average capacity utilization of these plants is quite low. In 2007, the plant load factor (PLF) of the captive plants was only at 41 per cent (see Figure 12.3). This is due to the fact that a substantial part of this capacity is used for back-up generation due to the unreliable grid supply.

Within industries also there is significant variation in captive capacity utilization. Metals, heavy engineering,

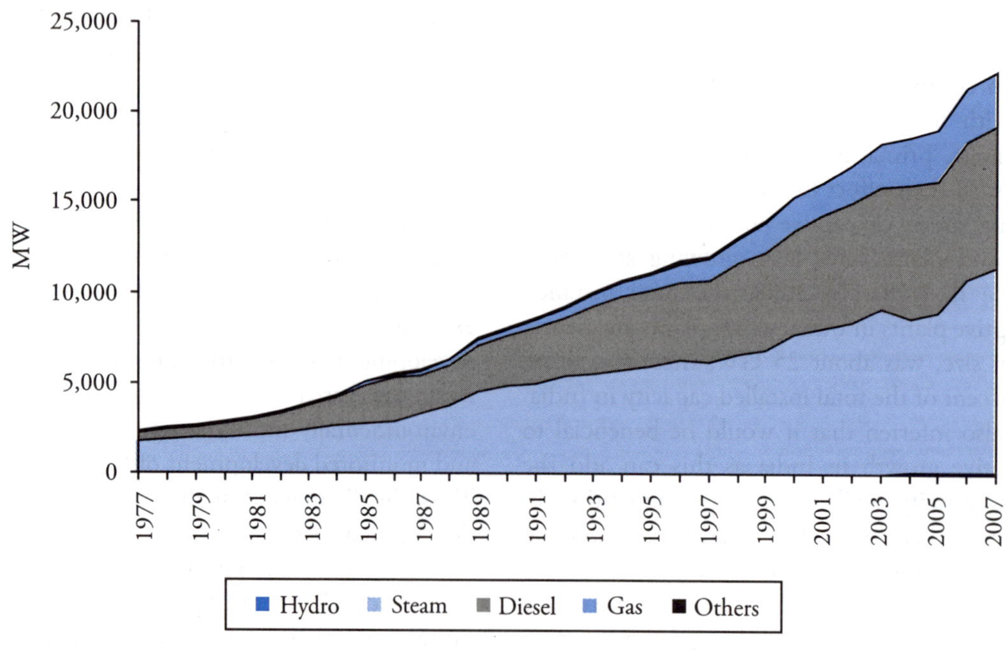

Figure 12.1 Growth in Captive Capacity in MW

Source: CEA (2008).

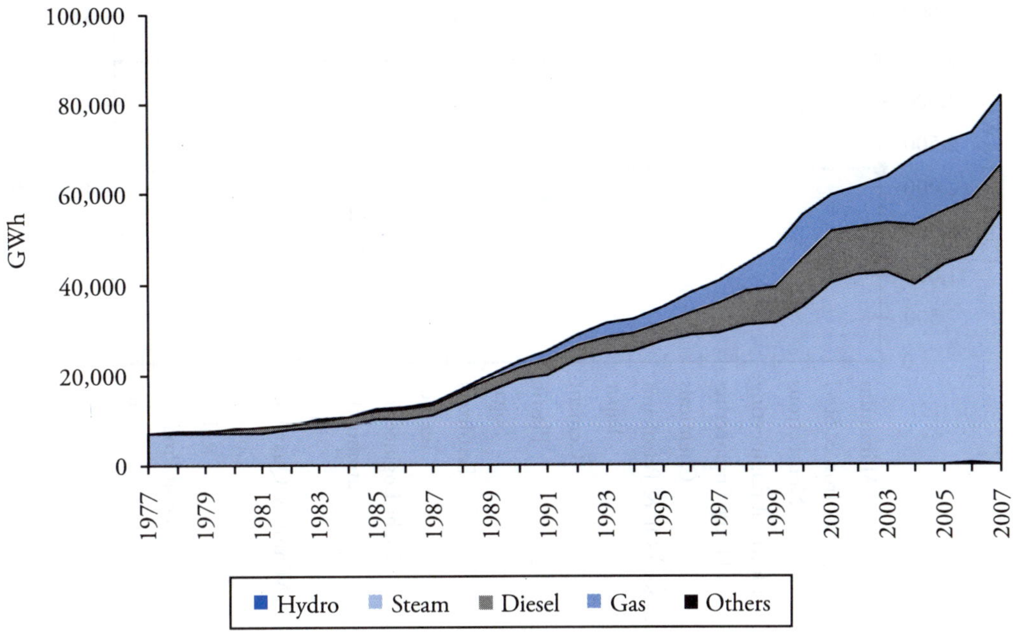

Figure 12.2 Growth in Captive Generation in GWh

Source: CEA (2008).

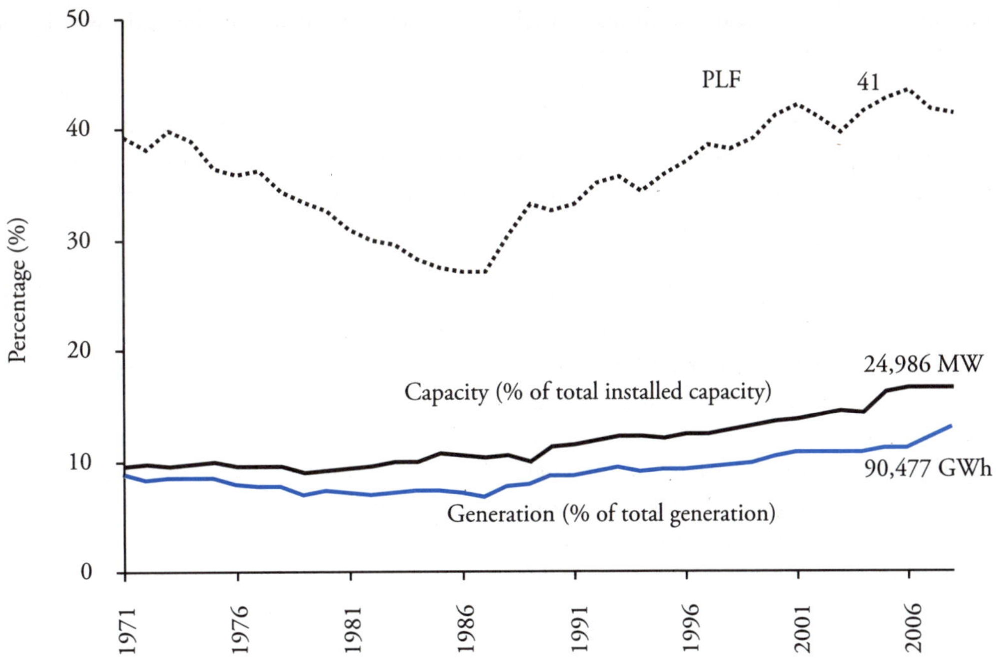

Figure 12.3 Captive Capacity, Generation, and Efficiency in 2008

Source: CEA (2009).

chemicals, petroleum, paper, and cement industries account for 70 per cent of the total captive capacity and 85 per cent of the generation. Through better coordination of the requirements of the industries and utilization of the captive capacities, around 55 TWh of surplus generation could have been available from the captive plants in 2007 (see Figure 12.4).

With reference to the fuel composition of the captive plants, coal comprises the major share in the fuel mix of the captive installed capacity although there has been rapid

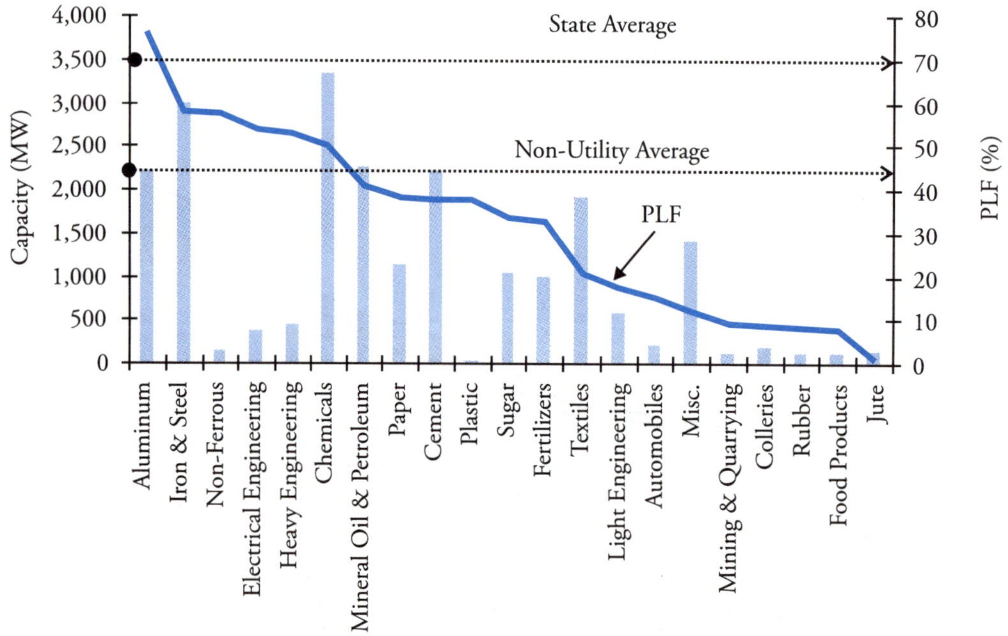

Figure 12.4 Captive Generation Capacity across Industries in 2007

Source: CEA (2008).

growth of gas-based captive plants. If the fuel mix across industries is examined, it becomes clear that industry fuel preferences are not very prominent, especially for coal and oil, where we find a spectrum of industries. However, markets for coal are yet to be fully developed and linkages with the coal mines are quite difficult to obtain within a limited time. On the other hand, oil-based captive generation has grown substantially, despite risks arising from volatility in prices since procurement of fuel is market-based and oil-based captive plants have a shorter gestation period for commissioning. Further, oil-based generating equipment are smaller in scale and quite easy to acquire. Thus, for captive plants not utilizing their full capacity, oil-based generation is sometimes preferred. But notwithstanding the demonstrated preference for coal- and oil-based captive plants so far, gas-based captive plants have also grown recently. However, the price volatility of gas and issues around its availability have been the major concerns in India.

Addressing Power Shortages

That captive plants are not operating to their full potential, and can contribute to greater economic gains, has been studied by researchers. Research drawing upon the experience of Gujarat shows that low PLF for each industry and collective PLF for all captive plants indicate a considerable dead weight loss from the under-utilized capacity (Morris 2003). Captive generation especially from large industries is in a position to supply to the grid as these industries are already connected to the grid. India's concern of electricity shortages could in part be addressed by better coordination of such industrial power surpluses. An example of this can be seen in the zero load shedding model in Pune, an innovative initiative introduced by the partnership between Industry Association, Distribution Utility, and Regulatory Commission with the confidence of the civil society (see Box 12.1).

The discussion so far has been referring to the captive plants above 1 MW. Information about captive plants below 1 MW is not so readily available in India. One such source is the information gathered from the manufacturers of small captive plants. However, such an estimate based on data provided by the manufacturers is expected to have a downward bias as it neither takes into account the contribution by local manufacturers nor does it account for the market for used capacities. The total capacity of such plants was about 24 GW in 2004—around 16 per cent of India's generating capacity, and most of these small plants were liquid fuel based (see Table 12.1). This indicates that captive plants—less than and the greater than equal to 1MW in capacity—together constitute a large pool of generation capacity, which could play a big role in meeting the electricity needs in the country.

Thus, the captive plants, whether grid-connected or stand-alone, could contribute towards greater availability of power in the system, either by increasing consumption from captive generation and drawing less from the grid,

Box 12.1
Zero Load Shedding Model in Pune

By 2005–6, the state of Maharashtra, which once boasted of surplus power availability, was reeling under an acute peak power deficit of 23 per cent (that is 3700 MWs). Pune, like many other cities in the state, faced regular load shedding for about 2–4 hours a day. With the objective of curbing the increasing electricity deficit, the Pune Chapter of the Confederation of Indian Industries (CII) had formulated a proposal (popularly known as the 'Pune Model') for using the under-utilized captive generation capacity of industries in Pune. The proposal was submitted to Maharashtra Electricity Regulatory Commission (MERC) for its consideration.

Pune faced an estimated a shortfall of 90 MW in the worst case scenario, while the top 30 industrial undertakings of Pune—which is home to major industries such as Tata Motors, Bajaj Auto, Bharat Forge, Kinetic Engineering, and DaimlerChrysler India—had unutilized captive capacity in excess of 100 MW.

The 'Pune Model', introduced in June 2006, involved industries with under-utilized captive power plants (CPPs) in Pune. The idea was that these industries would generate and consume additional captive power to the extent of the scheduled load shedding, so that equivalent grid power is made available to other consumers. To get uninterrupted power, the consumers would have to bear the incremental cost of generation by CPPs to the extent of the difference between the variable cost of generation by CPPs and the average High Tension (HT) industrial tariff. MERC conducted a public hearing and on 2 March 2006 issued an Order setting the (normative) variable cost of generation at Rs 8.24/KWh for light diesel oil (LDO)-based CPPs and at Rs 11.04/KWh for high speed diesel (HSD)-based CPPs. The model works through cooperation and coordination among the consumers of power, owners of CPPs, power distribution utility, and the Regulatory Commission.

There were issues around reliability charges to be paid by the consumers for the better reliability of power provided by the above mechanism. MERC approved Rs 0.42/KWh to be levied on the consumers of Pune Urban Circle excluding domestic consumers consuming up to 300 KWh/month. MERC, by exempting small domestic consumers (consuming up to 300 KWh/month) from paying a reliability charge, brought benefits to nearly 6 lakh consumers of the total 8 lakh consumers in the Pune Urban Circle. Industries were also required to pay reliability charge without any preferential treatment. The rate and terms of reliability charge for enjoying zero load shedding were acceptable to all stakeholders. From 4 June 2006, the model became operational and led to zero deficits over a considerable period of time.

The principles under which the model was proposed are given below:

- Users must be willing to pay a premium for reduced or no load shedding and the incremental cost should be borne by the beneficiaries (that is consumers) and not by the distribution company or the government;
- Load shedding mitigation should not be at the expense of any community;
- There must be enough idle captive power capacity to meet the entire unmet demand or at least a significant part of it;
- It should operate within the framework of governing laws and regulations.

Source: IDFC (2008).

thereby releasing more power into the grid, or by directly injecting surplus captive power into the grid.

Environmental Implications

Captive generation has some specific economic advantages compared to the grid. On-site power production has the advantage of avoiding transmission and distribution costs especially considering that, in India, considerable amount of the power generated is lost as transmission and distribution losses. Besides the economic advantages, captive generation could also contribute towards protecting the environment. To the extent that captive generation

Table 12.1 Sale of Captive Plants less than 1 MW from 1990 to 2004

Manufacturer	*Total Capacity (MW)*	*Number*	*Max Unit Size (MW)*	*Min Unit Size (MW)*	*Average Size (MW)*
Birla Power Solutions Ltd	508	457,210	0.001	0.001	0.001
Kirloskar Oil Engines Limited	22,138	354,200	0.063	0.063	0.063
Man B & W Diesel	14	18	0.900	0.700	0.767
Rolls-Royce Energy System	9	31	0.290	0.290	0.290
Tractors India	887	2,703	1.000	0.210	0.533
Wartsila India Ltd	29	49	0.980	0.315	0.695
Summary	23,585	814,211	1.000	0.001	0.440

Source: CEA (2005).

contributes to improving access to electricity and replaces less efficient use of energy (that is, wood, dung-cakes, kerosene, etc.), the resultant impact on environment is positive.

However, the present pattern and growth of captive generation in India rakes up some issues, highlighted below, which may be environmentally onerous and may place a major impediment along the path to low carbon economic development.

- Small plant size: Despite the advantages, the growth of captive plants may be a concern for a clean environment. A large number of the small-capacity captive plants have been added and the size of the plant has a definite influence on specific carbon emissions. As shown in Figure 12.5, specific emissions gradually decrease with higher plant sizes. Also, emission control equipments are often not installed in small captive plants and emission from widely dispersed large number of small-capacity plants are difficult to monitor. Figure 12.5 captures the declining trend of specific CO_2 emissions (primary vertical axis) with increasing plant size (horizontal axis) and notes that majority of the captive plants (number of plants denoted by secondary vertical axis) due to their smaller sizes may be prone to higher specific emissions. A detailed study of emissions from such captive plants needs to be undertaken to reach a definitive conclusion about the linkage between plant size and emission intensities of captive plants.
- Fuel mix: Apart from size, the fuel mix of captive plants is carbon-intensive as large generating capacities are coal- and diesel-based. Emission neutral technologies like hydro and renewable constituted only 0.6 per cent of the total captive generation in 2007, when grid supplied renewable energy and hydro generation was 18 per cent (see Figure 12.6).

Lower cost of coal-based generation with increasing availability of coal linkages has been steadily pushing the fuel mix of the captive plants towards coal-based generation. Since 85 per cent of the total captive capacity additions are expected to be coal-based (Crisil Research 2009) (see Table 12.2), such bias for fossil fuel-based captive capacity addition would worsen the fuel mix. A

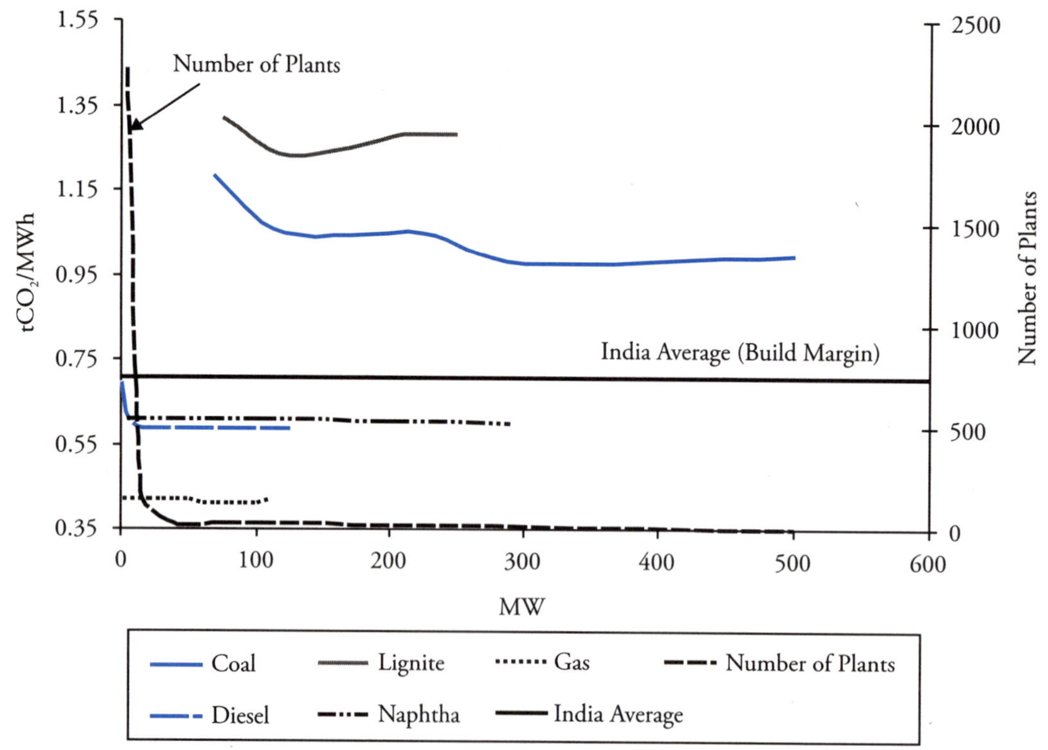

FIGURE 12.5 Specific CO_2 Emissions and Number of Plants More Than 1 MW in 2007

Note: The CEA database provides assumptions by capacity for units in the build margin where data was not provided by station, and not specifically for captive units.

Source: CEA, CO_2 Baseline Database, November 2009 and Infraline.

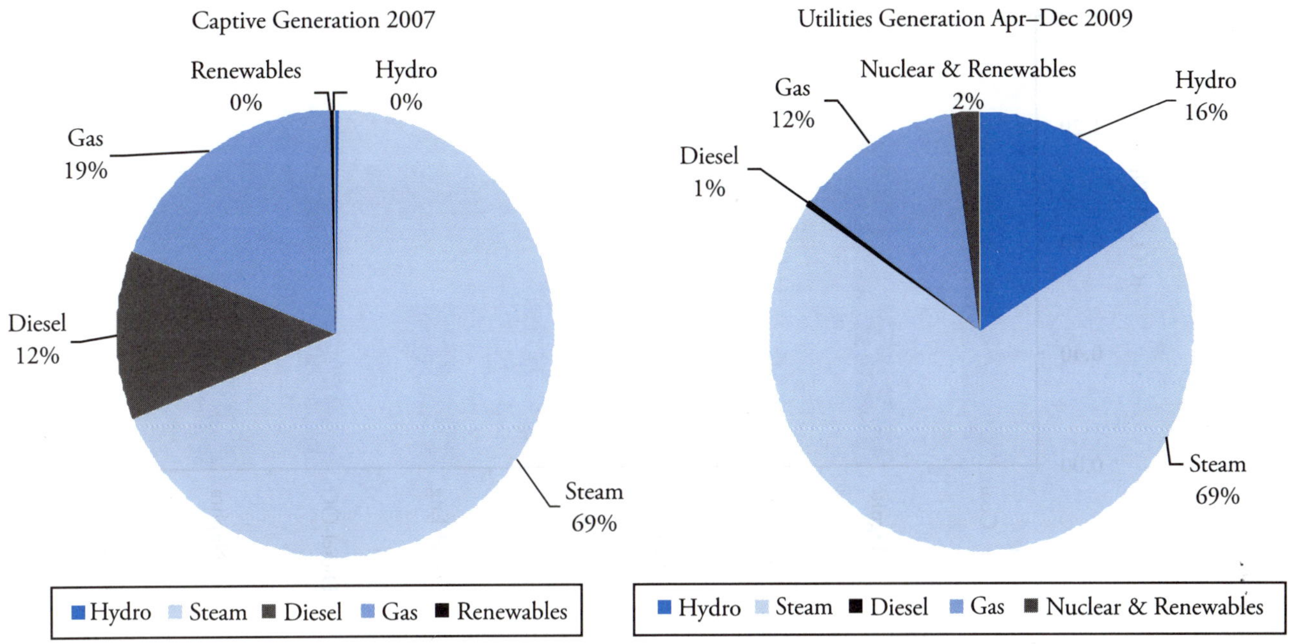

Figure 12.6 Comparison of Fuel Mix of Captive Plants and India Average

Source: CEA (2010).

shift towards less emission intensive fuel mix would help overcome the roadblock in transiting towards a low carbon economy.

Table 12.2 Fuel-wise Cost of Generation

Fuel	*Rs/KWh*
Coal/Steam/Gas	2.3
Diesel/Furnace Oil	6.3
Wind/Bagasse/ Waste	2.7

Source: Crisil Research 2009.

- Partial loading: Emission intensity of smaller plants running at low PLF is expected to be higher than larger plants operating at optimal loading. The energy conversion efficiency is dependent on plant operation and dispatch (Ministry of Power 1997). Running on partial loads have also been cited to be reasons for achieving higher heat rates (DVC 2005). Studies have reported that partial loading could result in an estimated impact of around 1–5 per cent on the heat rate (Lars-Erik Schöring 2004), and that a PLF below 70 per cent could increase the value of heat rate by 50 kcal/kWh (Presentation by Tata Power Company Limited).[2] Thus, impact of partial loading and low PLF on heat rates translates into higher emissions (see Figure 12.8).
- Emission control: Emission control technologies in small captive plants are not always economically viable and the distributed proliferation of the small captive plants makes emission monitoring by authorities difficult. However, this is not the case with large coal-based captive plants of sizes above 100 MW that comprised half the total captive generation in 2008 (see Table 12.3). Notwithstanding the muted effect on emission of the large plants, the growing pool of small fossil fuel-based captive plants is an imminent threat to the local and global environment and a major impediment to realizing sustainable low carbon economic development.

Way Forward

Proliferation of captive capacity is inevitable in the medium term for a resource constrained growing economy, but this poses challenges to low carbon growth. Policymakers have to recognize this dilemma of dualism and carefully address the multi-faceted issues around captive generation. Besides the bias of fuel mix towards coal and oil, the key to higher emission intensity of captive plants is found in operational inefficiency arising from partial loading and sub-optimal utilization of the plants. It could be argued that the solution may be sought in aggregation

[2] Tata Power Company Limited (2003), 'Discussion on Terms and Conditions of Power Tariff: Generator Perspective', Jamshedpur Division, 12 November 2003.

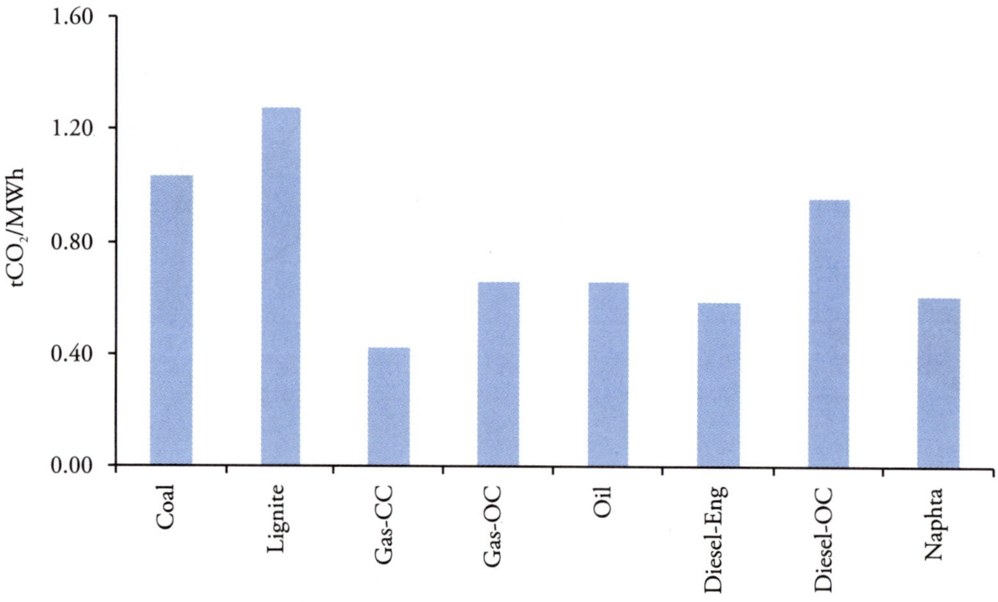

FIGURE 12.7 Specific Emissions (based on assumptions)

Source: Based on CEA Assumptions for utilities, 2009.

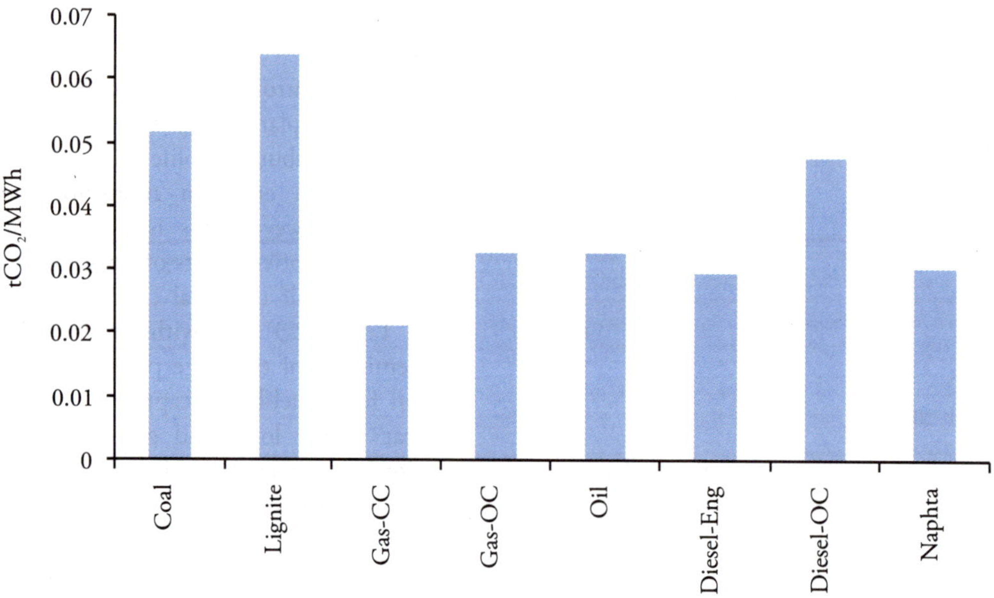

FIGURE 12.8 Additional Emissions for 5 per cent Impact on Heat Rates

Source: Based on CEA Assumptions[3] for Utilities 2009, and author's analysis.

and coordinated operation of captive capacities. Thus, through crafting of innovative solutions and progressive policies, besides ensuring austere governance and implementation practices, growth in captive capacity and generation could be better aligned with the a low carbon economic development.

Some of the measures for ameliorating the emission intensity of fossil fuel-based captive capacity addition and generation are:

- Encouraging larger plant sizes through group captives: Metal and chemical industries account for over

[3] CEA: CO_2 Baseline Database, Version 5.0, November 2009. The analysis assumes 5 per cent increase in heat rates across all fuel categories and projects the marginal increase in CO_2 emission intensities.

TABLE 12.3 Generation Details of Captive Plants above 1 MW in 2008

Range of Unit Capacities (MW)	*No. of Industries*	*Capacity (MW)*	*Generation (GWh)*	*Percentage of total Captive Generation*
01 to < 10	2,347	6,838	8,603	10
10 to<20	195	2,831	6,913	8
20 to < 30	88	2,245	8,525	9
30 to < 40	36	1,267	5,289	6
40 to < 50	27	1,228	5,660	6
50 to < 100	35	2,341	11,095	12
100 & Above	31	8,236	44,392	49
Total	2,759	24,986	90,477	100

Source: CEA (2009).

half the captive power generation in the country. An estimated 14 GW of capacity is expected to be added over 2008–14 with 75 per cent of capacities in the metal industry, and 60 per cent of these additional capacities are likely to be based in eastern India (Crisil Research 2009). Information asymmetry and absence of coordination between industries may not result in an environmentally optimal solution of setting up a large group captive plant. Thus, there may be a need for the government to identify newly growing clusters within specific sectors like metals and chemicals and set up mechanisms to encourage group captive plants. There are examples of established clusters, particularly in the metals industry.[4] Such mechanisms are quite evident in case of SEZs where fiscal benefits are applicable and these plants are allowed to sell power to other industries within the SEZ subject to certain conditions.

- Formulating a model captive power policy for removing barriers and encouraging sale of surplus power to the grid: Around 19.5 GW (as of March, 2007) of captive power is connected to the grid (Crisil Research July 2009) which can create considerable opportunities for sale of surplus power. Most states have their own policy or approach towards treatment of captive power with extensive inter-state variations. Several of these state policies inflate the cost of captive power through mechanisms like higher rates of electricity duty, minimum demand charges for grid support, uneconomical wheeling charges and losses, cess on captive power generation, high entry tax on heavy fuel oil, and high sales tax. Thus, there might be a case for setting up of a model captive power policy which the states could adopt to provide a level playing field to captive generators. The implementation of this would be similar to the CERC tariff regulations which are incorporated in spirit by the states, the model PPA, and the model competitive bid guidelines. A policy environment that is conducive would encourage captive power developers to set up large plant sizes and achieve higher plant utilization through sale of surplus capacity or increasing self-consumption.
- Reducing cross subsidy charges: Power tariffs in India chargeable to industrial, commercial, and household consumers are among the highest in the world in PPP[5] terms. Consequently, there is constant pressure exerted upon electricity regulators to ensure that tariffs for state distribution utilities are not raised further (Planning Commission 2005). It may be important to rationalize retail tariffs by reducing cross subsidy elements in tariffs so that industries can get back to the grid and

Box 12.2

A unit can be set up within the SEZ to generate power as a product or have a captive power plant and will be located in the processing area.

Such a power plant will be entitled to all the fiscal benefits covered under Section 26 of the SEZ Act, including the benefits for initial setting up, maintenance, and the duty free import of raw materials and consumables for the generation of the power in such plants. Such a unit can supply power to other SEZ units subject to certain conditions.

Source: Excerpts from 'Guidelines for Power Generation, Transmission and Distribution in Special Economic Zone (SEZs)', Ministry of Commerce and Industry, February 2009.

[4] Refer to http://www.nif.org.in/bd/list_industrial_clusters

[5] Purchasing Power Parity.

also facilitate open access to encourage higher capacity utilization. This is likely to have a two-fold advantage of curbing the rapid proliferation of captive plants and also encouraging the sale of surplus captive power through open access at reasonable open access charges. In a favourable open access situation, better plant utilization is likely to enhance operational efficiency, which, along with deceleration of fossil fuel-based captive capacity addition can have a positive effect on the environment.

- Designing distinct policies based on plant sizes: Large captive plants (25 MW and above), which are more efficient and less carbon-intensive than smaller captive plants, could be encouraged through appropriate policy to further the sale of surplus power from the captive plants to the grid in a cost-effective manner. However, smaller plants which have come up primarily as back-up power facilities need to be treated differently and encouraged to meet peak power demand through self generation to lessen the burden on the grid. With increasing capacity addition and improvement in quality of grid power, the need for such back-up power may go down in the future. Categorization of large and small captive power needs to be studied and implications thought through carefully for formulating distinct and targeted policies.
- Encouraging renewable and low carbon technology: The fuel mix of captive plants shows a strong bias for coal, lignite, and diesel, with coal-based captive plants envisaged for the future. Presently, the share of hydro or renewables in installed captive capacity is almost negligible. Although low carbon gas-based captive plants are in operation, issues around the availability of gas and volatility in gas prices have been assuming greater importance. Besides encouraging renewable energy for distributed power back-up or stand-alone facilities to replace or complement smaller sized fossil fuel-based captive power units, there should be ample thrust on technological innovations in diesel generators (Powerline, 2008).

Large group captive capacities that are more efficient and thus less carbon-intensive should be encouraged so that plant capacities are better utilized and surplus power from these captive plants supplied to the grid. The rapid proliferation of captive plants of all sizes could be checked and environmental damage substantially restrained, by accelerating the pace of removing retail tariff distortions and improving the quality of power supply to consumers. All of these would restrain paying consumers from leaving the grid and encourage erstwhile consumers to migrate back to the grid. Further, taking policy measures to promote rapid development of renewable energy and hybrid low-carbon technologies as back-up and stand-alone power sources would assist in reducing the carbon footprint of captive power generation.

References

Banerjee, R (2006). 'Comparison of Options for Distributed Generation in India', *Energy Policy*, 34(1), January.

Barnes, D.F., J. Halpern (2000). *Subsidies and Sustainable Rural Energy Services: Can we create incentives without distorting markets?*, Energy Sector Management Assistance Programme (ESMAP) report.

Central Electricity Authority (2005). *Report on Tapping Surplus Power from Captive Power Plants*, Planning Wing, August.

——— (2008). 'Captive Electricity Generation Plants (Non-utilities)', *General Review 2008*, Chapter 4.

——— (2009). 'Captive Electrical Energy Generation Plants Non-utilities', *General Review 2009*, Chapter 5, May.

——— (2010). *Electrical Energy Generation during the month of December, 2009 and period April-December'09*. Operation Performance Monitoring Division, CEA/OPM/PPA/3/1/2009, 5 January 2010.

Crisil Research (2009). *Power Annual Review*.

——— (2010). *Power Monthly*, January.

DVC (2005). 'Reason for Variation of PLF, SOC, APC & Heat Rate from CERC Norms for Bokaro 'B' Thermal Power Station', Petition No. 66/2005, Appendix vii.

Hansen, Christopher Joshi (2008). 'Bottom-up Electricity Reform using Industrial Captive Generation: A Case Study of Gujarat', Oxford Institute for Energy Studies, India, March 2008.

IDFC (2008). 'Innovative Partnership Approach to Mitigating Load Shedding: The "Pune Model" and Beyond', *Policy Group Quarterly*, 2 December 2008.

Indiastat, Power Sector Database, available at http://www.indiastat.com

Infraline, Power Sector Database, available at http://www.infraline.com

Joseph, Kelli L. (2010). 'The Politics of Power: Electricity Reform in India', *Energy Policy*, 38(1), pp. 503–11, January 2010.

Lars-Erik Schöring (2004). 'Lifecycle Costs—The Driver for Power Plant Investment Decisions', *Energy News*, 18, February 2004, Wartsila, Finland.

Ministry of Power (1997). 'Guidelines for Inviting Tariff Based Bids', D.O No. A-53/95-IPC-I, 3 June 1997, *Government of India*, New Delhi.

Ministry of Power (2003). *Discussion Paper on Rural Electrification Policies*, November, *Government of India*, New Delhi.

Morris, S. (2003). 'Restructuring Gujarat Electricity Board', in J. Ruet (ed.), *Against the Current: Organisational Restructuring of State Electricity Boards*, New Delhi.

Planning Commission (2005). *Draft Report of the Expert Committee on Integrated Energy Policy*, New Delhi: Government of India, December 2005.

Powerline (2008), *Design Improvements: Technological Advances to Reduce Diesel Engine Emissions*, July 2008.

Shukla, P.R., Debashish Biswas , Tirthankar Nag , Amee Yajnik, Thomas Heller, and David G. Victor (2004). 'Captive Power Plants: Case Study of Gujarat, India', Programme on Energy and Sustainable Development Working Paper 22, Stanford University, March 2004.

Tata Power Company Limited (2003). *Discussion on Terms and Conditions of Power Tariff: Generator Perspective*, Jamshedpur Division, 12 November.

13 Implementing Clean Coal Technology in India

Barriers and Prospects

Malti Goel

Introduction

It is not use of coal, but how coal is used that must be the focus of action.

—World Coal Institute

Coal as a fuel meets 29 per cent of the global primary energy needs and 39 per cent of the global electricity requirements. The total global coal resource is estimated to be 11,000 billion tonnes (Bt) and the extractable reserve at 909 Bt is less than 10 per cent. In 1992, about 2,000 million tonnes (Mt) of coal was used for 850 GW of electricity production worldwide. Total coal and lignite production in 2007 rose to 6,475 Mt. Coal productions in select countries and share of coal in electricity generation are shown in Table 13.1. Evidently, coal is a key fuel option to overcome energy shortages in the foreseeable future.

As world's third largest producer of coal, India has a share of about 8 per cent of the global coal reserves.[1] The resources, however, are much less, at about 2.5 per cent of global resources. The coal inventory for India as on January 2010, down to the depth of 1200 m is shown in Figure 13.1. Total coal resources and recoverable reserves are 270.9 Bt and 92.4 Bt respectively. Over 90 per cent of proven reserves are available up to a depth of 600 m. The majority of these (almost 96 per cent) belong to the Permian category (Gondwana coal). The remaining are in Jurassic, Cretaceous, and Tertiary categories. The total coal-bearing area is estimated to be 16,000 sq km, mostly in the south-eastern and north-eastern parts of the country. The lignite resource is 39 Bt with recoverable reserves of 3.9 Bt. It is found mainly in Tamil Nadu, with small quantities in Rajasthan, Kerala, Jammu & Kashmir, Pondicherry, and Kutch regions of the north-west.

Table 13.1 Coal Production and its Share in Total Electricity for Selected Countries

Country	*Coal production in 2006 (Mt)*	*Share of coal in electricity generated in 2007 (in per cent)*
PR China	2380.0	81
USA	1053.6	49
India	447.3	68
Australia	373.2	76
Russia	309.8	70
South Africa	256.9	94
Germany	197.2	49
Poland	156.1	93

Source: World Coal Institute (2008).

Nearly 85 per cent of coal produced in India is for electricity generation. Coal-based power generation capacity at 81000 MW in 2009 constituted about 53 per cent of the total installed capacity at 153,000 MW and will

[1] A reserve is that part of resources that is extractable with existing technology.

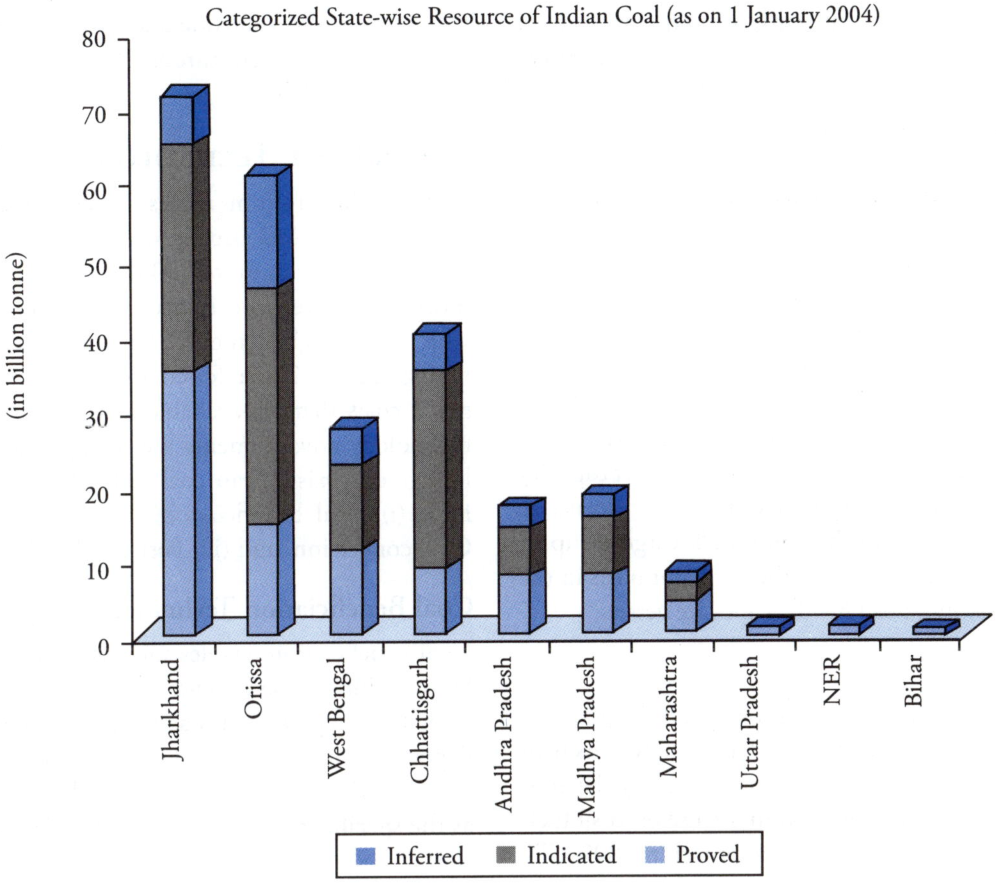

FIGURE 13.1 Coal Resources and Reserves in India

Source: State-wise Breakup of Indian Coal Resource.

continue to retain its dominant share in the decades to come. Total coal requirement for 2024–5 has been assessed as 1267 Mt with indigenous production of 1086 Mt. Coal use implies emission of high levels of carbon dioxide, oxides of sulpur, and oxides of nitrogen, as well as huge solid waste generation. One tonne of coal combustion per day (equivalent to about 0.4 GW of installed electricity capacity) generates 0.9 tonne of carbon dioxide. Inert matter is intermeshed with coal structure, which is difficult to remove and gets converted into ash during combustion.

Coal Energy in India

India has a vast energy infrastructure of coal, starting from coal mining to extraction, and coal transport to coal utilization in power plants.

Coal Extraction

Coal extraction deploys both underground and open-cast mining techniques. Underground mining allows access to deeper coal seams (up to 600 m depth). The techniques widely used for underground mining are board and pillar, arc's wall shearer, shortwall and longwall face mining. Hydraulic mining, shield mining, and blasting gallery mining have also been tried for increasing coal production. Other specialized techniques need to be pursued for improvement in productivity and conservation of resources.

Open-cast mining, on the other hand, is a technique for mining at shallow depths of up to 150 m through removal of overburden. Large-scale blasting and emulsion-based composite explosives are used for breaking the ground. Coal is extracted using a combination of scraper, dragline and shovel dumpers. Open-cast mining consumes a comparatively large surface area of the earth, leading to increasing risk of land subsidence and land degradation. The coal quality is also inferior. This aspect needs to be addressed.

Coal Transport

Coal, a bulk commodity, is transported from the mine to the place of its utilization using surface transportation and is a high energy consuming process. Rail over road is the preferred mode of coal transport and constitutes a significant part of coal delivery. It is said that transporting the annual production of coal would require as many numbers of rail wagons as required to encircle the earth once. About 56 per cent of the country's coal is transported by rail, 19 per cent by road, and 23 per cent by other means.

Application of coal water slurry transported through underground pipelines, wherever feasible, can reduce the need for surface transportation infrastructure and is also environmentally less onerous. Ways to minimize long distance transport need to be look into. Global coal movement depends on ships, and with growing coal imports in India it is crucial that the existing port capacity is expanded and infrastructure of Offshore Stockyard & Berths (OSBs) created, for handling bulk cargo of up to 4 to 5 Mt at a time. Presently, of the 12 major ports in the country, only Mundra can handle cape-size vessels.

Coal Power

In view of India's rapid economic growth at 8–10 per cent, the energy requirement to meet the basic needs of its people is also growing. Power generation is majorly dependent on coal. The projected growth in the use of fossil fuels in 2031–2 (the installed capacity approaching 800 GW as per the Integrated Energy Policy of India 2006) indicates coal requirements for three different scenarios—coal dominant, reference, and renewable dominant scenarios, with coal demand in 2031–2 expected to grow up to 2.6 Bt, 2.0 Bt, and 1.6 Bt respectively.

Power generation is the major source of carbon emissions, which accounted for about 38 per cent of total GHG emissions in 2007. Emission from a power plant depends on total generation, fuel consumption efficiency, and fuel quality. Of the 200 thermal power plants of different size and capacity about 40 per cent are older than 20 years and would cause more pollution. Most of the installed coal-based power plants up to 500 MW are based on pulverized fired units. A few circulating fluidized bed boilers using high sulphur lignite are also being operated.

The clean coal technology is of the utmost importance because: (i) coal is abundant and will remain a major source of energy for future years, (ii) emission from coal-based generation is a matter of serious concern. Thus, clean coal research has begun to:

- Improve the quality of non-coking coal at the pre-combustion stage for use in power generation by value addition,
- Adopt new coal combustion and conversion technology for improving efficiency of coal utilization, and
- Reduce carbon dioxide and other pollutant emissions in the environment through Renovation and Modernization (R&M).

Clean Coal Technology for Power

Coal produced from mines is termed as run-of-mine (ROM) coal. Coal usually occurs as large-size shales of 200 mm, found at up to 500 m depth and has mineral or inorganic matter as extraneous and inherent impurities, which needs to be removed. For commercial applications, high grade coal is a preferred option, but it is generally low grade coals that are available in large quantities. Hence, technology advancements are taking place in the use of low grade coals. Clean coal technologies are categorized into: (i) Coal beneficiation, (ii) Coal combustion, (iii) Coal conversion, and (iv) Post-combustion.

Coal Beneficiation Technology

Coal beneficiation enables value addition in coal, mainly by reducing the percentage of ash generated on combustion. Each type of coal has its own 'washability' criteria, depending on the chemical composition of coal. Extraneous impurities are easier to remove by mechanical means as the specific gravity of coal is lower than the impurities, so that upon washing, these impurities sink while the coal floats on the water surface. However, a part of extraneous impurities is intimately inter-meshed with ROM coal and is difficult to remove only by mechanical means. It requires chemical and biological methods of cleaning. Therefore, both dry and wet coal beneficiation technologies have evolved. Coal is broken down into specified sizes according to the washing technology applicable. Coarse coal is handled by dry separation in air jigs or hydraulic jigs, while cyclones and concentrators are used for medium-size coal, and coal fines are separated by flotation or agglomeration. By-products of the beneficiation process are clean coal, middling, and rejects. In a dry cleaning process, water and energy use is conserved. Techniques for dry coal cleaning and coal particle size are provided in Table 13.2.

In the case of coal containing heavy metal as intermeshed impurities, only 7 to 8 per cent reduction in ash is possible through conventional methods of beneficiation. Advanced techniques of coal cleaning such as heavy media cyclone, barrel-cum-cyclone, and vorsyl separator are customized to suit such types of indigenous coal. In a wet process, water or a dense medium like oil is used for preparing finely meshed coal (Table 13.3). Higher efficiency can be achieved by washing as compared to dry cleaning.

For difficult-to-wash coals, advanced coal beneficiation technologies under development include enhanced gravity

TABLE 13.2 Dry Coal Beneficiation

Dry Process	*Principle*	*Particle Size*
Photometric Ore Sorter	Difference in light reflectance coal and mineral water	100–50 mm
Dry Shale Extractor	Difference in specific gravity of coal and impurities	50–20 mm
Dry Separator by Dr Otto-gold	It is also based on specific gravity principle and uses vibrating screens	35–15 mm
Radiometric Mass Determination cum Automatic Removal of Stone/Shale (RAMDARS)	It uses radioactive attenuation to determine different specific gravities for separation	~ 100 mm

TABLE 13.3 Wet Coal Beneficiation Processes

Wet Process	*Principle*
Baum Jig	Medium and coarse coal are layered by specific gravity with the help of water propelled through a fixed sieve. Particle size (50–20 mm)
Batac Jig	Improvement on Baum Jig, uses automatic controls and can be used for both coarse and fine coal washing (20–0.5 mm).
Water Cyclone	Cyclone washer uses a centrifugal force which can be up to 1000–2000 times greater than 'g'.
Heavy Media Cyclone	For imbedded impurities in coal, use of oil as heavy media in place of water. Particle size (13–0.5 mm). Reduction in coal size gives better efficiency.
Spiral Concentrator	Under the influence of centrifugal force, coal particles migrate to the outer rim of the spiral while denser impurities go to the inner part and get discharged in two separate streams.
Vorsyl Separator	Improvement on spiral concentrator with a vortex finder which prevents short-circuiting of the feed directly into the overflow. More suited to fine coals of 3 mm to 0.15 mm in size.
Froth Flotation	It relies on hydro-phobicity properties of coal and is suited for coal fines of <0.5 mm. Chemical reagents are used to enhance recovery of coal. Coal has a naturally oily surface and when air bubbles are passed, coal particles form bubbles and are buoyed to the surface as froth. The two main techniques are: mechanical cell flotation and column flotation. Column flotation uses long columns with air sparger and allows extended retention time in the cell for achieving higher efficiency.
Oleo Flotation	Similar to froth flotation but uses high doses of specified oils such as diesel oil or tar oil. It requires very fine mesh of coal 0.1 mm and is not suitable for low grade coals.
Oil Agglomeration	Finer coal particles get agglomerated, forming large globules that become oil-coated coal particles and coalesce. Globules are easier to separate while tailings remain in water as sludge.

separators, multi-stage density separators, and microbial leaching.

In India, coal beneficiation has been a key infrastructure issue between coal producers and coal users. The policy guidelines restricting the use of unwashed coal in thermal power plants situated more than 1,000 km away from the mine site as well as those located in critical, sensitive, and urban areas were introduced in 1997. Advanced coal cleaning processes to suit the indigenous coal for power generation have been developed. These are cost-effective and can reduce the ash content by about 10 per cent or more. Use of washed coal is expected to reduce CO_2 emissions from 0.326 to 0.266 kg/kWh of electricity generation, besides other benefits. Research has been initiated and field trials were made for ROMJIG and RAMDARS systems for cleaning and deshaling of coal at the Bina and Yellandu mines, respectively. From a coal handling plant producing 4.5 Mt coal per annum installed at Bina, it was reported that for coal having up to 44 to 45 per cent ash, the ROMJIG can give 67 per cent yield with ash content of 31.6 per cent. Field trials were initiated to demonstrate the application of vorsyl separators for recovery of clean coal from middling and rejects from Dugda Coal Washery. Coal majors have targeted the use of 100 per cent washed coal in thermal power generation by 2017.

Coal Combustion Technology

Pulverized Coal (PC) firing is the oldest method of thermal power generation. Hot flue gases are used to heat water in a boiler. The steam produced is used to drive the steam turbine. The waste heat from the turbine is allowed to condense. It can use any type of coal and is relatively insensitive to the quality of coal burnt. Until the twentieth century most thermal power generation around the world was from direct combustion of coal in boilers. In India too, most coal-based power generation with installed capacity up to 500 MW is based on pulverized coal-fired units, while some use gas turbines. Average gross efficiency of generation from coal-based power plants is 30.5 per cent.

Efforts have been made to render coal combustion more efficient and less polluting. Fluidized Bed Combustion (FBC) uses a fluidized bed of fine coal particles suspended in air. At high pressures solid coal behaves like a fluid and allows rapid transfer of heat. The efficiency of the burning process gets enhanced because the motion of coal brings a constant supply of hot particles to the surface. The heat is extracted and utilized in a conventional power generation cycle. It works at lower temperatures than the Pulverized Fuel (PF) process, and hence, reduces NOx emissions in the atmosphere.

Two operating versions of FBC are Circulating Fluidized Bed Combustion (CFBC) and Pressurized Fluidized Bed Combustion (PFBC). In Circulating Fluidized Bed Combustion coal particle size is reduced to 0.07–0.3 mm and the fluidization velocity is kept at 5–10 m/sec, so that the particles are ablated in the steam gas. Since the gasifier is compact, higher heat release rate per unit area can be achieved. The CFBC can utilize low grade coal with high ash, or even lignite, and has been adopted in India. Pressurized Fluidized Bed Combustion uses crushed coal with a limestone suspension as a sorbent (to absorb the sulphur content in the coal). As air pressure inside the boiler is increased to 16 to 20 bars at a temperature around 850°C, the limestone sorbent captures the sulphur in the coal and forms a dry paste, which gets collected at the bottom of the boiler and can be removed. This technique is particularly suitable for high sulphur coals.

Super-Critical combustion and Ultra-Super-Critical combustion are thermo-dynamic cycles that improve thermal efficiency of coal combustion. A steam cycle with pressure above 226 bars and temperature above 537°C is called supercritical. Ultra-super critical combustion technology, operating at 357 bars/625°C, is also being developed. It is expected to achieve 55 per cent efficiency by 2020.

In India CFBC has been developed for high ash coals having high heat value less than 3000 kcal/kg. The first CFBC boiler of 175 t/h capacity was commissioned by BHEL at Sinarmas Pulp and Paper (India) Ltd. in Pune. It has proved to be a promising technique for increasing efficiency of power generation, and its use in commercial systems is growing rapidly. India has also embarked on a major plan to introduce super-critical combustion technologies. Nine super-critical coal pulverization units of 660 MW, in addition to seven ultra mega-power plants using super-critical technology, are in different stages of construction.

Coal Conversion Technologies

The third category of clean coal infrastructure comprises the technology of converting coal into gas through gasification and into oil through liquefaction. Coal conversion processes reduce pollution and increase efficiency, but adds to infrastructure needs for coal suppliers/users.

Coal Gasification

Coal gasification is considered an important strategy for low carbon energy development. The product of the gasification process is a producer gas, which is a mixture of carbon monoxide, hydrogen, and some methane. It can be utilized in ways similar to natural gas in an environment-friendly manner. Its calorific value (33.12 MJ/cu. m.) is lower than natural gas (49.0 MJ/cu. m.). Gasification reactors are designed to suit coal characteristics. Three well-known configurations are the fixed bed, fluidized bed, and entrained bed systems.

- *Fixed Bed Gasifier* reactor has different zones for each operation such as drying, devolatilizing, gasification, and combustion. Coal of 10–50mm size is fed from the top and air or oxygen is blown through the fuel bed. The crude gas leaves the gasifier from above. This type of gasifier obviates the need for a heat exchanger, has lower oxygen consumption, and has the lowest energy requirement of all gasification processes. This technology has been commercialized and about 200 fixed bed gasifiers are operating around the world. The best-known name commercially is Lurgi Process or British Gas Lurgi.
- *Fluidized Bed Gasifier* works on the counter-current principle and allows coal particles to move vigorously. It consists of a vertical cylindrical refractory lined vessel with recycle cyclone. The temperature in the reactor goes up to 850–1,050°C. It is a non-slagging gasifier and has been tested with all types of coal and lignite, and is found attractive for high ash coals as well as high reactive coals. The chemical reaction in this gasifier is accelerated by turbulent mixing and close contact. There are no separate de-gasification and gasification zones. Dust-laden gas leaves the reactor at the top, and is cooled and purified before use.
- *Entrained Bed Process* is the third configuration. Finely ground coal of 0.1 mm is entrained at high temperatures of the order of 1,400 to 1,600°C. Coal gasifies instantly and volatile matter in coal also contributes to the gas at

the reaction temperatures. The product gas has almost 80 per cent of the energy of the feed coal. The ash in the coal melts and runs down the refractory-lined walls of the gasifier as liquid slag in the water tank. Different versions of entrained bed gasifiers have been developed as Koppers-Totzek and five different versions of it are Shell, Texaco, Dow, Prentflo, and Destec.

The first coal gasification test facility in India came up when a 10 MW captive power plant used gas from coal washery rejects by Bharat Heavy Electricals Ltd. (BHEL) at the TISCO Jamadova Colliery in 1987. A number of trials have been made subsequently. Fertilizer plants at Ramagundum and Talcher installed entrained bed gasification technology for utilizing indigenous coal for production of ammonia. However, these plants have encountered some practical difficulties. From the experience gained from operating and testing facilities, two CFB gasifiers of 390 tonnes/(t/h)/capacity have been installed successively at Gujarat Industries Power Co. Ltd. for their Surat Lignite Power Plant (SLPP). The Neyveli Lignite Corporation Ltd. has also installed a circulating fluidized bed gasifier based on the Wrinkler process to demonstrate the use of lignite. Coal India and Gas Authority India Ltd. have jointly started work in 2010 to set up a large surface coal gasification plant.

Coal Liquefaction

Coal liquefaction is possible by raising the hydrogen-to-carbon ratio. It can be achieved either by direct conversion or by indirect conversion of coal through the gasification route. In the direct process hydrogen is dissolved in coal in the presence of a catalyst and the process is known as hydrogenation. In the indirect method, coal is first gasified and the hydrogen produced during gasification is converted to oil in a catalytic converter. This produces hydrocarbons such as methanol, ethanol, and diesel oil and methane-rich gas as by-products. The genesis of the indirect process (called Fischer–Tropsch Synthesis) took place as a result of the discovery by F. Fischer and H. Tropsch in 1925.

The most important property of coal in order to predict liquid yield from coal is the percentage of volatile material in it. The ratio of liquid yield from coal varies between 35 and 45 per cent. One tonne of coal can produce about one to three barrels of oil and 200 to1,000 cu.m. of gas. Wide ranges of by-products are obtained in different liquefaction processes. These can be used as chemical feedstock or for industrial process heating. The biggest coal liquefaction plant based on the Fischer–Tropsch synthesis is operated by South Africa Synthetic Ltd. at its Sasol Plant. It has a production capacity of about 150 thousand barrels of oil per day.

In India, laboratory-scale investigations on coal liquefaction began in the 1950s at the Indian Institute of Technology, Kharagpur, with the objective of developing indigenous catalysts. In the Fischer–Tropch synthesis 'syngas' was first produced using fixed bed gasification process at 800–900°C. A number of chemicals as catalysts were tested, including zeolite supported iron catalyst and resulted in the output of 4 litres of oil per day. Coal liquefaction research has also been pursued in R&D laboratories on a bench scale unit of 2 kg/h. Indian Oil Corporation Ltd. at Duliajan, in Assam has put up a pilot plant for conversion of low sulphur Assam coal to oil in 2005. Assam coal with its low ash content show better liquefaction characteristics. A contract has been signed recently with Coal India to set up a commercial-scale coal liquefaction plant of 3.5 Mt per annum coal capacity.

Post-combustion Technology

Post-combustion technology is the fourth stage alternative in which end-of-pipe pollutants such as SOx, NOx, and CO_2 are captured and removed from the atmosphere. Desulphurization and de-NOx operations have been tested in conventional power generation plants. Advanced clean coal technologies (CCT) are also perspective greenhouse gas mitigation technologies. These are discussed below. The CO_2 capture technologies are also discussed.

Perspective Clean Coal Technology

Advanced CCTs for substantive improvement in coal combustion efficiencies, underground coal gasification, methane extraction from coal bed and mines, and CO_2 sequestration are to be pursued in mission mode. These advanced CCTs are:

- Combined Cycle Technologies
- Underground Coal Gasification
- Coal Bed Methane
- Molten Carbonate Fuel Cell
- Magneto Hydro Dynamics
- Advanced Combustion Technologies
- Carbon Capture and Storage

Combined Cycle Technologies

Co-generation in the power sector has been suggested as means of reducing emissions of pollutants and achieving better energy output. Co-generation technologies could be:

- A topping cycle, in which electricity is generated first and waste heat utilized later.

- A bottoming cycle, in which heat utilization is followed by electricity generation.
- A combined cycle, which uses both topping and bottoming cycles for achieving maximum efficiency. Examples of combined cycle power generation techniques are IGCC, IGHAT, and PPCC, etc.

Integrated Gasification Combined Cycle (IGCC) has two main components: (i) Coal gasifier system and (ii) Combined cycle power generation cycle, with gas turbine and steam turbine for coal gas and steam, respectively. Coal is gasified in the presence of oxygen/air under high pressure (30 bars) maintained above 1000°C. Synthetic or syngas comprising mainly of CO and H_2 is produced, which needs to be cooled and cleaned of impurities before it is burnt in the gas turbine. The heat from the gasifier and hot gases is recovered in the heat recovery steam generator and used to run the steam turbine in a combined cycle. Mineral matter in the coal is separated as slag from the bottom of the gasifier. The overall efficiency is high and pollution is less due to reduction in emission of NOx, SOx, and CO_2. The first IGCC plant of 250 MW capacity using the shell gasification process came up in 1994 in the Netherlands at Buggenum. So far 28 demonstration and pilot plants of capacity up to 300 MW have been installed worldwide and a few others using coal or refinery residue are in the pipeline. Efforts to commercialize IGCC are on.

In 1988, India became the first country in Asia to construct a 6.2 MW IGCC demonstration plant. This closed loop combined cycle unit with air-blown fluidized-bed gasifier was put up by BHEL. It was unique in terms of testing coal with up to 40 per cent ash at temperatures of 960°C and 1050°C at 0.8 MPa in a fluidized bed gasifier. These early studies are forming the basis of scale-up and a demonstration power plant of 125MW capacity is planned to be set up in the near future. Gujarat Sanghi Steam Works and Ahmedabad Electric Co., have also developed IGCC technology.

Integrated Gasification Humid Air Turbine (IGHAT) is an advanced version of the IGCC technology. It uses a humid air turbine and intercoolers on a multi-stage compressor, to produce low grade heat. Warm water is used to humidify air in the turbine. The latent heat in the moist air is released and provides increased mass flow, resulting in higher efficiency. The IGHAT cycle is proposed to eliminate the steam turbine and utilize heat to warm water in various heat recovery sections. A combined process of integrated gasification with humid air turbine increases the net power output, thereby reducing emissions.

Pressurized Pulverized Coal-fired Combined Cycle (PPCC) uses pulverized coal firing in gas turbines. The gas is cleaned at very high temperatures of 1400–1600°C and a high pressure of 18 bar. The molten ash accumulates on the edge of the slagging chamber due to the centrifugal force. Low grade fuels, including biomass or lignite, or a mixture of both, can be used to enable combined heat and power generation. In combined heat and power generation with a waste heat recovery system, the efficiency is expected to reach 46–47 per cent, along with reduction of CO_2, NOx, and SO_2 by 10, 20, and 30 per cent respectively. The economics and efficiency of five main advanced clean coal technologies is depicted in Table 13.4.

Table 13.4 Expected Efficiency, Cost of Clean Coal Technologies, and Future Projections

Technology	*Installed Capacity in MW*	*Efficiency in the year in per cent*		*Capital Cost in ECU /kW*	
		2000	*2030*	*2000*	*2030*
Ultra Super-critical (USC-PF)	650	44	49–52	1268	968
IGCC	760	46	50–53	1370	900
IGHAT	400	40	44–46	1300	900
PFBC	550	43	44–46	1030	900
PPCC	40	46	50–52	1200	950

Underground Coal Gasification

Underground coal gasification (UCG) is *in-situ* gasification of coal/lignite deposits to produce clean energy in the form of gaseous fuel from unmineable, deep coal seams. The UCG research began in Russia in 1931 based on the principle of creation of a sustained burn-zone inside the coal bed and recovery of gas through injection of fluid to create an artificial fracture. It requires creation of enough permeability in the coal seams so that a stream of air could flow from one point to another, allowing combustion to take place. The coal is then ignited at either end to allow for burn-zone growth in the upstream direction. Desirable drilling depths for UCG are in the range 100 to 600 m to extract energy from coal seams that are too thick or too thin. The gas can be burned as fuel directly. The process of gas recovery is similar to oil or gas recovery from the interior of the earth. Four major technical steps involved in UCG recovery are:

- Drilling a pair of vertical holes or breaking the ground with explosives
- Linking boreholes by reverse combustion, horizontal drilling, or high power lasers

- Igniting coal seam using Controlled Refractory Injection Point (CRIP) technology
- Injecting gasifying fluids such as air, oxygen, or steam for the recovery of coal gas.

Though technology- and cost-intensive, UCG has tremendous economic significance; it does not require coal beneficiation and there is no problem of ash disposal. Through this method huge quantities of coal deposits located at great depths, which cannot possibly be extracted by conventional coal mining methods, can be utilized. The technology has been pursued in several countries, including India. In India prospects of development of UCG technology are high, with total energy potential of UCG estimated at 15,000 billion cu. m. of gas. Gujarat coal and lignite deposits with an estimated resource of 63 billion tonnes, the South Karanpura coal fields, as well as the lignite fields in Rajasthan appear suitable for this from geological and hydrological survey data considerations. Detailed physico-mechanical measurements and borehole data have also been acquired for carrying out feasibility studies at promising lignite sites.

Coal Bed Methane

Coal bed methane (CBM) is a process of recovering methane gas trapped inside the coal seam, as coal matures. The gas is attached to coal at the molecular level and is not a free gas. Almost all coal deposits contain methane in some quantity, which is released when coal is extracted, or even after the mine is abandoned or closed. During underground coal mining, it is considered a serious hazard as it may explode and cause fire. Five major geological formations containing coal bed methane content are shown in Table 13.5. Methane content can vary from 2 to 20 tonnes of coal. It is highest in Permo-carboniferous coal deposits and minimum in Tertiary coals. World coal bed methane extractable resources are assessed at about 135 Terra cu. m.

Table 13.5 Methane Content in Different Coal Types

Geological Coal Category	*Methane content in cu.m./tonne*
Permo carboniferous	20
Perminian (Gondwana)	8.5
Jurassic	5.5
Cretaceous	10.5
Tertiary	2.8

For CBM recovery, water in the coal bed must be removed so as to reduce the pressure on methane molecules. Different methods are adopted for extracting methane. If a source is detected in an operational mine, conventional techniques such as open hole, vertical jet slot, hydraulic fracturing, and perforation type of drilling at the coal seam depths, can be used for draining the gas before the mining starts. In an abandoned mine, carbon dioxide sequestration by pumping flue gas from a power plant (containing CO_2) into the coal seam under pressure is being considered a possibility. The carbon dioxide molecules get attached to coal and the trapped methane molecule is released. Those mines graded as saturated CBM reservoirs require better understanding of the reservoir mechanism for a controlled drainage of gas, as they may contain five times the amount of gas available in an ordinary coal mine. With the advancement in the technology of gas recovery from underground, CBM mining is becoming feasible. Several coal basins are currently being developed for CBM around the world.

Coal found in India mostly belongs to the Gondwana, Cretaceous, and Tertiary deposits, which contain medium level methane. Gondwana coal deposits may have 8.5 cu. m. of CBM per tonne of coal, while Tertiary deposits of coal have 2.8 cu. m. per tonne. Coal India has offered 26 blocks for CBM exploration covering 13,600 sq. km. of area with estimated CBM reserves of 1,374 billon cu. m. The first CBM recovery was demonstrated in 2009 with the Great Eastern Energy Corporation Ltd. (GEECL), an energy company signing contract for commercial production from the Raniganj coalfields near Burnpur. Recovery of coal mine methane (CMM) has been attempted for producing 500 kW of power through underground boreholes in Bharat Coking Coal Ltd.

Molten Carbonate Fuel Cell

Molten Carbonate Fuel Cell (MCFC) technology uses fuel cell, an electrochemical device that converts chemical energy directly to electrical energy. It derives its name from the electrolyte used—a molten mixture of lithium and potassium carbonates. The direct current (DC) output of the fuel cell is converted to alternate current (AC), through a DC-to-AC converter. The product of coal gasification is used to generate electricity without going through mechanical conversion. Overall efficiency is expected to be of the order of 55 per cent. The waste heat from the hot fuel cell gas stack exhaust can be recovered in the bottoming cycle and used to produce additional electricity. In this process CO_2 emissions from coal use are considerably reduced.

The first pressurized MCFC stack was successfully tested in 1980 in Japan. IGFC of 100 kW was demonstrated at the Kawageo Thermal Power Station in 1990s.

The Kentucky Pioneer Energy project has subsequently operated a 2 MW carbonate fuel cell in USA. Integrated with an IGCC plant, IGMCFC is under development. Research and development of 1 kW MCFC using coal gas was also initiated in India.

Magneto-hydro-dynamic Power

In a magneto-hydro-dynamic (MHD) power system exceedingly high temperatures are needed so that the fuel gets ionized. In the presence of oxygen-enriched air, at high temperatures of 2,000°C coal gas turns into plasma gas and electrical energy is produced without using a mechanical turbine. The construction of a generator requires a long duct or channel with both side walls made of metal. The bottom is made of an insulator. The electrically conducting plasma gas fluid is passed through a duct. A strong transverse magnetic field applied across the duct, induces a magnetic field in the moving fluid. According to Faraday's law a moving conductor in a magnetic field produces an electric current in a direction perpendicular to the direction of motion. When the electrical power density of the plasma gas is equal to the maximum achievable power density, the efficiency of the MHD generator becomes 50 per cent. Higher efficiency can be obtained if the waste heat coming out of the duct is further utilized to run a steam turbine.

The feasibility of a coal-based MHD generator has been established. Cost-effective, high-strength magnets capable of generating a high magnetic field are the prime requirements for commercial deployment. The length of the generator decreases as the magnetic field increases. Three types of MHD generator cycles have been conceptualized: (i) open cycle, (ii) close cycle, and (iii) liquid metal generator. Development of high temperature superconducting magnets and attainment of high temperatures are some of the challenges which are being addressed. MHD research facilities exist in Russia (then USSR), as well as in many other countries, namely, USA, Germany, Australia, Poland, China, Japan, the Netherlands, and India. In India, an experimental 5 MW water-gas fired open cycle generator was built in collaboration with USSR at Tiruchirapally a few years ago at the Bhabha Atomic Energy Research Centre jointly with other academic and research institutions.

Advanced Combustion Technologies

In oxy-fuel technology coal combustion takes place in the presence of 100 per cent oxygen. Combustion in pure O_2 results in CO_2/H_2O mixture in the flue gas with CO_2 content up to 90 per cent. The CO_2 can be sequestered without stripping from the flue gas stream. A further advantage revealed in pilot-scale tests is substantially reduced NO_x emissions. For coal-fired combustion, the oxy-fuel technology was suggested in the1980s. However, there are no full-scale plants using oxy-fuel combustion in operation yet. *The cost of producing oxygen for combustion is high.* Theoretical studies combined with laboratory and pilot-scale studies (typically 30–100 MWe) have been announced or are planned. With the introduction of CO_2 sequestration technology, oxy-fuel has become the centre of renewed interest. In India BHEL proposes to establish a pilot plant on oxy-fuel combustion. Sufficient experience exists in the Indian industry on atmospheric or circulating fluidized bed coal combustion processes to be able to integrate these efforts towards oxy-fuel and make it a business proposition.

Another promising development in coal combustion that needs to be mentioned is Chemical Looping technology. This has a fuel recycle option, while reducing the cost of oxygen separation. Chemical Looping has two reactors; a fuel reactor, where a metal oxide is reduced by reaction with coal. Reduced metal oxide is circulated to an air reactor where it is oxidized and regenerated. Exit gases from the fuel reactor contain CO_2 and H_2O, from which pure CO_2 can be separated, while H_2 is combusted. Flue gas from the air reactor contains N_2 and unreacted O_2. Tested on the laboratory scale, Chemical Looping in a circulating fluidized bed combustion process (which has already been tested on indigenous coal) appears to facilitate a better CO_2 capture option as compared to IGCC. However, this area needs further investigation.

Carbon Capture and Storage Technology

CO_2 Sequestration—Carbon Capture and Storage (CCS) technology is one of the emerging clean coal technologies to meet the global emission stabilization targets while meeting the national energy needs. It involves capture of CO_2 in the atmosphere and its permanent fixation away from the atmosphere. If the power plant and the storage sites are not near each other, it will involve transport of CO_2 in liquid form over longer distances. Essentially, the CCS has three main components, starting with capture of CO_2 in the atmosphere emitted from large point sources; fixing it or transporting it to a possible location where it can be safely stored; and finally process of fixation.

Recent developments and progress made in CCS technology are discussed below.

Carbon Capture

CO_2 capture technology as an end-of-pipe solution to power generation is based on chemical absorption, membrane separation, physical adsorption, and cryogenic separation methods. Chemical absorption process requires the use of chemical solvents. Mono-ethanolamine (MEA), diethanolamine (DEA), mixed amines, and tertiary amines have been investigated. Notwithstanding the regenerative capability of the solvent, the energy penalty and additional equipment requirements for circulating large volumes of liquid absorbents add significantly to the cost, thus limiting applications of the process.

Physical processes are based on cryogenic cooling or solid adsorbents. Solid adsorbents have better promise as they reduce regeneration and recirculation costs and increase binding capacity for CO_2. The adsorption of CO_2 gas by use of molecular sieves (zeolites) is based on significant intermolecular forces between gases and surfaces of certain solid materials. Both Pressure Swing Adsorption (PSA) and Temperature Swing Adsorption (TSA) have been attempted; however, the efficacy of the process depends on plant parameters with variation in pressure in one case and temperature in other. These early efforts are aimed at development of cost-effective regenerative adsorbents and membrane materials.

CO_2 Bio-Sequestration

Application of the flue-gas treatment using algae bio-processes for the absorption of CO_2 is a growing field of research. Triangular air-lift bioreactors have been designed as the most suited for algae growth. From the first series of experimental data obtained for two different algal species in a pilot-scale unit supplied with flue gases from a small power plant, removal efficiency of CO_2 was reported as approximately 80 per cent. Preliminary cost analysis suggested that micro algae biofixation from a 550 MW coal-fired power plant could sequester 25 per cent of the CO_2 cost-effectively, if the value recovered from the harvested algae was priced at approximately $100 per tonne. Design of a solar bioreactor has been proposed that uses computational fluid dynamics. In this case scaling-up can be done much more easily than using algae biofixation, which requires thousands of acres of space to soak up the CO_2 from one coal plant.

Terrestrial Sequestration

The terrestrial biosphere is estimated to sequester large amounts of carbon dioxide and is thought to be one of the most cost-effective means of reducing atmospheric levels of CO_2. Terrestrial storage would result in afforestation and can also enhance crop productivity. Advance crop species and cultivation practices could be designed to increase the uptake of CO_2 by terrestrial as well as coastal ecosystems through enhanced rate of photosynthesis. Studies are underway to optimize resource use with a view to quantifying the impact of defined changes in land use on carbon sequestration. Assessment of carbon pool and sequestration in the soil and vegetation in the forest ecosystems of Manipur and north-eastern India reveal that soil carbon stock ranged from 27.73 to 48.03 tonnes of carbon per hectare and emission of carbon dioxide from the soils varied from 1.697 to 4.462 tonnes of CO_2 per hectare per year in different forest ecosystems. The carbon stock in the vegetation ranged from 9.89 tonnes of carbon per hectare to 295.50 tonnes of carbon per hectare in the different forest types of Manipur. The study shows that soil carbon pool and emission of CO_2 are highly influenced by vegetation types and environmental factors.[2]

CO_2 Storage

The idea to cage CO_2 in natural geological surroundings for its storage has taken shape as a means to permanently removing it from the atmosphere. Both active and passive underground trapping of CO_2 are envisaged. It can be done by burying it in deep saline aquifers and in rocks and minerals. Rapid developments are taking place in evaluation of results of CO_2 storage in the underground deep aquifers and in the sedimentary basins under the sea bed. Sleipner, Norway has achieved tremendous success in this. It has injected 1 Mt of CO_2 every year in saline aquifers under the sea bed, since 1996. To understand the reaction taking place between CO_2 and mineral rocks, active storage in basaltic rocks is being pursued for better integrity for CO_2 storage. Calcium and magnesium silicates react to form carbonate minerals. A process of geochemical trapping can effectively eliminate risk of CO_2 leakage. Each geological setting is different and underground CO_2 trapping studies require geomorphology studies. There is a need to develop methodologies for long-term tracking of CO_2, once injected.

Energy Fuels by CO_2 Sequestration

The process of underground storage of CO_2 and consequent changes in the viscosity of fluids in depleting oil reservoirs can provide additional fuel for energy. The CO_2 will mix with the crude and by changing the oil

[2] Yadava (2010).

properties will help flush out remaining reserves making it flow easily. At the surface the gas mixture containing both CO_2 and natural petroleum gas will have to be separated from the oil before it is sent for refining. The stripped CO_2 can be recycled back into the oil fields to extract more oil. CO_2 management through this approach will be a highly challenging task. It will have to be adopted when all the conventional methods of enhanced oil recovery have failed. A CO_2-EOR (CO_2-Enhanced Oil Recovery) project designed to minimize CO_2 emissions back to the atmosphere with appropriate incentives would have an important role in assuring energy security. Like oil fields, unmineable coal seams can also prove to be potential reservoirs for CO_2 storage. On average three molecules of CO_2 are absorbed for displacing one molecule of methane (CH_4). By injecting CO_2 in coal seams, coal bed methane recovery can be enhanced.

Globally, research in CCS has grown by almost 100 per cent in the past five years as compared to first five years of the current decade. In India, research is still in its infancy. Under the National Programme on CO_2 Sequestration (NPCS), research started in DST in 2006; the following thrust areas are identified:

- CO_2 Sequestration through Micro-algae Bio-fixation
- Carbon Capture Process Development
- Terrestrial Agro-forestry Sequestration Modelling Network
- Policy Development Studies

CCS Policy Development Studies

Towards policy development studies, the feasibility of CO_2 sequestration in deep underground saline aquifers and inter-layered sedimentary sequences in denser low-permeability basalts and the sequential basalt are being tested. CO_2 sequestration through mineralization has been proposed in certain rocks such as basalts and laboratory studies conducted in select regions of the Deccan Volcanic Province have shown formation of secondary carbonates on the surface upon reaction with CO_2 in the super-critical phase (Prasad et al. 2008). Recent experiments are reported in the southwest Atlantic sector jointly by the National Institute of Oceanography, India and the Alfred Wegener Institute, Germany. LOHAFEX (LOHA—iron, FEX—Fertilization Experiment) experimentally tests the efficacy of iron fertilization in southern oceans by CO_2 sequestration. Exploratory investigation of gas hydrates as future CO_2 absorbers in the marine environment, as well as modelling and simulation studies for producing diethyl ether as fuel are underway.

There is a need to begin geo-modelling of terrestrial and geological sequestration of CO_2. In terrestrial sequestration, development of technologies for quantifying carbon stored in a given ecosystem and manipulation of ecosystems to increase the carbon sequestration rate beyond current conditions require modelling research. For underground sequestration modelling of geo-chemical, geophysical and hydrodynamic trappings processes, which are unique to local condition, form a pre-requisite for CO_2 storage site-selection.

Capture and Storage Costs

CO_2 capture results in significantly high energy penalty in a power plant and reduces it by as much as 15 per cent. The estimate of cost of post-combustion CO_2 capture and storage has also been worked out. Best available technology suggests $40–80 per tonne CO_2. The application of CCS may however double the cost of electricity generation, depending on the technology used. The CO_2 capture is estimated to cost about 70 to 80 per cent of the total cost. A comparison of recovery and capture cost according to capture technology used is given in Table 13.6.

In transportation, pipeline costs are $ 2–8 per tonne and injection costs are of the order of $5–20 per tonne. Storage capacity of different underground locations and cost is shown in Table 13.7.

In a conventional coal-based plant CO_2 is captured from the outgoing flue gas, which comprises many other impurities. But in IGCC for CO_2 capture, the syngas produced in the gasifier is passed through a water shift

Table 13.6 Economics of Post-combustion CO_2 Capture Options

Technology/Parameter	*CO_2 recovery (in per cent)*	*CO_2 purity achieved (in per cent)*	*Energy penalty (in per cent)*	*Capture cost \$/tonne CO_2*
Chemical absorption	90	> 98	36	47
Physical adsorption	90	44	47	61
Membrane separation	90	43	52	78

Source: IPCC report (2005).

Table 13.7 Storage Capacity of CO_2 in Possible Underground Locations and the Cost per Tonne*

Probable storage site	*Potential CO_2 storage capacity in Gt*	*IEA* Estimates of storage in \$/t*
Depleted oil fields	126	Net cost saving
Depleted gas fields	800	7–17
Unmineable coal beds	150	20
Deep saline formations	400–10,000	5–17

Source: *IEA—International Energy Agency.

reactor and converted into CO_2 and H_2. The CO_2 is then separated (present in high concentration) and can be fixed away from the atmosphere at the pre-combustion stage itself. This reduces the cost of capture and also the energy penalty. Preliminary economic assessments of capture costs show that IGCC costs become 63 per cent higher with capture than without capture. (For IGCC and high ash coal without capture, cost is 21 per cent higher than pulverized coal firing and 12 per cent higher than ultra-super-critical.)

Large-scale CCS projects are infrastructure-intensive. The plants are located farther than possible locations for storage. We cannot afford such a steep increase in the price of electricity, unless learning curves bring down the cost through R&D support and success is achieved in the recovery of a value added products through CO_2 sequestration.

CCT Roadmapping Studies in India

In India, thrust to R&D on Coal Beneficiation, Coal Gasification, Liquefaction, and IGCC began early in 1980s. A Pre-Combustion Technology Assessment Study conducted by the Technology Information, Forecasting and Assessment Council (DST) in 1996. It provided specific insights into measures to be adopted by power companies and other major coal-consuming industries like steel and cement for technology up-gradation. Joint technology research in sectoral applications began. The in-depth study on Clean Coal–Energy Cycle was conducted in the Department of Science & Technology in 2006 with the aim to give thrust to R&D and developing a future road map for CCT (see Box). These efforts have culminated into giving importance to introduction, adaptation, and development of clean coal through policies and programmes. A National Clean Coal Technology Centre (NCCTC) as a Centre of Excellence for continuance of dedicated research and development on indigenous coal and application of CCTs has been set up.

Proposed CCT Roadmap

A time-bound CCT Road Map drawn to establish the required R&D infrastructure for implementing it with the ultimate goal of achieving emission-free electricity generation. The proposed is as follows:

Ongoing and near-term (up to 2012):

- Improved coal recovery, coal beneficiation, reduction in cost.
- More emphasis on fluidized bed combustion; super-critical power plant boilers, IGCC demonstration.
- Enhanced energy recovery from coal: CBM, CMM, etc.
- Pilot scale studies on coal liquefaction.

Medium-term (2012–17):

- IGCC, PFBC, Ultra-super-critical power plants.
- Enhanced energy recovery from coal: CBM, UCG.
- Commercial-scale coal liquefaction.
- Zero Emission Technologies (ZETs) pilot scale.
- Carbon sequestration pilot scale.

Long-term (2017 and beyond)

- Zero Emission Technologies (ZETs)—commercialization.
- Carbon sequestration demonstration plant.
- IGFC and production of hydrogen fuels from coal.

Source: CCT Initiative—Roadmap for future development, CCT DST-BHEL Workshop, 26–7 Ocotober 2006.

Barriers to Implementation

On a world-wide basis, prospects of CCT are good in view of the advantages such as higher efficiency of power generation and lower GHG emissions per kW of installed capacity. The clean coal technology has been advancing rapidly to achieve goals of zero emission technology. In India efforts towards clean coal technology development began more than two decades ago, but have not kept pace with the global developments. Research efforts carried out in the country for the past several years have shown that as compared to IGCC, the quality of coal requirement in CFBC is less demanding. Yet IGCC has been given highest attention. There have been other barriers and constraints in the advancement of CCT, such as (i) High cost involved to support development of Clean Coal Technology to proving stage, (ii) Amenability of advanced technologies to available coal with high ash content (iii) Inadequate R&D infrastructure in academic institutions and national laboratories, (iv) Lack of academic–industry interaction for new coal-based technology, (v) Constraints in development of coal blocks in the absence of adequate equipment infrastructure and (vi) lack of sufficient coal evacuation facilities, among others.

Although policies have been introduced from time to time suggesting creation and implementation of R&D Fund for energy, key questions are: who should invest and why invest in clean coal technology development, is it the responsibility of the coal producer or coal user? Capacity building efforts have also not kept pace with the rapid developments taking place elsewhere. Moreover, many CCTs are proprietary and protected by strong patent regimes. New coal technologies are not proven and involve higher capital investment. In the absence of appropriate marketing strategies for adoption of clean coal for power generation, many new researches have not moved out of the laboratory.

Conclusion

This article provides brief description of various coal processes and technologies, explores early initiatives, bottlenecks and current status of clean coal technology in India. Coal is a dominant resource for electricity in India. At present nearly 85 per cent of the coal produced is consumed in the power sector. Opportunities are explored in coal extraction, coal transport, and coal beneficiation and critical clean coal technologies with the progress made in them are described. Research efforts have been initiated in India in almost all coal utilization technologies. Carbon capture and storage research has also begun as CCT enabler, its policy and cost implications are discussed. A clean coal technology R&D roadmap for identifying near and medium-term priorities towards zero emission technology as long-term solution is presented.

The challenge of implementing CCT on large scale however, remains as daunting as ever. There are many barriers. Coal gasification and coal liquefaction are less pollution emitting technologies, but for their implementation on industrial scale a number of trade-offs between financial and technological considerations continue, mainly arising from quality of coal resource. There are financial, infrastructural, and regulatory barriers to be tackled in almost entire coal chain starting from coal extraction to coal utilization and pollution abatement.

Way Forward

Nevertheless prospects of CCTs are becoming high as a result of global warming concerns. Actually both local as well as global environmental concerns can be addressed better through the use of CCT. The costs are coming down, although it may take long to establish their economic competitiveness. A long-term clean coal policy to address the issues of installation of thermal power plants based on CCTs, R&D, and transfer of technology are imperatives for growth. Most CCTs are research intensive and are still evolving, therefore, joint research ventures should be considered for technology transfer. In super-critical and ultra-super-critical coal fired plants, much higher efficiency can be achieved. The super-critical technology is already under development in our country. These efforts need to be augmented for ultra-super-critical combustion capabilities.

Technology Transfer under Climate Protocols

To address climate change concerns, CCTs have come up with new agenda for growth towards low carbon economy. Adoption of CCT offers a unique opportunity for technology transfer. The mechanisms introduced under the Framework Convention on Climate Change (FCCC) are Kyoto Protocol, Emissions Trading, and Clean Development Mechanism among others. New mechanisms like NAMAs have been proposed. The CCT can become an instrument for transfer of technology in such bilateral and international agreements.

To fully exploit potential of CCT, appropriate policy incentives and more capacity building efforts are must. An integrated inclusive growth perspective would be required in their adoption, aiming at full utilization of by-products at each stage. Different entities and stake-holders would need to work together for realization of this goal. Hence, there is a need for strategic planning to achieve clean energy infrastructure-based growth.

References

CCT Initiative—Roadmap for future development (2006). CCT DST-BHEL Workshop, 26–7 October.

Goel, Malti (2007). 'Barriers to Deployment of Clean Coal Technology: Key Issues and Perspectives', 6th Annual Conference on Carbon Sequestration, 7–11 May, Pittsburg, USA.

———(2008). 'Carbon Capture and Storage, Energy Future and Sustainable Development: Indian Perspective', in Malti Goel, B. Kumar, and S.N. Charan (eds) *Carbon Capture and Storage R&D Technologies for Sustainable Energy Future*, Narosa Publishing House, New Delhi, pp. 3–14.

———(2009). 'Recent Approaches in CO_2 Fixation Research in India and Future Perspective towards Zero Emission Coal Based Power Generation', *Current Science*, 97, pp. 1625–33.

Goel, Malti (2010). 'Perspectives in CO_2 Sequestration Technologies and An Awareness Programme', in S.Z. Qasim and Malti Goel (eds). *CO_2 Sequestration Technologies for Clean Energy*, Daya Publishing House, p. 205.

——— (2009). 'Climate Change, Carbon Capture and Storage Technologies and Carbon Trading', in B. Das, S.K. Ghosh, S.K. Banerjee, H.S. Ray, and S.P. Mukherjee (eds), *Carbon Capture, Sequestration & Trading*, Indian Association for Productivity, Quality Reliability (IAPQR), Kolkata, pp. 1–20.

——— (2010). 'Technologies for Carbon Dioxide Sequestration', in Krishan Saigal (ed.), *Climate Change: The Human Aspect*, Kalpaz Publications, New Delhi, pp. 71–90.

Government of India and Ministry of Coal (2006). *Integrated Energy Policy 2008*, Report of the Expert Committee, Annual Report, Government of India.

Intergovernmental Panel on Climate Change (IPCC) (2005). Bert Metz, Ogunlade Davidson, Heleen de Coninck, Manuela Loos, and Leo Meyer (eds), Cambridge University Press, United Kingdom, p. 431.

International Energy Agency (2008). *Carbon Capture and Storage Technologies.*

Majumdar A.K., H. Shah, and J.P. Burnwal (2006). 'Comparative Study on Magnetite Medium Stability in a Vorsyl Separator and in a Heavy Medium Cyclone', *Coal Preparation*, 26, pp. 165–79.

Ministry of Power (2008). *All India Electricity Statistics*, General Review, CEA, Government of India.

Prasad P.S.R., D. Sarma, L. Sudhakar, U. Basavaraju, R.S. Singh, Z. Begum, K.B. Archana, C.D. Chavan, and S.N. Charan (2008). 'Geological Sequestration of Carbon Dioxide in Deccan Basalts: Preliminary Laboratory Study', *Current Science*, 996, pp. 288–91.

'Recent Developments in Carbon Dioxide Capture Materials and Processes in Energy Industry' (2009). in N.R. Neelameggham, R.G. Reddy, C.K. Belt, and E.E. Vidal (eds) *Energy Technology Perspectives: Conservation, Carbon Dioxide Reduction and Production from Alternate Sources*, JWS Wiley Publications, pp. 53–62.

State-wise Breakup of Indian Coal Resource (2010). Available at http://www.gsi.gov.in and http://www.coal.nic.in.

Verma V.S. (2010). 'CO_2 Mitigation: Strategies and Issues', in S.Z. Qasim and Malti Goel (eds), *CO_2 Sequestration Technologies for Clean Energy*, Daya Publishing House, New Delhi, p. 205.

World Coal Institute (2008). *Coal Statistics*, available at www.worldcoal.org.

Yadava P.S. (2010). 'Soil and Vegetable Carbon Pool and Sequestration in the Forest Ecosystems of Manipur', in S.Z. Qasim and Malti Goel (eds), *CO_2 Sequestration Technologies for Clean Energy*, Daya Publishing House, New Delhi, p. 205.

14 The Nuclear Energy Imperative

Addressing Energy Poverty, Energy Security, and Climate Change in India

Manpreet Sethi*

India's Energy Reality—the 'Burning' Issues

India is severely energy deficient—more than half its rural households are resigned to darkness after sundown; cities suffer long and frequent power cuts. Per capita power availability in India at 631 kilo watt hour (kWh) is way below the world average.[1] This compares poorly with global statistics of 17,179 kWh in Canada, 13, 338 kWh in USA, or 5,644 kWh in Italy, and even 1,300 kWh in China.[2] This has both a direct and indirect impact not only on the quality of life but also on the overall economic growth potential and the national development index.

In addressing the challenge of energy poverty, it is imperative for the government to pay adequate attention to the overall picture of sources of energy available to the country and their advantages and limitations. For instance, it would be counter-productive for the nation to solely invest in those energy sources which do not come with the assurance of secure supplies, or those that raise national vulnerability by increasing dependence on unreliable and unstable supplier nations, or cause significant environmental pollution. Therefore, the energy demands need to be met through safe, reliable, secure, and environmentally sustainable fuel sources. This obviously calls for a diversification of energy sources. At the moment, India draws the bulk of its electricity from thermal sources, especially coal. In fact, 55 per cent of the country's total commercial energy need is met by coal-fuelled electricity generation. Hydro power comes a distant second at about 25 per cent, and then renewable sources provide another small share of the electricity at about 15 per cent. Finally, nuclear reactors provide 3 per cent of the total electricity generation. Despite its rather meagre contribution, nuclear energy holds substantive promise from the perspective of meeting India's humungous energy needs in a secure and sustainable low carbon way.

This article examines the role that nuclear power could play in assuring India with a level of energy security, and

* Manpreet Sethi has written extensively in national and international journals on nuclear power, proliferation, and disarmament. She is the author of *Nuclear Strategy: India's March towards Credible Deterrence* (2009), *Argentina's Nuclear Policy* (1999), editor of *Towards a Nuclear Weapons Free World* (2009) and *Global Nuclear Challenges* (2009) and co-author of *Nuclear Deterrence and Diplomacy* (2004).

[1] Union Power Minister Mr Shinde in a reply to a question in the Rajya Sabha and as reported in 'Per Capita Power Consumption in India', http://www.inrnews.com, 20 August 2007.

[2] International Energy Agency (2006).

even energy independence,[3] in an environmentally sustainable manner. It explores the advantages of investing in nuclear expansion, which is today possible with the conclusion of the Indo-US civilian nuclear cooperation agreement that has opened the prospects of India's participation in international nuclear commerce. It highlights the advantages, some of them unique to this country, of adopting nuclear power as a major input to the future energy mix. It also examines the challenges that lie ahead in the expansion of nuclear power.

While the primary focus of the paper is on nuclear energy, it nevertheless is premised in the belief that there is need for growth and development of *all* energy sources, existing and potential, to power India's socio-economic growth and development. The country's energy requirements are so huge that it cannot afford the luxury of banking on only one or two fuel sources to power its future.

Among the challenges facing an emerging India, two could particularly derail the process of its rise to being a significant power in the region and beyond, and they are interconnected. The first is widespread social disharmony as a result of skewed economic development and unmet aspirations of a growing and an increasingly aware population. The resulting discontentment coupled with growth of sub-nationalism, opportunistically exploited by vested interests of domestic and external adversaries could severely strain the country's socio-politico-economic fabric. Hence, it is important to comprehend the criticality of inclusive social and human development along with economic growth to ensure societal peace and national security.

The second challenge arises from the sheer shortage of electricity that drives the economic growth and development. It is widely accepted that electricity has a direct connection with development and per capita energy consumption is a parameter for calculating the human development index. Therefore, it is hardly surprising that energy and the ability of a nation to access it from reliable, secure, sustainable, and safe sources tops national priorities everywhere. Energy poverty is obviously a handicap that a nation aspiring to fast-track development and growth can ill afford. This is even more important for a nation like India that expects a phenomenal growth in its energy demand, estimated to be between 6–10 per cent per annum during the first quarter of the twenty-first century. The power policy of India promises electricity availability to all by 2012.[4] This appears practically impossible given that the present total power generation of about 157 GW is woefully short of the demand that is growing by the day. In fact, India's power generation capacity was calculated to be 68 per cent below the target that had been set for 2009.[5]

For this situation to substantially change, the absolute amount of electricity generated by India would have to at least double by 2020, double again over the next ten years, and be close to ten times the figure today by 2050. According to Dr Kakodkar, Chairman, Atomic Energy Commission, even if India's per capita energy consumption was to rise to 5,000 kWh (which would still be about one-third the current consumption figures in Canada or the USA), the country would suffer an energy deficit of 412 GW by 2050.[6] As is evident, the deficit itself is likely to be close to three times the current total power production!

The Expert Committee on Energy constituted by the Government of India estimated in 2006 that India's power needs would be about 960 GW by 2031–2, assuming a GDP growth rate of 9 per cent.[7] Later developments such as the global financial crisis and the consequent economic downturn have brought down the expected rate of growth of the Indian economy to 7 per cent per annum. Even at 7 per cent the vulnerabilities that will accompany large-scale energy import dependence are clearly evident.[8] A stark contrast in this sector is evident when one compares India with the rapid strides that China is making. It is today the fastest growing generator of electricity in the world. New generation capacity that China will add to its existing capacity in 2010 alone will exceed the total installed capacity of Brazil, Italy, and Britain, and these are nations with fairly large generation capacities themselves.[9]

It is obvious that energy poverty alleviation has to remain a critical priority for India if it is to realize its aspiration of emerging as a major power. Energy security through the expansion of generation capacity not only bolsters national confidence and pride, it also enables further growth and development. Secure and abundant

[3] Former President A.P.J. Abdul Kalam often talked of energy independence as the 'nation's highest priority'. See his address at Kudankulam Nuclear Power Project on 22 September 2006 as reproduced in *Nuclear India* (2006).

[4] Srinivasan (2005).

[5] *livemint.com* (2009).

[6] Kakodkar (2008).

[7] Aiyar (2008).

[8] India's energy imports are discussed in a subsequent section of this paper.

[9] *Economist* (2010). China is in fact slated to produce more power annually than America, the current leader, by 2012.

availability of electricity to run modern economies makes a nation an attractive investment destination. In this regard, it would be useful to cite a statement made in the context of China, 'Cheap, reliable electricity is one reason why China remains the *preferred destination* for manufacturing even as its wages rise above those in such countries as Bangladesh, Indonesia, the Philippines and Vietnam'.[10]

The Government of India, therefore, must urgently focus on meeting the enormous energy requirements of the country. This would call for cultivating a diverse mix of energy sources that pragmatically balance considerations of cost, uninterrupted availability of fuel, and environmental impact. It is important that every potential source of energy be optimally used and the menu of options be as varied as possible so as to minimize risks of disruption arising from shortages, price fluctuations, or political manipulations.

Sources of Energy in India: the Present Scenario

For India, which together with China accounts for 45 per cent of the increase in global primary energy demand, nuclear power holds tremendous promise. Much like the rest of the world (except perhaps France and Japan), the bulk of India's existing power generation capacity exists in the thermal sector. In fact, nearly 65 per cent of the total energy generation of India is met from coal, oil, and gas. The worrisome part is that India imports these traditional fossil fuels in large quantities to meet its energy demand, increasing its vulnerability to global mood swings. For a large and rapidly developing country like India, bulk imports of fuel are neither affordable nor strategically prudent. Moreover, with increasing worldwide competition for non-renewable hydrocarbons, their prices can only be expected to rise and this will remain a cause of concern for the future.

India has reasonable coal reserves, which according to British Petroleum estimates, comprise 8 per cent of the world total. The country is the fourth largest producer of coal and lignite in the world (after the United States, China, and Australia).[11] However, India's coal reserves are of low quality (with high ash content and low calorific value) concentrated in select pockets of the country. This necessitates haulage of coal over long distances, which not only raises cost but also ties down the transportation network. In fact, transport costs raise the cost of coal three times from when it comes out of the mine. Nevertheless, at present, coal remains the dominant fuel. This, however, entails the large-scale imports of coal annually. In fact, the Sankar Committee set up to recommend measures to meet the demand-supply gap had estimated import of 30–40 million tonnes of high-grade coal by 2011–12.[12] However, coal imports have far exceeded that figure in 2010 itself. According to the chairman of Coal India Ltd., in 2009, India's coal imports stood at 59 million tonnes and 'should be around 100 million tonnes' for the year ending 2011.[13] If the time horizon is stretched to 2050, *without adding nuclear energy to the Indian energy basket*, then coal imports would have to be to the tune of 1.6 billion tonnes.[14] The enormity of these figures and the gravity of the situation are self-evident.

India's oil consumption in 2009 was about 2.67 million barrels per day, having doubled from the figure in 1992.[15] As the Indian economy continues to grow even modestly at 7 per cent per annum, the oil requirement of the country is expected to double again from the present consumption figures by 2030.[16] In 2006, India was the seventh largest net importer of oil in the world. With 2007 net imports of 1.8 million bbl/d, India is currently dependent on imports for 68 per cent of its oil consumption. The EIA expects India to become the fourth largest net importer of oil in the world by 2025, behind the United States, China, and Japan.[17] Crude oil prices are unlikely to fall below $50 per barrel in the coming few years even though they have come down from the high peak of $135 per barrel earlier in 2008. This has enormous implications not only for the strain it causes on the Indian exchequer, but also on the strategic autonomy of the nation. It may be recalled that France and Japan realized their vulnerabilities during the oil shock of 1973 and thereafter pursued strategies to secure their energy supplies on a war footing.

[10] Ibid. Emphasis added.

[11] Tata Energy Research Institute (TERI) (2003), http://www.teriin.org/energy/Indian energy sector.htm

[12] *Hindu* (2007).

[13] Lomax (2010). India is presently importing its coal from Australia, Indonesia, South Africa, and more recently Colombia.

[14] As estimated by Kakodkar (2008), footnote 6.

[15] At 2.67 million barrels per day, India's oil consumption was actually less than in 2008 which had peaked at 3 million barrels a day but fell due to the economic slowdown. For more on this see India Energy data provided by US Energy Information Administration at http://www.eia.doe.gov/cabs/India/Oil.html

[16] EIA (2007).

[17] Ibid.

Fast track expansion of nuclear power generation emerged as the solution for them.

The third source of thermal power generation is natural gas. The use of this fuel for energy generation is expected to increase substantially in the coming years. But, given the limited domestic availability of natural gas vis-à-vis the demand, it will have to be sourced from outside through elaborate and long-distance pipelines and LNG shipments. These will bring their own risks of terrorism, piracy, and environmental spills. While 'peace pipelines' is politically a laudable concept, it has enormous economic and security implications, especially for India since the pipelines will have to pass through politically unstable nations that harbour open hostility towards India.

Efforts to harness viable renewable energy resources continue to increase the share from such sources, as wind, biomass, solar, hydro, in the total energy generation portfolio. Research and development efforts are being encouraged in renewable energy technologies, which include such sources as tidal and geothermal energy. However, except for hydro power in the few places where it is plentiful, none of these has presented itself as being suitable, intrinsically or economically, for large-scale power generation where continuous, reliable power supply is needed and it is well known that reliability and evenness of electricity supply is even more critical for an increasingly digitized information society. Development of energy efficient technologies and measures has to continue. But, these efforts cannot be expected to be able to meet the enormous energy demand and can only be complementary to the addition of new generation capacities.

In a scenario where the domestic deficit on fuel sources exists, nuclear energy emerges as a promising energy source. Nuclear power can significantly supplement electricity availability and hence ease the heavy dependence on hydrocarbons. As has been stated earlier, the cases of France and Japan amply prove this. France today generates 80 per cent of its electricity from nuclear energy. Meanwhile, Japan had managed to reduce its oil imports from 80 per cent in 1970s to 56 per cent by 1990s and today sources 30 per cent of its electricity from nuclear power, though it has no indigenous uranium sources.[18]

Nuclear Energy and Increasing Environmental Consciousness

If the growing Indian economy continues to rely on traditional thermal energy sources, carbon emissions would significantly rise and environmental consequences like greenhouse effect, global warming, and climate change would progressively become a serious cause for concern. Thermal power plants pose the problem of GHG emissions that cannot be wished away despite technology improvements and implementation of stringent environmental measures. Rather, pollution is sure to increase with the upsurge in energy production from thermal plants. Table 14.1 estimates CO_2 emissions from different energy sources in order to illustrate that coal, oil, and gas remain major sources of carbon emissions, while nuclear and other renewable energy sources figure around the lowest.

As is evident, nuclear power emits the least amount of greenhouse gases bettered only by wind energy. Given these figures, it is obvious that the strategies and technologies adopted by countries with large energy requirements will have critical implications for local and global environment. Illustratively, France, which meets 42 per cent of its primary energy consumption from nuclear energy has the lowest per capita carbon dioxide emission in Europe.

At present, India's per capita carbon emissions stand at 1–1.2 tonnes[19] compared to 20 tonnes per capita in the US.[20] This is not in the least due to exceptionally good energy policies and practices but due to the fact that a large proportion of the Indian population is denied access to power. This is about to change and should too, if India expects to grow and emerge as a power to reckon with globally. The least it can do is provide energy access to its people. With continued urbanization, a shift from non-commercial to commercial fuels, increased use of motorized vehicles, and prolonged use of older and inefficient coal-fired power plants, India's emissions are expected to

Table 14.1 Carbon Dioxide Emissions from Power Technologies in g/kWh

Coal	*Advanced Coal*	*Oil*	*Gas*	*Nuclear*	*Biomass*	*Hydro*	*Wind*
960–1,300	800–860	690–870	460–1230	9–100	37–166	2–410	11–75

Source: Banerjee (2001).

[18] Singh (1999).
[19] Ministry of Finance (2010).
[20] A report by Hinkle Charitable Foundation.

increase and nearly triple by 2030.[21] In fact, according to the US Department of Energy, between 2001 and 2025, India's carbon emissions will grow by 3 per cent annually, twice the predicted emissions growth in the US, making India the third largest air polluter after the US and China by 2015 itself.[22] If India is to avoid this dubious distinction, then a conscious decision must be taken to switch to more environmentally sustainable energy technologies, such as nuclear power.

Global Interest in Nuclear Energy

Nuclear power today accounts for 15 per cent of global electricity generation[23] and the world now has more than half a century's experience in handling this technology which is equivalent to over 14,000 reactor years; expertise and confidence in the area has steadily grown.[24] Furthermore, rising oil prices and growing environmental concerns over the last decade have led to a reconsideration of sustainable energy fuels. In this milieu, nuclear power has resurfaced as a keen contender for large-scale energy generation. Thus, even in the US, after a period of low interest in new nuclear construction, studies such as the one conducted by the Massachusetts Institute of Technology, indicated the need for renewed emphasis on the role of nuclear power for energy security.[25] After nearly three decades of no new nuclear plants (though upgrades of existing plants continued), the US Nuclear Regulatory Commission (NRC) today has licence applications for 20 new plants pending before it. Even as the NRC hires more people to help cope with the application rush, new factories are being set up to fabricate parts and components of nuclear plants.

Likewise, in Europe too, a report prepared for the European Economic & Social Committee, which advises the European Commission, emphasized that Europe needed nuclear power.[26] Consequently, some of the EU members, such as Italy and Germany that were not in favour of nuclear energy, are reconsidering their phase-out policies. The UK plans to build four more nuclear plants with help from France, with the first one likely to be operational in 2017.

Meanwhile, China has emerged as the fastest growing nuclear power generator and if its ambitious plans are realized, then it will be the largest producer of nuclear energy at 130 GW by 2030.[27] In fact, of the 55 GW of additional installed nuclear generating capacity projected for Asia, 24 GW is projected for China, 12 for India, and 12 for South Korea.[28] China currently has 21 nuclear power plants simultaneously under construction, more than in any other nation at any point in time in the past. As they attain criticality over the next ten years, China would have spent $150 billion to increase its nuclear capacity nine-fold.[29] According to OECD estimates, if the nuclear activity planned over the coming decades remains on track, nuclear reactors would supply a fifth of the total electricity generated worldwide by 2050.[30]

Nuclear Energy in India: Dispelling the Myths and Misconceptions

Several analysts have argued that given India's limited and low-grade uranium reserves, the development of the nuclear programme beyond 10,000 MWe would imply increasing dependence on uranium imports. However, this viewpoint tends to overlook the logic of India's three-stage nuclear power programme that envisages large-scale utilization of India's significant thorium reserves. It is in order to tide over the transition from fast breeder reactors to the thorium cycle that India needs uranium. Therefore, unlike the case of coal or oil or gas, where imports appear to be a permanent reality, uranium dependency would be for a limited period of time till India graduates to the thorium cycle.[31]

What is the contemporary Indian situation on the nuclear energy front? At present, India produces 4,340

[21] Ministry of Finance (2010).

[22] Figures as cited by Condoleezza Rice, Remarks at the Senate Foreign Relations Committee on the US India Civil Nuclear Cooperation Initiative, 5 April 2006. Available at US State Department website.

[23] This has dropped from 16 per cent in 2005 as a result of six of Japan's nuclear power plants remaining shut as a consequence of the earthquake early in 2008 and several of France's reactors going in for simultaneous repairs.

[24] World Nuclear Association (2009a).

[25] MIT Study (2004).

[26] 'EU Report Supports Nuclear Role', *Nucleonics Week*, 2004.

[27] At present, the US is the largest producer of nuclear power at 98 GW. At present, China has 11 operational nuclear power plants that provide 1.3 per cent of its total generating capacity.

[28] World Nuclear Association (2009b).

[29] Slater (2010).

[30] Patel (2008).

[31] For a detailed techno-scientific explanation of the three stages of the programme, see http://www.dae.gov.in

MWe from its 17 operational nuclear power plants. This amounts to about 2.9 per cent of the total generation capacity of the country. With the recent opening of India to international nuclear commerce, it is expected that there may be a surge in nuclear generation capacity in the coming decades.

It is worthwhile to examine the much debated issue of the economics of nuclear energy. Traditionally, nuclear power has been considered an expensive energy source given the high capital cost and long gestation periods required for building power plants. But recent empirical data indicates otherwise. Nuclear power has long been proven a viable economic option in terms of Long Range Marginal Cost (LRMC), or for power supply at locations far away from coal reserves, particularly if hydel sources are also not available in these areas.[32] In fact, a comparative techno-economic analysis that accounts for location of coal mines, transportation of fuel, availability of railroads, ash content, and associated environmental impact and necessary mitigation measures, etc., skews the cost benefit in favour of nuclear energy. Even if the cost of uranium has doubled in the last few years, yet given that fuel costs for nuclear plants are a minor proportion of total generating costs, in contrast to coal or gas-fired plants, the long-term economics of nuclear plants work out better. Also, the fuel's contribution to the overall cost of the electricity produced is relatively small, so that even a large fuel price escalation has relatively little effect. For instance, typically a doubling of the uranium market price would increase the fuel cost for a light water reactor by 26 per cent and the electricity cost about 7 per cent (whereas doubling the gas price would typically add 70 per cent to the price of electricity from that source).[33]

In fact, contemporary trends such as low interest rates, high oil prices, improvements in nuclear plant capacity factors,[34] reduction in construction time, etc., have further rationalized the per unit cost of nuclear electricity. In fact, the construction and cost experience of Tarapur Atomic Power Plant (TAPP) 3 and 4, among India's latest nuclear plants is illustrative of this. Not only have these plants been constructed in record time but also at a cost lower than expected. According to the Chairman of the Nuclear Power Corporation of India Ltd. (NPCIL),[35] the two units were built in five years at a cost of Rs 6,100 crore against an approval of Rs 6,525 crore. Modern systems of construction and resource management have indeed contributed to the economics of nuclear power.

At the same time, newer methods of cost calculation that include 'external costs' of health and environment tilt the balance further in favour of nuclear energy. Unlike thermal plants where the waste generated is so much more, nuclear power internalizes the cost of spent fuel management, plant decommissioning, and waste disposal. An EU study estimated that inclusion of health and environment costs would double the EU price of electricity from coal and increase that from gas by 30 per cent.[36] The cost of nuclear power is further enhanced once carbon dioxide emissions begin to carry a significant 'price'. Emission trading provides incentives for investment in carbon-free electricity technologies, and this improves the economics of nuclear power considerably.

Nuclear Energy for India's Energy Security

With experience of over half a decade in the field of nuclear technology, India, in the words of Dr Chidambaram, former Chairman, AEC, is 'the only developing country that has demonstrated its capability to design, build, operate and maintain nuclear power plants, manufacture all associated equipment and components, and produce the required nuclear fuel and special materials'. Indeed, India can claim to have experience in construction, operation, and maintenance of a varied range of nuclear power plants—Light Water Reactors (LWR), Pressurized Heavy Water Reactors (PHWR), Fast Breeder Reactors (FBR), and Advanced Heavy Water Reactors (AHWR). Having gathered several years of reactor experience in PHWR operations, India has now entered the commercial demonstration stage of the FBR programme with installation of the first prototype FBR of 500 MWe at Kalpakkam. Further, India is an emerging leader in the development of reactor and associated fuel cycle technologies for thorium utilization. A 30 kW (Th) research reactor, KAMINI, has

[32] Alagh (1997).

[33] World Nuclear Association (2010).

[34] Power plant reliability is measured by capacity factor, or the percentage of electricity actually produced compared to the total potential electricity that the plant is capable of producing. On this parameter, nuclear power plants have shown out as the most reliable sources of electricity production, with average capacity factors exceeding even 90 per cent in many countries, compared to only 68 per cent for coal, 35 per cent for natural gas, and 34 per cent for oil. Capacity factors for renewable energy sources are also low at about 30 per cent.

[35] A public sector undertaking of the Department of Atomic Energy (DAE) that is tasked with the designing, construction, and operation of nuclear power reactors.

[36] For more on this see section 'External Costs', in WNA, footnote 30.

been operational since 1996 and is one of a kind globally operating with uranium-233 based nuclear fuel along with thorium.

Indian nuclear plants have also achieved many international benchmarks. For instance, in 2002, the average capacity factor of Indian PHWRs was more than any reactor in the US. At the end of September 2002, Kaiga Atomic Power Station (KAPS) recorded a capacity factor of 98.4 per cent during the preceding 12 months and became the best performing PHWR among 32 reactors worldwide.[37] In 2009, the Nuclear Fuel Complex at Hyderabad made history of sorts by supplying 11,016 fuel rods from the imported natural uranium to NPCIL in a record time of six months. This fuel was meant for the three reactors at Rajasthan which are now under IAEA safeguards.[38]

While the Indian uranium reserves at about 0.8 per cent of the world are considered to be insufficient for a power programme more than 10,000 MWe if the uranium is used on once-through basis and then disposed of as waste, India has planned for spent fuel reprocessing to complement its nuclear fuel resources. The first stage of this programme involves using the indigenous uranium in PHWRs. The second stage utilizes the spent fuel of PHWRs after reprocessing to extract Pu 239. This is then used in FBRs to breed additional fissile nuclear fuel, plutonium, and uranium-233. In the third stage, thorium and uranium-233 based AHWRs will be able to meet the long-term Indian energy requirements. Thus, the available uranium will eventually be used to harness the energy contained in non-fissile thorium, of which India possesses about 32 per cent of the world's reserves or 360,000 tonnes of high-quality thorium, but which needs plutonium to kick-start fission.

Envisaging the crucial role that rapid addition of nuclear power generation could play in easing the overall energy deficit in the coming years, the government has been able to achieve exceptionalization for India from NSG guidelines that had long prohibited any transfer of nuclear material or technology to India until it accepted NPT membership as a non-nuclear weapon state and opened all its nuclear facilities to full scope safeguards. An opportunity to bypass this requirement presented itself in 2005 when President Bush offered to abandon the long-standing US nuclear policy towards India in favour of a constructive engagement in civilian nuclear cooperation. Intense and unprecedented negotiations between India and US over 2005–08 that traversed many steps and crossed several hurdles finally culminated when President Bush signed HR 7081 US-India Nuclear Cooperation Approval and Non-proliferation Enhancement Act in October 2008. This has opened a range of opportunities for the Indian nuclear power programme that had been the hamstring for international cooperation since May 1974. The opportunities, particularly in four dimensions of the Indian programme, are worth examining.

Fuel Availability

Lack of uranium to power the Indian nuclear reactors stood out as the most serious constraint that had begun to hamper the functioning of Indian reactors over the last few years. It is common knowledge today that through most of 2008, the Indian power plants had to run at half their capacity levels owing to inadequate availability of nuclear fuel. In fact, the Nuclear Fuel Complex itself that manufactures the fuel rods for the Indian nuclear reactors operated at less than 50 per cent of its capacity due to the shortage of uranium in 2008. This situation arose out of two factors: firstly, though the country's uranium reserves estimated at 61,000 tonnes had been calculated by the DAE to be enough for 10,000 MW power generation for 40 years, the uranium prospecting, mining, and milling had been relatively ignored over the last few decades. Since 1968, the Uranium Corporation of India Ltd. (UCIL) has been commercially producing and processing uranium ore mainly from the mines at Jaduguda, Bhatin, Narwapahar, and Turamdih, all located in Singbhum district of Jharkhand. This was sufficient for the operating power plants and research reactors until fast-track power plant construction started from the mid-1990s onwards. Thereafter, a mismatch developed between uranium demand and supply. Secondly, over the decades, the uranium reserves have depleted and the ore at Jaduguda mines is presently being obtained at much deeper levels than earlier. This pushes up the cost of recovery of uranium, which in the case of India is always high because of low concentration of uranium in the ore. Indian ore has low uranium content of about 0.6 per cent as compared to some Australian, Canadian, and Kazakh ores containing up to 15 per cent of uranium.

To meet the projected demand of the nuclear power programme, UCIL is exploring uranium deposits in Andhra Pradesh and Meghalaya, besides other areas of Jharkhand. Progress in this direction, however, has suffered due to opposition from the local populace and non-governmental activists in the regions. Therefore, in order to tide over the domestic uranium crunch, one of the relatively immediate

[37] Parthasarthy (2008).

[38] Article in *Business Standard* (2009).

benefits of the recent nuclear cooperation agreement is to access uranium from the international market at competitive prices for a programme that has planned at least five more indigenous power plants in the near future. It is interesting to note that uranium prices that had peaked in 2007 at $ 136 per lb U_3O_8 had fallen to $ 44.50 per lb U_3O_8 in 2009.[39] India has already procured uranium from France, Russia, and Canada, leading to a 15 per cent increase in reactor capacity factors.[40] UCIL would also be able to bid for uranium prospecting or mining in other resource-rich regions of the world. It has already concluded an agreement with Mongolia for capacity creation in Ulan Bator's nuclear sector and uranium mining. With Namibia, Gabon, Kazakhstan, and Russia too, India has arrived at uranium mining or supply arrangements.

Import of Larger Reactors and Export of Smaller Ones

The Tarapur Atomic Power Plant (TAPP 3), India's sixteenth nuclear reactor, went critical on 14 May 2006. With this, India's indigenous nuclear programme demonstrated the capability to construct and operate PHWR of capacity size 540 MWe. TAPP 3 and 4 are today India's largest capacity reactors, with all the other indigenously built plants being of capacity 220 MWe. In the future, NPCIL has plans to standardize 700 MWe plants that it has the capability to build. Larger reactors obviously offer economies of scale and having developed a mature expertise and technological and industrial base, India has felt the need to move on to larger capacity generations.

The Koodankulam plants being acquired from Russia are of 1,000 MW. The predominant reactor capacities in many of the countries that are advanced in nuclear technologies average at least 1,000 MW; majority of the reactors in France have a capacity of 1,300 MW. With the opening of international cooperation, India has the opportunity to import larger reactors to augment its generating capacities.

Meanwhile, given the interest in nuclear energy for peaceful purposes in many smaller countries, particularly in South-east Asia, India has an opportunity to export its 220 MWe reactors that would be ideally suited for their smaller electricity grids. These reactors have proved their competitiveness in capital as well as unit energy costs and have a demonstrated record of safe operations. India also has the capability to emerge as a low-cost manufacturing hub for nuclear component supplies to the resurgent nuclear industry worldwide. For instance, companies like L&T can export nuclear reactor building skills and/or operation and maintenance services. The firm has already formed alliances with many of the leading nuclear technology providers, such as Atomstroyexport, Atomic Energy of Canada Ltd, US-based Westinghouse Electric Co, which is owned by Japan's Toshiba Corp, and GE-Hitachi Nuclear Energy, with the aim of producing components and equipment for their reactors. It has also set up a $ 463 m joint venture with NPCIL to provide heavy forgings and generators for nuclear reactors.[41] GE Hitachi Nuclear Energy Ltd. and Westinghouse Electric Co. also plan to use India as a low-cost supplier of nuclear parts for exports to the US and Europe. Other Indian companies such as Reliance Power, NPCIL, and BHEL announced plans to invest $ 50 bn in the next five years to expand their nuclear manufacturing base. In particular, BHEL is looking to spend $ 7.5 bn in just two years to build the factories needed to supply 1,600 MW reactors.[42]

Participation in International Projects

It is in recognition of India's nuclear expertise that India was invited to participate in the multinational International Thermonuclear Experimental Reactor (ITER) being built in Cadarache, France to harness energy from nuclear fusion. Indian research in fusion had in any case been underway for the past two decades at the Institute for Plasma Research at Gandhinagar. India had planned to build an ITER scale reactor by 2030.[43] Participation in the global project will enable it to leapfrog in technology, while making a value addition to the multinational effort. India is also member of the IAEA's International Project on Innovative Nuclear Reactors and Fuel Cycles (INPRO) activity and is participating in eight of the 12 collaborative projects under INPRO's phase II programme. This programme seeks to build innovative energy systems which are not only more proliferation resistant but have better safety, economics, and waste management; these are crucial for the sustained growth of nuclear power. Interestingly, research on such reactors is exploring closed fuel cycles and seriously considering reprocessing technologies as a means of extracting greater energy and reducing waste. India is among the handful of countries that have

[39] 'Uranium Mining Issues: 2009 Review'. Available at http://www.wise-uranium.org/uissr09.html, updated February 2010.

[40] Balaji (2010).

[41] Fenwick (2010).

[42] Ibid.

[43] *Hindu* (2006).

mastered the plutonium reprocessing technology and has lots to offer from its experience. Meanwhile, Indian nuclear scientists have a chance to interact with the best of their fraternity elsewhere, an exchange that has been denied to them since the late 1970s.

Tiding over Delays in Moving to Thorium Cycle

India's development of the thorium cycle has now completed nearly 40 years of work on the concept and demonstrated feasibility through the successful operation of a research reactor since 1996. Of course, problems of high cost and technical complications in fuel fabrication because of high radioactivity of U-233 and reprocessing required to move to the thorium fuel cycle still persist. But then, India is among the very few countries pursuing this technology. Even the World Nuclear Association, which is dedicated to the promotion of nuclear technology, sees little scope of development of this technology as long as abundant uranium is available. However, given the peculiarities of the Indian resource base, Dr Homi Bhabha had prescribed a three-stage programme for the country that would culminate with the exploitation of India's large thorium reserves. There is, nevertheless, a logical technical progression that is required of the PHWR and FBR stages in order to reach an optimal level of fissile material build-up that would then make the use of thorium feasible and effective. While R&D continues to reach the thorium utilization stage from multiple directions, including the use of Accelerator Driven Systems (ADS), these are pioneering technologies that India is struggling with alone. Therefore, there can be no pre-determined dates for the advent of the third stage. Estimates vary from 2020 to 2040. In the meantime, the import of reactors from abroad would not only help India in quicker accumulation of requisite fissile material but also help narrow the widening demand-supply gap in an environmentally friendly way.

Grappling with Challenges

Even though it makes eminent sense for India to not only keep the option of nuclear power expansion open, but to press for it urgently, there are certain limiting factors that must be grappled with.

The (DAE) is estimated to have a work force of 70,000 experts today. Given the additions planned to nuclear generation capacity, it is understood that the need for more nuclear scientists, engineers, craftsmen, construction managers, plant operators, and maintenance personnel would significantly swell in the coming years. The AEC has a Nuclear Training School that has until now been in charge of manpower development. However, with the need for rapid and increased numbers, it would be a challenge to recruit, educate, train, and retain technical personnel especially at a time when the private nuclear industry is also expected to be expanding worldwide. To strengthen research at universities, the DAE provides grants for projects through the Board for Research in Nuclear Sciences. A DAE Graduate Fellowship Scheme for IITs has existed since 2002 to promote collaborative research. IIT Kanpur already offers a course in nuclear engineering and technology, and so does Chennai since 2009. Concerted efforts towards creation of a trained manpower pool will be required from academic institutions and the DAE to have sufficient number of nuclear experts available for future expansion plans.

Given the high technology content, and the sensitive and precise nature of materials, equipment, and processes involved in nuclear power generation, it is imperative for the Indian manufacturing industry to keep pace with advancing nuclear science and technology. In fact, this challenge could be turned into an opportunity by the industry, given that the global nuclear renaissance is exposing the inability of manufacturers worldwide to meet the growing demand for reactor components and systems. For instance, the US does not have the capability to domestically manufacture ultra large forgings that exceed 350 tonnes. These are necessary for making reactor vessels and its global suppliers are the Japan Steel Works that has the capacity to make five to six such forgings every year. Given the small number of suppliers for such high-end products, it is natural for their manufacturing capacities to be booked years in advance.

Given India's cost-competitiveness, reasonably high engineering and technological skills supplemented by innovative techniques, the country could emerge as a hub of nuclear components and graduate slowly to more complex and high-end products over the years. With the opening of international nuclear trade with India, Indian companies have the possibility to enter into joint ventures or technical collaborations with global nuclear manufacturing majors. This could not only support the Indian nuclear expansion but also enable exports. The government could help build an enabling environment for the Indian industry by drafting necessary policies to this effect. For instance, just as there are offsets in the defence industry, a similar provision may be worked into the commercial contracts for import of nuclear reactors, making it mandatory for the seller to enhance the capability of Indian companies active in the field. It would also be of great value if the indigenous component of every new power plant is kept at a high level by sourcing equipment, components, and labour from the domestic market.

This would not only enable cost benefits but also provide a fillip to the domestic industry and help provide employment to large numbers.

The existing Atomic Energy Act, 1962 does not allow private players into the field of nuclear power generation. Until now, this has been the exclusive preserve of state-owned companies. With the opening of the sector to international markets, it is now necessary to amend the Act in order to allow listed public sector and private companies to set up and operate nuclear reactors.[44] The National Thermal Power Corporation (NTPC), the largest Indian power company, has already proposed a joint venture with imported technology to set up and make operational a 2000 MWe nuclear power plant by 2017.[45] Besides, many private companies such as Jindal Steel and Power Ltd., Tata Power Ltd., Reliance Power Ltd. have expressed a desire to step into the field. Also, several multinational companies would be encouraged to bid for the multi-billion nuclear reactors market in India.

However, in order to enable this, India would also have to enact nuclear liability laws to safeguard against the eventuality of an accident. This is certainly a concern for American private companies more than for the state-owned enterprises of France or Russia who have sovereign immunity. Nevertheless, India will be required to sign the international legal framework for nuclear accidents, namely the Convention on Supplementary Compensation that covers claims through a global fund to pay victims.[46] Moreover, government support will also be necessary to provide risk insurance for companies building nuclear reactors, which would cover events beyond the control of the owner, including regulatory and litigation delays.

Given the sensitive nature of the technology and materials in use at a nuclear power plant, these have existed in a heavily regulated environment to guard against possible threats, natural and man-made, to their safety and security. For a sustainable and safe expansion of the nuclear power programme, ample attention must therefore be devoted to the correct and quick implementation of necessary regulatory and environmental procedures. These are extremely essential because any accident at a nuclear site would have repercussions on the growth of the global nuclear industry. Therefore, safety of operating nuclear power plants (NPPs) and periodic and stringent rule-based evaluation are of vital importance in order to minimize and possibly obviate any danger to plant workers or the public. In fact, for every nuclear plant that is built and operated, the society needs assurance that the facility:

- Will not suffer an accident leading to large radioactive radiation.
- Will not pollute the environment during its routine operations.
- Will ensure and account for long-term storage and safe disposal of radioactive waste.

The guarantee of these assurances requires deployment of effective measures at all stages—design, site selection, operation, and decommissioning—of the development and operation of the nuclear plant. At the same time, relevant regulatory bodies need to be instituted to oversee and assess the implementation of safety measures against different parameters so that the individual, society, and the environment can be protected against radiation hazards. From the moment of site selection to the actual construction of the plant, a number of other mandatory requirements of seeking environmental clearances, rehabilitation of displaced populations from exclusion zones, development of infrastructure etc. are required to be undertaken. While India's AERB has performed this task well in the past, as the pace of nuclear activity rises, it might be necessary to expand the regulatory organization through additional induction of trained manpower so as not to develop bottlenecks on issues of requisite licensing, while simultaneously ensuring that the most stringent standards of safety and security are maintained.

Yet another significant obstacle to rapid and large-scale nuclear power expansion is public perception of this source. Unfortunately, there is very little awareness of the stringent safety regulations enforced and followed in the design, construction, and operation of power plants, or of the safety record of India's power plants of nearly three and a half decades. Neither is there adequate knowledge of the fact that natural radiation in some cases exists at scales that are several times that in the vicinity of a power plant ordinarily. Fortunately, the nuclear industry is extremely conscious of the dangers involved in its activities and

[44] Interestingly, the US Atomic Energy Act, 1946 was revised in 1954 to permit private sector involvement in reactor development, though the Congress retained ownership over nuclear fuel. The 1954 Act also established the AEC as the agency to oversee reactor construction and use. This distinguishes the manner in which the nuclear power generation is regulated as compared to conventional electricity production.

[45] World Nuclear News Overview (2008).

[46] This convention will come into force once five or more nations that collectively have 400,000 MWe of installed capacity ratify it with the IAEA. Four have already done so—US, Morocco, Argentina, and Romania totalling a capacity of 319,256 MWe.

hence takes sufficient precautions to obviate chances of an accident.[47] It is well aware of the fact that any accident anywhere in the world would have an adverse impact on the global nuclear programme. Hence, complacency in the nuclear power plant operations cannot be tolerated and India must keep its safety record unblemished if it is to reap the true potential of nuclear energy.

The other major aspect of nuclear energy that causes public concern is that of waste management and disposal of spent nuclear fuel. Fortunately for India, this is not such a big challenge since it follows a closed fuel cycle in which the nuclear fuel after being used once is not immediately disposed of as waste. Rather, the spent fuel is reprocessed to extract plutonium for the second stage of the reactors and the products left only after reprocessing constitute waste. High level waste is then vitrified and stored underwater. The US has been following a once through fuel cycle since the 1970s when President Carter had put a stop to reprocessing due to proliferation concerns. However, now grappling with the issue of spent fuel management, the US is showing an interest in returning to the closed cycle. Meanwhile, on the domestic front the public relations department of the DAE must step up its efforts to better educate the public on the advantages and risk mitigation endeavours of the atomic establishment in order to develop the ground for greater exploitation of nuclear energy.

Conclusion

Nuclear technology in India has reached a state of self-reliance. India today has nearly 300 reactor years of safe nuclear power generation. Kaiga 2 set a record by registering 529 days of uninterrupted run during August 2006–January 2008; 17 operating reactors and six more under construction indicate a high level of nuclear activity that will only pick up in the coming years as more fuel and technology is inducted into the domestic programme. The Indian nuclear power programme has also moved into the second stage of development wherein a Prototype FBR is now under construction, and research and development for AHWRs is under way. India today has the capacity, technology, and the will to expand its nuclear power programme. International cooperation would facilitate the availability of environmentally sustainable energy to India well in time to avoid stagnation of human development.

We are witnessing a moment in history that has opened new vistas for the country's energy scenario. It is the bounden duty of the nation to use this to its own advantage after a careful consideration of risks and vulnerabilities. As has been indicated earlier in the paper, the energy choices before India from indigenous sources are severely limited. Large-scale imports of coal, oil, and gas raise dependence and hence the vulnerabilities of the nation. This is particularly uncomfortable for a country that is economically on the ascendant and cannot afford to be choked on energy. Renewable energy offers an attractive alternative and the country has exploited its hydel potential. However, both the hydroelectric plants and wind farms also come with the problems of environmental displacement and rehabilitation, besides being poor sources of base load electricity. Solar energy, of course, is plentiful in India but its commercial viability for large-scale electricity generation and storage are issues that still demand more R&D. The government needs to invest in this in order to find a long-term energy solution in solar power. In the meantime, nuclear energy presents itself as a commercially proven and environmentally sustainable, large-scale electricity source. With the opening of the international market to India, this is an opportune moment to undertake its rapid expansion through import of nuclear fuel as well as large capacity reactors. However, as India embarks down this road, three caveats are in order:

- Nuclear safety and security must remain topmost priority for the nuclear establishment. It cannot afford an accident of any sort.
- Investment in R&D in the third stage of the nuclear programme that will enable the utilization of indigenous thorium should be accelerated so that uranium dependency can be obviated in the future.
- Greater public awareness on the merits of nuclear energy in India's energy mix must be generated. While none can deny the risks involved in nuclear fission, the investments made in the safety processes and regulatory procedures to minimize these must be adequately brought out. The government must also encourage transparency in calculating the costs of nuclear electricity generation, which ample studies have proven is cost competitive in many scenarios.

If human development, economic growth, and environmental sustainability are taken as essential parameters for these decisions, then there is a case for nuclear expansion for electricity generation, especially as part of the

[47] For more on the safety aspects of the Indian power programme, see Sethi (2006).

strategic imperative to develop as wide a diversification of the Indian energy basket as possible.

India, today, adds about 30–35 GW of power capacity every five years, which is half the planned amount. In order to add 60 GW every five years for the next 25 years, the right choices must be made now. For sustained progress to usher in a resurgence in civil nuclear power, realistic action will be necessary on several fronts: a supportive policy environment, including legislative changes, commensurate industrial investments, linkages with university, and training institutes for manpower requirements and support from the academic and strategic community to monitor trends and identify limitations to forewarn against possible dangers. A comprehensive policy on its expansion must be urgently drafted and implemented if India is not to let unavailability of power stand in the way of its economic growth and development.

The IAEA Director General, El Baradei, once rightly pointed out, 'Disparity in energy supply, and the corresponding disparity in standards of living, in turn, creates a disparity of opportunity, and gives rise to the insecurity and tensions....' India cannot afford such fissures.

Therefore, the imperative of nuclear energy for addressing the current and projected energy deficit and ensuring long-term energy security, while simultaneously addressing environmental issues, can afford to be dismissed only at India's own peril. Energy poverty and its concomitant implications stare the nation in the face. Nuclear energy, if produced safely, offers promise. The requirement hence is to fast-track civilian nuclear expansion while maintaining the highest standards of nuclear safety and security. Today's India has to carefully make the right choices to assure the future generations of a brighter and secure tomorrow.

References

Aiyar, Swaminathan Anklesaria (2008). 'Nuclear Power Gives Energy Security', *The Times of India*, 20 July.

Alagh, Yoginder K. (1997). 'Economics of Nuclear Power in India', *Nu-Power International*, 11 (1–3), pp. 22, January–March.

Balaji, Fakir (2010). 'As Fuel Supplies Resume, India's Nuclear Power Output Up', http://thaindian.com, 11 January.

Bannerjee, Rangan (2001). 'Assessment of Role of Renewable Energy Technologies', Greenhouse Gas Pollution Prevention Project—Climate Change Supplement, The Louis Berger Group Inc. Global Environment Team, 14 February, available at http://www.climatechangeindia.com/gep_ccs/.

Business Standard (2009). 'NFC Despatches Fuel Bundles to Newly Built RAPS Unit 6', 3 December 2009.

Economist (2010). 'Lights and Action: Electricity and Development in China', 29 April 2010.

Energy Information Administration (2007). Office of Integrated Analysis and Forecasting, Department of Energy, *International Energy Outlook*.

'EU Report Supports Nuclear Role' (2004). *Nucleonics Week*, 29 January.

Fenwick, Samuel (2010). 'India's New Nuclear Build: Coming in from the Cold', *Industrial Fuels and Power*, 7 May.

Hinkle Charitable Foundation. 'How Do We Contribute Individually to Global Warming', Report 5, available at http://www.thehcf.org/emaila5.html

Hindu (2010). 'India will Join ITER next month in Brussels', 26 April 2006.

'India's Power Generation Capacity 68% below Target in FY'09' (2009). *livemint.com*.

International Energy Agency (2006). *Key World Energy Statistics*.

'India to Broaden Corporate Base for Nuclear Power' (2008). *World Nuclear News Overview*, 31 October.

'India will join ITER Next Month in Brussels', *Hindu*, 26 April.

Kalam, A.P.J. (2006). 'Energy Independence', *Nuclear India*, 40 (5–6), pp. 2–3, November–December.

Kakodkar (2008). 'Uranium Import can Stave Off Looming Energy Crisis: Kakodkar', *Hindu Business Line*, 5 July.

'Lights and Action: Electricity and Development in China', *Economist*, 29 April.

Lomax, Simon (2010). 'Indian Coal Imports May Rise to 100 Million Tons on Power Demand', *Bloomberg Business Week*, 20 May.

Ministry of Finance (2010). *Economic Survey of India (2009–10)*, Government of India, New Delhi.

MIT Study (2004). 'The Role of Nuclear Power', MIT, Massachusetts.

'NFC Despatches Fuel Bundles to Newly Built RAPS Unit 6' (2009). *Business Standard*, 3 December.

Patel, Tara (2008). 'Nuclear Reactors May Supply a Fifth of Power by 2050', *Bloomberg Business Week*, 16 October, available at http://www.bloomberg.com

Parthasarthy, K.S. (2008). 'Nuclear Growth Despite Fuel Resource Constraints', *Navhind Times*, 6 June.

'Sankar Panel Suggests Recast of CIL' (2007). *Hindu*, 1 June.

Sethi, Manpreet (2005). 'Go for Nuclear Power' (2005). *The Times of India*, 24 October.

——— (2006). 'Nuclear Safety: Critical for Future Nuclear Expansion', *Air Power Journal*, 3(4), (Winter 2006).

Singh, Jasjit (1999). 'Growing South Asian Interests in the Persian Gulf Region: Problems and Opportunities', *Strategic Analysis*, 23(9), December.

Slater, Tom (2010). 'Sick of Coal, China Boosts its Nuclear Goals by 50%', 24 March, available at http://green.venturebeat.com/2010/03/24/sick-of-coal-china-boosts-its-nuclear-goals-by-50-percent/

Srinivasan, M.R. (2005). 'The World's Energy Resources and Needs', *Nuclear India*, 39 (1–2), July–August.

Tata Energy Research Institute (TERI) (2003). *Indian Energy Sector*, March, available at http://www.teriin.org/energy/Indian energy sector.htm

'Uranium Import Can Stave Off Looming Energy Crisis: Kakodkar', *Hindu Business Line*, July.

US Energy Information Administration, available at http://www.eia.doe.gov/cabs/India/Oil.html

World Nuclear Association (2009a). 'External Costs', 29 March.

——— (2009b). 'Nuclear Power in the World Today', March, available at http://www.world-nuclear.org

——— (2010). 'The Economics of Nuclear Power', http://www.wna.org, April.

World Nuclear News Overview (2008). 'India to Broaden Corporate Base for Nuclear Power', 31 October 2008.

Section IV

Transport Infrastructure

15 Reconciling Economic Growth with Low Carbon Mobility in India

Addressing the Challenges

Kaushik Ranjan Bandyopadhyay

Introduction

Transport plays a crucial role in development and constitutes a significant share of world energy consumption. Transportation primarily relies on petroleum, which supplies nearly 95 per cent of the total energy use of world transport and accounts for nearly 60 per cent of oil consumption. Hence, the transport sector has also been largely responsible for the pollution and GHG emissions.[1]

In 2005, the total final consumption of petroleum products for the world was 3,420 million tonnes of oil equivalent (mtoe), of which 60.4 per cent was consumed by the transport sector (see Table 15.1). Table 15.1 further delineates that within the transport sector, road transport consumes the largest share of 76.0 per cent.

Of the GHG emissions from the transport sector, carbon dioxide (CO_2) comprises the lion's share.[2] In 2005, the share of CO_2 emission from the transport sector was about 23 per cent of the world's energy-related CO_2 emissions (see Figure 15.1). Further, among all the end-use sectors, the growth of transport-related CO_2 emissions has been highest over the past three decades (see Figure 15.2).

Emerging Asian economies,[3] led by India and China, are projected to account for much of the future growth in oil consumption and GHG emissions. A recent study by Timilsina and Shrestha (2009) on CO_2 emissions from transport sector in Asia reveals that income and population growth accounts for the largest share of growth in CO_2 emissions in India and China.[4] According to projections made by the Asian Development Bank (ADB), these two countries are expected to account for

Table 15.1 World Petroleum Products Consumption by the Transport Sector, 2005

Sector	*Mtoe*	*Percentage*
Road	1571	76
World marine bunkers	171	8.3
International aviation	140	6.8
Domestic aviation	106	5.1
Domestic navigation	36	1.7
Rail	35	1.7
Pipeline transport	5	0.2
Others	3	0.1
Total transport	2067	100

Source: IEA (2007b).

[1] Kahn et al. (2007).

[2] Other GHGs include methane (CH_4), nitrous oxide (N_2O), HFCs, PFCs, and SF6.

[3] Includes Bangladesh, Bhutan, Cambodia, People's Republic of China (PRC), India, Indonesia, Lao PDR, Malaysia, Nepal, Pakistan, Philippines, Sri Lanka, Thailand, and Vietnam.

[4] The study took into consideration the annual time series data over the period 1980 to 2004.

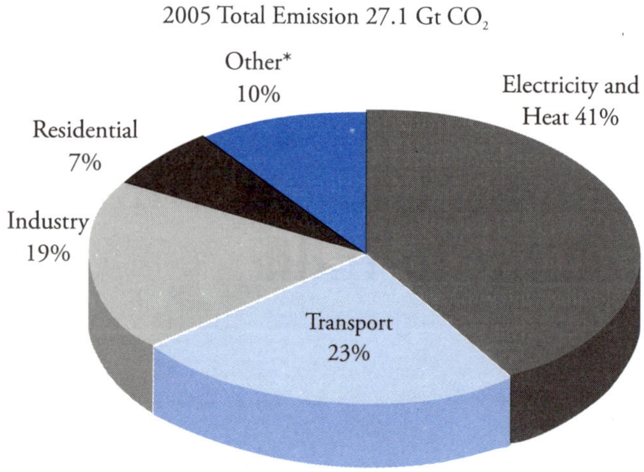

Figure 15.1 World CO_2 Emission by Sector (2005)

*Other includes commercial/public services, agriculture, forestry, fishing, energy industries other than electricity and heat generation, and other emissions not specified elsewhere.
Source: IEA (2007c).

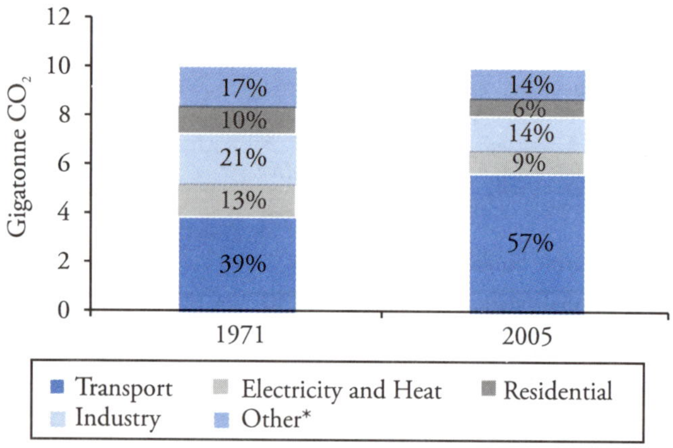

Figure 15.2 CO_2 Emissions from Oil Combustion

*Other includes commercial/public services, agriculture, forestry, fishing, energy industries other than electricity and heat generation, and other emissions not specified elsewhere.
Source: IEA (2007c).

45 per cent of the total world increase in oil use through 2025.[5] IEA (2008) in their simulation exercise also indicates that the lion's share of the increase in oil demand from the transport sector for the period 2006 to 2030 will come from India and China.

Figure 15.3 provides the transport CO_2 emissions across modes for 2005. This shows that road transport is the largest contributor to emissions, and within this the key contributors are on-road vehicles such as cars and light duty vehicles (LDVs) that is four-wheeled vehicles (including sports utility vehicles, small passenger vans with up to eight seats), and trucks. Between 1990 and 2005, CO_2 emission from the world transport sector rose by 37 per cent. During the same period, road transport emissions increased by 29 per cent in the industrialized countries and 61 per cent in other countries, which includes primarily the developing countries.[6]

The Intergovernmental Panel on Climate Change (IPCC) in its fourth assessment report (AR4) advises that to avoid worst impact of climate change, global CO_2 emissions must be cut by at least 50 per cent. Transport has a very significant role to play in realizing that goal. Although all the modes of transport have to take part in emission reduction, as evident from Figure 15.4 the major onus would be on road transport. Thus, this paper focuses on challenges and opportunities of reducing energy consumption and CO_2 emissions from road transport in India.

Challenges in Reducing Energy Consumption and CO_2 Emissions from India's Road Transport Sector

Road transport in India has emerged as the dominant segment with a share of 4.5 per cent in India's GDP as of 2006–7. From 2000–1 to 2006–7, the road transport sector as a component of GDP recorded an annual average growth rate of 9.4 per cent, and thus higher than the overall GDP growth rate of GDP of about 6.9 per cent.[7] The challenges in reducing CO_2 emissions and hence ensuring low carbon mobility could be clubbed under four broad categories: (1) controlling travel and freight activity (A); (2) influencing modal mix and hence modal shift (S); (3) reducing energy intensity (I) of modes; and 4) reducing carbon content or carbon factor of the fuel (F) used. This framework was suggested by Schipper et al. (2000) and is referred to as the ASIF framework.[8]

Challenges in Controlling Travel and Freight Activity in India (A)

Urbanization and Rapid Motorization

Economic growth in most of the developing nations including India has been largely propelled by urban

[5] ADB (2006).
[6] IEA (2007d).
[7] RBI, *Handbook of Statistics for the Indian Economy*, available at: www.rbi.org.in
[8] Schipper et al. (2000).

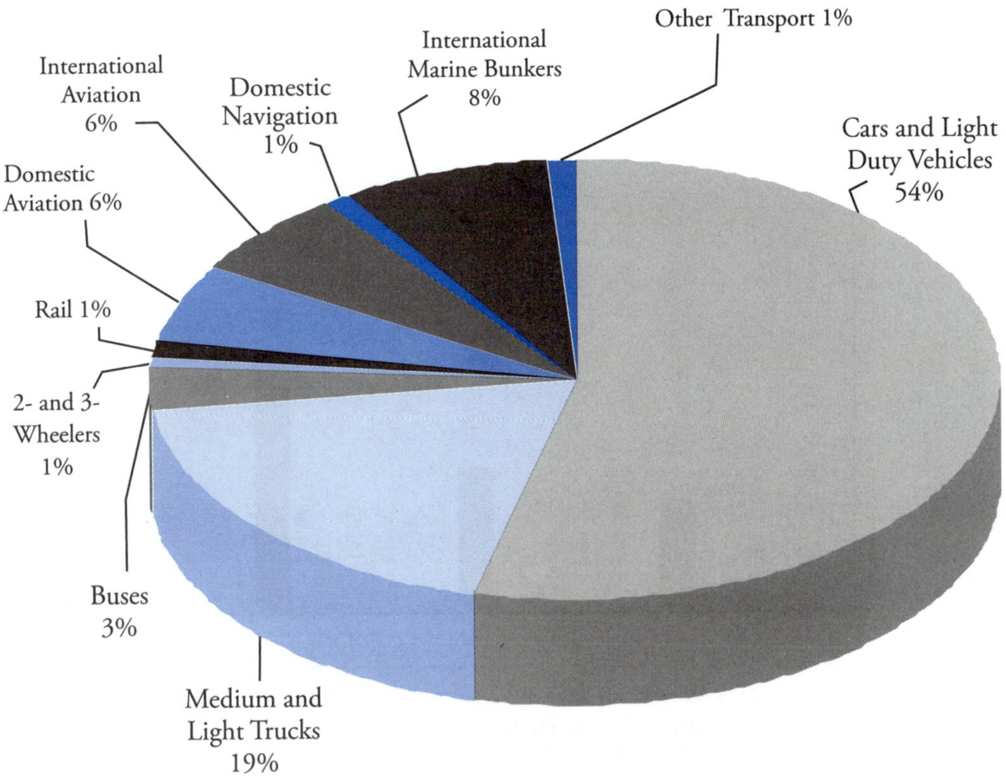

FIGURE 15.3 Modal Shares of Transport CO_2 Emissions (2005)

Source: IEA (2007c).

economic activities, which provide the bulk of employment opportunities. The ADB has projected that nearly 38 per cent of India's population will live in cities by 2025.[9] Going by the Indian census, the number of cities with populations above 1 million (or million-plus cities) increased from 12 in 1981 to 35 in 2001. The growing urban population has led to de-densification of cities, with rapid growth in suburban areas. This de-densification has resulted in rising demand for travel as longer distances are required to be travelled to access jobs and basic services.[10] The rising travel demand could hardly be served by the prevailing unattractive and inadequate public transport system, which inevitably led to an increasing dependence on personal vehicles.

Further, post-liberalization of the Indian economy, a number of new firms entered the automobile sector and introduced a large variety of cars in different segments (small, medium, and large) and two-wheelers. The wide choice of vehicles along with the easy financing schemes available at competitive interest rates increased the sale of private vehicles during 1990s and afterwards. Way back in 2004–5 the number of cars sold in the country exceeded one million and the number of two-wheelers exceeded six million.[11] Figure 15.4 shows the vehicle fleet projections in India till 2025 by ADB.

This is clearly a matter of serious concern. Although an on-road car consumes less energy and emits less CO_2 per vehicle km as compared to a high-capacity public transport, the energy intensity and CO_2 emission per passenger km for the former is much higher than that of the latter (as illustrated in Table 15.2).[12] As India shifts to a higher growth trajectory, the ownership of personal vehicles, especially cars, will continue to grow at a rapid pace driven by rising per capita incomes and growing urbanization coupled with rising aspirations of the middle class. The problem might get compounded with increasing consumer preferences for larger personal vehicles, fitted with highly energy-intensive power steering, and

[9] ADB (2006).

[10] Kahn et al. (2007).

[11] Available at: http://www.siamindia.com/scripts/domestic-sales-trend.aspx

[12] Vehicle kilometre is the unit of vehicle traffic and one vehicle kilometer means one kilometre traversed by the vehicle. Passenger km is the unit of passenger traffic and is measured by multiplying vehicle km with occupancy ratio (no. of occupants in the vehicle).

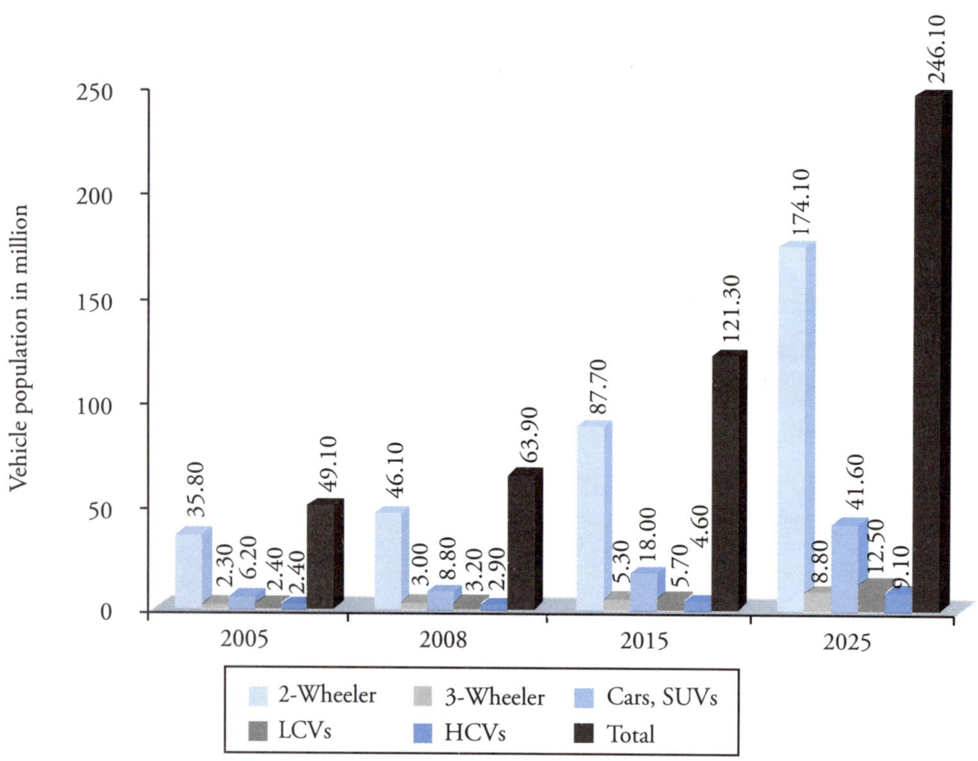

Figure 15.4 Projections of Vehicle Fleet

Source: ADB (2006).

air-conditioning, leading to higher energy consumption and associated emissions.

Table 15.2 Energy Intensity and CO_2 Emission for an On-road Passenger Vehicle across All Modes of Road Transport in India (as of 2004–5)

Modes	*Energy Intensity (in MJ/passenger km)*	*CO_2 emissions (in kg)*
Cars	0.864	0.058–0.064
2-wheelers	0.476	0.032–0.036
3-wheelers	0.580	0.039–0.043
Buses	0.137	0.009–0.0102

Note: MJ-Mega Joule; CO_2 emissions have been computed for the uncertainty range of CEF factors provided in IPCC Guidelines, 2006.

Source: Calculated by the author using data on passenger traffic for 2004–5.

Motorization of Rural Transport

The Government of India has undertaken an ambitious programme named Prime Minister's Gram Sadak Yojana (PMGSY) aimed at connecting all villages with all weather roads by 2012. While this will definitely provide easy access to schools, post offices, and hospitals and help in faster movement of the rural people and products to bigger markets or mandis, this will give rise to demand for motorized transport, both passenger and freight, (like tractor-trailer and three-wheeler) in place of non-motorized modes (like bullock-carts and camel-carts). While this development is desirable, rather inevitable, if no efforts are made to increase the fleet of public transport in rural areas or augment energy efficiency of these motorized modes, then fuel consumption and CO_2 emissions will increase and jeopardize low carbon road transport mobility.

Increase in Freight Traffic

In the aftermath of economic reforms and industrialization in the developing world coupled with globalization, freight traffic is increasing with growing demand for increased speeds and reliability. Freight movement in developing countries is largely by road though some countries have well-developed railway networks. For instance, in China, while inland water transport and railways contribute significantly to freight movement, the share of road transport is on the increase. Similarly, in India, road is the dominant mode of transport and the share of railways is shrinking. The share of inland water transport and coastal shipping in India is also insignificant. Furthermore, heavy-duty trucks used in India and most developing countries are largely two axle vehicles which are not fuel efficient.[13] Additionally, most of these trucks are overloaded and frequent detention at various check points leaves the vehicles idling, adversely affecting both fuel efficiency and operational efficiency. This causes further increase in consumption of fuel and concomitant rise in CO_2 emissions.

Distorted Transport Planning

Transport planning and markets in India and other developing countries are usually distorted with a strong bias towards increased usage of personalized modes. For example, motorists are rarely charged the full costs of congestion, road space, parking, and air pollution. Public policies usually tend to favour personalized modes and the bulk of public expenditure in most cities has been on expanding roads and highways infrastructure to cater to the needs of these personalized modes.[14]

Structural Challenges in Modal Shifts (S)

Marginalization of Public Transport

Between 1951 and 2006 the vehicle population grew at CAGR of nearly 11 per cent. However, the share of buses in total registered vehicles has declined from 11.1 per cent in 1951 to 1.1 per cent as in 2006.

This marginalization of public bus transport reflects major social and economic changes. The demand for speed, service quality, convenience, flexibility, and availability favoured adoption of the private mode as the main mode of transport. In addition to this, government regulation and control have exacerbated the poor operational and financial performance of publicly owned bus transport services in the country, resulting in increasing reliance on private modes of passenger transport as against public transport. Some major reasons for the poor performance of the public sector transport are the high staff cost and loss on account of low user charges and concessions in fares provided to various special and vulnerable categories of commuters (such as students, freedom fighters, etc.), which are not compensated for by state or central governments. Furthermore, operation on economically unviable routes coupled with high rates of taxation renders the public transport system in India financially unviable. Figure 15.5 indicates the contribution of different taxes to the total operating cost of a bus.

Although buses carry 40 to 60 per cent of total trips in some large cities of India, their fleet is in want of moderni-

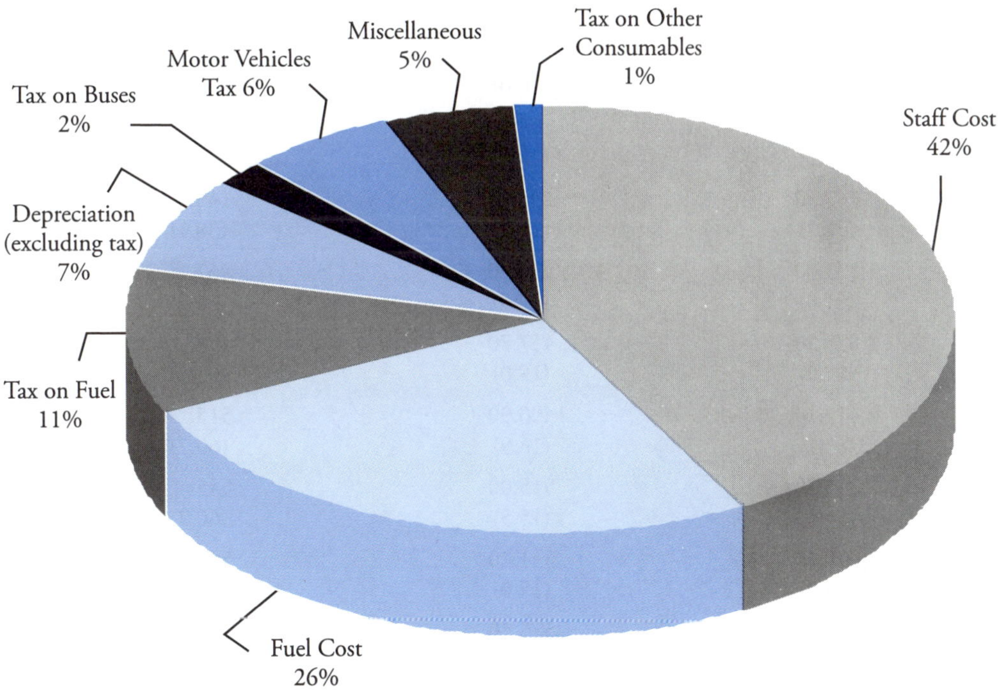

FIGURE 15.5 Contribution of Different Taxes to the Total Operating Cost of a Bus

Source: Kharola and Tiwari (2008).

[13] Trucks on a single frame with two axles and dual rear wheels. Multi-axle trucks may consist of both single and more units. In case of multi-units, one unit is a tractor or straight truck power units.

[14] Sundar and Dhingra (2008).

zation and strengthening in order to reduce emissions. A good public transport system is desirable since it provides more capacity at less marginal cost; produces less emission per passenger km travelled; and reduces congestion on roads by weaning away personal vehicle users.

Relative Decline in Rail Transport Share in both Intra-city and Inter-city Passenger and Freight Traffic

Table 15.3 provides a summary of the total road-based and rail-based passenger and freight traffic from 1971 to 2006. Although during this period, the total population registered a growth of around 98 per cent, absolute road-based passenger traffic increased from 210 billion passenger km to 4,252 billion passenger km in India, which is an overwhelming 1924 per cent rise at a CAGR of nearly 9.0 per cent per year. The absolute road-based freight traffic grew from 48 billion tonne km to 659 billion tonne km, indicating a phenomenal growth of nearly 1281 per cent at a CAGR of around 8 per cent per year. However, the rail-based passenger and freight traffic lost their shares to road-based passenger and freight traffic.

Railways are a relatively benign mode of transport as compared to road transport when considered in terms of energy intensity and emission. The Asian Institute of Transport Development (AITD)[15] conducted a comparative assessment of rail and road transport in India from perspectives of social and environmental sustainability. The study observed that the energy consumption on different inter-city rail sections in the case of freight traffic varied between 10.28 to 25.01 per cent of the energy consumed by road transport in parallel stretches of state and national highways. In the case of passenger transport, the energy consumption on rail varied between 78.77 to 94.91 per cent of the energy consumed by road transport (see Figures 15.6 and 15.7). Furthermore, land requirement for road corridor has been observed to be two and a half times that of the rail corridor.

Table 15.3 Road-based and Rail-based Passenger and Freight Traffic

Year	*Road-based Passenger Traffic*	*Rail-based Passenger Traffic*	*Road-based Freight Traffic*	*Rail-based Freight Traffic*
	(billion passenger km)		*(billion freight km)*	
1970–71	210.00 (64.0)	118.10 (36.0)	47.7 (30.1)	110.7 (69.9)
1980–81	541.80 (72.2)	208.60 (27.8)	90.9 (38.1)	147.7 (61.9)
1990–91	767.70 (72.2)	295.60 (27.8)	145.1 (38.1)	235.8 (61.9)
1999–2000	1,831.60 (81.0)	430.70 (19.0)	467 (60.5)	305.2 (39.5)
2000–1	2,075.50 (82.0)	457.70 (18.0)	494 (61.3)	312.4 (38.7)
2001–2	2,413.10 (83.1)	1490.90 (16.9)	515 (60.7)	333.2 (39.3)
2002–3	2,814.70 (84.5)	515.00 (15.5)	545 (60.7)	353.2 (39.3)
2003–4	3,070.20 (85.0)	541.20 (15.0)	595 (61.0)	381.2 (39.0)
2004–5	3,469.30 (85.8)	575.70 (14.2)	646 (61.3)	411.3 (38.7)
2005–6	4,251.70 (87.4)	615.60 (12.6)	658.9 (60.0)	441.80 (40.0)

*Figures in the parenthesis indicate percentage share.
Source: Government of India (2009).

[15] AITD (2002).

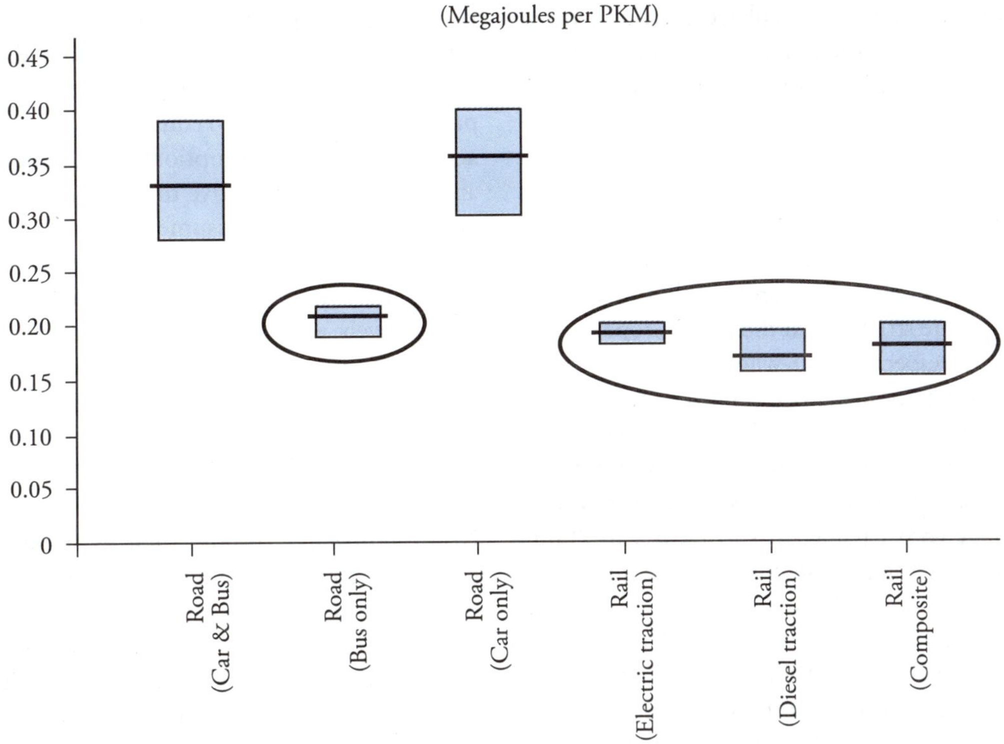

FIGURE 15.6 Energy Consumption: Inter-city Passenger Road and Rail

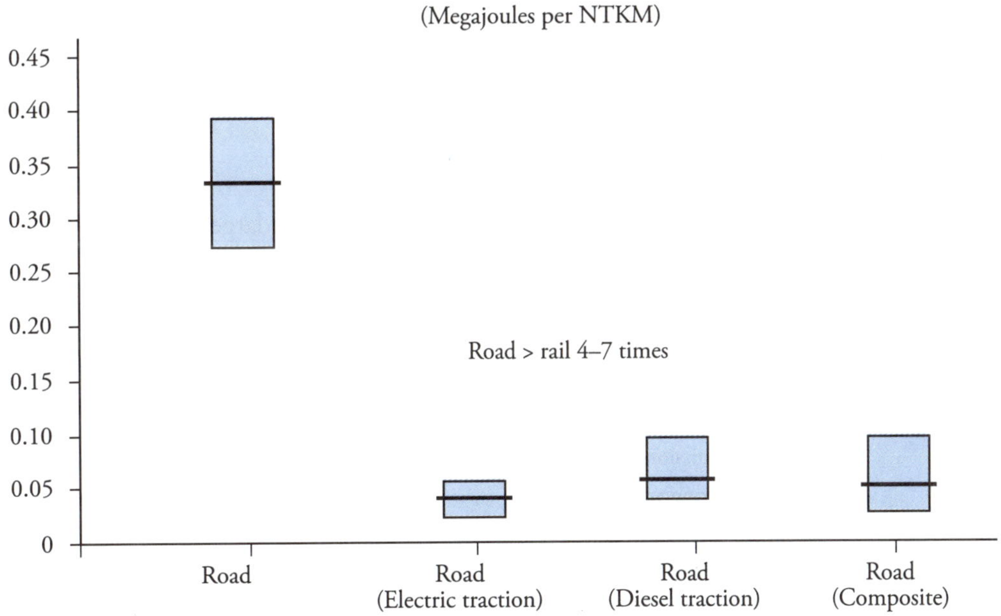

FIGURE 15.7 Energy Consumption: Inter-city Freight Road and Rail

Source: AITD (2002).

Challenges in Reducing Energy Intensity (I)

Poor Standards of Fuel Efficiency and Emission

Appropriate fuel efficiency and vehicle emissions standards designed for new and in-use vehicles and well-designed and functional inspection and maintenance (I and M) programmes are important elements of an overall strategy to reduce vehicle emissions and air pollution.

Developed countries such as USA, Europe, Japan, Australia, and South Korea have regulations for the automobile industry where the regulated metric involves either fuel economy of vehicles, fuel consumption of vehicles, CO_2 emission from vehicles or a combination of fuel economy and CO_2 emissions over a targeted period of time (see Table 15.4). Among the developing countries, only China introduced regulations to improve fuel efficiency in 2005. India is only in the process of designing fuel efficiency standards for motorized vehicles.

With regard to emissions standards, while India's two-wheeler standards are stricter than those in Europe, it lags behind Europe in respect of four-wheelers. Furthermore, the national roadmap for fuel quality and vehicle emission standards is selective and focuses only on the larger cities and neglects the rapidly motorizing medium and small towns. Pan-India emission standards were introduced with Bharat Stage (BS) I (equivalent to Euro1) in 2000. BS II (equivalent to Euro II) standards came into force in India in 2005, and BS III (equivalent to Euro III) standards were introduced in 2005 across 11 cities to be extended nationwide by 2010. BS IV (equivalent to Euro IV) standards are scheduled for introduction in 13 major and more polluted cities by 2010 but no date has yet been set for introducing Euro IV equivalent standards in the rest of India. With regard to inspection and maintenance system the large population of private passenger vehicles in Indian metropolises is not yet covered by any mandatory requirement of periodic fitness certification. What exists in practice is a simple Pollution Under Control (PUC) check which was introduced in 1991 for all on road vehicles.

Price Distortions in Automobile Fuel

The phase of rapid growth of the Indian economy, especially in the new millennium, coupled with the policy of regulating retail prices of petrol and diesel to insulate from international oil price fluctuations, has led to an unabated increase in consumption of automobile fuel. High fuel prices send out signals to consumers that they need to take action to reduce consumption. Thus, removing that signal also removes the incentive to invest in more fuel efficient vehicles and makes consumers vulnerable to future price increases. Further, keeping fuel prices insulated from international oil price fluctuations usually tends to benefit the relatively well-off passengers primarily in the densely populated cities as the propensity for personalized modes like cars tends to be considerably higher among them.[16]

Declining Share of Non-motorized Transport (NMT)

Non-motorized transport such as walking and cycling have zero emissions. These have been in use in many developing countries including China, Colombia, Chile, Africa, and India. However with the easy availability of motorized transport and safety concerns in walking and cycling, there has been a marked shift away from non-motorized transport. Many cities rely on para-transit vehicles like auto-rickshaws and mini-buses to satisfy unmet travel demand. Generally, these vehicles are fuel inefficient and lead to higher emissions.

Challenges in Reducing Carbon Content of the Fuel (F)

Heavy Dependence of Transport on Oil

Transport has the largest share of oil use in India (see Table 15.5). Moreover nearly 96 per cent of the total commercial energy used in the transport sector comes from oil

Table 15.4 Worldwide Automobile Efficiency or GHG Standards

Country/Region	*Regulated metric*	*Expected reduction in CO_2 per-distance emissions**
European Union	CO_2 emissions (CO_2/km)	40% reduction, MY 2008–20
United States	Fuel economy (miles/gallon) GHG emissions (CO_2e/mile)	20% reduction, MY 2011–16
Japan	Fuel economy (km/L)	19% reduction, MY 2010–15
China	Fuel consumption (L/100km)	12 % reduction, MY 2008–15
California	GHG emissions (CO_2e/mile)	25% reduction, MY 2008–16
Australia	Fuel consumption (L/100km)	10% reduction, MY 2004–10
South Korea	Fuel economy (km/L) CO_2 emissions (CO_2/km)	13% reduction, MY 2012–15

Note: *Expected reduction in CO_2 reduction pertains to different test driving cycles for different countries.
@ MY stands for measurable year.
Source: Bandivadekar (2009).

[16] See Bandyopadhyay (2010a; 2010b).

(see Table 15.6). Given the fact that imported crude provides for more than 75 per cent of the refinery throughput for meeting domestic oil consumption in India; the risk exposure to volatility in international crude prices is high. High volatility creates uncertainties making it non-conducive for fresh investments to pour in and often leads to delay in major investments in new oil production and refining capacity besides acting as a deterrent to investment in fuel efficient car technology.[17]

Absence of Adequate Low Carbon Substitutes

The substitutes for oil in road transport are currently inadequate and not always commercially viable. Although in 1998, the Supreme Court mandated conversion of all public buses in Delhi to CNG and for subsequent conversion of all Government of India vehicles to CNG, no road map has been constructed towards that end due primarily to dearth of an adequate natural gas supply. Until recently, the primary source of natural gas in India has been the offshore western coast of Arabian Sea (South Bassein), which has also started depleting. The pumping of natural gas by Reliance Industries Limited (RIL) and Oil and Natural Gas Corporation (ONGC) from the D-6 field in the Krishna-Godavari (KG) basin of Bay of Bengal has just begun[18] and it is only after adequate gas distribution network and infrastructure are put in place in all the cities that can one expect the dependence on petroleum to come down.

The government has been encouraging the use of biofuels and has set a target of blending 20 per cent ethanol with gasoline by 2017 under the National Biofuel Policy. However concerns related to the trade-offs that may arise with respect to availability of land, food-crop production, land-use changes, and bio-diversity and above all, availability of feedstock, remain in order to raise the blending to the targeted level. In addition, the ability of biofuel to reduce greenhouse gases is still contested by scientists around the world. Electricity is the cleanest and cheapest fuel for transport but it is yet to draw adequate appeal in terms of commercial viability due to high up-front cost involved in purchase and replacement of the batteries, lack of adequate mileage, and dearth of adequate charging facilities. However, electricity sourced from thermal power plants running largely on inferior quality coal does not save in terms of CO_2 emissions and thus the electricity generated cannot be considered as a low carbon source.

Institutions and Governance-related Challenges

Transport planning and management in urban areas necessitates a holistic and coordinated approach. However, in most developing countries, including India, there is a plethora of impediments to a coordinated approach due

TABLE 15.5 Sectoral Distribution of Oil Use in India
(as percentage share of total oil use across sectors)

Year	*Industry*	*Transport*	*Agriculture*	*Commercial & Public Services*	*Residential Households*
1971	24.5	37.4	4.3	0.8	21.6
1990	22.9	45.1	0.4	3.1	23.8
2005	17.9	33.3	5.6	0.4	19.7

Note: The shortfall of the row sum from 100 is to be imputed to non-energy use of energy resources or use by other sectors.
Source: Adopted from Sengupta (2007); originally computed using different volumes of Energy Balances of Non-OECD Countries published by IEA.

TABLE 15.6 Sector-wise Oil Application in India
(as percentage of total final commercial energy use in a sector)

Year	*Industry*	*Transport*	*Agriculture*	*Commercial & Public Services*	*Residential Households*
1971	19.3	45.8	63.6	27.8	64.8
1990	17.0	88.9	4.7	47.2	79.6
2005	26.6	95.8	41.5	–	63.0

Source: Adopted from Sengupta (2007); originally computed using different volumes of Energy Balances of Non-OECD Countries published by IEA.

[17] See Bandyopadhyay (2008; 2009b).
[18] See Bandyopadhyay (2009a).

mainly to dearth of appropriate institutional arrangements and linkages.[19] The authorities and associated responsibilities pertaining to transport planning and management are often fragmented and divided between and within the state and city governments. Furthermore, these authorities also lack the necessary power, resources, and capacity to address problems of congestion, air pollution, and GHG emissions. A particular challenge in institutional development for sustainable transport in developing countries is posed by the large share of para-transit modes in public transport.[20] These modes operate in the (semi) informal sector and are not easy to integrate in governmental programmes for fleet renewal to reform the transport sector in order to make it less carbon intensive.[21]

Addressing the Challenges

Transport is considered to be a major plank for pro-poor economic growth, especially in developing countries like India. Therefore, putting a cap on transport growth is neither feasible nor desirable. Hence, as India continues to grow on a higher trajectory in future the demand for transport will also increase concomitantly. Thus, the key challenge that the policymakers in India are encountering is to decouple economic and social development from the inevitable increase in energy consumption and CO_2 emissions that arises due to rapid growth of transport.

A stand-alone policy of reducing GHG emissions (especially CO_2) from the transport sector may not appeal significantly to policymakers and other stakeholders because the cost involved is considerably high. Hence, initiatives to restrain CO_2 emissions from transport need to be aligned closely with overall strategies to reform the sector and should essentially be recognized as co-benefits rather than as a primary goal. In view of this, a meeting was held in Bellagio in May 2009[22] leading to the formulation of a common policy framework on sustainable low carbon transport for developing countries aimed primarily at the road transport. The framework recognized an integrated multi-pronged approach based on co-benefits and underscored sector-wide re-orientation of the transport sector, combining policies and measures aimed at (a) avoiding or reducing travel or need to travel (b) shifting to more environment-friendly or energy efficient modes and (c) improving efficiency of motorized modes. This approach is more popularly known as the Avoid-Shift-Improve framework.

Reduce Travel or Need to Travel

Integration of Land Use and Transport Planning

Integrating land use planning with transport planning is key to reducing GHG emissions. Travel can be reduced when various forms of land use such as residential houses, shops, public services, etc. are mixed and located in close proximity of one another. Density of an area is crucial for emission reduction. Where low density leads to heavy dependence on private vehicles and higher energy demand, areas with higher density reduce travel needs and emissions. Demand for transport in the high-density centres is more easily served by public transport as it is cost-effective due to reasonable load factor or occupancy ratio. Instances of such integration of land use and transport planning can be drawn from the city of Toronto in Canada.[23] Proper land use planning can also provide for pedestrian footways and cycle paths and encourage the use of NMT modes.

Promoting use of Alternatives to Travel

Use of communication and information technologies can help avoid or reduce the need to travel. For instance, introduction of the 'Easy Bill' facility in Delhi and some other cities has helped citizens pay most of the utility bills at nearby centres at convenient hours. Similarly, in Bangalore, the government of Karnataka has set up one-stop facility for citizens of Bangalore to access information and pay all government and municipal bills. Some corporate organizations, especially in developed countries, have 'work from home' programmes which reduce travel demand. However, in order to implement these initiatives universally and successfully, well-knit information and communication networks should be put in place on a priority basis.

[19] Sundar and Dhingra (2008).

[20] In South Asia this includes the motorized three-wheeled rickshaws, locally assembled jeepneys, and buses built around imported second-hand truck engines in the Philippines, and the Bemo in Indonesia.

[21] Because they operate in the informal sector they often do not keep formal books, or have formal franchises, or pay taxes on a regular basis which can be a guarantee to benefit from financial assistance programmes.

[22] http://www.sutp.org/slocat/about/bellagio-process/targets-and-progress/

[23] Driven by the increasing concerns for climate change, the City of Toronto recognized the importance of transit in its Official Plan called the Toronto Transit City, which said, 'No new roads will be built in Toronto. Instead, all growth in travel demand is to be carried on transit.' (for more details see http://www.transitcity.ca/media/TransitCity_fullreport.pdf)

Regulatory Instruments

Regulatory instruments can be used to discourage travel or deny access to certain traffic or vehicles. Some regulatory measures that already exist, especially in developed countries, include:

- *Physical restraint measures*: City authorities can implement physical restraints like restricting access for certain private vehicles. One such measure is the restriction on plying of vehicles on certain days, depending on their registration plate number. This has been widely implemented in Athens, Manila, Mexico City, Seoul, etc. The benefits of this measure include reduction in congestion, increase in speed, and saving in fuel consumption. However the measures may not be without leakages, as evinced by the example of Hoy no Circulan (a day without a car) in Mexico City.[24]
- *Traffic management measures*: Traffic management measures are used to smooth traffic flows, improve fuel efficiency and reduce emissions. Among traffic signal systems, the most efficient is the area traffic control system where signals are coordinated across a whole network. In developed countries, traffic management has achieved emission reduction by around 2–5 per cent. In developing countries, this measure can help achieve higher reduction in fuel consumption and emissions. It has also been estimated that effective land use planning together with better traffic management schemes (like the Intelligent Transportation System) can bring about energy savings of 20–30 per cent for public transport[25] due to better planned trips and smooth vehicle movement. For example, Hong Kong's Intelligent Transportation System (ITS) project after its completion in 2010 is expected to modernize the traffic operations on major highways, road tunnels, and urban roads.[26]
- *Regulation of parking*: Restriction of parking space supply can make car use unattractive and encourage modal shift. Planning authorities can also involve employers and commercial establishments in reducing private parking space reserved for their employees or customers. Citywide initiatives involving private entities are likely to be more successful compared to restrictions imposed only on publicly provided parking.
- *Speed restrictions*: To reduce GHG emissions, governments may prescribe minimum and maximum speed limits for vehicles.
- *Inspection, maintenance, and certification*: An effective inspection and certification programme coupled with driver training and adequate maintenance can bring about 2–17 per cent reduction in fuel consumption and GHG emissions.[27]

Economic Instruments

The primary objective of economic instruments is to discourage the use of private vehicles or encourage more efficient use of transport through levy of charges or taxes. Various economic instruments are discussed below:

- *Road pricing and congestion charging*: In general, road pricing increases the cost of running a vehicle and thereby encourages the use of alternate modes. Implementing agencies usually have two options- (1) introducing national road pricing where charges are applied on long-distance highway use; and (2) introducing local road pricing schemes that cover only city-centre areas. To reduce peak period traffic, road pricing rates can be fixed at a higher rate for peak periods. The scheme could be highly effective in reducing GHG emissions. Box 15.1 illustrates the experiences of Singapore, South Korea, and London in implementing road and congestion charges. Interestingly, Delhi High Court has also come out with a ruling in February 2010 in support of congestion charges for car owners passing through congested areas of the city.[28]
- *Fuel taxation*: Fuel taxes can increase the price of travel and consequently affect individual travel behaviour. This can reduce the number of vehicle kilometres travelled. Since fuel taxation is proportional to fuel consumption, this could provide an incentive to purchase fuel-efficient vehicles. Either way, it will help in reducing GHG emissions. However, care should

[24] Towards the early 1990s, Mexico City started a programme called 'Hoy no Circulan' under which cars could not be allowed to be driven for a day in a week depending on the last number of the licence plate. However World Bank research (Eskeland and Feyzioglu 1995) indicates that this measure was not successful in saving fuel consumption. The outcome was just the opposite, as the measure led to an increase in purchase of second-hand cars with a different last number on the licence plate. This example shows how 'leakages' may occur if measures are implemented without careful planning to anticipate possible outcomes.

[25] Dalkmann and Brannigan (2007).

[26] For more details see: http://www.roadtraffic-technology.com/projects/hong-kong

[27] ADB (2006).

[28] Garg (2010).

Box 15.1

Road Pricing and Congestion Charging in Singapore, South Korea, and London

Singapore: Singapore's cordon pricing measure, an Area Licensing Scheme (ALS), covers a 7.5 square km restricted zone in downtown Singapore. The restrictions are applied during the morning peak, between 7:30 and 10:30 hrs. Access to the restricted zone is made possible through the purchase of daily or monthly licences at post offices and kiosks outside of the zone. Since 1989, access restrictions have been extended to carpools and trucks (which were previously exempt under the scheme). Singapore's ALS has been successful in reducing motorized traffic within the zone by 50 per cent, and private car travel by 75 per cent. The speed of the traffic has also been increased from approximately 18 to 30 km/h. The scheme was complemented by the doubling of parking charges.

South Korea: Road pricing was introduced to the #1 and #3 tunnels linking downtown Seoul (South Korea) to the southern part of the city. Both corridors experienced high volumes of private vehicle traffic, leading to heavy congestion. Private cars with three or more passenger, buses, vans, and trucks were exempt from the 2,000 won charge (US$2.20), as was all traffic on Sundays and national holidays. The road pricing schemes resulted in a 34 per cent reduction in peak period passenger vehicle volumes in the two years following implementation. Average travel speeds also increased by 50 per cent, from 20 km/h to 30 km/h. As it was not an area-wide charging scheme, traffic volumes increased on alternate routes up to 15 per cent. However, average travel speeds also increased as a result of improved flows at signalled intersections and increased enforcement of on-street parking rules on alternative routes.

London: The London Congestion Charge came into effect in February 2003. The Charging Zone covers an area in Central London (which was extended in 2007), and drivers of non-exempt vehicles must pay a charge of £8 (US$16) per day to enter and travel within this zone. The scheme is enforced by a network of Automatic Number Plate Recognition (ANPR) cameras that monitor vehicles entering and circulating within the Charging Zone. The scheme has resulted in an estimated 19 per cent reduction in traffic related CO_2 and a 20 per cent reduction in fuel consumption.

Source: Adapted from Dalkmann and Braningann (2007).

be taken to remove any distortions that may exist in the fuel taxation system that discriminates against any particular fuel leading to pricing anomalies or generate perverse incentives.

- *Vehicle taxation*: Vehicle taxes are regarded as an 'access fee' to use the road network. Charges vary with vehicle type, vehicle size or emissions, and noise levels. If tax rates are differentiated according to fuel consumption, this will encourage sale of fuel-efficient vehicles. However, this tax does not necessarily ensure efficient operation of the vehicles. Additional measures would therefore, be required to promote energy efficient vehicles through levy of fuel taxation. However due care needs to be taken to see that the axe of vehicle tax does not fall on the public transport system as that would frustrate the very objective of moving towards a low carbon transport.
- *Parking pricing*: This instrument increases the cost of using a vehicle by raising the cost of parking. This can be expected to substantially reduce parking demand compared to a free parking regime.

Information Instruments

Information instruments include awareness campaigns, mobility management, and driver education and training. Marketing of sustainable transport system requires public awareness and acceptance of the negative impact of certain transport systems and practices. Therefore, there is need for information instruments to spread these messages. For instance, Colombia and Mexico have implemented 'car-free days', banning cars from entering the city on certain days. In India, the city of Ahmedabad has also initiated car-free days recently. This can be coupled with promotion of alternate mode choices such as public transport, cycling, or walking. Education through schools or dissemination of information through places of employment can also be useful in raising awareness. Improving fuel efficiency is also possible through education and training of drivers that facilitates behavioural change with regard to speed, braking and acceleration, engine idling, carrying capacity, and vehicle condition (vehicle age, oil and air filters, maintenance of engine and tyres). Estimates show that the fuel savings through this measure are in the range of 10–15 per cent.[29]

Shift to Environment-friendly Modes

Improve the Share of Public Transport

The expansion of public transport in the form of large capacity buses, light rail transit, and suburban rail or

[29] Dalkmann and Brannigan (2007).

metro is a feasible option for transport sector.[30] The IPCC recognizes the preservation and augmentation of the market shares of low emitting collective transport modes as a worldwide mitigation option. However, public transport should be accessible, affordable, and reliable if it is to replace private vehicles.

Improvement of public transport is possible through expansion of systems or services and/or improvement in operation of systems and services pertaining to public transport. The expansion of services can include dedicated lanes, express bus services, and local bus services. Operational improvements may include splitting of routes, increased vehicle frequency, coordination of routes through integrated ticketing. Services may also be improved through provision of passenger amenities.

The Bus Rapid Transit (BRT) System, Transmilenio,[31] Bogota in Colombia is one of the most successful models of BRT passenger transport system. Some features of BRT systems include exclusive right of way lanes, rapid boarding and alighting, free transfers between lines, pre-board fare collection and fare verification, enclosed stations, clear route maps, real time information displays, automatic vehicle location technology to manage vehicle movements, modal integration at stations, effective reform of the existing institutional structures for public transit, clean vehicle technologies, and excellence in marketing and customer services. Table 15.7 delineates the broad characteristics and CO_2 impact estimates for selected international BRT systems. In India, the first BRT corridor was opened in Delhi. Surveys among the users of the BRT indicated general satisfaction with the service provided despite the shortcomings in the original design and its implementation. In Ahmedabad, the city residents have embraced their new Janmarg BRT system; around 18,000 daily passengers use Janmarg to commute to work, to school, and elsewhere. Janmarg uses innovative central median stations pulled away from the junctions. Bus stations feature passive solar designs, an inexpensive way to keep stations naturally cool. The city is making efforts to be a leader in sustainable transport, providing high-quality pedestrian facilities in some corridors, as well as bicycle lanes.

Promote NMT

Shorter trips are best performed by NMT. These modes can be promoted through provision of cycling and walking tracks and through road safety measures; appropriate pricing of individual vehicle use and fuels; regulation of polluting motorized modes; and use of information and awareness campaigns (see Box 15.2). In this light, in a recent landmark judgment dated 10 February 2010 (in response to petitions filed against the cap of 99,000 three-wheeler cycle rickshaw licences imposed by the Municipal Corporation of Delhi in 1997), the Chief Justice bench of the Delhi High Court saved an important non-motorized mode from near extinction by removing the restriction on the number of licences that can be issued to the rickshaw pullers. The bench also stated that confiscation and scrapping of cycle rickshaws are against the law.[32]

Table 15.7 Characteristics and CO_2 Impact Estimates for Select BRT Systems

	Reported Data and Estimates from Studies						*IEA estimates based on car-taxi vehicle km reduction in studies*	
	BRT line distance (km)	*Percentage shift from car/taxi to BRT*	*Vehicle travel reduction (million km)*	*Million vehicle km saved per km BRT*	*CO_2 reduction per km per year (in tonnes)*	*Total CO_2 reduction per year (in tonnes)*	*Calculated CO_2 savings (tonnes/year)*	*As a percentage of reported CO_2 savings*
Bogota	84	9	435.0	5.2	2,940	247,000	83,520	34
Mexico City	20	6	23.0	1.2	900	18,000	4,416	25
Pereira	30	16	54.5	1.8	900	27,000	10,464	39
Chongqing	82	21	495.3	6.0	3,171	260,000	95,098	38

Source: IEA (2009a: Table 5.16).

[30] Kahn et. al (2007).

[31] Transmilenio in Bogotá consists of a BRT system which is being implemented gradually since the end of 2001. It currently transports more than 2 million passengers daily. Transmilenio reduces emissions per passenger trip compared to the traditional transport system due to the use of new and larger buses, mode switching due to increased attractiveness of public transport (around 10 per cent of Transmilenio would have used taxis or passenger cars in absence of the system) and improved bus occupancy rates. (Grutter 2007 and 2008).

[32] *The Hindu* (2010).

Box 15.2
Non-motorized Modes in Developing Countries

China: In China, bike mode share increased in cities until the early 1990s, accounting for nearly 30 to 70 per cent of all trips. However, bike use fell sharply in the Southern and Eastern provinces in the late 1990s. Wealthier residents have upgraded to taxis, mopeds, or motorcycles. Bicycle use has declined largely due to public policies banning their use on major arterials, and upgrading major urban arterials to high speeds. Bicycle lanes have also been removed. Road safety is another important barrier to increasing cycle use in China. Cyclists are often forced out of or on to the road by cars parked or driving in cycleway. Traffic deaths have doubled between 1990 and 2000, with cyclists accounting for 38 per cent of fatalities (approximately 38,000).

Colombia: Bogotá has been successful in increasing bike use from 0.58 to 4.0 per cent of all trips through improvements to cycling infrastructure; 330 km of new fully grade-separated bicycle lanes were constructed over three years, coupled with other complimentary bicycle measures. Following the implementation of cycling and other mode improvements, a study was undertaken in Bogotá involving interviews with 12,000 homes. Respondents were asked which works had improved their quality of life during the previous five years. The responses were as follows: parks (73.4 per cent), bicycle paths (68.6 per cent), pedestrian overpasses (67.8 per cent), roads (66.1 per cent), the Transmilenio BRT (64.8 per cent), sidewalks (64.5 per cent), public libraries (55.5 per cent), and public schools (37.9 per cent)

Chile: Experience in Santiago with a cycling project revealed that a 3 per cent decrease in car and taxi travel as a result of modal shift to bicycle is expected to reduce CO_2 emissions by 126,000 tonnes a year (approximately 1.15 per cent).

Africa: The implementation of 60 km of bikeways as part of a network in Tamale, Ghana, accounted for 65 per cent of transport trips. The network was fully integrated with the town and with other transport modes, such as taxis and lorries, which are used for long-distance travel.

Source: Dalkmann and Brannigan (2007).

The High Court bench also mandated the formation of a special task force to explore all questions pertaining to road traffic in the city aimed at minimizing congestion, reducing pollution levels from vehicles, and ensuring equitable access to all classes of vehicles that ply on roads (including non-motorized transport such as bicycles and cycle rickshaws).

Shifting Freight Traffic from Road to Energy Efficient Modes

One of the most pressing needs in the freight transport sector in developing nations, including India, is to increase the share of railways and inland transport in freight traffic. Although large investments are being made in developing alternate modes in many developing countries in order to augment the carrying capacity, these investments are not always coupled with endeavours to make these modes cost and energy efficient, attractive, and capable of meeting consumer requirements. In this context, adequate insights could be gained from the Marco Polo model of freight shift in modal transportation in Europe (see Box 15.3), which shows how targeted policy interventions including fiscal incentives can make the desired low carbon oriented inter-modal freight shifts possible.

Improving Vehicle Technology and Energy Efficiency

Variation in GHG emissions is contingent upon the nature of fuels and technologies used. Thus, technology solutions for vehicles usually underscore two possible areas of improvement with respect to GHG emissions: 1) reducing the carbon content of fuel (say by altering the mix of fuels actually used) and/or 2) by influencing the intensity with which fuels are used.

This could be achieved by promoting and providing incentives for use of road-friendly and fuel-efficient vehicles by introducing appropriate fuel efficiency standards; making superior quality fuel adequately available for transport vehicles; and putting in place appropriate regulatory policies to check fuel adulteration. However, in order to tap the full potential of technological improvements, especially in passenger transport, these measures should be supplemented with policy instruments that focus on promoting modal shifts and reducing overall travel time.[33]

[33] However, it should be recognized that the overall growth in travel and freight activity, which increases at a rapid pace in developing countries, may offset the gains from new technology or technological upgradation. This rebound effect occurs if automobile fuel prices are regulated, leading to a pure income effect of lowered fuel cost which might offset any saving in consumption or reduction in emissions. This is true in India also where the high carbon automobile fuel prices remain within the regulated domain under administered prices.

Box 15.3
Marco Polo Model

The Marco Polo programme (Marco Polo I) was launched in 2003 to improve sustainability and efficiency of the transport sector. The programme provides subsidy to transport service operators to facilitate a shift from the road to more environment-friendly modes of transportation, such as short sea shipping, rail and inland waterways, or to a combination of modes of transport in which road journeys are as short as possible. The intent is to support intermodal freight transport initiatives and alternatives to road-only transport in the early stages until they become commercially viable. The subsidy was provided at the rate of 1euro per 500 tonne km shifted off the road. The programme had envisaged to shift the expected increase in international road freight traffic of 12 billion tonne kms (btkm) per year to cleaner modes during the period 2003–10. It was also estimated that every 1 euro of subsidy to Marco Polo would generate at least 6 Euros in social and environmental benefits.

Marco Polo II, which pertains to the period 2007–13, is more ambitious than its predecessor. It has a larger budget and supports two new types of actions (the motorways of the seas and traffic avoidance measures) over an extended area that includes neighbouring non-EU countries. In all, Marco Polo provides support for five distinct types of action which are as follows:

Modal shift actions: Shift as much freight as economically meaningful under current market conditions from road to short sea shipping, rail and inland waterways.

Catalyst actions: Change the way non-road freight transport is conducted in the EU. Support provided to innovative proposals aimed at overcoming structural market barriers in European freight transport.

Common learning actions: Enhance knowledge in the freight logistics sector and foster advanced methods and procedures of cooperation in the freight market.

Motorways of the sea actions: Similar to modal shift actions, but specific to sea mode.

Traffic avoidance actions: Integrate transport into production logistics. This should lead to a reduced freight transport demand by road having direct impact on emissions. It is emphasized that actions of this type shall not adversely affect either output or the labour workforce.

For more details see : http://ec.europa.eu/transport/marcopolo/home/home_en.htm

Further, from a low carbon perspective, electric vehicles (EVs) and hybrid electric vehicles (HEV) should be promoted in India on a priority basis as they are cleaner than diesel and gasoline powered vehicles despite the fact that electricity generation in India would take long to become less GHG intensive (see Box 15.4). In fact EVs are already being produced on a mass scale in India in the form of two-wheeled bikes and scooters and the four-wheeled light duty vehicles are expected to catch up soon. Globally, HEVs (using both petrol and electric propulsion systems) compared to EVs are expected to capture the market sooner as these vehicles do not require refuelling or charging infrastructure. Although both EVs and HEVs have great potential in India, policy support is crucial for making them cost-competitive. Expanded use of EVs and HEVs would require better understanding of consumer needs and desires. Measures to influence greater penetration might include fiscal and purchase incentives besides influencing the driving range, which presently is a major constraint with electric two-wheelers and four-wheelers. Moreover, continuous support needs to be provided for research, development, and demonstration so as to reduce battery cost and ensure adequate supply of materials for battery manufacture. Industry and governments must also work in tandem towards prioritizing international collaboration that can facilitate research programmes aimed at accelerated deployment of smart grids and vehicle-grid interface for fuelling electric vehicles.[34]

Role of Finance and Pricing in Executing the Avoid-Shift-Improve Framework[35]

Current mainstream financing mechanisms and pricing practices in developing countries, including India, are not aligned with sustainable transport systems. Pricing does not capture the full costs of transport (economic, social, and environmental), and investment (public and private, domestic and foreign) is skewed towards carbon-intensive private motor vehicles. Hence price structures for transport activities ought to be reformed to encompass the full cost to society, including congestion, accidents, infrastructure wear and tear, GHG emissions, and noise and air pollution externalities.

[34] The paragraph draws largely on IEA (2009a) and Chattopadhyay (2010).

[35] This section draws heavily on Leather (2009); Huizenga and Bakker (2009).

Box 15.4
Prospects and Challenges of Electricity-Driven Vehicles in India

Electric vehicles (EVs) use an electric motor for propulsion with rechargeable batteries for electricity storage. Unlike conventional gasoline- or diesel-powered vehicles, battery-powered vehicles do not have an internal combustion engine (ICE), the drive train, and a fuel tank. Since the EVs do not burn fossil fuels they generate zero emission of pollutants. However the life-cycle emissions will depend on whether the power used has been generated from fossil fuels or renewable sources. In terms of fuel efficiency, the electric motor converts 75 per cent of the chemical energy from the batteries to power the wheels as compared to ICEs which only convert 20 per cent of the energy stored in gasoline. Furthermore, compared to oil, the cost of electricity is much less, hence, the operating cost per kilometre is far lower than that of a gasoline-driven car. Hybrid electric vehicles (HEV) use both ICE and electric propulsion systems, with adequate battery capacity to store the electricity generated by the engine or by brake-energy regeneration. The batteries power the motor when necessary, provide auxiliary motive power to the engine, and even allow the engine to be turned off at low speeds. In these vehicles, the electric motor usually provides a boost to start-up and is recharged during vehicle operation. The process results in considerable improvement in fuel economy and thus reduces fossil fuel consumption and CO_2 emissions. A plug-in hybrid vehicle (PHEV) is essentially a HEV with additional batteries and a plug. This gives the vehicle an ability to use electricity from the grid to move the vehicle.

In India, although electricity-driven vehicles are produced mass scale in the form of two-wheeled bikes and scooters, the four-wheeled LDVs are yet to catch up. For instance, in the two-wheel segment, Yo bikes (from Electrotherm, a Gujarat- based company) offers two scooterettes and four bike models with motor powers ranging from 200–250W. The light vehicles can run at a top speed of 25km/hr and up to a range of 75 km on a full charge of six to eight hours. In the electric car segment the pioneer has been Reva Electric Car Company (RECC) since 1994, which produces the two-seater electric car named Reva.

Most Indian cities are characterized by congested roads, low vehicular speeds, and limited distances that make them leading contenders for the current fleet of electric-run vehicles. India is also uniquely and favourably positioned for these vehicles because of hardware availability, low labour cost, low manufacturing cost, low start-up cost, availability of R&D facilities in the auto component industry, and a potentially large domestic market. Further, electric vehicles need little maintenance as they do not have oil filters, air filters, spark plugs, or radiators. Despite these advantages and environmental benefits, EVs have remained a non-starter and are yet to pick up the required sales.

A recent study by Frost & Sullivan shows that EVs is just catching-on in the country. The study released in February 2010, however, reveals that due to post-purchase concerns like battery life, distance travelled, maintenance cost, acceleration, and top speed, only 7 per cent of Indian vehicle-owners may purchase an EV in future and may be willing to pay a low premium over the base price for those vehicles. Concerns regarding EVs are high prices due to high battery prices; limited driving range; lack of charging infrastructure; slow improvement in technology, durability of batteries; inadequate government support; and regulatory challenges.

The limited driving range being offered at present by the EVs, although suitable for Indian driving conditions, curtails the driving freedom of consumers. Further, the battery needs replacement every two to three years, which adds to the cost. As it may not be very easy to decouple vehicle purchase costs from the battery cost, it is an imperative that the battery technology be developed such that EVs as a whole become competitive. Several battery technologies exist at present. Lithium ion batteries have a clear edge over other battery technologies but are exorbitant and need rapid innovation to make lighter and cheaper batteries without compromising on storage capacity, performance, and durability. Further, outdoor charging facilities are almost absent in Indian cities, except for some localized voluntary initiatives that are grossly inadequate to cater to the EVs plying on the roads.

A key challenge is the disposal and recycling of the batteries. The technology currently used in India is the lead acid battery, which is relatively cheap; but lead being hazardous needs special care in terms of disposal or recycling. The Battery Management and Handling Rules 2001 require the lead battery manufacturers to recollect 90 per cent of their used batteries but there are no safeguards to ensure that the batteries are returned at the end of their life to the official recyclers to abate contamination.

Besides, effective regulations pertaining to road-worthiness and safety features are lacking with respect to EVs. The bigger and more established automobile companies do adhere to some standards of their own. However, in the absence of stringent testing procedures or certification processes, the smaller and more unorganized players are taking advantage by only importing and selling e-bikes in India. They lack the post-purchase service back-up, have little regard for quality, and are mostly unable to provide spare parts. These factors invoke a negative feeling in the consumer's mind and act as a deterrent to the growth of e-bikes industry

Although India has been recognized globally as a growing hub of electricity-driven vehicle production, Indian manufacturers contend that the support is inadequate and mainly confined to sporadic fiscal support. For instance, the centre waived the excise-duty on battery operated vehicles in 2008. This was followed by similar concessions in Chandigarh (which offered a subsidy of 15 per cent on battery operated vehicles), Bengaluru (which offered 4 per cent VAT waiver for initial five years after the launch and registration), West Bengal, Madhya Pradesh, Kerala, and Gujarat (where VAT rates for EVs were brought down to 4 per cent). Delhi also announced a 29.5 per cent discount on all EVs. Besides, the buyer of EV is given 15 per cent subsidy on the base price, 12.5 percent VAT refund, and 2 per cent concession on road tax and registration expenses. Some cities offer refund of road tax

(*contd.*)

Box 15.4 (*contd.*)

and registration charges. Furthermore, the Union Budget 2010 has provided a boost to EVs by removing customs duties levied on imports of critical components.

In view of these concerns and roadblocks, the coming decade would be really crucial for garnering policy support in two primary areas: ensuring the cost-competitiveness of vehicles and providing for adequate recharging infrastructure. Research, development, and demonstration should essentially emphasize reduction of battery costs. The government besides providing fiscal support should also provide non-fiscal support by installing adequate charging infrastructure in public places like parking lots, malls, office complexes etc. Parking lots could also be made free for these vehicles and the cars could be allowed to enter car-free zones in order to generate or increase awareness about these greener modes. The government also needs to collaborate with the industry in order to develop performance metrics for some key attributes like driving range and battery requirements in order to ensure that these vehicles achieve their true potential. Additionally, the government should continue to promote renewable energy more aggressively so that the electricity-driven vehicles become green in the true sense in the future.

Sources: Basu (2009); Chattopadhyay (2010); Environment Pollution (Control and Prevention) Authority (2009); Frost and Sullivan (2010); IEA (2009b).

There is abundance of both traditional and innovative financing mechanisms to fund low carbon transport. Transport-oriented financial mechanisms which feed into public sector funding (in particular fuel tax, vehicle tax, and road pricing) have the potential to play a central role in reducing motorized trips, shifting modes and improving the efficiency of various modes. However, most of these instruments are not used to their fullest in supporting a sustainable transport system, and financing mechanisms especially designed for climate change mitigation like CDM (Clean Development Mechanism) are also limited in their use in transport sector.[36]

Other important financial initiatives pertaining to low carbon future include Global Environment Facility (GEF);[37] and Clean Energy Financing Partnership Facility (CEFPF) established by ADB as a special fund in 2007. GEF's support to the transport sector focuses on technological solutions and various non-technology options, such as planning, modal shift to low-GHG-intensive transport modes, and promotion of better managed public transit systems. As for CEFPF out of 17 projects pertaining to energy efficiency and fuel switch that were financed under this facility, there was only one transport-related project (energy efficiency in railways).[38] Furthermore, in 2008, the World Bank established the Climate Investment Fund (CIF) in cooperation with the multilateral Development Banks. Two strategic funds were also set up under the umbrella of CIF. They are—a) Clean Technology Fund (CTF) and b) the Climate Change Fund. The CTF was designed to fill an immediate financing gap before further details of the future climate regime are worked out, and the fund was seeking to demonstrate how financial and other incentives could be used to scale up clean technology deployment and transfer. For the transport sector it focused on modal shift, fuel economy, and fuel switch.[39] Various programmes are also being considered under CTF in Vietnam, Philippines, South Africa, Mexico, and Thailand that include BRT, rail systems, vehicle technology, and biofuels components.[40] However, it is too early for a performance assessment of all the aforementioned innovative funds.

As far as the project-based CDM is concerned it is unlikely to play a major role in a shift to sustainable transport systems under the existing rules, although the

[36] The current under-representation of the transport sector can be explained by the following barriers: 1. The difficulty in determining additionality, for example, due to the small share of CER revenues in the total project cost; 2. Complexity in establishing the baseline scenario, due to the fact that transport projects contribute to a multitude of goals; 3. Emissions from individual sources are relatively small and dispersed, making monitoring difficult; 4. Extensive linkages to other economic activities (makes it more difficult to give boundaries to a project); 5. Transport's strong relationship with human behaviour (which can make evaluation difficult); 6. Lack of uniformity in Methodology Panel's recommendations. (for more details see UNEP 2009; Huizenga and Bakker 2009).

[37] GEF was set up to fund projects and programmes aimed to protect the global environment. In principle, GEF only provides co-funding, that is, a significant contribution to the projects financing needs to come from other sources. Such financing can either come from the national government or from other donor agencies. The financing may be also done by providing 'in kind' work resources (for example, preparation of the transport planning administration), credits, and loans (for more details see Huizenga and Bakker 2009).

[38] ADB (2008).

[39] World Bank (2008).

[40] World Bank (2009).

programme of activities-based CDM may result in some opportunities. Discussions are however on for a reformed version in the form of policy-based or sectoral CDM or the replacement of CDM with some other emission offset mechanism that could eliminate the current difficulties pertaining to its project-based nature. Other financial mechanisms that have put in a larger share of their resources in the transport sector, both for lending and grants, are primarily directed towards development or upgradation of road infrastructure. However, since the turn of the century a new trend has evolved to perceive transport more holistically and invest more in modal shift. Such investments could be utilized more effectively if combined appropriately with technology cooperation, institutional strengthening, and capacity building.

While pursuing new and improved financing mechanisms is important, such initiatives also need to be matched by efforts to reform mainstream investments and financial flows into transport, which includes transport taxes, official development assistance (ODA), export credits and private investments.

Low Carbon Transport: Recent Initiatives by Indian Government

The Indian government has taken a number of national policy initiatives that recognize some components of the Avoid-Shift-Improve framework in order to address some of the challenges described in the preceding section. Box 15.5 gives a snapshot of these initiatives.

In terms of financing initiatives to bring about changes at the local level with support of strategic plans and programmes at the national level, the Jawaharlal Nehru National Urban Renewal Mission (JNNURM) in India provides a great example. JNNURM provides financial assistance as soft loans, grant-cum-loans or grants to Urban Local Bodies and parastatal bodies via state-level nodal agencies in return for formulating City Development Plans (CDPs) and detailed project reports for urban infrastructure development. Furthermore, grants for urban buses have recently been made available, subject to the set-up of Dedicated Urban Transport Funds at state and city levels (see Box 15.6 for further details).

Conclusion

It is indeed encouraging to observe that many of the potential policies and measures under Avoid-Shift-Improve framework are already well known and have been tested in specific countries and cities in the developing or developed world and can be relatively easily replicated or scaled up. The Indian policymaking, both at the national and sub-national levels, has also internalized some components of this approach. However the financial, technological, and institutional resources are yet to be fully reoriented towards an integrated and holistic Avoid-Shift-Improve framework.

Box 15.5
Indian Government Initiatives that Addresses Some Components of the Avoid-Shift-Improve Framework

National Urban Transport Policy (NUTP), 2006

- Aims to integrate land use and transport planning
- Facilitates investment in and promotion of public transport and encourages non-motorized modes
- Develops transport projects focused on equitable allocation of road space
- Promotes clean vehicles
- Aims to raise resources through innovative financing mechanisms
- Focuses on building capacities

National Action Plan on Climate Change (NAPCC), 2008

- Suggests early introduction of fuel economy standards
- Promotes investments in high-capacity public transport systems
- Suggests introducing transport pricing measures to influence purchase of vehicles on the basis of their energy efficiency
- Envisages a ban on abandoning of old vehicles, fixing responsibility on the last owner of the vehicle to hand over the vehicle at the end of its life to specific collection centres to be nominated by the government.
- Encourages setting up of demonstration centres to take up recycling of vehicles, especially two-wheelers
- Encourages energy R&D in Indian railways
- Promotes use of coastal shipping and inland waterways, encourage rail-based movement instead of long-distance road-based movement

Source: http://pmindia.nic.in/climate_change.htm ; www.urbanindia.nic.in/policies/TransportPolicy.pdf

Box 15.6
Transport Funds in India

Examples of local transport funds exist in India, where recently, two urban areas have adopted such an approach. In Surat, vehicle taxes, parking charges and advertisement fees are fed into a dedicated urban transport fund, which is used to support its urban mobility plan, including the expansion of bus services and modifying three-wheelers to power on CNG. In Pimpri-Chinchwad, a 130 km BRT network is being developed using urban transport fund, funded by fares, monthly passes, advertisement and land related taxes (for example, development rights around the BRT corridor, and property tax). India has also initiated the JNNURM which, at the national level provides assistance to megacities in their efforts to improve urban infrastructure. Sustainable transport is included in this scheme. The philosophy behind the JNNURM is one of cost-sharing between national and local level, in design, construction and operation of infrastructure. Recently, as part of the GoI's economic stimulus package, a one-time assistance grant of $58 billion has been provided to the states under the framework of the JNNURM for the purchase of urban buses. This provision is subject to various conditions, including the setting up of a dedicated Urban Transport Fund at both the state and the city levels. Revenue sources suggested for the fund at state level include sales tax on petrol, vehicle registration fees, renewal fee for driving licences, congestion taxes and green taxes. The fund at the city level includes betterment levies on land, parking fees, property development taxes, and advertisement revenue.

Source: Leather (2009).

An important issue that deserves attention is that climate change does not seem to be the key driver of transport policies and projects in developing countries. This is because the potential financial earnings from GHG reduction tend to be significantly lower than other earnings or cost savings associated with a good transport policy or project that addresses local benefits, such as reduced traffic congestion and air pollution. Thus these local negative spillovers still play a much bigger role in development of transport polices and investments than climate change mitigation.

In this context, it should be recognized that the transport policies and programmes can have: (a) *Benefits*—the primary goal of policies and project (for example, reduced traffic congestion), (b) *Primary co-benefits*—other benefits that directly result from transport policies or projects (for example, GHG and air pollution reduction), or (c) *Secondary co-benefits*—benefits that indirectly result from transport policies or project (for example, reduced health impact and costs from air pollution). A holistic implementation of the Avoid–Shift-Improve approach will be able to foster a synergy of these benefits and variegated co-benefits. But the implications of benefits and co-benefits may be different for different nations depending on the initial condition or the state of affairs under which such approach is being implemented. Thus there is no 'one-size fits all' kind of tailor-made solution that could be applied universally. It is rather essential to go in for a needs-based combination of policies. For instance, in developing cities that are dominated by a large number of old highly polluting vehicles, policies focusing on *improvement* based on technological solutions tend to have relatively high co-benefits. Similarly, in densely populated cities in developing countries that are yet to develop a strong planning capacity, planning instruments such as efficient mix of land use-transport-environment can bring about higher co-benefits. Likewise, in developing countries where the lion's share of the pollution and emission is attributed to freight transport, regulatory and planning instruments targeting the freight sector can bring relatively large and immediate co-benefits. These examples should not, however, be taken to imply that other instruments or policies pertaining to the Avoid-Shift-Improve approach are of least importance. The moot point is a minimum essential level of implementation of all the components or policies pertaining to this approach needs to be ensured at the first instance but depending on the state of affairs or specific needs in some countries or cities, particular components could be given more or less attention. However, the speed and level of implementation would largely be contingent upon concomitant efforts made in developing awareness level among the masses; reforms and coordination in nature of policies and institutions; invoking high degree of transparency and accountability; and finally the efforts undertaken in augmenting capacity and resources.

Institutional development, in particular, in support of low carbon urban transport is crucial and includes—(a) clarification of institutional mandates at all geographical levels (local, sub-national, national, regional, and global) (b) strengthening of institutional capacities within all sectors (government, civil society, academia, and private sector), and (c) improved coordination and cooperation between different sectors at, and between, different geographical levels. The requirement of improved coordination applies especially to integration of land use and transport planning and should essentially be directed towards development of comprehensive transport systems, rather than individual, ad-hoc, projects.

Furthermore, private sector participation in the provision of low carbon transport products and services needs to be encouraged as the private sector is better at mobilizing investments required to support the implementation of low carbon transport policies. Experiences from developed countries indicate the importance of a transparent and predictable regulatory framework to promote private sector involvement. Therefore in order to facilitate increased private sector participation appropriate regulatory frameworks need to be developed in the first place. The same applies to the civil society which can help mobilize support for policy development and implementation, follow-up of policy commitments made by governments, and flag problems before they become unmanageable. The absence of effective and transparent public consultation mechanisms will ultimately slow down decision-making and its implementation and might reduce the rate at which changes in behaviour are adopted.

Developing countries like India and China should play a key role in applying the co-benefits approach and make their transport system sustainable and low-carbon through a combination of policy instruments, institutional capacity development, appropriate pricing mechanisms, and mobilizing financial resources. However in order to implement the co-benefits approach, it should also be integrated in a more structured and quantified manner in policy analysis and the feasibility studies of programmes and projects. This is more likely to happen if co-benefits are fully recognized and internalized in the post-2012 climate agreement.

References

Asian Development Bank (2008). *Clean Energy Financing Partnership Facility - Semi Annual Progress Report, January–June,* Philippines: Asian Development Bank, available at: http://www.adb.org/Documents/reports/CEFPF/CEFPF-Semiannual-Progress-Report.pdf

——— (2006). *Energy Efficiency and Climate Change Considerations for on-road Transport in Asia,* Asian Development Bank, Philippines.

Asian Institute of Transport Development (AITD) (2002). *Environmental and Social Sustainability of Transport: Comparative Study of Rail and Road,* Asian Institute of Transport Development, New Delhi.

Bandivadekar, A. (2009). 'Review of Fuel Economy/Greenhouse Gas Standards Worldwide', presentation at the GFEI (Global Fuel Economy Initiative) Symposium held in New Delhi, 25 November.

Bandyopadhyay, K.R. (2008). 'OPEC's Price-making Power', *Economic and Political Weekly,* 43 (46), pp. 18–21.

——— (2009a). 'Adding KGs to GDP', the *Financial Express,* 4 December.

——— (2009b). 'What will oil do in 2010?', the *Financial Express,* 30 December.

——— (2010a). 'Fossil Fuel Subsidy Reform in India', Policy Brief 45, Research and Information System for Developing Countries, New Delhi, January, available at www.ris.org.in/pb45.pdf

——— (2010b). 'Crude logic lies in decontrol', the *Financial Express,* 4 February.

Basu, Agnimirh (2009). 'Unorganized Players give e-bike a Bad Name', *Down to Earth,* August 16–31.

Chattopadhyay, Vivek (2010). 'e Driven', *Down to Earth,* Centre for Science and Environment, Delhi, February 1–15.

Dalkmann, H. and C. Brannigan (2007). 'Transport and Climate Change', Module 5e in *Sustainable Transport: A Sourcebook for Policymakers in Developing Cities,* GTZ, Germany: available at http://www.sutp.org

Environment Pollution (Control and Prevention) Authority (2009). 'Learning from Practice: Examples of Fiscal Reform in Cities to deal with Pollution and Congestion', Briefing paper 2b, Government of Delhi, February.

Eskeland, G.S., and T. Feyzioglu (1995). *Rationing Can Backfire, the Day 'Without a Car' in Mexico City,* World Bank, Washington DC, December.

Frost and Sullivan (2010). 'Voice of Indian Automotive Customers 2009: Evaluation of Power train Technologies in Vehicles', Frost and Sullivan, Mumbai, February.

Garg, Abhinav (2010). 'Delhi High Court moots congestion fee on cars', the *Times of India,* 11 February 2010.

Government of India (2009). *Road Transport Yearbook 2006–07,* Ministry of Shipping, Road Transport, and Highways, New Delhi.

Grutter, Jurg M. (2008). 'CDM transport projects up and coming', *JIKO Info,* 6(3), pp. 1–6.

——— (2007). 'CDM in the transport sector', Module 5d in *Sustainable Transport: A Sourcebook for Policymakers in Developing Cities.,* GTZ, Germany, available at http://www.sutp.org

Huizenga, C. and S. Bakker (2009). 'Applicability of post 2012 Climate Instruments to the Transport Sector', Draft Interim Synthesis Consultants Report, Asian Development Bank, Philippines, December.

International Energy Agency (IEA) (2007a). *CO_2 Emissions from Fuel Combustion: 1971–2005,* IEA, Paris.

——— (2007b). *World Energy Statistics and Balances,* IEA, Paris.

——— (2007c). *CO_2 Emissions from Fuel Combustion: 1971–2005,* IEA, Paris.

——— (2007d). *World Energy Outlook,* IEA, Paris.

——— (2008). *World Energy Outlook,* IEA, Paris.

——— (2009a). *Transport Energy and CO2: Moving Towards Sustainability,* IEA, Paris.

International Energy Agency (IEA) (2009b). *Technology Roadmap: Electric and Plug-in Hybrid Vehicles (EV/PHEV)*, IEA, Paris.

Kahn, R.S., S. Kobayashi, M. Bouthe, J. Gasea, D. Greene, D.S. Lee, Y. Muromachi, P.J. Newton, S. Plotkin, D. Spering, R. Wit, and P.J. Zhou (2007). 'Transport and its Infrastructure', in Metz, B., O.R. Davidson, P.R. Bosch, R. Dave, and L.A. Meyer (eds.) *Climate Change 2007: Mitigation*, Contribution of Working Group III to the Fourth Assessment Report of the Intergovernmental Panel on Climate Change (IPCC), Switzerland 2007.

Kharola B.S. and G. Tiwari (2008). 'Urban Public Transport Systems: Are the Taxation Policies Congenial for their Survival and Growth', *Economic and Political Weekly*, 43(41), October, pp. 41–7.

Leather, James (2009). 'Rethinking Transport and Climate Change', Draft Sustainable Development Working Paper, Asian Development Bank, Philippines, September.

Schipper, L, C. M-Lilliu, and Roger Gorham (2000). *Flexing the Link between Transport and Greenhouse Gas Emissions: A Path for the World Bank*, IEA, Paris, June.

Sengupta, R., 'High Economic Growth, Equity and Sustainable Energy Development of India', Discussion Paper Series, 213, Research Institute of Economics and Business Administration, Kobe University, Japan, December, available at http://www.rieb.kobe-u.ac.jp/academic/ra/dp/English/dp213.pdf

Staff Reporter (2010). 'Task Force to find solution to Delhi's Traffic woes', the *Hindu*, 11 February 2010.

Sundar, S., and C. Dhingra (2008). 'Reducing Transport CO_2 Emissions in Emerging Economies', Paper presented at the Second Annual Conference of the International Transport Forum, Leipzig, Germany.

Timilsina, G., and A. Shrestha (2009). 'Why have CO2 emissions increased in the transport sector in Asia? Underlying Factors and Policy Options', *Policy Research Working Paper*, 5098, World Bank, Washington DC.

United Nations Environment Programme (UNEP) (2009). 'CDM Pipeline', Risø, Denmark: UNEP, 1 December, available at www.cdmpipeline.org

World Bank (2008). *Clean Technology Fund*, World Bank, Washington DC, available at http://siteresources.worldbank.org/INTCC/Resources/Clean_Technology_Fund_paper_June_9_final.pdf

———— (2009). *Transport Lending Trends 1996–2007*, World Bank, Washington DC, available at http://go.worldbank.org/KM9OPODLQ0

World Business Council on Sustainable Development (WBCSD), (2004). *Mobility 2030: Meeting the Challenges to Sustainability*, WBCSD, USA.

16 Putting Urban Transport Sector on a Low Energy and Low Carbon Path

A Focus on the Passenger Transport Sector in Million-Plus Cities

Akshima T. Ghate and Sanjivi Sundar

Key Transport Issues in Million-Plus Cities

India is urbanizing at an unprecedented pace and the process of urbanization in the country has been primarily large city oriented (Kundu 2006). In 2001, almost two-thirds of the urban population was concentrated in 441 large cities with over 0.1 million population and the remaining in 4,720 small cities and towns. Within these 441 large cities, the 35 million-plus cities alone had a share of about 37 per cent of the total urban population (GoI 2001). The number of million-plus cities is expected to increase to about 75 by 2021 (NIDM 2001).

The unplanned growth of the million-plus cities in the absence of integrated land-use and transport planning coupled with inadequate public transport and poor infrastructure for non-motorized transport (NMT) has led to an exponential growth in personal vehicles.

Lack of Integrated Land use and Transport Planning

Million-plus cities clearly call for more urban space to address the needs of their increasing population. It is well recognized that the land-use planning in these cities needs to respond to this challenge and deliver efficiently organized, compact urban spaces where residential areas, work-places, education, recreation, shopping, etc., are within close vicinity and where mobility needs can be addressed by public transport or non-motorized modes. However, land-use planning and transport planning have not been adequately integrated in Indian cities.

The National Urban Transport Policy (NUTP) does recognize that transport planning has been historically neglected by urban planners while drawing up strategic development and land-use plans (GoI 2005). While it stresses upon the need for integration of the two, million-plus cities continue to develop the two plans in isolation. Urban planning and land-use planning as they are practised in Indian cities seek to address current transport demands through specific projects and do not attempt to shape the structure of the city and influence its future growth on a sustainable basis.

Inadequate Public Transport and NMT Infrastructure

The public transport system in Indian cities has not been able to keep pace with the increasing demand for urban transport. The public modes in most Indian cities constitute only 2–3 per cent of the entire vehicular fleet (TERI 2008a). According to a study by Wilbur Smith Associates Pvt. Ltd. (WSA) and the Ministry of Urban Development (MoUD) in 2008, the four largest cities in the country, that is, Mumbai, Delhi, Kolkata, and Chennai, showed a negative growth rate in the bus fleet size from 2000 to 2007. In most cities, dedicated public transport is absent and a combination of para-transit modes like jeeps, autos, etc., serve the purpose. Dedicated city bus services are known to operate only in 17 cities; rail transit exists only in Mumbai, Delhi, Kolkata, and Chennai where metro rail services cater to around 7 million trips per day (Singh 2005). Some other cities also have limited suburban rail systems, serving a part of their population's trip demands.

Inadequate and poor quality of public transport has led to increasing use of personalized vehicles. According to the WSA and MoUD (2008) study for 30 select cities[1] in India, while there has been a continuous decline in the share of public transport from 1994 to 2007, the share of personalized modes, specifically two-wheelers, has increased at the rate of 12 per cent per annum. Large cities in the country are witnessing the falling share of NMT in the absence of good-quality and safe infrastructure. Roads in the cities have inadequate facilities for pedestrians, cyclists, and cycle rickshaws; pavements are fast disappearing and even where they exist, they have been transformed to parking places for private vehicles. The mode share of cycling has dropped from 25 per cent in 1994 to 15 per cent in 2007 in these 30 cities. Cities face the huge challenge of arresting this declining share of public transport and NMT modes in favour of personal modes.

Rapid Motorization and Increasing Share of Private Vehicles

Most large cities have witnessed an exponential growth in the number of motorized personal vehicles. The growth in motor vehicles in the six metropolitan cities (Bangalore, Chennai, Mumbai, Delhi, Hyderabad, and Kolkata) has been almost four times the growth of population during 1981 to 2001 (Agarwal 2006). The modal split of on-road vehicles in metropolitan cities when compared to the rest of the country indicates the heavy concentration of private motor vehicles in metropolitan cities. As shown in Figure 16.1, these metropolises accounted for about 53 per cent of the total cars and 31 per cent of the total two-wheelers in the country in 2001 (MoRTH 2003). The car and two-wheeler ownership in metropolitan cities is much higher than in the rest of the country. Car ownership in metropolitan cities in 2001 was 29 cars per 1,000 persons as compared to three cars per 1,000 persons in the rest of the country. Similarly, the two-wheeler ownership in these cities was much higher than in the rest of the

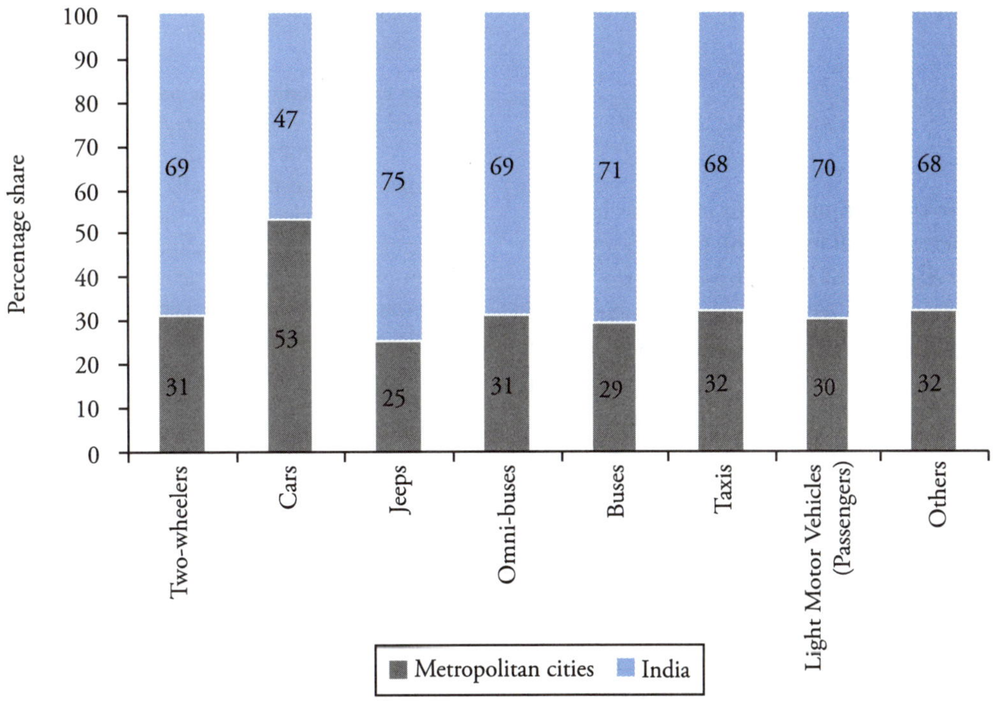

Figure 16.1 Comparison of Share of Vehicles Registered in Metropolitan Cities with the Rest of the Country in 2001

Source: MoRTH (2003).

[1] Mumbai, Kolkata, Delhi, Bangalore, Chennai, Hyderabad, Ahmedabad, Pune, Surat, Kanpur, Jaipur, Nagpur, Varanasi, Patna, Kochi, Bhopal, Agra, Madurai, Gangtok, Panaji, Shimla, Pondicherry, Bikaner, Raipur, Bhubaneswar, Chandigarh, Hubli Dharward, Guwahati, Amritsar, and Trivandrum.

country (Figure 16.2). Vehicle ownership in these cities has increased with rising household incomes, aspirations for better quality of life, enabling a market environment for vehicle purchase, increasing trip lengths, and inadequate public transport services. The heavy concentration of private motor vehicles in metropolitan cities has been one of the key reasons for congestion, increased travel times, pollution, and accidents.

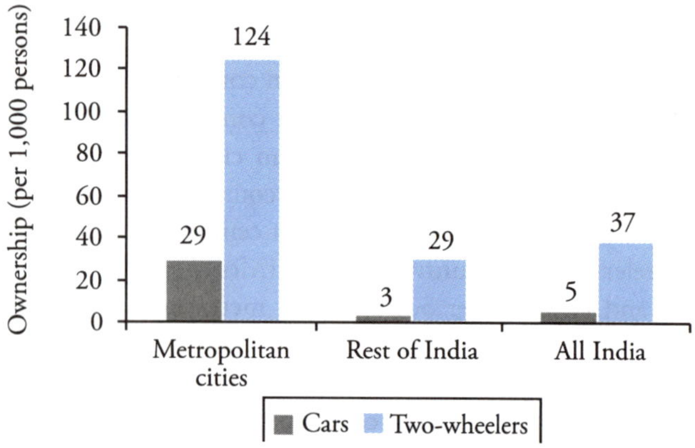

FIGURE 16.2 Car and Two-wheeler Ownership in 2001

Source: MoRTH (2003).

Implications of the Current Trend of Urban Transport Growth on Energy Consumption and CO2 Emissions

Transport sector growth in million-plus cities has led to a growing dependence on fossil fuels, which is also reflected in the total energy demand of the transport sector in the country. The sector is the second largest consumer of commercial energy after industry. About 98 per cent of the energy demand of the sector is met through petroleum fuels and the rest by electricity (TERI, various years). The share of transport in petroleum consumption is expected to increase significantly in the future, which will increase dependency on oil imports.

This poses a serious challenge in the context of energy security and climate change. The recently announced NAPCC recognizes this and has a dedicated sub-mission on urban transport focusing on a low energy and low carbon growth path for the transport sector in cities.

Measuring the Energy Consumed and CO_2 Emissions Produced from Passenger Transport Activities in Million-plus Cities

There are several pan-India studies such as TERI (2007), TERI (2006a), TERI (2006b), and IEA (2007) that specifically focus on quantifying energy use and CO_2 emissions from the transport sector. Such studies use different methods to estimate the transport sectors' energy use and CO_2 emissions. These include spreadsheet models, accounting, and simulation software like the Long Range Energy Alternatives Planning (LEAP) Model, analytical frameworks like ASIF (prepared by the International Energy Agency), energy-technology-economy linear programming models like MARKel Allocation (MARKAL) model, detailed sectoral analysis, activity analysis models, etc. However, we are not aware of studies specifically carried out to measure city-specific or area-specific (that is, urban-rural)

Box 16.1
Million-plus Cities

The 23 million-plus cities considered in this paper are:

City	Population in 2001 (millions)
1. Greater Mumbai	6.4
2. Kolkata	13.2
3. Delhi	12.8
4. Chennai	6.4
5. Hyderabad	5.5
6. Bangalore	5.7
7. Ahmedabad	4.5
8. Pune	3.8
9. Surat	2.8
10. Kanpur	2.7
11. Jaipur	2.3
12. Lucknow	2.3
13. Nagpur	2.1
14. Patna	1.7
15. Indore	1.6
16. Vadodara	1.5
17. Bhopal	1.5
18. Coimbatore	1.5
19. Ludhiana Municipal Corp.	1.4
20. Kochi	1.4
21. Vishakapatnam	1.3
22. Varanasi	1.2
23. Madurai	1.2

Note: Except Ludhiana, the population of each city refers to the urban agglomeration size.

Sources: GoI (2001); Kundu (2006); and MoRTH (2009).

As per the Census of India (GoI 2002), there were 35 million-plus cities in 2001. Ideally, all these 35 cities should be considered while estimating energy and CO_2 emissions from passenger transport activities in million-plus cities of the country. However this paper considers only 23 of them while estimating energy and CO_2 emissions because city-wise time series vehicle registration data is available only for these 23 cities.

energy consumption levels and CO_2 emissions in India. An attempt has, therefore, been made to quantify the energy and CO_2 impacts of passenger transport activities in 23 million-plus cities[2] in respect of which time-series data is available (see Box 16.1). Even with only 23 of the 35 million-plus cities under consideration, the share of energy use and GHG emissions of these cities is substantial. A spreadsheet model was prepared to carry out this estimation. The broad framework of the spreadsheet model is described in Figure 16.3.

Motorized transport activities in cities occur through diverse modes which vary in terms of their energy consumption levels and CO_2 emissions due to differences in vehicle technology, type of fuel consumed, vintage, and average daily use in terms of kilometres travelled. To ensure that all these variables are considered while calculating energy use and CO_2 emissions from passenger transport activities in the 23 million-plus cities, a distance-based approach was used. This approach uses distance-based fuel consumption and CO_2 emission factors for different types of vehicles, fuels, and technologies. Transport activity data is estimated in terms of vehicle kilometres and distance-based factors applied to estimate energy consumption and CO_2 emissions levels. The methodology and data used for these estimations are further explained in the next sections.

On-road Vehicles in Metropolitan Cities

The total motor vehicles registered in 23 million-plus cities in 2001 are shown in Figure 16.4. However, the actual number of vehicles on the roads could be less. In India, personal vehicles that is cars, jeeps, and two-wheelers are registered only once at the time of purchase. There is no record of these vehicles going off the road due to age.[3] To calculate the approximate number of on-road vehicles in these cities, an average age of 15 years for cars and two-wheelers was assumed and the on-road fleet for 2001 was estimated (Figure 16.4).[4] These on-road vehicle numbers were considered while estimating energy consumption and CO_2 emissions in the 23 million-plus cities. Passenger transport vehicles other than cars, jeeps, and two-wheelers, that is, taxis, buses, and three-wheelers are registered every year till they are road-worthy; we therefore consider the on-road vehicles in these categories to be equal to the registered motor vehicle numbers as given by MoRTH.

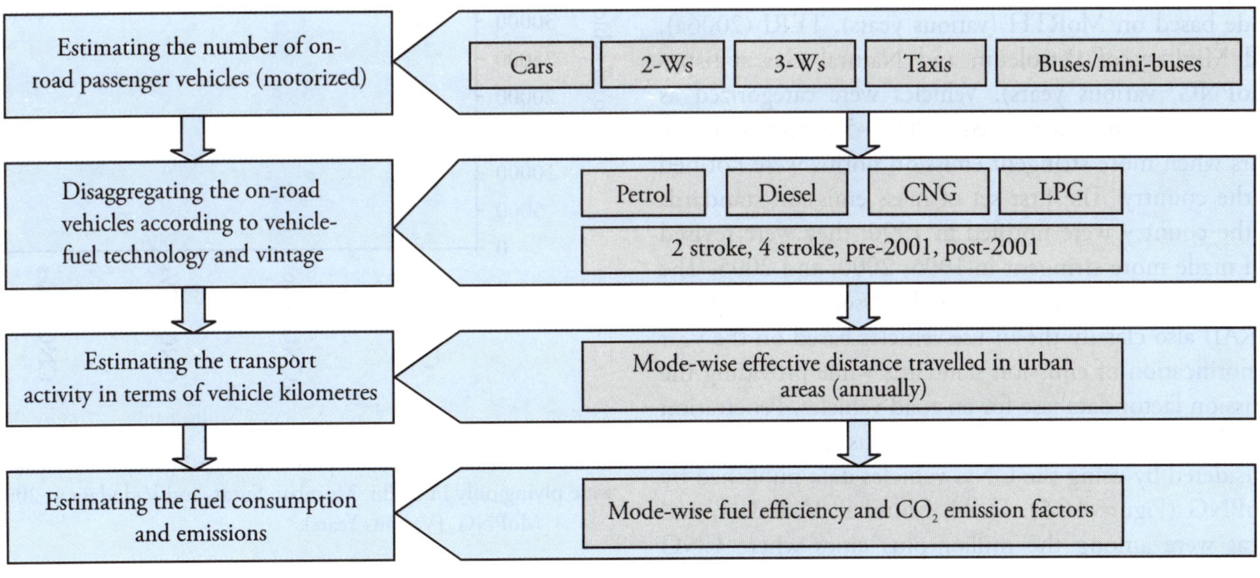

Figure 16.3 Framework for Estimating Energy Consumption Levels and CO_2 Emissions from Passenger Transport Activities in Metropolitan Cities

Source: Authors' own.

[2] Greater Mumbai, Kolkata, Delhi, Chennai, Hyderabad, Bangalore, Ahmedabad, Pune, Surat, Kanpur, Jaipur, Lucknow, Nagpur, Patna, Indore, Vadodara, Bhopal, Coimbatore, Ludhiana Municipal Corp., Kochi, Vishakapatnam, Varanasi, and Madurai.

[3] Also, some cars and other vehicles may be plying in other cities and towns. However, there are no means of calculating these in a systematic manner.

[4] 1986 was considered as the base year to estimate on-road vehicles in 2001.

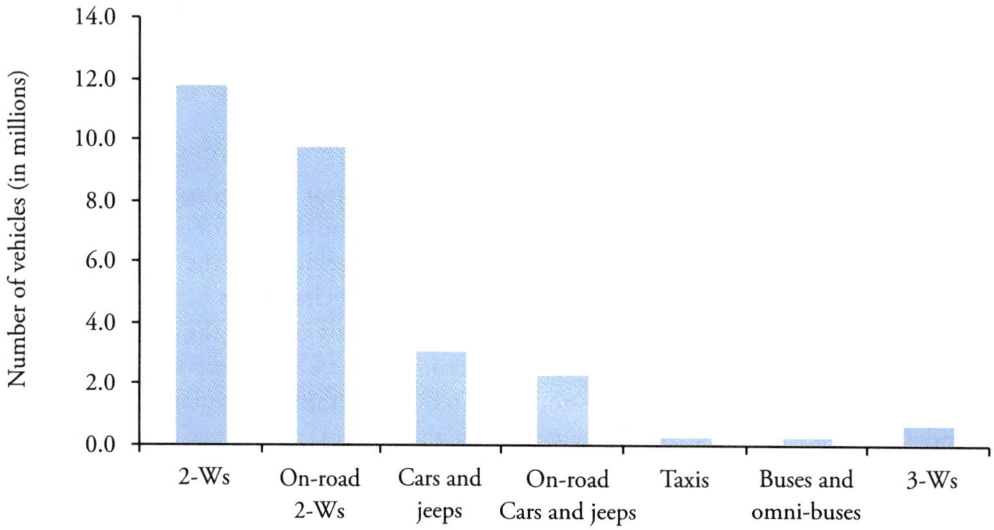

Figure 16.4 Registered and On-road Passenger Vehicles in Million-Plus Cities, 2001

Source: MoRTH (various years) (On-road vehicles were estimated by authors).

Technology Penetration

Vehicle technology has improved over a period of time to meet the increasingly stringent emission norms and adopt new fuels like CNG. Assumptions regarding the penetration of improved technologies have been made based on MoRTH (various years), TERI (2006a), and Ministry of Petroleum and Natural Gas statistics (MoPNG, various years). Vehicles were categorized as pre-2001 and those registered in 2001–5 as these were the years when more stringent emission norms were notified in the country. The first set of mass emission standards in the country were notified in 1990; they were revised and made more stringent in 1996, 2000, and 2005. The CPCB and Automotive Research Association of India (ARAI) also classify the in-use vehicles based on the year of notification of emission standards while providing the emission factor database for on-road vehicles. Penetration of CNG vehicles in the million-plus cities was duly considered by using the CNG vehicles data published by MoPNG (Figure 16.5). Delhi, Mumbai, Vadodara, and Surat were among the million-plus cities where CNG vehicles started plying 2000 onwards. The total number of CNG vehicles in these four cities in 2001 is shown in Figure 16.5.

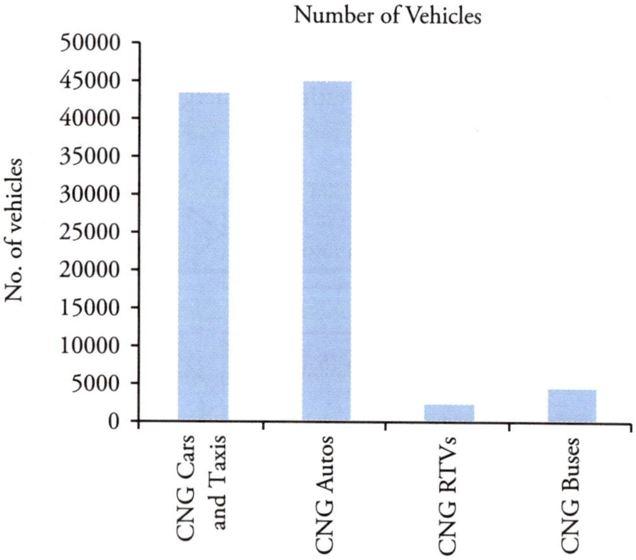

Figure 16.5 Total CNG Vehicles in Million-plus Cities in 2001

Note: Out of the 23 million-plus cities considered, CNG vehicles were plying only in Delhi, Mumbai, Surat, and Vadodara in 2001.
Source: MoPNG, (Various Years).

Annual mileage

The annual mileage of the on-road vehicles in 2000 was based on a CPCB report titled 'Transport Fuel Quality for Year 2005'. The yearly increase in vehicle mileage after 2000 was estimated based on the Planning Commission (2002). Table 16.1 gives the annual mileage figures for different modes in 2000 and the yearly mileage increase assumed from 2000 onwards.

Fuel Consumption of Vehicles and CO_2 Emission Factors

Data on distance-based fuel consumption and CO_2 emission factors for different vehicle and fuel technologies of different vintages was compiled from TERI (2006a), ARAI (2007), and Society of Indian Automobile

Table 16.1 Annual Mileage of Different Modes

Mode	*Average annual mileage (kms) in 2000*	*Yearly increase in annual mileage (kms)*
2-Ws	10,000	130
Car	15,000	100
Taxis	30,000	–
3-Ws	40,000	–
Bus/Mini-bus	60,000	400

Sources: CPCB (2000) and Planning Commission (2002).

Manufacturer's (SIAM) fuel economy brochure.[5] ARAI (2007) is a recently completed study conducted by Automotive Research Association of India and co-ordinated by CPCB. The study provides emission factors which have been worked out through emission tests on vehicles carried out on the basis of vehicle categories, vintages, and engine cubic capacities (see Table 16.2).

As stated earlier, the time periods used to classify vehicle technologies have been chosen in accordance with the emissions tightening programme in the entire country. It was observed that technology improvements brought about to meet the emission norms have also resulted in fuel efficiency improvements.

Based on the number of on-road vehicles estimated, technology penetration, annual mileage, fuel consumption, and CO_2 emission factors discussed in the previous sections, the energy consumption levels and CO_2 emissions were estimated for the 23 metropolitan cities using the equations given in Box 16.2. The energy and CO_2 emission results for these cities are discussed in the next section.

Table 16.2 CO_2 Emission Factors for Different Vehicle-Fuel Technologies

Technology/model	*CO_2 emissions (g/km)*
2-W 4s pre-2001	22.8
2-W 4s 2001–5	25.9
2-W 2s pre-2001	22.6
2-W 2s 2001–5	25.8
Car/taxi petrol pre-2001	97.1
Car/taxi petrol 2001–5	131.9
Car/taxi diesel pre-2001	147.6
Car/taxi diesel 2001–5	155.7
Car/taxi CNG pre-2001	149.4
Car/taxi CNG 2001–5	137.4
Taxi CNG 2001–5	137.4
Taxi LPG pre-2001	130.9
Taxi LPG 2001–5	140.1
Bus diesel	869.1
Bus CNG	806.5
Mini-bus diesel	365.8
3-W 4s petrol pre-2001	77.1
3-W 4s petrol 2001–5	62.7
3-W 2s petrol pre-2001	54.5
3-W 2s petrol 2001–5	62.4
3-W CNG pre-2001	57.3
3-W CNG 2001–5	67.7
3-W LPG pre-2001	54.6
3-W LPG 2001–5	68.2
3-W diesel pre-2001	130.2
3-W diesel 2001–5	173.9

Note: The emission factors estimated from ARAI (2007) are the average of all vehicle-fuel technologies available within a mode.
Source: ARAI (2007).

Energy Consumption Levels and CO_2 Emissions from Passenger Transport Activities

Estimated fuel consumption in 2001 due to the on-road motorized vehicle fleet in the 23 million-plus cities is given in Figure 16.6. The amount of fuel consumed in these cities for passenger transport activities was of the order of 12.6 MTOE in 2001, of which diesel accounted for 50 per cent followed by petrol (42 per cent), and CNG (8 per cent). The CO_2 emissions from passenger transport activities in these 23 million-plus cities were of the order of 18.9 MT in 2001.

The energy consumption estimates for on-road passenger transport activities in the 23 million-plus cities were compared with energy consumption of transport sector at the all-India level as estimated in TERI (2006a) and Bose (2006). As per TERI (2006a), 34.0 MTOE is estimated to be consumed for the total transport activities in the country in 2001. Bose (2006) estimated that the total energy consumption for all on-road transport activities in 2000 was 29.0 MTOE and CO_2 emissions were 81.3 MT. As per our estimates, energy consumed for on-road passenger transport activities in the 23 million-plus cities in 2001 was 12.6 MTOE and CO_2 emissions were 18.9 MT.

The above comparison indicates that even 23 of the 35 million-plus cities have a significant share in energy consumption and CO_2 emissions from the passenger transport activities in the country. It is acknowledged that there may be differences in basic assumptions and data

[5] http://www.siamindia.com/default.aspx

Box 16.2
Energy and CO_2 Emission Estimation

1 Estimating mode-wise vehicle kilometres (kms)
For year 'x',
$$VKM_{M1} = V_{M1} X D_{M1}$$
where,
VKM_{M1} = Annual vehicle kms for mode 'M1' in year 'x'
V_{M1} = Total number of on-road vehicles for mode 'M1' in year 'x'
D_{M1} = Annual mileage per vehicle for mode 'M1' (in kms) in year 'x'
M1 = Cars, M2 = Two-wheelers, M3 = Three-wheelers, M4 = Taxis, M5 = Buses, M6 = Mini-buses

2 Estimating total fuel consumption from passenger transport activities (TOE)
For year 'x',
$$Fuel_{M1} = VKM_{M1} X FE_{M1}$$
where,
$Fuel_{M1}$ = Total annual fuel consumption for mode 'M1' in year 'x' (TOE)
FE_{M1} = Fuel economy of mode 'M1' (TOE/km)

Note: The fuel economy numbers in litres and cum were converted to TOE units using the fuel specific calorific values

3 Estimating total CO_2 emissions from passenger transport activities (kg)
For year 'x',
$$CO_{2M1} = VKM_{M1} X EF_{M1}$$
where,

CO_{2M1} = Total CO_2 emissions for mode 'M1' in year 'x' (kg)
EF_{M1} = CO_2 emission factor for mode 'M1' (kg/km)

4 Total fuel consumption for year 'x' (in TOE) = $Fuel_{M1} + Fuel_{M2} + Fuel_{M3} + Fuel_{M4} + Fuel_{M5} + Fuel_{M6}$

5 Total CO_2 emissions for year 'x' (in kg) = $CO_{2M1} + CO_{2M2} + CO_{2M3} + CO_{2M4} + CO_{2M5} + CO_{2M6}$

Source: Authors' own.

sources of these different studies. However, a comparison gives some basic understanding of the share of passenger transport activities of these cities as compared to the rest of the country.[6] These numbers highlight the need for concerted effort and strategies to reduce energy consumption and CO_2 emissions.

The energy and emission estimates discussed previously would be even higher if the impacts of poor road conditions, congestion, and idling, which are important issues in urban areas, were to be considered. However, there is hardly any consolidated data on the impact of these factors. A study undertaken by the Central Road Research Institute (CRRI) and Petroleum Conservation Research Association (PCRA) estimated the total fuel loss per day due to idling of vehicles at traffic intersections in Delhi.[7] As per the estimates in this study, about 320 kilolitres of petrol and 100 kilolitres of diesel is being burnt every day due to idling of vehicles at the intersections. The idling due to traffic jams on roads would further increase this number. Additionally, the poor road conditions and congestion on roads lead to slow journey speeds in the large cities, which in turn has implications in terms of increased fuel consumption and emissions.

The previous analysis clearly highlights the significant share of the million-plus cities in the energy consumption and CO_2 emissions from the total on-road passenger transport activities in the country. As these cities grow, the mobility needs of their residents will increase. Transport

[6] The estimates made in this paper are based on the assumption that all on-road vehicles in the 23 million-plus cities are plying in those cities for intra-city movement. It is acknowledged that the all-India CO_2 emission numbers for passenger transport activities also include inter-city movement of vehicles for passenger transport. However, in the absence of data available to estimate this inter-city passenger transport movement, the distinction between intra-city passenger movement and inter-city passenger movement in all-India numbers could not be made. This is acknowledged as a limitation while comparing CO_2 emissions of 23 select cities with all India numbers. In fact, if inter-city movement is excluded and only intra-city movement is considered, the share of the million-plus cities would be even more.

[7] http://www.pcra.org/English/transport/CRRIstudy.htm, last accessed on 18 December 2009.

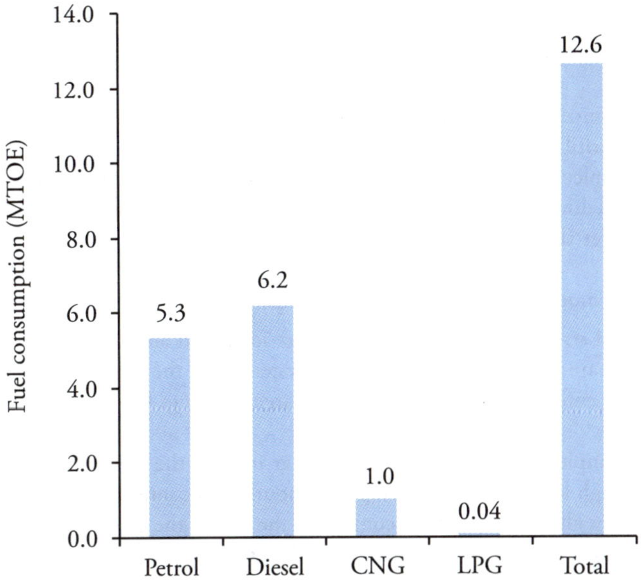

FIGURE 16.6 Estimated Fuel Consumption from Motorized Transport Activities in 23 Million-plus Cities (2001)

Source: Authors' own.

Box 16.3
Key Transportation Planning Principles—
Integrated Land-use Planning

'Planners who care about sustainability integrate land-use planning with transportation and air-quality decision making. They focus on moving people on their feet, on bikes, on transit rather than just moving cars.

This type of planning often uses the "five-minute rule"—all destinations are within a five-minute walk. Streets, paths, and businesses are attractively designed, so people enjoy their journey.

With good land-use planning, communities can reduce reliance on single-occupancy vehicles and reduce the number of vehicle miles travelled. Reducing both of these factors will, in turn, help achieve improved air quality.'

Source: http://www.smartcommunities.ncat.org/transport/trintlu.shtml, last accessed on 11 December 2009.

growth is necessary to sustain economic growth which in turn leads to an increase in transport demand. It is, therefore, all the more necessary for these cities to create transport capacity by adopting a sustainable low carbon path. The next section focuses on the key approaches and strategies for promoting a low energy and a low carbon intensive path for the growth of the transport sector in these cities.

Low Energy and Low Carbon Growth of the Transport Sector in Million-plus Cities: Key Approaches and Strategies

The million-plus cities of the country need to rethink their transport plans and projects from the perspective of their energy and CO_2 emission impacts. The cities need to adopt the 'Avoid, Shift, and Improve' approach in transport planning as advocated by the ADB in its draft 'Action Plan to Make Transport in Developing Countries More Climate-Friendly' and reiterated by the Bellagio Declaration[8] in May 2009. The 'Avoid, Shift, and Improve' framework relevant in the context of urban transport sector of large Indian cities is discussed next.

AVOID: Reducing Transport Demand

The vibrant socio-economic life in large cities creates a huge demand for mobility for work, recreation, education, and shopping. This creates immense pressure on the transport infrastructure in these cities. Cities need to tackle the problem at the root by trying to 'avoid' increased demands for mobility. This can be done in two ways:

- by reducing the number of trips and
- by reducing the length of trips

The two key instruments to do this are integration of land-use and transport planning, and the use of information technology (IT) as a substitute for physical mobility.

Integrated Land-use and Transport Planning

Population pressure in most of the million-plus cities in the country has led to a low density horizontal spread of the built-up area or urban sprawl. This is primarily owing to the failure to integrate land-use and transport plans for these cities. The planners in these cities need to understand the relationship between different land uses that affect travel behaviour and need to plan for new developments that are transit-oriented and facilitate walking and cycling. Even in retrofitting of existing development these goals should be kept in mind (see Boxes 16.3 and 16.4).

Using IT to Reduce Demand for Physical Transportation

'Virtual Mobility refers to the use of the new Information and Communications Technologies (ICT) as an alternative to physical mobility. It is about using ICT as the

[8] http://www.slocat.net/bellagio-process/targets-and-progress/, last accessed on 18 February 2010.

Box 16.4
Integrated Land-use and Transport Planning and a Dedicated Public Transport System in Curitiba

The transportation system in Curitiba, as it exists now, has evolved since the late 1960s when the master plan for the city was formulated. The master plan proposed a change in the urban form of Curitiba from radial to linear. The plan utilized integrated land-use, road and public transport systems as tools to implement this principle. The city planners, unlike in many other Latin American cities at that time, did not embark on brutal reconstructions of the city's downtown area or large-scale highway constructions; rather they used integrated land-use and transport planning as a tool to meet the challenge of growing urban limits and the resultant transportation demand (Friberg 2000).

The key features of Curitiba's public transport system that make it a model for many other cities are summarized below:

1. Creation of a road hierarchy and land control system—Five arterial structural growth corridors were identified and developed to dictate the growth pattern of the city. These structural corridors are composed of a triple road system with the central road with two restricted lanes dedicated to express buses. Zoning laws are enforced along these corridors; large buildings holding high density of people are permitted along these corridors.
2. Integrated system—Curitiba's transport system comprises three complementary levels of service that include the feeder lines, express lines, and inter-district routes. The feeder lines passing through lower density outlying neighbourhoods connect with the express system along the structural corridors. The inter-district routes allow passengers to connect to the axis of the express lines without entering the central city area. The system encompasses transfer terminals, express routes, direct routes using boarding tubes, feeder and inter-district routes supplemented by central city routes, neighbourhood routes, night routes, special education routes, and pro-park routes which collectively make up Curitiba's Mass Transit System (MTS).
3. Integrated fare system—The city has introduced automatic combined ticketing. Revenue sharing between bus companies is based on the number of kilometres travelled by vehicle type for any given company. The system is financed by the bus fares without any public subsidies.
4. Bus and transfer terminal design—Buses are designed with three doors, two doors for exiting and a front door for boarding, turbo engines, lower floor levels, wider doors, and a convenient design for mass transit. Curitiba has also developed boarding tube stations to increase convenience and boarding efficiency. Provisions have been made for the convenience of disabled and elderly passengers.
5. Information system—Station and route maps are provided at each tube station.
6. Regular maintenance and renewal of fleet after every ten years ensures good condition of buses and helps keep down the air pollution levels.

Source: Friberg (2000).

means of "getting to" activities that would previously have required transport."[9] Government authorities responsible for traffic management may engage with businesses to encourage a tele/e-work culture and flexi-work hours and also encourage them to develop sustainable mobility plans for their staff.

Bangalore One is such a programme that was launched in Bangalore city; a TERI study in 2008 analysed the possible impacts of the initiative on travel demand in the city (Box 16.5).

SHIFT: From Personal Vehicles to Public Transport and Non-motorized Modes

Increasing use of personalized transport is one of the key reasons for the growing urban transport problems including that of increased energy consumption. A shift from personal vehicles to other mass transit and non-motorized modes is necessary to reduce energy demand from cities. The largest cities in the country, that is, Delhi, Mumbai, Bangalore, Hyderabad, Chennai, and Kolkata are making huge investments into high capacity public transport. However, capacity enhancement must be accompanied with measures that discourage the routine use of personal vehicles and encourage the increased use of public transport and NMT modes. A few measures that can encourage such travel behaviour are (GTZ 2009):

- Road/congestion pricing
- Fuel pricing
- Parking policies and pricing
- Vehicle use restrictions
- Road space reallocation
- Priority for bus and non-motorized modes
- Clustered land uses
- Flexible work hours and telecommuting
- Travel planning information

[9] http://www.virtual-mobility.com/, last accessed on 6 December 2009.

Box 16.5
Bangalore One (B1) Initiative

The vision of the B1 Project is to provide to the citizens of Karnataka, all G2C (government to citizen) one-stop services and information of departments and agencies of central, state, and local governments in an efficient manner through easy access to a chain of computerized Integrated Citizen Service Centres (ICSCs) and through multiple delivery channels like electronic kiosks, mobile phones, and the internet. In addition to providing easy and speedy access of services to people, the project impacts the number and length of road trips in the city. At present there are 16 hi-tech integrated citizen service centres in the city. The government of Karnataka (GoK) has decided to establish 15 additional service centres in different parts of the city and provide 24 basic services of eight government departments participating initially in the B1 Project. Travel demand is reduced because:

- People can either sit at home and avail these services through online portals, or
- They can combine many services and perform them together rather than making separate trips for all services individually.

Length of trips reduces as the destination points change from centrally located government offices to locally distributed citizen centres. Quantification of impact of B1 transactions on city roads is difficult but the growth in number of users of B1 facilities can help us understand the quantum of trips being altered due to B1 services (Figure 16.7).

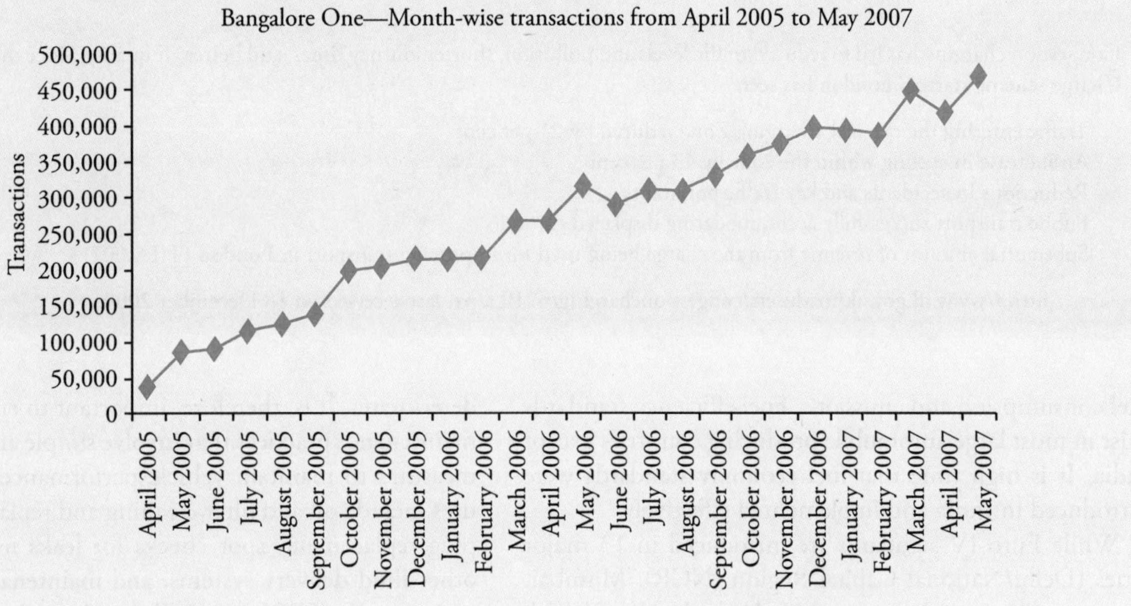

FIGURE 16.7 Month-wise Transactions Performed through B1 Citizen Service Centres in Bangalore

Source: Bangalore One Department (E-governance Secretariat), Bangalore.

Figure 16.7 shows the month-wise transactions being performed through B1 citizen service centres during 2005–7. Transactions have increased rapidly and consistently since the inception of the project. These transactions by B1 users may have helped to reduce some load on the roads of Bangalore by either reducing the need to undertake trips or by reducing the length of trips being undertaken. E-governance can serve as an effective tool/measure to solve the challenges of physical mobility indirectly. If its role in doing so is recognized and valued then such objectives may be integrated into the inherent designing of such programmes.

Source: TERI (2008b).

World experience has shown that an effective shift to public transport can occur only if transport demand management measures are adopted in tandem with increased provision of public transport (see Box 16.6). While with increasing per capita incomes and growing aspirations the ownership of private vehicles cannot be easily discouraged, it is possible to discourage the routine use of personal vehicles through an intelligent combination of interventions listed above.

IMPROVE: Using Efficient and Clean Vehicles and Improving the Traffic Movement in Cities

Clean and efficient vehicle technology needs to be used both for private and public modes in order to reduce their

Box 16.6
Congestion Charge in London

London suffered the worst traffic congestion in the UK. It was estimated that the city lost between £2–4 million every week in terms of time wasted due to congestion. The Mayor of London, who was appointed in 2000, enacted a scheme to meet the travel demands of the city. He introduced the Congestion Charge in 2003, as a part of a wider, comprehensive transport strategy. Vehicles, which drive within a clearly defined zone of central London between the hours of 07:00 and 18:00, Monday to Friday, have to pay an £8 daily Congestion Charge. Payment of the charge allows one to enter, drive within, and exit the Charging Zone as many times as one wishes on that day. The aim is to reduce traffic congestion and improve journey times by encouraging people to choose other forms of transport if possible. All funds raised from Congestion Charging are spent on London's transport facilities. Congestion charging thus contributes directly to the achievement of four transport priorities, as set out in the Mayor's Transport Strategy:

- to reduce congestion;
- to make radical improvements in bus services;
- to improve journey time reliability for car users; and
- to make the distribution of goods and services more efficient.

Impacts

Congestion charging has led to reduced traffic levels and pollution, shorter journey times, and better air quality. Since the Congestion Charge scheme started, London has seen:

- Traffic entering the original Charging Zone reduced by 21 per cent
- An increase in cycling within the zone by 43 per cent
- Reductions in accidents and key traffic pollutants
- Public transport successfully accommodating displaced car users
- Substantial amount of revenue from the charge being used for improving transport in London (TfL 2007)

Source: http://www.tfl.gov.uk/roadusers/congestioncharging/6710.aspx, last accessed on 18 December 2009.

fuel consumption and emissions. Fuel efficiency standards exist in most large automobile producing countries except India. It is high time that fuel economy standards were introduced in India and implemented effectively.

While Euro IV standards are introduced in 13 major cities (Delhi/National Capital Region (NCR), Mumbai, Kolkata, Chennai, Bangalore, Hyderabad, Ahmedabad, Pune, Surat, Kanpur, Agra, Sholapur, and Lucknow) from April 2010 and Bharat Stage III standards for the whole country are expected to be implemented by October 2010, no date has been fixed for the introduction of Euro IV norms for the rest of the country. It is important to define the roadmap for emission standards for these cities and the rest of the country to ensure progressive reduction of vehicular emissions and improvement in air quality all over the country. Given that India is emerging as a major exporter of cars conforming to the more stringent standards set in Europe it should be possible for the Indian auto industry to meet more stringent emission standards provided they are given adequate time and appropriate fuels are made available.

It is also critical to monitor the performance of the fleet by ensuring a proper inspection and maintenance regime for in-house vehicles in cities. It is obvious that with age and increased use, the performance of vehicles deteriorates. It is, therefore, important to encourage good maintenance practices that involve simple and inexpensive measures to maintain vehicle performance. These measures include oil and filter cleaning and replacement, spark plug replacement, spot checks for leaks in the fuel and other fluid delivery systems, and maintenance of correct tyre pressure (TERI 2006). To inculcate the habit of good vehicle maintenance it is important to develop robust inspection and maintenance systems for Indian cities. The Pollution Under Control (PUC) certificate systems now in place in Indian cities are woefully inadequate and serve little purpose. India cannot become a modern automobile nation unless it has a modern inspection and certification regime.

In addition to introducing a robust regime of fuel efficiency standards, emission norms, and inspection and maintenance certification regimes, cities also need to encourage the use of alternate fuels and clean vehicle technology. Successfully implemented clean technologies include hybrid cars, electric cars and two-wheelers, and flexi-fuel cars, cars, and three-wheelers using CNG and LPG. It should be possible for India to replace 50 per cent of motorized vehicles using fossil fuel by electric vehicles drawing electricity from renewables by 2050.

Improving the fuel efficiency of public transport modes is also very important from the energy and emissions perspective. It is vital to improve the fuel vehicle technology of buses used in the cities. A few cities like Delhi, Mumbai, and Surat have switched to a public transport system using CNG; a few others like Bangalore are testing the use of biofuels like ethanol in public buses to reduce their energy and emission impacts.

As discussed previously, congestion and idling leads to increased fuel burning and emissions in cities; an efficient traffic management system, therefore, is critical to ensuring minimum delays, less congestion, and optimal journey speeds. A number of technologies packaged together, also known as Intelligent Transport System (ITS) can play an important role in delivering such an efficient system in cities. A few cities like Hong Kong, Shanghai, Singapore, etc., are using ITS to improve their traffic flow. In India, Association For Intelligent Transport Systems (AITS) India has been established to foster the development and deployment of ITS in the country.[10] It is important to implement ITS based traffic management in our cities as manual management and simple measures cannot adequately help in improving the deteriorating traffic conditions.

Impacts of the 'Avoid, Shift, and Improve' Approach on Energy Consumption and CO_2 Emissions

The Avoid, Shift, and Improve approach recommended in the previous section would contribute to:

- Reduction in private vehicles on-road,
- Increase in public transport and NMT ridership, and
- A cleaner vehicle fleet.

These in turn would have a significant impact on the energy consumption levels and CO_2 emissions produced. As per TERI, 2006, the number of vehicles in the country will increase to about 670 million by 2030 at a GDP growth rate of 8 per cent in a business as usual (BAU) scenario, which is about the number of cars now in the world. As per this study, if the share of buses is increased to 75 per cent by 2030 and private vehicles and IPT modes meet the remaining 25 per cent of the travel demand, the fuel demand would decrease by 21 per cent and CO_2 emissions by 20 per cent as compared to the BAU scenario. Another TERI study, indicates 18 per cent reduction in motor fuel demand by 2030 as compared to the BAU if buses meet 70 per cent of the total road passenger travel demand in 2030 (TERI 2007). According to this study, if fuel efficiency of vehicles can be improved by 5 per cent and 20 per cent in 2015 and 2030, respectively, for the vehicles registered after 2010, a reduction of about 17 per cent is achievable in motor fuel consumption by 2030 as against the BAU scenario. Integrated land-use and transport planning can also reduce transport energy demand by 20 per cent by 2030 (TERI 2007). These numbers indicate the impact of different interventions on energy and CO_2 reduction. If these interventions are taken together, the reduction in energy use and CO_2 emissions could be very significant. It should be possible for India to achieve a significant reduction in CO_2 emissions from the urban transport sector by 2050.

Way Forward for the Indian Cities

It is important that cities in India recognize energy use and CO_2 emissions from their transport sector as a key issue of concern demanding immediate and proactive action. Urban transport plans and projects need to be viewed from this perspective. NAPCC also advocates the same through its sub-mission on urban transport. It suggests that better urban planning and a modal shift to public transport along with long-term transport plans are necessary to facilitate the growth of cities in a manner that is not hostile to the environment. The plan specifically lays emphasis on extensive public transport facilities and non-motorized modes in urban areas in order to discourage the use of personal motorized vehicles. It also draws attention towards initiating a switch to clean fuels, retiring old polluting vehicles, strengthening mass transportation, and promoting use of electric vehicles. The plan suggests some technical, fiscal, and policy actions to direct transport growth towards the path of sustainability. The roadmap outlined by NAPCC will be instrumental in achieving low carbon growth in future as the policies for the transport sector can be expected to be in line with recommendations of NAPCC. The NUTP also envisages integrated land-use transport planning, public transport, and NMT in cities.

This paper establishes that even 23 of the 35 million-plus cities have a significant share in energy consumption and CO_2 emissions by the transport sector, and if they were to adopt the interventions suggested above, they could make an equally significant contribution towards reducing energy consumption and CO_2 emissions. They need to be encouraged and adequately funded to meet their growing transport demands on a low carbon path. First, a good database should be established in all cities in order to assess past trends and make future projections

[10] http://www.itsindia.org/aitsindia/index.htm, last accessed on 19 December 2009.

accurately. Second, the cities need to develop inventories of their current energy consumption levels and CO_2 emissions and establish a base line. Third, they need to be encouraged to draw up or reboot their mobility plans and projects to meet growing transport needs based on the 'avoid, shift, and improve' approach. Fourth, cities should be encouraged to commit to a progressive reduction in the rate of growth in fossil fuel consumption and emissions, and monitor the impact of their policies and projects on fuel consumption and CO_2 emissions. Such an approach would help the country to reduce oil imports and meet the voluntary targets set for reducing CO_2 emissions. At a time when climate change is dominating the world agenda, it is important that cities in India respond to this challenge and work towards putting their transport sector on a sustainable low carbon path. This would be in India's national interest.

References

Agarwal, O.P. (2006). 'Urban Transport', in 3iNetwork, *India Infrastructure Report 2006*, Oxford University Press, New Delhi, India, pp. 106–29.

Automotive Research Association of India (ARAI) (2007). 'Emission Factor Development for Indian Vehicles', Draft report on as a part of Ambient Air Quality Monitoring and Emission Source Apportionment Studies. Project Rep No.: AFL/2006–07/IOCL/Emission Factor Project/Final Rep, ARAI, Pune.

Bangalore Department (E-governance Secretariat). Primary data collected from Bangalore1 Department (E-governance Secretariat), Bangalore, for a TERI study.

Bose, R.K. (2006). *Transport Sector and Climate Change in India: Forecast and Policy Recommendations.* Presented at Regional Workshop on 'Climate Change Mitigation in the Transport Sector' held at ADB Headquarters, Manila, 24–25 May 2006, available at http://www.cleanairnet.org/caiasia/1412/articles-70731_climate.ppt.

Central Pollution Control Board (CBCP) (2000). *Transport Fuel Quality for Year 2005.* Delhi.

Friberg, L. (2000). 'Innovative Solutions for Public Transport; Curitiba, Brazil', in Pink/Anna (ed.) *Sustainable Development International,* 4th Edition, ICG Publishing, Brighton, pp. 153–6,

Government of India (2001). *Census Handbook,* Registrar General and Census Commissioner, Government of India (GoI), New Delhi.

——— (2005). *National Urban Transport Policy,* Ministry of Urban Development, Government of India (GoI), New Delhi.

Deutsche Gesellschaft für Technische Zusammenarbeit (GTZ) (2009). *Transportation Demand Management. Division 44, Water, Energy and Transport,* B. Jain Publishers (P) Ltd., New Delhi.

International Energy Agency (2007). *World Energy Outlook 2007: China and India Insights.* International Energy Agency (IEA), Paris.

Kundu, A. (2006). 'Trends and Patterns of Urbanization and their Economic Implications' in 3iNetwork, *India Infrastructure Report 2006,* Oxford University Press, New Delhi, pp. 27–41.

Ministry of Petroleum and Natural Gas (MoPNG) (various years). *Indian Petroleum and Natural Gas Statistics,* Government of India, New Delhi.

Ministry of Road Transport and Highways (2009). *Road Transport Year Book (2006–07),* Government of India, New Delhi.

——— (2003). *Road Transport Year Book 2000–01,* Government of India, New Delhi.

——— (Various Years). *Road Transport Year Book/Motor Transport Statistics of India,* GoI, New Delhi.

National Institute of Disaster Management (NIDM) (2001). *Urban Risk Management.* Presented in Thematic Cluster J: Emerging Issues and Concerns at The Second India Disaster Management Congress held between 4–5 November 2009.

Planning Commission (2002). *Vision 2020 Transport prepared by Mahesh Kapoor,* GoI, New Delhi.

——— (2006). *Integrated Energy Policy: Report of the Expert Committee,* GoI, New Delhi,

Singh, S.K. (2005). 'Review of Urban Transportation in India', *Journal of Public Transportation,* 8(1).

TERI (2006a). *National Energy Map for India: Technology Vision 2030.* Report prepared by TERI for the Office of the Principal Scientific Adviser, The Energy and Resources (TERI) and Office of the Principal Scientific Adviser, Government of India, New Delhi.

——— (2006b). *Energy Efficiency and Climate Change Consideration for On-Road Transportation in India. (TERI Report No. 2005UG27),* The Energy and Resources Institute (TERI), New Delhi:

——— (2007). *Motor Fuel Demand and Auto Fuel Policies in India,* The Energy and Resources Institute (TERI), New Delhi.

———(2008a). *The Energy Data Directory and Yearbook 2007,* The Energy and Resources Institute (TERI), New Delhi.

——— (2008b). *Mobility for Development—Case Study in Bangalore,* The Energy and Resources Institute (TERI), New Delhi.

——— (various years). *The Energy Data Directory and Yearbook,* The Energy and Resources Institute (TERI), New Delhi.

Transport for London (TfL) (2007). *Central London Congestion Charging—Impacts monitoring Fifth Annual Report, July 2007,* Transport for London, London.

Wilbur Smith Associates Pvt. Ltd. and Ministry of Urban Development (2008). *Study on Traffic and Transportation Policies and Strategies in Urban Areas in India: Final Report,* Ministry of Urban Development and Wilbur Smith Associates Pvt. Ltd., New Delhi, May.

17 Pollution-Energy-Carbon Intensity of Urban Transport in India

Dynamics of Government Policy Intervention

Rita Pandey

Introduction

Growing oil consumption and its rising import share have triggered serious debates in many developed and developing countries on appropriate governmental intervention in stimulating fuel efficiency. Besides the macro-economic impact associated with oil price shocks, there are other externalities associated with oil consumption: burning of fossil fuels has a bearing on GHG emissions as well as other regulated emissions; imperfections in fuel efficiency markets due to consumer short-sightedness or technology spill-over effects may eventually lead to insufficient investments towards improving the fuel efficiency.

All over the world, the transport sector claims a significant share in the total demand for fuel. With sprawling cities the world over, distances between home, place of work, and services are increasing as is the demand for urban transport. Further, poor, inconvenient, and often time-inefficient and uneconomical public transportation as well as rising income levels in big cities create demand for private vehicles, which in turn results in increased demand for transport fuel.

Recognizing the important environmental and social benefits of reducing fuel consumption in the transport sector, governments in a number of countries in North America and Europe have taken measures to encourage improvement in the fuel economy of new vehicles. Examples include the Corporate Average Fuel Economy (CAFE) programme in the US and the Tax for Fuel Conservation (TFC) in Ontario, Canada. While CAFE follows a regulatory approach to achieving improvement in fuel performance of new vehicles, TFC involves an economic incentive to the purchasers of 'fuel efficient' vehicles and penalty on 'fuel inefficient' vehicles. Although TFC was the first feebate of its kind, the model has since been adopted elsewhere in Maryland and California. Also, vehicle manufacturers in France have taken upon themselves to voluntarily work towards improving fuel efficiency. A variety of other approaches such as subsidies/grants for research and development (R&D), insurance reforms, and fuel taxes have been strategically put forward in the literature in this regard.

The Tax for Fuel Conservation Programme, which is based on the US Energy Tax of 1978, began as a tax on fuel-inefficient vehicles in 1989. After a brief period of consensus building amongst representatives of the auto industry, the Canadian Auto Workers' Union, car-dealers, and environmental groups, the TFC was born in 1991. It is a feebate system, which taxes fuel-inefficient vehicles and rebates USD100 to the most fuel-efficient cars (under 6 L/100, km) (Barg et al. 2000: Table 17.1). The Ministry of Finance in Ontario administers the tax. The TFC programme was implemented for energy conservation and to reduce the environmental impacts of energy use by vehicles, particularly atmospheric pollution (NOS, VOCs, and COS).

It is reported that approximately 90 per cent of all cars in the market fall in the USD75 tax bracket, and neither a USD75 tax nor a USD100 rebate represents a significant portion of the total price of purchasing a new

Table 17.1 Tax for Fuel Conservation (TFC) 1991

Highway Fuel Consumption Tax Ratings (L/100 km) SUVs	*Tax/Rebate (VSD)*	*Passenger Vehicles*
Less than 6.0	(100)	0
6.0–7.9	75	0
8.0–8.9	75	75
9.0–9.4	250	200
9.5–12.0	1,200	400
12.1–15.0	2,400	800
15.1–18.0	4,400	1,600
Over 18.0	7,000	3,200

Source: Barg et al. (2000).

vehicle. Sales figures show that while there has been a shift towards fuel-efficient cars, there has simultaneously been an increase in the popularity of 'dirty' sport utility vehicles (SUVs). To what extent these two trends counteract each other in Ontario is not clear. A November 2000 guess estimate of revenues from TFC (Barg et al. 2000) put the total between USD40 and USD50 million per year respectively.

Given the low rates of tax and rebate, TFC acts more as a revenue-raising instrument with little or no impact on consumer behaviour.

The CAFE, first enacted by the US Congress in 1975, was intended to improve the average fuel economy of cars and light trucks (trucks, vans, and sport utility vehicles) sold in the US in the wake of the 1973 Arab oil embargo. Historically, it is the sales-weighted harmonic mean fuel economy, expressed in miles per gallon (mpg), of a manufacturer's fleet of current modal year passenger cars or light trucks with a gross vehicle weight rating (GVWR) of 8500 pounds (3856 kg) or less, manufactured for sale in the US.

The CAFE programme requires automobile manufacturers to meet standards for the sales-weighted average fuel economy of their passenger vehicle fleets: current standards are 27.5 mpg for cars and 20.7 mpg for light duty trucks. A 2002 report of the National Academy of Sciences on the effects of the CAFE standard found that in its absence, and with no other fuel economy regulation substituted, motor vehicle fuel consumption would have been approximately 14 per cent higher than it actually was in 2002. This is an encouraging finding favouring fuel economy regulation.

On 19 December 2007, the US passed the Energy Independence and Security Act, which aimed at improving vehicle fuel economy. The Act set a goal for the national fuel economy standard of 35 mpg by 2020. This would increase the fuel economy standards by 40 per cent and save billions of gallons of fuel. This standard is the first standard that has been set above the CAFE since it was created in 1975.

Studies that have analysed the economic efficiency and environmental effectiveness of both CAFE and TFC are discussed further in the chapter.

The Fuel Efficiency Debate in India

The Indian transport sector already consumes nearly one-fourth of the total commercial energy, and almost half of the total petroleum products in the country.[1] Energy demand from urban transport in Delhi alone is expected to increase three-fold over the next decade. It is reported that explosive growth in personal transport will dominate the increase in transport-related energy demand in the future. The compound annual rate of growth of vehicles during 1990–1 and 2001–2 was 9.2 per cent. The rate of growth was the highest for two-wheelers (9.7 per cent), followed by cars, jeeps, and taxis (8.6 per cent), others including tractors, trailers, three-wheelers, and other miscellaneous vehicles (8.0 per cent), goods vehicles (7.4 per cent), and buses (6.4 per cent). In the absence of public policies to encourage mass passenger transportation, the shares of two-wheelers and cars are likely to increase over time with the higher rate of growth in gross domestic product and also preferences towards a personal mode of transportation.

Considering the vast potential of energy savings and benefits of energy efficiency, the GoI enacted the Energy Conservation Act, 2001. The Act aims to promote end-use energy conservation and efficiency improvements. The Act also provides for the legal framework, institutional arrangement, and a regulatory mechanism at the central and state level to embark upon an energy-efficiency drive in the country. The focus of the Act, however, is only on electricity. It is significant to note that under the Indian Industry Programme for Energy Conservation (IIPEC),

[1] The steady growth in GDP and purchasing power of the Indian population has resulted in a corresponding growth in consumption of petroleum products in India. Over 70 per cent growth in road transport vehicles during the last five years is particularly significant in this regard. Moreover, in 2004–5, private vehicles constituted 82 per cent of the total vehicle sales (78.6 per cent two-wheelers and 13.44 per cent four-wheelers).

the Task Groups for textile, cement, pulp and paper, fertilizer, chlor-alkali, and aluminum have been formed. The transport sector/automobile industry is not included under the IIPEC.

The issue of promotion of fuel efficiency in automobiles was, however, discussed by the Expert Committee on Auto Fuel Policy in India (GoI 2002). Though the Committee recognized the merit of fuel efficiency of vehicles; no specific recommendations were made for bringing in fuel economy regulations. It is believed that this was largely under pressure from the vehicles manufacturers' lobby that put forth before the Committee the conventional wisdom that there is no relationship between fuel economy and motor vehicle emissions. Harrington (1997), however, rejected this argument. This argument also overlooked the potential benefits of resource conservation and GHG reduction that would subsequently result from improvement in fuel efficiency.

The Report of the Expert Committee on Auto Fuel Policy recommended various regulatory, fiscal, and institutional measures for containing vehicular emissions in India in a phased manner. In order to address the issue of fuel economy of vehicles, the Committee suggested a mandatory voluntary declaration of fuel economy by the manufacturers for each model 'to enable informed customer choice' (GoI 2002). The fact that such voluntary measures are not sufficient to address issues of fuel-inefficient vehicles on Indian roads came to sharper focus in a recent study on taxation of polluting inputs and outputs (Chelliah et al. 2007). This study shows how close we are to a worsening fuel economy. As of today, a large number of car models fall in the fuel economy range of 12–16 km/litre and their engine capacity ranges from 796 cc to 1,800 cc, with most models in the 796 cc to 1,400 cc range. But already a dramatic shift is evident towards mid-engine capacity (1,000–1,700 cc), a trend that is expected to only accelerate in the medium term. This segment is likely to dominate the Indian car market—already the combined share of the total sales in this segment has increased from 44.5 per cent in 2001 to 63.3 per cent in 2003 (ICRA 2003). The study thus observes that there is a need to simultaneously reduce the pollution-energy-carbon intensity of urban transport vehicles by sending appropriate signals through a system of incentives/disincentives.[2]

Moreover, since the regulation for enhanced environmental compliance in a phased manner (from 2005–10) has been enacted in India, environmental performance is likely to be the major factor prompting change in automobile technology in India. Therefore, this would be the right time to set the target for improvement in the fuel economy of vehicles. The objective of this chapter is to revisit this debate with a view to examine the rationale of policy intervention to encourage fuel economy of vehicles and identify appropriate policy measures for reducing pollution-energy-carbon intensity of transport in India.

Policies and Measures to Stimulate Fuel Economy

Despite a continuing need for fuel conservation in transport and curbing local and global emissions, India has not implemented any policy to increase the energy efficiency of road transport, notwithstanding the Energy Conservation Act passed in 2001. A number of policies could produce higher fuel economy, reduce oil use, and lower local regulated and GHG emissions.

Rationale

Discussion on the rationale of encouraging fuel economy of automobiles in the literature brings out the following concerns favouring government intervention (Portney et al. 2003; Greene et al. 2005; and Harrington 1997):

- Need for saving fuel;
- Environmental consequences; both local and global emissions; and
- Imperfect markets for improvements in fuel economy.

Need for Saving Fuel

The energy consumption in the domestic transport sector is increasing rapidly in the country because of the increased demand for passenger and freight transport, increasing private ownership of vehicles, and the substitution of road transport for rail or water transport for the movement of goods. India is an oil-importing country. Production of crude oil in India constitutes less than one-third of the total consumption demand. This gap is growing rapidly, resulting in an increase in the oil imports bill. Recognizing that oil dependence needs to be checked, the government strategically responded by setting up the Petroleum Conservation Research Association (PCRA).

One of the main objectives of the PCRA is to function as a *think tank* for the Government of India in terms of proposing policies and strategies on petroleum conservation and environment protection to reduce excessive

[2] The Report does not consider commercial freight and passenger vehicles as they have only a few models falling within a narrow band of variation in terms of fuel economy.

dependence on oil. PCRA plays the role of a catalyzing agency for achieving petroleum conservation in the transport, agriculture, industry, and domestic sectors. The major thrust areas of activities undertaken by PCRA in transport include driver training programmes, model garages, emission check programmes, engine replacement schemes, and mass awareness programmes. The inter-ministerial working group has identified a saving potential of 20 per cent in the transport sector (PCRA 2006). The current efforts alone may not be sufficient to realize this potential. Instead, it would require a sustained policy targeting behavioural attributes—driving habits, miles driven, good maintenance, etc., and determinants of choice of vehicle based on fuel economy, power, weight, and size.

Arguably, there are costs of our oil dependency including macro-economic effects of oil price volatility. The vulnerability of oil-importing countries to increase oil prices depends on the degree to which they are net importers of oil and the oil intensities of their economies. Since developing countries are less able to weather the financial turmoil wrought by higher oil-import cost, adverse economic impact is more severe than for developed countries. In India, the oil-import bill was as much as three per cent of GDP in 2003. A recent study (IEA 2004) estimated that loss of GDP in Asia would average around 0.8 per cent following a USD10 per barrel oil price increase. With the per capita consumption level in India being only about 60 per cent of that in China in 2001; a strong growth potential exists in India, particularly given the projections for higher GDP growth and a large population base of over a billion. The only way to insulate the economy from these disruptions is to reduce fuel intensity.

Environmental Consequences

The primary environmental justification for governmental intervention to reduce fuel consumption is concern about emissions produced from burning of oil—which have implications for future global climate change—and local regulated emissions. The former is of greater concern because unlike other auto emissions, abatement technologies do not exist for CO_2 emissions, so emissions are proportional to fuel use. A wide range of estimates of the economic impacts of future climate change on human health, agriculture, etc., is available in the literature. Apart from GHGs, fuel consumption results in emission of other regulated pollutants, namely carbon dioxide (CO_2), hydrocarbon (HC), and the oxides of nitrogen that create airborne particulates. Those opposing government intervention for fuel economy argue that since tail-pipe emissions in India are regulated, better fuel economy has no direct effect on pollutant emissions. This, however, is not correct. Emission standards in India for new vehicles are specified in terms of gram per kilometre rather than gram per litre of fuel. Thus, specification of standards assumes a fuel economy value based on some criteria not published by the regulators. Thus, the requirement that all vehicles meet a common emission standard based on gram per kilometre distorts the link between fuel economy and emissions both in new and on-road vehicles. Harrington (1997) shows that better fuel economy is strongly associated with lower emissions of CO_2 and HC and that the effect gets stronger as vehicles age. By the time vehicles get to be a decade old, fuel economy is a major factor in explaining emissions. The study also shows that a gram per gallon model is far more successful in explaining deterioration in vehicle emissions than a gram per mile model. This result has important policy implications for the methods used in estimating vehicle emission inventories as well as setting vehicular emission standards.

Imperfect Markets

A particularly contentious issue is whether the market can provide an optimal level of fuel economy or is government intervention required even in the absence of emissions or oil-dependency externalities. Technological solutions for improvement in fuel economy involve costs. Increase in costs to be paid upfront and the benefits in terms of future fuel savings is one set of determinants of demand for fuel economy. The other determinant is consumer preference for vehicle weight, power, and other design features which affect fuel economy of vehicles.

Many engineering studies suggest a wide range of technological possibilities for improving fuel economy that could pay for themselves in the vehicles' life-time through fuel savings (National Research Council 2002). The pertinent question then is: why vehicle manufacturers do not adopt the technologies that would pay for themselves? This can happen due to two reasons. First, when consumers undervalue potential fuel savings either due to short horizons (lack of information), or because they are uncertain about future fuel prices. This is a possibility in India, as it is not mandatory to put stickers on vehicles revealing fuel economy although this has been recommended by the government-appointed Expert Committee (GoI 2002). Presence of consumer myopia justifies a corrective action through government intervention.

Second, vehicle manufacturers perceive that consumers value fuel economy less than they actually do. In an oligopolistic automobile industry, as in India, profit-maximizing manufacturers can undersupply vehicle attributes even when potential buyers value them. Today, most fuel-efficient cars and two-wheelers available in India are twice and one and a half times more fuel efficient, respectively, over the current fleet average. This indicates there is substantial scope for improvement in fuel economy in other vehicles available in the market, and points to the need to investigate approaches such as mandatory fuel efficiency standards and consumer information programmes to realize CO_2 reduction more fully and harness potential fuel efficiency improvements. Significantly, enactment of CAFE in the US dramatically improved the fuel economy of vehicles (Greene et al. 2005).

Another potentially significant market failure arises from inadequate incentives for R&D into vehicle fuel economy. There is evidence to suggest that the social returns to R&D may exceed the private return (Mansfield et al. 1977).

Policies and Measures

A number of policies and measures have been used for stimulating transport fuel economy in various countries. These can broadly be grouped into price measures such as higher fuel prices/taxes, higher tax/fee on fuel-inefficient vehicles such as TFC; and non-price measures such as CAFE. The main role of public policy measures is to create the necessary conditions to encourage and speed up the development and production of fuel-efficient vehicles at affordable prices; increasing awareness about individual and national benefits of fuel efficiency; and risk sharing with producers and consumers of fuel-efficient vehicles. These can take several forms: energy efficiency regulation, fee, rebate, tax credit, etc.

The two criteria of environmental effectiveness and acceptability provide a broad framework for evaluating instruments of choice. In this chapter, these criteria have been used in examining the results of the studies reviewed here. On the basis of the discussion of these results, some inferences have been drawn about the choice of appropriate instruments. With regard to the first criterion, in many instances, it is difficult to provide precise and also comparable quantitative estimates because of data or informational limitations. For instance, evaluation of environmental effectiveness requires detailed information on baseline environmental parameters. For practical purposes, it is often necessary to rely on the strategically approximate estimates of environmental impacts of a particular instrument.

If information on baseline emissions factors and reduction in emissions due to application of a given policy were to be obtained from different studies—these may not be comparable on account of variation in the sample size of the studies, methods employed in analysis, different-weights employed in aggregating various pollutants, test procedures and cycles, emission characteristics of the vehicle stock, and, of course, assumptions employed in different studies. Such data limitations, however, are extremely difficult to overcome. Therefore, this chapter examines and discusses simulation studies that compare some of these alternate instruments.

The second criterion reflects the fact that instrument choice is also a political process and policymakers need to consider the practicalities of building political support as an integral part of policy formulation. However, political acceptability is only one of the several reasons why a policy may face problems of implementation. In this context, the relevant interest groups that should accept the policy include polluters, victims, environmental groups, and the voting and tax-paying people.

Fuel Pricing

In principle, an increase in fuel tax/price would provide an incentive both to increase fuel economy and reduce vehicle travel. However, in reality, besides the fact that most governments find it difficult to implement higher taxes on fuel (effectively increasing fuel prices) owing to the presence of a powerful constituency lobbying against higher taxes, this may not always be the most effective policy measure especially in dealing with market failures such as consumer myopia, oligopolistic structure of the auto industry, and inadequate R&D incentives for fuel economy. For instance, if consumers do undervalue fuel savings, an important implication for policymaking is that fuel taxation would have a smaller impact on improvement of fuel economy *vis-à-vis* fuel economy regulation. Shifting the price signal from fuel to the price of vehicle should then be more effective than a fuel tax. Also, Nivola and Crandall (1995) have identified a number of obstacles to higher fuel taxes in the US. These include high levels of vehicle ownership, poorly developed public transport system, and promotion of low density development. In India also, the poorly developed public transport system, fast growth in vehicle sales in the last four to five years, and the impact of fuel price corrections on the Consumer Price Index (CPI) are some of the factors which make the increase in fuel prices difficult. In fact, when the international prices of crude went up in 2007 and 2008, the government lowered taxes and effectively subsidized fuel. Taxation of fuel then appears to be just a component of various policies and measures of promoting fuel economy because of its much larger socioeconomic aspects, but it certainly determines the effectiveness of such policies and measures.

Fuel Economy Standards and Feebates

Little is known about how consumers estimate the value of improved fuel economy and factor that information into their vehicle buying decisions in most countries. Studies in the US show that the consumers undervalue the true economic value of fuel saving. For, they reckon only first three years or first 50,000 miles of fuel saving when considering the value of higher fuel economy (German 2002 and Patterson 2002). In another survey (Patterson 2002), when consumers were asked what they would be willing to pay for a doubling of fuel economy, the responses implied a much higher (five years) pay-back period as compared to three years in the earlier two studies. It could well be that the apparent undervaluing of fuel economy is a result of bounded rational behaviour. Further, consumers may not find it worth the effort to fully investigate the costs and benefits of fuel economy (Greene 1996).

However, if consumers undervalue fuel savings, there are several important implications for policymaking. Increasing the price of fuel would have a smaller impact on fuel economy. Setting fuel economy standards would be a more effective approach because regulation circumvents market failure. Shifting the price signal from fuel to the price of the vehicle should also be more effective than fuel tax. Vehicle prices appear to play an important role in their purchase decisions and this should motivate manufacturers to accurately weigh the costs and benefits of increasing fuel economy so as to avoid fees and capture rebates.

This clearly suggests that a system of rebates for high fuel-economy vehicles should be an effective fuel economy policy. To date, this has been used only in Canada and Austria. The essential elements of a feebate system are a pivot point that divides vehicles into two groups based on fuel economy—vehicles falling in one group are charged a fee and those in the other receive a rebate; and a rate that specifies the fee or rebate as a function of distance from the pivot point. A single pivot point can be used for all vehicles or they can be divided into classes (for example, passenger cars and light trucks) and different pivot points assigned to each class.

A key advantage of feebates over fuel economy standards is that they provide a continuing incentive to increase fuel economy as the new technologies are developed (Gordon and Levenson 1989). Disadvantages of feebates include the possibility that they will be perceived as a kind of tax and that they will undoubtedly confer different benefits and costs on different manufacturers. The first disadvantage can be mitigated by designing feebates to be revenue neutral. The second disadvantage can be mitigated by establishing different feebate schedules for different vehicle classes.

Previous Studies of Feebates

Greene et al. (2005) presents a comprehensive review of previous studies of feebates here. Previous studies are also reviewed here with a view to find answers to the following:

- Whether feebate was effective in encouraging fuel economy; and
- Whether it produced technological innovation.

A comprehensive study (Davis et al. 1995) for the US found that adoption of fuel-economy technology accounted for about 90 per cent of the overall increase in fuel economy brought about by feebate systems. Changes in consumers' choices (shifting sales towards higher fuel-economy vehicles) were always considered a minor factor.

A potential feebate system for Canadian vehicles based on GHG emissions was assessed in a study for the Canadian government (HLB Decision Economics Inc. 1999). One of the objectives of the study was estimating the effect of a Canada-only feebate system versus a harmonized US–Canada system. The study concluded that the latter was more cost-effective with a marginal benefit of US two dollars per tonne versus marginal cost of USD60 per tonne of GHG reduced in the case of the former.

Feebates for reducing CO_2 emissions from cars in Europe were evaluated by Koopman (1995). The study divided cars into five classes: small, medium, and large petrol vehicles, plus diesel, and liquid petroleum gas (LPG). The feebates approximately equal to about USD700–1175 per 0.01 gallons per mile produced an estimated reduction of 11.8 per cent in fuel use and in CO_2 emissions of 10 per cent. Another study (DRI 1991) in the US which evaluated a feebate system and a gas-guzzler tax found, like Davis et al., that the overwhelming majority of the fuel saving from feebates came from the adoption of fuel-efficient technology by manufacturers (mix shifting never accounted for more than 18 per cent of the increase). Greene et al. (2005) assessed feebates using recent data for the US and found that a feebate rate of USD500 per 0.01 gallons per mile produces a 16 per cent increase in fuel economy, while a USD1000 per 0.01 gallons per mile results in a 29 per cent increase, even if consumers count only the first three years of fuel savings. Unit sales decline by about 0.5 per cent but sales revenue increases because the added value of fuel-economy technologies outweighs the increase in sales. In all cases, a vast majority of fuel economy increase is due to the adoption of fuel-economy technologies rather than shifts in sales.

Other Economic Measures Targeting Cars

A study conducted by the World Energy Council (WEC 2001) surveyed 50 member countries to identify policy measures which have been effective in encouraging fuel efficiency of vehicles. The measures discussed in the report, however, pertain mainly to cars. This section summarizes some of the major findings of the report. The report observes that the share of car-related expenditure in household budgets (around 15 per cent) suggests that economic measures should have an influence on the key factors which affect energy use and CO_2 emissions by cars: ownership levels, annual usage, and specific consumption/emissions.

Incentives for Scrapping Old Cars: These incentives often have a double objective: to accelerate the renewal of the car fleet to stimulate the car industry; and to remove old cars from the fleet as they are usually fuel-inefficient and have a high level of emissions. It is usually a temporary measure implemented over one to two years. Such a measure has been implemented in about 10 countries (see Annexure 17A.1). Evaluations show that this measure accelerates the renewal of the fleet, but may have unintended side effects, including 'free riders' and a shift to bigger cars.

Subsidies for Clean and Efficient Cars: Subsidies for clean and efficient cars are not so common: only 10 countries in the sample provide subsidies to buyers of electric or CNG cars (Annexure 17A.1). The main objective is to reduce the price of these cars, which are more expensive to buy but have lower utilization costs. A second objective is to create a market for such cars, so as to reduce the production cost through increased production levels.

Car Ownership Tax: The second level of taxation is on car ownership. Consumers will take an annual registration tax into account in their car buying decisions (whether a new or a used car). The main advantage of such a tax is its visibility. Because it is not associated with any other payment, people are aware of the level of the tax, and car manufacturers take it into account in their strategy.[3] In most countries, this tax varies according to an index representative of the power of the car, which has a link with fuel consumption. On the other hand, this link is not absolute and in a few cases a more powerful engine may be more efficient. A move towards more explicit consideration of CO_2 emissions can be observed in a few countries.

Road Pricing: Road pricing and tolls for road use are never in place on the total territory of a country. Tolls are generally limited to certain freeways. Toll freeways are important in France, Italy, and Spain, for example, but freeways are generally free of charge in countries such as the Netherlands, the UK, and Germany. Moreover, there is generally a free-of-charge alternate road in countries for toll freeways. Road pricing occurs only in a few countries (Norway and Singapore) in some urban areas such as Singapore, Oslo, Trondheim, and Bergen. Road pricing may have some effect on CO_2 emissions, because it leads to smoother traffic flow. On the other hand, people may divert their journeys from these areas, which are generally high-density zones, and drive more elsewhere. There is no clear evidence to assess the effect, which is in any case limited.

Car Purchase Tax: Some countries levy a value added tax (VAT), and registration fees on purchase of a new car. The latter can either be one time or an annual fee. This is very often the case in car-producing countries, such as France, Germany, the UK, and Italy. It is now also the case in Sweden, where a specific tax on car purchases existed up to 1997.

In other countries, there may be a specific tax on car purchases such as the 'gas-guzzler tax' in the United States, designed to restrain sales of high-consumption cars. Car manufacturers have the ability to adapt to the requirements of the regulations through technology, and the effect is relatively limited because only a few cars are affected. In other cases, such taxes result from long-term policies designed to deter people from buying a car—this is the case in Singapore, Denmark, Norway, and Finland, and also in some developing countries where cars are an important component of imports. Even though these taxes may be based on technical characteristics, their level is mainly dependent on the vehicle's price. The pre-tax price of the car reflects indirectly the level of consumption, since consumption is related to weight and power.

There is some concern about unintended effects from such taxes. First, high taxes can deter consumers from buying new cars, and thus the penetration of new technologies is slower. Second, a high level of tax on car purchases concentrates the new car market on the most affluent part of the population, whose tastes may be more oriented towards higher consumption of cars. Furthermore, there is evidence to show that there is a wide

[3] In France, for example, a significant step in the ownership tax at the eight fiscal horse power threshold has been an incentive for car manufacturers, and for consumers to choose cars under the threshold.

variation in the specific consumption of cars falling in a category (compact, mid-size, large, and SUV), suggesting that price-based taxation is a poor proxy for CO_2 taxation. Difference in fuel economy (litres per 100 km) between the best and worst gasoline sub-compact, compact, mid-size, large and sport utility vehicles was 3.8, 4.1, 4.7, 4.8, and 8 respectively (IEA 2004). Thus a more direct consideration of specific consumption should contribute more effectively to fuel economy and the limitation of CO_2 emissions. However, in Europe, some countries (such as Austria) integrate fuel consumption or CO_2 emissions as a component of the basis for taxation. Some others (such as France) offer subsidies for LPG or electric cars (Annexure 17A.1).

Fuel economy cost curves presented by Fulton (2004) show the cost of introducing better technologies for a given type of vehicle. Fulton estimates that for Denmark, Germany, and the US, fuel economy for new cars as high as two litres per 100 km is achievable for as little as USD600 (before tax) per car. Market studies show that consumers do not necessarily take this trade-off into account, because their own discount rate is quite high (a 20 per cent figure is estimated).[4] As a result, car manufacturers do not introduce these technologies at the optimal rate.

Taxation on Motor Fuels: There are large differences between countries in the taxation of motor fuels, both gasoline and diesel. In Europe, such taxes are definitely much higher than in the rest of the world for three reasons:

- Most European countries are oil importers;
- Revenue from motor fuel tax is an important source of income for government budgets; and
- There is a strong commitment to meet Kyoto targets, and one way to do this to regularly increase the tax on motor fuels (by adding CO_2/environmental taxes to the existing taxes on fuels).

The last phenomenon is clear in Denmark, Germany, the UK, and to a lesser extent in the Netherlands and Austria.

The level of fuel taxes can be compared to an index of national wealth (for example, per capita GDP) to appreciate their weight. This indicator shows a clear hierarchy: it is lowest for the US, followed by Australia and Canada, and then Switzerland; the 15 European Union (EU) countries follow thereafter. Countries from Central and Eastern Europe have a ratio at least twice as high as the EU, which may explain the lower level of car ownership and use.

Many studies (Goodwin 1988; Orfeuil 1990; and Johansson and Schipper 1997) have demonstrated a link between the quantity of fuel used and its price over time. Their results are consistent, and converge towards a long-run elasticity of fuel consumption to a fuel price of -0.7. While the short-term elasticity is not very high (between -0.2 to -0.3), the long-term elasticity is quite significant: in the long run, a 10 per cent increase in the price of motor fuel leads to a one per cent reduction in the car stock, a two per cent reduction in the mileage per car, and a four per cent increase in fuel efficiency (that is, a total reduction in consumption of seven per cent). The intervals of variation around the median of these estimates are relatively large, which means that other components of policy (other types of fiscal and non-fiscal measure) are of importance as well.

Other Measures: Two other fiscal measures are discussed, even though no international comparison is available. The first is income tax relief related to journeys to work. In France, wage earners have the option to deduct from their taxable income either a standard deduction of 10 per cent or their real cost of commuting. Commuting distances up to 40 kms are accepted without discussion, and distances over this limit have to be justified. The majority of wage earners use the standard deduction. These rules differ from one country to another, and some governments, such as the Netherlands and the UK, have limited the relief either in terms of distance or by allowing it for public transport use only.

The second is policy towards company cars. Companies are important players in new car markets, both for their own needs and to provide employees with cars as a part of their remuneration. In the UK, around 50 per cent of new cars are bought by companies. Cars are kept by companies for two to three years, and are then sold to individual buyers. As the criteria of companies in choosing cars may be different from those of individuals, this may lead to an upsizing of the car fleet.

Summarizing the findings of this review, following observations can be made.

- Even though there are limitations to empirical findings, the basic conclusion is that the consumer is

[4] For example, a car consuming one litre less per 100 km, driven for 15 000 km/year for 10 years will provide (at USD1 per litre), a USD1500 saving. This saving is USD1200 at a discount rate of five per cent, USD750 at a discount rate of 20 per cent.

responsive to price signals at every level. From a policy perspective, the European situation is far from optimal. While car manufacturers in the US have a homogeneous market, those in Europe face a range of quite different taxation regimes. Because purchase taxes are concentrated on small markets (high-price segment), and are not directly related to fuel consumption, they do not provide an effective incentive for manufacturers to promote better technologies.

- According to the European Automobile Manufacturers Association Agreement, CO_2 emissions of new cars were planned to decrease from 185g/km in 1995 to 140 g/km in 2008. Comparison of 1995 and 1999 values suggests that European manufacturers are on track. However, this does not ensure a parallel decrease in total fuel consumption, since some type of rebound effect may occur. Taxes on car purchases and ownership should depend, at least partly, on specific consumption. This would help car manufacturers to comply with their commitment, and probably to go further.
- In cases where new technology would not prove sufficient and/or would be too expensive, restrictions on the introduction of new cars with high-specific consumption could be considered ('gas guzzler' taxes, prohibition of vehicles with maximum speed above a threshold, etc.). Another direction could be explored at the level of usage, by cancelling income tax relief linked to commuting, at least in situations where public transport is a potential alternative.

A Case for Purchase Tax on New Vehicles Based on Fuel Economy in India

The share of new vehicles introduced every year is about one-tenth of the stock of vehicles in use. The Government of India has taken a number of steps to control vehicular emissions. These include improvement in fuel quality, introduction of CNG as cleaner auto fuel in some identified cities, setting a retirement age for commercial vehicles, and laying down a road-map for implementing vehicular emission norms for new vehicles.

These interventions do not target fuel economy of vehicles. The present tax policy in India also does not take into consideration the energy efficiency of vehicles. It may be noted that petroleum is an exhaustible resource and India, at present, meets 73 per cent of its petroleum demand via imports, which is expected to go up to 85 per cent by 2020. Hence, some discouragement for the use of hydrocarbons is in order.

Raising tax on auto fuels is an obvious candidate. However, tax burden on petroleum products in India is already quite high. According to the Sixth Report of the Standing Committee of the Parliament on Petroleum and Gas, which submitted its report recently, taxes and duties levied on these products, including levies by the states, are the highest in the world, that is, at about 132 per cent of the basic price.

In line with the changes in the international price of crude oil and other macroeconomic considerations, the government has made appropriate changes in custom and excise duty of petroleum products from time to time. Unfortunately, these so far appear *ad hoc*, lacking in transparency and indicating no proper direction or purpose. For instance, while the government wants to subsidize retail prices of kerosene and domestic LPG, it does not do it entirely through budgetary support. Oil companies are made to bear a substantial portion of it by cross-subsidizing these products through higher prices of auto fuels.

It is, therefore, time that the government formulated a comprehensive strategy to deal with rising crude prices. The strategy should include not only a pragmatic pricing policy for petroleum products, but also long-term measures to take care of the country's energy security. Keeping prices artificially low will result in inefficient energy use. According to the International Energy Agency (IEA), the energy intensity of the Indian economy is nearly three times that of developed countries. Hence, all efforts are needed to ensure that the energy intensity is reduced through technological improvement and increased productive efficiency. According to energy experts, the price signals in the economy should be used to trigger inter-fuel substitution and curb unnecessary use of energy in a big way.

In many OECD countries, taxes on motor vehicles have been restructured to incorporate environmental concerns, while also fulfilling the basic objectives of revenue. Further, there is evidence (IEA 2004; WEC 2001; GoI 2002; and Greene et al. 2005) in support of the introduction of measures to encourage fuel economy of vehicles. Furthermore, India is in a high growth phase of demand for fuel, it already has high dependence on oil imports and regulations for enhanced environmental compliance are already in place. These regulations are likely to drive the change in automobile technology in India. In view of all these factors, this is perhaps the opportune time to set targets for improvements in fuel economy of vehicles by sending appropriate signals through a tax on purchase of vehicles which would, at least partly, depend on vehicle fuel efficiency.

Basis for Vehicle Purchase Tax[5]

In theory, the tax should be equal to the marginal environmental damage costs. An adequate estimate of marginal environmental costs is difficult to obtain. There exists only one example—the UK land-fill tax, introduced in October 1996—which is explicitly based on an estimate of the damage costs. In view of the non-availability of reliable estimates of marginal environmental damage costs, incentive effects and revenue raising become underlying criteria in setting environmental taxes. According to Ribeiro et al. (1999), two other criteria may substitute the theoretical criterion of tax rate being equated to marginal environmental damage costs. These are environmental effect (that is, the effect of tax on environmental pollution) and incentives effect (that is, a comparison with the marginal pollution-abatement costs, or as a proxy, the average abatement costs of the measures taken by the tax payers). The first criterion directly attempts to trace the contribution of the tax to the monitored pollution reduction, while the second criterion endeavours to establish incentives for tax payers to change their behaviour in a way that is more favourable to the environment often by adopting abatement measures.

Since the road-map of emission norms for new vehicles has been set in India, it is expected that the issues in emission performance of new vehicles would be taken care of. It may, however, be noted that two vehicles of the same class/type (say passenger cars) may conform to a given emission standard (specified in g/km), say Euro II, yet total emissions of these vehicles (including GHG emissions) may be at variance if fuel consumption (per km) of these vehicles varies. This is both because fuel efficiency may deteriorate over a period and that the emission factor itself depends on the efficiency of fuel combustion as well as fuel efficiency of the vehicle. Thus, the fuel economy of vehicles is of great significance both for fuel conservation as well as GHG and local regulated emissions.

Setting the Rate of Tax

The incentive structure can be linked to:

- the cost of upgrading the engine technology, and
- the benefits derived from such upgradation, which is sum of health damage cost forgone due to less fuel burnt per km and resultant lower emissions.

The incentive structure can also be a weighted average of both the above factors. However, there is very sketchy or no information available on both aspects. As far as vehicle technology is concerned, there is no information available in the public domain on cost requirements to bring about better fuel economy for different models and all categories of vehicles.

The calculation of benefit in terms of health cost forgone is difficult due to non-estimation of dose-response functions in the Indian vehicular pollution context through epidemiological studies. Indian data in regard to the proportion of vehicular emissions-related morbidity and its impact on health are insufficient. Therefore, a differential tax structure is being suggested based on the fuel economy of different types of vehicles complying with various Euro norms.

The fact is that only private vehicles have been considered for purchase tax in this chapter.[6] This is mainly because commercial vehicles such as buses, trucks, three-wheelers, and light commercial vehicles currently have only a few models and these fall within a narrow band of variation in terms of fuel economy. Further, in the case of heavy duty vehicles, fuel economy data in km/litre is not available as the heavy engines are tested separately on the engine dynamometer and fuel consumption is recorded in grams per kilowatt hour. In the private vehicle category, two-wheelers, cars, and jeeps have been considered. Although fuel economy achieved by certain two-wheelers in India is comparable/superior to that achieved in other countries for the same class of vehicles, there is a lot of scope for improvements in view of the entry of a large number of motorbikes in India.

Data on fuel economy of vehicles have been obtained from Society of Indian Automobile Manufacturers (SIAM). Fuel economy data are based on Type Approval Tests conducted under controlled environment. On-road fuel consumption of vehicles would depend upon factors such as traffic conditions, vehicle condition, and driving habits. Since the proposed tax directly targets the fuel consumption of vehicles, it may be more appropriate to call it a 'resource tax'. In addition to conservation of resources, the resource tax would have an impact on emissions of both local and global pollutants. The resource tax factor has been derived on the basis of categorization of vehicles based on fuel economy. The Society of Indian

[5] Sections on 'Basis for Vehicle Purchase Tax', Setting the Rate of Tax', and 'Rates of Resource Tax' of this chapter draw heavily from Chapter 4 in Chelliah et al. (2007).

[6] In the eight major cities in India, the traffic load in terms of vehicle kilometres per day is mainly (70–80 per cent) constituted by private automobiles (cars and two-wheelers). In each of the eight cities, the largest single contributor to the traffic load is two-wheelers (GoI 2002: 72).

Automobile Manufacturers has provided data for a few makes of two- and four-wheelers. These data are for Bharat Stage II vehicles. Data on passenger cars and jeeps show strong negative correlation between engine capacity and fuel economy of the vehicles, indicating that the fuel economy of vehicles decreases with an increase in engine capacity. The following main observations can be made on the basis of data provided by SIAM:

- Vehicles reporting fuel economy less than 10 have engine capacity of 2000 cc and above;
- Of the four makes of vehicles falling in the fuel economy range of 10–12, three have engine capacity of 2300 cc and above. One has engine capacity of around 1800 cc. This suggests that the vehicle technology is an important determinant of fuel economy, although engine capacity of vehicles also has a strong bearing on their fuel economy;
- A large number of vehicles are in the fuel economy range of 12–14 km per litre. Many of these have engine capacities below 1800 cc. Some vehicles, however, have higher engine capacity; and
- Fuel economy category of 14–16 km per litre also has a large number of vehicles. Most of these, however, have engine capacities that are less than 1500 cc.

There is a large concentration of vehicles in the fuel economy range of 12–16 km per litre. Engine capacity of most of these cars range between 1000 cc and 1800 cc. The trend towards higher engine capacity is already evident in the figures for FY 2003. This trend is likely to accelerate in the medium term. Eventually, the 1000–1700 cc segment is likely to dominate the Indian car market (the combined share of the total sales in this segment increased from 44.5 per cent in FY 2001 to 63.3 per cent in FY 2003) (ICRA 2003).

Rates of Resource Tax

The proposed resource tax rates for two-wheelers, passenger cars, and jeeps are given in Table 17.2. The resource tax factors are arrived at based on fuel economy slabs. This tax factor has been computed as follows. The resource tax factor for the best fuel economy category is taken as 1 for both cars and two-wheelers. For the next fuel economy category, the resource tax factor for two wheelers is calculated as 61/1x55 (where 55 is the average of the fuel economy range in this category). Similarly, the resource tax factor for the next category of two-wheelers would be 61/45. There is no resource tax for the most fuel-efficient vehicle. The rate of resource tax increases as the fuel economy of vehicles decreases. For the worst fuel economy categories for two-wheelers and passenger cars/jeeps, the resource tax is proposed to be at three per cent and five per cent respectively, on factory price of vehicles before excise tax (central) is levied.

The resource tax for the next fuel economy category for two wheelers is calculated as (3x1.33)/1.5. The rate of resource tax in this case works out to 2.66. For ease of implementation, this has been rounded off to 2.5 (see Table 17.2: column 4, row 2). The rate of resource tax for other categories has also been rounded off to keep the tax rate structure simple. Similarly, for passenger cars and jeeps, the slab exceeding more than 18 km to the litre has a resource tax factor of 1 and for the slab less than 10 km per litre, the tax factor is fixed at 1.67. The best fuel-economy passenger cars and jeeps would be exempt from the resource-tax. For the least fuel-efficient category, the tax rate is five per cent.

The rates indicated below clearly show that what is aimed at is differential taxation to induce the incidence effect as well as higher rate corresponding to higher cost. Since the central value added tax (CENVAT) rate is already high, the resource tax rates are pitched low.

Table 17.2 Rates of Resource Tax

Vehicle	*Fuel Economy (km/litre)*	*Resource tax Factor*	*Rate of Resource tax (per cent)*
Two-wheelers	0–40	1.5	3.0
	41–50	1.33	2.5
	51–60	1.09	2.0
	61 and above	1	–
Passenger Cars/Jeeps	<10	1.67	5
	10–14	1.25	3
	12–18	1.11	2
	>18	1	–

Source: Author's own estimates.

Conclusion

It is being increasingly recognized in India that there is a need to implement measures to reduce energy intensity in various sectors including transport. The inter-ministerial group has identified energy-saving potential of up to 20 per cent in the transport sector. Fuel saving has implications not only for resource conservation but also for reduction in local regulated emissions and greenhouse gases. This chapter revisits the vehicle fuel economy debate in India to assess whether government intervention is necessary to stimulate the fuel economy in India and what form should it take. It reiterates that since the regulation for enhanced environmental compliance is already in place, environmental performance is likely to be the major factor prompting change in automobile technology in India. This is, therefore, the right time to set the target for improvement in fuel economy of vehicles by sending appropriate signals through a differentiated tax on vehicles. Technological innovations targeting emission standards and fuel economy standards simultaneously might turn out to be more cost-effective *vis-a-vis* when this will be attended to one by one.

The chapter recommends a differentiated tax on purchase of new vehicles based on fuel economy of vehicles. Rates of tax have been suggested for two categories of vehicles: passenger cars, jeeps, etc. and two-wheelers. Each vehicle category is sub-divided into three classes for tax purposes. With further growth in the auto industry both in size and the range of models, we may graduate to the modified CAFE.

It is also being observed here that emission standards in India for new vehicles are specified in terms of gram per kilometre rather than gram per litre of fuel. Thus, specification of standards assumes a fuel economy value based on some criteria not published by the regulators. Further, the requirement that all vehicles meet a common emission standard based on gram per kilometre distorts the link between fuel economy and emissions both in new and on-road vehicles. This has important policy implications for the methods used in estimating vehicle emission inventories as well as setting vehicular emission standards.

References

Barg, Stephan., A. Duraiappah, and S.V. Exan (2000). *Economic Instruments for Environmental Policy Making in Ontario,* Research Paper #2, International Institute for Sustainable Development, December.

Chelliah, R.J., P.A. Appasamy, U. Sankar, and Rita Pandey (2007). *Ecotaxes on Polluting Inputs and Outputs*, Academic Press, New Delhi.

Davis, W.B., M.D. Levine, K. Train, and K.G. Duleep (1995). 'Effects of Feebates on Vehicle Fuel Economy, Carbon Dioxide Emissions, and Consumer Surplus', DOE/PO-0031. Office of Policy, US Department of Energy, Washington, DC, February.

DRI (1991). *An Analysis of Public Policy Measures to Reduce Carbon Dioxide Emissions from the US Transportation Sector*, Standards and Poors, Lexington, MA.

Fulton, Lew. (2004). *Reducing Oil Consumption in Transport: Combining Three Approaches*, Report no. EET/2004/01, Paris.

German, J. (2002). *Honda of America*, Ann Arbor, MI.

Goodwin, P.B. (1988). 'Evidence on Car and Public Transport Elasticities', TSU Paper 427, Oxford University, UK.

Gordon, D., and L. Levenson (1989). *Drive: A Proposal for California to Use Consumer Fees and Rebates to Reduce New Motor Vehicle Emissions and Fuel Consumption*, Applied Science Division, Lawrence Berkeley Laboratory, Berkeley, CA, July, p. 131.

Government of India (GoI) (2002). *Expert Committee Report on Auto Fuel Policy*, Government of India, New Delhi.

Greene, David L., P.D. Patterson, M.Sing, and J. Li (2005). 'Feebates, Rebates, and Gas-Guzzler Taxes: A Study of Incentives for Increased Fuel Economy', *Energy Policy*, 33, pp. 757–5.

Greene, David L. (1998). 'Why CAFE Worked', *Energy Policy*, 26(8), pp. 595–614.

——— (1996). *Transportation and Energy*. The Eno Transportation Foundation, Inc., Washington DC.

Harrington, Winston (1997). 'Fuel Economy and Motor Vehicle Emissions', *Journal of Environmental Economics and Management,* 33, pp. 240–52.

HLB Decision Economics, Inc. (1999). 'Assessment of a Feebate Scheme for Canada', Final Report (Draft) prepared for Natural Resources, Canada.

ICRA (2003). *ICRA Industry Watch Series*, ICRA Information, Grading and Research Service, ICRA Ltd., New Delhi (www.icraindia.com).

IEA (2004). *Analysis of the Impact of High Oil Prices on the Global Economy*, IEA, Paris.

Johansson, O. and L. Schipper (1997). 'Measuring Long Run Fuel Demands of Cars', *Journal of Transport Economics and Policy*, 30(1), pp. 277–92.

Koopman, G.J. (1995). 'Policies to Reduce CO_2 Emissions from Cars in Europe: A Partial Equilibrium Analysis', *Journal of Transport Economics and Policy*, 30 (1), pp. 53–70.

Mansfield, Edwin, J. Rappaport, A. Romeo, Samuel Wagner, and G. Beardsley. (1977). 'Social and Private Rates of Return from Industrial Innovations,' *Quarterly Journal of Economics,* 16, pp. 221–40.

National Research Council (2002). *Effectiveness and Impact of Corporate Average Fuel Economy (CAFE) Standards*, National Academy Press, Washington, DC.

Nivola, Pietro, and Robert Crandall (1995). *The Extra Mile*, The Brookings Institution, Washington, DC.

Orfeuil, J.P. (1990). 'Tax Regimes and Co_2 Emissions', available at http://www.wec.org.

Patterson, P. (2002). *Personal Communication, Office of Energy Efficiency, and Renewable Energy*, US Department of Energy, Washington, DC.

Petroleum Conservation and Research Association (PCRA) (2006). *Annual Report*, Ministry of Petroleum, Government of India, New Delhi.

Portney, Paul R., Ian W.H. Parry, Howard K. Gruenspecht, and W. Harrington (2003). 'The Economics of Fuel Economy Standards,' *Journal of Economic Perspectives*, 17(4), pp. 203–17.

Ribeiro, M.T., K. Schlegelmilch, and O. Gee (1999). 'Environmental Taxes Seem to be Effective Instruments for the Environment', in Thomas Sterner (ed.), *The Market and the Environment—The Effectiveness of Market-Based Policy Instruments for Environmental Protection,* Edward Edgar, UK and Massachusetts, USA, pp. 184–6.

World Energy Council (WEC) (2001). *Energy Efficiency Policies and Indicators*, World Energy Council, UK.

ANNEXURE 17A.1

TABLE 17A.1 Overview of Fiscal Measures on Cars

OECD Countries: Europe

	Purchase Tax(1)	*Annual Registration Tax* †	*Incentives for Car Scrapping* ‡	*Incentives for Clean/Efficient Car*
Austria	λ	λ		4
Belgium	λ	λ		
Denmark	λ λ	λ	4	4
Finland	λ λ	λ		
France	μ		T	4
Germany	μ	λ		
Greece	λ	λ	4	
Italy	λ	λ	T	
Ireland	λ	λ	T	
Portugal	λ	μ	P	
Spain	μ		4	
Sweden		λ	T	
Netherlands	λ	λ		4
UK	μ	λ		
Norway	λ λ			
Switzerland		λ		4[1]
Turkey	λ	λ		
Czech Rep.				
Hungary	λ	λ	4	
Poland				
Slovakia		4		

(†) λ: Average tax
λ λ: Very high tax
μ: Low tax
(‡) T: Terminated; P: Planned

Asian and Pacific

	Purchase Tax	*Annual Registration Tax*	*Incentives for Car Scrapping*	*Incentives for Clean/Efficient Car*
Australia			P	
Canada	4	4	4	
Japan	4	4	T	4
Korea	4	4		
Mexico	4			
USA[2]		4		4

[1] Only in one community as a pilot project.

[2] There exists purchase tax and annual registration tax in some states.

Non-OECD Countries/Economies

	Purchase Tax	*Annual Registration Tax*	*Incentives for Car Scrapping*	*Incentives for Clean/Efficient Car*
Chile		4		
Colombia		4		
Hong Kong, China	4	4	4	4
Indonesia	P			
Malaysia	4	4		
PNG		4		
Russia		4		
Taiwan, China	4	4	4	4
Bulgaria	4	4		
Estonia	4	4		
Latvia		4		
Romania	4	4		
Slovenia	4	4		
Egypt	4	4		

Note: No tax or incentives in India, Peru, Philippines, Peru, Vietnam, Lithuania, Algeria, Cameroon, and South Africa.
Source: WEC (2001).

18 Carbon Dioxide Emission Reduction Potential from Civil Aviation Sector

A Case Study of Delhi–Mumbai Air Route

Yenneti Komalirani and Joshi Gauravkumar

Introduction

Air transport is an important marker of modern society and plays an integral role in the development of the economy. Since its advent in India in December 1912, the sector has witnessed 5 to 8 per cent growth in demand per annum. Aviation is a major contributor to the economic and social well-being of India, connecting it to the world as a trading nation, and fostering economic growth and prosperity. With the phenomenal growth[1] of the sector, its environmental impact has also intensified simultaneously. Aviation is increasingly being singled out as a major source of GHG emissions, a significant contributor to global climate change, and a source of air pollutants. It has been said that one person flying in an airplane for one hour is responsible for the same GHG emissions as a typical Bangladeshi leading his life through a whole year (Beatrice Schell).[2]

> Human-generated emissions at the Earth's surface can be carried aloft and affect the global atmosphere. The unique property of aircraft is that they fly several kilometers above the Earth's surface. The effects of most aircraft emissions depends strongly on the flight altitude and whether aircraft fly in the troposphere or stratosphere. The effects on the atmosphere can be markedly different from the effects of the same emissions at ground level... The rate of growth in aviation CO_2 emissions is faster than the underlying global rate of economic growth, so aviation's contribution... to total emissions resulting from human activities is likely to grow in coming years.
>
> —Intergovernmental Panel on Climate Change (IPCC)[3]

At present, domestic aviation is included in the system of national GHG inventories on which the Kyoto GHG reduction targets and the Climate Change Bill's targets are based, but there is no agreed methodology as to how these should be assigned to individual countries. Against the background of significant growth in air travel and aviation markets, and as a result of government and public focus on climate change and its consequences, airlines are coming under increasing pressure to reduce their GHG emissions.

An aircraft typically cruises at an altitude of 8 to 13 kilometres, where it releases several types of gases and particles from fuel combustion, which alter the composition of the atmosphere and contribute to the climate change (Box 18.1). The impacts of gases emitted by the sector are captured in Table 18.1.

According to IPCC, the contribution of CO_2 is 2 per cent and NOx is 8 per cent of the global anthropogenic gases at present but will increase if the aviation sector

[1] Two billion passengers have travelled by air in 2007 with 8 million out-bound passengers and 43 million domestic passengers in India according to ICAO (International Civil Aviation Organization).

[2] Schell (2001).

[3] IPCC (2000).

continues to grow. The impact on global warming is expected to be more severe as the gases are released at higher altitudes. According to IPCC data, the transport sector accounts for 13 per cent of the total global GHG emissions out of which aviation accounts for 2 per cent (Figure 18.1). However, there are sufficient uncertainties around these estimates to support conjectures that the impact may actually be much more. Currently, the estimates of emissions by the sector are estimated to be 1.48 billion tonnes by 2025, which exceeds the estimates made in 2004 by about 1.3 billion tonnes. Kenneth Button and Roger Stough[4] review and assert that the aviation emissions affect not only the environment but also the industry and society as a whole.

> Box 18.1
> How Does Aviation Contribute to Climate Change?
>
> Aviation emissions arising from the combustion of kerosene include:
>
> - Carbon dioxide (CO_2);
> - Water vapour (H_2O, which leads to the formation of contrails and cirrus cloud at high altitudes);
> - Nitric oxide and nitrogen dioxide (or NOx, which forms ozone, a GHG, at high altitudes);
> - Particulates (soot and sulphate particles); and
> - Other compounds including sulphur oxides, carbon monoxide, hydrocarbons, and radicals such as hydroxyl.
>
> *Source*: Federal Aviation Administration (2005).

Globally, the world's 16,000 commercial jet aircraft generate more than 600 million tonnes of CO_2, the world's major GHG, per year. Indeed aviation generates nearly as much CO_2 annually as that from all human activities in Africa (Aviation Environment Federation 2000).[5]

Even if you only fly once a year you can generate a significant amount of greenhouse pollution. For example a passenger taking a long haul flight from the UK to the USA can produce as much carbon dioxide as a motorist driving in the UK for a whole year.[6] The report on 'Aviation and global climate change' of AEF, also says that for a typical journey under 500 kilometres, say London to Amsterdam, the amount of CO_2 produced per passenger is 0.17 kilogram per kilometre for air travel, 0.14 kilogram per kilometre for travel by car; 0.052 kilogram per kilometre for rail and 0.047 kilogram per kilometre by boat.

Background on Aviation and GHG Emission Projections

According to IPCC's summary of predictions of emissions,[7] GHG emissions from the sector are slated to double by 2050 (Table 18.2). Due to this projected increase in emissions, the 'radiative forcing'[8] of aviation emissions may rise by a factor of 4–2 by 2050 over 1992.

Table 18.1 Gases Emitted from Aviation and their Impact on Atmosphere.

Gas	*Impact*
CO_2	Long-lived GHG. Contributes to global warming
O_3	Lifetime weeks to months. Product of NOx emissions plus photochemistry. The effect of O_3 is high at subsonic cruise levels and causes radio-active reactions at those levels
CH_4	Lifetime of ~10 years. Aircraft NOx destroys ambient CH_4
H_20	The effect is small because of its small addition to natural hydrological cycle. Triggers contrails, but actual contrail content is from the atmosphere
Sulphate	Scatters solar radiation to space. Impact is one of cooling
Soot	Absorbs solar radiation from space. Impact is one of warming
Contrails	Reflect solar radiation, have cooling effect; but reflect some infrared radiation down to earth, that has a warming effect; but net effect is one of warming
Cirrus	Contrails can grow to larger cirrus clouds (contrail cirrus), which can be difficult to distinguish from natural cirrus. Generally warming effects

Source: Federal Aviation Administration (2005).

[4] Stough (2000).
[5] Aviation Environment Federation (2000).
[6] Refer to footnote 10.
[7] IPCC (2000). http://www.grida.no/publications/other/ipcc%5Fsr/?src=/climate/ipcc/aviation/index.htm
[8] The radiative forcing index is the measure of total effect of climate change. It is measured for Aviation as the ratio of total RF to that of CO_2= $(CO_2+O_3+CH_4+H_2O+\text{contrails}+\text{Particles})/CO_2$.

TABLE 18.2 Summary of Predictions of Emissions to 2015 and 2050

	CO_2	NOx
Average of estimates for 1992	476 MT	1.78 MT
Average of 2015 forecasts	1232 MT	4.04 MT
Per cent of change 1992–2015	258 per cent	226 per cent
Average of 2050 forecasts	2808 MT	7.33 MT
per cent of change 1992–2015	227 per cent	181 per cent
Per cent of change 1992–2050	588 per cent	411 per cent

Source: IPCC (1999).

The International Energy Agency (IEA) in its World Energy Outlook 2006 forecasts the growth of transportation and aviation fuel consumption and GHGs for the period of 2004 to 2030. The IEA provides two forecasts—the reference scenario and the alternative policy scenario.

According to IEA, global transportation emissions are expected to increase by about 40 to 60 per cent depending on the assumptions made in each forecast (Table 18.3). Although the aviation sector is expected to grow more than the road sector (76 per cent to 91 per cent compared with 38 per cent to 53 per cent), aviation energy consumption is expected to still remain at 15 per cent of total transportation energy demand. GHG emissions from aviation would also remain at about 15 per cent of transportation GHG emissions (Table 18.3).

The fleet of aircraft is expected to grow more rapidly in non-OECD countries, especially in China, India, and Latin America. Global GHG emissions from the transport sector are expected to remain the same as today, at 14 per cent assuming BAU forecasts (Stern 2007). This implies that aviation's share of global GHG emissions would remain the same, at least under the reference scenario. Under the many assumptions that the IEA has made regarding the alternative policy scenario, aviation's share would increase from about 1.6 per cent to 3 per cent, reflecting the wider range of policies under consideration in other sectors.

According to a study by Transport Canada, total revenue passenger-kilometres grew at an average annual growth rate of 4.3 per cent for all commercial air transport services between 1992 and 2004 (Table 18.4). By 2030, the Canadian aviation sector alone would account for 0.045 per cent of global GHG emissions, similar to today's share. Boeing forecasts that the GHG emissions would grow to 33 Mt and account for 0.054 per cent of global GHG emissions as compared to about 0.043 per cent today. Airport Council International (ACI) forecasts that GHG emissions would grow to 27 Mt by 2030, an increase of 51 per cent. All the studies project substantial increase in GHG emissions from the sector and hence it is imperative that at least unnecessary emissions are avoided wherever feasible.

AVIATION IN INDIA: THE DELHI–MUMBAI CONNECT

Indian aviation has experienced a revolution in the last five years. Domestic traffic has tripled, whereas the international traffic has doubled. In fact as pointed out earlier, much of the projected increase in the global aviation sector is expected to come from expansion of the sector in developing countries such as India and China. According to Airports Council International projections, India would be the third largest aviation market in the world by 2027 in terms of passengers handled (Table 18.5).

Both policymaking as well as execution in the Indian aviation sector is still fairly weak on aspects driving effective reductions in GHG emission. This paper studies ways in which benefits of GHG emission reduction can be captured through improvements in operations. After careful study of the quantum of emissions, the possible airline strategies for dealing with this problem are assessed;

TABLE 18.3 Derived from IEA 2006, Mtoe refers to Megatonnes of Oil Equivalent

	2004	*2030 Ref. Scenario*	*Percentage share of total*	*Percentage increase 2004–2030*	*2030 Alternative policy*	*Percentage share of Total*	*Percentage increase 2004–2030*
Total Energy (Mtoe)	1,970	3,085	100	57	2,804	100	42
Road	1,567	2,401	78	53	2,519	77	38
Aviation	238	454	15	91	419	15	76
Other	165	230	7	39	226	8	37
GHGs (Mt)	5,289	8,287			7,336		

Source: IEA (2006).

Table 18.4 Canadian Aviation GHGs Forecasts (Mt)

Forecasts	*2004*	*2030*	*Increase (in percent)*	*Share of global GHGs in 2030 (in percent)*
Transport Canada	18.2	39.4	116	0.065
ACI	18.2	27.5	51	0.045
Boeing	18.2	32.9	81	0.054

Sources: Derived from Canada Aviation & GHGes, Transport Canada.

at the next stage, sustainable, long-term solutions for airlines are identified.

This study focuses only on the commercial airlines (Civil IFR flights), which cover the ordinary passenger aircraft on the Delhi–Mumbai route.[9]

According to the data provided by the Official Airline Guide (OAG) in September 2007 the Delhi–Mumbai route in India is the sixth busiest route in the world and the busiest route in India contributing to over 50 per cent of the total Indian air traffic. It is said to be the third busiest route in Asia-Pacific after the Sydney–Melbourne route. The route also enjoys load factors between 75–80 per cent through the year.

The total distance from Delhi to Mumbai is 722 miles. This is equivalent to 1,163 kilometres or 628 nautical miles. The travel direction from Mumbai to Delhi is in the direction of the north (22 degrees from North). A typical flight between Mumbai and Delhi would have a flying time of about 1 hour 27 minutes. This assumes an average air speed for a commercial airliner of 500 mph, which is equivalent to 805 kilometres per hour or 434 knots. The exact flight time may vary depending on wind speeds.

Estimates of *Down to Earth*[10] show that the average fuel wastage per flight operating on this route is around 30–40 per cent. This route has over 40 flights that operate about 80 trips between Mumbai and Delhi every day. Each trip from Mumbai to Delhi is estimated to consume Aviation Turbine Fuel (ATF) to the tune of 4,500 kg. Apart from the ATF that is being used for a journey through the route, each plane has to carry 2,200 kg to 2,400 kg extra ATF to be consumed during the extra hour that the aircraft may have to hover over the destination airport waiting for runways and air-bridges to be cleared. Aviation fuel, which is a form of kerosene, produces about 2.158 kg of CO_2 emissions per litre.[11] In terms of emission, the 115,000 extra litres of fuel burnt every day between Delhi– Mumbai due to poor traffic and congestion management translates to

Table 18.5 Growth of Aviation in India

2007			*2012*			*2017*			*2027*		
Rank	*Country*	*Passengers (millions)*	*Rank*	*Country*	*Passengers (millions)*	*Rank*	*Country*	*Passengers (millions)*	*Rank*	*Country*	*Passengers (millions)*
1	USA	1,450	1	USA	1,552	1	USA	1,790	1	USA	2,345
2	China	297	2	China	497	2	China	792	2	China	1,708
3	UK	243	3	UK	282	3	UK	324	3	India	581
4	Spain	210	4	Spain	251	4	Spain	294	4	UK	409
5	Japan	204	5	Japan	228	5	India	274	5	Brazil	407
6	Germany	186	6	Germany	218	6	Japan	259	6	Spain	370
7	France	140	7	India	176	7	Germany	252	7	Japan	330
8	Italy	129	8	France	168	8	Brazil	224	8	Germany	311
9	Brazil	120	9	Brazil	165	9	France	192	9	France	242
10	Canada	101	10	Italy	154	10	Italy	180	10	Italy	233
11	Australia	101	11	Australia	131	11	Australia	154	11	Australia	209
12	India	100	12	Canada	125	12	Canada	147	12	Mexico	206

Source: CAPA (2009).

[9] The air traffic is often divided into four categories: Civil IFR (Instrumental Flight Rules) flights; Civil VFR (Visual Flight Rules) flights, also called general aviation; Civil Helicopters; and Operational Military flights.

[10] 'Suspended Animation', *Down to Earth*, 29 February 2008.

[11] Greener by Design (2005).

248.2 tonnes of CO_2 being pumped into the atmosphere, which is equivalent to the pollution caused by 161 small cars running for a year. In terms of costs, this wastes Rs 44 lakh per day as it costs Rs 1 lakh for a plane to hover an extra hour during a flight.

There are two different types of traffic on this route.

- *Direct flights (Delhi–Mumbai)*[12]
- *Hopping or indirect flights (Delhi–X–Mumbai)*[13]

There were about eight airlines in operation in the study period in the route. They are S2 (Jetlite), G8 (Go Air), IT (Kingfisher), 6E (Indigo), 9W (Jet Airways), DN (Kingfisher Red), and SG (Spice Jet).

Data Assumptions

- Traffic data pertains to 2005–9 for the route (direct and via) and 2007–9 for other routes in the country.
- All the airlines are either departing from or arriving at the Delhi Airport (IGIL).
- There are several other flights, which are moving on the route via different cities. Some other flights continue after Mumbai. The flight routes mentioned below are flights departing from Delhi and travelling via other routes to Delhi or flights departing from Delhi and travelling through Mumbai to other places of the country, that is, all the flights considered have linkages through Delhi–Mumbai. The major hopping flight routes considered at the study period on this route are as mentioned below:

Composition of Routes

Direct Flights

Direct flights between Mumbai and Delhi at 77,357 greatly outnumbered the indirect flights at 16,124 in the period 2005–9 (Table 18.7).

Table 18.8 shows the year-wise trends in direct flights on this route between 2005 and 2009. The number of

TABLE 18.6 Major Hopping Flights on Delhi–Mumbai Route

Departure	*Destination*
Delhi–Ahmedabad–Mumbai	(DEL–AMD–MUM)
Delhi–Bhubaneswar–Hyderabad–Mumbai	(DEL–BBI–HYD–MUM)
Delhi–Vadodara–Mumbai	(DEL–BDQ–MUM)
Delhi–Bhopal–Indore–Mumbai	(DEL–BHO–IDR–MUM)
Delhi–Mumbai–Bangalore	(DEL–MUM–BLR)
Delhi–Vadodara–Mumbai–Bangalore	(DEL–BDQ–MUM–BLR)
Delhi–Hyderabad–Bangalore–Mumbai	(DEL–HYD–BLR–MUM)
Delhi –Mumbai–Coimbatore–Kozhikode	(DEL–MUM–CJB–CCJ)
Delhi –Mumbai–Cochin	(DEL –MUM–COK)
Delhi–Chandigarh–Mumbai	(DEL–IXC–MUM)
Delhi–Aurangabad–Mumbai	(DEL–IXU–MUM)
Delhi–Jaipur–Mumbai	(DEL–JAI–MUM)
Delhi –Mumbai–Chennai	(DEL–MUM–MAA)
Delhi –Mumbai–Trivandrum	(DEL–MUM–TRV)
Delhi–Jaipur–Udaipur–Mumbai	(DEL–JAI–UDR–MUM)
Delhi–Chandigarh–Mumbai	(DEL–IXC–MUM)
Delhi –Mumbai–Coimbatore	(DEL–MUM–CJB)
Delhi–Udaipur–Mumbai	(DEL–UDR–MUM)

Source: Analysed by the authors from data on flight details of Airports Authority of India (AAI) for the period 2005–9.

[12] The direct flight is the flight travelling directly without any halt.

[13] Indirect flight is the flight travelling via another city with a halt.

Table 18.7 Composition of Flights in the Study Route (2005–7)

Routes	*Arrivals*	*Departtures*	*Total*
Delhi–Mumbai All Indirect Flights	6,942	9,181	16,124
Delhi–Mumbai Direct Flights	24,821	52,536	77,357
Total	31,763	61,717	93,481

Source: Analysed by the authors from data on flight details of the Airports Authority of India (AAI) for the period 2005–9.

Table 18.8 Year-wise Growth on the Route (Direct Flights)

Routes	*Total no. of flights*	*2005–6*	*2006–7*	*2007–7*	*2008–9*
MUM–DEL	77,357	13,681	18,573	12,745	34,703

Source: Analysed by the authors from data on flight details of Airports Authority of India (AAI) for the period 2005–9.

flights took a dip in the year 2007–8 and then almost trebled in 2008–9 over the previous year.

Indirect or Hopping Flights

There are about 20 via routes covering the Delhi–Mumbai sector. Mumbai–Goa and Mumbai–Ahmedabad with 2,534 and 1,619 flights come second and third respectively to the Delhi–Mumbai connect in terms of traffic (Figure 18.1). Indirect flights also witnessed a dip in 2007–8 followed by a steep increase in 2008–9 similar to trends in direct flights.

Comparison with Major Metros in India

Figure 18.2 shows that traffic between Delhi and other major metros of India increased in 2008–9 over 2007–8. When compared with other metro pairs with arrival or destination being Delhi, it is clear that the Delhi–Mumbai route enjoyed a maximum of 42,256 flights

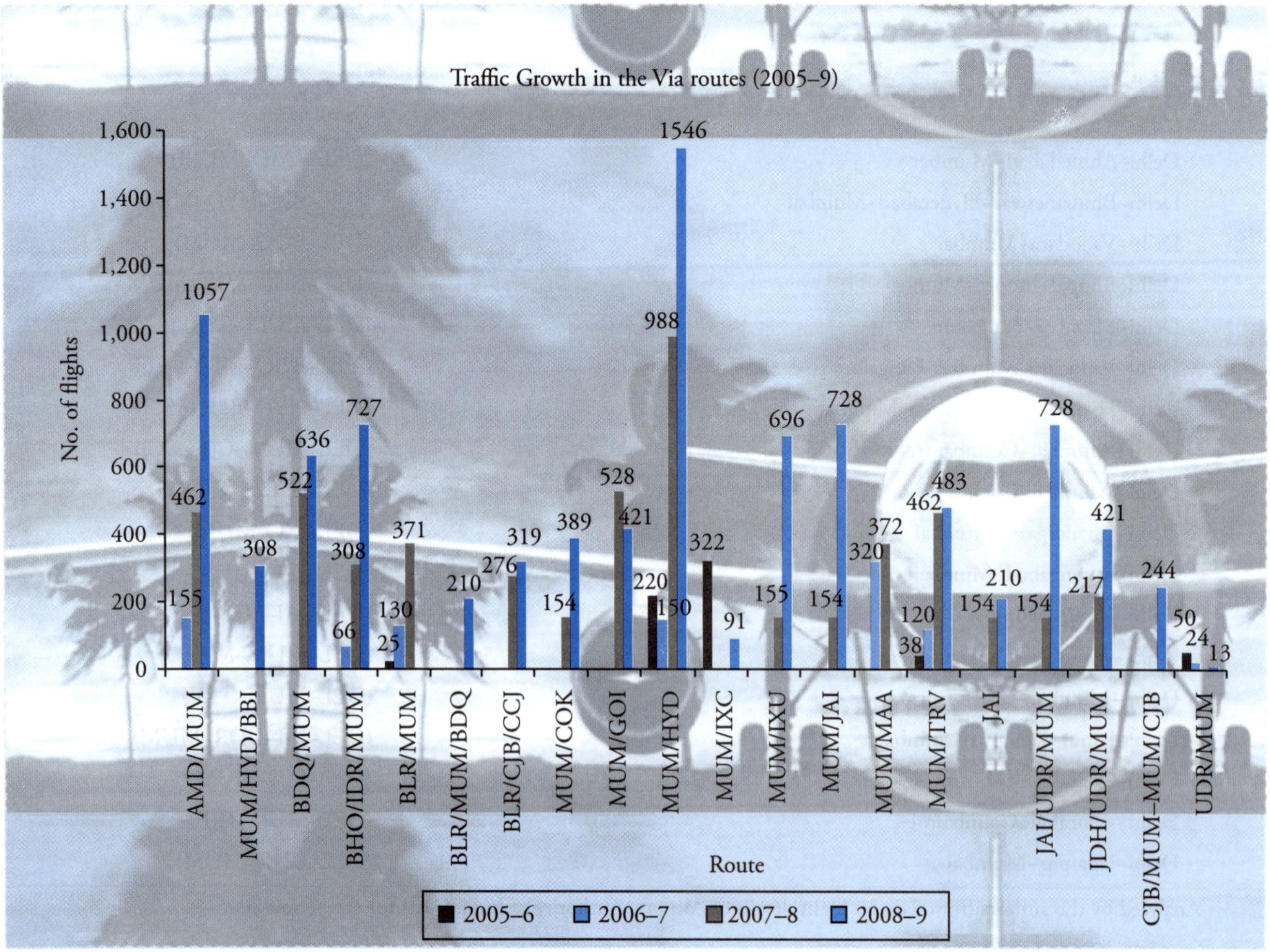

Figure 18.1 Traffic Growths on the Indirect Routes

Source: Analysed by the authors from data on flight details of the Airports Authority of India (AAI) for the period 2005–9.

during 2007–9. Delhi–Bangalore followed second with 26,562 flights.

Emissions Estimate for the Route

Exhaust emissions from aviation arise from the combustion of jet fuel (jet kerosene and jet gasoline) and aviation gasoline.[14] They arise during the two activities mainly, that is, during the Landing/Take-off (LTO) cycle and cruising (Figure 18.3).

- *LTO cycle* defined in ICAO (1993) includes all the activities of the aircraft near the airport that take place below the altitude of 3,000 feet (1,000 m). This therefore includes taxi-in and out, take-off, climb-out, and approach landing.
- *Cruise* is defined as all the activities of the aircraft at altitudes above 3,000 feet (1,000 m). Cruise, in the emission inventory methodology, includes climb to cruise altitude, cruise, and descent from cruise altitudes.

Exhaust emissions contain many gases apart from the GHGs which have potential of both warming as well as cooling, but a major proportion of the emission is CO_2 (See Box 18.2).

Emission calculations are based on the assumptions in Table 18.9.

The growth rates for emission projection for 2025 are taken from two sources. In Scenario-1, the growth percentage is as per the Ministry of Civil Aviation, India (MoCA) and Scenario-2 is as per the GDP growth rate of the country multiplied with aviation elasticity of GDP growth. It is said that the aviation growth is expected to be twice that of the overall GDP growth rate (McKinsey Global Institute 2007).

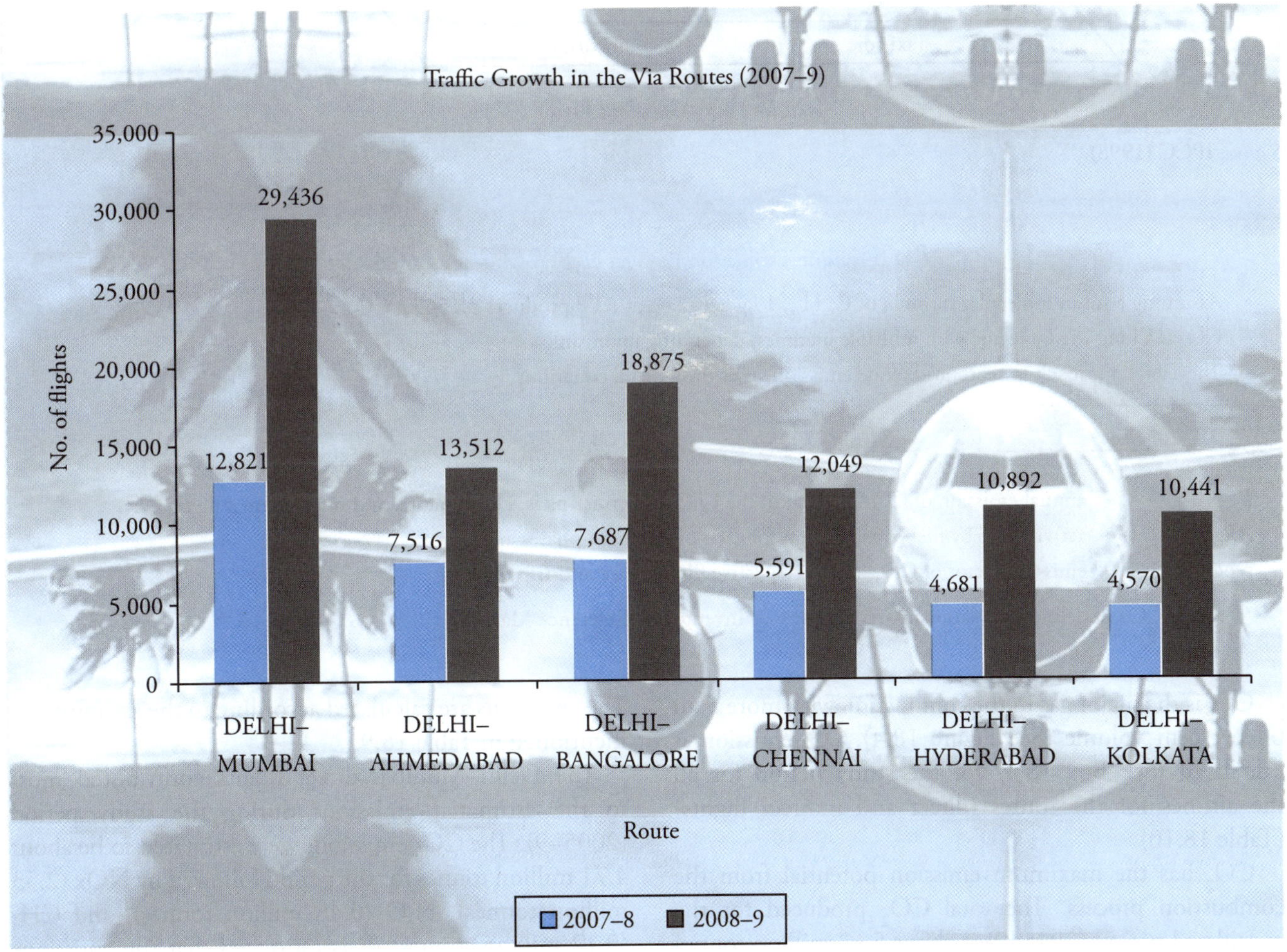

Figure 18.2 Comparison of the Major Metros with the Route for the Period 2007–9

Source: Analysed by the authors from data on flight details of Airports Authority of India (AAI) for the period 2007–9.

[14] A fuel used only in small-piston engine aircraft, and which generally represents less than 1 per cent of the fuel used in aviation.

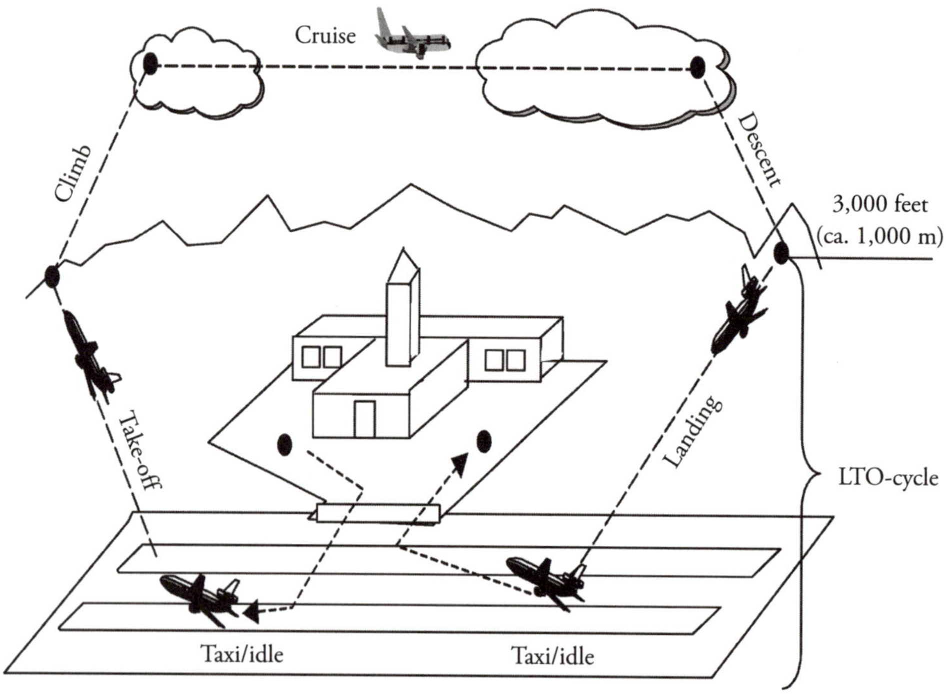

FIGURE 18.3 Standard Flying Cycles

Source: IPCC (1998).

Box 18.2
CO_2 Emission Estimation Product of Kerosene Combustion

- Assuming a mean molecular formula of $C_{12}H_{23}$, 1 kg kerosene or ATF produces 3.156 kg CO_2.
- CO_2 is a long-life molecule with multiple lifetimes, depending upon sinks.
- The Tier 1 approach for carbon-dioxide emissions uses the general equation;

$$E_{CO_2} = AR_{fuel\ consumption} \times EF_{CO_2}$$

where:

E_{CO_2} = annual emission of CO_2 for each of the LTO and cruise phases of domestic and international flights
$AR_{fuel\ consumption}$ = activity rate by fuel consumption for each of the flight phases and trip
types EF_{CO_2} = emission factor of CO_2 for the respective flight phase and trip type

Source: IPCC Guidelines on National Greenhouse Gas Inventories. Reference Manual.

CO_2 is the major gas in the combustion with more than 60 per cent volume (See Figure 18.4). CO_2 emission is calculated (See Box 18.3) for the study period for all the airlines for the routes (direct and indirect flights) (Table 18.10).

CO_2 has the maximum emission potential from the combustion process. The total CO_2 produced for the considered period (2005–9) is about 5.62 million tonnes not considering the delays and other external factors. The Delhi–Mumbai route has the maximum number of flights and hence generates the maximum emission.

All indirect flights were considered separately as emissions vary with flight paths and likely fuel consumption. The emissions are calculated according to the assumptions mentioned in Table 18.9.

The Delhi–Mumbai direct flights contributed most to the estimated emissions during the study period (2005–9). The CO_2 emissions were estimated to be about 4.71 million tonnes for the period followed by NOx (2.53 million tonnes), N_2O (0.48 million tonnes), and CH_4 (0.12 million tonnes). It is estimated that the emissions were less in 2007–8 as the number of flights decreased (See Figure 18.5).

The Delhi–Mumbai indirect flights were 16,124 during the period (2005–9). The estimated CO_2 emissions were about 0.90 million tonnes for the period followed by

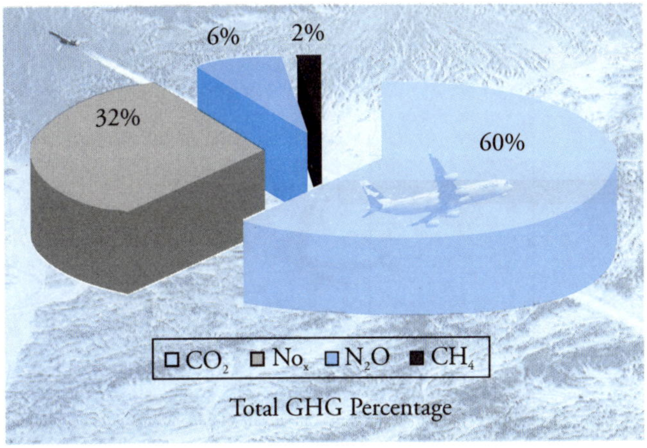

Figure 18.4 Share of CO_2 in the GHGs Produced

Note: The estimate of total CO_2 produced is the sum for the period (2005–9).

Source: Analysed by the authors from data on flight details of Airports Authority of India (AAI) for the period 2005–9.

Box 18.3
Tier-1 Method

The Tier-I method is the simplest method of IPCC methodologies *(Tier-1: Purely fuel-based, Tier-2: Simple LTO cycle-based, Tier-3: detailed individual aircraft based)* and is based on the aggregate figure of fuel consumption for aviation to be multiplied with average emission factors. The emission factors have been averaged over all flying phases based on an assumption that 10 per cent of the fuel is used in the LTO phase of the flight.

Emissions = Fuel Consumption * Average Emission

The following are the default emission factors:

CO_2 : 19.5 tonnes C/PJ;
CH_4 : 0.5 kg/PJ, and
N_2O : 2 kg/PJ

Source: IPCC Guidelines on National Greenhouse Gas Inventories. Reference Manual.

NOx (0.48 million tonnes), N_2O (0.09 million tonnes) and CH_4 (0.02 million tonnes). But unlike the direct flights, indirect flights emissions were increasing (See Figure 18.6).

Factoring in direct as well as indirect flights, the average emissions were estimated to be 61 tonnes CO_2e/flight, 33 tonnes CO_2e/flight (NOx), 6 tonnes CO_2e/flight (N_2O) and 2 tonnes CO_2e/flight (CH_4) respectively.

Both types of flights were used to project the emissions for 2050 on the route as well as to extrapolate for the country as a whole (See Figure 18.7).

Table 18.9 Assumptions for Calculating Emissions

Assumptions		
Fuel Consumption of Aircrafts	Units	Value
Total Fuel Consumption for Airbus	kg/hr	
Total Fuel Consumption for Boeing	kg/hr	
Total Fuel Consumption for ATR	kg/hr	
Total Fuel Consumption for CRJ2	kg/hr	
Average fuel consumption	kg/hr	
Emissions factors (IPCC,1996)		
Tier-1 CO2	CO2 e	19.5
Tier-1 Nox	CO2 e	10.5
Tier-1 N2O	CO2 e	2
Tier-1 CH4	CO2 e	0.5
RFI		2.5
Growth rate for emissions projection (MoCA)		
Till 2015 growth	%	12
Till 2025 growth	%	13
Till 2050 growth	%	15
Growth rate for emissions projection (GDP)		
Till 2015 growth	%	12
Till 2025 growth	%	13
Till 2050 growth	%	15
According to McKinsey Global Institute		
GDP growth rate till 2005	%	6
GDP Growth rate till 2025	%	7.3
GDP Growth rate till 2050	%	7.3

Note: The assumptions as shown in Table 18.9 are taken from various sources as cited. The emission factors are considered for the Tier-1 method as the emission calculation is carried out by the Tier-1 method (IPCC 2006).

Source: Assumptions of the authors based on the IPCC Reference Manual for Emission Factors, discussions with airlines for fuel consumption, McKinsey Global Institute and Ministry of Civil Aviation projections on the growth of the aviation sector for emission projections.

GHG Emission Projections

Having estimated the emission levels on the route, we proceed to calculate GHG emission projections for the Delhi–Mumbai route. The emission projections were made to estimate the growth of the emissions on the route and for the sector in India in a Business as Usual scenario.

For the projections, two scenarios were considered.

- Growth of the sector according to the estimations of the MoCA
- Growth of the sector according to the growth of the GDP growth (McKinsey Global Institute and International Energy Agency)

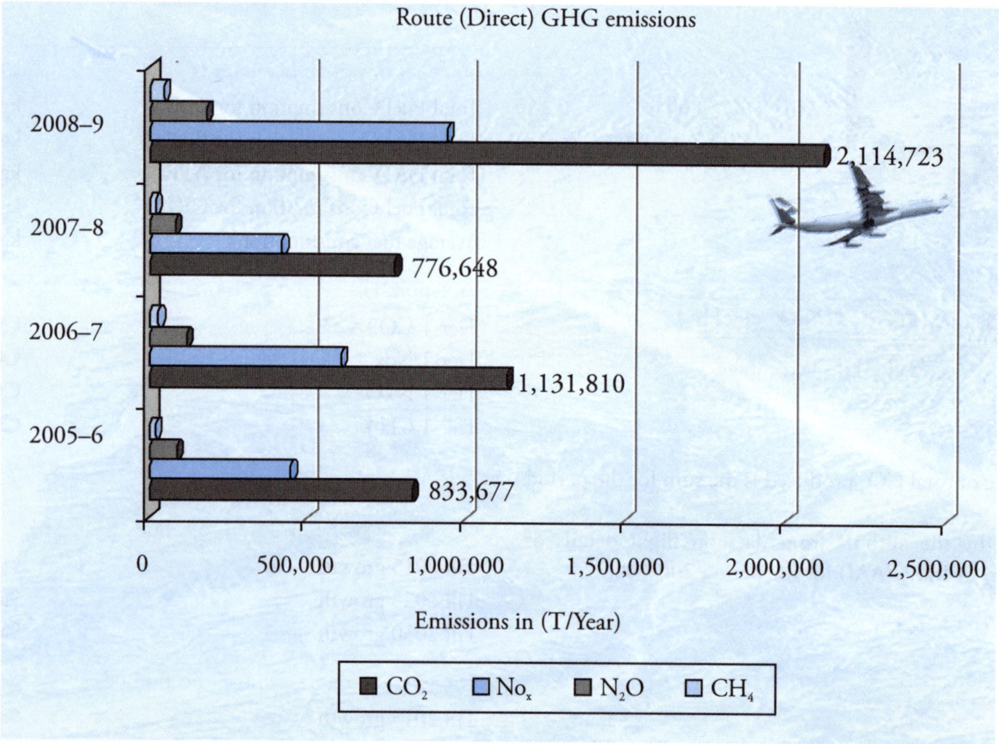

FIGURE 18.5 Delhi–Mumbai Direct Route Emission Growth Annually

Source: Analysed by the authors from data on flight details of the Airports Authority of India (AAI) for the period 2005–9.

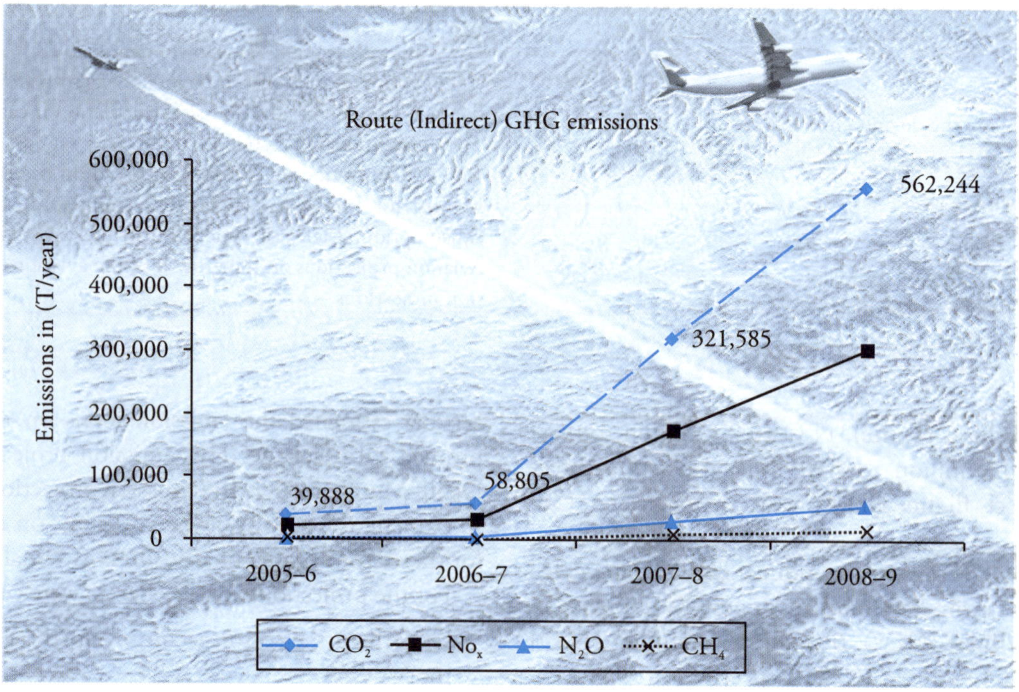

FIGURE 18.6 Delhi–Mumbai Via Route Emissions Annually

Source: Analysed by the authors from data on flight details of the Airports Authority of India (AAI) for the period 2005–9.

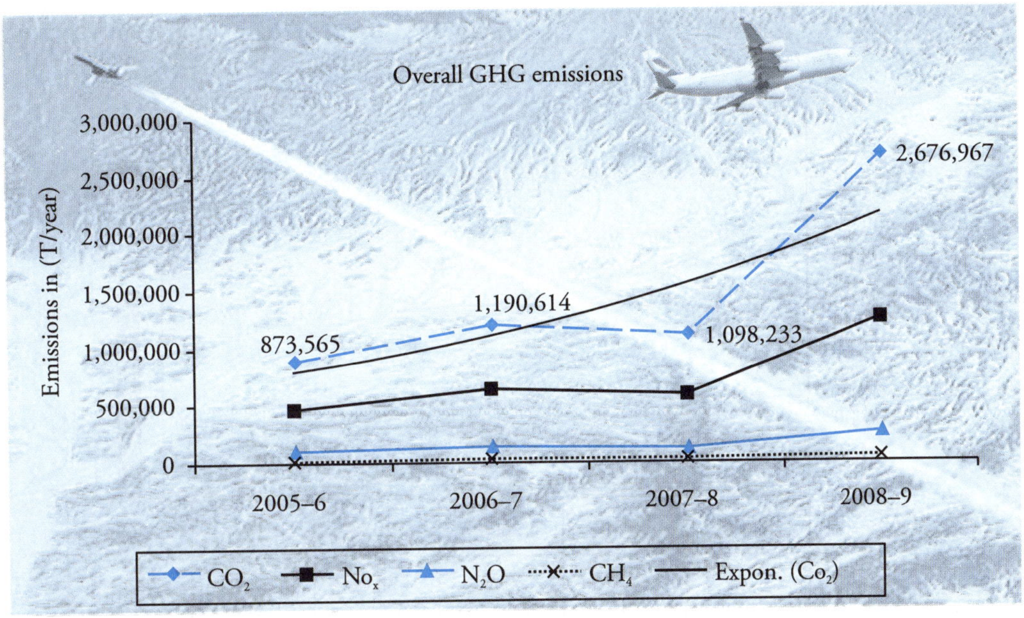

FIGURE 18.7 Annual Growth Rate of the GHG Emissions in the Route

Source: Analysed by the authors from data on flight details of the Airports Authority of India (AAI) for the period 2005–9.

The emissions shown in the particular year are for the year and are not cumulative.

The scenarios are explained in detail as below:

Scenario-1: Growth Based on Estimations of the MoCA

In this scenario, the growth of the sector was based on growth estimations of MoCA—12 per cent till 2015, 13 per cent till 2025, and 15 per cent till 2050—for the aviation sector in India as a whole.

In Scenario-1, the growth was extrapolated for the emission projections in 2050. The country-wide growth rate was assumed to hold for the Delhi–Mumbai route in this exercise, which may be an upward biased estimate as the two cities are already extensively served and the percentage increase may be less on this route. The emissions were calculated and projected for the route as a whole, not considering the direct and indirect flights separately. In this case, the projections suggest that, the emissions would increase from 2020, as the overall sector growth rate is expected to increase from 2020. It is estimated that the total emissions in 2030, 2040, and 2050 would be 28 million tonnes, 114.52 million tonnes, and 463 million tonnes respectively (See Figure 18.8).

Scenario-2: Growth of the Sector Based on GDP Growth Estimates of McKinsey Global Institute and IEA

In this scenario, the growth of the sector was calculated based on of the expected growth the GDP of India as estimated by McKinsey Global Institute and IEA. McKinsey Global Institute and IEA estimate that the average annual GDP growth of India would be in the range of 6 per cent till 2015, 7.3 per cent till 2025, and 7.3 per cent till 2050.

It is assumed that the aviation sector would grow at a rate that is twice the rate of growth of GDP of the country.[15]

Emission projections for Scenario-2 up to 2050 assume that the growth assumptions of GDP for India are applicable throughout the projection period upon emissions as well. Under this scenario, it is estimated that the GDP growth of India will stabilize after 2015 at 7.5 per cent per year till 2050 (as per IEA and McKinsey projections). In this case the analysis shows that the emissions will increase from 2020 as the overall sector growth rate tends to increase from 2020.

The total emissions on the Delhi–Mumbai route will increase from 3.89 million tonnes in 2020 to 7.88 million

[15] According to International Air Transport Association (IATA 2008b).

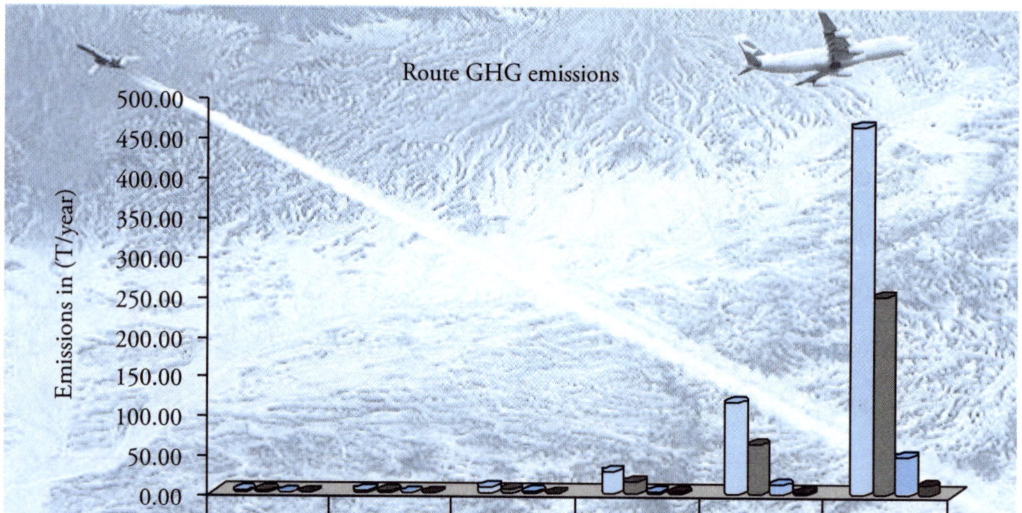

	2009	2010	2020	2030	2040	2050
CO_2	1.82	2.01	7.00	28.31	114.52	463.31
No_x	0.98	1.08	3.77	15.24	61.67	249.47
N_2O	0.19	0.21	0.72	2.90	11.75	47.52
CH_4	0.05	0.05	0.18	0.73	2.94	11.88

Figure 18.8 Emissions Projection of Delhi–Mumbai Direct Flights (Scenario-1)

Source: Analysed by the authors based on the civil aviation projections of the Ministry of Civil Aviation.

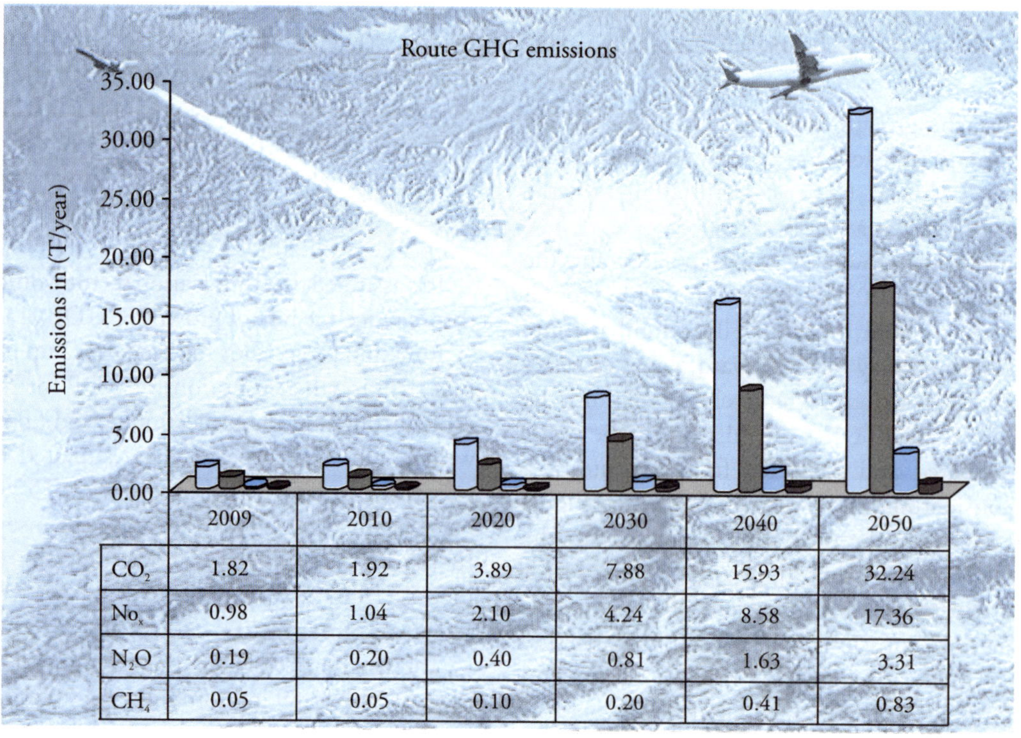

	2009	2010	2020	2030	2040	2050
CO_2	1.82	1.92	3.89	7.88	15.93	32.24
No_x	0.98	1.04	2.10	4.24	8.58	17.36
N_2O	0.19	0.20	0.40	0.81	1.63	3.31
CH_4	0.05	0.05	0.10	0.20	0.41	0.83

Figure 18.9 Emission Projections of Delhi–Mumbai Direct Flights (Scenario-2)

Note: It is said that Civil Aviation sector grows twice the GDP growth rate.

Source: Analysed by the authors based on the GDP projections of India by McKinsey Global Institute.

tonnes in 2030, 15.93 million tonnes in 2040, and 32.24 million tonnes in 2050 respectively (See Figure 18.9). The MoCA estimates prove to be much higher than that of McKinsey as the scenarios and assumptions were different and hence the two projections are not comparable. But considering the fact that the sector is growing by leaps and bounds, any strategy proposed must provide long-term solutions.

Strategies for Emission Reduction Worldwide

'*The airline industry is in crisis. With a fuel bill of US$190 billion—one third of its costs—saving fuel is a matter of survival.*' (IATA 2007)

The emission reduction options can be mainly categorized into:

- Technology Management
- Operations Management
- Economic Instruments

This section of the paper discusses the emission reduction strategies used internationally and proposes operational strategies, which can be implemented in Indian conditions and reduce the emissions in India significantly.

Mitigation measures to manage aviation emissions include changes in aircraft and engine technology, fuel, operational practices, besides regulatory and economic measures.[16]

- Aircraft and Engine Technology Options: Technology advances have substantially reduced emissions per passenger-kilometre. Research programmes addressing NOx emissions from supersonic aircraft are also in progress. However, there is potential for further improvement. Any technological change involves balancing across a range of environmental impacts. To be seriously considered as a mitigation strategy, improved technology options must be both cost-competitive and offer significant reductions in GHG emissions. Assuming that the emission reduction goals can be achieved through new technology, fleet replacement worldwide with the new technology can take up to a decade. Several technological improvements exist to improve aircraft aerodynamics, such as applying laminar flow control (LFC) to an aircraft to reduce drag and, as a result, fuel consumption.[17] More radical innovations include blended wing body aircraft that not only reduce drag but allow the entire aircraft to generate lift, as opposed to just the wings.[18] More fuel-efficient engines and incorporation of super-lightweight materials, such as fibre-metal laminate, into the airframe offer additional avenues to improving aircraft efficiency.[19, 20]
- Fuel Options: Although alternative fuels have lower net GHG emissions than traditional petroleum-based aircraft fuel,[21] there are no practical alternatives to kerosene-based fuels for commercial jet aircrafts as in the near future. Biofuels, Fischer-Tropsch fuels,[22] and liquid hydrogen could all present feasible alternatives in the future. Yet as with other sectors, alternative aviation fuels face numerous challenges with respect to their production, distribution, and cost, and it is not entirely clear what quantity of these fuels will be available and when, or what magnitude of GHG benefits can ultimately be achieved by using them (IPCC 2007). Additionally, to significantly contributing to GHG mitigation, the lifecycle carbon footprints of these fuels needs to be significantly lower than the conventional fuels they replace. Jet aircraft require fuel with a high energy density, especially for long-haul flights and these alternative fuels like biofuel contain a low-energy-density which would be a limitation over jet fuels. The only feasible options for 'drop-in'

[16] IPCC (2000).

[17] Laminar flow control (LFC) refers to technologies that modify the aircraft's boundary layer (the layer of air that clings to the surface of the airframe). LFC increases fuel efficiency by reducing turbulence in this layer. There are two types of LFC technology: passive and hybrid. Passive LFC reduces aerodynamic drag by modifying the air-wing interaction through the shape of the front of the wing. Hybrid LFC removes a portion of the boundary layer (for example, through slotted or porous wing designs) to reduce drag.

[18] Liebeck (2004).

[19] Karagozian (2006).

[20] Greener by Design (2005).

[21] While the direct GHG emissions from combustion of biofuels or Fischer–Tropsch fuels will be similar to or the same as the direct GHG emissions from combustion of traditional petroleum-based aviation fuel, such alternative fuels can have significantly lower net lifecycle GHG emissions since they can be manufactured from biomass feedstocks so that, in effect, combustion of such alternative fuels emits CO_2 that was earlier absorbed from the atmosphere by the biomass feedstocks.

[22] Fischer–Tropsch synthesis of transportation fuels involves gasification of a carbon-containing feedstock (for example, biomass, coal) and production of a synthetic crude oil, which can then be processed into refined liquid fuel products.

replacements to petroleum-based jet fuels include hydroprocessed renewable jet fuel (HRJ)[23] and Fischer–Tropsch (FT) fuels. Other fuel options, such as hydrogen, may become viable in the long term because these fuels do not present an immediate alternative, and their adoption presents only in a long-term path towards lower carbon flight.

- Operational Options: Improvements in air traffic management (ATM) and other operational procedures could drive 8 to 18 per cent reduction in aviation fuel burn. A large majority (6 to 12 per cent) of these reductions can come from ATM improvements, which are anticipated to be fully implemented in the next 20 years. All engine emissions will be reduced as a consequence.
- Regulatory, Economic, and Other Options: Although improvements in aircraft and engine technology and ATM efficiency can bring some environmental benefits, these cannot fully offset the impact of the projected growth in aviation. Policy options to reduce emissions include more stringent aircraft engine emissions regulations, removal of subsidies and incentives that have negative environmental consequences, market-based options such as environmental levies (charges and taxes) and emissions trading, voluntary agreements, research programmes, and substitution of aviation by rail and coach. Most of these options would lead to increased airline costs and fares.

Operational Strategies Used Internationally

Cairns and Newson (2006) have showcased several ways of reducing aviation emissions based on improvement in operations.

One of the key strategies prevalent internationally involves ATM aimed at reducing inefficiencies in flight patterns and encouraging flight patterns that take into account prevailing atmospheric conditions in order to minimize the impacts of non-CO_2 emissions from aviation.

It has been estimated that improvements in ATM could lead to increases in energy efficiency, estimated to be in order of 6 to12 per cent (Cairns and Newson 2006; IPCC 1999). Three major international ATM initiatives have been identified—A Single Sky for Europe; an efficient Pearl River Delta in China; and a Next Generation Air Traffic System in the US (IATA 2007).

Other improvements in operational efficiency include:

- Increasing load factors;
- Eliminating non-essential weight;
- Optimizing aircraft speed;
- Continuous Descent Approach
- Limiting use of auxiliary power (for example, for heating and ventilation);
- Reducing taxiing.

Operational Strategies under Consideration in India

There are various measures for GHG emission reduction under consideration by various stakeholders of civil aviation like the DGCA, airlines etc. These various measures are discussed here under.

- DGCA: The Directorate General of Civil Aviation (DGCA), the regulatory authority in India has set up an Aviation Environmental Unit to address problems faced by the sector and provide feasible solutions to the end-users. The unit has the responsibility of providing technical guidance on issues such as fuel conservation, emission reduction, and noise abatement. The unit is also conducting general awareness programmes for the people working in the aviation community through a lecture series. DGCA has also advised the airlines and air navigation service-providers to create environment cells in their respective organizations. Besides DGCA, the airlines, the air navigation agency, and others have also initiated measures aimed at improving fuel efficiency and reducing emissions.
- Airlines: The airline operators always have incentives to bring about improvements in fuel efficiency of their respective fleets. They have already started targeting reduction in fuel consumption by adopting better operational procedures such as minimum usage of Auxilary Power Units (APU),[24] reduced flap take-off and landings, idle reverse on landing, proper flight planning system, adhering to proper maintenance of aircraft, weight reductions in cabin equipment, catering services, avoiding carrying extra fuel on board, etc. Similar exercises are being adopted towards noise

[23] Hydroprocessing plant- or animal-based oil is similar to the process of conventional crude oil refining. First, the oil is 'hydrotreated' by adding hydrogen, which increases the oil's hydrogen-to-carton ratio. Then, the molecules that result are 'cracked', yielding a finished jet fuel product.

[24] The primary purpose of an aircraft APU is to provide power to start the main engines. It is a small engine, situated at the base of the tail of a plane (in most cases) that can be turned on if ground support is not offered. The APU is also used to start the engines of the plane as this requires a great, sudden burst of power which, in some cases, the standard battery alone cannot supply.

abatement in terms of minimum usage of thrust reversal, low-noise low drag approaches, steep climbing during take-off, etc. Airlines are also advised to develop Balanced Approach Procedures for minimizing noise during landing. The fuel efficiency litres/Revenue Tonne Kilometres (RTK) data from airlines operating at international sectors have been collected and analysed. Airlines are working to bring the current fuel efficiency of their fleet close to world average (ICAO 2009a).

- Air Navigation Service-provider (ANS): Consistent high growth rate of civil aviation in India coupled with the emergence of new airlines with fleets of new generation aircraft has necessitated rapid up-gradation of facilities, procedures, and infrastructure at all airports. The ANS are also contributing to this national endeavour through implementation of Performance-based Navigation (PBN) procedures for optimizing airspace utilization and enhancing airport capacity by taking advantage of airborne capabilities and Global Navigation Satellite Systems (GNSS) (ICAO 2008). PBN represents a shift from sensor-based to performance-based navigation. It specifies performance parameters in terms of accuracy, integrity, availability, continuity, and functionality in the context of a particular airspace and aircraft Area Navigation (RNAV) system. RNAV can be defined as a method of navigation that permits aircraft operations on any desired course within the coverage of station-referenced navigation signals or within the limits of a self-contained system capability, or a combination of these. Performance requirements are identified in navigation specifications, which also define the choice of navigation sensors and equipment that may be used to meet the performance requirements. The development of the PBN recognizes that advanced aircraft RNAV systems are achieving a predictable level of navigation performance accuracy which, together with an appropriate level of functionality, allows a more efficient use of available airspace (ICAO 2010). For sustained effort in implementing PBN procedures at all airports and airspace in India, a PBN Implementation Roadmap of India has been established with the objective to accrue quantifiable benefits to the stakeholders in terms of fuel savings, reduction in emissions, capacity enhancement, and improved access to the airport. PBN RNAV-1 Standard Instrument Departures (SIDs)[25] and Standard Terminal Arrival Routes (STARs)[26] have been made operational at Mumbai, Delhi, and Ahmedabad airports since August 2008.[27] PBN RNAV-1 SIDs and STARs have been developed by AAI-India with the assistance of Mitre for Chennai and Hyderabad and have been operational since 2009. The implementation of PBN at these airports has reduced the flight distance (Great Circle Distance) leading to reduction in annual fuel consumption. This reduction in fuel consumption has reduced the quantity of carbon emissions. Further, plans for implementing Continuous Descent Approach (CDA) at major airports of India are under consideration (ICAO 2009b).
- International Air Traffic Association (IATA): More efficient operations with regard to fuel conservation can save up to 6 per cent according to IPCC. Inefficiency in the ATC can add 12 per cent to 18 per cent in fuel bills and IATA estimates that within India, a streamlined ATM system can cut airlines' fuel bills and thus emissions by more than 50 per cent. IATA publishes best-practice guidelines and its Green Team is advising carriers on implementation. Airlines are trying to reduce weight by removing items such as in-flight magazines, pillows, and blankets; more regular cleaning and in the case of Japan Airlines, encouraging passengers to visit the bathroom just prior to boarding (IATA 2008). According to IATA estimates in 2005, adopting such measures could have reduced 11 million tonnes in emissions by 2008.

Operational Strategies Proposed for India

After studying the various operational strategies available globally and under consideration in India, the following operational strategies have been proposed for India as it is found that these strategies are viable economics and in applicability. The emission reduction potential has also been studied by adopting these strategies for the Delhi–Mumbai air route.

[25] A SID, or Standard Instrument Departure, defines a pathway out of an airport and onto the airway structure. A SID is sometimes called a Departure Procedure (DP). SIDs are unique to the associated airport.

[26] A STAR, or Standard Terminal Arrival Route ('Standard Instrument Arrival' in the UK) defines a pathway into an airport from the airway structure. STARs can be associated with more than one arrival airport, which can occur when two or more airports are in close proximity (for example, San Francisco and San Jose).

[27] SIDs and STARs are procedures and checkpoints used to enter and leave the airway system by aircraft operating on IFR flight plans. There is a defined transition point at which an airway and a SID intersect.

Continuous Descent Approach (CDA)

For approaches into busy airports, stepwise descent profiles are standard practices. However, it is recognized that the CDA allows considerable fuel savings (with associated reductions in CO_2 emissions). In addition, the noise footprint is considerably reduced and the chances of encountering a wake vortex from another approaching aircraft are reduced. In this the aircraft, instead of descending using the conventional step method, descends from a high altitude moving towards the ground steadily (See Figure 18.10).

When the aircraft uses the stepped approach, it joins 'stacks'[28] at different levels. The CDA method removes the need for stacks, and therefore reduces the chances of the aircraft encountering wake vortices from other approaching aircraft. About 300–1,000 pounds (135–450 kg) of fuel can be saved per flight per landing or 1 tonne of CO_2 and further reducing noise and emissions further.[29] For different kinds of aircraft, the saving potential varies. For example: CDA saves—for a Boeing B-767 around 165 kg fuel or 525 kg CO_2 per arrival. CDA also reduces nitrogen oxides (NOx) pollutants by 30 per cent at 3,000 feet and below. Figures 18.6 and 18.7 depict CDA (green flight path) and stepped approach (red flight path) graphically.

The table below (Table 18.10) shows the amount of fuel saved by applying CDA in the Delhi and Mumbai airports. The fuel saved is thus from the Delhi–Mumbai routes on the basis of actual fuel used and emissions calculated in the route.

Some instances of successful implementation of CDA are presented below.

- Louisville International Airport in Kentucky: At Louisville International Airport in Kentucky (Clarke et al. 2004), it was found that noise in the proximity of the airport dropped between 3.9 and 6.5 decibels with the use of CDA as opposed to the stepped approach.
- Mather Airport, Sacramento County Airport System: Noise produced by Boeing 757 and Boeing 767 approaching the airport was measured prior to, during, and after the implementation of the CDA (ESA 2006). The results are presented in Tables 18.11 and 18.12.

CDA significantly reduced aircraft noise levels on a single-event basis as UPS's[30] Boeing 757 aircraft approached Mather Airport. The average reduction at each of the measurement sites was a palpable 4 decibels. The reduction in noise levels (again on a single event basis) for the ABX's Boeing 767 during CDA was not as consistent as the UPS 757, but that is to be expected as the ABX's CDA is in the early stages of development and implementation. Noise reduction is a good indirect measure of fuel

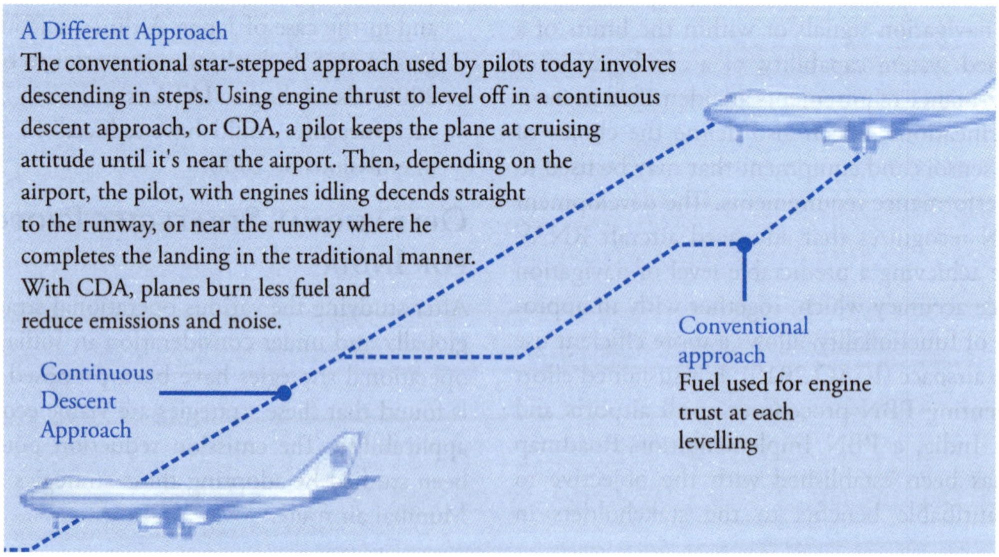

Figure 18.10 Continuous Descent Approach Method

Source: Air Transport Association, European Air Traffic Management.

[28] Normally an altitude of 6,000 or 7,000 feet. Stack basically mean altitudes in aviation terms

[29] *FAA Flight Plan.* Washington DC: The Federal Aviation Administration. FAA (2008).

[30] United Parcel Service.

TABLE 18.10 Emission Reduction Potential and Fuel Saving through CDA for the Delhi–Mumbai Air Route

	2005–6	*2006–7*	*2007–8*	*2008–9*
Fuel efficiency by continuous descent arrival (kg)	22,392,114	31,949,497	21,122,127	48,495,104
Reduction of cost of fuel after continuous descent approval (million USD)	15,249	23,962	19,538	33,025
CO_2 emission reduction potential (T)	1,091,616	1,557,538	1,029,704	2,364,136
Total CO_2 emission reduction (T)	109,327	155,990	103,127	236,772
Total cost of fuel saving (million US$)	1,527	2,400	1,957	3,308

Note: Cost of total fuel saved (million $)	9,191
Total CERs generated(T)	605,216
@' price of 13$/T $ generated	7,858,734
@' price of 13$/T million $ generated	8

The CER price of 13$/T is taken as of the January 2009 price.
Source: Analysed by the authors from the example of Boeing B-767 provided above in the text.

TABLE 18.11 Number of CDA and Non-CDA UPS Boeing 757 Aircraft Arrival Noise Events

Site No.	*Non-CDA*	*CDA*	*Total*
1	52	38	90
2	70	41	111
3	67	33	100
4	74	34	108

Source: ESA (2006).

TABLE 18.12 Number of CDA and Non-CDA UPS Boeing 767 Aircraft Arrival Noise Events

Site No.	*Non-CDA*	*CDA*	*Total*
1	22	8	30
2	30	7	37
3	34	7	41
4	40	7	47

Source: ESA (2006).

efficiency and is desirable by itself to reduce noise pollution in areas close to the airport.

- CDA at Schiphol Airport, Amsterdam: CDA has been in use at Schiphol Airport, Amsterdam during night hours on a single runway for some time now. The National Aerospace Laboratory of France studied FMS[31] data of actual flights on Boeing 747–400 and Boeing 737–300/400 2000 to compare CDA procedures with conventional procedures to demonstrate the substantial environmental benefits of the CDA. Noise footprints (65 dB(A)) were found to be 30–55 per cent smaller (about 30 sq. km for B747 and 15 sq. km for B-737). Fuel consumption during the last 45 kilometres of the flight was about 25–40 per cent lower (approximately 400 kg for B-747 and 55 kg for B-737).

Differences were found to be mainly due to the presence of a horizontal segment in conventional approaches. Conventional 3,000-ft approaches in general show larger fuel consumption when compared to 2,000-ft approaches with equal length of the horizontal segment. This is mainly caused by the difference in Instrument Landing System (ILS)[32] flight path length. Noise areas for 3,000-ft approaches are in general smaller than for 2,000-ft approaches at comparable horizontal segment lengths. Despite the longer distance with higher thrust settings along the ILS glide slope, the higher altitude seems to over-compensate for this unfavourable effect.

Implementing CDA in India

There is an easy way to implement CDA today—it is a simple clearance by ATC[33] instructing individual flights to 'descend and maintain [assigned altitude] at the pilot's discretion' in a way that does not force the aircraft to level

[31] The Flight Management System is a specialized computer system that automates a wide variety of in-flight tasks, reducing the workload on the flight crew to the point that modern aircraft no longer carry flight engineers or navigators.

[32] An instrument landing system (ILS) is a ground-based instrument approach system that provides precision guidance to an aircraft approaching and landing on a runway, using a combination of radio signals and, in many cases, high-intensity lighting arrays to enable a safe landing during instrument meteorological conditions (IMC), such as low ceilings or reduced visibility due to fog, rain, or blowing snow.

[33] Air Traffic Control.

off at an interim altitude assignment. This will allow the pilot to start descent at the profile that is optimal for fuel savings. Although there are huge environmental benefits of the CDA, it should be noted that for the introduction of CDA in daytime operations, improved ATC concepts are necessary in order to satisfy, or even increase, the present day approach capacity of conventional procedures.

Optimizing Routes and Air Traffic

Required Navigation Performance (RNP) is a type of Performance Based Navigation (PBN)[34] system that allows an aircraft to fly a specific path between two three-dimensionally defined points in space (See Figure 18.11). Global ATC community devised this system to increase ATC's capacity to handle the anticipated demand of the traffic along with airspace user requests to reduce flight time and save money. This can be useful for en route descents, terminal manoeuvring areas, and final approaches where the systems would speed schedules and flying times according to prevailing winds.

RNP can assist in aircrafts' approach and departure procedures in busy airports. It can reduce delays resulting from shorter arrivals for RNP aircraft. It also maximizes use of the onboard navigational capability of the modern aircrafts. Integration of RNP into the ATM system provides greater flexibility to balance operational requirement with community expectations. RNP also facilitates a CDA. Non-RNP flights following an RNP aircraft benefit from reduced delays derived from the shorter RNP approach. In response to the growing demands, the International Civil Aviation Organization (ICAO) has specified that RNP is an essential element of communications navigation surveillance/air traffic management (CNS/ATM) and is encouraging early implementation in the en route environment.

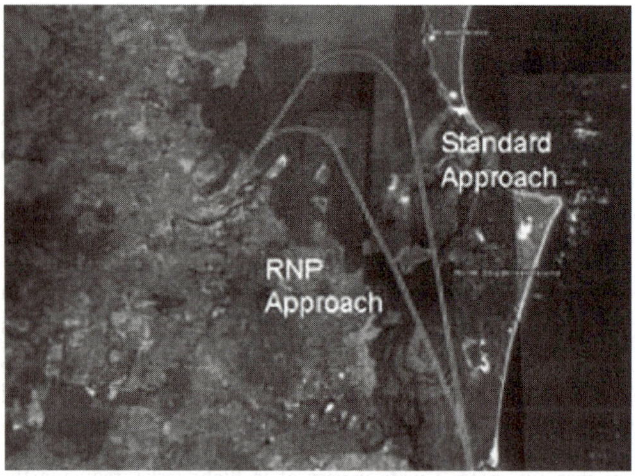

Figure 18.11 RNP Approach Shows System

Source: Brisbane Green Project 2007.

The Brisbane Green Project with an RNP has saved 650,000 kg of CO_2 emissions in the first year alone with a fuel saving of 200,000 kg for a year. The total number of track miles saved during Stage1 is estimated to exceed 17,300 nautical miles. The RNP path ensures that the low-level final approach is conducted over the river and industrial areas. It also ensures increased safety in all weather conditions. By optimized routes systems, the aircraft can become 12 per cent more fuel-efficient (Brisbane Green Project 2007).

Introducing RNP in India

The following enhancements would reduce the fuel significantly, further minimizing the costs and emissions (See Table 18.13).

Enhancements to the Air Traffic Management and Air Navigation Systems:

- More fuel-efficient approaches and overall routing
- Reduced vertical and horizontal separation minima—expanding available airspace through tighter spacing, thus giving airlines a greater choice among fuel-efficient routes and altitudes.

Improving Air Traffic Management (ATM) to Reduce Delays in India

As mentioned earlier, India suffers serious lacunae in its operational management system; per day cost of poor ATM on the Delhi–Mumbai route could be of the order of INR 44 lakh.[35] Clearly, there is ample scope for improvement. After studying the existing operational measures under consideration in India for Air Traffic management, it is found that proper ATM can have a great impact in reducing the delays and further saving the fuel used, emissions, and the cost incurred in the delays.

Table 18.14 presents information on delays on the Delhi–Mumbai route in a day (2008–9). The figures are based on calculations, the methodology for which has been explained earlier.

According to the analysis, there are about 80 flights a day on this route. Around 40 of these 80 flights are in the air during peak hours. Considering that peak hour flights are usually delayed by half an hour, it is apparent that

[34] PBN system is explained under the Air Navigation Service-provider Section of the measures under consideration.

[35] 'Suspended Animation', *Down to Earth*, 29 February 2008.

Table 18.13 Emission Reduction Potential and Fuel Savings by the RNP for the Delhi–Mumbai Air Route

	2005–6	*2006–7*	*2007–8*	*2008–9*
Fuel efficiency by optimizing routes and air traffic (kg)	21,678,556	30,931,379	20,449,039	46,949,736
Reduction of cost of fuel after optimizing routes and air traffic control (million US$)	14,763	23,199	18,915	31,973
CO_2 emission reduction potential (T)	1,056,830	1,507,905	996,891	2,288,800
Total CO_2 emission reduction (T)	144,113	205,623	135,940	312,109
Total cost of fuel saving (million US$)	2,013	3,163	2,579	4,360

Note: Cost of total fuel saved (million USD)	12,116
Total CERs generated (T)	797,785
@' price of 13$/T US$ generated	1,844,479,345
@' price of 13$/T Million US$ generated	1,844

The CER price of 13$/T is taken as of the January 2009 price.
Source: Analysed by the authors from the example of the Brisbane Green Project 2007.

Table 18.14 Delays on the Delhi–Mumbai Route for a Typical Working Day for the Financial Year 2008–9

Total average flights/day	80
Considering delays in peak hours, avg. flights delayed in a day	40
As per *Down to Earth*, delay in peak hours (mins)	30
Avg. fuel consumption in the route(kg)/flight	1,813
Total fuel use in the route (kg)/day	145,000
Average CO_2 emissions per day (T)	7,069
Fuel use in delay hours (kg)	625
Total fuel use in delay (kg)	25,000
Average delay CO_2 emissions per day (T)	1,219
% of delay emissions to total emissions	14.71

Source: Author's own (as per author's analysis).

50 per cent of the traffic on this route is never on time; the international standard is about 12 per cent. Hence, in order to achieve international standards, the route needs to increase efficiency by 75 per cent.

Analysis presented in Table 18.15 shows that if ATM is more efficient and delays reduced by 75 per cent, India can match international standards and save fuel to the tune of 18,797 kg per day, saving $ 10 million. About 916 tonnes of CO_2 emission can also be prevented per day by optimizing the delays in the route.

Other Measures

Apart from the above mentioned measures, a few other measures are also proposed which have to be studies in detail for their applicability for Indian conditions. The measures are as explained below:

- *Flex Tracks, User Preferred Routes (UPRs), Dynamic Re-routes:*
  - Flex tracks permit air-carriers to make the best use of tailwinds or avoid headwinds in flight planning. Flex tracks challenge the ATC system each day with widely varying routes, but the savings for airlines are enormous. The initiative came out of the Australian Air Traffic Management Strategic Plan issued in 2002 as part of the country's commitment to implementation of ICAO's global plan for future ATM.
  - UPRs are customer designed for each individual flight in order to meet the specific needs of the aircraft for that flight, including fuel optimization, cost-index performance, or military mission requirements. UPRs are calculated based on factors such

Table 18.15 ATM System for Fuel Efficiency and Emission Reduction (Per day)

Air Traffic Management	*Average Fuel conserved (kg)*	*Average CO_2 emissions reduced (T)*	*Average Cost saved (million USD)*
100 per cent reduction in delays	25,000	1,219	14
75 per cent reduction in delays	18,797	916	10
50 per cent reduction in delays	12,500	609	7

Source: Analysed by the authors from study of *Down to Earth* (Refer to footnote 20).

as forecasted winds, aircraft type and performance, convective weather, and scheduling requirements. While flex tracks do not provide the same level of efficiency to individual aircraft that can be achieved in a UPR system, a flexible track system may be the most efficient solution. For example, in the oceanic environment, UPRs can create problems in sequencing aircraft, forcing some to fly at sub-optimal flight levels.

  - Dynamic Airborne Re-route Procedures allow aircraft to adjust their present position to a new point in order to realize savings in fuel or time. This is coordinated by the airlines with the flight crew, and sent to air traffic control as a request to change route from the aircraft.

- *Implementing Advanced Navigation Capabilities, RNAV-RNP*
  - Required Navigation Performance (RNP) of Aircraft Navigation (RNAV) is a type of PBN system that allows an aircraft to fly a specific path between two three-dimensionally defined points in space. A navigation specification that includes a requirement for on-board navigation performance monitoring and alerting is referred to as an RNP specification. One not having such a requirement is referred to as an RNAV specification. (For more details on RNP refer to optimizing routes and air traffic section above). Integration of RNP into the ATM system provides greater flexibility to balance operational requirements with community expectations.
    - Gate to Gate Management initiatives which take into account potential delays along the entire route (aircraft do not take off if congestion is expected at destination) to prevent unnecessary holding patterns; aircraft in holding patterns at lower altitudes can burn five times as much fuel a at cruising heights.
    - Improved arrival/departure routes and profiles (for example, secondary radars installed at Delhi, Mumbai, Ahmedabad, Nagpur enabled ATCs to provide direct routings, improved route structure for improved air capacity due to direct routings which makes the aircraft spend less time in the air, burn less fuel, and emit less CO_2).
- *Optimizing Airport Operations through Collaborative Decision Making:*
  - Collaborative Decision Making (CDM) is a joint government/industry initiative aimed at improving air traffic management through increased information exchange among the various parties in the aviation community. The CDM programme is made up of representatives from the government, general aviation, airlines, private industry, and academia who are working together to create technological and procedural solutions to traffic flow problems that face the National Airspace System (NAS).
  - Improving airport infrastructure to support optimum capacity.
  - Most airports need to have spare capacity, and it says that much of the existing capacity remains unused at the typical busy hour traffic levels earlier.[36] Significant effort needs to be devoted to taking every last scrap of capacity out of the existing infrastructure, and develop much more infrastructure to handle the increasing traffic in the future years.
- Economic regulations for the airports and air navigation services.
- Creating a transparent and supportive regulatory regime on air traffic management.
- Developing an equitable fiscal environment (for example, tax on fuel).
- Investing in appropriate airport infrastructure.
- Building an efficient airspace and air traffic management system.
- Training the workforce that will drive the industry.

Summary and Conclusions

Aviation is increasingly being singled out as a major source of GHG emissions, a significant contributor to global climate change, and a source of air pollutants. From the study it was observed that aviation contributes to 2 per cent of global CO_2 emissions and 13 per cent of transport emissions and 8 per cent of global NOx emissions. Aviation's CO_2 emissions rose by 4.5 per cent, from 675 to 705 million tonnes from 2000–4. For the same period fuel wastage increased about 13 per cent, reaching 18 per cent fuel use from the sector. Apart from the above mentioned findings, the other major findings from the research are as mentioned below:

- Aviation is a major contributor to the economic and social well-being of India; connects India to the world as a trading nation and fosters economic growth and prosperity.
- It provides access to remote communities where air transport may be the only realistic option.

[36] ICAO (2009a).

- The aviation sector internationally is growing at 5 per cent per annum (PA)
- Aviation emits gases like CO_2, CH_4, NOx, N_2O, soot, contrails and cirrus which have much more impact than the other sectors.
- Aviation's share of GHGs has not grown since 1990 although aviation has grown substantially.
- Aviation energy consumption is 15 per cent of total transport sector.
- There are many uncertainties in estimating emissions as the level of understanding of all the gases is not known. Gases like soot, contrails, and cirrus which have much more impact are not known.
- There is a scientific concern that, despite the very low levels of GHG emissions from commercial aircraft operations, the standard cruise altitudes of those aircraft could compound the effects of their GHG profile through a process that is commonly referred to as radiative forcing. Notably, there is significant uncertainty within the scientific community as to the extent and relevance of this process on the overall GHG footprint of the industry. The most recent IPCC report of 2007 concluded that contrails contribute a small radiative forcing impact with a low level of scientific understanding. It is essential that more scientific resources be devoted to this particular factor in the overall debate in order to better understand and respond to this issue.
- According to predictions of IPCC, CO_2 is to be increased by 258 per cent (1991–2015) and NOx would increase by 411 per cent for the same period. It is also predicted that CO_2 would and NOx would increase by 588 per cent and 411 per cent (1992–2050) respectively.
- The IEA forecasts that GHGs from the sector would increase by 90% by 2030 without any policy implications taken.
- It was also found that there are various concerns and developments in mitigation of aviation emissions globally and in India. The following points are the crucial concerns in aviation emissions. These concerns are important to be considered for improving the civil aviation sector and the emission reduction potential from the sector in India.
- The history of emission reduction strategies for started way back in 1969 although a proper framework to reduce emissions started only in 1997 after the inclusion of domestic aviation in the Kyoto Protocol.
- Framework for mitigation of emissions although included in the Kyoto Protocol, the sector is working only under ICAO to meet the targets.
- There is no proper legal framework for emission reduction for the sector.
- NATCOM is the only framework to reduce emissions from other sectors other than aviation in India.
- Several steps by various governments and airlines have been taken since Kyoto, but there is no international framework for the emission reduction.
- USA and UK have been the leaders in emission reduction from aviation.
- There are no policy frameworks for the emission reduction internationally or in India.
- Despite its insignificance Indian aviation has grown in leaps and bounds with more than 12 per cent annual growth in the fleet.
- The air traffic is growing at an average of 5 per cent annually with around 8 per cent growth in 2008
- India ranks third in the world for addition of new flights increasing domestic passengers.
- Severe delays with 50 per cent of the traffic getting delays at the major airports due to lack of infrastructure, mechanisms, and management systems to reduce delays, traffic control or slot management for the sector.
- There is no placed methodology or framework for the emission reductions in India.

It was also observed that there is significant potential in emission reduction, fuel saving, and further cost saving in implementing various proposed operational strategies. Operational improvement-based three strategies proposed for India, have been suggested after studying various operations strategies and these operational strategies have been selected for their applicability to Indian conditions. These could significantly reduce emissions and improve the overall efficiency on the Delhi–Mumbai route:

- ATM to reduce delays: The effective ATM can save fuel worth 10 million $ and further international standard of 12 per cent can be achieved by this mechanism.
- Continuous descent approach can save about 605,216 CERs and fuel worth 8 million $.
- Optimizing route can also save about 797,785 CERs and fuel worth 1844 million $.

Operational procedures can improve the overall fuel efficiency of the sector and reduce the emissions. Thus by improving the routes approaches and departures, there could have been fuel savings up to 12,116 million $ during the study period for the study route.

References

Air Transport Action Group (2008). '*The Economic and Social Benefits of Air Transport*', available at http://www.atag.org, last accessed on July.

Aviation Environment Federation (2000). *Aviation and Global Climate Change,* AEF, London.

Brisbane Green Project 2007: Airservices Australia (2007). *RNP Project: Brisbane Green Stage One Report.*

Busink, F.W. (2000). 'Environmental Benefits of Continuous Descent Approaches at Schiphol Airport Compared with Conventional Approach Procedures', National Aerospace Laboratory, Nice, France.

CAPA (2009). *China and India Domestic Traffic Soars,* Centre for Asia Pacific Aviation (CAPA), India.

Cairns, S. and C. Newson (2006). *Smart Carbon: Potential Emissions Savings from Smarter Choices,* Report for the Department for Transport, United Kingdom.

Clarke, J.P.B, N.T. Ho, L. Ren, J.A. Brown, K.R. Elmer, K.O. Tong, and J.K. Wat (2004). 'Continuous Descent Approach—Design and Flight Test for Louisville International Airport', *Journal of Aircraft,* 41(5), pp. 1054–66.

ECA Airports (2006). *Mather Airport Continuous Descent Approach–Noise Analysis Report,* The Sacramento County Airport System, Sacramento.

Environmental Finance (2008). Voluntary Carbon 2008. Climate Change, Offsets and the Carbon Markets, Special Report, February.

ESA (2006). *Mather Airport Continuous Descent Approach (CDA),* The Sacramento County Airport System, California.

Eyers, C.J., P. Norman, M. Plohr, S. Michot, K. Atkinson, and R.A. Christou (2004). '*AERO2K Global Aviation Emissions Inventories for 2002 and 2025*', QINEYIQ/04/01113, United Kingdom.

Federal Aviation Administration (2005). *Aviation & Emissions—A Primer,* Office of Environment and Energy, United States of America, January.

——— (2008). *FAA Flight Plan,* The Federal Aviation Administration, Washington DC.

Gold Standard, available at http://www.cdmgoldstandard.org.

Greener by Design (2005). *Mitigating the Environmental Impact of Aviation: Opportunities and Priorities,* Report of the Greener by Design Science and Technology Sub-Group, Royal Aeronautical Society, United Kingdom.

Hamilton, K., E. Stewart, and S. Waage (2006). Offsetting Emissions. A Business Brief on the Voluntary Carbon Market. Ecosystem Market Place and Business for Social Responsibility.

IATA (2008a). 'Building a Greener Future', April, available at http://www.iata.org, last accessed on 15 September 2008.

——— (2008b). 'History and Development of International Aviation', available at http://www.iata.org/about/history_3.htm, last accessed on 4 November 2008.

——— (2007). *State of the Air Transport Industry—64th Annual General Meeting,* Montreal, June.

International Civil Aviation Organization (2007). 'Aviation Environment Outlook', August 2008, available at http://www.icao.org.

——— (2008). *Air Navigation Services Providers (ANSPs) Governance and Performance,* Conference of the Economics of Airports and Air Navigation Services, Montreal.

——— (2009a). 'Measures Adopted by Civil Aviation Sector in India', Director General of Civil Aviation, Montreal, Canada.

——— (2009b). 'Proposals for Strategies and Measures to Achieve Emissions Reduction's', 1033 Civil Aviation Sector in India, Montreal, 7–9 October 2009.

——— (2010). ICAO Performance BasedNavigation (PBN) Programme, available at http://www2.icao.int/en/pbn/pages/introduction.aspx

International Energy Agency (2006). *World Energy Outlook,* Paris.

IPCC (1998). 'Aircraft Emissions' in *Good Practice Guidance and Uncertainty Management in National Greenhouse Gas Inventories,* Institute for Global Environmental Strategies.

——— (1999). *Aviation and the Global Atmosphere: A Special Report of IPCC Working Groups I and III,* by J.E. Penner, David H. Lister, David J. Griggs, David J. Dokken, and Mack McFarland (eds), Cambridge University Press, Cambridge, United Kingdom and New York, NY, USA, June 1999, p. 373.

——— (2000). *Special Report on Aviation and the Global Atmosphere,* The Hague, November, available at http://www.grida.no/publications/other/ipcc%5Fsr/?src=/climate/ipcc/aviation/index.htm

——— (2007). 'Changes in Atmospheric Constituents and in Radiative Forcing', in S. Solomon, D. Qin, M. Manning, Z. Chen, M. Marquis, K.B. Averyt, M. Tignor, and H.L. Miller (eds), *Climate Change 2007: The Physical Science Basis—Contribution of Working Group I to IPCC Fourth Assessment Report,* Cambridge University Press, UK and New York, p. 129.

Jacobs Consultancy Canada Inc. (2007). 'Canadian Aviation and Greenhouse Gases–Literature Review' Jacobs Consultancy, Ontario.

Karagozian, A., W. Dahm, E. Glasgow, R. Howe, and I. Kroo (2006), *Technology Options for Improved Air Vehicle Fuel Efficiency: Executive Summary and Annotated Brief,* United States Air Force Scientific Advisory Board, Washington DC.

Kim, B., G. Fleming, S. Balasubramanian, A. Malwitz, J. Lee, J. Ruggiero, I. Waitz, K. Klima, V. Stouffer, D. Long, P. Kostiuk, M. Locke, C. Holsclaw, A. Morales, E. McQueen, and W. Gillett (2005). *SAGE: The System for Assessing Aviation's Global Emissions.* FAA-EE-2005-01, USA.

Kolmuss, A., H. Zink, and C. Polycarp (2008). *A Comparison of Carbon Offset Standards,* WWF, Germany.

Kolmuss, A. and J. Lane (2008). Carbon Offsetting and Air Travel. Part 1: CO_2- Emissions Calculations.

Liebeck, R.H. (2004). 'Design of the Blended Wing Body Subsonic Transport', *Journal of Aircraft*, 41(1), pp. 10–25.

Mckinsey Global Institute (2007). 'Next Big Spenders: India's Middle Class', *Business Week*, 19 May 2007.

Schell, Beatrice (2001). *European Federation for Transport & Environment*, Ninth Session of the United Nations Commission on Sustainable Development Multi Stackholder dialogue segment, New York.

Senguttuvan, P. (2008). *Global Trends in Air Transport: Traffic, Market Access & Challenges,* Delhi International Airport Private Limited, Indira Gandhi International Airport, New Delhi, India.

Stern, J. (2007). *World Energy Outlook 2007*, International Energy Agency (IEA), Paris.

Stough, K.B. (2000). *Air Transport Networks–Theory & Policy Implications,* Edward Elgar Publishing Ltd, Northampton.

UK House of Commons Environmental Audit Committee (2007). The Voluntary Carbon Offset Market, para 32, p. 19.

19 Multi Modal Transport in a Low Carbon Future

Sanjiv N. Sahai and Simon Bishop

Introduction

This essay investigates the role of an integrated multimodal transport system in a low carbon future. Drawing heavily on the case of Delhi, the chapter addresses the question: how far can multimodal transport help achieve a low carbon future while fostering economic progress and social equity? Two papers that have been reviewed here have both quantified carbon emissions reductions associated with a shift towards multimodal transportation. One of them refers specifically to the potential impact of a transformation in Delhi, while the other is a case of actual transformation from Bogotà, Columbia.

Despite the rhetoric, and the odd case of cities like Bogotà, the direction of travel in most cities of the world is towards a series of uncoordinated, ad-hoc interventions that help to facilitate transport disintegration, a move away from public transport, walking, cycling, and other non-motorized modes to greater dependency on private, motorized vehicles. The paper will seek to identify and establish the magnitude of these challenges and, drawing as far as possible on best-practice case studies, discuss possible ways to address them.

'Multimodal transportation' is a scientific term for something really quite simple; journeys that involve some kind of transfer from one type of travel or 'mode' to another. Even if one is travelling by car or motorcycle for example, a journey is likely to involve a short walk at the start and end points. However, trips by public transport, principally bus and Metro, typically involve a longer walk trip to access or egress them and here multimodality comes into its own. There may also be public transport journeys that involve a combination of more than two transit modes, a walk trip followed by a bus trip, then a Metro trip, and finally a cycle-rickshaw trip, for example.

To facilitate multimodality of the type needed to encourage public transit usage, a number of different kinds of integration are required:

- Integration with land-use planning
  - Building public transit links first and then developing high-density, mixed land-use around them thereby reducing the need to travel, especially by private vehicles
- Integration within and between different modes of transport
  - *Physical Integration*—facilitating direct, comfortable, convenient, and safe access to public transport (providing safe, direct road crossings, tree-shaded paths, refreshments, cycle and rickshaw parking, differently abled pavements and access points)
  - *Fare Integration*—Enabling the public transit user to pay ONCE for a journey involving different transport
  - *Route Integration*—Facilitating logical interchange points where passengers are able to transfer from one vehicle or mode to another conveniently and safely
  - *Information Integration*—Enabling a 'one-stop-shop' for public transit users, cyclists, and walkers to gain information on any journey they wish to conduct using these modes
  - *Institutional Integration*—Ensuring that different public transit providers see themselves as part of a network and provide links to other types of transit, walking, and cycling

Policy Integration with Environment, Health, Education, and Economy

Public transport starts with a disadvantage compared to the door-to-door flexibility of private transport. So there must be good reasons to set about creating a multimodal system. Climate change is conceivably one of those reasons. According to the UK's Chief Scientist, David King:

'*Climate change is the most severe threat the world is facing today, more serious even than the threat of terrorism.*'

The transport sector is responsible for approximately 25 per cent of total greenhouse gas emissions globally and is the fastest growing sector source worldwide. Between 2007 and 2030, global emissions from transport are expected to rise by 80 per cent. Three quarters of the contribution is expected to come from road transport (IPCC 2007).

Urban transport emissions are likely to be especially problematic in the Asian context due to growing city populations, rising incomes leading to higher demand for personal, motorized mobility, and the disproportionate climate change impact of short journeys due to inefficient engine use (Bannister 2008).

Compared to a 2.1 per cent increase per annum in greenhouse gas emissions from transport in the developed world, developing country emissions are expected to rise at a rate of 3.5 per cent a year to 2030 (IEA 2002). As India and China race to catch up with the 2.5 tonnes of carbon emitted per head in Europe or 5.5 tonnes per capita emitted in the US, the stabilization targets worldwide are 0.5 tonnes, similar to that of India now. The scale of the challenge looks insurmountable.

Transport and Climate Change in Delhi

The Development of Urban Form

With a population of 17 million, rising at a compound rate of 4 per cent a year, Delhi provides a very good vantage point from which to view the threat, not only because its transport system is not presently integrated but also because it is the capital city of a country that is home to more than one sixth of the world's citizens (*Economic Survey 2009–10*).

Since 70 per cent of the urban environment in Asian cities that will exist by 2050 has not yet been built, there are opportunities to develop sustainably and get ready for the transformation needed to cope with climate change challenges associated with rapid economic development (Penalosa 2008). Any successful attempt to create a multimodal transport system in India's capital city is likely to influence policy and practice in other parts of India with potentially enormous implications for developing a low carbon pathway in transport and the built environment.

Delhi also typifies an urban structure being replicated in other Asian cities that have been booming economically for the past 20 years since economic liberalization. Unlike older cities in Europe and the US that built a central business district (CBD) in an age before mass motorization based around extensive rail networks, Delhi has no clearly identifiable CBD. As Map 19.1 shows, a number of subsidiary centres dot the landscape. These are sprawling outwards, characterized by mixed use, quite low population density and generate comparatively modest trip lengths, the majority being less than 10 km. In this context the city is becoming heavily reliant upon more flexible, low-cost transport, principally cars and motorcycles.

Road Infrastructure Development: Implications for Multimodality

As the city sprawls so does demand for mobility increase. Trip demand is expected to rise from approximately 20 million per day now to 29 million by 2021 (RITES 2005).

To cater to this demand, Delhi already owns a higher number of vehicles than the next three Indian metropolises combined—presently more than 6 million with approximately 1,100 more being added each day. In addition to the emerging urban layout described above (Map 19.1), part of the explanation rests upon GDP, rising on average between 10 and 12 per cent per year. Average incomes are now over $2,000 per annum, the level at which most countries start buying into greater personal mobility, motorcycles, and cars (Dargay and Gately 2007). Yet there remains significant room for market growth. According to the RITES study, approximately half of all Delhi households still do not own a car or motorcycle (*Economic Survey 2009–10*; RITES Ltd and TERI 2010).

Ironically, on the ground is little room to accommodate future growth. Delhi already has one of the most capacious road networks in the world with 21 per cent (28,000 km) of the city's total area under tarmac and little room for further expansion. In the 25 years from 1971–2 Delhi's road network grew 3.7 times while the number of vehicles grew by more than 25 times. Offering less than 6 km per 1,000 vehicles, the road network in Delhi is rapidly becoming inadequate to the task of catering for the expanding number of vehicles (*Economic Survey 2009–10*) (see Figure 19.1).

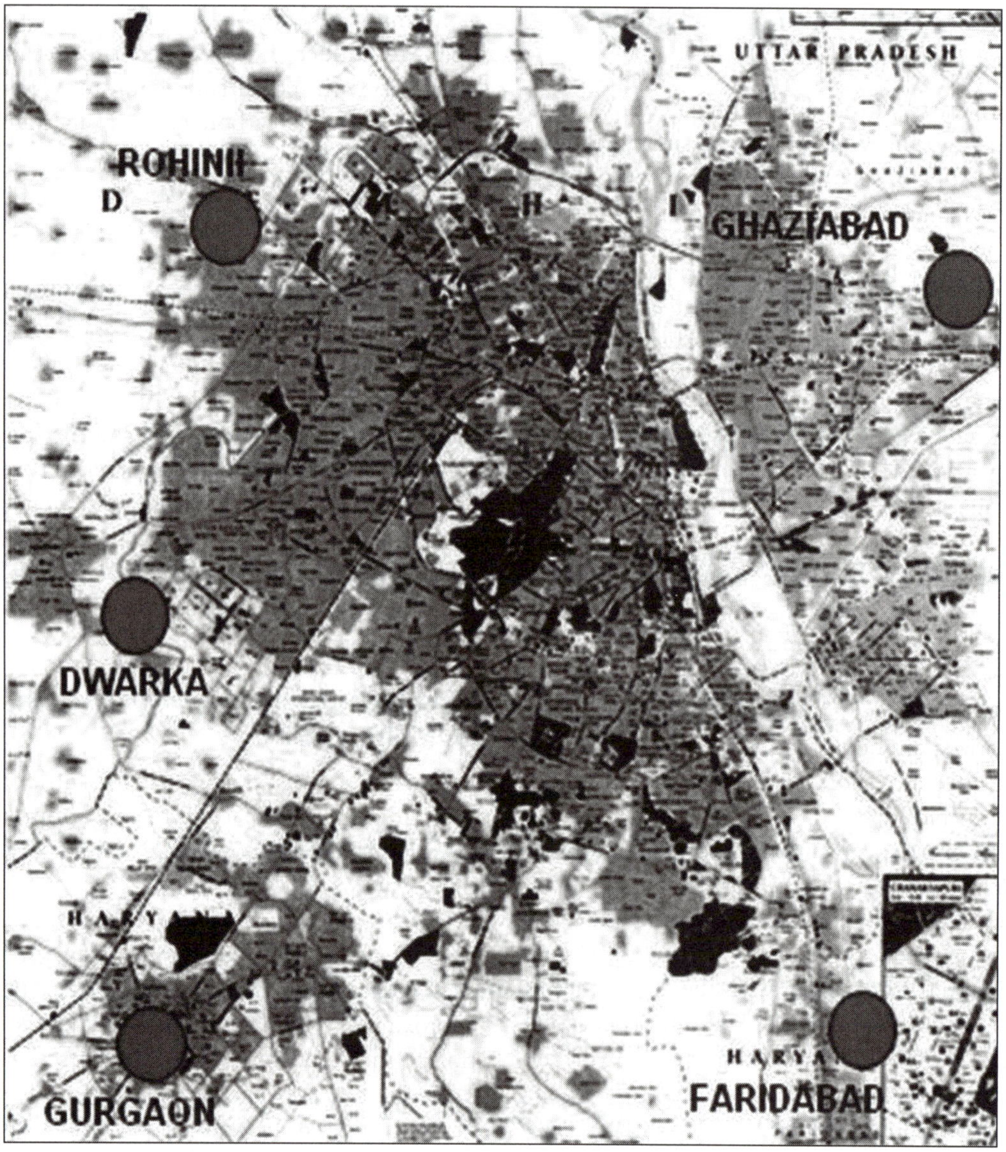

Map 19.1 Delhi's 5 Satellite Cities

Source: Delhi Integrated Multimodal Transit Systems (DIMTS).

The graph encapsulates the first major policy response to rising transport demand: 'keeping private motorized vehicles moving' through widening and flyover construction to reduce bottlenecks as and when they arise. The City Development Plan is investing more than half its transport budget into flyovers and road capacity enhancement schemes (Arora 2010).

Less Modal Choice Implies Higher Carbon Trips

A focus on road capacity enhancement contrasts significantly with two of the key objectives of the Ministry of Urban Development (2006), firstly, to establish an 'equitable allocation of road space' and secondly, to prioritize non-motorized and public transport. Harm is also caused to another key objective; to create a multimodal transport system. In Delhi, for instance, including public transport, more than three quarters of trips in the city involve a walk or cycle trip, as shown in Figure 19.2. Over 75 per cent of access and egress trips to Metro stations are 'non-motorized' (RITES Ltd and TERI 2010).

Preserving a high non-motorized share, especially for short distance trips of 5 km or less should be a priority in any low carbon transport strategy (55 per cent of trips in Delhi are less than 5 km). The table below, taken from the US Bureau of Energy Efficiency, compares energy consumption of different means of transport (see Table 19.1). Although there are caveats associated with comparing the energy consumption of different modes,

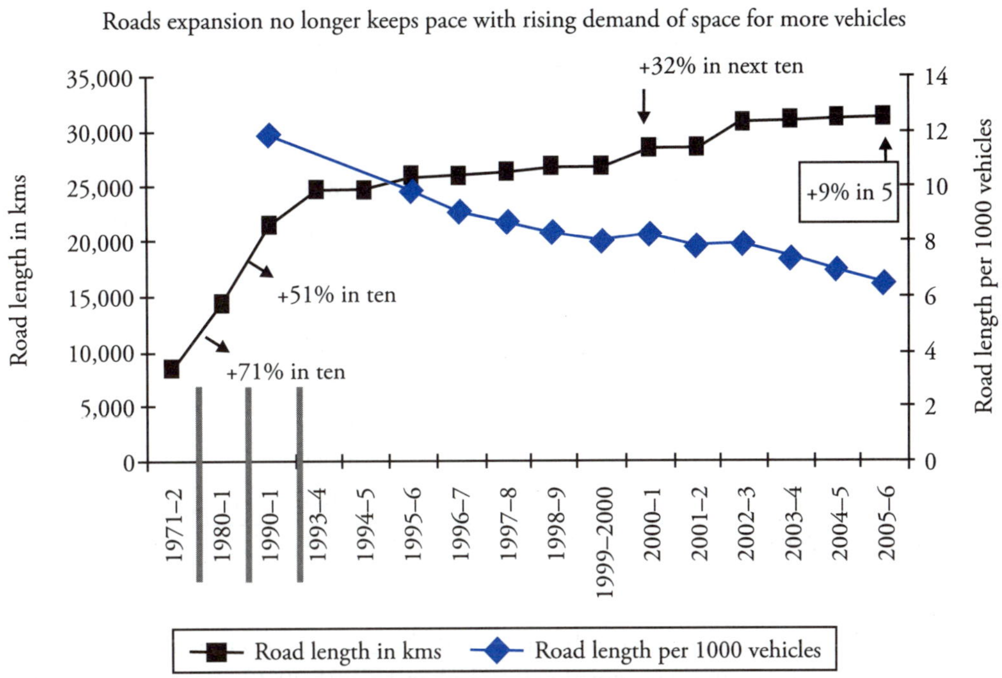

Figure 19.1 Expansion Struggling with Rising Space Demand

Source: Environment Pollution (Control and Prevention) Authority (2009).

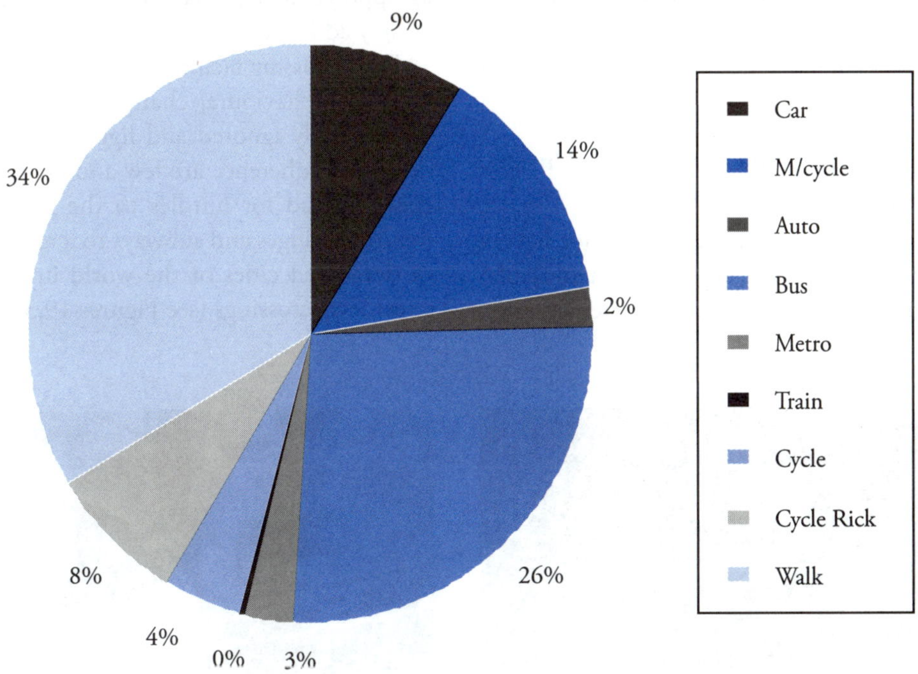

Figure 19.2 Low Carbon Transport Journeys in Delhi, 2008

Source: RITES Ltd and TERI 2010.

not least in a different country, what is interesting to note is that ridership of a bus needs to be at least 10 passengers in order to consume the energy at a rate equivalent to an average car.

In Indian cities like Delhi the picture is more favourable to lower carbon bus use, with an average of 50 passengers using one at any given time, combined with the fact that all buses in Delhi run on CNG. However, carbon dioxide

Table 19.1 Comparative Fuel Efficiency of Different Transport Modes

Transport mode	*Average passengers per vehicle*	*BTU per passenger-mile*	*MJ per passenger-kilometre*
Vanpool	6.1	1,322	0.867
Efficient Hybrid	1.57	1,659	1.088
Motorcycles	1.2	1,855	1.216
Rail (Commuter)	31.3	2,996	1.964
Rail (Transit Light and Heavy)	22.5	2,784	1.825
Rail (Intercity Amtrak)	20.5	2,650	1.737
Cars	1.57	3,512	2.302
Air	96.2	3,261	2.138
Buses (Transit)	8.8	4,235	2.776
Personal Trucks	1.72	3,944	2.586
Cycle	1	183	0.12

Source: US Department of Energy (2006).

emissions per passenger kilometre are still likely to be at least one fifth that of an equivalent averagely occupied car given the fact that average vehicle weight in Delhi is less than the US average.

Walking a kilometre, on the other hand, consumes only 0.330 MJ of food energy. Cycling uses even less energy, 0.12 MJ per km (183 BTU/mi), less than a quarter of the energy needed to carry a passenger one kilometre by bus in Delhi.

Walking (or cycling) to Public Transport is Unsafe, Consumes Unnecessary Time and Effort

Presently 40 per cent of roads in the city do not have a pavement refuge and those that do exist are often unusable, especially by the mobility impaired due to extremely high kerb heights, encroachments, and obstructions (RITES Ltd and TERI 2010). Reported road deaths are another deterrent, topping 2000 a year, with the majority of victims being pedestrians (55 per cent). Road planning is undertaken by citywide agencies and the needs of local, as opposed to regional, road planning requirements are weakly addressed.

Road crossing facilities are ripe for an upgrade; as is the need for behavioural change in drivers. Zebra crossings are routinely ignored and light controlled crossings that do secure adherence are few and far between; a penchant exists instead for hurdles to the mobility impaired like foot overbridges and subways that are now being removed in developed cities of the world in favour of accessible, street level crossings (see Figures 19.3(a) and 19.3(b)).

Figure 19.3(a) A Family Trying to Cross a Road to Change Bus

Source: Centre for Science and Environment Photo Library, 2009.

Figure 19.3(b) Buses Don't Stop at the Stop

Though similar in geographical size to London, Delhi possesses approximately 750 pedestrian light controlled crossings compared to 6,500 in London. Vehicle movement is prioritized over public transport users by allowing 'free left turns' at most junctions. In this scenario, given a choice in travel mode, who is not likely to opt for a car or motorcycle?

Figure 19.4 showcases the effect of private vehicle-based development, showing the impact of installing an elevated road in Ashram Chowk on the Ring Road in Delhi. Designed to reduce congestion by allowing signal-free movement, the road elevation makes local journeys nearly impossible to conduct by non-motorized means. Everyone is forced into a motorized vehicle even for short journeys and bus stops are difficult to reach too.

Buses are an Option of Last Resort

With worsening travel conditions for pedestrians, as also most other public transport users, the use of the bus is taking a nosedive. In the last eight years the number of person trips in Delhi has increased by 22 per cent. While the city has seen a marginal shift in person trips to the new Metro service, this has been more than cancelled out by a fall in the order of 17 per cent in the total number of trips in the capital that are taken by bus. In 2008, 46 per cent of trips were taken on public transport compared to 60 per cent in 2001.

Such trends are resulting in an increasingly poor level of service for motor vehicles too. The level of service for public and privately owned motorized vehicles is falling in Delhi, which a few salient statistics clearly show. According to a recent RITES Study (RITES Ltd and TERI 2010):

- Traffic speeds are now less than 30 kmh on 70 per cent of the road network,
- Traffic capacity is exceeded on 44 per cent of network
- On another 19 per cent of network 'nearly' exceeds capacity

A Losing Battle against Climate Change

In a study of 87 cities in India, which included analysis of cities of over 5 million population as a special category (Delhi, Bangalore, Kolkata, and Mumbai), Wilbur Smith Associates used a calibrated urban transport model to establish the possible implications. The study concluded that failure to make any improvement to the existing situation in these cities will lead to a continued decline in bus patronage, falling as low as 25 per cent of modal share by 2030 (Wilbur Smith Associates 2009).

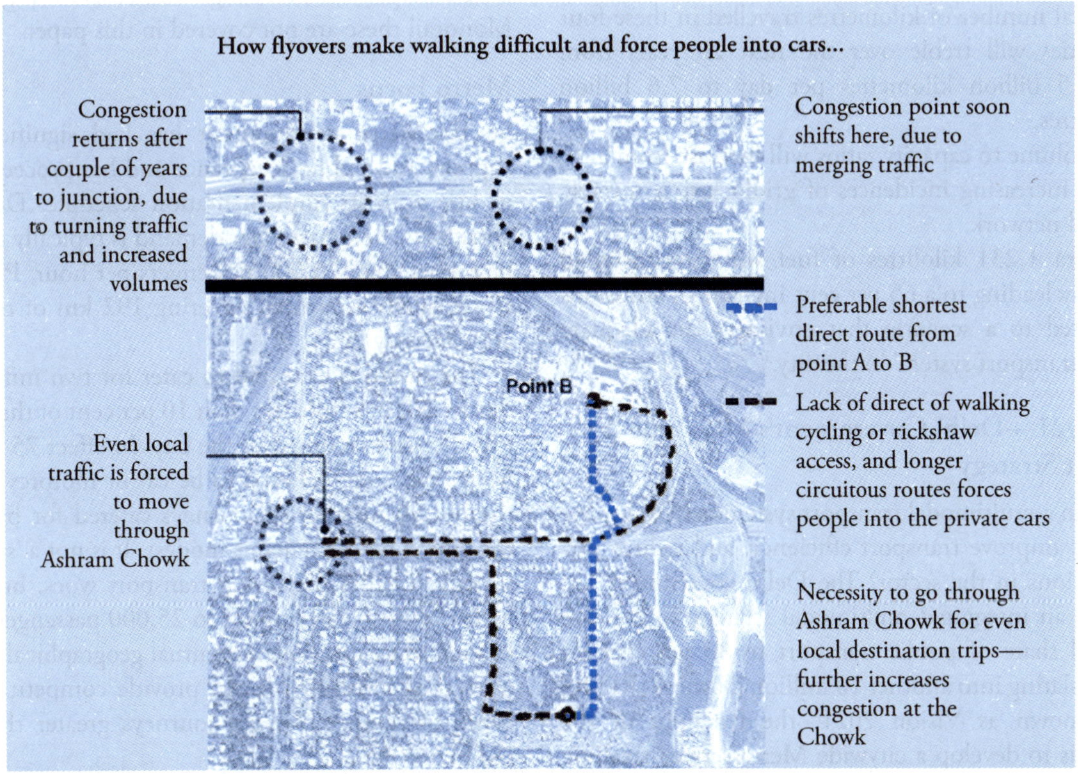

Figure 19.4 How People are Forced to Use Motorized Vehicles for Short-distance Trips—Ashram Chowk Flyover, New Delhi

Source: Solving Congestion through Transit Oriented Development, Romi Roy 2009.

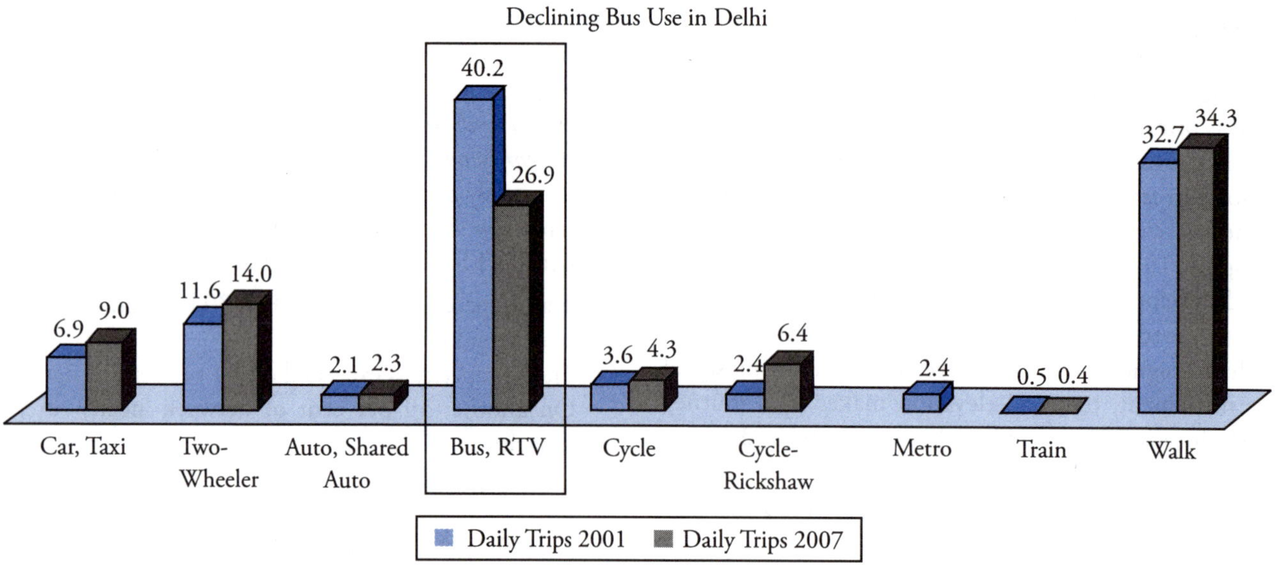

Figure 19.5 Declining Bus Use in Delhi, 2001–8

Note: Modal Split—Per cent of Person Trips in Delhi* (Figures in per cent).
Source: RITES Ltd and TERI (2010).

At the same time average trip lengths will rise from around 10 km now to 15 km by 2030. This, combined with increasing number of trips per capita, implies that:

- The total number of kilometres travelled in these four megacities will treble over the next 20 years from over 2.5 billion kilometres per day to 7.6 billion kilometres.
- Road volume to capacity ratios will increase from 1.21 to 2.9, increasing incidences of gridlock to a severely strained network.
- An extra 1,231 kilolitres of fuel will be consumed each day leading to a 65 per cent increase in emissions compared to a scenario that envisages 'an adequate public transport system' in the city.[1]

Vision 2021—Delhi Government's Multimodal Transport Strategy

So how can a multimodal transport system help to reverse this trend, improve transport efficiency, and reduce carbon emissions in the sector? The Delhi government has developed an integrated multimodal strategy to increase the modal share of public transport to 80 per cent by 2021 translating into another 10 million journeys (RITES 2005). Known as Vision 2021, the lynchpin of the approach is to develop a citywide Metro service rivalling that of London in size, buttressed by a series of bus priority corridors covering nearly 300 km, Light Rail Transit, and Monorail (see Map 19.2). Since feasibility studies have emerged with very high unit costs for Light Rail and Monorail these are not covered in this paper.

Metro Focus

So far Metro development has had significant media support and public acceptance and has proceeded closely in line with its implementation schedule. Designed for corridors where passenger demand is typically expected to be higher than 25,000 passengers per hour, Phases I and II are nearly complete, covering 192 km of the 413 km envisaged by 2021.

The metro is expected to cater for two million trips a day by 2010, a little less than 10 per cent of the total daily trip demand recorded in the city. In effect 75 per cent of Metro users are believed to be car or motorcycle owners, the overall number of journeys catered for by Metro in the city therefore remains modest. It is not a 'silver bullet' to solve Delhi's increasing transport woes, but given its high capacity (carrying up to 25,000 passengers per hour in each route direction), eventual geographical scope, and unrivalled reliability, it can provide competitive journey times for longer distance journeys greater than 10 km (RITES 2005).

[1] Adequate public transport includes: bus modernization and augmentation including terminals and bays, improved interchange facilities, junction improvements, on-street parking management, safe crossing facilities, and cycle tracks.

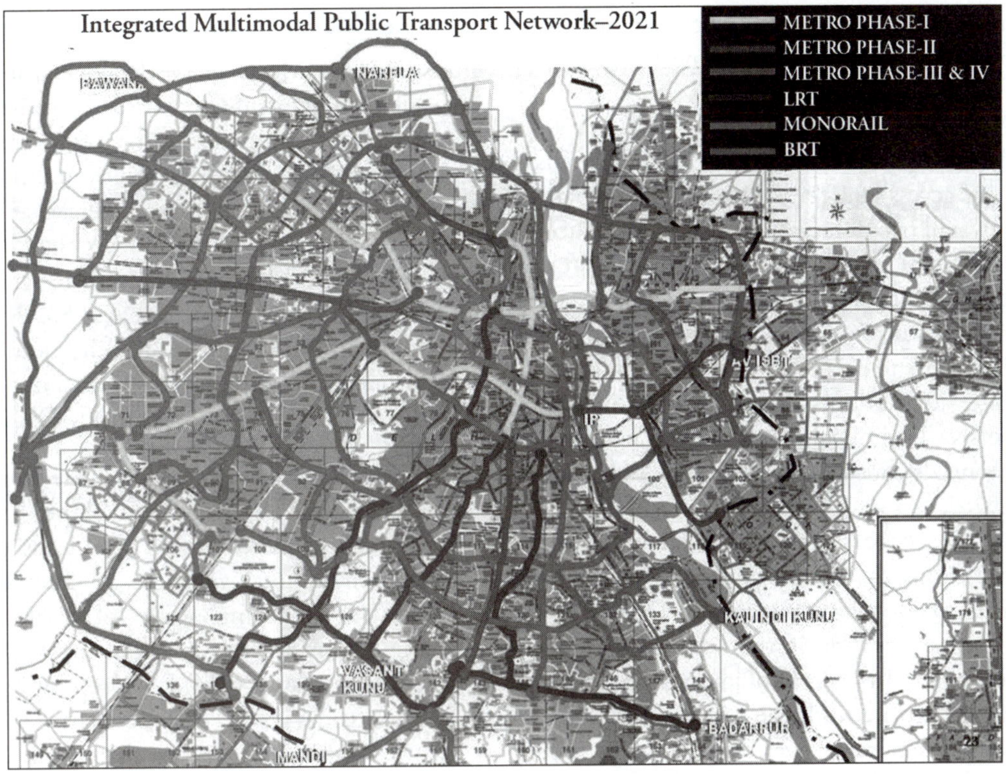

Map 19.2 Vision 2021 Public Transport Network

Source: RITES (2005).

The Limits of Metro in a Multimodal Low Carbon Transport City

Yet an analysis of Metro networks in worldwide cities shows that the Metro faces considerable hurdles to ramping up its patronage to levels reaching 20 per cent of modal split. In Delhi actual Metro patronage is consistently less than figures predicated by advocates making a case for investment in this transport mode. With Phase II of the Delhi Metro nearly complete (126 km by June 2010 out of 189 km by September 2010), ridership hours around 5 per cent of all trips in the city (1.1 million), less than the number taken by cycle rickshaw. This compares with a 1995 prediction for over 3 million trips to be undertaken by the Metro on Phase I (65 km) by 2005 alone (Comptroller and Auditor General, India, 2010). The Metro is highly capital-intensive, costing INR 187 billion in the first two phases alone (DMRC 2008). Each passenger trip is subsidized to over Rs 100 (Mohan 2008). Nearly three quarters of the city's public transport budget for the City Development Plan currently finds its home in Metro expenditure but these loans are granted on the condition that ridership will eventually be high enough to pay them back. In this respect the Metro charges a rate of nearly Rs 3 per kilometre (Arora 2010). The Metro must compete with the door-to-door convenience and marginal cost of using a bus and a motorcycle which are Rs 1.25 and Rs 1 per kilometre respectively.

Climate also plays a role in limiting Metro catchments; 48 per cent of Delhi residents are beyond the 500 metre catchment area considered desirable to encourage use of public transport. Like many other cities in South Asia, for seven months of the year the soaring temperatures in Delhi are punishing. Evidence from temperate, western countries shows that people are unwilling to walk more than five minutes to a public transit stop, a factor which is increased for the Metro due to the extended time and effort in using steps and escalators to access and egress from the train. In a city like Delhi the 'willingness to walk' to public transit is, if anything likely to be much less and compounded by safety and access concerns highlighted earlier.

Car parks can be provided for vehicles, but these can only ever cater for a small number of the required number of metro passengers (2,000 or so long-stay commuter cars compares unfavourably with an *hourly* Metro capacity of 25,000 trips). Personal vehicle access to Metro stations is also likely to generate localized congestion, increase the overall carbon emissions for each journey, and can only serve one half of the access or egress trip. Only 3 per cent of trips to Metro stations are currently by car, a figure that is not likely to change significantly in the near future.

Bus Travel in a Low Carbon Transport City

Whilst the Metro can offer time savings on longer distance trips where access and egress times form a smaller portion of the overall trip duration, the 'workhorse public transit system' in Delhi needs to be low cost to cater for a large cohort on low incomes (Delhi's average per capita income is still less than $6 a day), highly flexible with stops and stations close to people's homes and workplaces, and able to cater for multiple origins and destinations with shorter trips. Traditionally, buses have been able to deliver these needs much better than fixed rail heavy transit systems.

Such a conclusion echoes a study of different cities in Latin America showing that Metro systems alone are not a sufficient means of effecting a modal shift. Despite having one of the largest networks in the world, the Mexico Metro caters for merely 14 per cent of journeys in the city. London, with a Metro network the size of Delhi's after completion handles an even lower proportion of trips. Extensive use of more flexible public and para transit options including buses, combined with land-use planning measures to create an environment-friendly network for pedestrians and cyclists would appear to be more essential components to reduce car use and carbon emissions from transport (Mohan 2008; BRT Planning Guide 2008) (see Figure 19.6).

Demand Management and Bus Prioritization

Investing in a Metro network alone brings with it no particular requirement to increase the efficiency of the road network, to cater for more trip demand using less space and energy. In the absence of any multimodal strategy to manage demand for private vehicles and to prioritize public transport, walking, and cycling, Metro facilities open up more space for private vehicles, making cars and motorcycles more convenient to use. Studies for the Asian Development Bank provide an indication of the scale of possible carbon dioxide savings from a bus-based strategy in India, Bangladesh and Sri Lanka (ADB 2006):

- Bangalore: An increase in bus share from 62 per cent to 80 per cent saves equal to 21 per cent of the fuel consumed in the base case. This leads to 23 per cent reduction in total vehicles and frees up road space equivalent to taking nearly 418,210 cars off roads. Carbon dioxide emissions can drop by 13 per cent. Particulate matter (PM) can drop by 29 per cent and nitrous oxides (NOx) by 6 per cent.
- Dhaka: An increase in bus share from 24 per cent to 60 per cent saves fuel equal to 15 per cent of the fuel consumed in the base case. This frees up road space equivalent to removing 78,718 cars from the roads. Carbon dioxide emissions drop by 9 per cent. PM can drop by 13 per cent and NOx less than 1 per cent.
- Colombo: An increase in bus share from 76 per cent to 80 per cent can save 104,720 tons of oil equivalent,

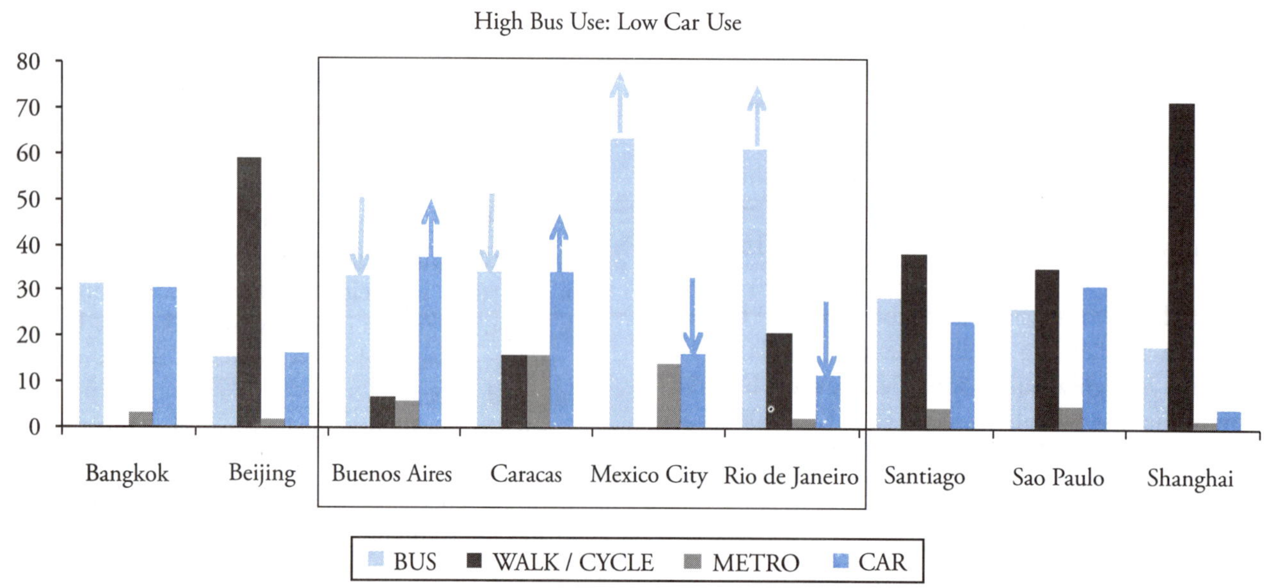

FIGURE 19.6 High Bus Use, Walking, and Cycling: Key Determinants of Reduced Congestion

Source: Deutsche Gesellschaft für Technische Zusammenarbeit (GTZ) and SUTP (2008).

or 3 per cent of the fuel consumed in the baseline case. This means a 5 per cent reduction in the total number of vehicles and frees up road space equivalent to removing 62,152 cars. (ADB 2006)

An Optimal Low Carbon Transport Strategy for Delhi

Using comparative risk assessment methodology researchers from Delhi and London carried out a study of five different greenhouse gas scenarios for a series of different transport investments in the two cities (The Lancet 2009). The study compared policy action to improve vehicle fuel efficiency combined with rail-based improvements to the same in enhancement of the bus network, restrictions on private vehicles, and higher standards of connectivity, safety, comfort, and access for pedestrians and cyclists.

The Delhi study used data from VIBAT and Wilbur Smith Associates to establish a baseline scenario of global emissions from the transport sector in 2004 (6.1 million tonnes carbon dioxide) and extrapolated this first to 2010 and then onwards to 2030 (Scenario 1) when the sector is expected to emit 19.6 million tonnes of carbon dioxide. This is a 526 per cent rise on 1990 carbon dioxide emissions levels in Delhi from the transport sector.

The baseline was then adapted to three different policy scenarios. Scenario 2 parallels the Delhi government's CNG initiative when all public transit vehicles were required to shift to liquid petroleum gas fuel in 2002 and subsequent requirements for vehicles to meet international EURO IV standards. The scenario assumes compliance with Euro VI standards by 2020 in line with all European countries. Efforts to up-scale the vehicle fleet are combined with significant investment to develop a citywide rail network like the Metro. The result for carbon dioxide emissions is a rise in the order of 447 per cent on 1990 levels, 73 per cent less than the baseline.

Scenario 3 of the Lancet study, meanwhile assumes a reversal in declining conditions for non-motorized transport (NMT) in Delhi, resulting in a marginal increase in walking trips and a doubling in the amount of cycle trips. Scenario 3 sees a halving in per capita carbon dioxide emissions in transport in Delhi compared to Scenario 2, achieved through restrictions on vehicle usage, ranging from road pricing and tolling to the application of tighter parking controls. Delhi is transformed from a city in which cycling and walking are a mode of necessity for those unable to afford a motor vehicle to a mode of choice. Bus trips increase marginally in Scenario 3, bucking the current downward trend. There is a significant increase in rail usage, paralleling again rising Metro patronage in Delhi. Scenario 3 sees a rise in carbon dioxide emissions in the order of 234 per cent on 1990 levels, a little more than half the amount secured through a vehicle technology and Metro focused approach.

Finally, Scenario 4 links measures implemented in Scenarios 2 and 3, seeing an increase in 199 per cent on 1990 levels of carbon dioxide emissions from the transport sector, something like a doubling on levels emitted in 2004. The results are shown in Table 19.2.

An important conclusion from the study is that *prioritization of walking and cycling and restricting vehicles through policy interventions like carbon rationing, road pricing, and traffic demand management, combined with improving conditions for those using public transport (Metro and bus), would reduce emissions more than twice as much as those from a strategy focused solely on vehicle efficiency improvements and Metro development.*

The strategy also achieves important co-benefits such as better health and improved quality of life. Health benefits include lower levels of chronic disease such as Type II diabetes and heart disease due to a combination of less airborne pollution and a fitter, more active, healthy

Table 19.2 Comparative Scenarios of Carbon Emission Mitigation Strategies in the Transport Sector, Delhi (2010–30)

	Aggregate Transport CO_2 Emissions	*Transport CO_2 Emissions Per Person (tCO_2/person)*	*CO_2 Emissions Increase on 1990 (%)*
2004 Delhi	6,146,651	0.4	97
2030 Scenario 1: BAU	19,550,693	0.8	526
2030 Scenario 2: Low Carbon Motor Vehicles (LCD)	17,069,668	0.7	447
2030 Scenario 3: Active Transport (AT)	10,458,736	0.4	235
2030 Scenario 4: Sustainable Transport (ST)*	9,327,207	0.4	199

Note: Delhi Population: 2004 = 14.8 million and 2030 = 26.0 million

* Sustainable Transport = LCD + AT

Source: Public Health Benefits & Strategies to Reduce Greenhouse Gas Emissions: Urban Land Transport (The Lancet 2009).

population. Decreasing road traffic also has a potential to reduce road accidents, although the study was not able to quantify this effect.

Bogotá, Columbia—Real-life Example of a Multimodal Transport System

It is also important to understand the costs and benefits of any strategy to mitigate carbon dioxide emissions. A study by Lloyd Wright and Lewis Fulton (Box 19.1), conducted in 2005 attempts to quantify these by drawing on empirical data from the transformation of public transport, walking and cycling facilities in Bogotá, Columbia enacted as part of 'Transmilenio' in 2000 (Wright and Fulton 2005). The authors set out to compare the costs and benefits of policies aimed at improving vehicle efficiency through fuel switching, on-board technology, lighter weight materials, and better maintenance with policies that target modal shifts secured through a multimodal transport network. Bus prioritization formed the lynchpin of the multimodal strategy supported by small, but influential investments in non-motorized transport.

Wright and Fulton started out by defining three different categories to isolate the relative impacts of fuel-based approaches and multimodal transport systems to carbon dioxide mitigation.

- The share of trips undertaken by each transport mode (car, motorcycle, bus, metro, cycle, walk, etc.) and the load factor or the number of passengers carried by a particular vehicle. Most of the subcomponents of this category have some influence on the modal choice of the consumer which is determined by considerations of convenience, safety, comfort, cost, and travel time.
- The distance travelled by each mode affected by network design and land-use planning applications.
- The application of technology to reduce emissions from improved engine design, better maintenance, vehicle weight, and driver behaviour.

As a preview to the study, the IEA (2002) found that an ordinary 120-seater diesel bus with a 50 per cent load factor carrying 8 per cent of its passengers who had switched from private vehicles could deliver reductions in carbon dioxides up to four times the emissions of a single bus. What was even more interesting was that the selection of bus engine technology had hardly any impact on the final outcome. It didn't matter if the bus was fitted with EURO I, II, or III technology, the savings in tailpipe emissions were completely overwhelmed by the effect of a modal shift.

Wright and Fulton also reviewed the impact of fuel switching policies and programmes of different governments to measure the costs and benefits of this approach to mitigate carbon dioxide emissions. The EU headed the list of big spenders on fuel switching research with an investment $3.7 billion on a 10-year programme. The expenditure on fuel switching vastly exceeded expenditure on targeting modal shifts despite a high degree of risk and uncertainty associated with investments in technology like fuel cell research.

The most tried and tested fuel switches, CNG, and hybrid fuel vehicles face problems as CNG is believed

Box 19.1
'Transmilenio'

A multimodal transport system

- Route integration is secured through a series of 'feeder routes' (309 km) linked to dedicated bus lanes (84 km).
- Physical integration with other modes has involved the construction of over 300 km of cycle routes complemented by improved pedestrian pathways and car-free pedestrian plazas linking to the BRT network directly, safely, and conveniently.
- Stations are built to minimize the distance travelled to change from a feeder to a mainline bus without needing to leave one interchange point.
- Land-use planning has been integrated requiring higher density, mixed land-use around bus stops and interchanges thereby facilitating more convenient travel by public transit.
- Demand management measures check the growth in private vehicle usage. Parking capacity has been reduced on streets served by the network and restrictions are placed on the number of cars entering the city by prohibiting vehicles with particular number plate combinations on alternate days.
- Fare integration is achieved through a system of common ticketing allowing those using feeder buses to travel on all buses without buying more permits to travel.
- Institutional reforms ensure that different public transit providers see themselves as part of a network and provide links to other types of transit, walking, and cycling.

Source: Wright and Fulton (2005).

to offer few discernible benefits in carbon dioxide reductions once methane leakages are considered. Hybrid vehicle technology has also under-performed in real life situations. Compared to manufacturers' claims of a 25 per cent baseline fuel reduction capability in Seattle, host to one of the largest hybrid diesel bus fleets in the world, actual emissions reductions were less than half those promised. Solely fuel-based approaches also ignore the additional social benefits of accident and congestion reductions.

Using data available from Transmilenio, Wright and Fulton built up a reference case based on a total of 10 million trips per day, less than half the number of a city like Delhi, but interestingly the number set to be switched to public transit by 2021. Each motorized trip was 10 km on average, if anything longer than the average trip distance in Delhi. Table 19.3 sets out the reference case, where, in comparison to Delhi, the majority of trips by bus are catered for by smaller minibuses but like Delhi are not segregated from ordinary traffic and constitute a similar modal share of the overall traffic mix.

No increase in the number of private vehicles was assumed over the 20-year period; this is clearly not realistic but it keeps the potential emissions reduction resulting from a mode switch more modest. The costs of mitigation were estimated to be $2.5 million for a km of BRT, $150,000 for a km of pedestrian improvements, and $100,000 for a km of cycle infrastructure. Low cost of infrastructure, means that Transmilenio operates without any subsidy, so none was included in the calculations.

Compared to the lowest cost fuel switching scenario in which $148 per tonne of carbon dioxide saved, the highest costs of a BRT mitigation package were less than $70 per tonne of carbon dioxide (see Table 19.4). With important lessons for Delhi, investment in cycle infrastructure alone to increase its mode share from 1 to 10 per cent of all trips, yielded carbon dioxide reductions at the lowest cost of $14 a tonne. In the case of targeted cycle track investment carbon dioxide savings from the baseline amounted to 4,160,400 tonnes alone.

Three times the amount of carbon dioxide a year was saved through the creation of a multimodal transport system grouping together walking and cycling with public transport. This is because the capture by one mode of a greater share of trips 'tends to suppress the other'. The lesson drawn is similar to that derived from the Lancet study. It is particularly important to include cycle and pedestrian improvements with bus network enhancements because a sole focus on buses will draw people from non-polluting transport onto buses, thereby reducing space for erstwhile motor vehicle users.

Reinforcing the earlier IEA study, Wright and Fulton found that very small reductions in car use in the order of one per cent could generate potentially large reductions in carbon dioxide in the order of one million tonnes over the 20-year period.

Delhi Bus Rapid Transit

As part of the Vision 2021 investment strategy, a total of six Bus Rapid Transit Corridors are slated for development in Delhi, each with the kinds of pedestrian and cycle facilities envisaged in the Wright and Fulton paper (see Map 19.3). These may help to transform the image of bus transport in the city by improving the speed, comfort, and status of this mode of transport. They may also herald something of a cycling renaissance and serve as a benchmark for future pedestrian facilities in the city, according to international experts.

Table 19.3 Transport Reference Case for Bogotá, 2001

Mode	*Mode Share (%)*	*Trips/Day (000s)*	*Passengers/ vehicle-km*	*Distance travelled/day (km 000s)*	*Fuel Consumption (litres/100 km)*	*CO_2 (kg)/ litre*	*CO_2/day (tonnes, 000s)*	*CO_2 over 20 years (tonnes, 000s)*
Automobile	20	2,000	0.15	13,333	10.8	2.42	1087.2	21,744
Motorcycle	4	400	0.105	3,809	2.2	2.42	63.2	1,266
Taxi	5	500	0.15	3,333	10.8	2.42	271.8	5,436
Minibus	50	5,000	1.3	3,846	30.3	2.87	1,043.5	20,870
BRT	0	0	5.2	0	64.1	2.87	0	0
Walking	20	2,000	1	150	0	0	0	0
Cycling	1	100	1	100	0	0	0	0
							2,465.8	49,315

Source: Wright and Fulton (2005).

TABLE 19.4 Carbon Mitigation Costs and Benefits of Different Transport Investment Strategies in Bogotá 2001–21

Scenario name (in per cent)	*Mode share (in per cent)*	*Carbon dioxide (CO_2) over 20 years (tonnes, 000s)*	*CO_2 reduced from the baseline (tonnes, 000s)*	*Cost of infrastructure (in US$)*	*Cost ($)/ tonne of CO_2*
BRT mode share increases from 0 to 5	Automobile 19 Motorcycle 4 Taxi 4 Minibus 48 BRT 5 Walking 19 Cycle 1	47,409.7	1,905.5	$125 million (50 km of BRT at 2.5 million/km)	66
BRT mode share increases from 0 to 10	Automobile 18 Motorcycle 4 Taxi 3 Minibus 45 BRT 10 Walking 25 Cycle 1	45,086.8	4,228.5	$250 million (100 km of BRT at 2.5 million/km)	59
Walking mode share increases from 20 to 25	Automobile 19 Motorcycle 4 Taxi 4 Minibus 48 BRT 0 Walking 25 Cycle 1				
Bicycle mode share increases from 1 to 5	Automobile 19 Motorcycle 4 Taxi 5 Minibus 48 BRT 0 Walking 18 Cycle 10	45,145.9	4,160.4	$60 million (500 km of cycleways at 100,000/km, plus $10 million promotional campaign)	14
Package: BRT, pedestrian upgrades, cycleways	Automobile 15 Motorcycle 3 Taxi 3 Minibus 34 BRT 10 Walking 25 Cycle 10	36,917.5	12,397.8	$370 million (BRT $250 million; footpaths $60 million; cycleways $60 million)	30

Source: Wright and Fulton (2005).

The Experience of Delhi's Pilot BRT Corridor—Ambedkar Nagar to Delhi Gate

One BRT is already in existence, a 14.5 km corridor running in South Delhi from Ambedkar Nagar to Delhi Gate, although only 5.8 km is currently operational. In contrast to the Metro, the Delhi BRT has been mired in controversy since it started in April 2008 despite witnessing an increase in bus patronage in the order of 10 per cent, bucking the citywide trend and a reduction in bus user travel time in the order of 33 per cent (Hidalgo and Pai 2009). In line with the Wright and Fulton study findings, another important benefit of the first corridor is the rising number of cyclists using its fully segregated lane. The number of cyclists using it has increased from 1,200 per hour to 2,800 during peak periods.

BRT, despite the controversies that surround it, remains a potentially cost-effective means of transport investment. Its true benefits will only begin to be realized once it becomes part of a more capacious public transport network. In comparison to the Metro, the total cost of

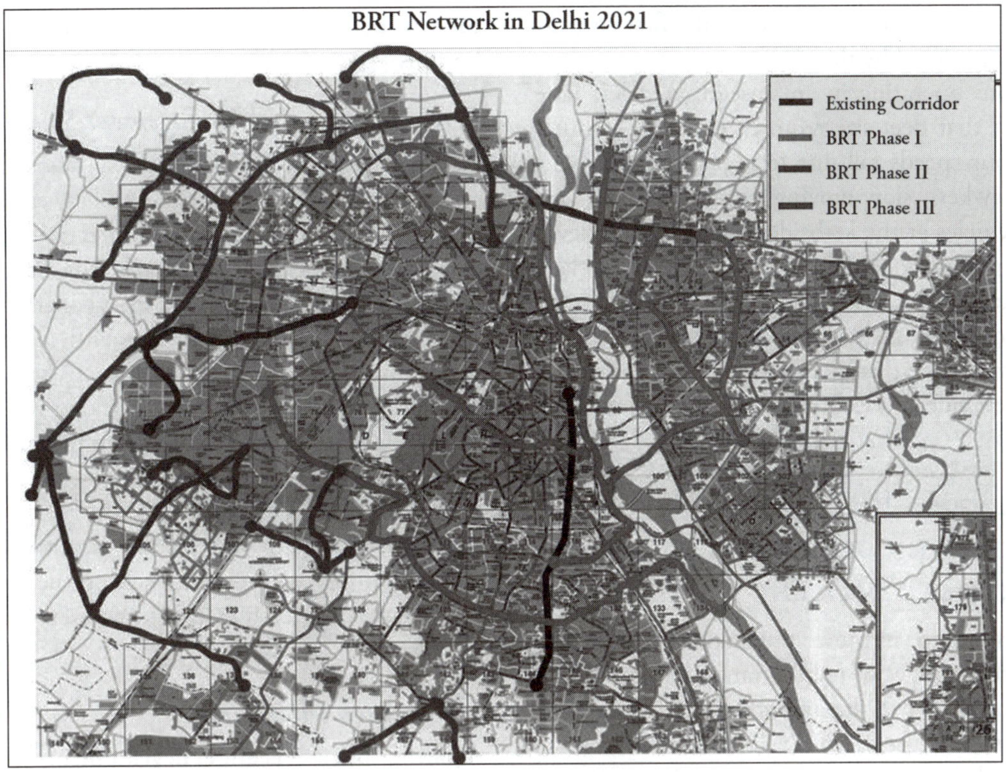

Map 19.3 Plan for Bus Rapid Transit in Delhi to 2021

Source: RITES (2005).

corridor construction was $48 million, an average of $3.3 million per kilometre. The Delhi Metro ranged from $25 million to $60 million per kilometre. Although the Delhi Metro has the capacity to cater for 25,000 passengers per hour during the peak period, the Delhi BRT already carries up to 12,000 passengers per hour at less than one tenth the capital cost. A fully fledged BRT akin to that operational in Bogotá could see this figure rise to 40,000 passengers per hour.

Challenges to Establishing a BRT Network

Issues associated with public acceptance and cultural change (the requirement that motorized vehicles stop at mid-blocks as well as at junctions to allow bus passengers to access the stops) set significant challenges to the ultimate success of BRT in Delhi from the outset.

Journey times for car users have increased by 14 per cent since the corridor began (EMBARQ 2009). In purely textbook terms the first corridor might have fitted the bill for conversion to BRT; a large number of buses, cycles, pedestrians, and a high number of personal vehicles that were ripe for segregation. Politically, however, the corridor was challenging.

Much of BRT's promised success rested on people being willing to switch to public transport to reduce dwell times in the mixed traffic lanes. That might have been possible if the whole network was able to capitalize on such an expectation. Despite the recent introduction of a new fleet of low-floor vehicles, outside the single BRT corridor buses remain stuck in traffic, unreliable, overcrowded and, overall a poor competitor to private vehicles that face subsidized parking costs and lower taxes than buses (see Corporatization of Private Stage Carriages in Delhi section below) (Narain 2009). Neither are there deterrent policy measures against using a car or motorcycle apart from congestion, something which experts acknowledge has a greater impact in effecting modal shift than supply side improvements alone (Dasgupta et al. 1994).

The government appears to remain a long way from asking the public to leave their vehicles at home and switch to the bus. Only 0.2 per cent of the City Development Plan is spent on raising public awareness on transport (Arora 2010).

A decision to now shift the second part of the BRT corridor for the final 7 km stretch from central lane to left lane operating could compromise operational efficiencies gained in bus speed and passenger throughput in the first corridor. There will be no physical segregation of the bus lane and it will almost certainly be shared with other vehicles. Despite the initial plan to develop six corridors of BRT by 2010, it is unlikely that even the first corridor will be fully operational by this time.

With the bus operating in an unsegregated left lane, experts suggest that fleet size requirements will as much as double as bus speeds fall due to greater friction with pedestrians, hawkers, slow-moving vehicles, parked, and left-turning vehicles at the kerbside leads to higher levels of unreliability. Audits conducted by engineers, cyclists, and the Traffic Police, of the constructed cycle lane on the new section of corridor from Moolchand to Delhi Gate also show service disruption as the need to put bus stops on the left side causes breaks in footpath and cycle track continuity.

Complementing BRT—The Corporatization of Private Stage Carriages in Delhi

Delhi is working to improve integration within and between different modes of public transit, integrate fares and routes, and improve the availability of information for public transport users. The 'vehicle' to achieve this restructuring is known as 'The Corporatization of Private Stage Carriage Services Scheme'.

Status of Bus Services in Delhi

Presently around half the bus services in Delhi are provided for by private contractors who typically own a very small number of buses. Each contractor operates his or her bus on individual routes, competing against 60 per cent of buses served by the state operator, Delhi Transport Corporation, and other private operators. As a consequence, the system is highly inefficient, encourages unsafe driving practices, and delivers few 'network' benefits. Only individually remunerative routes are operated by private operators. Less remunerative routes are sometimes served by the state-run DTC. However, like many other state-run transport companies there are weak incentives to provide efficient services. Recently a Comptroller Auditor General (CAG) report found that less than three quarters of DTC kilometres are actually run, a figure that has been falling for a number of years.

Bus Network and Management Reform Measures

The corporatization scheme aims to group cohesive bus networks into 17 area-wide clusters, each of which will be run by one operator for a contractual period of 10 years. The number of routes operated will increase from an estimated 500 actually run now to 657, thereby bringing the network within 500 metres of every home in Delhi. With the aim of reducing unsafe driving practices the operator will be paid according to the number of kilometres he runs.

Performance-based Management System

Compared to the state-run DTC buses, however, final operator payments will depend on how each bus performs in accordance with a pre-determined timetable. Operators with 'No shows' and late buses will either forfeit their payment or be renumerated less than those arriving on time, serving passengers in line with a number of pre-determined standards. Performance will be measured through an on-board GPS bus tracking system linked to a Central Control Room that records individual data.

Intermodal Integration

A smartcard system will enable passengers to 'touch in' and 'touch out' of each bus, ending the requirement for time-consuming cash transactions every time passengers interchange.

Information Integration

A journey planner is under development, presently piloted on over 200 buses using the Bus Rapid Transit corridor in Delhi, which will use mobile phone and internet technology to feed real-time travel information to bus users. The first bus cluster of 17 has already been awarded and a further four more are currently out for tendering.

Walking and Cycling in a Low Carbon Transport System

Greater attention to improving NMT facilities could have a serious impact on the Delhi transport sector's contribution to climate change as the Lancet study clearly showed. Even a shift from a bus to a bicycle or foot can reduce carbon dioxide emissions more cost-effectively than the introduction of fuel-efficient vehicle technology. Early morning and evening commuting trips could be made feasible during summer months with the availability of better street infrastructure including high levels of tree shading, work showers, changing rooms, cycle parking, and a supportive management.

A number of different NMT initiatives are currently coming together under a combination of a pro-active stance taken by the Delhi Metro and the manager of Delhi's BRT corridor, DIMTS, and a desire to 'beautify' and 'streetscape' for the Commonwealth Games. The latter involves the application of new Pedestrian Design Guidelines which have adopted the highest possible standards for pedestrian facilities and are mandatory to follow (UT and TC 2009). Both cycle sharing and these new 'showcase' pedestrian and cycle infrastructure projects have the potential to demonstrate the role that an NMT could play in reducing carbon dioxide emissions in the city.

Cycle Sharing Schemes in Delhi

The first initiative is a cycle sharing scheme that involves installing hire bicycles near to BRT stops and Metro stations. The idea is that people could use this means of zero carbon transport to undertake a motorized public transport connecting trip or as an alternative to short-distance journeys often undertaken by car or motorcycle (see Figure 19.7).

The most successful international cycle sharing scheme is run by the advertising company, JC Decaux, in Paris for the municipal government, with other, smaller schemes in Lyon, Berlin, Vienna, and Barcelona.

In Paris a total of 20,600 bicycles are used every day by over 81,126 people. Even assuming that a modest 20 per cent of customers would have otherwise used a car to travel an average of 7.5 km (half now using a bus for 10 km and half using the cycle alone for 5 km) this is a reduction in vehicle kilometres in the order of 121,680, all that would have been driven in the central urban area and most at peak travel times when carbon dioxide emissions per passenger km would have been at their highest due to high levels of congestion (Schlebusch 2010).

Ignoring the scale differences between the two schemes for a moment, an examination of the utilization rate and the fare structure shows that Delhi's scheme is not currently securing maximum usage of its cycles, many remain parked in outlying areas to be returned only when the user makes a return trip to the station (see Table 19.5).

The Paris scheme, on the other hand, has cycle stations installed at destination and origin points away from the public transit stop or station and provides a financial incentive for cycle sharers to utilize the bicycle for a short trip before it deposited at the drop off point. This enables the user to drop off the cycle thereby making it available for another user. The results are shown in the comparative

Figure 19.7 Cycles for Hire Outside Delhi Metro Station and BRT Stop

Source: Schlebusch (2010).

Table 19.5 Comparative Assessment of Cycle Hire Schemes in Delhi and Paris, 2008

System/City	*Paris*	*Delhi*
Number of Bicycles	20,600	130
Number of Stations	1,451	13
Number of Daily Customers (Average)	80,126	150
Duration of Trip (Average)	18 mins	174 mins
Bicycle Occupancy Per Day (Average)	3.89	1.16
Fare Structure	Free—first 30 mins	Rs 10 first 4 hours
	1 Euro—31–60 mins	Rs 5 each extra hour
	2 Euro—61–90 mins	
	4 Euro—Each extra 30 mins	

Source: Schlebush (2010).

utilization rates of both schemes. Other advantages of the Parisian system that Delhi would do well to replicate include: easy booking option for cycles over the internet or by mobile, and a strong brand identity through the choice of a modern bicycle that is distinctive comfortable and attractive to ride.

Despite this, a survey of the Delhi Cycle Sharing Scheme conducted by the German Development Agency, GTZ shows that the scheme has great potential to substitute for short-distance trips by car and motorcycle. The user survey found that two thirds had an above average education level, an average income of up to Rs 5,000 per month, and half-owned a car or a motorcycle but were not using it because 'a bicycle is (more) convenient' (Schlebusch 2010).

Streetscaping and Beautification for the Commonwealth Games

As part of the preparations for the Commonwealth Games a number of streets have been earmarked for high-quality pedestrian and cycle infrastructure development. Although the work is not yet complete at many of the locations it is already possible to see that a high degree of professionalism has been applied at the design stage to ensure that facilities are *direct, safe, attractive,* and *comfortable* to use. Adherence to Delhi's Pedestrian Design Guidelines is part of the way towards achieving these goals.

In the context of cycle infrastructure one of the key challenges remains in incorporating these new facilities into a clearly legible network, which fits with existing (and future) travel patterns. The GIS maps 19.4, 19.5, and 19.6 compare the existing routes provided by municipal agencies, including new facilities being developed for the Commonwealth Games with those that might be considered in any way 'usable' and finally with existing cycle flows. The first map (Map 19.4) shows that, according to the municipalities' definition of a cycle track, there already exists a fairly large number of tracks in the city. At the same time there are significant gaps between them, making them difficult to use.

The second map (Map 19.5) shows cycle routes that were audited by experts in a recent evaluation exercise. Compared to the first map, the number of cycle tracks that were deemed relatively free of encroachments, direct, comfortable, safe, and attractive was quite limited. Most

Map 19.4 Existing Cycle Tracks in Delhi

Source: New Delhi Municipal Corporation, Public Works Department, Municipal Corporation of Delhi, March 2010.

Map 19.5 Fully Segregated Cycle Tracks in Delhi Identified Through Audit

Source: Schlebusch (2010).

tracks given by the agencies were service lanes only, many filled with parked vehicles and all without any signage indicating their status.

The final map (Map 19.6) is useful, illustrating as it does roads with substantial cycle flows. Comparing cycle flows to existing and usable cycle lanes, however, indicates that current facilities need to be linked to a series of new cycle tracks in areas where cycling has a higher modal share and aligned further with cycling origin and destination patterns. Linkages also need to be made with public transit interchanges with facilities for cycle parking. This is not to undermine the usefulness of currently existing tracks as they are situated in central areas with a comparatively well-off population who must form part of a new target group to start cycling as a healthy activity.

However, more effort and investment clearly needs to be made in other parts of the city to improve conditions for cyclists if modal share is to be maintained in this transport mode. According to a recent study of the City Development Plan, 0.8 per cent of Delhi's transport budget is dedicated to NMT infrastructure and 0.5 per cent to pedestrian facilities (Arora 2010). If the National Urban Transport Policy headlines on securing an 'equitable allocation of roadspace' with priority given to non-motorized modes is to be realized on ground, significantly greater effort will be needed to create a multimodal transport system to encourage people to walk, cycle, and use public transport.

Conclusions

The potential role of small-scale, local transport schemes which provide travel options for those walking and cycling for short trips and as a means of accessing motorized public transport has not yet been realized in India as a very good means of reducing carbon dioxide emissions. Local planning is weak.

A transport network based on buses, para transit, and with greater attention placed on making streets pedestrian and cyclist-friendly will reduce carbon emissions more than a strategy focused on the Metro and improving fuel efficiency of vehicles alone. In the end the growing size of population in megacities in India is likely to mean that both strategies will be needed but presently investment is heavily skewed to heavy infrastructure whilst pavements, road crossings, cycle facilities, pedestrian, and public transport interchanges are neglected.

The argument that 'a good public transport system is needed before demand management measures can be

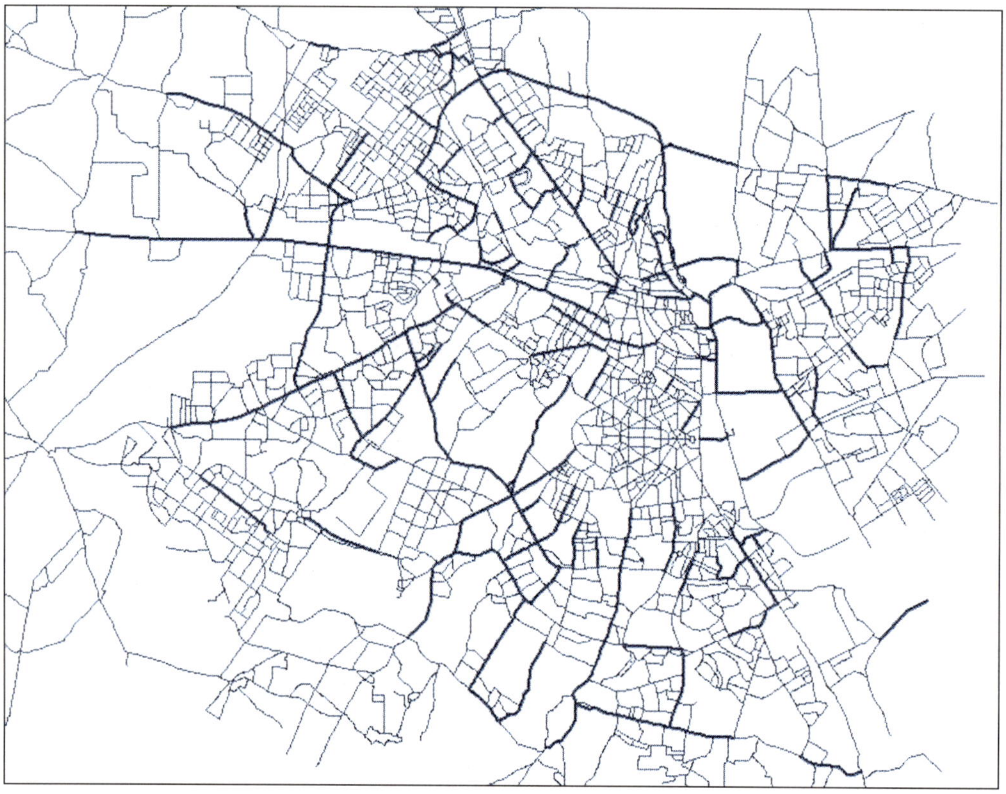

Map 19.6 Roads with 'Significant' Cycle Flow (over 10 per cent of mode share)

Source: RITES Ltd and TERI (2010).

introduced' does not hold. Measures are urgently needed to reduce the need to travel, increasing not only the supply of public transit but also the quality of public transport, while simultaneously introducing incentives to use it: higher parking charges, road pricing, equitable taxation between modes, etc.

Although many politicians and bureaucrats have been attracted to Bogotá as a successful model of how to achieve transport improvements while reducing carbon dioxide emissions, Bogotá worked because the Mayor, Enrique Penalosa, had a clear vision of what he wanted to achieve and stuck doggedly to the task despite powerful opposition from vested interests. A strong political leadership is an essential prerequisite for a multimodal transport system.

Greater capacity and skills needs to be developed amongst public agencies on how to design multimodal streets and roads. Whilst Delhi has witnessed some very innovative cycle and walking schemes emerging in preparation for the Commonwealth Games, they are not integrated with pedestrian and cycle networks at a local and then a city-wide level. There is no programme to promote cycling and walking as 'responsible', 'high status' means of transport. Likewise rickshaws are banned on most roads. Quality standards for rickshaws are absent and these vehicles are rapidly becoming antiquated and perceived as part of the problem rather than as part of the solution to transport woes.

Recommendations

- Creation of a Unified Metropolitan Transport Authority with responsibilities for land-use planning and transport investment with the mission of securing Transit Oriented Development through a new 'Road Users Act', a Transport Strategy and Plan that is fully funded, time-bound, and 'owned' by the Mayor.
- Re-balancing of investment in line with recommendations of the National Urban Transport Policy towards public transit, walking, and cycling and away from road capacity enhancement schemes in urban areas.
- In medium- to large-scale cities, higher levels of investment in Bus Rapid Transit and a faster approach to implementation involving the creation of a body, supported in law, solely responsible for BRT in the city.
- Modernization of bus vehicles focused on medium- to large-scale cities to be combined with structural reform

to management of bus operations. Private corporations invited to run area-based franchises as part of a bus network better integrated with other walking, cycling, other buses, and Metro services. Private corporations to be a 'public sector comparator'. If public bus operations do not improve, privatize them.

- Creation of an NMT Centre of Excellence, part of the Urban Metropolitan Transport Authority (UMTA) mooted for Delhi and tooled with adequate funding to invest in cycle and walking infrastructure. Infrastructure planning only approved with cycle and pedestrian plans (at local and network planning levels).
- Standards of design to accord with those of the Pedestrian Design Guidelines set by the United Traffic and Transportation Centre (UTTIPEC) in Delhi and forthcoming Indian Cycle Design Guidelines based on Dutch CROW Cycle Design Manuals.
- A significant thrust towards greater road safety, including the development of targets for the NMT Centre of Excellence and targets for the Traffic Police to reduce road casualties while increasing cycling and walking mode share. Traffic Police to be re-named 'Transport Police'.
- Local bodies to be consulted on measures to improve road safety in their area and to be involved in small-scale, adequately resourced local transport (walking/cycling/public transport access) audits, improvement, and road safety schemes.
- Introduction of a suitable methodology and plan to alter streets in line with the Pedestrian Design Guidelines: better quality street furniture, including tree shading, spaces for hawkers to provide road users with refreshments, spots to congregate, and take a breather away from traffic.
- Introduction of demand management schemes to encourage use of public transport, walking and cycling such as road pricing, stricter parking control, and removing subsidies on fuel and parking.
- As investment in public transport, walking and cycling facilities grow, with greater efforts to explain policy changes to the public through a series of carefully targeted campaigns.

References

Arora, Anvita (2010). 'The Demand Perspective of Low Carbon Transport: The Need for Socio-Economic Impact Assessment of Urban Transport Projects', UNEP Workshop Promoting Low Carbon Transport in India, February.

Asian Development Bank (2006). *Energy Efficiency and Climate Change: Considerations for On Road Transportation in Asia.*

Bannister, David (2008). 'Cut the Commute and Fly Less Too', *Civil Society*, 5(11), September–October.

Comptroller and Auditor General of India (2010). *Report into Phase I of the Delhi Metro.*

Dargay, Joyce and Dermot Gately (2007). 'Vehicle Ownership and Income Growth Worldwide—1960–2030' *The Energy Journal*, 28(4), pp. 143–70.

Dasgupta, M., R. Oldfield, K. Sharman, and V. Webster (1994). *Impact of Transport Policies in Five (UK) Cities*, Project Report 107, Transport Research Laboratory, Crowthorne, Berks.

Delhi Metro Rail Corporation (2008). *Annual Report 2008*, National Capital Region Planning Board, Ministry of Urban Development, Government of India, New Delhi.

Deutsche Gesellschaft für Technische Zusammenarbeit (GTZ) and SUTP (2008). *Bus Rapid Transit Planning Guide*, The Institute for Transportation and Development Policy (ITDP), United Nations Environment Programme, the Hewlett Foundation, and Viva, New York, June 2007.

Environment Pollution (Control and Prevention) Authority (2009). Briefing Paper 5, Delhi, 5 February 2009.

Economic Survey (2009–10) (2010). Ministry of Finance, Government of India, New Delhi.

Hidalgo, D. and M. Pai (2009*). Review of Delhi BRT Corridor*, EMBARQ.

International Energy Agency (2002). *World Energy Outlook.* Paris.

IPCC (2007). *The Fourth Assessment Report on Climate Change*, Intergovernmental Panel on Climate Change.

Ministry of Urban Development (2006). *National Urban Transport Policy*, Union Government of India, New Delhi.

Mohan, D. (2008). 'Metros, Mythologies and Future Urban Transport', *TRIPP Report*, 08–01, Transportation Research and Injury Prevention Programme, Indian Institute of Technology, Delhi, New Delhi.

Narain, Sunita (2009). 'In Poverty and in Wealth', *Business Standard*, 26 February 2009.

Penalosa, Enrique (2008). 'Create Public Spaces to Bring Equality and Joy', *Civil Society*, 5(11), September–October.

RITES Ltd (2005). *Integrated Multi-Modal Public Transport Network for the National Capital Territory of Delhi.*

RITES Ltd and TERI (2010). *Traffic and Transport Demand Study for the National Capital Territory of Delhi.*

Roychowdhury Anumita (2009). *Seeking Solutions to Air Pollution, Congestion and Climate: The Role of Transportation & Mobility*, Centre for Science and Environment.

Schlebusch, Sebastian (2010). Bicycle Sharing in Delhi, Presentation by Sebastian Schlebusch, GTZ Research Student) (forthcoming).

The Lancet (2009). *'Public Health Benefits & Strategies to Reduce Greenhouse Gas Emissions: Urban Land Transport'*, 374(9705), December.

US Department of Energy (2006). *US Transportation Energy Data Book.*

United Traffic and Transportation (Planning and Engineering) Centre (UT and TC) (2009). *Pedestrian Design Guidelines*, Delhi, November 2009.

Wilbur Smith Associates (2008). *Study on Traffic and Transportation Policies and Strategies in Urban Areas in India* for Ministry of Urban Development, Government of India.

Wright, L. and L. Fulton (2005). 'Climate Change Mitigation & Transport in Developing Countries', *Transport Reviews*, 25(6), pp. 691–717, November.

20 Urban Transport and Climate Change

Issues and Concerns in the Indian Context

Dinesh Mohan

Introduction

From the genesis of human history until about the seventeenth century AD, man had to perforce limit his 'innate desire for more', simply because excess consumption automatically translated to more manual labour. Human beings could travel only thus far, live in houses that were only that big, own only those many clothes, and eat and store only certain foods in certain amounts. Life was constrained by the capacity of the individual to toil for his basic needs. The Industrial Revolution changed all that. Machines created scope for processed foods, large-scale housing, readymade clothes, and effortless travel. Somewhere on the way this also transformed the concepts of 'need' and 'greed' as they were generally understood. The world view changed—mankind was lulled into believing that the Earth can provide endless resources and science and technology has solutions to every emerging problem without constraint. Most of the responses world-wide to the urgent warnings by the Intergovernmental Panel on Climate Change (IPCC 2007) are rooted in this belief that is willing to belie all evidence to the contrary in a sort of self-defeating march to destruction (Stern 2005; Spence 2009).

Unending problems of traffic congestion, carbon dioxide (CO_2) emission, road traffic injuries, and pollution in cities around the world have forced us to re-evaluate both our favourite theories as well as our long-standing practices. Professor Hermann Knoflacher of the Technical University in Vienna warns us that 'car traffic is cooling social relationships by heating up the atmosphere!' (Knoflacher 2007a). Voices like his are not alone or new. Professor Banister (Oxford University) argues that 'the belief that technology provides the solution is misplaced, as technological innovation can only get us part of the way to sustainable transport. Significant reductions of CO_2 emissions in transport can only be achieved through behavioural change. There is little sign that people are aware of the scale of the challenge, or prepared to make the necessary changes' (Banister 2009).

Their concern arises from the fact that large cities, more so in high- income countries, have not even attempted to address these problems at the scale that they should in order to enable us to tackle the future. Almost all cities in the world face severe congestion on arterial roads. During peak hours, car speeds average up to 10–15 kilometres per hour in cities such as London, Paris, Tokyo, Dhaka, Delhi, Nairobi, Kuala Lumpur, Lagos, and Karachi. Evidences from cities such as London, Paris, and New York indicate that public transport use is above 60 per cent only in the small inner city cores where parking services are limited and prohibitively expensive; the roads too are perpetually full with average speed seldom crossing 15 kilometres per hour (World Business Council for Sustainable Development 2001; Mohan 2008a). In the rest of the city cores, use of private transport is generally more than 60 per cent as roads are less crowded and there is easy availability of parking space. Empirical evidence suggests that car use (not ownership) is low only when walking and bicycling trips form a significant proportion of all trips (greater than 30 per cent) in cities such as Amsterdam (see Table 20.1).

Table 20.1 Modal Share of Trips by Different Modes of Transport in Medium-sized Cities in Europe

	Model share per cent		
City	*Car+MTW*	*PT*	*W&C*
Bristol, UK	65	12	23
Leeds, UK	61	36	3
Nantes, France	58	14	28
Helsinki, Finland	54	20	26
Marseille, France	53	12	35
Edinburgh, UK	52	29	19
Newcastle, UK	48	19	33
Brussels, Belgium	44	18	38
Frankfurt, Germany	42	21	37
Stuttgart, Germany	36	25	39
Amsterdam, Neth's	32	16	52

Note: MTW—Motorized two-wheeler, PT—Public transport, W&C—Walking and cycling
Source: Adapted from Commission for Integrated Transport, UK, 2001)

Urban transportation policy reports prepared by consultants in most countries assume that car use can be reduced just by providing more public transport facilities and assert that if their prescriptions are followed, 70 to 80 per cent of the trips would then be taken by public transit. The fact is that no city in the world has accomplished this feat! In the richest cities of India, that is, Mumbai and Delhi, recent estimates suggest that car trips constitute less than 10–15 per cent of all trips. In all other Indian cities, this proportion would be lower (Wilbur Smith Associates 2008). Additionally, the share of public transport in these two cities is certainly higher than most of the cities in Europe or North America. Therefore, it is difficult to imagine how car and motorcycle use can be contained as we get richer, if the international experience is anything to go by. Obviously, business as usual and copycat emulation of rich cities is not going to help.

Current concerns with climate change and CO_2 emissions have focused global attention on the accelerated growth of motor vehicles in India and China. However, this fact must be viewed keeping in perspective the overall international situation. According to the Stern Report (2007) projections for transport-related CO_2 in 2030, India remains as a minor contributor (Figure 20.1).

In addition, as the Spence (2009) Report indicates, emerging countries such as India are likely to take their time over adopting mitigation policies because growth concerns are still an overwhelming priority in these economies. According to Spence's calculations, per capita CO_2 emissions from India and China may take a slow growth path almost to the 2030s before declining. In all high-income countries, however, serious carbon reduction would have to start immediately (Figure 20.2). Stern (2007) also believes that 'de-carbonizing' transport would be essential for achieving a low carbon future:

> Whilst transport is likely to be largely oil-based in 2050, it is important for it to de-carbonize in the longer term if stabilization at 550 ppm CO_2 emission (CO_2e) to be achieved. For example, in the period beyond 2100, total greenhouse gas (GHG) emissions will have to be just 20 per cent of current levels (around 5 $GtCO_2e$, which is roughly the same as today's emissions from agriculture). *It is impossible to imagine how this can be achieved without a de-carbonized transport sector.*
>
> Road transport is likely to be de-carbonized before aviation. *Biofuels and hybrid electric/ICE technologies are already feasible for the roll out in road transport vehicles*... road transport would probably be the first transport mode to adopt hydrogen technology, although as the technology developed, it could potentially be ready for use in other modes' [Emphasis added].

Saul Griffith and his team (www.wattzon.com) have introduced an innovative method of energy use calculations which includes both daily activities and the embodied energy in one's possessions. Using these principles, Griffith calculates figures based on average energy use per day for different regions of the world and he comes up with 1,450 watts per person for Asia, 5,400 watts for Europe, and 11,400 watts for north America. If we were to apply his *calculator* to an upper middle-class Indian commuting to work by car and owning a refrigerator, air-conditioner, microwave, etc., we would get energy consumption of about 5,000 watts per person (similar to the European average). The same statistic for an Indian lower middle-class individual who commutes by bus stands at around 1,000 watts; a poor individual bicycling to work consumes less than 1,000 watts a day.

If we take these energy consumption estimates and the Stern and Spence reports as a starting point for a discussion on CO_2 mitigation and adaptation policies for Indian urban agglomerations, we should consider the following:

- India as a whole can afford to increase the total energy use for some time, provided this overall increase is accompanied by decrease in energy consumption by the higher socio-economic groups who are operating domestically at average European levels of energy consumption;

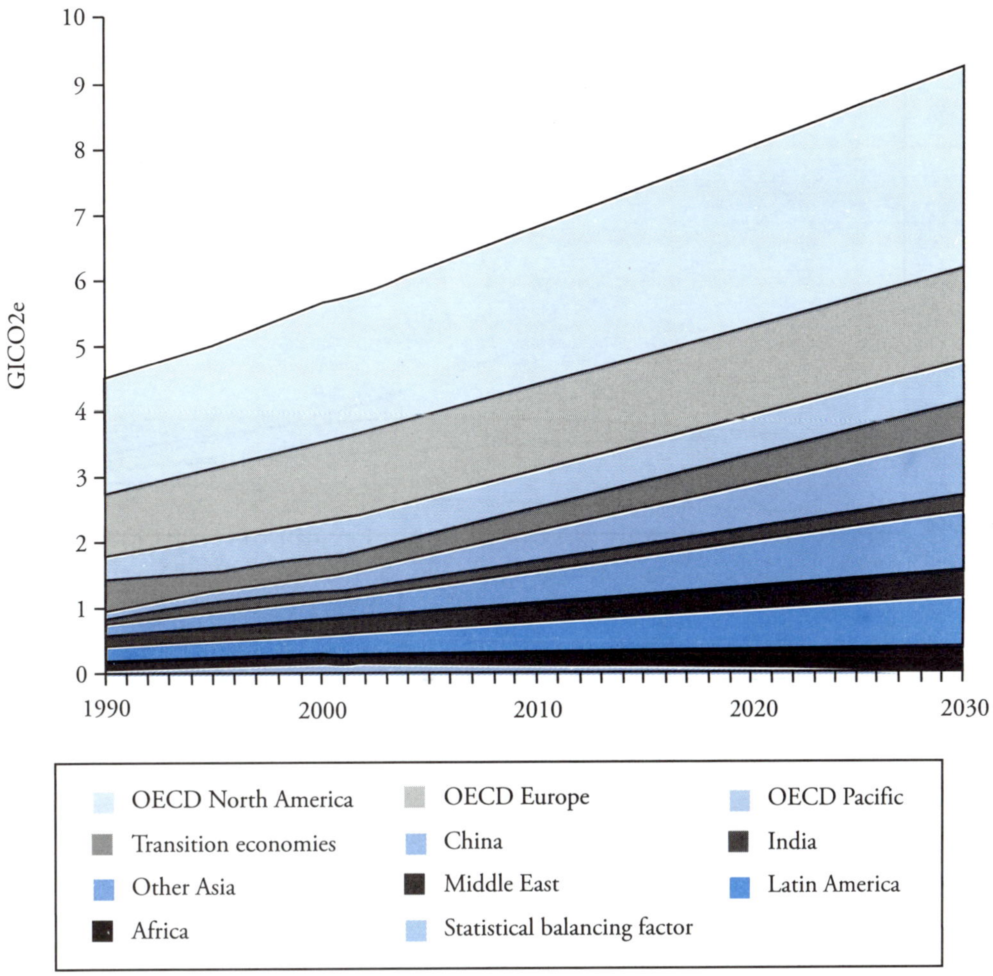

FIGURE 20.1 Country-wise Transport Emissions, 1930–2030

Source: Stern (2007).

- Increases in energy consumption of the bottom 60–70 percentile of the Indian urban population should emanate from fulfilment of food and housing needs rather than transport. The upper third of the income groups will probably have to reduce energy consumption in all walks of life; and
- A 'de-carbonized' transportation future is imperative. Since de-carbonized technologies do not seem to have emerged as cost-effective solutions, the appropriate 'de-carbonized' options for Indian cities will have to aim towards city plans that can facilitate an increase in the modal target share of both walking and cycling.

Future policymaking must leverage what is positive about our cities at present, and catalyze change in a way that majority of the people perceive it to be in their self-interest. What has to be ensured is that urban transportation planners do not move towards infrastructure development that will fix our future to high energy use and CO_2 emission paths. This change will not be easy as traditional mobility planning embedded in textbooks promotes capital-extensive projects that are also attractive as symbols of progress and profitable for large consultancy/contracting/manufacturing corporations world-wide. Transformational policymaking will only come about if majority of city residents are convinced that their current and future mobility/accessibility needs can be met at lower risk levels, at lower costs, and within a wide choice-set.

OLD CITIES VERSUS NEW

Most cities of the twenty-first century are growing under circumstances that are very different from those before the twentieth century. Most large cities in high-income countries (HIC) grew to their present size between 1850 and 1950. Technological developments were critical in changing the shape and form of the city. Car ownership started increasing in the 1920s, but most families did not own a car until the middle of the twentieth century. By

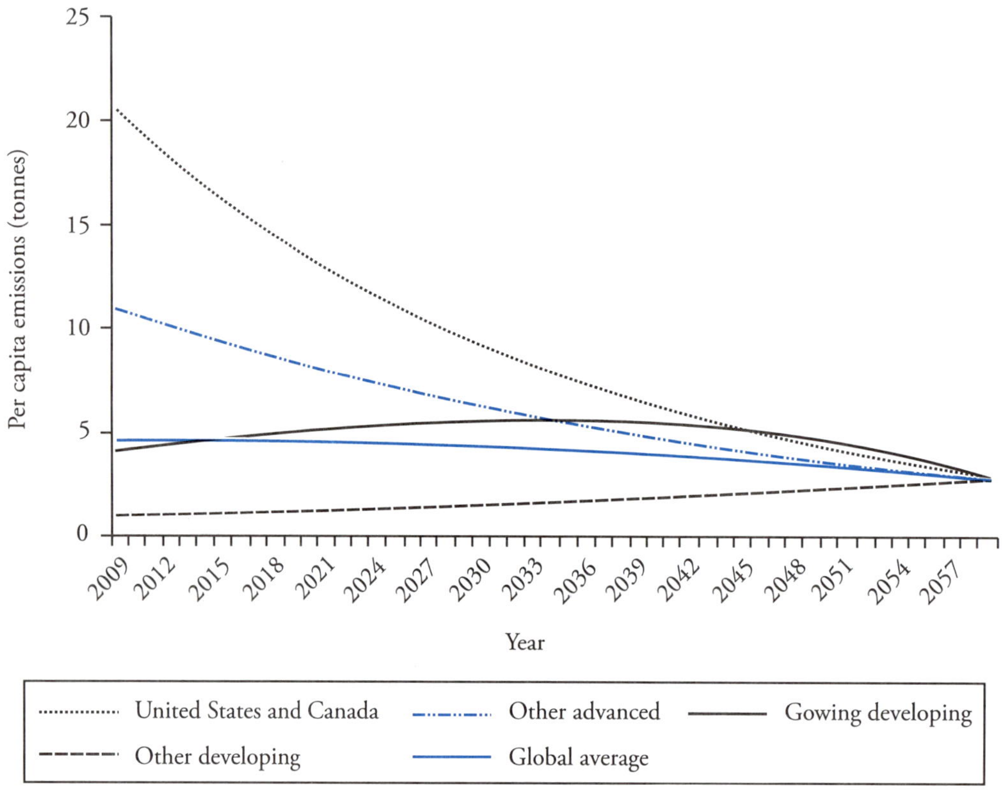

FIGURE 20.2 Per Capita Emissions on Path to Safe Target

Note: India is included in the 'growing developing' curve.
Source: Spence (2009).

then the essential land use and transportation patterns of large cities in HICs were well set with large central business districts (CBDs). This encouraged building of high capacity grade-separated metro systems; and the transport system encouraged densification of CBDs as large numbers of people could be transported to the centre of the city. Low car ownership among the middle class determined the widespread use of public transport and the resultant city form.

On the contrary, cities that have grown since 1950 do not have the characteristics of strong CBDs in any part of the world. In fact, cities in most non-OECD countries have expanded after 1960 and most have multiple business districts. In the past two decades, motorcycle ownership has increased substantially in many cities, and as a result, a significant proportion of families own either a car or a motorcycle even at low per capita income levels of about USD 1,400 per year (Mohan et al. 2009). Such high levels of private vehicle ownership did not occur historically in HICs until incomes there were much higher. Therefore, the high ownership of motorcycles, non-availability of funds to build expensive grade-separated metro systems, and official plans encouraging multi-modal business activities in cities have resulted in the absence of dense high population CBDs and city forms which encourage 'sprawl' in the form of relatively dense cities within cities.

Most middle class families did not own air-conditioned cars with stereo systems in HICs before 1970. The cars were noisy and occupants were exposed to traffic fumes as windows had to be rolled down. Under such conditions, the train was much more comfortable. On the other hand, brand new, silent, stereo-equipped air-conditioned cars are being sold in countries such as India today at prices as low as INR 200,000 and second-hand cars for quarter the price. This has made it possible for the middle-class first-time car owner to travel with comfort, which the Europeans had not experienced till the late twentieth century. Air-conditioned, comfortable, safe, and quiet travel in cars with music in hot and tropical climes cannot be matched by public transport. Owners of such vehicles would rather brave traffic congestion than tackle the heat and dust of a typical Indian summer while jostling in public transport.

Availability of motorcycles further reduced the middle-class demand for public transport. In addition, it has pegged fare levels that can be charged by public transport operators. It appears that public transport cannot attract these road users unless the fare is less than the marginal cost of using a motorcycle. At current prices, this amounts to less than INR 1.00 per kilometre. The only option available is to design potentially cost-efficient public transport systems that come close to matching this price.

Cities in low- and middle-income countries that have strategically grown after the 1950s seem to be different in character with multiple business districts, mixed land use (largely by default, illegally), relatively short-trip distances, and a large share of the walking population and public transport, even if the latter is not provided by the city authorities. This is because a large proportion of the population still cannot afford motorized forms of transport and live close to their place of work, legally or illegally, as shown in a detailed study of commuting patterns in Mumbai (Baker et al. 2005). When public transport is not provided officially, informal systems comprising mini-buses, three-wheelers, and vans operate semi-legally or illegally, and provide a majority of the motorized trips. No city in India is without such systems. It is also clear that no city in the country has been able to build a metro system that attracts public transport passengers substantially. This is partly because no city that has strategically grown after 1950 has a large and dense central business district.

Way Forward

For the issues outlined above, finding a resolution in the future indicates that certain challenges will need immediate attention, both in theory as well as design: road safety, incorporating informal activity on roads, reduction of crime by innovative design of road space and street furniture, and equal spread of low-income people in all parts of the city. People in the lower income group provide skills and services that are needed by the industrial, service as well as domestic sectors, and therefore, can find employment within short distances where they live. If they are not allowed to live within the city parameters, we force them to travel longer distances. There is ample evidence to illustrate the mismatch between current urban planning methods and the growing transportation problems (Banister 2005; Dora 1999; and Preston and Raje 2007). Unless we understand the basic nature of problems faced by our cities, the adverse impact of growing mobility on the environment and safety would continue to multiply in future. Whether people opt to walk, bicycle by choice or use public transport is influenced by risk perceptions of being involved in traffic crashes, being bothered, attacked or threatened on the road or in the bus, and also the attractiveness of the route and facilities en-route (Alm and Lindberg 2009; Schlossberg et al. 2007; Boer et al. 2007; Trim 2006; Cozens 2008; Cozens et al. 2004; Rodriguez et al. 2009).

Road Safety

Deaths and injuries due to road traffic accidents are a serious problem in all low- and middle-income countries (LMICs) (Peden et al. 2004). Even in high-income countries, pedestrians and bicyclists generally face higher crash risks than car occupants (Jorgensen1996; Pucher and Dijkstra 2000; Scientific Expert Group on the Safety of Vulnerable Road Users [RS7] 1998). According to one estimate, losses due to road traffic injuries in LMICs may be comparable to those due to pollution (Vasconcellos 1999). The safety record of bus transit operations has been reasonably good in most cities of the world as compared to other modes of transport. Yet people prefer to use their cars and motorcycles if affordable and convenient to do so. The main problem of safety as perceived by commuters is not as a passenger inside the bus, but as a pedestrian or bicyclist going from the destination to the bus stop or vice versa. A study of risks due to road traffic injuries faced by Copenhagen road users in different modes concluded: 'there is no reason for a traveller to choose a bus instead of a car from the point of view of his own safety,' and that 'from a social point of view, there would be a safety benefit through a change of car driving into bus driving' (Jorgensen1996). These conclusions were based on the fact that the risk of death per trip for a bus user was very high on access trips.

For public transport users, each trip involves two access trips which could be non-motorized modes—walking or cycling. In addition to other concerns, commuters will chose to walk or use the bicycle only if these modes are safer than other modes. Therefore, it is important to understand the factors influencing safety of road users with special reference to pedestrians in Indian cities and others around the world.

Figure 20.3 shows road traffic fatality risk per million persons in different cities plotted against per capita income of the country in which they are located, and Figure 20.4 shows fatality rates in Indian cities that had a population of 1 million or more in 2001 (Mohan 2007 and 2009). These data show that the risk varies by a factor of 20 between the cities with the lowest risk and the highest risk. Detailed analyses for factors associated with crashes for different cities are not available. However, some general observations can be made for the patterns implicit in Figure 20.3. Some characteristics are summarized below:

- The highest fatality rates seem to be experienced by cities in the mid-income range of USD 2,000—10,000 per person per year; and
- There is a great deal of variation even in those cities where the per capita income is greater than USD

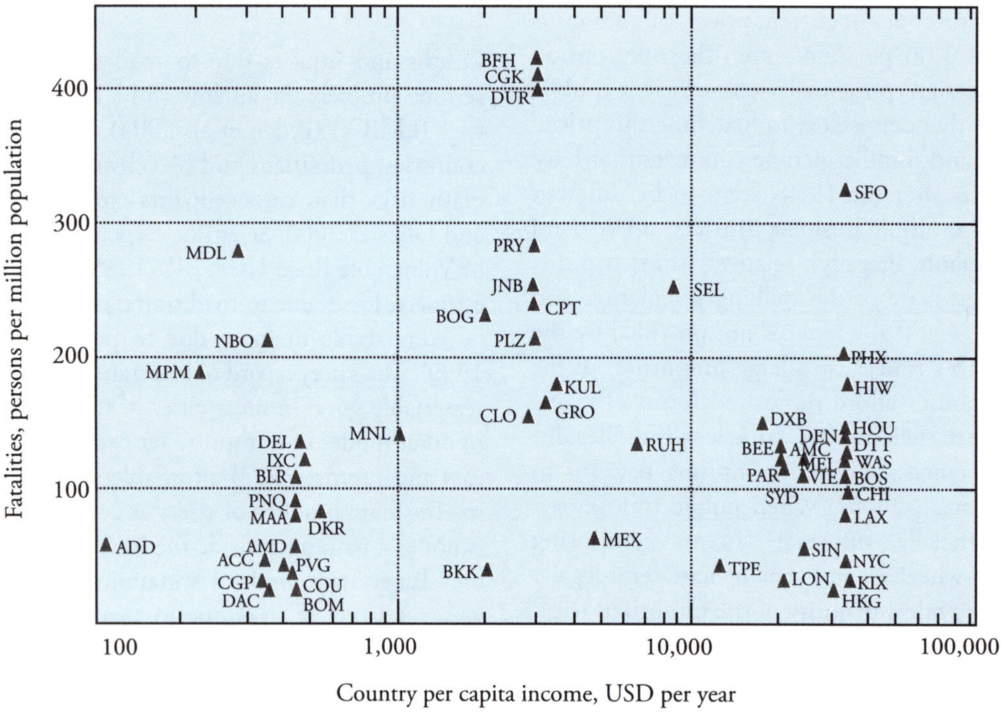

FIGURE 20.3 Road Traffic Fatality Risk per Million Persons in Different Cities by Per Capita Income in US Dollars (City Identifiers are Respective Airport Codes)

Source: Mohan (2007).

20,000 per year. At highest levels of income, the cities with the lowest rate, Tokyo (TYO), London (LON), and Hong Kong (HKG) have rates that are about 20 times lower than Phoenix (PHX) in the United States of America (USA);

- In cities with very low per capita income, the differences between the lowest and the highest is also a factor of about 20; and
- The lowest and highest rates in LMIC and HIC cities seem to be similar.

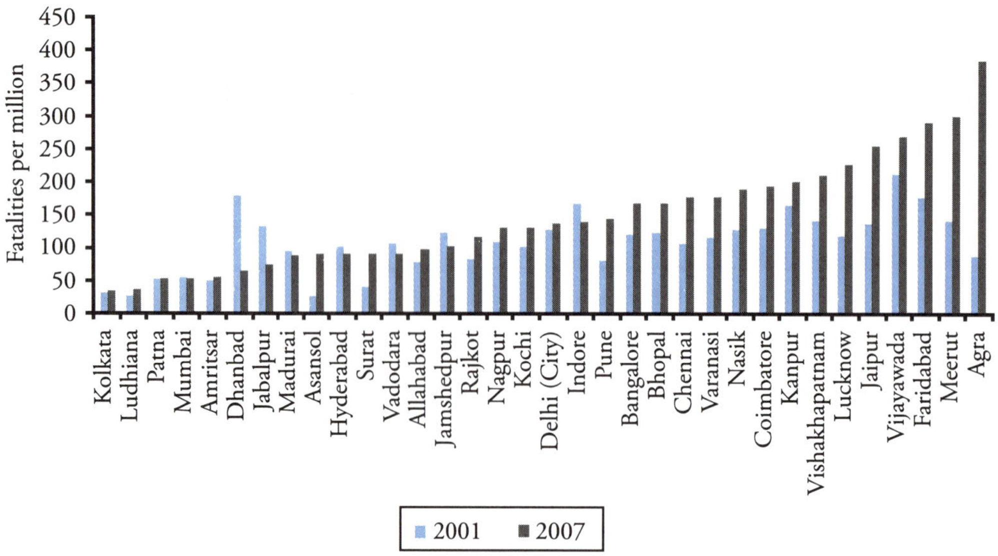

FIGURE 20.4 Traffic Fatality Rates in Indian Cities with Populations of At Least One Million in 2001

Source: Mohan (2009).

The data for Indian cities (Figure 20.4) shows that only eight of the cities did not experience an increase in fatality rates. The highest increase was 550 per cent in Asansol (West Bengal), with an overall average for all cities of 5.5 per cent compounded annually. This is quite an alarming situation, as at this rate the city death rate per million persons will double in 12 years. Since a vast majority of the victims in these cities consist of vulnerable road users, one possible cause could be increase in vehicle speeds (Mohan et al. 2009). The probability of pedestrian death is estimated at less than 10 per cent at impact speeds of 30 km/h and greater than 80 per cent at 50 km/h, and the relationship between increase in fatalities and increase in impact velocities is governed by a power of four (Leaf and Preusser 1999; Koornstra 2007). Small increases in urban speed levels can increase death rates dramatically.

Indian cities are also characterized by a high road presence of buses and trucks and this has been investigated in a detailed conflict-analysis study (Tiwari et al. 1998). The authors have mentioned in their report that these vehicles have to use the kerbside lane in the city and often come into conflict with pedestrians, cyclists, and motorized two-wheelers, as they are present in the same space on the road. This frequently results in fatal crashes because of the absence of dedicated bicycle paths and adequate space for pedestrian movement. Therefore, urban safety policies should accord highest priority to pedestrian and bicycle separation lanes from motor vehicles and speed control on main arterial roads. Conflict of pedestrians and bicyclists with buses can only be removed on arterial roads when buses are given a dedicated lane through the centre of the road. On all collector streets and residential areas, traffic calming would be essential.

Safety of road users in general and pedestrians in particular has not been maximized given the present state of knowledge among road engineers and urban planners. Land use policies that encourage greater use of cars per day and transportation policies that promote personal transport increase exposure rates and thus the overall risk of death and injury.[1] Once such systems are in place, it is difficult to reduce death rates per capita. These issues have to be examined in detail so that we can plan for safer cities in the future in addition to improving vehicle and infrastructure-related technologies. This would be essential for Indian cities which are expanding rapidly. For sustainable transport policies, it would be essential that these cities are not locked into systems that encourage high speeds and greater use of personal transport per day.

Crash Rates and City Structure

In the absence of detailed traffic modal share and speed and crash information, we can only have informed guesses on what is happening in all these cities included in Figures 20.3 and 20.4 respectively. International data show that per capita income is not the only determinant of road fatality rates, as these rates can vary by a factor of three across the richest nations. We also know that improvements in the crash-worthiness of vehicles, use of seatbelts and airbags and other safety devices can reduce fatality rates by 30 to 70 per cent, alcohol control by about 30 to 40 per cent (Peden et al. 2004), and that enhancement in road and infrastructure facilities can lead to an increase in fatalities (Noland 2003). However, the variations in rates across the world and in India can be in the range of factors of five or more. This seems to suggest that city structure, modal share split, and exposure of motorists and pedestrians may have a greater role in determining fatality rates than vehicle specifications and road design alone.

Therefore, the results from the analysis of city data seem to suggest very strongly that cities with high motor vehicle fatality rates are those where exposure and speed levels of motorists are high, and pedestrian fatality rates can be low if pedestrian exposure is low. Within the USA, where incomes, availability of technology, knowledge, and road design and vehicle specifications can be similar across cities, these differences in speed levels and exposure are probably accounted for by the structure of cities. At the international level, cities that have modernized and expanded in the past few decades are those in the per-capita income range of USD 1,000–10,000, and these are the cities with very high fatality rates (Durban, Johannesburg, Tehran, etc.). Typically, these cities have built wide avenues and high-speed corridors within the city. In India, Delhi has a high fatality rate, and Mumbai and Kolkata low fatalitry rates. Here also, Delhi has much faster vehicular traffic than Mumbai and Kolkata and a lower density of through-traffic streets. It is possible that the high growth rates in road traffic injuries/fatalities experienced by Agra, Meerut, Faridabad, Vijayawada, Jaipur, and Lucknow could be due to the introduction of high-speed roads and flyovers in and around these cities.

With the same proportion of land devoted to road space, we can have large blocks with fewer arterial roads or smaller blocks with a larger number of arterial streets. In the former type of cities, the avenues would be wider

[1] This holds true even though risk rates per km travelled by personal mode may be low because greater travel distances lower risk per km (Elvik and Truls 2004). This tends to offset the advantages gained by provision of safer cars and roads.

than the latter. If the arterial streets are wide, it encourages high-speed levels during off-peak hours, resulting in high pedestrian and bicycle crash fatality rates. High pedestrian and bicycle fatality rates discourage use of non-motorized modes and public transport. For these reasons, planners in the Netherlands make the following recommendations (SWOV 2004):

A road categorizing has been chosen in sustainable safety that concentrates on the cars driving through on motorways and other main roads. Through traffic is kept out of the residential areas and slower speeds are ensured, especially by speed reducing measures. The reduction of through traffic and driving speeds are indispensable for a successful residential area. Both road safety and the quality of life (noise level, being easy to cross the road, and emission quantity) benefit. *However, if a 30 km/h area is larger than 1 km², it leads to a lot of traffic on the surrounding through-roads. We recommend taking this into account by limiting Zones 30 to smaller than 1 km², or by adapting surrounding roads, especially their ease of crossing over.* We also recommend a traffic structure using 'limited access' for a Zone 30. This favours all aspects: road safety, quality of life, accessibility, and construction and maintenance costs. [Emphasis added]

The different ways in which local streets can be organized is shown in Figure 20.5 (SWOV 2004). The report states that road safety in residential areas is best served by a system based on entry limitations and speed; and this is so in the case of organic structure and limited access. The quality of life and accessibility are optimal in a grid system because the traffic is dispersed over many streets. The construction and maintenance costs of the traffic structure are the most favourable for the 'limited access' because of the short total road length in the area. If the features of these structure types are totalized, the 'limited access' scores positively in all aspects. These designs have been experimented within Europe. Much more detailed design work will have to be done to adapt these principles for Indian neighbourhoods where use of motorcycles is much higher.

Dense layout of streets, lower speed levels, and smaller neighbourhoods are also supported by other studies by emphasizing the positive role played by higher density of public transport networks. In a recent study, a statistical analysis was done for 23 urban districts of the German capital of Berlin (Reckien et al. 2007). They found that the

... number of jobs per district and the share of the well-off population can best describe the CO_2 emissions from traffic in Berlin. Also the number of residents, the total built area, the number of cars, and the amount of traffic area are positively related to the dependent variable. **Therefore, the possibilities to reduce CO_2 emissions from road traffic for urban planners seem limited: a restriction of space dedicated to traffic and a change of transport means for commuting represent leverage points**, according to the analysis. The other significant indicators are less able to be influenced by local and regional decision-makers—an alteration in the means of mobility to less CO_2 emitting alternatives is needed if CO_2 emissions from road traffic are extensively to be decreased. [Emphasis added]

Yves Crozet, summarizing the issues concerning economic development and the role of travel time states:

the travel time budget issue is central to understand the challenges of sustainable urban transport... that is to say that instead of trying to improve the average speed of urban trips, public policies have to focus on accessibility... **The main learning of the accessibility concept is that, in urban areas, it is more important to have higher density than higher speed and especially higher road speed** (Crozet 2009). [Emphasis added].

A study on excess commuting concludes that

in terms of the sensitivity analysis, the results suggest that public transport users could achieve dramatic savings on their commute if the density of that network was increased considerably Thus, as the complexity of commuting increases, the role played by public transport in servicing revised patterns of trip making will be undermined unless significant improvements are made to the density of that network (Murphy 2009).

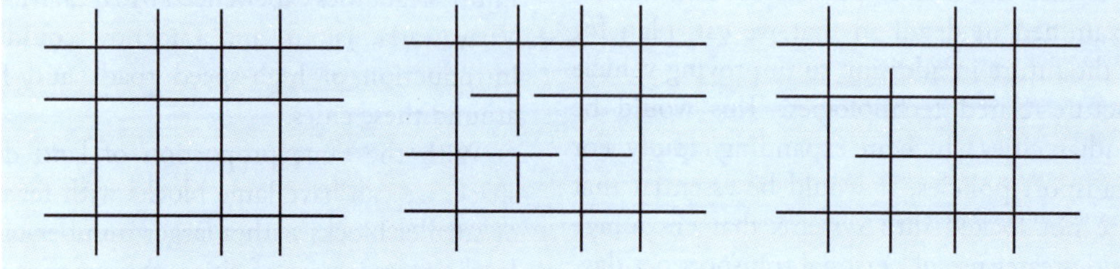

FIGURE 20.5 Traffic Structures, Grid or Lattice (Left), Organic or Tree (Centre), Mixed or Limited Access (Right)

Source: SWOV (2004).

Many studies also show that for parents of children in urban and rural areas alike, concern about traffic crashes/fatality rates are the main reason for not allowing a child to walk to school. For parents in urban areas, concern for a child's security from attack is also a major consideration, whereas for parents in rural areas this does not appear to be such a significant factor (DfT 2006). In Indian cities, this probably holds much more importance, considering the number of middle-class children who are not even allowed to walk home alone from the bus stop.

When a large number of commuters are dependent on personal motor vehicle use for their essential needs, the system creates a political demand for greater provision of facilities for their vehicles and adequate road space. This in turn can make it difficult for the political system to be harsh on drivers in terms of speed enforcement, restrictions on road widening, and controlling drinking and driving. In this situation, not only do people tend to use their vehicles for short trips, but also demand facilities that reduce the trip time for long trips.

It seems that if we have to promote walking, bicycling, and public transport use, we will have to make traffic safety a priority along with city structure designs that incorporate the following:

- Street design ensuring safety of non-motorized modes;
- Vehicle speed control by street design and ultimately ITS control on vehicles;
- Denser layout of through traffic streets with narrower cross-sections;
- Smaller size of residential neighbourhoods; and
- High-density public transport networks.

Crime and Transport

Crime and fear of crime affects travel choice significantly and acts as a major barrier to the use of public transport, cycling, and walking. It is also clear that just depending on more aggressive street policing is not very effective in reducing crime in neighbourhoods or in reducing the perception of risk, especially among women. Forty eight years ago, in her book *The Death and Life of Great American Cities*, author Jane Jacobs suggested that crime could be reduced by having 'eyes on the street' (Jacobs 1961). By 'eyes on the street' Jacobs meant shops on ground floors abutting the sidewalk, abundance of kiosks and cafés, and a vibrant walking atmosphere. A report from UK suggested that 'there might be as much as a 15 per cent increase in passengers for all rail journeys if a range of anti-crime initiatives were successfully implemented' (Crime Concern and Transport and Travel Research, 1997, cited in Cozens et al. 2004).

Reviews of environmental criminology literature indicate that mixed-use developments with the rich and poor living in close proximity have been associated with reduced levels of crime only if pedestrian volumes are high and there are many 'eyes on the street'. Many urban planners, street furniture, and public facility planners are also working on designs that automatically reduce incidence of crime and perception of risk by all road users (Cozens et al. 2004; Cozens 2008). An example of this approach is shown in Figure 20.6. Before and after studies revealed that reduced fear of crime and higher levels of consumer confidence had an effect of 33 per cent increase in annual passenger flows on the local commuter trains. Principles used in such designs include the following:

- Natural Surveillance: The placement of physical features, activities, and people in such ways as to

FIGURE 20.6 A Typical Brick Shelter Found on a Valley Lines Railway Station in South Wales, UK (left) and a Redesigned Transparent Shelter (right)

Source: Cozens (2004).

maximize visibility. This also involves the lighting of public spaces and walk-ways at night.

- Natural Access Control: The physical guidance of people entering and exiting a space by the judicial placement of signs, entrances, exits, fencing, landscaping, and lighting.
- Territorial Reinforcement: The use of physical attributes that express ownership such as fences, pavement treatments, artwork, signage, landscaping, and placement of buildings.
- Image/Maintenance: Allows for the continued use of space for its intended purpose and serves as an additional expression of ownership. This also involves supporting a positive image through the selection of materials, design, and scale.

However, the authors warn us that the variety of crimes, number of different settings in the transport system, and the diversity of victim types effectively means that 'we cannot therefore, identify with reasonable certainty, any specific tactic against specific crimes, that can be said to 'work' across similar settings in other cities,' and that 'approaches need to be tailored to specific local circumstances.' Much more attention needs to be given to this aspect of urban space design and planning as it will ultimately lead to greater adoption of sustainable forms of transport.

Further, street designs in many Indian cities do not allow for shops and businesses abutting the sidewalk because buildings have a mandatory set-back from the street. On the other hand, we have 'eyes' on all these streets where hawkers and vendors are able to exist in our cities. These vendors also serve a potential social need and provide employment and basic needs in terms of nutrition, for example, to city dwellers. Without them, our streets would not provide the relative crime-free atmosphere we have. These vendors thus emerge as an essential part of our transportation planning process.The social need for street vendors has been stressed by many researchers (Yatmo 2008; Tinker 1997). It is not very difficult to plan for them, as every road needs a tree line that occupies a corridor of 1–1.5 m of space on the pedestrian path. Vendors only need 1–1.5 m and they can occupy spaces between trees without bothering pedestrian traffic. There can be many other approaches and street designs to achieve a similar outcome, and we must evaluate all the different designs available in real world settings. However, it is important to develop street design standards by strategically incorporating street vendors as an essential component.

Indeed, if the various new concepts representing strategies for creating truly sustainable and liveable communities need to be successful, they must at least consider the evidence relating to crime and the fear of crime in a more systematic manner, thereby balancing more effectively the diverse issues and needs within the community.

Conclusions

There has been a great deal of discussion in recent years around policies that will help us reduce personal transport use. The most common solutions proposed are: (i) high-density cities with a very dense core, (ii) land-use planning promoting mixed use, (iii) short-trip distances, and (iv) transit-oriented development. Indian cities already incorporate the first three options except the existence of dense central business districts (Mohan 2008b; Tiwari 2007; Badami et al. 2007; Tiwari 2009). However, a purely technical approach to transit-oriented development (actually implying high-speed grade-separated rail systems) has also been a target of criticism by many researchers (Banister 2009; Zhao et al. 2009; Knoflacher 2007b; Bertaud 2004; Crozet 2009; Crotte et al. 2009; Siemiatycki 2006; Winston and Maheshri 2007). The consensus that seems to be emerging among this group of scholars is that fixed line grade-separated systems are far too expensive, not cost-effective, do not attract enough passengers, are not very friendly to desirable urban forms, and encourage sprawl by allowing fast transport over long distances.

It is the last point which becomes even more important in the face of climate change. Zhao et al. (2009) assert that:

> based on the results of a correlation analysis, findings suggest that home-based job proximity has the strongest significantly negative relationship with average community commuting time. In fact, the results of a two-step regression analysis suggest that 68.6 per cent of the changes in average commuting time are explained overwhelmingly by the home-based job proximity variable ... current urban policy, which relies predominantly on ambitious and expensive programmes of transport infrastructure provision must be rethought in Beijing. Improving the jobs-housing balance through the implementation of compact land development may be an alternative to reducing overall commuting duration [Emphasis added].

Crozet (2009) is quite clear on this issue and states that high speed systems will further encourage sprawl and greater energy consumption, and hence, '*Public Transit (PT), even if the commercial speed is rather low, is probably the only way to improve urban accessibility and urban attractiveness in a sustainable way.*'

This leaves us in a very comfortable situation to move our policies in directions which support relatively dense cities within cities, with small neighbourhoods, and dense networks of medium-capacity surface public transport systems. But, none of this will succeed if the safety of pedestrians and bicyclists is not assured. Therefore, traffic safety for non-motorized road users is an essential (not sufficient) condition for carbon control.

References

Alm, C. and E. Lindberg (2009). *Public Transportation in the City—Do People Avoid Travelling Because They Feel Unsafe?* (Rep. No. VTI meddelande 941), Swedish National Road and Transport Research Institute, Linkoping.

Badami, M.G., G. Tiwari, and D. Mohan (2007). 'Access and Mobility for the Urban Poor in India', in A.A. Laquian, V. Tewari, and L.M. Hanley (eds), *The Inclusive City: Infrastructure and Public Services for the Urban Poor in Asia,* Woodrow Wilson Press, Washington DC.

Baker, J., R. Basu, M. Cropper, S. Lall, and A. Takeuchi (2005). 'Urban Poverty and Transport: The Case of Mumbai' (Rep. No. World Bank Policy Research Working Paper 3693), The World Bank, Washington DC.

Banister, D. (2009). 'Cities, Mobility, and Climate Change', (Rep. No. 2nd Annual TRIPP Lecture, TRIPP-RP09-01), Transportation Research and Injury Prevention Programme, Indian Institute of Technology, New Delhi.

——— (2005). *Unsustainable Transport: City Transport in the New Century*. Routledge, New York.

Bertaud, A. (2004). 'The Spatial Organization of Cities: Deliberate Outcome or Unforeseen Consequence?' (Rep. No. Paper WP—2004–01), Institute of Urban and Regional Development, Berkeley.

Boer, R., Y. Zheng, A. Overton, G.K. Ridgeway, and D.A. Cohen (2007). 'Neighborhood Design and Walking Trips in Ten US Metropolitan Areas', *American Journal of Preventive Medicine,* 32, pp. 298–304.

Cozens, P., R. Neale, J. Whitaker, and D. Hillier (2004). 'Tackling Crime and Fear of Crime While Waiting at Britain's Railway Stations', *Journal of Public Transportation,* 7, pp. 23–41.

Cozens, P.M. (2008). 'New Urbanism, Crime, and the Suburbs: A Review of the Evidence', *Urban Policy and Research,* 26, pp. 429–44.

Crime Concern and Transport and Travel Research (1997). *Perceptions of Safety from Crime on Public Transport,* DETR, London.

Crotte, A., Noland, R.B., and Graham, D.J. (2009). 'Is the Mexico City Metro an Inferior Good?', *Transport Policy,* 16, pp. 40–5.

Crozet, Y. (2009). 'Economic Development and the Role of Travel Time: The Key Concept of Accessibility', in (pp. 1–22). Gothenberg: Volvo Research and Educational Foundations.

DfT (2006). *Personal Security Issues in Pedestrian Journeys,* Department for Transport, London.

Dora, C. (1999). 'A Different Route to Health: Implications of Transport Policies', *British Medical Journal,* 318(7199), pp. 1686–9.

Elvik, R. and Vaa Truls (2004). *The Handbook of Road Safety Measures,* Elsevier, Amsterdam.

IPCC (2007). *Climate Change 2007: Synthesis Report,* Intergovernmental Panel on Climate Change, Geneva.

Jacobs, J. (1961). *The Death and Life of Great American Cities,* New York, Random House.

Jorgensen, N.O. (1996). 'The Risk of Injury and Accident by Different Travel Modes', in *International Conference on Passenger Safety in European Public Transport,* European Transport Safety Council, Brussels, pp. 17–25.

Knoflacher, H. (2007a). 'From Myth to Science', *Seminar,* 579, pp. 40–4,

——— (2007b). 'Success and Failures in Urban Transport Planning in Europe—Understanding the Transport System', *Sadhna—Academy Proceedings in Engineering Sciences,* 32, pp. 293–308.

Koornstra, M. (2007). Prediction of Traffic Fatalities and Prospects for Mobility becoming Sustainable-safe', *Sadhna—Academy Proceedings in Engineering Sciences,* 32, pp. 365–96.

Leaf, W.A. and Preusser, D.F. (1999). *Literature Review on Vehicle Travel Speeds and Pedestrian Injuries,* (Rep. No. DOT HS 809 021), National Highway Traffic Safety Administration, US Department of Transportation, Washington, DC.

Mohan, D. (2007). 'Traffic Safety as a Pre-requisite for Sustainable Urban Transport: An International Analysis', *Journal of the Eastern Asia Society for Transportation Studies,* 7, pp. 2907–17.

——— (2008a). 'Mythologies, Metro Rail Systems, and Future Urban Transport', *Economic and Political Weekly,* 43, pp. 41–53.

——— (2008b). 'Traffic Safety and City Structure: Lessons for the Future', *Salud Publica de Mexico,* 50, pp. S93–100.

——— (2009). 'Road Accidents in India', *Journal of International Association of Traffic and Safety Sciences,* 33, pp. 75–9.

Mohan, D., O. Tsimhoni, M. Sivak, and M.J. Flannagan (2009). *Road Safety in India: Challenges and Opportunities* (Rep. No. UMTRI-2009-1), The University of Michigan Transportation Research Institute, Ann Arbor, MI.

Murphy, E. (2009). 'Excess Commuting and Modal Choice', Transportation Research Part A,–*Policy and Practice,* 43, pp. 735–43.

Noland, R.B. (2003). 'Traffic Fatalities and Injuries: The Effect of Changes in Infrastructure and Other Trends', *Accident Analysis And Prevention,* 35, pp. 599–612.

Peden, M., R. Scurfield, D. Sleet, D. Mohan, A.A. Hyder, and E. Jarawan, and C. Mathers (2004). *World Report on Road Traffic Injury Prevention,* World Health Organization, Geneva.

Preston, J. and F. Raje (2007). 'Accessibility, Mobility, and Transport-related Social Exclusion', *Journal of Transport Geography,* 15(3), pp. 151–60.

Pucher, J. and L. Dijkstra (2000). 'Making Walking and Cycling Safer: Lessons from Europe', *Transportation Quarterly,* 54, pp. 25–50.

Reckien, D., M. Ewald, O. Edenhofer, and M.K.B. Ludeke (2007). 'What Parameters Influence the Spatial Variations in CO_2 Emissions from Road Traffic in Berlin? Implications for Urban Planning to Reduce Anthropogenic CO_2 Emissions', *Urban Studies,* 44, pp. 339–55.

Rodriguez, D.A., E.M. Brisson, and N. Estupinan (2009). 'The Relationship between Segment-level Built Environment Attributes and Pedestrian Activity around Bogota's BRT Stations,Transportation Research Part D', *Transport and Environment,* 14, pp. 470–8.

Schlossberg, M., A.W. Agrawal, K. Irvin, and V.L. Bekkouche (2007). *How Far, by Which Route, and Why? A Spatial Analysis of Pedestrian Preference* (Rep. No. MTI REPORT 06–06). Mineta Transportation Institute College of Business, San José State University, San José.

Scientific Expert Group on the Safety of Vulnerable Road Users (RS7) (1998). *Safety of Vulnerable Road Users* (Rep. No. DSTI/DOT/RTR/RS7(98)1/final). Organisation for Economic Co-operation and Development, Paris.

Siemiatycki, M. (2006). 'Message in a Metro: Building Urban Rail Infrastructure and Image in Delhi, India', *International Journal of Urban and Regional Research,* 30, pp. 277–92.

Spence, M. (2009). *Climate Change, Mitigation, and Developing Country Growth* (Rep. No. Working Paper No. 64), The World Bank on Behalf of the Commission on Growth and Development, Washington DC.

Stern, N. (2007). *The Economics of Climate Change: The Stern Review,* Cambridge, Cambridge University Press, UK.

SWOV (2004). *Zone 30—Urban Residential Areas,* Leidschendam: Institute for Road Safety Research (SWOV).

Tinker, I. (1997). *Street Foods: Urban Food and Employment in Developing Countries,* Oxford University Press, New York.

Tiwari, G. (2007). 'Urban Transportation Planning', *Seminar, 579,* pp. 45–8.

——— (2009). 'Public Transport Research Challenges in India', in Gothenberg: Volvo Research and Educational Foundations.

Tiwari, G., D. Mohan, and J. Fazio (1998). 'Conflict Analysis for Prediction of Fatal Crash Locations in Mixed Traffic Streams', *Accident Analysis and Prevention,* 30, pp. 207–15.

Trim, A. (2006). 'Morice Town Home Zone', in N. Stamatiadis, and B. Psarianos (eds), *International Perspectives on Urban Street Design—Proceedings of the Context-Sensitive Design Workshop* (Transportation Research Circular E-C097, Transportation Research Board, Washington, DC.

Vasconcellos, E.A. (1999). 'Urban Development and Traffic Accidents in Brazil', *Accident Analysis and Prevention,* 31, pp. 319–28.

Wilbur Smith Associates (2008). *Study on Traffic and Transportation Policies and Strategies in Urban Areas in India—Final Report,* Ministry of Urban Development, Government of India, New Delhi.

Winston, C. and V. Maheshri (2007). 'On the Social Desirability of Urban Rail Transit Systems', *Journal of Urban Economics,* 62, pp. 362–82.

World Business Council for Sustainable Development (2001). *Mobility 2001: World Mobility at the End of the Twentieth Century and Its Sustainability,* WBCSD, c/o E&Y Direct, Geneva.

Yatmo, Y.A. (2008). 'Street Vendors as 'Out of Place' Urban Elements', *Journal of Urban Design,* 13, pp. 387–402.

Zhao, P., B. Lu, and G.J.J. Linden (2009). 'The Effects of Transport Accessibility and Jobs and Housing Balance on Commuting Time: Evidence from Beijing', *International Planning Studies,* 14, pp. 65–83.

Section V

Urban Infrastructure

21 Carbon Emissions, Climate Change, and Impacts in India's Cities

Kala Seetharam Sridhar

Introduction

The Intergovernmental Panel on Climate Change concluded in 2007 that warming of the climate system is now 'unequivocal', based on observations of increases in global average air and ocean temperatures, widespread melting of snow and ice, and rising global average sea levels (IPCC 2007). According to the National Oceanic and Atmospheric Administration's (NOAA's) *State of the Climate Report 2007* and the National Aeronautics and Space Administration's (NASA) *Surface Temperature Analysis 2007*, the eight warmest years on record since 1850 have all occurred since 1998, with the warmest year being 2005.

According to the IPCC (2007):

- The warming trend is seen in both daily maximum and minimum temperatures, with minimum temperatures increasing at a faster rate than the maximum temperatures.
- Land areas have tended to warm faster than ocean areas and the winter months have warmed faster than summer months.

One of the expected impacts of climate change on South Asia is a general increase in both the mean minimum and mean maximum temperatures by two to four degrees centigrade (Sharma et al. 2006). A 10 to 15 per cent increase in monsoon precipitation in many regions, a simultaneous precipitation decline of 5 to 25 per cent in semi-arid and drought-prone central India, and a sharp decline in winter rainfall in northern India is also projected (Ramesh and Yadava 2005). In this chapter, we focus on carbon emissions, climate change, and their economic and ecological impacts on India's cities.

Most studies to date focus on coastal areas, given their vulnerability to climate change (Hunt and Watkiss 2007). Many coastal cities are in fact threatened by swelling sea levels and ironically, it is estimated that by 2015, 21 of the world's megacities will be in coastal locations (Kreimer et al. 2003), thus intensifying the threat perception. However, there is a near absence of studies on inland cities. Further, most of the studies so far are qualitative rather than being based on empirical analysis; and this is no doubt due to the paucity of data. Finally, most studies confine themselves to a single issue arising out of climate change, most commonly sea-level rise, whereas the impact of climate change is a multi-dimensional phenomenon.

In this chapter, we first discuss how urban areas can become growth centres for an economy. Following this, we discuss the relationship between urbanization and climate change. We also provide a description of the carbon footprint of Indian cities, based on the scant evidence thus far. The reverse impact of climate change on the ecology and the economy of a city is the next level of discussion here.

Based on the above, we make a case for developing urban infrastructure to enable low carbon urban growth and summarize some of the mitigating strategies cities in India have been adopting, including initiatives that are part of the Asian Cities Climate Change Resilience Network (ACCCRN). Finally we summarize and end the chapter with concluding remarks.

Urban Areas as Engines of Growth

The year 2007 has been described as the tipping point in human history with half the world's population living in urban areas for the first time. Urbanization in India has been closely following this global trend. According to the 2001 Census, India had a population of 1,027 million with approximately 28 per cent (or 285 million people) living in urban areas. This share of urban population is predicted to increase to about 40 per cent by 2021. According to international experience, urbanization picks up pace after the proportion of urban population reaches 25 per cent. In India, urban population at 29 per cent indicates that this is a statistic that may be expected to increase at an alarming rate in the near future.

Cities are always the hubs of economic growth and urban areas contribute close to half of India's gross domestic product today. It is estimated that by 2011, urban areas would contribute about 65 per cent of the GDP of India (Ministry of Urban Development 2006). Evidence at India's sub-national level shows that more urbanized states (such as Maharashtra, Karnataka, and Gujarat) recorded more than 100 per cent growth in their per capita net state domestic product (at current prices) during 1993–4 to 2002–3.

However, this higher productivity seen in urban areas is contingent upon the availability of quality infrastructure services. Urban economic activities are dependent on infrastructure, such as power, telecom, roads, water supply, and mass transportation, coupled with civic infrastructure, such as sanitation and solid waste management. Adequate infrastructure is not only necessary for increasing productivity, but also for raising the general quality of living. So, the overall growth of urban GDP cannot be separated from the delivery of public services or strategies to improve them.

Economic growth often implies the conversion of rural land for urban uses (residential, commercial, and industrial) as regional economies undergo a transition from an agrarian base to urban-based industry and services. Rural development cannot be a substitute for healthy urbanization. This process occurs in urban areas of developing countries undergoing structural economic changes. Presumably, in the initial phases, when urbanization rates and per capita income increase at roughly the same rates, productivity increases reflect shifting resources from rural activities with lower productivity gains. In later phases, rapid productivity gains reflect mainly improvements within industries and services (Romer 1986; Lucas 1988; and Quigley 1998).

At a global scale, changes in information, production, and transportation technologies have had profound effects on urbanization. To the extent that these changes substitute for geographic proximity, they have vastly reduced the need for face-to-face communications (Gasper and Glaeser 1998; Sridhar and Sridhar 2003) and have greatly increased the mobility of goods, services, labour, technology, and capital throughout the world. This marked increase in the pace of globalization has spurred rapid economic growth in many developing countries.

Annez and Buckley (2009) confirm a strong link between rapid growth and a structural shift from agriculture to urban activities (manufacturing and services) in the sectoral composition of GDP growth across countries. Across the developing world, the urban sector drives growth: according to the National Research Council (2003), 86 per cent of the growth value-added in developing countries' GDP between 1980 and 1998 came from services and manufacturing. A large body of literature explains why industry and services locate in cities. Duranton (2009), Quigley (2009), and Venables (2009) discuss the role of agglomeration economies and the functioning of labour markets in cities, highlighting both productivity impacts and linkages with the growth process. Lucas (2004 and 2007) explicitly considers how urbanization affects the growth process through the enhanced flow of ideas and knowledge due to agglomeration in cities. As Quigley (2009) points out, the fundamental question in urban economics is why people voluntarily live in close proximity to one another when there are costs to competing for land. The simple answer has two parts: efficiency gains and consumption benefits.

In developing countries, poor transportation and communication infrastructure tend to magnify the advantages of cities over the countryside. The importance of the informal sector may distinguish cities in developing countries from those in developed countries. In fact, the little evidence available on agglomeration economies in the informal sector suggests that it also benefits from agglomeration and that informal operators generally have a positive impact on their formal sector counterparts through supply of inputs.

We thus have plenty of evidence to support that urban areas are growth centres for any economy in general and India's economy in particular. Further, we discuss the role of cities in climate change and the impacts of the carbon footprint[1] on the ecology and economy of cities, following which we examine the evidence regarding the carbon footprint of Indian cities in the context of their contribution to economic growth.

[1] A carbon footprint is defined as the total amount of greenhouse gases produced to directly and indirectly support human activities, usually expressed in equivalent tonnes of carbon dioxide (CO_2).

Impact of Cities on Climate Change

Given that half of the world's population started to live in cities by 2007, it is no exaggeration to say that the battle against climate change will be won or lost in our cities. To the extent that cities promote use of cars, urban sprawl is also often associated with climate change. That is, the wider the sprawl, the greater the use of cars and carbon emissions. Energy consumed in heating and lighting of residential and commercial buildings generates nearly a quarter of GHGs globally and transport contributes 13.5 per cent, of which 10 per cent is attributed to road transport (McCarney 2009). We can safely assume that a sizeable portion of this volume of emissions is generated in cities. According to the Clinton Foundation, large cities are responsible for about 75 per cent of the GHGs released into our atmosphere.[2]

In this context, it is useful to study how Indian cities have contributed to climate change through carbon emissions. The primary impact of carbon emissions on cities is through the modes of transport used. In a simple analytical framework, Grazi and Waisman (2009) account for external (costs) benefits of land use and transport that reflect the (dis) economies arising from agglomeration. The spatial disaggregation of national into city economies is a major outcome of this research that goes beyond the scope of climate change analysis.

There is very little empirical information available on carbon emissions in Indian cities. Box 21.1 discusses a South Asian regional initiative to develop an overall regional approach and consensus for addressing urban climate change. As reported in the box, under the project, the International Council of Local Environmental Initiatives (ICLEI), South Asia, associated with 54 local governments in the South Asian region (including 41 cities from India) to collect city energy consumption and related carbon emissions inventory data of the participating cities.

Based on a cursory examination of the per capita carbon emissions across metropolitan and non-metropolitan cities (see Table 21.1), we find that the average per capita carbon emissions are higher in the metropolitan cities of India (being 1.19 tonnes per capita as compared to only 0.90 tonnes per capita in the non-metropolitan cities) as we would expect, and the national average is 0.93 tonnes per capita. This is because larger cities have more industries and other polluting activities such as emissions from public and private transport. However, the corporation level emissions as a percentage of city-level emissions are much higher in the non-metropolitan areas than in the metropolitan areas. Corporation-level emissions include those emanating from street lighting, water supply and sewage systems, transportation, building, and other facilities. While this finding is interesting, this is plausible because smaller city corporations lack the adequate technology to minimize their carbon emissions in the provision of various public services such as water supply, sewerage, street lighting, and transportation.

The carbon emissions in Indian cities are also lower than what we observe internationally across a group of selected cities (see Figure 21.3). It should be mentioned that among these cities, apart from Sao Paulo and Rio de Janeiro in Brazil and Shanghai in China, which can be compared to Mumbai, other cities are not comparable directly with Indian cities in terms of their landscape or level of development.

Having said this, internationally, Palo Alto, California, USA, leads the pack with emissions amounting to nearly 12 tonnes per capita, followed by Toronto, Canada (at 9.6 tonnes per capita). Only seven of the 41 Indian cities studied by ICLEI have per capita emissions greater than Sao Paulo's 1.5 tonnes per capita.[3]

However, some caveats of the data from the ICLEI study should be noted. Their data do not include major cities such as Delhi and Mumbai, which might be contributing significantly to carbon emissions. However, the city corporations in these cities may also be contributing less through their provision of urban services such as water supply, sewerage, street lighting, and sanitation, if we were to assume that they have access to better technology than some of the smaller cities.

Impact of Climate Change on Cities

Not only do cities and urbanization impact climate change, but also, the question of whether climate change has impact on cities (the meticulous reader has to note that climate change may also have impacts not only on cities, but also on rural areas through their effects on increased or decreased rainfall which have impacts on agricultural output). Since cities have a high concentration

[2] On the other hand, cities are viewed as playing a positive role in mitigating the negative impacts of climate change. The OECD is actively working with governments to highlight the role of cities to deliver cost-effective policy responses to climate change. An analysis of emissions inventories (Dodman 2009) shows that—in most cases—per capita emissions from cities are lower than the average for the countries in which they are located. Similarly Satterthwaite (2008) suggests that the contribution of cities to global anthropogenic greenhouse gas emissions is often overstated.

[3] These are Faridabad (Haryana), Jaipur, Kolkata, Ranchi, Gurgaon, Vishakapatnam, and Jamshedpur. See Table 21.1.

of population density and economic activity, they are vulnerable to climate change. India's cities are characterized by high density of population, housing stock, and poor infrastructure, which make them all the more vulnerable to climate change. Given that the most valued infrastructure is usually located in cities, the economic and social costs of climate change will be much higher in cities. For example, cities house valuable communications infrastructure as they do physical infrastructure such as buildings, roads, bridges, and flyovers. Hence, any climate change impacts in the form of damage will be quite expensive. For instance, Kumar, Jawale, and Tandon (2008) estimate that the economic damage (this includes only building-foundation damages for the period till 2050 due to sea-level rise) to Mumbai, as a result of climate change, could amount to Rs 1,501,725 crores.[4]

Climate change impacts the physical assets used within cities for economic production, the costs of raw materials and inputs to economic production, the subsequent costs to businesses, and thus output and competitiveness. For instance, at India's sub-national level, an annual Gross State Domestic Product (GSDP) compression of about two per cent has been estimated for Gujarat, of which drought makes up 57 per cent, cyclone and storm surge

Box 21.1
The International Council of Local Environmental Initiatives

The International Council of Local Environmental Initiatives (ICLEI)–South Asia recently completed a project on the 'Energy and Carbon Emissions Profiles of 54 South Asian Cities'. The study gathered data from the engineering and administrative departments of the participating Urban Local Bodies (ULBs) to assess the energy consumption by them for services rendered to the citizens across the city.

This report by ICLEI–South Asia provides an inventory of the energy status and carbon emissions of 54 South Asian cities, including 41 cities from India, based on the city energy consumption and related carbon emissions inventory data. Analysis of the collected information was performed by ICLEI using the Harmonized Emissions Analysis Tool (HEAT, http://heat.iclei.org/), a unique and customized emissions calculation tool/software for ULBs/local governments. The final result was arrived at through a rigorous and structured feedback process by engaging engineering and administrative staff, followed by the involvement of municipal leaders, relevant institutions, and ministries.

Table 21.1 summarizes the per capita carbon emissions in the selected Indian cities, extracted from the ICLEI report. Further, in the report, for every city, energy consumption by category is given—residential, commercial, industrial, transportation, waste, and others. In addition to per capita carbon emissions, the report has the entire (absolute) consumption of electricity of 2007–08 for every city. Every city corporation's emission is given in detail by sector. For every selected city, the city level and corporation level carbon emission patterns are summarized with the help of pie charts.

Figure 21.1 summarizes the emissions by the sector in the selected Indian cities. It shows that the majority of the emissions are industrial in nature, followed by residential emissions (at 28 per cent) and then transportation (which contributes 24 per cent of all emissions).

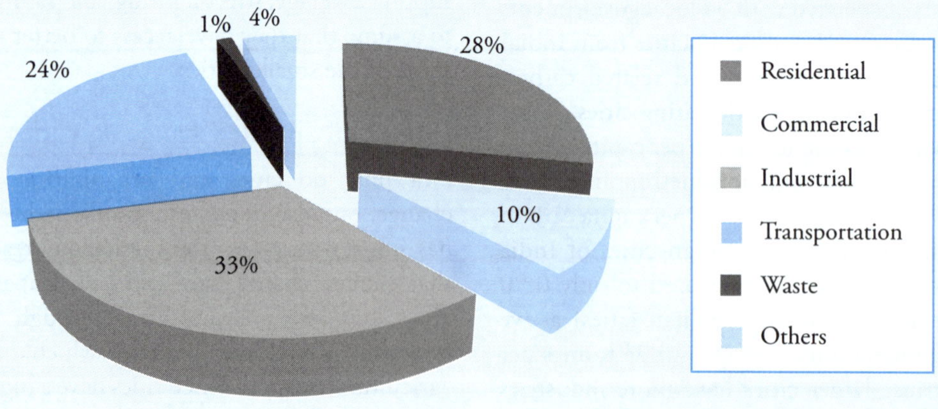

Figure 21.1 Sector-wise Emissions in the Selected Indian Cities, 2007–8

(contd.)

[4] They also estimate damages of climate change in Mumbai due to dislocation caused by flooding (Rs 407.6 crores), material damage to low-lying areas due to extreme events (Rs 6,413 crores), mortality costs due to extreme events of flooding (Rs 3,050 crores), disability-adjusted life years (DALYs) lost due to diseases like malaria, diarrhoea, and leptospirosis (Rs 3,153 crores), and tourism losses in the form of fewer tourists visiting Mumbai (Rs 1,963,500 crores).

Box 21.1 *(contd.)*

Figure 21.2 summarizes carbon emissions (in absolute terms) in the selected Indian cities. In absolute terms, the highest emissions are in Kolkata, followed by Vishakapatnam and Agra.

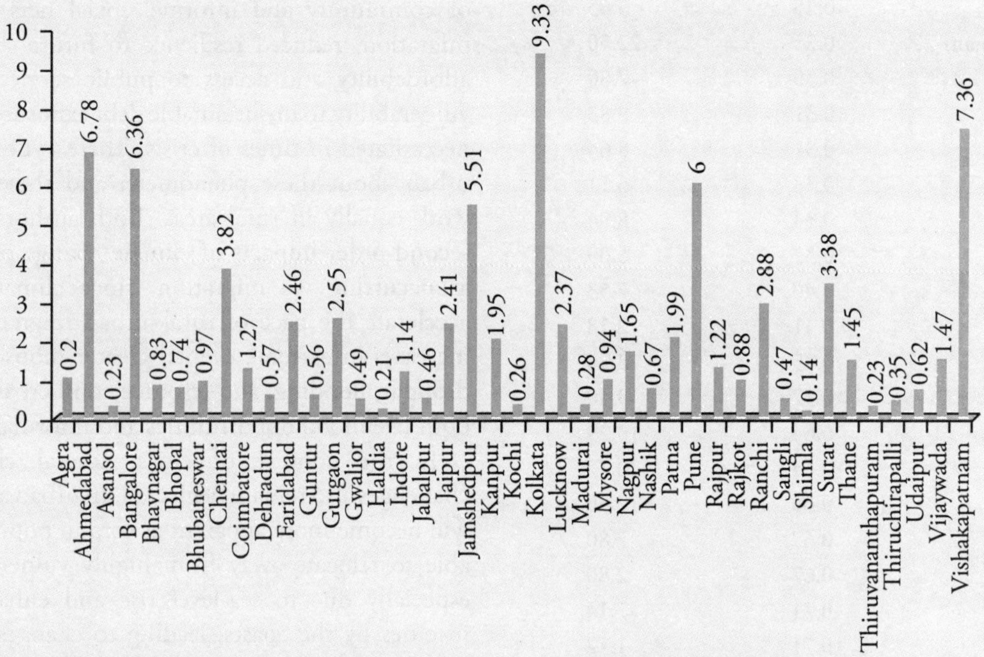

FIGURE 21.2 Carbon Emissions in 41 Indian Cities, 2007–8 (in Million Tonnes)

Based on this data, cities developed plans to combat climate change at the local level. These actions included efficient water usage, effective solid waste management, generating clean energy, and to thereby decrease air pollution. A survey was also carried out to gather feedback and comments of the cities on the analyses, which were then incorporated into the final report.

The following action plans were suggested and discussed with cities (through sample surveys) to reduce carbon emissions in their cities in the following broad areas:

- Street lighting EE programme which has high potential of energy savings (20–5 per cent).
- Building and facilities energy efficiency programme.
- Pumping system-efficient projects for water supply and drainage pumping stations.
- Residential/commercial and industrial sectors.
- Transportation system.
- Public awareness.
- Others—Integration of renewable energy (RE) and EE measures in public places.

Source: Energy and Carbon Emissions Profiles of 54 South Asian Cities, ICLEI—South Asia.

12 per cent, and inland flooding five per cent over a 100–year time horizon (Revi 2008). A recent report using data collected over 193 years shows that since the 1960s, there has been a dip in India's annual rainfall. For instance, in the plains of Kerala, peak rainfall declined from at least 3,700 mm received in the 1920s and 1930s to around 2,800 mm in the 1960s, a fall of 24 per cent. The Kerala State Planning Board's Compendium of Environment Statistics finds that as of 2003, the state's annual rainfall fell nearly 17 per cent short of the normal rainfall from 1990 to 2003. In the plains of Punjab, there is a similar fall, from 1,100 mm in the early years of the twentieth century to around 687 mm, now registering a decrease of 37.5 percent.[5] Part of this could probably be attributed to global warming.

Cities in developing countries face more risks of economic and social catastrophes due to their relative lack of resources to adapt and mitigate. Mukhopadhyay and

[5] http://www.livemint.com/2008/08/17233753/India8217s-fluctuating-rain.html

Table 21.1 Carbon Emissions in India's Cities

City	*CO_2 emission Per Capita (tonnes)*	*Corporation level emissions as % of City-level Emissions*
Asansol	0.25	3.63
Thiruvananthapuram	0.25	22.50
Jabalpur	0.30	7.80
Bhopal	0.31	8.83
Madurai	0.31	8.64
Tiruchirapalli	0.33	6.11
Nashik	0.34	8.94
Gwalior	0.37	6.09
Kochi	0.40	7.53
Indore	0.41	2.28
Kanpur	0.45	3.20
Sangli	0.52	3.40
Agra	0.64	10.29
Lucknow	0.64	20.77
Shimla	0.66	12.50
Nagpur	0.67	7.80
Rajkot	0.67	2.80
Dehradun	0.71	7.14
Guntur	0.71	1.72
Mysore	0.72	6.80
Udaipur	0.76	6.33
Bengaluru	0.82	4.14
Patna	0.83	7.10
Bhubaneshwar	0.84	1.17
Vijayawada	0.90	1.20
Chennai	0.91	2.68
Surat	0.91	3.48
Haldia	0.95	NA
Bhavnagar	1.11	2.39
Thane	1.15	2.88
Ahmedabad	1.20	2.91
Pune	1.31	2.16
Raipur	1.32	1.85
Coimbatore	1.37	0.67
Faridabad	1.58	2.06
Jaipur	1.63	4.22
Kolkata	1.83	2.15
Ranchi	1.97	0.06
Gurgaon	2.13	0.27
Vishakapatnam	2.25	0.32
Jamshedpur	2.76	NA
Average, all	0.93	5.30
Average, Metros	1.19	10.39
Average, Non-metros	0.90	4.72

Source: ICLEI-South Asia, Energy and Carbon Emissions Profiles of 54 South Asian Cities, 2009.

Revi (2009) highlight the multiple ways in which climate change can impact Indian urban residents through loss of livelihood opportunities (including housing and assets) and income, loss in terms of health or ability to work, of community and informal social nets due to forced migration, reduced resilience to future shocks, reduced affordability and access to public services, and greater vulnerability to unsustainable debt exposure, that could be necessitated in times of crisis. There is nothing uniquely urban about these phenomena and these channels can work equally in rural areas. Both authors also mention second-order impacts of climate change on Indian cities as occurring via migration, since climate change can accelerate the pace of rural–urban migration, driven by increases in extreme events, greater monsoon variability, drought, flooding, and resource conflict, as well as loss of both livelihood opportunities and informal social nets.

In the context of cities, several climate-induced challenges also remain neglected. In urban areas, inequities will become more apparent as certain populations are less able to relocate away from highly vulnerable locations, especially due to sea-level rise and enhanced flooding in cities by the coasts, leading to changes in the spatial distribution and density of both formal and informal settlements. Degradation of building and infrastructure materials is also projected to occur. As warmer temperatures extend into higher latitudes, diseases that have long been considered eradicated may re-emerge; and new diseases may also be experienced. The health ramifications could be serious. The gap between water supply and demand is also projected to increase as drought-affected areas expand and the episodes of floods intensify.

Overall, climate change and increased climate variability will alter the environmental baseline of urban locales, such as the temperature regimes and precipitation patterns. Shifts in climate and increased frequency of extreme events have direct impacts on water availability and quality, flooding and drought periodicity, and water demand amongst a host of conditions. These dynamic changes will affect system processes within multiple sectors in cities interactively, increasing the uncertainty under which urban managers and decisionmakers must operate (Mehrotra et al. 2009).

Economic costs of climate change in cities need to 'bracket' for uncertainty and assess both intra- and inter-sectoral and systemic risks to address direct and indirect economic impacts. Risk frameworks tend to fall broadly into three categories or groups. The first group stems from the work of climate scientists associated with the IPCC and focuses primarily on climate hazards—variances in mean and extreme climate parameters, collectively referred to as

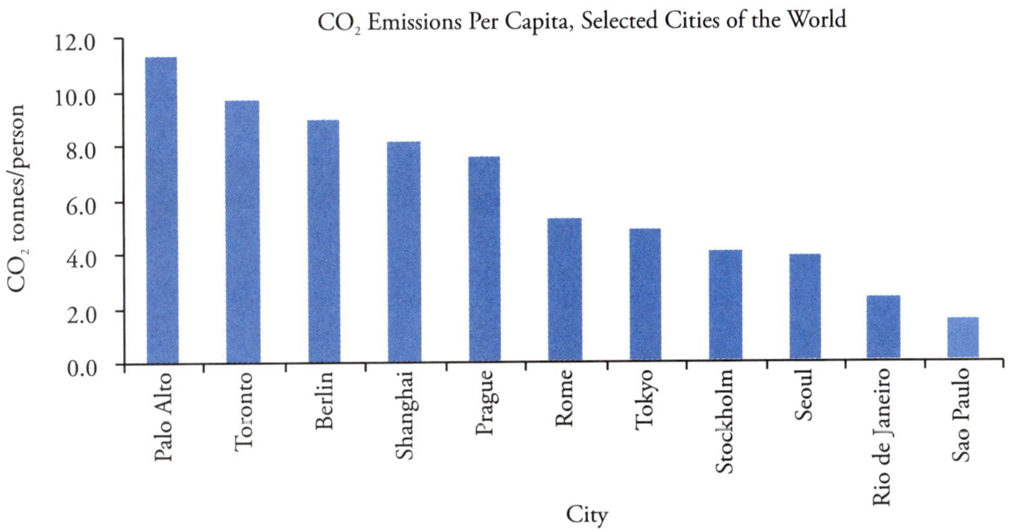

FIGURE 21.3 Carbon Emissions in Cities Around the World

Source: McCarney (2009).

climate hazards. The second group emerges from the work of planners and policymakers, such as those associated with UN Habitat's *The Cities in Climate Change Initiative* (CCCI) or the World Bank. The World Bank's East Asia Unit's recent analysis summarized in the *Climate Resilient Cities: A Primer on Reducing Vulnerabilities to Disasters*, focuses on vulnerabilities—essentially city characteristics that determine the susceptibility a city has to climate change. The third group of risk frameworks focuses on economic analysis of climate impacts, such as the OECD reports.

Much of the risk associated with climate change in cities is concentrated among low-income households, as described by Aromar Revi for India and Patricia Romero-Lankao for Latin America.[6] The cities most at risk are those which:

- lack the ability to avoid the direct or indirect impacts because of their location—on the coast, by rivers, or where cyclones or hurricanes are common. For example, as Mehrotra et al. (2009) point out, each year New York City is susceptible to mid-latitude cyclones, which peak from November to April. These storms contribute greatly to coastal erosion of vital wetlands that help defend areas of the city from coastal flooding. Tropical cyclones (hurricanes) also have the potential to reach New York City usually during the months of August to September. There is some indication that intense hurricanes will occur more frequently in the future, but this, as they point out, is an area of active scientific research.
- are likely to be most affected by the impacts because of their physical form—poor-quality buildings and lack of water supply and storm drainage infrastructure. Nothing can explain this better than the floods that occurred in Mumbai on 26 July 2005, aggravated by the poor and inadequate drainage system of Mumbai, which was not capable of carrying even half the amount of water per hour on the day the disaster took place in the city. Further, the mangroves that existed along the banks of the Mithi River and Mahim Creek have been destroyed over time to make way for the construction of new buildings.
- are least able to cope with the impacts due to a lack of local government capacity and funding to rebuild or repair damage, restore services, and support households to rebuild homes and livelihoods. The example here is of Mumbai again, which experienced floods in 2005. One of the factors that had an adverse impact on the floods was the rapid growth and development of the northern suburbs of the city which lacked proper control and planning on the part of the city's municipal authorities.

The urban populations most at risk are those who are:

- least able to avoid the direct or indirect impacts, because, for example, they live in poor-quality homes

[6] http://www.id21.org/insights/insights71/art04.html

and in areas with inadequate drainage systems, and are unable to move or change jobs if climate change threatens their livelihoods.

- most vulnerable to the impacts, such as infants and elderly people who are less able to cope with heat waves or unable to flee quickly when a disaster is imminent.
- least able to cope with illness, injury, or premature death; or loss of income, livelihood, or property.

Mitigating Strategies in Urban India

Many cities have the potential, and indeed are becoming, key actors in global mitigation efforts, as will be discussed in Chapter 23 in this Report. McCarney summarizes five sectors which can help mitigate the negative effects of climate change—energy supply, transport, buildings, industry, and waste. The Vienna City Council adopted the city's Climate Protection Programme as a framework for its Eco-Business plan[7] and as a result, the city reduced its solid waste output by 109,300 tonnes; toxic solid wastes by 1,325 tonnes, and carbon dioxide emissions by 42,765 tonnes.

This climate protection programme, described in detail in Box 21.2, saved a total of 138.7 million Kwh of energy and 1, 325,000 cubic metres of drinking water. The Eco-Business plan is also now being implemented in Chennai, India, and Athens, Greece.

In India, the ACCCRN aims to catalyze attention, funding, and action on building climate change resilience for the poor and vulnerable by creating robust models and methodologies for assessing and addressing risks through active engagement and analysis of cities. Gorakhpur, Surat, and Indore have taken up pilot projects for adaptation and mitigation of the impact of climate change in their cities. Indore, Madhya Pradesh, which has been affected by climate change in the form of rising temperatures and increasing incidence of non-monsoon drought, has identified potential pilot activities such as underground water storage and a volunteer-based water supply availability tracking system.

At the sub-national level, various pollution control boards and several city corporations have taken the lead in reducing carbon emissions. For example, various carbon emission-reducing processes such as the use of methane gas emanated from 180 million litres per day (MLD) sewerage plant, the Gyaspur landfill site and the process of burning waste-beads to produce electricity are gaining carbon credits in the Ahmedabad Municipal Corporation (AMC). Technologies involved in cutting electricity consumption in street lights, use of LED (light emitting diodes) lighting source, the BRTS mass transit system, green technologies and e-governance are part of this process. There are several private firms helping the AMC trade in carbon credits such as United Phosphorus, Creative Technologies, and Excel Technologies. These bodies would trade carbon credits generated out of using 1,900 tonnes of waste for green processes. AMC has agreements with the three companies with a 60 to 40 per cent profit-sharing arrangement for carbon credit trade. Gujarat Urban Development Corporation (GUDC) is the main agency for the carbon credit trade in the state of Gujarat.[8]

The ICLEI project (see Box 21.1) aims to illustrate local criteria pollutants and CO_2 emissions from India's growing transport sector using available data, and to provide policies and measures that will prevent future undesirable consequences of motorization. ICLEI has also initiated a programme on carbon emission reduction through city-level local action plans by integrating RE and EE measures into city activities funded under the Climate Change and Energy (CCE) programme of the British High Commission by UK's Foreign and Commonwealth Office's Global Opportunity Fund (GOF). The project is aimed at promoting greater use of renewable energy and more efficient use of energy to help address climate change and ensure energy security and a low carbon future for Indian cities.

So it appears that while urbanization and climate change are inextricably related, some attempts are being made by Indian cities to cope with this phenomenon. However, in order to do this, municipal finances are a constraint. In this volume, the chapter by Annez and Zuelgaray examines the impact of high-cost carbon on municipalities' finance, and concludes that raising energy prices will create an adverse fiscal shock for local governments, the magnitude of which will depend on the structure of spending.

Conclusions

This chapter has initiated discussing issues as to how urban areas can become growth centres for an economy. Following this, the relationship between urbanization and

[7] Examples of some activities included under a typical eco-business plan might be to rebuild and renovate buildings with green materials to reduce energy usage, reduce the energy consumption of appliances as well as heating, lighting, and cooling systems with the use of Light Emitting Diodes (LEDs) and replacement of incandescent lights with compact fluorescent lamps (CFLs).

[8] http://timesofindia.indiatimes.com/city/ahmedabad/City-has-lowest-carbon-emission-Study/articleshow/5121470.cms, retrieved 10 February 2010.

Box 21.2

KLiP—Vienna's Climate Protection Programme

Vienna's climate protection programme known as Klip Vienna (KlipI), was enacted in 1999 by the city council and is valid until 2010. KliP's goal of preventing an increase in annual emissions of CO_2 equivalents by 2.6 million tonnes by 2010 was achieved in 2006. So far, the city has successfully avoided an annual emission of 3.1 million tonnes of CO_2 equivalent. Now, Vienna's climate goal is a 21 per cent reduction in per capita greenhouse gas emissions by the year 2020 from the base year of 1990. This is achieved through the measures of KliP II.

The update of the 1999 KliP I consists of 37 sets of measures with a total of 385 individual measures in the following five fields of action:

- Energy production.
- Use of energy.
- Mobility and city structure.
- Procurement, waste management, agriculture and forestry, and nature conservation.
- Public relations.

Actions in the context of energy production are primarily supply-related projects that reduce CO_2 emissions produced by power generation and district heating and cooling that Vienna can influence directly. With respect to the use of energy, the focus is to encourage end-consumers to use energy in the most efficient way, particularly with regard to measures taken for energy efficiency in buildings. This comprises all aspects of energy use that are necessary for constructing and maintaining buildings. In addition, there are also measures for public lighting, equipment using combustion engines, and electric devices. Actions with respect to mobility and town structure, relate to the objective of reducing, both directly and indirectly, greenhouse gas emissions generated by transport. Measures include promotion of bicycling, walking, public transport, and car pooling. In addition, this demand-orientated strategy has been supplemented with restrictions on using modes of transportation that cause environmental and climactic damage. The Viennese population has the opportunity to better combine various types of transportation to best fit their mobility needs. Finally, public relations guidelines for the entire climate protection programme have been developed. The measures in this field aim to inform the Viennese population and other relevant stakeholders. They endeavour to induce climate-friendly behaviour by raising awareness.

The implementation of the planned measures will allow Vienna to prevent an additional annual emission of 1.4 million tonnes of greenhouse gases in the period from 2009–20.

Climate Protection in Vienna: Precise Measures with Precise Targets

Increasing the share of district heating to 50 per cent: This goal will be reached by the continuous development of 'Wien Energie District Heating' via the expansion of the heating network, increasing energy efficiency, and the use of renewable energy.

Further promotion of thermal rehabilitation of residential buildings: There is great potential in the field of thermal rehabilitation of residential buildings, especially concerning the subsidy programme Thewosan. The subsidy guidelines will be adapted and the statutory provisions (for example, building code) will also be changed, further tightening prescriptive limits for new buildings and for the thermal rehabilitation of buildings.

Expansion of public transportation, reduction of passenger car traffic and promotion of public transport, bicycles, and walking. In future, particular attention will be paid to the use of bicycles. Efforts will also be made to make walking more attractive. This will provide a vital contribution in reducing greenhouse gas emissions. In addition, one may also expect that greenhouse gas emissions produced by Viennese passenger car traffic will significantly decrease due to advances in automotive technology and accompanying measures.

More than doubling of the amount of final energy produced by renewables compared to 1990: All the different options available to the City of Vienna and its municipal enterprises shall be utilized to make use of the various kinds of renewables within the urban area as well as within.

Creation of a plan for the secure supply of energy: Energy efficiency and renewable energy sources will be focus areas by adopting clearly defined measures for reducing energy demand by improving final energy efficiency and increasing the use of renewable energy.

The current organizational and operational structure in the field of climate protection in Vienna will be retained to reach the targets in the best manner possible.

Source: http://www.wien.gv.at/english/environment/klip/

climate change has also been discussed here. In this, we first highlighted how cities contribute to climate change and provided a description of the carbon footprint of Indian cities. Also in discussion were issues such as the reverse impact of climate change on the ecology and the economy of a city. Based on the above, we make a case for developing urban infrastructure to enable low carbon urban growth and summarize some of the mitigating strategies cities in India have been adopting to adapt to climate change.

References

Annez, Patricia C., and Robert M. Buckley (2009). 'Urbanization and Growth: Setting the Context', in M. Spence, P.C. Annez, and R.M. Buckley (eds), *Urbanization and Growth*, The World Bank, on behalf of the Commission on Growth and Development, Washington, DC, pp. 1–46.

Dodman, David (2009). *'Blaming Cties for Climate Change? An Analysis of Urban Greenhouse Gas Emissions Inventories',* Environment and Urbanization, 21(1), pp. 185–201, http://eau.sagepub.com/cgi/content/abstract/21/1/185, Retrieved 15 February 2010.

Duranton, Gilles (2009). 'Are Cities Engines of Growth and Prosperity for Developing Countries?', in M. Spence, P.C. Annez, and R.M.Buckley (eds), *Urbanization and Growth*, The World Bank, on behalf of the Commission on Growth and Development, Washington, DC, pp. 67–114.

Gasper, J. and E.L. Glaeser (1998). 'Information Technology and the Future of Cities', *Journal of Urban Economics*, 43, pp. 136–56.

Government of Kerala (2004). *Compendium of Environment Statistics*, Directorate of Economics and Statistics, Thiruvananthapuram, Kerala, June.

Grazi, F. and Henri Waisman (2009). 'Climate Change and Urban Economic Development: A CGE Analysis', Paper Prepared for the World Bank's 5th Urban Research Symposium Cities and Climate Change: Responding to an Urgent Agenda Marseille, France, 28–30 June.

Hunt, A., and P. Watkiss (2007). 'Literature Review on Climate Change Impacts on Urban City Centres: Initial Findings'. ENV/EPOC/GSP(2007)10. OECD, Paris, France.

IPCC (2007). 'Summary for Policymakers', in S. Solomon, D. Qin, M. Manning, Z. Chen, M. Marquis, K.B. Averyt, M.Tignor, and H.L. Miller (eds), '*Climate Change 2007: The Physical Science Basis, Contribution of Working Group I to the Fourth Assessment Report of the Intergovernmental Panel on Climate Change*', Cambridge University Press, Cambridge, UK and New York.

Kumar, Rakesh, Parag Jawale, and Shalini Tandon (2008). 'Economic Impact of Climate Change on Mumbai, India', *Regional Health Forum,* 12 (1),pp. 38–42.

Kreimer, A., M. Arnold., and A. Carlin (eds) (2003). 'Building Safer Cities: The Future of Disaster Risk', *Disaster Risk Management Series No. 3,* World Bank.

Lucas, Robert E., Jr. (2007). 'Trade and the Diffusion of the Industrial Revolution', Frank D. Graham Memorial Lecture, Princeton University, Princeton, New Jersey, March.

——— (2004). 'Life Earnings and Rural–Urban Migration', *Journal of Political Economy,* 112 (1, pt. 2), S29–59.

——— (1988). 'On the Mechanics of Economic Development', *Journal of Monetary Economics,* 22 (1), pp. 3–42.

McCarney, P. (2009). 'City Indicators on Climate Change: Implications for Policy Leverage and Governance', Paper Prepared for the World Bank's 5th Urban Research Symposium on Cities and Climate Change: Responding to an Urgent Agenda, Marseille, France, June 28–30.

Mehrotra, S., Claudia E. Natenzon, Ademola Omojola, Regina Folorunsho, Joseph Gilbride, and Cynthia Rosenzweig. (2009). 'Framework for City Climate Risk Assessment', Paper Prepared for the World Bank's 5th Urban Research Symposium on Cities and Climate Change: Responding to an Urgent Agenda, Marseille, France, June 28–30.

Ministry of Urban Development and Ministry of Urban Employment and Poverty Alleviation. (2006). 'Toolkits for the Jawaharlal Nehru National Urban Renewal Mission (JNNURM)', New Delhi.

Mukhopadhyay, Partha and A. Revi. (2009). 'Keeping India's Economic Engine Going: Climate Change and the Urbanization Question', *Economic and Political Weekly,* 54 (31), pp. 59–74.

National Research Council (2003). *Cities Transformed: Demographic Change and Its Implications for the Developing World. Panel on Urban Population Dynamics*, in Mark R. Montgomery, Richard Stren, Barney Cohen, and Holly E. Reed (eds), *Committee on Population, Division of Behavioral and Social Sciences and Education*, National Academies Press, Washington, DC.

Quigley, J.M. (2009). 'Urbanization, Agglomeration and Economic Development', in M. Spence, P.C. Annez, and R.M. Buckley (eds), *Urbanization and Growth, Commission on Growth and Development,* The World Bank, Washington DC.

——— (1998). 'Urban Diversity and Economic Growth', *Journal of Economic Perspectives,* 12 (2), pp.127–38.

Ramesh, R. and M.G.Yadava (2005). 'Climate and Water Resources of India. Physical Research Laboratory', *Current Science,* 89 (5), pp. 818–24, 10 September.

Revi, Aromar (2008). 'Climate Change Risk: An Adaptation and Mitigation Agenda for Indian Cities', *Environment and Urbanization*, 20(1), pp. 207–30, April.

Romer, Paul (1986). 'Increasing Returns and Long-Run Growth', *Journal of Political Economy,* 94 (5), pp. 1002–37.

Satterthwaite, David (2008). 'Cities' Contribution to Global Warming: Notes on the Allocation of Greenhouse Gas Emissions', *Environment and Urbanization, 20(2),* pp. 539–49, http://eau.sagepub.com/cgi/content/abstract/20/2/539 retrieved 15 February 2010.

Sharma, S., S. Bhattacharya, and A. Garg (2006). 'Greenhouse Gas Emissions from India, A Perspective', *Current Science,* 90(3), pp. 326–33, 10 February.

Sridhar, Kala Seetharam and V. Sridhar (2003). 'The Effect of Telecommuting on Suburbanization: Empirical Evidence', *Journal of Regional Analysis and Policy*, 33(1), pp. 1–25.

Venables, A. (2009). 'Rethinking Economic Growth in a Globalizing World: An Economic Geography Lens'., in M. Spence, P.C. Annez, and R.M. Buckley (eds), *Urbanization and Growth,* The World Bank (on behalf of the Commission on Growth and Development), Washington, DC, pp. 47–66.

22 Low Carbon Intensity Urban Planning Strategies for India

Part 1 The Growing Cities of India: Towards Sustainability and Emission Reduction

Ramakrishna Nallathiga

Urbanization in India

India has been progressively changing from a rural to an urban society. While only 11 per cent of the total population constituted city dwellers in 1901, this statistic stood at around 28 per cent in 2001.[1] It is said that in the next 20 years (starting 2008), the urban population will rise to around 250 million, in contrast to an increase of 230 million between 1971 and 2008. Much of the urbanization has been taking place in million-plus cities, whose share of the total urban population had risen from 32 to 38 per cent during 1991–2001. The number of million-plus cities in fact went up from 23 to 35 during this period and is estimated to increase to 68 by 2030. Urban centres are abuzz with economic activities and consequently, driving economic growth; economic value addition of cities to GDP has risen from 46 per cent in 1990 to 54 per cent in 2001 and further expected to rise to almost 70 per cent by 2030 (MGI 2010).

Much of the analysis, research, discussion, and debate around urbanization are confined to emerging trends, patterns, and their implications for policymaking in terms of: (a) rural-urban migration of population, employment structures, and the impediments to urbanization/urban growth patterns emerging from current policy and institutional framework; (b) demographic burden on urban infrastructure service provisioning by urban local governments and para-statal agencies; (c) the positive linkages of urbanization with the national economy in terms of the rising contribution of urban areas to economic development; and (d) the rising social and environmental costs of urbanization.

As cities expand, the implications of urbanization on the provision of infrastructure services, energy consumption, GHG emissions, and decline of natural resources as well as the governance and institutional frameworks has caught research and policy attention. The spatial aspects of urban growth and its linkage to a low carbon trajectory require further attention to determine how to foster and sustain the linkage.

Spatial Patterns of Urban Growth

Data on spatial dimensions of urban growth are not directly collected, collated, and released by the Census of India. The Census measures of population in 'core city' and 'out-growths' may be used to make distinctions across spatially different units within urban agglomerations. The following is an attempt to compare and analyse the

[1] The Census defines an area of human settlements as urban if all the following criteria are met: (a) the number of people is more than 5,000 (b) 75 per cent of the total workforce is engaged in non-agriculture activity. There exists a difference in urban area and population data, as the Census of India collects the data at the block level and aggregates them at the district level, whereas the urban local governments record area and population within their boundaries/city limits.

growth of the core city and peripheral areas[2] of urban agglomerations, which provides some broad directions, in terms of the constraining factors of urban population growth, especially that of rural-urban migration, employment generation, and the absorption of relatively cheaper labour from rural hinterland. These growth patterns are also linked to resource and energy consumption (thereby, to carbon emissions) via the suburban sprawl.[3]

Of the 35 million-plus Indian cities, most cities have either growing cores and peripheries or declining cores and peripheries (see Table 22.1.1). A few cities show a declining core and growing periphery pattern while only Bangalore shows a growing core and declining periphery pattern.

Table 22.1.1 Matrix of Growing/Declining Core and Periphery

	Growing Core	*Declining Core*
Growing periphery	Agra, Amritsar, Dhanbad, Indore, Jabalpur, Jamshedpur, Kanpur, Patna, Pune, Rajkot, Surat	Delhi, Ahmedabad, Asansol, Coimbatore
Declining periphery	Bangalore	Greater Mumbai, Kolkata, Chennai, Allahabad, Bhopal, Hyderabad, Kochi, Lucknow, Madurai, Meerut, Nagpur, Nashik, Vadodara, Varanasi, Vijayawada, and Vishakapatnam

Notes: 1. City agglomerations are placed in terms of growth/decline during 1981–91 and 1991–2001.
2. Jaipur, Faridabad, and Ludhiana do not have any urban agglomeration.
Source: Sivaramakrishnan and Kundu (2007).

The relative decline of core cities in terms of population growth is attributed to an already large population base of core cities, the lack of infrastructure and amenities, the rising costs of living, and the stringent land laws (Sivaramakrishnan and Kundu 2007). Even cities like Jamshedpur and Asansol, which are now attaining the status of metro cities, had fast growing peripheries in 2001. Migration of the population from the central city to suburban areas/neighbouring cities resulting in simultaneous growth and decline of large cities has been observed in some Asian countries and is termed as the 'doughnut effect'. It is attributed to the middle-income groups moving to suburban areas or neighbouring cities for better as well as affordable living conditions in those locations (UN Habitat 2008).

Most of the million-plus cities are multi-municipal agglomerations comprising a large city as the core with one or more small urban areas (outgrowths) in the periphery, and they show a vivid population share and growth pattern.

Table 22.1.2 shows the growth rate of the core city and outgrowths. Outgrowths appear to fare better than the city even in terms of the growth rate. This is probably because much of the rural-urban migration (unskilled to semi-skilled workers) gets concentrated in these areas; and, to some extent, population with skill-sets that are employed in the city, which cannnot afford the high living costs of the city, lives here. Some production/business activity that generates employment is also found in the outgrowths as the core city gets choked or land values are too high. The choking of cities is often a reason offered by the cities to align their city development plans in favour of 'decongestion' of the core city and encouragement of sub-urbanization (as in the case of Delhi, Mumbai, Kolkata, and Chennai) without any planning done for the development of suburban or ex-urban/peri-urban areas. Several SEZs are located in such outgrowths so that they remain connected to and utilize the strengths of core city such as specialized skill-sets, logistical hub advantages, and economies in the concentration of firms into clusters.

Sub-urbanization and suburban population growth at a considerable pace, when compared to that of the core city, result in increases in the number of vehicles on the roads than otherwise. Most of the 35 million plus population cities have been experiencing a rapid rise in vehicular ownership in the last two decades as per the statistics of the Ministry of Surface Transport. As motor vehicle statistics are collected and maintained at the overall city level, it is not possible to dissect the vehicle ownership and travel patterns in the core city and suburban towns. It can, however, be asserted that sub-urbanization increases the travel miles per vehicle due to the rise in not only the

[2] Here, the core city refers to the city within municipal limits, while the peripheral area/periphery refers to the urban areas outside municipal limits but within the urban agglomeration.

[3] Urban sprawl refers to the patchy and disconnected expansion of urban areas that begins with unplanned land development without any relation to the city in terms of civic infrastructure and other services. Some typical features of urban development characterized as urban sprawl include single use zoning, low density land use, discontiguous development, and automobile dependent communities.

TABLE 22.1.2 Growth Rates of City and Outgrowths Population of Select Cities

Metro city	*Growth rate during 1991–2001*		
	UA	*City*	*Outgrowth*
Greater Mumbai	2.65	1.84	5.25
Delhi	4.27	3.14	9.39
Kolkata	1.83	0.40	2.69
Bangalore	4.52	4.90	3.79
Chennai	0.48	0.94	–0.72
Ahmedabad	3.16	2.03	8.71
Hyderabad	2.45	1.53	4.21
Pune	4.18	4.95	2.74
Kanpur	2.86	3.05	0.18
Surat	6.35	4.97	34.07
Lucknow	3.11	3.15	1.75
Nagpur	2.47	2.36	6.20
Bhopal	3.19	3.04	–
Ludhiana	2.95	2.95	–
Patna	4.50	4.15	6.12
Vadodara	2.85	2.39	6.92
Nashik	1.63	5.30	–11.42

Source: Author's own. (Computed by author based on the data compiled from Census papers.)

commuting trips to the central city for work but also to the nearby/local centres for other purposes. The increase in number of vehicle miles travelled (VMT) comes at the cost of greater emissions in many cities due to limited carrying capacity of roads and congestion on them. The high levels of emissions in the major cities of India are indicative of the congestion (MoEF 2009).

Sustainable City Development

Conventionally, the development of cities is considered to be dependent on the web of economic activities, the availability of skill-sets- and the productivity of capital and labour. National economic policies and priorities largely determine the formation of skill-sets and the availability of capital. With the unleashing of the forces of globalization and liberalization, economic development is nearly synonymous with urban development, particularly in developing countries (Zetter 2002). In its quest for economic development, environmental sustainability (resource and energy use efficiency, and minimization of deleterious environmental consequences) is deprioritized in developing countries, and their development policies aimed at promoting economic development by improving the investment climate (Hassan and Zetter 2002). While economic policy is formulated at the national level, at the local level, the patterns of urban development can be made sustainable through deliberate choice of local policies, which may also be guided by an overarching national policy.

Cities are key contributors to carbon emission and climate change because most human and economic activities are concentrated there and much of the built form exists there. Cities also influence energy and land-use patterns of the surrounding and hinterland population through livelihood and quality of life linkages. Cities have a larger ecological footprint as compared to non-urban areas.[4] An ecological footprint can be an important indicator of the appropriateness of a city's development pattern—the greater the footprint of a city, the greater is its impact on the hinterland and its resources. Measurement of the ecological footprint of a city helps city administrations to benchmark, re-define their development path, and work out the strategies that promote development which causes the footprint to shrink rather than enlarge.

The sustainability of urban growth is contested along three dimensions: economic, environmental, and social sustainability. Growing cities require adequate provision of civic infrastructure services (water supply, sanitation, roads, street lighting, and solid waste management) and other amenities by concerned local authorities. With swelling populations, both capital operation and maintenance expenditure requirements rise. With limited revenue sources of local authorities, the heightening mismatch of revenue and expenditure leads to concerns about servicing a growing population and ensuring the sustainability of service delivery.[5] Second, the environmental consequences of urbanization and urban population growth include air as well as noise pollution from poor traffic conditions, exhaustion of renewable resources like groundwater due to excessive withdrawal, increased public health hazards, and an adverse impact on biodiversity and

[4] Rees and Wackernagel (1996) developed the ecological footprint concept—the area of land needed to provide the necessary resources and to absorb the wastes generated by a community. India's ecological footprint of 0.8 global hectares per capita is well below the global average of 2.2 ha/ca (CII-GFN 2006).

[5] Jawaharlal Nehru National Urban Renewal Mission (JNNURM), the biggest intervention made by the Government of India, is essentially aimed at correcting the fiscal gap and to promote urban development under partnership between it and local and state governments.

natural resources[6] due to unfettered expansion of the city into hinterlands. Resource and energy requirements of the growing urban population are much higher than the rural areas and regions outside them. Large volumes of water, coal, and gas are utilized directly or indirectly by cities. While many of the solutions for sustainable development lie in the long-term spatial planning and governance of cities, the seeds of pursuing a low carbon growth agenda in cities can be sown into urban management practices as well as planning policy choices. Urban environmental management[7] involves integration of a 'green agenda' into urban development through appropriate strategies and plans that become integral to the development of cities within their planning and governance framework. We discuss some such management practices next, followed by a discussion on longer term trajectories for low carbon urban growth.

Urban Environment Management: Integrating Climate Change with Growth Agenda of Cities

Specific interventions to reduce carbon emissions through actions at the unit/project level or the local level may involve voluntary initiatives of citizens or restrictive measures of governments. These approaches are sometimes distinguished as: (a) *preventive approaches* targeting emission reduction through voluntary actions, land use, and development planning; (b) *mitigative approaches* using specific regulations, technologies, and policies to influence production and consumption. Green management actions can reinforce the low carbon agenda, if they are well cast based on the synergistic linkages between the two. At the city level, the scope for synergy and integration exists in all major sources of pollution and emissions. The choice of the urban growth pattern/form that minimizes resource consumption may also result in reduced carbon/GHG emissions.

Integrated Planning

Urban Environmental Management Plans (EMP) lay emphasis on interventions that lead to improved public health and promotion of the natural urban environment and green infrastructure through planning policy. They lay down the framework for spatial planning with coordination between central and local governments and for involving public, voluntary, and community sectors. For a structured approach towards lowering the carbon intensity of city development, an EMP has to be integrated with energy, transport, infrastructure, and other sector policies. The process begins with establishing the baseline environmental conditions in urban areas in terms of the measurements on various parameters of major environmental components—air, water, land, energy, biota, socio-economic, and built environment. Improving or maintaining the existing baseline environmental condition without impeding growth is the overall objective of an urban EMP. It goes beyond implementing existing environmental legislation, to establish a continual, measurable improvement in the urban area's environmental performance, to achieve a concrete impact on the quality of life in cities, and lead to a reduction of the ecological footprint of cities. Thus, an EMP should support a more comprehensive or holistic urban policy, tackling contradictions due to the compartmentalization of sectoral policies for the necessary dialogue between the sectors of environment, economy, physical planning, and land development. Box 22.1.1 presents the case of Kanpur city, where the EMP, however, remained/confined to paper and to the generation of maps.

Box 22.1.1
Environmental Management Plan for Kanpur

The Central Pollution Control Board (CPCB) undertook a pilot study to introduce spatial planning approaches to achieve environmentally sustainable development. It included preparation of the city profile, assessment of environmental quality, and identification of hot-spots for environmental management plans. It adopted GIS tools for generating a series of thematic maps for representation of information for quick and realistic decision-making. The EMP made a few prescriptions such as:

- Realignment of a major rail track
- Industrial emission control
- Green Area Development
- Water and drainage improvement
- Liquid and solid waste management

Source: Babu and Kumar (2002).

[6] These impacts and the resulting status of urban environment have been well documented in the *State of Environment 2009* brought out by the Ministry of Environment and Forests, Government of India. The consequences of these impacts on the urban living environment and quality of life have been well documented and discussed in environmental economics and policy literature.

[7] An Environmental Management Plan (EMP) is defined as: a strategic document that sets out the short-, medium-, and long-term environmental objectives and policies for an urban area, which defines a clear vision and the overall strategy and action plan to achieve quantifiable objectives and targets, as well as timetables, which are necessary to guide and steer management decisions (European Commission 2007).

Pollution Abatement Strategies

The conventional approach to pollution abatement at the local/city level involves following measures that can potentially reduce GHG emissions when applied stringently, but the outcomes depend upon enabling factors present within the systems of national and local government:

- Vehicle emission standards
- Mandatory devices for emission control
- Improved vehicle inspection and maintenance
- Vehicle retirement/replacement
- Alternative fuel use
- Improved fuel quality and/or efficiency

Box 22.1.2 showcases an experience of integrated strategy for air pollution and emission reduction in the case of Mumbai.

Resource Conservation Strategies

Conservation of natural resources of the city can lead to substantial savings on future investments that would have to be made for transporting such resources from distant locations in the event of scarcity induced by population pressure and climate change. For instance, cities like Chennai, Hyderabad, and Bangalore have taken steps towards conservation of fresh water. Likewise, development and protection of parks not only improves the local environment (through green spaces) but also the global environment (by acting as emission sinks). Box 22.1.3 presents a case study of Hyderabad where public parks were revived and maintained by the local community, corporates, and other stakeholders.

Long-term Solutions: Sustainable Urban Growth Patterns

Scale economies and efficiencies in organization make urban centres the hub of development, growth, and areas of dense human settlement. However, if the city growth consumes resources (including energy) and generates wastes in excess of manageable proportions and its spatial growth pattern is found to be reinforcing the same, then such development has direct implications for long-term sustainability. Public service (including transport) provisioning to the population, and competing demands between the city and suburbs pose serious challenges. Moreover, the fragmentation of functions with differential services to suburban areas could lead to unwanted social segregation of people and raise governance issues of public service delivery and management. Multiple authorities of different jurisdictions such as notified areas or cantonments could lead to a multiplicity of actors with overlaps, accountability ambiguities, and gap areas, compounding the challenge. Finally, the loss of rural land and landscape in the suburban and peri-urban areas result in a host of environmental and social stress points.

Patterns of urban growth that lead to the development of urban sprawl, or sub-urban sprawl, raise questions of

Box 22.1.2
Particulate Matter Reduction Action Plan in Mumbai

Mumbai has set an example of air quality management and pollution reduction, which are strategized through a set of policy instruments, institutional mechanisms and interventions for improved air quality, with funding support of the World Bank under the Mumbai Urban Transport Project (MUTP Phases I and II).

Under MUTP I, the emission generation process was examined, emissions were quantified, and health cost estimated. It was confined to measures to improve traffic conditions and to restrain the entry of highly emitting vehicles.

Under MUTP II, a long-term sustainable programme of urban transport, a Particulate Matter (PM) reduction action plan was prepared by the Mumbai Metropolitan Region Development Authority (MMRDA) to identify the strategies for emission reduction/pollution abatement. Based on the emission per unit of fuel used, targeting was done as following for the priority of action:

- Targeting most polluting vehicles (emission per km)
- Targeting most used vehicles (vehicle miles travelled per year)
- Targeting the vehicles with high growth rate

The PM action plan comprised three major strategies:

- Structural controls consisting of fuel and its quality, vehicles and technology, vehicle inspection and maintenance, roads and traffic control
- Non-structural controls consisting of policy interventions and public processes
- Institutional needs consisting of macro- and micro-planning, data collection and monitoring, implementation, and Information, Education, and Communication (IEC)

Source: NEERI (2004).

Box 22.1.3
Fund Your Park Initiative of Hyderabad

In a move to transform Greater Hyderabad into Greener Hyderabad, the Greater Hyderabad Municipal Corporation (GHMC) began a greening programme through avenue plantation, upgradation of existing parks, and developing new parks from 1999 onwards. It took an innovative approach in engaging key stakeholders of the city—the community, corporates, and business houses in the development and maintenance of parks.

Fund Your Park Concept

'Fund Your Park' is an innovative partnership programme of GHMC for sustained maintenance of parks and other green cover through the expanded scope of Public Private Partnerships (PPP). GHMC identified city-level parks, colony parks, theme parks, central medians, and traffic islands for redevelopment, refurbishment, and improved maintenance under this programme. Empanelled landscape architects/designers provided both concept and detailed design along with estimates for development and maintenance of the identified parks. These development/maintenance models for the specified parks were then put up for sponsorship in lieu of the advertisement rights.

GHMC planned to refurbish ten major city-level parks with new attractions that would enhance the ambience and aesthetics and improve the outlook of the park. It also planned improvement of around 250 colony parks and 2,200 open spaces.

Advertisements have been integrated into park design through specifications of design at all locations within the proposed park development in terms of harmony with the concept/theme of the park, by specifying the size, shape, material, ground clear height, colours, etc., for each of the advertisement hoardings proposed in different locations. The advertisement rights were initially for a period of one to three years as per the terms and conditions subject to payment of a specified amount towards the development and maintenance.

Source: GHMC.

sustainability. Map 22.1.1 shows how the growth of the national capital of Delhi has been sprawling into suburban and peri-urban development during the last few decades. The progression of built-up areas from 1986 to 1993 to 1999 clearly demonstrates the discontiguous development that is characteristic of the urban sprawl. Most of the Indian cities exhibit similar patterns of growth around the core city in the process of urbanization. Growth patterns of outward expansion or increasing sub-urbanization/peri-urbanization of the population are unsustainable not only due to ecological inefficiencies but also due to the pressure on shifting the organization of basic urban services like water supply and sewerage, transportation infrastructure, and social and commercial services from central cities to the distant periphery, negating the economies of scale in urbanization (Duany et al. 1999).

Emphasis on choosing an appropriate spatial growth pattern for a city, well-guided public policy (including planning policy), and appropriate governance and institutional framework may largely set the city growth pattern on a sustainable development path and can avoid/reduce emissions from dwellings and transport.

Compact City Development and Smart Growth

Planning policies that set the right development direction and strategies that define the right mix of activities can influence spatial urban growth and organization of human settlements and activities. Compact city development and/or smart growth form one strand of approaches that have the potential to play an important role in city/local environmental management, based as they are on premises of avoiding or reducing carbon/GHG emission potential by organizing city space better so as to minimize vehicular emissions from automobiles, residential resources, and energy consumption (see Box 22.1.4).

Compact city and smart growth models are consistent with neo-modern formulations of sustainable urban development that require conservation of material, energy, and the environment through spatial organization of cities. These models typically cover three aspects (Kaji 2004): (i) *Urban form:* Highly dense settlements with less dependence on automobile ownership and use, and demarcation of clear boundaries from surrounding areas (ii) *Spatial characteristics:* Mixed land-use with diversity of life and clear identity (ii) *Social functions:* Social fairness in interactions in dense settlements, self-sufficiency in daily life, and independence of government. A number of spatial models have been suggested to achieve environmental sustainability goals in terms of compact city structure depending upon the specific context, development stage, and features of cities (Owens 1985):

- Central core city structure: a primary spatial structure with development in concentrated rings around the centre.
- Star shape structure: a spatial structure with several nodes or centres, which is appropriate when there are

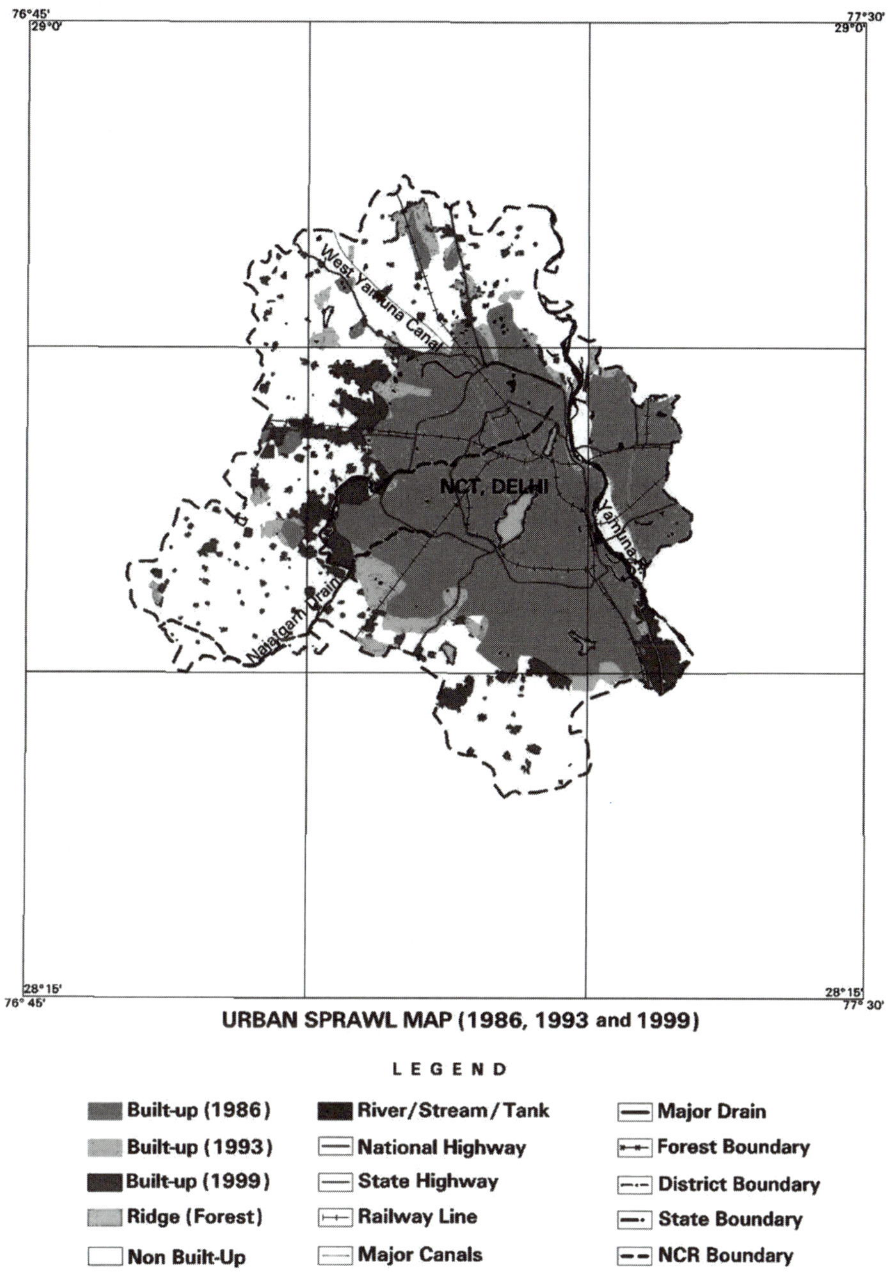

Map 22.1.1 Urban Sprawl Map

Source: Land-use map (NCR-PB), IRS-1B (LISS III) of 1993, IRS-ID (LISS III+PAN) of March 1999, Limited Ground Truth, Base details of 1993 (NCR-PB) and updated to 1999 for National Capital Region Planning Board, New Delhi by NRSA/DOS 2000.

many urban areas in a region with overlapping influence zones.

- Satellite city structure: a counter magnet(s) that only serve(s) as potential traps for absorbing the immigrant population, which have also been used recently as special areas to promote selective or wholesale economic growth.
- Galaxy structure: a spatial structure that is less compact in spatial organization but uses gravity concepts to define the flow of economic activities.
- Linear city structure: a spatial structure that is efficient on a small scale (for example, Curitiba) but that can support city development if combined with density.
- Multi-pole structure: a poly-centric spatial structure with each node/centre having a large influence area and connectivity through regional transport.

Box 22.1.4
Compact City and Smart Growth Definition

'Compact city' refers to urban land planning with a focus on higher density and better accessibility, which reduces automobile dependency. Dantzig and Saaty (1974) first made an effort to define it in term of components like high-density settlements, less dependence on automobiles, clear boundary from surrounding area, mixed land-use, diversity of life, clear identity, social fairness, self-sufficiency of daily life, and independency of governance (Kaji 2004).

'Smart growth' is a general term for land-use practices that create more accessible land-use patterns which reduce the amount of travel needed to reach goods and services (Litman 2003). They refer to what can be termed as guided growth of the cities towards efficiency, equity, and sustainability, which are well-examined by Burchell and Mukherji (2003).

Sub-urbanization and urban sprawl are widely prevalent in all cities but have received more attention in cities from the developed world. Although there is general consensus on the need to avoid sub-urbanization, the means of addressing it through growth management and control policies is contested, especially with respect to the effects of growth management on housing options (Nelson et al. 2002) and economic development (Staley and Gilroy 2002). Compact city development and smart growth have emerged as a consensual choice among policymakers. The cities in the East (for example, Singapore, Hong Kong, Tokyo, and Bangkok) are often cited as examples of how they have been able to sustain high densities in the cities without intruding into much of the hinterland in terms of land, water, and energy.[8] There is a general agreement that it is important to structure policies and strategies towards proactive urban planning rather than excessive regulation of urban development.

Urban Planning Policy and Practice in India

Unfortunately, much of the urban planning policy and practice in India is pre-occupied with following the Victorian model of 'city beautiful', which practises the divide of current occupants of the city from future occupants through the prescription of high standards (of open space, setbacks, recreational space, etc.). In the process, town planning deviates from its basic objective of providing space for living to the rural migrants through the organization of systems and services. Several cities have prescribed 'rigid zoning', that do not permit certain activity within the reserved premises, whereas the need emerging is mixed land-use. Low development densities so that city authorities can save on public services has resulted in human settlements much beyond city boundaries (edge-city), entailing long commutes to workplaces, as well as poor service delivery institutions in far-flung areas (Nallathiga 2004). In fact, the choice of low development density itself is contested on the grounds of being used as a fiscal or manipulative tool by local governments (Phatak 2002).

Apart from the prescription of low density, several cities follow decongestion policies, and subscribe to the dispersal of population and industrial activity, which creates suburban chaos. Most cities are plagued by a host of land-use and development control regulations, for example, permitted activity, plot setbacks, floor area ratio (FAR) or floor space index (FSI), which impact choice of housing, built space, and mobility (Bertaud 2002). Mumbai, for example, has a plethora of local and state government regulations that led to the development of a very highly constrained land market, which further reduce housing and living options for the urban poor; reforms in this sector have long been called for (Nallathiga 2002; Bombay First—McKinsey 2003). Box 22.1.5 summarizes the findings of a parametric study of such impacts. Faulty land-use regulations and a general lack of understanding of ownership rights intensify the challenge of regenerating our existing cities.

The simulation modelling of various types and placement of density over space suggests that high development density can be achieved in a variety of ways, but the choice of city form is an important factor that also determines the resulting vehicle flows (and, thereby, emissions) as well as built environment (Bertaud 2003). Therefore, both development planning and regulation can play an important role in the outcomes. Further, the choice of appropriate modes of transport is also determined by the residential density, that is, unless a very high density of population exists in a city, public transport cannot be built and run in a fiscally sustainable manner. Therefore, while the cities have to be planned to be built in appropriate urban forms using high development densities along with mixed use zoning, the suburban growth has to be planned and well connected/linked to public services, including mass urban transport.

In India, urbanization has been largely parallel with urban area expansion, particularly in the last couple of

[8] However, this theory has been debated afresh with the citation of omissions and survey of the cities in the West (Jenks and Burgess 2000).

> **Box 22.1.5**
> **Land-use Regulation Impacts on Land and Housing Options in Cities**
>
> There is a widespread usage of land-use regulations in Indian cities in the form of permitted development density (maximum allowed FAR/FSI) and prevalence of the Urban Land Ceiling Regulation Act (ULCRA), which has resulted in more sub-urbanization and peri-urban growth of urban agglomerations. It is hypothesized that these regulations have affected cities adversely (Nallathiga 2005). A study conducted by Sridhar et al. tests this hypothesis and assesses whether competition among services in the suburban areas result in better services; whether people follow jobs or jobs follow people in the process of sub-urbanization; and whether literacy and skill-sets play a role in the sub-urbanization process.
>
> The study finds that while all forms of sub-urbanization are influenced by these variables, it is highest in the case of household sub-urbanization. Urban spatial structure is determined to a good extent by historical forces. While employment sub-urbanization is driven by the combination of cost advantages and skill-set availability, the pre-existing population is also an important factor of the relocation of firms, that is, jobs follow/lag population in suburban areas.
>
> *Source*: Sridhar (2009).

decades. Several cities have not made any formal plans or institutional arrangements to take care of the peripheral areas around the core city, which have led to wide disparities between core urban and peri-urban areas (Dupont 2005). They have adopted low density standards that do not allow compact housing development, thereby, contributing to the sub-urbanization, peri-urban development, and urban sprawl development. Only recently, the Master Plan of Delhi recognized this anomaly and attempted to relax these standards. Indian cities, other than Mumbai, also lack the high speed (rail) transport corridors that make compact city development possible without compromising mobility needs. Nevertheless, with advancements in construction technology, it is now possible to develop compact vertical structures accommodating higher densities.

Compact City Form of Urban Development in India: Some Requisites

Achieving compact city development and smart growth of cities require some enablers, as are listed below:

Flexibility in Planning

Planning has to be flexible enough to accommodate development demands systematically, to pave the way for appropriately delineated zones that can absorb high densities. Steps in this direction include developing a fair degree of understanding of the land market, incorporating mixed land-use, discarding rigid rules/regulations that are weak in enforcement and perverse in impacts, realistic building regulations, and development controls.

Planning Policy Steering Urban Development

The urgent need for a coherent national urban and/or planning policy that gives direction to the need for pathways of sustainable urban development and appropriate growth patterns of cities is obvious. In spite of the Taskforce on Urbanization Report in 1985, no attempt has been made to formulate some template of urban planning policy, to spell out the basic objectives and principles of planning.

Regional/Metropolitan Planning

As cities expand, neighbouring urban areas come under their influence zones, and the need for service provision, shelter, and transport arises. Pro-active planning of the entire metropolitan region needs to be mainstreamed to take care of the requirements of the rising population in the region both through earmarking and development of such land as well as exploiting the areas with high development potential, without increasing the ecological footprint.

Density Planning of the Cities

It may be useful to demarcate zones with high development potential in cities, for example, buffer areas of transport corridors, and prescribe higher density so that there is supply of built space to the growing population. Density increase is best achieved if development areas are located in areas that are well-served by public transport (Petersen 2002; Newman and Kenworthy 1999).

Strong Mass Urban Transport and Fiscal Resources

Implementation of high density urban planning would require additional land and property acquisition for the green belt, zoned areas, public transit, artery roads, walking, and biking streets, etc. and construction and maintenance of infrastructure. If land-use planning takes a long-term perspective and plans for compact cities, it not only saves on additional investments on infrastructure but also makes the mass urban transport feasible.

Right Set of Complementary Local Policies

Integrated land-use and transport planning and policy are part of international standard practice. Singapore shows the example of the effect of this kind of policy mix.

Governance and Institutional Arrangements

Strong political will and support from citizens of the city and agglomerations is needed to promote compact development (Litman 2003). Since each city has its own background and conditions, the impacts of major transport and other urban infrastructure decisions on urban development, and the resulting travel patterns, should be carefully considered while preparing regional transport plans. The planning framework should be realistic in terms of what government can achieve (ADB 2003). The formation of the Metropolitan Planning Committee (MPC) as enshrined under 74th Constitutional Amendment Act 1992 is a first step in that direction. In addition, a supporting executive body of a Metropolitan Authority needs to be created, but which exists only in Kolkata.

Conclusion

The challenge of urbanization in India is well acknowledged, but the scale and quantum of resources required in order to sustain it have been brought out by the study of McKinsey Global Institute, which also provided a template for realigning urban development in order to achieve sustainable growth. In a similar vein, sustaining the energy and quality of living demands of urbanization calls for realigning urban growth in line with the low carbon path and sustainable development. At present, the 'doughnut' pattern of development, suburban sprawl, and the resulting increased energy demands of Indian cities may result in uncontrolled carbon emissions and very poor quality of environment unless they adopt a different growth pattern. Compact city development and smart urban growth are models worth emulating, at least for the adoption of underlying principles into planning policies and designs as well as regulatory and governance frameworks. Integration of environmental and climate change goals and their achievement through sustainable urban growth patterns are expected to improve long-term sustainability of urban development.

References

Asian Development Bank (2003). *Transport Planning and Traffic Management for Better Air Quality: Policy Guidelines for Reducing Vehicle Emissions in Asia,* ADB, Manila.

Babu, N.R. and A. Kumar (2002). 'Environmental Management Plan for Kanpur Urban Area', *GIS Development,* available at http://www.gisdevelopment.net/application/environment/conservation/envm0002pf.htm accessed on 3 January 2010.

Bertaud Alain (2002). 'The Economics of Land Use Planning and Regulation', available at http://alain-bertaud.com/images/AB_India_Urban_Reform.doc

——— (2003), 'The Spatial Organization Of Cities: Deliberate Outcome Or Unforeseen Consequence?', Background paper for Dynamic Development in a Sustainable World, World Development Report 2003 available at http://www.alain-bertaud.com/image/AB_The_Spatial_organisation_of_cities_Version3.pdf

Bombay First—McKinsey (2003). *Transforming Mumbai into World Class City,* Report submitted to Government of Maharashtra, Mumbai

Burchell, R.W. and S. Mukherji (2003). 'Conventional Development vs Managed Growth: The Costs of Sprawl' *American Journal of Public Health,* 93(9), pp. 1534–40.

Confederation of Indian Industry (CII)-Global Footprint Network (GFN) (2006). *India's Ecological Footprint: A Business Perspective,* Report published by CII-GFN.

Dakal, Shubhankar (2004), 'Urban Energy Use and Greenhouse gas Emissions in Asian Mega Cities: Policies for Sustainable Future', Institute of Global Environmental Studies, Japan.

Dantzig, G.B. and T.L. Saaty (1974). *Compact City: A Plan for a Livable Urban Environment,* W.H. Freeman & Co, San Francisco, California.

Duany, A., E.P. Zyberk, and J. Speck (1999). *Suburban Nation: The Rise of Sprawl and the Decline of American Dream,* North Point Press, New York.

Dupont, Veronique (ed.) (2005). 'Peri-urban Dynamics: Population, Habitat and Environment on the Peripheries of Large Indian Cities', CSH Occasional Paper No. 14, Centre des Sciences Humaines (CSH), New Delhi.

European Commission (2007). *Urban Environmental Management Plan: Benefits for Local Authorities,* NS, CMW, available at http://www.cowiprojects.com/4CountryEnvironmentalProject/project_documents/UrbanEnvironmentalManagementPlans-Background_FINAL_20-02-07.pdf

Hassan, Al-Motaz and R. Zetter (2002). 'Sustainable Development: Between Development and Environmental Agendas in the Developing World' in R. Zetter and R. White (eds) *Planning in the Cities: Sustainability and Growth in the developing world,* ITDG Publishing, London.

Jenks Michael and Rodd Burgess (2000). *Compact Cities: Sustainable Urban Forms for Developing Countries,* Spon Press, London.

Kaji, H. (2004). 'Compact City and Sustainable Urban Form: Is Compact City Approach Appropriate as an Urban Development Policy for Cities in Developing Countries?', Institute of Global Environmental Studies (IGES), Japan, available at http://web.sfc.keio.ac.jp/unodb/fasid/lec_note/1201p.pdf, accessed on 14 September 2004.

Litman, T. (2003). 'Smart Growth: More Efficient Land Use Management'. *TDM Encyclopedia*.

Ministry of Environment and Forests (MoEF) (2009). State of the Environment Report India 2009, available at http://moef.nic.in/downloads/home/home-SoE-Report-2009.pdf

MGI (2010). *India's Urban Awakening: Building Inclusive Cities and Sustaining Economic Growth*, McKinsey Global Institute (MGI) Report, April, available at http://www.mckinsey.com/mgi/reports/freepass_pdfs/india_urbanization/MGI_india_urbanization_fullreport.pdf, accessed on June 2010.

Nallathiga, R. (2005). 'Regulatory Impacts on Land and Housing Markets in Mumbai', *Nagarlok* 37(3), pp. 50–65.

——— (2004). 'The Impacts of Density Regulation on Cities and Markets: Evidence from Mumbai', *International Journal of Regulation and Governance,* 5(1), pp. 13–39

———(2002), 'Land Use and Housing in Mumbai: A Review of the Status and the Need for Reforms', *The CITY* I (4), pp. 25–9.

NEERI (2004). *Particulate Matter Reduction Action Plan for Greater Mumbai,* Final report submitted to MMRDA, February 2004

Nelson, A.C., R. Pendall, D.J. Dawkins, and G.J. Knaap (2002). *The Link Between Growth Management and Housing Affordability: The Academic Evidence,* Discussion Paper prepared for Brookings Institution Center on Urban and Metropolitan Policy, Brookings Institution, Washington DC, available at http://smartgrowthamerica.org/growthmang.pdf

Newman, P. and J. Kenworthy (1999). *Sustainability and Cities: Overcoming Automobile Dependence,* Island Press, Washington DC.

Owens, S. (1985). *Energy and Urban Form,* Pion Press, London.

Petersen, R. (2002). *Land Use Planning and Urban Transport. A Sourcebook for Policy Makers in Developing Cities,* Deutsche Gesselleschaft fur Technische Zusammenarbeit (GTZ), Eshborn.

Phatak, V.K. (2002). 'The Use of Floor Space Index in the Development of Land and Housing Markets in Mumbai', *The CITY* I(4), pp. 6–9.

Rees, W. and M. Wackernagel (1996). *Our Ecological Footprint: Reducing Human Impact on the Earth,* New Society Publishers, Gabriola Island, British Columbia.

Sivaramakrishnan, K.C. and A. Kundu (2007). *Handbook of Urbanization in India,* Oxford University Press, New Delhi.

Sridhar, Kala Sitaram (2007). 'Density Gradients and their Determinants: Evidence from India', *Regional Science and Urban Economics* 37(2007), pp. 314–44

——— (2009). 'Impact of Land use Regulations: Evidence from India's Cities', *Urban Studies* 20(10), pp. 1–29.

Staley, S.R. and L.C. Gilroy (2001). '*Smart Growth and Housing Affordability: Evidence from Statewide Planning Laws*', Policy Study 287, Reason Public Policy Institute, USA

UN Habitat (2008). *State of the World's Cities 2008/09: Harmonious Cities,* Earthscan Publishers, London.

Zetter, R. (2002). 'Market Enablement or Sustainable Development: The Conflicting Paradigms of Urbanization', in R. Zetter and R. White (eds) *Planning in the Cities: Sustainability and Growth in the Developing World.* ITDG Publishing, London.

Part 2 Climate Change and Urban Planning Strategies for India

Sweta Byahut

This chapter discusses some of the regional climate protection initiatives adopted across the world by cities in the US, UK, and Latin America, and the implementation challenges faced by them. There are several innovative and successful examples from these cities, which are striving to becoming carbon-neutral by reducing their energy and oil dependency. In this part of the chapter we examine some of them. Another aspect discussed is the role of networking and coalition building by municipal governments, as this is one of the key strategies that cities are adopting to increase their political influence in climate politics. Based on the learning from international experience, the paper highlights key lessons for incorporating climate protection strategies into the Indian urban planning context.

Experience of Cities in the US

In the US, the climate protection movement is bottoms up and community-driven. Cities, counties, and states have been leading the efforts on climate protection, as there is a lack of meaningful federal action or policy on climate. The understanding of local to global causes and effects of climate change has induced many local governments in the US to adapt their policy to the climate agenda. Urban planning adaptation and mitigation measures of climate change are being incorporated in the design of American cities, neighbourhoods, buildings and streets, and overall city planning.

Current knowledge on urban development and climate protection promotes strategies like mixed use development and strong employment centres to reduce the amount of travel as measured in vehicular miles travelled (VMT). VMT growth in the US has cancelled out substantial gains achieved by vehicle fuel economy improvement—since 1980 average VMT grew at thrice the rate of population growth and twice the growth in the number of registered vehicles; 28 per cent of all GHG emissions in the US emanated from the transportation sector in 2006. The US transportation sector has a disproportionate effect on global climate change—the population of the US is only 5 per cent of the world's population, but it owns one-third of all vehicles which contribute up to 45 per cent of total CO_2 emissions from cars worldwide (US DOT A 2009; Handy and Krizek 2009).

California's landmark Global Warming Solutions Act of 2008 SB32 mandates regional planning to consider climate impacts of all land-use decisions. This Act sets the 2020 greenhouse gas emissions reduction goal into law. It directs the California Air Resources Board to begin developing early actions to reduce GHG emissions while also preparing a scoping plan to identify how to reach the 2020 limit. These reduction measures are to be adopted at the start of 2011. Opportunities also exist for hybrid-electric vehicles, but their market penetration is limited by costs and technology constraints. Policymakers agree that the US needs a three-pronged strategy for GHG reduction from vehicles: increased vehicle fuel economy, reducing the carbon content in fuel, and reducing the amount of driving (Ewing et al. 2008; Stone et al. 2009).

Cities are increasingly focusing on compact urban development as a key climate protection strategy and the emerging belief is that the long-term solution is to alter urban development patterns in a way that reduces the need for people to drive.

With changing demographics and an aging society, residential preferences are leaning towards city living focusing towards inner city regeneration. There has been a resurgence of growth in central cities due to an increasing movement back to the cities from the suburbs; it is projected to increase metropolitan growth and urban re-concentration (Stone et al. 2009; Leinberger 2005). There is increased application of Smart Growth strategies like green building, increasing densities, public transit, and fuel efficient cars as core activities in climate protection. Cities adopt Smart Growth policies as they are aware that they will accrue tangible and localized co-benefits. Climate benefits are usually linked with other environmental benefits and improve the overall quality of life factors by reducing congestion and air pollution, making downtowns more vibrant, creating walkable neighbourhoods, and resulting in an overall healthier society.

As many as 30 US states and hundreds of cities and counties have prepared detailed Climate Action Plans (CAPs) that have set time-bound GHG emissions reduction targets over the last decade. These plans include specific measures for compact land-use planning, mass transportation, energy-efficient building andinfrastructure, and policy intervention (Wheeler 2008). Many cities and states have drawn technical support from ICLEI's Cities for Climate Protection (CCP) campaign or the US Mayors' Climate Protection Agreement. It is important that cities see the economic benefits of climate protection measures like energy savings, and social benefits like equity and safety, for them to buy into the plans. CAPs set emissions-reduction targets based on GHG inventories and identify a range of actions to achieve it. The main implementation hurdle with many CAPs is that they are not incorporated within mainstream comprehensive planning and remain separate planning documents.

Large cities of India need to proactively prepare long range and detailed CAPs that lay out specific carbon reduction targets within a timeframe, and undertake policy goals and actions across different sectors to achieve them. It is commendable that the Delhi government has recently come out with the Climate Change Agenda for Delhi 2009–12 that lays out the green development path for the region (Government of Delhi 2009). However, the overall capacity and resources of most local governments, as well as their access to information, tools for carbon reduction planning and better practice is limited. The feasible alternative lies in integrating climate concerns into statutory planning processes like the Development/Master Plans, and sectoral infrastructure planning for water management, energy, and transportation.

Spatial planning in most Indian cities is determined through Development/Master Plans, usually prepared within a well-defined legislative framework. Climate concerns need to be firmly entrenched within the mainstream planning processes like the Development/Master Plans as well as mandatory for consideration in all large development projects, as we saw in the UK model. A major problem with the Development/Master Plans is that they tend to ignore real estate market demands (Bertaud 2002). Development plans need to encourage redevelopment and investment in the inner cores of the cities and help bring back/retain the commercial importance of the city centres, which has been gradually moving to the newer peripheral developments in larger metropolitan areas. This would enable us to take advantage of public infrastructure already available and invest in modern public transit.

Box 22.2.1
Smart Growth Strategies

Smart Growth strategies have been essentially designed to combat sprawl, and the negative externalities associated with it like air pollution, congestion, and inner-city decline. These strategies include inner-city redevelopment, mixed land-use, taking advantage of compact and transit oriented development, creating walkable neighbourhoods, developing a strong sense of place and attractive communities, providing a variety of transportation choices, and preserving open spaces and environmental areas. It therefore presents many opportunities for reducing VMT-related energy consumption and GHG emissions.

Proactive, sustained Smart Growth measures have been adopted in many cities, the best known example being of Portland, Oregon. The Portland Metropolitan Authority has deliberately contained development within its growth boundary for several decades now. It has been defining infrastructure priority areas and providing transportation options to its residents. These 'growing in, not growing out' policies have helped reduce per capita vehicle trips by 17 per cent and have helped stabilize Portland's GHG emissions at 1990 levels despite a 16 per cent population rise (Condon et al. 2009). Smart Growth policies in Portland has worked due to a strong state legislation on growth management, as well as a very strong regional planning authority Metropolitan Planning Office (Metro), that oversees land-use and transportation planning in three counties and 24 cities. Metro strongly mandates high density housing and mixed use developments along transit corridors.

Planners face many challenges in implementing Smart Growth which include: dealing with negative perceptions associated with central cities like inadequate safety, underperforming schools, housing inaffordability, lack of large open spaces, and other complex socio-economic problems, all of which have led to strong preferences for suburban living. Critics of Smart Growth have also highlighted issues of gentrification and housing inaffordability, increased congestion and air pollution, increasing property taxes, rising transportation costs, and reduction of open spaces due to densification measures. High fragmentation of local governance makes adoption of regional Smart Growth policies difficult, and usually there is a lack of political will for implementation.

Source: Condon et al. (2009).

Box 22.2.2
PlaNYC 2030

The most successful of these CAPs is the ambitious New York Strategic Plan PlaNYC 2030 that mandates a 30 per cent reduction in GHG emissions by 2030 for New York City through 127 projects, regulations and innovations like controlling sprawl, densification, brown-fields development, efficient transportation, clean energy, and greener buildings through a comprehensive planning process for climate protection, including assessment of risks, costs, and potential solutions for adapting to climate change (The City of New York A 2007). The plan sets concrete goals and public funding commitments, for example: investments of $200 million a year from both the city and state to create a financing authority that would ensure implementation of major projects, develop and open 290 schoolyards as playgrounds, plant more than 1 million trees over the next decade, cultivate mussels to reduce river pollution and commit funding to clean up 7,600 acres of brown-fields and many more. Sixteen specific transportation actions include elimination of city sales taxes on energy-efficient hybrid vehicles, increasing the number of bike paths, improvements in express bus service and up-gradation of public transit in neighbourhoods with limited access to the subway, expansion of ferry services, more stringent traffic violation enforcement, and installation of an intelligent transportation system.

In November 2007, the City Council passed Local Law 55 that codifies PlaNYC's goal of reducing citywide GHG emissions by 30 per cent below 2005 levels by 2030. This helps ensure that the commitment to addressing climate change continues despite administrative changes. The law requires the city to reduce the carbon footprint of municipal buildings and operations much faster, by 30 per cent by 2017 (The City of New York B 2008). One of the important achievements is the passing of a law by the City Council to permanently establish an Office of Long-Term Planning and Sustainability within the municipal government. The city has also established the new Office of Environmental Remediation to manage its brown-field policy. Annual progress reports as well as a set of online sustainability indicators are also mandated by law.

Results show that per capita energy consumption is declining, more people are using transit and are biking, and GHG emissions reductions are meeting their annual targets. Since 2007 when the plan was launched, New York City has completed 19 re-zonings that direct development to public transit, in addition to creating a major bicycle network, enacting clean air laws for school buses, and an advanced green building legislation (The City of New York C 2010). However, due to political hurdles, New York City failed to implement the most contentious proposal of $8-a-day congestion pricing charge (modelled on the one implemented in London in 2003) proposed for people driving cars into Manhattan, aimed to reduce traffic and auto emissions while raising money for transportation projects. Despite strong support and clearance from the NY City Council, and success in building unprecedented coalition of supporters, the critical congestion pricing component was not implemented by the New York State Legislature. The city had relied heavily on this to finance many other transportation planning projects. Implementation of several other capital infrastructure works that depend on huge financial commitments from the state and federal governments will prove challenging.

Sources: The City of New York A (2007); The City of New York B (2008); and The City of New York C (2010).

Experience of Cities in the UK

Overall, the climate strategy in Europe is comprehensive, well developed, usually centralized, and very well integrated within several national planning frameworks. In UK, for instance, sustainable cities have been promoted as a desirable goal in a comprehensive manner, right from the central level. Scale of planning, multilevel governance, and political issues play an important role in defining successes in creating sustainable cities. Policy recognizes that spatial planning plays a significant role in minimizing the causes and consequences of climate change (Bulkeley 2006). In the UK, a comprehensive planning policy for sustainable development has been developed since the 1990s in the spheres of the land-use planning system, transport planning, regional planning and housing. These policies determine achievable targets to meet their Kyoto Protocol targets on time, and climate protection considerations are central to the overall strategy for sustainable urban development (DEFRA 2009). The Climate Change Act of 2008 makes UK the first country to have a legally binding long-term framework to cut carbon emissions, and to have created a framework for building UK's ability to adapt to climate change. UK is required to reduce its GHG emissions by 34 per cent from 2018–22 and by at least 80 per cent by 2050, and the UK Low Carbon Transition Plan lays down the sharing of the carbon budget between government departments such that all departments are involved in reducing emissions.

Local governments in the UK are required to consider the implications of land-use planning on climate change in their policy and planning processes. Targets are translated into practice by a multi-pronged approach that includes requirements of on-site energy generation for large developments and managing land-use to reduce energy demand by determining location and travel needs, inner city densification, addressing flooding risks in land-use planning using the precautionary principle, and a code for sustainable buildings (DEFRA 2009). UK's National Climate Policy is now increasingly focused on adaptation that requires all major infrastructure projects, regional strategies and local development planning to account for the changing climate. Planning includes preparation of surface water management plans for high priority areas, higher water efficiency standards, and heat losses and gains in the building code for residential buildings. Overall in the UK, significant planning focus is concentrated on the impacts of climate change (Bulkeley 2006).

There are many challenges in the UK planning framework as there are tensions between the economic, social, and environmental dimensions of sustainable urban development, local versus national priorities, and technical concerns as well (Bulkeley and Betsill 2005, Kern and Bulkeley 2009). Interpretation and implementation of sustainable urban development goals vary significantly across local governments. Urban governance of climate protection also depends on the local–state relations and networks formed at various scales. For instance, policy guidance to local authorities stresses reducing emissions through compact development and land-use and transportation planning, and the need to reduce travel distances, but development policies stress location of industries away from the city centres. Policymakers also point out the lack of knowledge or experience among local officers and councillors about the issues involved as a major challenge. Local authorities usually lack capability to model and monitor resource flows, assess sustainability indicators, and there is a growing gap between the rhetoric of sustainable cities and the reality of land-use and transportation planning (Bulkeley and Betsill 2005). Also, the policy guidance recommends soft approaches like encouraging developers to take action for sustainable energy use rather than requiring them to do so. This does not provide the local authorities with any teeth for implementation as they play a more enabling role rather than a regulatory role, which is not as effective. Sustainability and energy use considerations cannot be used to refuse development proposals as they cannot carry any weight. Further, despite direct linkages to the European Union, the local authorities are not able to bypass the political constraints of the national government.

With increasing economic growth in India, anticipated new development must be directed, and not allowed to go out of control. Urban planning and intervention can play a significant role in both adaptation and mitigation of climate change. There needs to be a greater understanding developed and the explicit and effective link between urban form and emissions reduction needs to be more strongly entrenched in the planning framework.

Box 22.2.3

Energy Efficient Building in UK Cities

Climate policy in UK cities also focus on the development regulation system where action is required at the level of individual development proposals that promote energy efficiency and sustainable construction and design (Rydin 2009). The impetus for this was provided in 2006 when it was announced that all new residential construction should be zero-carbon by 2016 and in the meantime all zero-carbon houses would be exempt from stamp duty. A similar ruling for non-residential construction was introduced in 2008 according to which all new non-residential buildings would be zero carbon by 2019 and such buildings would be exempt from stamp duty (Rydin 2009). Significant departmental reorganization at the national level has resulted in the new Department of Energy and Climate Change to enable nationwide implementation of climate policies.

The Code for Sustainable Homes is a government-supported rating system for assessment of all new housing. The houses are rated for their performance on a set of eight criteria that includes energy/CO_2 emissions, water efficiency, building materials, surface water run-off, waste, pollution, health and well-being, management, and ecology. In 2003 the municipality of Merton implemented the 'Merton Rule' that stipulates that 10 per cent of the all new major building's energy needs must be met by onsite renewables. The purpose of the Merton Rule was to reduce reliance on fossil fuels as well as aid in the development of a renewable technology market to deliver these products at a lower cost (Rydin 2009). Now almost 200 local governments have adopted it and it has been included in the UK government's national planning policy. Renewable sources may be solar panels for water heating, photovoltaic cells for energy generation, wind turbines or biomass combined heat, and power plants.

At the municipal level there are still many challenges that include overcoming the knowledge gap amongst planners who have limited knowledge of sustainable construction and design technology. There is scope for significant learning in the planning profession towards understanding sustainable design and construction and quantifying accurately, GHG reductions that can be achieved from it. There is problem of enforcement as this is under-resourced. In 2006–7 there were more than 5,500 enforcement notices issued, out of which about a 1,000 were contravention notices more relevant to sustainable construction concerns (Rydin 2009). Another concern is that the number of new buildings anticipated to be added over a period of time is comparatively less and policies need to comprehensively increase the energy efficiency of existing buildings as well. Overall in the UK, sustainable design and construction has a major role to play in achieving the larger climate agenda.

Source: Rydin (2009).

Climate protection strategies in cities should focus on strengthening the planning legislation and strengthening the development regulation to ensure construction of energy efficient building. Urban planning systems must also invest in urban infrastructure and public transportation in order to reduce GHG emissions and congestion. Local and regional development authorities must consider the overall energy consumption in urban planning and the decision-making process.

Experiences of Latin American Cities

In the developing world, the urban transportation sector is going through an explosive growth of private vehicles, with two-wheelers and four-wheelers choking the roads. Increasing incomes and demand for travel will further aggravate the problem. Such development is leading to severe congestion on city roads, air pollution and related health impacts, and increasing levels of GHG emission.

Bogotá in Colombia and Curitiba in Brazil are two well-known examples of sustainable urban planning in Latin America, and very relevant to the Indian planning context. These cities are comparable to many Indian cities where thousands of new vehicles are added everyday on the roads that cancel out emissions reductions through fuel and vehicle efficiency. They have successfully integrated transportation planning with land-use planning using the Bus Rapid Transit System (BRTS) and shown that it is possible to reduce emissions through innovative transportation initiatives. This is important because transportation emissions represent the fastest growing source of GHG emissions (Wright and Fulton 2005). The Bogotá and Curitiba BRTS examples are discussed in Box 22.2.4 below, adapted from the analysis by Wright and Fulton (2005).

The success of the Curitiba and Bogotá public transportation systems lies in the fact that they are highly integrated with the land-use and arterial road systems that are organized around key structural axes. This provides direction and intensity to the overall urban development pattern. In Curitiba, the highest intensity of commercial and residential land-use is concentrated along a two-block distance from the structural spines. Curitiba has ensured that the BRTS is socially just by implementing a single-fare scheme that provides the poorer people living on the

Box 22.2.4
Bus Rapid Transit Systems in Bogotá and Curitiba

Wright and Fulton (2005) provide a detailed account of how the BRTS in Bogotá and Curitiba help cut GHG emissions and the content of this box is adapted from their work. In Bogotá, the planning programmes have been undertaken by the city since 2000 and in Curitiba since 1974. These have successfully transformed the two cities into showcases of modern city planning. In Curitiba, planning initiatives by the local government contribute to mitigation of GHG emissions. One key strategy was to channel growth along major transportation corridors supported by the creation of a fast and comfortable mass transportation system that resulted in reduced traffic congestion and reduced transportation time for people. This also provided added health benefits like significant reductions in air and noise pollution. A BRTS uses an exclusive right-of-way lanes for buses, providing the performance and facilities of a rail-based transit system but at a fraction of a cost. The Bogota TransMileno BRTS phase I of 41 km was built at a cost of $5.3 million/km, whereas elevated/underground rails systems cost anywhere from $50 million to over $200 million/km.

Both the Curitiba and Bogotá systems have gained public transportation ridership shares over the years by focusing on saving travel time, comfort, security, and cleanliness. It is critical to ensure that the performance of the BRTS is at par with the modern rail systems and incorporate features like exclusive right-of-way lanes, state-of-the-art technology, and automation that is convenient for the passengers, as well as enclosed stations that are safe and comfortable, clear route maps and signage, and real-time information displays, modal integration, and clean vehicle technologies. Bogotá's system is supported by measures like new cycle-paths, pedestrian facilities, major feeder networks, and car restriction measures like car-free events. In 2005, the 58 km system moved over 800,000 passengers a day, operating without subsidies, and using Euro II or Euro III articulated buses through private financing.

GHG emissions are reduced by increasing the share of public transport ridership, constructing segregated bus lanes that provide fast movement without delays, pre-boarding fare collection that reduces idling time, replacing four to five older buses with one articulated bus each and enforcing emission standards, use of GPS technology in fleet management, and encouraging Transit Oriented Development (TOD) along the corridors. Parallel land-use planning is undertaken to support the successful implementation of transportation projects. Curitiba modified its zoning to permit only high-rise development along the BRTS corridors and densification of commercial, office, and residential sectors has led to reductions in travel distance and frequency. In Bogotá there has been densification and large-scale commercial development around bus stations and along the corridor, and there has been an upswing in the property market and land prices as well. However, full replication of the Bogotá and Curitiba examples is uncertain in other cities. There was a very high degree of political will exhibited by these two cities, and continued transportation policy support over several administrations.

Source: Wright and Fulton (2005).

city's edge with a cost-effective means of transportation. Approximately 2 million people use the system daily.

Larger transformation of Bogotá involved the makeover of derelict vacant and illegally occupied lands (for instance, lands under bridges and sidewalks) into vibrant public places. Over 1,200 parks covering 280 hectares have been built or restored in the process, many pedestrian zones created, and tens of thousands of trees planted on sidewalks. The Bicycle Master Plan of Bogota delineates 350 km of bicycle paths out of which 270 km were completed by 2003. Cars are further discouraged by prohibiting on-street parking in many areas, which has enabled the pedestrians to reclaim the city. Revising land-use zoning laws to enable greater mixed use developments along places that are easily accessible by public transit is necessary to increase ridership and provide cheaper transportation options to the poor. Interconnectedness between different modes of transportation like subway, light rail, buses, and para-transit modes is necessary for ensuring smooth, convenient, and affordable travel.

Role of Climate Protection Networks

The climate change debate has moved beyond the scientific proof of climate change to the manner of implementation at different levels of government, and commitments/mandates needed in different spheres of carbon reduction. As the need to work at different aspects of multilevel governance becomes clearer, the role of cities is appearing to be more and more critical. The role of cities is expanding in the highly urbanizing and globalizing world. New importance accorded to the local context is resulting in stronger local and regional governance. Cooperation, network building, and inter-municipal dialogue with other cities at national, regional, and global levels is one of the key actions being taken by local governments. Cities multiply their effectiveness by being part of larger national or Transnational Municipal Networks, forming coalitions that use their combined synergy to address climate protection, learn from each other, and maximize their collective influence in global environmental politics (Betsill 2001; Selin and VanDeveer 2007; Toly 2008).

Participation in most of these networks requires a commitment from cities to prepare climate plans. In the US, more than a thousand cities have signed onto the US Mayor's Climate Protection Agreement. The Sierra Club's Cool Cities programme is also popular. Hundreds of others reaffirm their commitments to reduce their carbon footprint through focused Climate Action Plans. In the US, policy changes in the public, private, and civil society sectors at the state, regional, and local levels are likely to have a strong influence in shaping the future comprehensive US federal policy on climate change (Selin and VanDeveer 2007). Similarly, in Europe more than 1,400 towns and cities are members of climate networks like the Climate Alliance, Cities for Climate Protection, the Energie-Cités, and the Covenant of Mayors onto which over 1200 cities have already signed. These transnational networks have developed a range of strategies for coping with the multilevel governance context within the EU. The ICLEI initiative described briefly in Box 22.2.5 below is particularly relevant in the case of India. More than 1,100 cities globally are a part of ICLEI's CCPs. Other initiatives like the International Solar Cities Initiatives, the World Mayors and Local Governments Climate Protection Agreement, and the C-40 Cities (part of the Clinton Climate Initiative) are also noteworthy. These networks are not interventionist in their approach, but rely on softer, laissez-faire approaches instead. Innovative approaches like certification of member cities, which are designed to improve internal governance, are also applied by some national municipal networks.

Conclusion

Most Indian urban planning policies encourage sprawl, motivated with a view to decongesting the city (Pucher et al. 2005). New development in India has been moving away from cities. Modern residential development as well as large-scale office complexes in the IT and ITES sectors are cropping up everywhere in the vicinity of cities like Hyderabad, Bangalore, Delhi, Mumbai, and Kolkata. Floor Space Index (or Floor Area Ratio) in Indian cities that regulates maximum achievable development on a parcel of land is unreasonably low in the centre of cities, encouraging development on the periphery and artificially limiting supply of serviced urban land (Bertaud 2002). Most Indian cities have an FSI/FAR ranging from 1.2–2.0, whereas comparable Asian cities have FSI/FAR ranging from 5.0–15.0. Freeing up prime urban land for higher development intensity would enable affordable housing and provide land for new developments close to the city centre. However, it must be noted that adequate municipal and transportation infrastructure are prerequisites for having a high FSI/FAR. An alternative for infrastructure-constrained Indian cities would be to focus on planned cohesive and contiguous development in cities, in line with the spatial planning in several cities of the UK. Efficient land utilization and allocation in core urban areas will rationalize land utilization in the centre of the city. Today, prime land in the centre of many cities is occupied by large institutional and government entities like the railways and ports, and many pockets of defunct industrial land and other non-performing uses

Box 22.2.5
ICLEI India CCP Programme

Networking can bring together cities and provides technical assistance in planning and adapting to climate change. Participation for Indian cities in climate coalitions needs to be scaled-up. A beginning has been made by the ICLEI Cities for Climate Protection—Indian programme targeting 16 cities presently. The CCP programme provides assistance to cities with technical support, information dissemination, and best practice documentation, transfer of technical knowledge and know-how on planning and design issues for climate mitigation and adaptation (ICLEI CCP programme India). It provides municipalities with a five-step model designed to reduce GHG emissions that entails technical support for the following five stages of climate planning: preparing an inventory of the GHG emissions from different sources and across time, setting a target of how much emissions reduction is desired, preparing a plan to reach the target, implementation of the plan, and monitoring improvement and making adjustments as needed. The programme focuses on energy efficiency and reduction, fiscal savings for local governments, and other long-term benefits, making it feasible for Indian cities to participate.

In India, the campaign additionally aims to 'to find innovative and cost-effective solutions to urban environment and energy management problems that also mitigate city-level GHG emissions.' (ICLEI CCP programme, India A). CCP India Phase I Cities are Kolkata, Ludhiana, Sangli, Vadodara, Jabalpur, Hyderabad, and Guntur. These were implemented in 2002–3 and were voluntary in nature. Various GHG emission reduction projects were implemented in the participating cities that include water pumping retrofit to reduce CO_2 emissions in Kolkata, energy efficient street lighting through power-savers and waterworks energy audit in Guntur, retrofit tubelight systems to reduce carbon emissions, design-based street lighting, solar water heating systems, and a public awareness campaign in Jabalpur, traffic junction design in Hyderabad and Jabalpur, and capacity building measures. In Phase II, the programme was extended to nine additional cities of Agra, Gwalior, Guwahati, Coimbatore, Shimla, Dehradun, Bhubaneshwar, Madurai, and Udaipur. Phase II cities have completed Milestone 1 (emissions inventory and forecasting) and are in the process of Milestone 2 (setting a reduction goal). The next three milestones to be undertaken by them are preparing a Climate Action Plan, implementing measures, and monitoring and verification.

Source: ICLEI CCP programme India.

exist that can be rationally redeveloped to provide land for affordable housing, modern transportation options, and infrastructure development. This would make use of already existing infrastructure in the centre of city areas. However, densification measures must be coupled with high capacity transportation systems, upgraded infrastructure, and public spaces. It would encourage compact development that will increase the viability of investing in public transit, bring origins and destinations closer, and reduce GHG emissions by reducing travel.

There are many ways Indian cities can promote compact development through spatial planning within its existing planning framework. Although the development contexts are very different for India, there is significant learning from international experience. We have enough knowledge available to us and can adopt appropriate models of development from best practices. There is much to be learnt from the US planning experience where states and cities have taken the lead in climate protection using spatial planning, policy intervention, and governance as they design and implement climate protection strategies.

The UK approach shows that it is possible to integrate climate change as a cross-cutting environmental issue at all scales of government—central, state, regional, and local, while carefully balancing economic, social, and environmental dimensions. Latin American cities present two successful examples of sustainable urban transportation and land-use planning that are also affordable options for Indian cities. Many technical and governance issues can be overcome through networking with other cities. Municipal coalitions can exercise collective action and maximize their effectiveness in policy implementation, and create new synergies with civic and non-governmental actors.

Climate concerns need to be fully integrated within the existing planning framework for the long-term sustainability of our cities. There is a renewed interest in the complex relationship between urban form, land-use and transportation, with its explicit link to global impact on climate change becoming apparent. A sustainable and compact urban development pattern that results in reduced need for people to use private transport, and investments in public transportation, will help reduce GHG emissions from urban areas. Sustainability planners believe that the battle for climate change will be won or lost in cities. In the context of climate change and its mitigation and adaptation measures, it becomes all the more imperative to hasten these reforms and plan for our sustainable urban future.

REFERENCES

Bertaud, A. (2002). 'India—Urban Land Reform', available at http://alain-bertaud.com/, accessed on 20 December.

Betsill, M. (2001). 'Mitigating Climate Change in US Cities: Opportunities and Obstacles', *Local Environment*. 6(4), pp. 393–406.

Bulkeley, H. and M. Betsill (2005). 'Rethinking Sustainable Cities: Multilevel Governance and The "Urban" Politics of Climate Change', *Environmental Politics,* 14(1), pp. 42–63.

Bulkeley, H. (2006). 'A Changing Climate for Spatial Planning' in 'Is the Issue of Climate Change too Big for Spatial Planning?' *Planning Theory and Practice*, 7(2), pp. 201–30.

'City BRTS best in South Asia, bags award' (2010), *The Times of India*, 14 January, available at http://timesofindia.indiatimes.com/city/ahmedabad/City-BRTS-best-in-South-Asia-bags-award-/articleshow/5442628.cms, accessed on February 2010.

Condon, P., D. Cavens, and N. Miller (2009). 'Urban Planning Tools for Climate Change Mitigation', Lincoln Institute for Land Policy, https://www.lincolninst.edu/pubs/1573_Urban-Planning-Tools, accessed on 10 December 2009.

DEFRA (2009). 'Adapting to Climate Change—UK Climate Projections', available at http://www.defra.gov.uk/environment/climate/documents/uk-climate-projections.pdf, accessed on 18 December 2009.

Ewing, R., K. Bartholomew, S. Winkelman, J. Walters, D. Chen (2008). 'Growing Cooler: Evidence on Urban Development and Climate Change', Urban Land Institute, Washington DC.

Government of Delhi (2009). 'Climate Change Agenda for Delhi 2009-2012', January, available at http://publicity.delhigovt.nic.in/public/eng/publication/climateChange0001, accessed on 18 December 2009.

Handy, Susan and Kevin J. Krizek (2009). 'The Role of Travel Behavior Research in Reducing the Carbon Footprint: From the U.S. Perspective', Resource Paper for the Triennial Meeting of the International Association of Travel Behavior Research, Jaipur, India

ICLEI CCP Programme India, (2009). Available at http://www.iclei.org/index.php?id=1092, accessed on 15 December 2009.

Janmarg–The eLifeline of Ahmedabad', Video recording by the Government of Gujarat and Ahmedabad Municipal Corporation, available at http://www.youtube.com/watch?v=l15OetusJj8&feature=related

——— (2010). Available at http://www.iclei.org/index.php?id=1095, accessed on 31 May 2010.

Kern, K. and H. Bulkeley (2009). 'Cities, Europeanization and Multi-level Governance: Governing Climate Change through Transnational Municipal Networks', *Journal of Common Market Studies,* 47(2), pp. 309–32.

Leinberger, Christopher (2005). *Turning Around Downtown: Twelve Steps to Revitalization*, The Brookings Institution, Metropolitan Policy Program.

New York Strategic Plan (2006). *PlaNYC 2030*, New York City, available at http://www.nyc.gov/html/planyc2030/html/plan/plan.shtml, accessed on 12 December 2009.

Pucher, J., N. Korattyswaropam, N. Mittal, and N. Ittyerah (2005). 'Urban Transport Crisis in India', *Transport Policy*, 12, pp. 185–98.

Rydin, Yvonne (2009). 'Sustainable Construction and Design in UK Planning' in S. Davoudi, J. Crawford, and A. Mehmood (eds) *Planning for Climate Change: Strategies for Mitigation and Adaptation for Spatial Planners*, pp. 181–90.

Selin, H. and S.D. VanDeveer (2007). 'Political Science and Prediction: What's Next for U.S. Climate Change Policy?', *Review of Policy Research,* 24(1).

Stone B., A. Mednick, T. Holloway, and S. Spak (2009). 'Mobile Source CO_2 Mitigation through Smart Growth Development and Vehicle Fleet Hybridization', *Environmental Science and Technology,* 43(6), pp. 1704–10.

The City of New York A. (2007). 'PlaNYC 2030: A Greener, Greater New York', available at http://www.nyc.gov/html/planyc2030/downloads/pdf/full_report.pdf

——— B. (2008). 'Climate Change: Our Progress', available at http://www.nyc.gov/html/planyc2030/downloads/pdf/progress_2008_climate_change.pdf, accessed on 30 May 2009.

——— C. (2010). 'Progress Report: PlaNYC 2030: A Greener, Greater New York', available at http://www.nyc.gov/html/planyc2030/downloads/pdf/planyc_progress_report_2010.pdf.

Toly, N.J. (2008). 'Transnational Municipal Networks in Climate Politics: From Global Governance to Global Politics', *Globalizations*, 5(3), pp. 341–56.

US Department of Transportation A (2009). 'The 'Carbon Footprint' of Daily Travel', *National Household Travel Survey*, March, available at http://nhts.ornl.gov/briefs/Carbon%20Footprint%20of%20Travel.pdf, accessed, February 2010.

Wheeler, S. (2008). 'State and Municipal Climate Change Plans: The First Generation', *Journal of the American Planning Association*, 74(4).

Wright, L. and L. Fulton (2005). 'Climate Change Mitigation and Transport in Developing Nations', *Transport Reviews,* 25(6), pp. 691–717.

23 Linking Regeneration and Business with Competitiveness for Low Carbon Cities

Lessons for India

Shaleen Singhal, Jim Berry, and Stanley McGreal

Introduction

Growing cities worldwide are making a substantial impact on carbon emissions with people living and working in urban areas in ever-increasing numbers. Progressive cities globally are trying to demonstrate that they can significantly reduce citywide carbon emissions while simultaneously promoting their economic competitiveness[1] where their governing bodies use their influence ingeniously in partnership with key stakeholders. These cities offer competitive advantages capturing opportunities for economic growth and development, attracting leading edge business, and advancing towards a low carbon economy. In contrast, the challenged cities are striving to negotiate their position in an increasingly complex and competitive global economy. Specifically, an integrated approach to regeneration/renewal[2] and business strategies related to the property sector are within the policy ambit that many cities globally employ to address the physical, infrastructure, ecological, social, and economic challenges which urban areas clearly face in the twenty-first century. The chapter builds upon the somewhat limited literature available in this area by examining the linkages between regeneration strategies and business strategies[3] in the context of promoting the low carbon agenda and competitiveness of cities. This is an important phenomenon which is gaining increasing attention within the policy and academic debate at the global level.

The purpose (and structure) of this chapter is to address a number of key objectives as follows:

- To understand the relationship between city competitiveness and low carbon growth and present an explanatory hierarchical model to showcase the synergies between city competitiveness, regeneration, business, and low carbon, and track the key linkages.
- To assess the evidence base in mature (UK and US) and emerging (China and India) economies to illustrate the usefulness of the hierarchical model and showcase some low carbon growth initiatives.

[1] Based on performance indicators such as 'quality of life'.

[2] Urban Regeneration as a term varies across countries and within the literature. It may be referred to as regeneration, renewal, redevelopment, and/or revitalization. Public policy response to urban problems stresses the important role of returning derelict land and buildings to productive use in a sustainable manner (Couch 2003).

[3] This research classifies urban regeneration strategies into key themes—such as local economic development, retail-led, property-led, culture-led, event based, and entertainment-led regeneration. Furthermore, the research classifies property-led business strategies into key themes—such as corporate social responsibility and socially responsible investment, tax-based mechanisms, and corporate real estate strategy (Singhal et al. 2009).

- To highlight the case for intensifying city competitiveness aligned with low carbon growth especially in an emerging economy such as India.

Competitiveness and Low Carbon Cities

The drivers and facilitating components of sustainable communities are globalization, international partnerships, and agreements stressing the significance of sustainable energy policies with environmental-led solutions, regeneration encapsulating economic, social, and environmental balance, and economic growth operating in synchronization with the design and construction of low carbon urban development schemes. In cities with a green agenda (also called competitive cities, as defined later in this section), particular focus has been on energy efficient property development, creation of high-quality infrastructure such as public transport, supply chain management for the movement of goods and products, and effective communication systems, while creating opportunities for a sustainable economy based on employment provision, income growth, and quality of life indicators. The necessary delivery mechanisms require a strong public and private sector commitment and policy stimulus supported by fiscal apparatus, regulatory support, business leadership, stakeholder engagement, and accountability in governance. The strategy also requires an aware and responsive community serviced by an education and skills base delivering inputs into the operational capacity of public-private partnership initiatives at the local level.

Resurgent cities are striving to create innovative strategies and solutions towards enhancing city competitiveness based on a low carbon agenda (Box 23.1 and Box 23.2). Figure 23.1 indicates the critical attributes of city competitiveness within a low carbon framework modelled on spatial planning policies, energy efficient built environments, quality employment and high income opportunities, and environmental-led energy conscious production. This combination of co-requisites can work to create the synergistic effects by enhancing competitive position within the urban hierarchy.

There are contrasting views concerning the phenomenon of city/urban competitiveness. While Krugman (1996) and Urwin (2006) claim that cities, regions, and nations do not compete, Malecki (2002) states that it is now common for cities, regions, and nations to evaluate, improve and publicize their competitive standing vis-à-vis other places. Porter (2008), explaining competition and value creation, highlights that nations must compete to maintain their existing prosperity. In the *absence of any accepted definition, this chapter defines competitiveness as a phenomenon that relates to cities striving to improve their performance by exploiting new opportunities for growth and development while counteracting their inherited problems in a sustainable manner, thus stressing the significance of operating within a low carbon environment.*

Box 23.1
Feasibility of Making the Thames Gateway a Low Carbon Development Area

In the UK, the Department of Communities and Local Government commissioned a low carbon feasibility study in 2006 to provide an evidence base of ongoing and future GHG emissions arising from activities in the Thames Gateway Area and to recommend interventions to enhance competitiveness for long-term growth. The methodological approach employed is based on the ISO 14040 Standard focusing on full life cycle carbon and GHG emissions assessment using the Integrated Resource Management (IRM) modelling approach over a period of 45 years (2005 to 2050). This study contributes to the debate on how GHGs should be measured and managed across sectors including energy supply; treatment of waste, foul and potable water; public and private transport, and logistics including movement of goods, and services. It is estimated through the IRM model that from the Thames Gateway under a 'business as usual' scenario (BAU), the 2005 baseline emissions of 13.8 Mt CO_2e will increase to approximately 28.6 Mt CO_2e by 2050. The emissions reduction intervention scenarios with per cent changes in emissions by 2050 are predicted as: BAU (+107 per cent), easiest level I (-18 per cent), more demanding level II (-52 per cent) and ambitious and challenging level III (-85 per cent). Under all scenarios, the use of energy in buildings accounts for the majority of the total emissions from all sectors, followed by (personal) transport-related emissions and logistics. The study therefore identifies level II and III energy interventions as the most effective strategy to reduce GHG emissions. The model predicts that the most effective interventions are switching to renewable energy sources along with community energy systems and enforcing zero carbon performance standards for new and existing buildings. Improvement in energy efficiency of appliances, de-carbonization of industrial processes, personal carbon accounting and extension of emissions trading schemes are advocated as important interventions (DCLG 2008). This low carbon feasibility study demonstrates adaptability for analysing other cities and regions by establishing a whole lifecycle perspective on sources and magnitudes of GHG emissions along with interventions to achieve climate change targets.

Source: DCLG (2008).

Box 23.2
Dundalk 2020—Creating a Sustainable Energy Community

Dundalk 2020, Ireland's first sustainable energy zone, aims to improve energy practices by demonstrating multiple renewable technologies and strategies for managing energy supply and demand to establish cross-border sustainable communities in Newry (UK) and Dundalk (Ireland). This project with commitment from the Sustainable Energy Ireland and a pro-active public-private-academic stakeholder model is successfully initiating a joint sustainable energy communities' programme across both jurisdictions (ICLRD 2009). The target increase in energy efficiency and the proportion of electricity and heat from renewable sources will reduce CO_2 emissions from the pilot Sustainable Energy Zone (SEZ) covering 4 km^2 by 10,000 tonnes each year from 2010. The SEZ includes mixed use development comprising residential, industrial, retail, commercial, leisure, education, hotels, and hospitals. Targets set for the Dundalk SEZ include improvement in energy efficiency by 40 per cent in residential, industrial, and commercial buildings; a minimum of 20 per cent of all energy used for heating homes and businesses to be generated by renewables; and a minimum of 20 per cent of all electricity used by businesses to be generated by renewables (SEAI 2010).

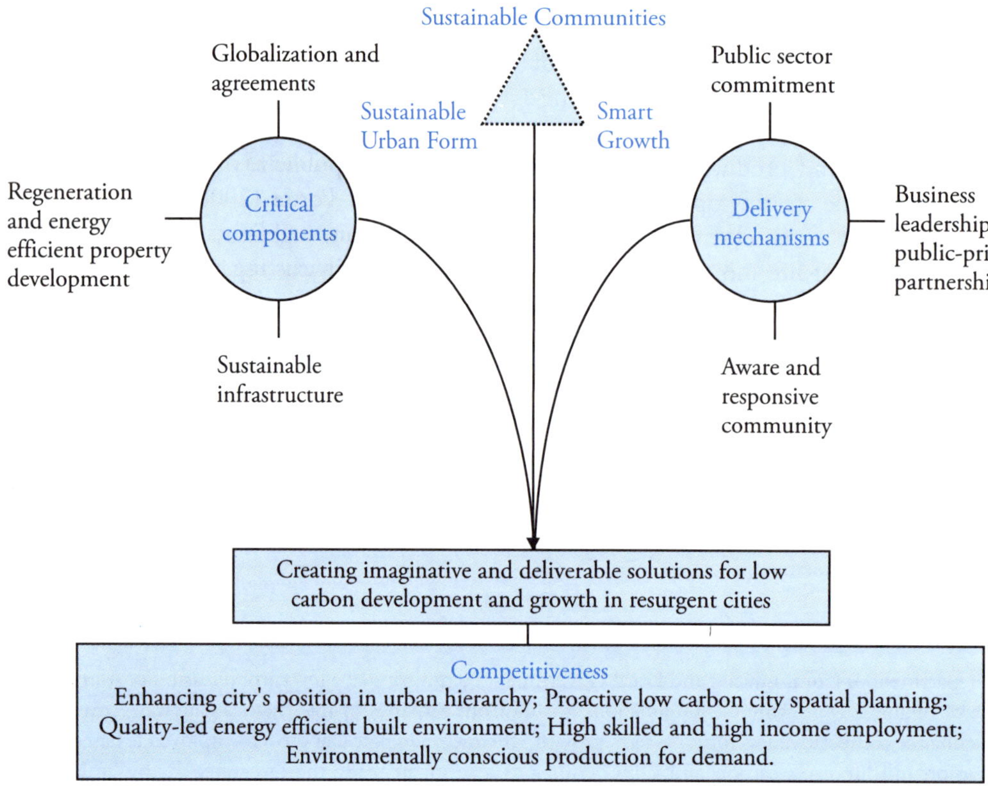

Figure 23.1 Competitiveness and Low Carbon Cities

Source: Author's own.

Hierarchical Model for City Competitiveness, Regeneration, and Business Strategies: Tracking Low Carbon Linkages

The linkages of regeneration and business strategies with the overarching component of city competitiveness are examined by developing a hierarchical model, shown in Figure 23.2, designed to consider the intricate interrelationships which drive city competitiveness. The hierarchical model has been then tested and weighted through the application of advanced analytical decision-making tools utilizing the Delphi technique and multi-criteria analysis (Singhal et al. 2009).

In Figure 23.2, the hierarchical model reinforces the connection of competitiveness with regeneration and business strategies through the identification of the upper level process components of public policy, resources, operating environment, and corporate governance. These components are underpinned by a set of six operational

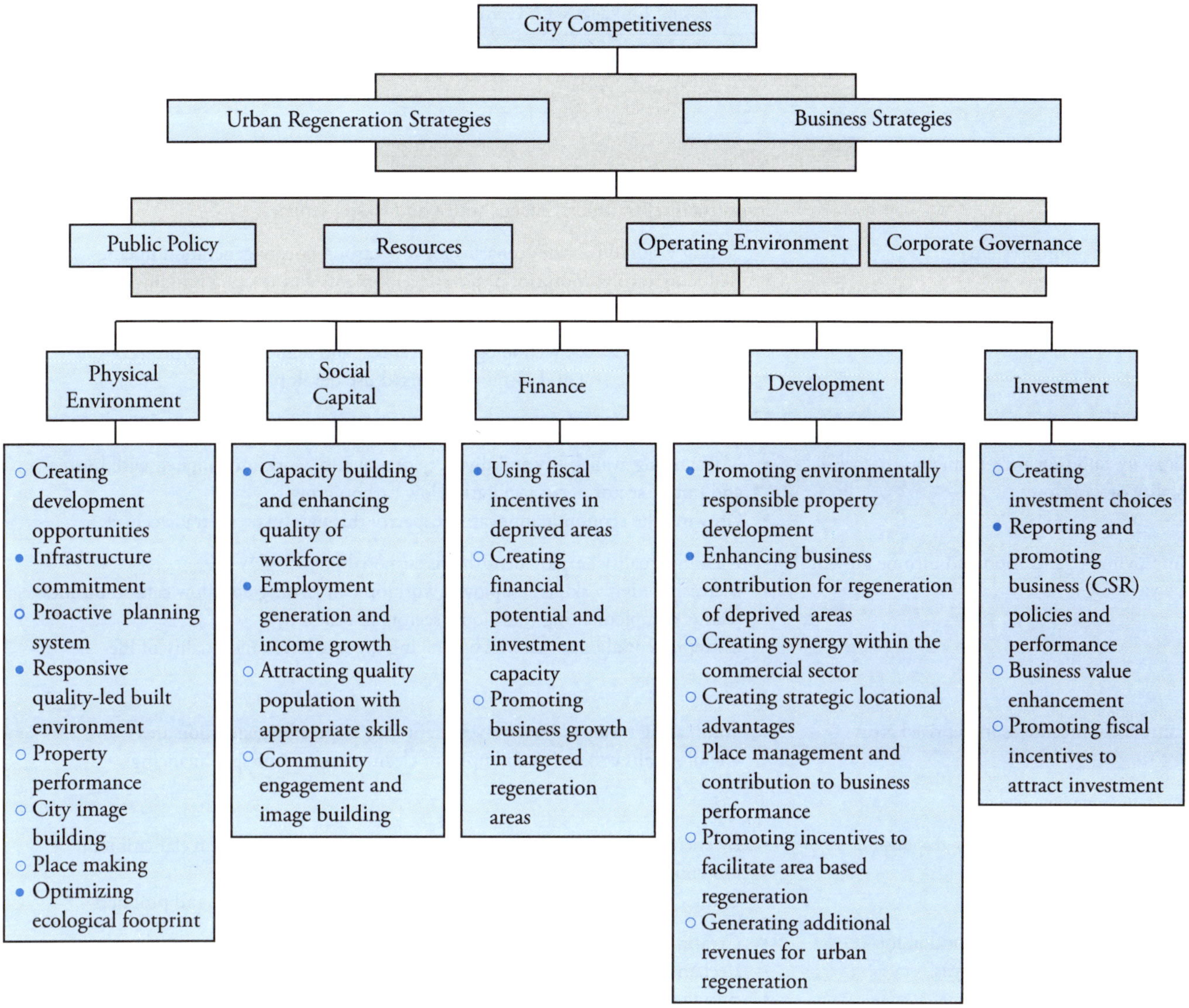

Figure 23.2 Model for City Competitiveness Based on Regeneration and Business Strategies

Source: Singhal (2009).

components of physical environment, social capital, finance, development, investment, and use, of which 12 key factors (marked by • on the model in Figure 23.2) can be identified that have a clear correlation with a low carbon agenda as detailed in Table 23.1.

The hierarchical model creates an interwoven set of linkages encapsulating the upper level process components and factors identified from regeneration and business, many of which can be related with low carbon. In this section, the linkage of competitiveness promoting the low carbon agenda in cities is explained through the key process components of public policy, resources, operating environment, and corporate governance. These are defined below.

Public policy captures the effect of good governance by public authorities through leadership, proactive decision-making, and stakeholder engagement with an enabling fiscal and regulatory framework to enhance the sustainability and competitiveness of cities for low carbon and balanced economic growth. Resources relate to the development of the human resource and social environment with funding arrangements to facilitate the delivery of regeneration and business strategies for competitiveness of low carbon cities. Operating environment outlines the creation of enabling circumstances for macro- and microeconomic conditions to attract socially and environmentally responsible investment for low carbon development opportunities. Corporate governance, in relation to social

Table 23.1 Critical Factors and Criteria Addressing Linkages with Competitiveness and Low Carbon Agenda in Cities

Component	*Criteria explaining the factors*
Factor	
Physical Environment	
Infrastructure commitment	By public and private sector to make cities climate-positive by constructing sustainable infrastructure (transport, energy, water, and waste) services
Proactive planning system	• Setting vision on future scenarios for low carbon energy generation in cities • Reducing carbon footprint of new developments and existing building stock
Responsive quality-led built environment	• By investing into renewable energy for built environment using innovative regulatory measures, technological advances, and demonstration projects • Creating successful and sustainable mixed use developments
Social Capital	
Capacity building and enhancing quality of workforce	• Maintaining availability and diversity of a quality workforce aligned with business and public sector needs facilitating low carbon growth • Growing the economic innovative capacity through financial/trade centres
Employment generation and income growth	• Creating quality employment that is sustainable • Increasing highly skilled employed workforce in leading-edge low carbon business sectors complementing traditional sectors of economy • Entrepreneurial opportunities enhancing income levels and quality of life
Finance	
Using fiscal incentives in deprived areas	• Stimulating business sector investment into targeted regeneration areas • Use of fiscal/tax benefits and upfront clean energy municipal financing
Development	
Promoting environmentally responsible property development	• By encouraging sustainable development principles including reclamation of brownfield and 'green' buildings • Using environmentally sustainable design, building practices, and products
Enhancing business contribution for regeneration of deprived areas	• Creating jobs in deprived city locations targeting local population • Reclamation of derelict land and development of energy efficient spaces • Business contribution for delivery of urban environmental services
Investment	
Reporting and promoting business policies and performance	• Reporting of business, social, ethical, environmental, and energy policies and CSR performance to stakeholders through CSR reports • Promoting business policies and performance to encourage a wider business response towards low carbon cities
Use	
Improving environmental performance and reporting	• Optimizing business resource consumption (energy, raw material, and water) • Minimizing business carbon and polluting emissions and waste generation • Promoting a business *green* image and reporting its performance
Responsiveness to customers and community quality of life	• Investing in society through improvement of essential local services • Improving quality of life of local community by enhancing employability, capacity building, and opportunities for income growth • Exploiting business capacity to build greener image of an area and creating neighbourhood pride by decisions to invest into low carbon initiatives
Supply chain management	Creating high-end infrastructure to facilitate energy efficient movement of goods and products through point of entry to distribution centres in a city for improving trade and economic potential of a region in a sustainable manner

Source: Authors' own.

responsibility, refers to maintaining a balance between economic, social, and environmental goals and between individual and communal goals through efficient use of resources, leadership, assurances, corporate structure and partnership arrangements with government and community to create low carbon cities. In the wake of the economic slowdown it is generally accepted that the public and private sectors will attach increasing importance to stimulate growth by promoting green industries involving proactive governance and entrepreneurship (Fuller et al. 2009; ICIC 2009; Kapoor and Singh 2009; TCPA and CHPA 2008; UTF 2005, and Couch 2003).

In order to illustrate these relationships further at a city level, the following section provides exemplars of best practice in terms of policies and procedures being adopted in both mature (UK and US) and emerging (China and India) economies. Though there is some progress in establishing strategies for low carbon growth, there is nevertheless a need to advance the implementation of policies at regional and local/city levels. Evidence indicates that some countries are addressing the challenges in an integrated sustainable way while other countries are in a transitional phase of integrating policy inputs, outputs, and actions through a coherent approach. While the hierarchical framework presented in this chapter is adaptable on a jurisdictional basis, the trajectories of performance on strategies, policies, and actions are at different stages of maturity across the international spectrum. Distinctions at a global level can be explained by variability of political endorsement, governance structures, leadership and capacity building, financial commitment, and technological development.

Evidence from Cities in the UK, US, China, and India

This section examines urban strategies in the UK, USA, China, and India for addressing the complex policy interrelationships involved in delivering low carbon growth aligned with the increasing need to develop and regenerate cities on the one hand and to actively involve public and private sectors in delivering on sustainability agendas on the other. The complexities have consequences for governance structures, institutional arrangements, and financial provision which influence decision-making at national, regional, and local/city levels. In order to appreciate these interrelationships this section focuses on the processes that operate in mature economies relative to the immature economies. In each country an interesting portfolio of practice-based support measures is being rolled out to address these complex relationships. Consideration is given to the four key process components referred to in Figure 23.2, namely, public policy, resources, operating environment, and corporate governance. Tracking the intricacies across these four criteria on a country basis will enable the theoretical perspective to be linked to the extent of low carbon city competitiveness and tested through a practice-based approach.

UK

Public Policy

In the UK there has been a conscious policy to put in place a good governance approach to sustainability in anticipation of reducing carbon. Public policy has emerged from proactive decision-making, partnerships between the public and private sectors, stakeholder engagement, and a fiscal and regulatory framework. The move to a low carbon economy has required the setting of five-yearly carbon budgets under the Climate Change Act 2008 and legally binding emission reduction targets for 2020 (34 per cent reduction in GHG emissions from the 1990 levels and 18 per cent reduction from the 2008 levels) and for 2050 (at least 80 per cent reduction in GHG emissions) (DECC 2009). A Low Carbon Cities Programme was initiated in 2008 funded by Defra[4] and delivered by the Carbon Trust and the Energy Saving Trust. The programme was initially piloted in the cities of Bristol, Leeds, and Manchester to develop citywide carbon reduction strategies with lessons being shared across all eight Core Cities including Birmingham, Liverpool, Newcastle, Nottingham, and Sheffield (LCCP 2010).

Bristol, Leeds, and Manchester with participation of key stakeholders and good governance arrangements, identified carbon saving options and developed tailored action plans for the respective cities. Bristol has been focusing on development of a sustainable Information and Communication Technology-based (ICT) strategy and evaluating the level of carbon emissions that can be attributed to ICT across a range of employers. Manchester[5] has been enhancing citywide awareness of climate change issues by utilizing the interest of the private and public

[4] Department for Environment, Food and Rural Affairs.

[5] The 'Mini-Stern for Manchester' report (Deloitte 2008) identified an economic opportunity of £20 billion at risk by 2020 for the Manchester City region for which the city region requires early action to control GHG emissions, encourage the use of low carbon alternatives, and increase adaptation to climate change. Subsequently, this is being targeted through various actions focusing on regeneration,

sectors (Core Cities 2010). Manchester City is targeting a reduction in CO_2 emissions by 41 per cent by 2020 from 2005 levels through engagement of individuals, neighbourhoods, and organizations in a process of cultural change embedding low carbon thinking (MCC 2009a). The Leeds City Region has been developing an 'urban eco-settlement' programme, aimed to build energy efficient homes, eco-towns in main regeneration areas, and enhance domestic energy efficiency across the sub-region.

Resources

The public policy approach employed in the UK is dependent upon the human resource commitment, social capital, and funding to facilitate the goal of a low carbon economy. To drive low carbon growth under the constrained economic conditions within the UK, emphasis is placed on making essential investment in energy, accessing finance for viable businesses to support high potential energy projects, encouraging innovation through business to develop new products and services, securing new energy infrastructure, and fostering innovative low carbon energy sectors. A new Low Carbon Investment Fund is being proposed to support sectors with high growth potential, demonstrate innovative technologies, and attract more mature industries to locate in the UK. Special focus is placed on the development of new skills and new jobs to support the key sectors, including low carbon through initiating new qualifications and apprenticeship frameworks, new adult advancement and careers services to support people to get jobs in low carbon and other emerging markets (HM Government 2009). It is estimated that a significant proportion of clean-energy jobs in the UK will be in the offshore wind industry and further spin-out jobs will arise in the manufacturing and installation stages of the supply chain (GCN 2010).

Operating Environment

The UK currently holds a 3.5 per cent share of the global market for low carbon and environmental goods and services, worth around £107 billion and employing 880,000 people. To expand the share and maintain the UK's competitive position, the focus is on innovation and demonstration in priority industries such as carbon capture and storage, and renewable and nuclear energy through business engagement. The new approach recognizes the need for the government to be pro-active and strategic in its role by addressing market failures and creating a favourable operating environment for business operations (HM Government 2009). For example the UK Low Carbon Industrial Strategy (2009) aims to lever industrial and business strength to tackle climate change while ensuring that businesses remain competitive and as efficient as possible. The UK's Budget Report 2010 provides an additional £400 million to support business investment in low carbon growth and help households reduce energy costs. At the city level, the Low Carbon Cities Programme promotes convergence of citywide low carbon strategies led by the public sector and supported by other major influencers of city carbon emissions such as large businesses, housing associations, community and voluntary groups in order to secure carbon reductions and savings (LCCP 2010). The need for concerted action in making the shift to a low carbon economy requires prioritization from politicians, and empowerment of consumers and business to actively engage in promoting green industries to grow (CBI 2007).

Corporate Governance

The Confederation of British Industry is encouraging businesses in the UK to measure and monitor their energy usage more, act to reduce energy consumption, and engage employees, customers, and supply chain operators in promoting energy efficiency (CBI 2010a). While the CBI has reported progress through business engagement on key indicators such as new low carbon infrastructure, nuclear power, EU emissions trading scheme, and aviation and shipping industries seeking ways to reduce emissions, the need to focus more on energy efficiency in the UK is a priority. The UK Department for Business, Innovation and Skills (DBIS) through a 'carbon reduction delivery plan' aims to demonstrate that carbon is central to businesses' long-term thinking (DBIS 2010). Several corporates are actively engaged in facilitating low carbon economic growth in the UK by focusing on various initiatives. Examples include Barclays Bank, which is providing support for carbon finance and emission trading (CBI 2010b). The Boots company is focusing on the measurement and reduction in the carbon footprint of a typical consumer product by engaging with companies in its supply chain and helping consumers to understand the carbon impact of its purchasing choices (CBI 2010c). Ford Britain is investing into a low carbon vehicle strategy partly

---

retrofitting, business alliance, low carbon energy infrastructure and communities, climate-change ready local development framework, awards, and greening the city and airport. These actions are aimed to enhance competitiveness by supporting the mainstream understanding, partnerships, vision, and capacity across Manchester (MCC 2009a and 2009b).

supported by government loan guarantees (The Manufacturer 2010). The DBIS and Department of Energy and Climate Change have launched a new skills consultation exercise to ensure that businesses are equipped and encouraged to take competitive advantage of the opportunities from sectors facilitating low carbon emissions by embedding the necessary skills (DBIS and DECC 2010). The significance of attracting investors to finance skills development and stakeholder engagement through business leadership and commitment of local authorities in cities has been emphasized (nef 2010).

US

Public Policy

In the US, the Environmental Protection Agency and the Department of Energy have created the State Energy Efficiency (SEE) Action Network with an aim of helping states in cost-effective energy efficiency improvements in homes, offices, buildings, and industry by 2020 through technical and policy support (USEPA 2010a). This network builds upon the goals of the National Action Plan for Energy Efficiency which is a public-private initiative. A report by McKinsey & Company (2009) indicates that the US economy has the potential to reduce up to 1.1 giga tonnes of GHG emissions annually, through the development of new no- and low-carbon energy sources.

To advance the goals of the Kyoto Protocol through leadership and action by American cities, the 'US Mayors Climate Protection Agreement' was launched in 2005 by Seattle Mayor, Greg Nickels. Under this agreement the participating cities commit to (i) meet or beat the Kyoto Protocol targets in their own communities; (ii) urge state governments, and the federal government, to enact policies and programmes to meet the Kyoto Protocol target suggested for the US, that is a 7 per cent reduction from 1990 levels by 2012; and (iii) influence the US Congress in the need for legislation supporting a national emission trading system (MCPA 2009). Lerch (2010) in the book *Post Carbon Cities: Planning for Energy and Climate Uncertainty*, highlights the need to create post-carbon communities with the goal to become resilient in a world of energy and climate uncertainty through adaptation and adoption of best practices.

Resources

Regulatory initiatives such as the American Recovery and Reinvestment Act, and the American Clean Energy and Security Act are expected to stimulate $150 billion clean energy investment and aim to create thousands of new jobs related to energy efficiency, renewable energy, and other green job sectors in the US and overseas. Furthermore, 'smart grid' projects linked to employing digital technologies and systems for transforming electricity generation, transmission, distribution, storage, metering, and grid maintenance in the US are estimated to require $1.5 trillion of investment over the next two decades that is likely to create significant job opportunities (GCN 2010; US Department of Energy 2009). Between 1998 and 2007, jobs in the clean energy sector in the US grew at a national rate of 9.1 per cent compared to traditional jobs which grew by 3.7 per cent only (Pew Charitable Trusts 2009).

Operating Environment

A low carbon economic tool has been developed by McKinsey & Company (2010) to allow the public sector, business leaders, and NGOs to understand the macro-economic impact of a wide range of energy and climate policies on GDP, jobs, and prices in the US at the state level by 2030. The United States Climate Action Partnership has been bringing together leading businesses and environmental organizations to push the US federal government for stronger national legislation facilitating significant reductions of GHG emissions (USCAP 2009). The city of Boston introduced the 'green building zoning standard' in December, 2006 to promote new green buildings and development, and greening the existing buildings to stimulate business growth and job creation (BRA 2006). New York State formulated a 'smart grid consortium' in 2008 to meet the sustainable energy needs of the state and enhance the competitiveness of key cities by retaining important businesses and quality jobs (NYS 2009). New York City, aiming to reduce GHG emissions in 2030 by 30 per cent from 2005 levels, is evaluating the potential of accommodating electric vehicles (NYC 2010) and Denver International Airport has installed a two-megawatt solar power system expected to generate over three million kilowatt hours of clean electricity annually (ICLEI 2008).

Corporate Governance

The US Environmental Protection Agency 'Climate Leaders' is an industry-government partnership working with a wide range of businesses to develop comprehensive climate change strategies under which businesses commit to reducing their impact on the global environment by completing a corporate-wide inventory of GHG emissions (USEPA 2010b). The International Energy Agency and the World Business Council for Sustainable Development, with 30 leading global companies, aim to support the transition to a low carbon economy through concrete actions. By promoting an international low carbon energy technology platform, the focus is on exploring possible partnerships and collaboration in the areas of technology roadmaps, technology financing, and overcoming barriers to technology diffusion (WBCSD 2010). General Electric's key growth strategy 'ecomagination' (WBCSD 2008), Intel's 'open energy initiative' (Intel 2010), etc., demonstrate how low carbon technologies are an integral aspect of their competitive strategy.

China

Public Policy

China's public policy aims to include low-carbon targets in its Twelfth Five Year Plan (2011–15) for national economic and social development in order to build an energy-saving and ecologically friendly society. The government, through technological and fiscal support policies, aims to promote the use of non-fossil and renewable energies (English News 2010). China's Renewable Energy Law, effective since February 2005, has set a legally binding target that by 2020, 15 per cent of all energy is to be generated from wind, biomass, solar, and hydro power energy as compared to the present 7 per cent (CSEP 2010a). A low carbon city initiative in China, supported by the World Wildlife Fund, China, aims to utilize the low carbon development model in different cities, thus facilitating energy efficiency improvement in the industrial, construction, and transportation sectors based on the development of renewable energy. The focus of this initiative is on research and implementation of policies contributing to low carbon development, capacity building, technology transfer and cooperation, new finance and investment instruments, sustainable trade opportunities, and improved public awareness for energy efficiency and renewable energy. The initiative aims to contribute to the national target of a 20 per cent reduction in energy density by decoupling economic development and CO_2 emissions, and promoting climate-friendly solutions for the key economic sectors in target cities. In the initial pilot stage, cooperative projects are being implemented in the cities of Shanghai and Baoding with plans to include the roll-out to other cities on a staged programme (*Chinadaily* 2009; WWF-China 2009).

Resources

China's targeted investment into renewable and new energy sectors indicates potential for the creation of 6.46 to 6.78 million jobs (most probably in the areas of research, manufacturing, installation, operation, and maintenance). A macro shift to the service sector would create up to 20 million jobs. These together are likely to create a net gain in jobs against the scenario of fewer jobs in traditional sectors due to China's commitment to lower energy use per unit of GDP by 2020. There is a need for government investment into skills and capacity building so that the workforce takes advantage of the potential renewable and new energy jobs (GCN 2010). According to the Pew Charitable Trusts (2009), China is fast approaching the top in terms of clean-energy investment compared to other economies. There is however the need for investment in China to focus more specifically on energy efficiency on the demand-side compared to the supply-side in order to improve competitiveness, and increase jobs and economic growth, while reducing public health and environmental costs from excessive reliance on coal (CSEP 2010b).

Operating Environment

China is building its first low carbon technology research, development, and promotion centre in Shanghai with joint financial support from the China Energy Conservation and Environmental Protection Group, Shanghai Yidian Holding Company, and Baoshan district. The centre aims to provide a platform to several businesses specializing in energy conservation and environmental protection to display energy-efficient and environmental friendly products, technologies, and techniques and also generate revenue through technology transfers, product marketing, and comprehensive services (CDM in China 2010). The National Development Reform Commission in China had initiated the 'Top-1,000 Programme' in 2006 aimed to reduce energy consumption in 1,000 of the largest enterprises that were consuming one-third of all China's primary energy. The programme realizes the need for reducing emissions from the industrial sector in China (Price et al. 2010). Many cities are building partnership arrangements between the public sector, business, and the community to promote low carbon development. The cities of Shanghai and Beijing, through a large-scale campaign '20 ways to 20%' supported by WWF-China, are bringing together government, media, scientific, and industrial communities to participate in conserving energy. This campaign, started in 2007, has been focusing on training, advertising, and efficiency contests to help China reduce energy use by 20 per cent, as outlined in its Elventh Five Year Plan. (WWF-China 2010). The city of Baoding is pro-actively enhancing networking on sustainable energy knowledge management and technology cooperation by investment in capacity building in city planning and exporting sustainable energy products. Best practice derived through the pilot projects in the cities of

Shanghai and Baoding is assisting in promoting the focus of a low carbon development policy in the capital city of Beijing (Ying 2009).

Corporate Governance

In China many state-owned enterprises and large business corporate-houses have been working in partnership with the government and community to support low carbon growth. The Gansu province has joined together with the state-owned enterprise, China Huadian Corporation, to work on energy development and construction of an energy base in the Hexi area of Gansu by optimally utilizing new and renewable energy resources in the region (GreenChinaTech.com 2010a). The Shanghai government is comprehensively integrating low energy solutions into the redesign of city development. As an example, the Huayuanfang Energy-Saving Industrial Zone, rebuilt from a previous automobile factory, and situated in downtown Shanghai, now hosts a number of new energy efficient projects and companies. Many businesses are responding by acting in favour of low carbon such as the China Huaneng Group which is advancing its clean energy production through carbon capture at its coal-fired power plants. In Shanghai, the priority is to increase energy efficiency of buildings and transportation through demonstration projects. For example, the furniture giant IKEA (Shanghai) is in the process of turning to clean energy and raising its energy efficiency goals by replacing the inefficient power equipment with energy-saving ones such as bulbs and air-conditioners (China View 2009). Corporate sector partnership arrangements to increase investment potential for low carbon growth are evident in China. The ZheShang Venture Capital and 27 partners have launched China's first private equity fund, the ZheShang Nuohai Low Carbon Fund, to focus on the country's low carbon economy. The fund is raising money for investments in fast-growing and innovative companies linked to energy conservation, environmental protection, and new energy sectors in China (GreenChinaTech.com 2010b).

India

Public Policy

In India, public policy is supporting the development of a 'low carbon strategy' through a 26-member 'low carbon expert group' constituted by the Prime Minister. This top-own process relates to the good governance approach to sustainability in the UK, a top-down support to states in the US, and the promotion of a low carbon growth agenda through the Five Year Plans in China. The low carbon strategy in India, promoted by the Planning Commission, comprises sector-specific, critical low carbon initiatives with a suggested timeline and targets. The strategy complements the National Action Plan on Climate Change[6] and aims to facilitate India's commitment to reduce the national energy intensity by 25 per cent by 2020 compared to 2005 levels (Worldwatch Institute 2010) that is comparable to the target of 20 per cent reduction in energy density by 2020 in China. Furthermore, the low carbon cities agenda is also being reinforced by the Government of India's programme on the 'development of solar cities'. The programme is to promote the use of renewable energy in urban areas by providing support to the municipal corporations for preparation and implementation of a road map to develop a network of cities as solar cities. The aim is to cut the demand for conventional energy at the end of 2012 by at least 10 per cent (PIB 2009; MNRE 2009).

Resources

The targeted renewable energy production in India indicates significant potential for job creation, particularly through the development of wind, solar PV, and bio-fuel markets. GCN (2010) has made optimistic assumptions about expansion in these three sectors to estimate that around 10.5 million new jobs are likely to be created. The majority of these jobs in India would link to the use of bio-fuels in rural communities and small and medium-sized industries with potential jobs related to research, manufacturing, O&M in China, energy efficiency in the US, and offshore wind industry in the UK. Other potential new jobs in wind power and solar PV are expected to contribute to the high-waged-high-quality jobs portfolio in India and leverage the advantages of a growing global market. The focus is on capacity building through investment in training to support the creation of highly skilled renewable energy jobs with the availability of a green workforce. India's commitment to low carbon economic growth is evident through the National Action Plan on Climate Change.

[6] The National Action Plan on Climate Change, initiated in June, 2008 by the Prime Minister of India outlines the existing and future policies and programmes to address climate mitigation and adaptation. The plan identifies eight core national missions that focus on solar energy, enhanced energy efficiency, sustainable habitat, water, sustaining the Himalayan ecosystem, green India, sustainable agriculture, and strategic knowledge for climate change (GoI 2008).

Operating Environment

Establishment of the high-profile low carbon expert group in India indicates the rising emphasis on low carbon growth, simultaneously addressing the country's energy security issue and stimulating the global community to reach a consensus on reducing carbon emissions (World-watch Institute 2010). In India the public sector's proactive engagement with the business community is vital to help establish the low carbon growth models at national and city levels as reflected through the Mayor's Climate Protection Agreement and Climate Action Partnership in the US and Low Carbon Cities programme in the UK. As an example in India, the solar cities programme is supporting the city of Nagpur to be developed as a model solar city by 2012. Nagpur city plans to meet up to 10 per cent of its energy demand from renewable energy sources and implement other energy efficiency measures to improve its low carbon rating. Business involvement for implementation of commercially viable technologies (solar thermal heating systems) supported through regulatory initiatives (building byelaws to make use of solar water heating systems mandatory for certain categories of buildings) are expected to play a key role in meeting this target for Nagpur city (TET 2009a). Various fiscal mechanisms such as property tax incentives for the users of solar water heaters being promoted by the solar city programme will further facilitate widespread adoption of technologies supporting low carbon growth. It is recognized that India has enormous potential to prosper from the new opportunities presented by the low carbon economy and to lead the agenda globally (Stern 2009).

Corporate Governance

The linkage between energy supply and other challenges such as poverty, environment, and water are recognized by the corporate sector in India. The corporate sector has a vital role in promoting a national approach with the public sector for scaling-up decentralized energy models in the cities in India (CII 2010; CII 2008) as reflected through the state-owned enterprises and large corporates in China, the Confederation of British Industry in the UK and the Environmental Protection Agency in the US. Many large businesses in India through their corporate social responsibility policies have facilitated a balance between economic, social, and environmental goals through effective leadership and partnership arrangements with government and communities to create low carbon growth. Two cities in India, Jaipur (as Mahindra World City) and Ahmedabad (as Godrej Garden City) have been identified by the Clinton Climate Initiative in partnership with the corporate sector as part of the 'climate positive development programme'. The focus of this initiative is on development of high efficienct, high performance 'green' buildings, clean energy generation, interconnected transport systems and land-use patterns, advanced and integrated waste management strategies, efficienct water systems, environmental performance, and integrated environmental and ecosystem management (CCI 2010; the *Hindu* 2009). The Mahindra World City spread across 300 acres aims to encourage property developers and the local government to work together to implement economically viable innovations into infrastructure and buildings (*TET* 2009b). The importance of corporate social responsibility of the large corporate players towards sustainable real estate development in India is a critical factor in property performance (JLLM 2007). The significance of attracting investment, skills, and technology for low carbon growth in the cities in India is demonstrated through innovative partnerships with business leadership models in China, the UK, and the US.

Cross Jurisdictional Impacts

Across jurisdictions, mega-regeneration projects are increasingly being utilized in enhancing the image and branding of cities through sustainable resource management modelled on the key process components of public policy, resources, operating environment, and corporate governance. The London 2012 Olympic Games is an inspired example, setting new benchmarks in sustainability through various phases of planning, funding, construction, and occupational after-use. This mega-project is a partnership between the public sector (Olympic Delivery Authority) and a private sector company (London Organizing Committee of the Olympic Games and Paralympic Games).The mission statement for climatic change is to minimize the carbon footprint of the Games and provide a platform for demonstrating long-term solutions for energy and water resource management, infrastructure development, transport provision, local and seasonal food production, and carbon impact mitigation and adaptation measures.The commitment is to achieve long-term sustainable regeneration utilizing a Master Plan framework promoting the legacy of the Olympic Park concept (ODA and LDA 2007). By creating world-class sporting facilities for London, the Games are regenerating the Lower Lea Valley area, providing new homes, work space, schools, health and other community facilities to enhance economic competitiveness and quality of life of citizens (LOCOG 2010).

Similarly in India, the Commonwealth Games 2010 development scheme has been constructed in Delhi reflecting an environment-led approach, including a series of green measures to enhance energy efficiency and air quality and to expand the city's forest cover. The potential positive impact is to highlight the environmental awareness of the scheme to the 14 million inhabitants of Delhi. The new measures under the 'XIX Commonwealth Games 2010 Delhi Ecological Code' provide guidelines on conserving biodiversity, energy efficiency, effective waste management, reduced air and noise pollution, and sustainable transportation. Specifically, the scheme is designed to reduce emissions and attain carbon neutrality through energy efficiency initiatives and use of clean fuel measures (CWG 2010a; UNEP 2010a). The legacy of the Games is to advance the city's competitiveness, create employment, increase investment, and transform the landscape through sustainable development by increasing the social, economic, and physical potential of areas such as East Delhi and the Yamuna riverfront (CWG 2010b).

In the US, the stadium for the Dallas Cowboys will be the first mega-sports project to gain recognition in the US Environmental Protection Agency's National Environmental Performance Track Programme (USEPA 2008). The City of Arlington will experience a significant contribution towards its environmental conservation efforts from the development that aims to reduce the environmental footprint through various 'green' environmental design, construction, and operational excellence measures. Exploring the same theme in Beijing City indicates that the 2008 Olympic Games focused on sustainability principles for the thematically planned 'Green Olympics' (UNEP 2007). The thrust was on building energy conservation through advanced architecture, a master plan for greening the city's landscape, sustainable sourcing of building materials for Olympic venues, water resource protection and reutilization, efficient disposal of solid waste, and implementation of noise control measures (Beijing 2008).

Conclusion

This chapter highlights that competitive cities are embracing a low carbon footprint. One way to enable city competitiveness and track whether a city is progressing along a low carbon growth path is through the hierarchical model proposed in this chapter.

The evidence drawn from across the four economies demonstrates the importance of public policy, resource allocation, operating environment, and corporate governance in transforming urban areas from grey to green while exploiting new opportunities for economic growth and development. Creating enabling capacity for businesses to operate in partnership with the public sector in promoting low carbon economies requires proactive strategic thinking, innovative fiscal incentives, institutional cooperation, and technological solutions.

Based on the evaluation of the criteria included in this chapter it is apparent that there are significant challenges for Indian cities at two levels. Firstly, there would appear to be differences between the status of mature versus emerging cities in terms of their progression towards a low carbon economy. Although there is clear evidence of strategic programme/policy-level arrangements in both mature and emerging cities to promote carbon efficiency, the operational mode and delivery of low carbon initiatives and their implementation at the city level in emerging economies needs comprehensive evaluation. Emerging evidence would tend to suggest that mature cities have workable case study exemplars and solutions whereas the emerging cities are at more formative stages in creating examples of excellence.

Secondly, in India specifically, there exists a need for a coherent approach to the formulation of a consistent strategy and operational framework to realize the low carbon development goal that has also been recognized by the Planning Commission. There are differences between the large metropolitan cities and the middle-tier cities,[7] with the latter making strides towards developing a low carbon strategy. The situation in the large metropolitan cities in India shows signs of strategic policy formulation and implementation of carbon neutral strategies. The middle-tier cities are faced with the challenges of balancing a rapid urbanization rate with sustainable infrastructure provision, quality investment by the private and public sector- and efficient use of social capital. However, there exists enormous potential for low carbon development in these cities particularly through integrated provision of urban development and transportation infrastructure.

According to Stern (2009), given its size and commitment to sustainable economic growth, India is in a strong position to set the agenda for the low carbon economy at the city level. Furthermore, the transition over the next two or three decades is likely to bring a period of dynamic innovation, competitiveness, and investment which will drive growth within a low carbon economy. Potentially,

[7] Large metropolitan cities in India such as Mumbai, Delhi, and Bangalore and middle-tier cities such as Jaipur and Lucknow (Singhal 2009).

the emerging economy of India could be a real market leader in the new technologies and take advantage of the opportunities involved in building modern infrastructure through innovative approaches such as the establishment of National Clean Energy Fund (GoI 2010); mobilizing financial resources for large-scale infrastructure and low carbon technology development (TCG 2010); and enhancing climate accountability (UNEP 2010b).

References

Begg, I. (1999). 'Cities and Competitiveness', *Urban Studies*, 36(5/6), pp. 795–810.

——— (2002). Introduction. 'Urban Competitiveness: Policies for Dynamic Cities', in I. Begg (ed.), *The Policy Press*, Bristol, pp. 1–31.

Beijing (2008). 'Green Olympics: Progress v Challenge', available at http://en.beijing2008.cn/12/12/greenolympics.shtml, last accessed on 6 May 2010.

Boston Redevelopment Authority (BRA) (2006). 'City of Boston to Become First Major City in Nation to Incorporate LEED Standards into Zoning Code', Office of the Mayor, City of Boston, Massachusetts.

Chinadaily (2009). Low-carbon urbanization way forward for China. http://www.chinadaily.com.cn/opinion/2009-11/30/content9075126.htm last accessed on 17 February 2010.

China Institute of City Competitiveness (2009). *Chinese City Competitiveness Report 2009.*

China Sustainable Energy Programme (CSEP) (2010a). 'Fact Sheet: China Emerging as New Leader in Clean Energy Policies', available at http://www.efchina.org/FNewsroom.do?act=detail&newsTypeId=1&id=107 as viewed on 9 April 2010.

——— (2010b). 'Underinvestment in Energy Efficiency', http://www.efchina.org FPubInfo.do?act=list&abb=About Us&sabb=2&pageno=3 as viewed on 12 April 2010.

China View (2009). 'Shanghai Leads China's Fight of Climate Change and Low-carbon Development', available at http://news.xinhuanet.com/english/2009-12/15/content_12651242.htm as viewed on 18 February 2010.

Clean Development Mechanism (CDM) in China (2010). 'China Builds First Low-carbon R&D Center in Shanghai', http://cdm.ccchina.gov.cn/english/NewsInfo.asp?NewsId=4357 as viewed on 14 April 2010.

Clinton Climate Initiative (CCI) (2010). 'Climate Positive'. http://www.clintonfoundation.org/what-we-do/clinton-climate-initiative/our-approach/cities/climate-positive as viewed on 13 February 2010.

Commonwealth Games (2010a). 'Striving Towards Consumption—Carbon Neutrality, The XIX Commonwealth Games 2010 Delhi Ecological Code. http://www.cwgdelhi2010.org/greengames/sites/default/files/eco-code%20pages%202.pdf, last viewed on 8 May 2010.

——— (2010b). Legacy of Delhi 2010. http://www.cwgdelhi2010.org/dcwg/index.php?q=node/707, last accessed on 8 May 2010.

Confederation of British Industry (CBI) (2010a). 'CBI Third Climate Change Tracker: Monitoring Progress Towards a Low-carbon Economy', The CBI Climate Change Board, p. 6.

——— (2010b). 'Barclays: Helping London Lead in Carbon Finance'. Case studies, available at http://climatechange.cbi.org.uk/case_studies/00361/ as viewed on 13 April 2010.

——— (2010c). 'Soaking up Emissions', available at http://climatechange.cbi.org.uk/case_studies/00221/ as viewed on 13 April 2010.

——— (2007). *Climate Change: Everyone's Business*, A report from the CBI Climate Change Task Force, pp. 54.

Confederation of Indian Industry (CII) (2010). 'Low Carbon Renewable Strategy Critical to India's Sustainable Energy Future—Dr Kirit Parikh'. CII news updates, Centralized Approach to Promote De-centralized Energy Models—Mr Suresh Prabhu, Chairman CEEW.

——— (2008). *Building a Low Carbon Indian Economy: Discussion Paper*, Energy Department, pp. 136.

Core Cities (2010). 'Low Carbon Cities Programme—Supporting Bristol, Leeds and Manchester in Developing City-Wide Carbon Reduction Strategies', available at http://www.corecities.com/dev07/News/newsletter/Low%20Carbon%20Cities%20Programme.htm as viewed on 5 April 2010.

Couch, C. (2003). 'Economic and Physical Influences on Urban Regeneration in Europe', in C. Couch, C. Fraser, and S. Percy (eds) *Urban Regeneration in Europe*, Blackwell Science Limited, Oxford.

Deloitte (2008). '"Mini-Stern" for Manchester: Assessing the economic impact of EU and UK climate change legislation on Manchester City Region and the North West.'

Department for Business, Innovation and Skills (DBIS) (2010). *BIS: Carbon Reduction Delivery Plan*. Department for Business, Innovation & Skills, Crown Copyright, URN 10/787, p. 75.

Department for Business, Innovation and Skills and Department of Energy and Climate Change (DBIS and DECC) (2010). 'Meeting the Low Carbon Skills Challenge: A Consultation on Equipping People with the Skills to take Advantage of Opportunities in the Low Carbon and Resource Efficient Economy', Crown Copyright, BIS/300/03/2010/NP, URN 10/849, p. 88.

Department for Communities and Local Government (DCLG) (2008). 'Feasibility Study to Examine Making the Thames Gateway a Low Carbon/Carbon Neutral Development

Area', Copyright, Queen's Printer and Controller of Her Majesty's Stationery Office, p. 164.

Department of Energy and Climate Change (DECC) (2009). *UK's National Strategy for Climate and Energy: Transition to a Low Carbon Society*, Her Majesty's Government, Crown Copyright 2009.

English News (2010). 'China to develop low-carbon economy: top economic planner', http://news.xinhuanet.com/english2010/china/2010-03/01/c_13193015.htm as viewed on 6 April 2010.

Fuller, M.C., S.C. Portis, D.M. Kammen (2009). 'Toward a Low-Carbon Economy: Municipal Financing for Energy Efficiency and Solar Power', *Environment: Science and Policy for Sustainable Development*, 51(1), pp. 22–3.

Global Climate Network (GCN) (2010). *Low Carbon Jobs in an Interconnected World: Global Climate Network*, discussion paper no. 3, p. 37.

Government of India (2010). 'Union Budget 2010–11', Speech of Pranab Mukherjee, Minister of Finance, 26 February 2010. http://indiabudget.nic.in/ub2010-11/bs/speecha.htm as viewed on 22 June 2010.

——— (2008). National Action Plan on Climate Change, Prime Minister's Council on Climate Change, Government of India, p. 50.

GreenChinaTech.com (2010a). 'Gansu and Huadian Group will jointly build low-carbon energy base'. http://www.greenchinatech.com/en/2010/03/09/gansu-and-huadian-group-will-jointly-build-low-carbon-energy-base/ as viewed on 10 April 2010.

———(2010b). 'First Private Low Carbon Fund Established in China', http://www.greenchinatech.com/en/2010/04/06/first-private-low-carbon-fund-established-in-china/ as viewed on 13 April 2010.

Her Majesty's Government (HM Government) (2009). 'Investing in a Low Carbon Britain', Crown Copyright. URN 09D/544, p. 44.

ICLEI (2008). 'Denver International Airport Installs Massive Two-Megawatt Solar System', http://www.icleiusa.org/success-stories/copy_of_clean-power/solar-power/denver-international-airport-installs-massive-two-megawatt-solar-system as viewed on 11 April 2010.

Initiative for a Competitive Inner City (ICIC) (2009). 'Initiative for a Competitive Inner City', available at http://www.icic.org/site/c.fnJNKPNhFiG/b.4173155/k.AFA3/About.htm as viewed on 26 September 2009.

Institute for Competitiveness (2009). *India City Competitiveness Report 2009*.

Intel (2010). 'Intel Open Energy Initiative', http://www.intel.com/technology/eco-technology/openenergy.htm as viewed on 6 April 2010.

International Centre for Local and Regional Development (ICLRD) (2009). *The Newry-Dundalk Twin City Region: Supporting the Implementation of Cross-Border Collaborative Frameworks*. Copyright, ICLRD, p. 37.

Jones Lang LaSalle Meghraj (JLLH) (2007). 'Sustainable Real Estate Development in India: The cost in difference' Advance, new knowledge first, Jones Lang LaSalle Meghraj.

Kapoor, A. and S. Singh (2009). *India City Competitiveness Report 2009*. Institute for Competitiveness, India.

Kitson, M., R. Martin, and P. Tyler (2006). 'The Regional Competitiveness Debate'. The Cambridge-MIT Institute report for The Programme on Regional Innovation, p. 14.

Krugman, P. (1996). 'Making Sense of the Competitiveness Debate', *Oxford Review of Economic Policy*, 12, pp. 17–25.

Lerch, D. (2010). 'The Future of Our Cities Lies in their Integration with the Environment', available at http://www.postcarbon.org/article/75766-the-future-of-our-cities-lies, last date of access on 25 February 2010.

Lever, W.F. and I. Turok (1999). 'Competitive Cities: Introduction to the Review', *Urban Studies*, Vol. 36, Nos 5/6, 791–3.

London Organizing Committee of the Olympic Games and Paralympic Games Ltd (2010). *London 2012: Sustainability plan summary—Towards a one planet 2012*. Copyright, LOCOG, pp. 12.

Low Carbon Cities Programme (LCCP) (2010). *Low Carbon Cities Programme*, *News Letter*, 3, available at http://www.lowcarboncities.co.uk/cms/assets/Attachments/LCCPNewsletter3FINAL.pdf as viewed on 22nd February, 2010.

'Low-carbon Urbanization Way Forward for China' (2009). *Chinadaily*, available at http://www.chinadaily.com.cn/opinion/2009-11/30/content_9075126.htm, as viewed on 17 February 2010.

Malecki, E.J. (2002). 'Hard and Soft Networks for Urban Competitiveness', *Urban Studies*, 39(5–6), pp. 929–45.

Manchester City Council (MCC) (2009a). *Manchester, a Certain Future: Our Collective Action on Climate Change*. City of Manchester, p. 55.

——— (2009b). *Manchester Climate Change: Call to Action*. Manchester City Council, p. 52.

Mayors' Climate Protection Agreement (MCPA) (2009). '1,000th Mayor Mesa, AZ Mayor Scott Smith signs the U.S. Conference of Mayors Climate Protection Agreement', available at http://www.usmayors.org/pressreleases/uploads/1000signatory.pdf, last date of access 16 February 2010.

McKinsey & Company (2010). *The US Low Carbon Economics Tool: Climate Change Special Initiative*, United States of America.

——— (2009). *Unlocking Energy Efficiency in the U.S. Economy*. McKinsey Global Energy and Materials, United States of America.

Ministry of New and Renewable Energy (MNRE) (2009). 'MNRE Programme on "Development of Solar Cities"', Guidelines for preparing master plan as per the prescribed format of MNRE. http://mnes.nic.in/pdf/city-guidelines.pdf as viewed on 20 February 2010.

New Economics Foundation (NEF) (2010). *Good Foundations: Towards a Low Carbon, High Well-Being Built Environment,* edited by Mary Murphy, new economics foundation, London, pp. 80.

New York State (NYS) (2009). *Strategic Smart Grid Vision and Technical Plan Report: Leading the Way to New York's Future.* Smart Grid Consortium, New York State.

New York City (NYC) (2010). *PlaNYC: Exploring electric vehicle adoption in New York City—A Greener, Greater New York.*

Olympic Delivery Authority and London Development Agency (ODA and LDA) (2007). 'Commitment to Sustainable Regeneration: Olympic, Paralympic & Legacy Transformation Planning Applications for the Olympic Park', *ODA and LDA*, 3, p. 40.

Parkinson, M. and M. Boddy (2004). 'Introduction. City Matters: Competitiveness, Cohesion and Urban Governance'. The Policy Press, Bristol, pp. 1–10.

Pew Charitable Trusts (2009). 'The Clean Energy Economy: Repowering Jobs, Businesses and Investments across America'. The Pew Charitable Trusts, p. 59.

Porter, M.E. (2008). *On Competition, Updated and Expanded Edition.* Harvard Business School Press, United States of America, available on http://www.amazon.com/Competition-Michael-E-Porter/dp/142212696X/#reader_142212696X.

——— (1998). *The Competitive Advantage of Nations,* Macmillan, London.

Press Information Bureau (PIB), (TCPA and CHPA) (2009). 'Development of solar city', http://pib.nic.in/release/release. asp?relid=50553&kwd= as viewed on 14 February 2010.

Price, L.X. Wang, and J. Yun (2010). 'The Challenge of Reducing Energy Consumption of the Top-1000 Largest Industrial Enterprises in China', *Energy Policy,* 38(8), pp. 1–29.

Singhal, S. (2009). 'City Competitiveness, Regeneration and Property-led Business Strategies', PhD Thesis, University of Ulster.

Singhal, S., J.N. Berry, and W.S. McGreal (2009). 'A Framework for Assessing Regeneration, Business Strategies and Urban Competitiveness', *Local Economy,* 24 (2), pp. 111–24

Sustainable Energy Authority of Ireland (SEAI) (2010). 'Dundalk2020'. http://www.seai.ie/Dundalk2020/ as viewed on 7 May 2010.

Stern, N. (2009). 'Climate Change, Internationalism and India in the 21st Century'. Jawaharlal Nehru Lecture by Nicholas Stern on 15 July 2009. London School of Economics, http://www.lse.ac.uk/collections/IndiaObservatory/pdf/Nehru_synopsis_22_July_09_Final.pdf as viewed on 12 April, 2010.

'The XIX Commonwealth Games 2010 Delhi Ecological Code'. http://www.cwgdelhi2010.org/greengames/sites/default/files/eco-code%20page%202.pdf as viewed on 8 May 2010.

——— (2010b). 'Legacy of Delhi 2010', available at http://www.cwgdelhi2010.org/dcwg/index.php?q=node/707 as viewed on 8 May 2010.

The Climate Group (TCG) (2010). 'Climate change and finance in India: banking on the low carbon Indian economy. The Climate Group, Indian Banks' Association and Price Waterhouse Coopers, p. 19.

The Economic Times (TET) (2009a), 'Nagpur to become India's First Solar City', available at http://economictimes.indiatimes.com/news/news-by-industry/energy/power/Nagpur-to-become-Indias-first-solar-city/articleshow/4149714.cms, last date of access 20 February 2010.

——— (2009b). 'Mahindra World Signs MoU with Climate Initiative'. http://www.mahindraworldcity.com/Docs/Jaipur/In%20the%20News/ET%20Chd%2021.05.09.pdf as viewed on 13 April 2010.

The Hindu (2009). 'Mahindra City to Set Eco Standards', http://www.thehindu.com/2009/06/08/stories/2009060857640700.htm as viewed on 18 February 2010.

The Manufacturer (2010). 'Low Carbon Boost for Ford', available at http://www.themanufacturer.com/uk/content/10333/Low_carbon_boost_for_Ford, lats date of access 13 April 2010.

The UK Low Carbon Industrial Strategy (2009). Department for Business, Innovation and Skills and Department of Energy and Climate Change, Crown copyright. URN 09/1058.

Town and Country Planning Association and the Combined Heat and Power Association (2008). *Community Energy Urban Planning for a Low Carbon Future,* RAP Spiderweb Ltd., Clowes Street, Hollinwood, Oldham, United Kingdom, available at http://www.tcpa.org.uk/data/files/ceg.pdf.

UK Budget Report 2010 (2010). 'Supporting low-carbon growth. In Budget Report 2010, Securing the recovery: growth and opportunity'. Presented to Parliament by The Chancellor of the Exchequer by Command of Her Majesty, Crown copyright 2010, pp. 105–18.

UNEP (2010a). 'The 2010 Commonwealth Games Go Green: Ecological Codes to Underpin Environmental Improvements for Delhi-Based Event', http://www.unep.org/Documents.Multilingual/Default.asp?DocumentID=612&ArticleID=6463&l=en as viewed on 7 May 2010.

——— (2010b). 'One Third of Countries Show Promising Gains in Low Carbon Economic Growth Since the Copenhagen Climate Accord', http://www.unep.org/Documents.Multilingual/Default.asp?DocumentID=620&ArticleID=6536&l=en as viewed on 22 June 2010.

——— (2009). 'UNEP and ICLEI Launch the Carbon Climate Centre'. http://www.unep.org/Documents.Multilingual/Default.asp?DocumentID=606&ArticleID=6422&l=en as viewed on 21 February 2010.

——— (2007). 'UNEP reaffirms support to "Green" Olympics in Beijing', http://www.unep.org/Documents.

Multilingual/Default.asp?DocumentID=498&ArticleID=5491&l=en as viewed on 6 May 2010.

United States Climate Action Partnership (USCAP) (2009). *Blueprint for Legislative Action: Consensus Recommendations for US Climate Protection Legislation,* United States of Ameruica.

Urban Task Force (2005). *Towards A Strong Urban Renaissance.* An independent report by members of the Urban Task Force chaired by Lord Rogers of Riverside.

Urwin, C. (2006). 'Urban Myth: Why Cities Don't Compete'. Discussion paper no. 5, Centre for Cities, Institute for Public Policy Research, www.ippr.org/centreforcities.

US Department of Energy (2009). 'Renewable energy and smart grids spurred by Economic Stimulus Act', http://apps1.eere.energy.gov/news/news_detail.cfm/news_id=12244 as viewed on 10 April 2010.

US Environmental Protection Agency (USEPA) (2010a). 'State Energy Efficiency Action Network', available at http://www.epa.gov/cleanenergy/energy-programs/seeaction/index.html, last date of access 7 April 2010.

——— (2010b). 'Climate Leaders', available at http://www.epa.gov/climateleaders/index.html, last date of access 8 April 2010.

———(2008). 'Dallas Cowboys' New Stadium Aims to Score Big with EPA's Premier Environmental Stewardship Program', available at http://yosemite.epa.gov/opa/admpress.nsf/d0cf6618525a9efb85257359003fb69d/f0d5181698f279c9852574e40050cb62!OpenDocument, last date of access 8 May 2010.

World Business Council for Sustainable Development (WBCSD) (2010). 'Concrete Action for Transition to Low-Carbon Economy', available at http://www.wbcsd.org/Plugins/DocSearch/details.asp?DocTypeId=251&ObjectId=Mzc4NDg as viewed on 6 April 2010.

——— (2008). 'Case Study: General Electric—Energy Efficiency as Strategy', available at http://www.wbcsd.org/DocRoot/fAk5htUjKvcua6Eep2wJ/GEfullcase_final.pdf as viewed on 11 April 2010, p. 4.

Worldwatch Institute (2010). Interview with Kirit Parikh on India's Low Carbon Growth Strategy, http://www.worldwatch.org/node/6384 as viewed on 6 April 2010.

World Wildlife Fund, China (WWF-China) (2010). Conservation programmes/Climate and Energy. http://www.wwfchina.org/english/sub_loca.php?loca=4&sub=96 as viewed on 6 April 2010.

——— (2009). 'Low carbon city initiative in China', http://www.wwfchina.org/english/sub_loca.php?loca=1&sub=96 as viewed on 15 February 2010.

Ying, S. (2009). 'A Tale of Two Low Carbon Cities'. 45th ISOCARP Congress 2009, http://isocarp.net/Data/case_studies/1416.pdf as viewed on 19 February 2010.

Zhilin, L., D. Yixin, D. Chang-gui, and Q. Ye (2009). 'Low-Carbon City: Concepts, International Practice and Implications for China,' *Urban Development*, 16 No. 06.

Section VI

Rural Infrastructure

24 Towards A Carbon-Neutral Rural India

Part 1 Challenges and Opportunities in Agriculture

Sreenath Dixit, J.V.N.S Prasad, B.M.K. Raju, and B. Venkateswarlu

Introduction

Environmentally sustainable social and economic development, a daunting challenge by itself is made more intimidating in the contemporary context as the threats posed by climate change loom large. That economic growth cannot solely guarantee poverty reduction and equality of opportunity is well-understood and accepted. Failure to safeguard the environment in the blind pursuit of economic growth eventually jeopardizes hard-earned economic and social achievements of any nation in the dynamic state of deepening and maturing economic development that India is today.

Climate Change: Implications for the Rural Sector

Nearly 70 per cent of the world's poor live in rural areas. With the global population reaching 9 billion by 2050 (even though most of the population increase will be in cities), the sheer number of poor people competing for the little infrastructure in rural areas will pose a serious challenge. Larger populations put more pressure on ecosystems and natural resources, intensifying the competition for land, water, and access to energy.

The process of development of rural areas is arduous. Enormous investments are needed to improve the quality of life of the rural poor. Climate change will affect numerous sectors and productive environments, including agriculture, forestry, energy, and coastal zones everywhere. The impact on developing economies will be more immediate, in part because of their greater exposure to climate shocks and in part because of their low adaptive capacity. Millions of people inhabiting the coastal ecosystems from Bangladesh to Florida will suffer as the sea level rises, inundating settlements and contaminating freshwater (Harrington and Walton 2008; IWM and CEGIS 2007). Greater rainfall variability and more severe droughts in semi-arid Asia and Africa will hinder efforts to enhance food security and combat malnourishment (Schmidhuber and Tubiello 2007). The melting of the Himalayan and the Andean glaciers—which regulate river flow, generate hydro power, and supply clean water to over a billion people—will threaten rural livelihoods and major food markets (Bates et al. 2008). Agriculture and the primary industries (including livestock rearing, fishery, etc.), which support most livelihoods in rural sector, are going to be hit hard as a consequence of climate change. Interestingly, this is also a sector that contributes to both emission and sequestration of carbon emissions. Out of nearly 2000 million tonnes of CO_2 eq. pa, enteric fermentation in ruminant livestock accounts for 212 and rice cultivation for 70. However forests and farmlands sequester 68 and 208, thus more or less neutralizing emissions caused by rural industries (INCCA 2007). The real concern however is loss of crop yield due to climate change. In China and Japan, yields of rice are likely to decline, while yields of wheat, maize, and rice in Central and South Asia will fall drastically (Cruz et al. 2007). Prospects for crops and livestock in rainfed semi-arid lands in sub-Saharan Africa are bleak, even before warming reaches 2–2.5°C above preindustrial levels (Easterling et al. 2007). This calls for decisive, immediate action even as the debate about the costs and benefits of climate change mitigation continues.

Implications for Rural India

India's post-1980 deceleration in growth of rice productivity (from the Green Revolution in the 1960s) is attributable not only to falling rice prices and deteriorating irrigation infrastructure, as previously postulated, but also to adverse climate phenomena resulting from local pollution and global warming (Auffhammer et al. 2006). Extrapolating from past variations in climate and agricultural outcomes, yields of major crops in India are projected to decline by 4.5 to 9 per cent within the next three decades, even allowing for short-term adaptation (Guiteras 2007). The implications of such climate change for poverty and GDP could be enormous given the projected population growth and the evidence that one percentage point of agricultural GDP growth in developing countries increases the consumption of the poorest third of the population by four to six percentage points (Ligon and Sadoulet 2007).

India has the responsibility of feeding a huge population while maintaining a healthy growth rate. Better application of known practices and fundamental transformations in natural resource management, energy provision, urbanization, social safety nets, technological innovation, and rural and urban governance are needed to meet the challenge.

Climate Change and Rural Infrastructure

Rural India has dismal infrastructure with huge potential for large investments in the sector. Investments on key rural infrastructure like roads and communication, drinking water and sanitation, education, social reforms, health, and agriculture have been the focus of successive governments both at federal and provincial levels. However, the stated emphasis has often been on employment generation rather than on asset creation (Donnges 2009). In the context of climate change and the vulnerability of poor rural communities to the changing scenario, there is a need to look into the gamut of rural infrastructure development from a different perspective. This includes some thought on how investments in this sector can reduce the vulnerability of the rural communities to the process of climate change and the adoption of new scientific tools, technology, and innovation besides dealing with adaptation to usher in new institutions and policies to govern change. The entire process demands resources and willingness to manage the required change. This chapter examines challenges and suggests opportunities for smart investments that can help reduce carbon footprints in an already energy-hungry infrastructure-poor sector.

Rural Infrastructure Development and Resource Management: Investment Justified

'Ecosystems are critical to people's livelihoods and they are also profitable, and they should be invested in as development infrastructure, just as you would invest in bricks, pipes and dams', said John Waugh, Senior Fellow, International Union for Conservation of Nature, as reported by Hagen in the UN Chronicle Online Edition (2007).

Box 24.1.1 discusses organic farming as an example of the myriad opportunities for carbon-saving rural investments. Investing in rural infrastructure has always made good business sense, with most studies reporting a high rate of return (World Bank 2003). The Operations Evaluation Department of the World Bank (2003) reported a higher economic rate of return for road projects, for example, 40 per cent in Bangladesh during 1996–2003 and 460 per cent in Togo during 1997–2003, than for energy projects, for example, 17 per cent in Uganda during 1991–2002 and 21 per cent in Lithuania during 1994–2003. The profitability of investments in rural infrastructure goes up when profitability is measured in terms of public benefits after consideration of externalities. Because of the public good characteristics of infrastructure investments, relying on the private sector is very likely to result in underinvestment. Even the public sector may not adequately invest in infrastructure if it fails to consider external effects of infrastructure (Pinstrup-Andersen and Shimokawa 2006).

Roads and communications, electrification, health, hygiene, drinking water and sanitation, education and agriculture have long been the key sectors of rural infrastructure. It is not a matter of debate any more as to whether to invest or not in these sectors, as evidence strongly suggests long-term positive impact on poverty reduction and growth. The question now is which subsectors are more potent when it comes to offsetting the carbon footprints left behind. One needs to think carefully and then put money in such areas so the process of development could provide a win-win solution in the face of climate change. Keeping this in mind, an attempt is made to examine opportunities for investing in developing infrastructure for wasteland management; rainwater management in rainfed areas, crop residue management; value addition; storage and distribution of agricultural produce; and energy efficiency in household and farm sectors. These

Box 24.1.1
Organic Farming

'Demand for organic foods is expanding between 5 and 20 per cent annually in the United States and Europe', said Virginia Barreiro of the World Resources Institute. About one third of the world's organically managed land is located in developing countries—located largely in Latin America followed by Asia and Africa in second and third place respectively. Countries with the largest area under organic management are Argentina, Brazil, China, India, and Uruguay. Global demand for organic products remains robust, with sales increasing by over five billion USD a year. Exceptionally high growth rates have led supply to tighten in almost every sector of the organic food industry: fruits, vegetables, beverages, cereals, grains, seeds, herbs, and spices. (Willer and Kilcher 2009). India is among the few countries with such a varied agro-ecosystem that offers opportunities for growing a range of crops—nutritive cereals (millets like ragi, bajra, Setaria, etc), medicinal plants, dyes, resins, besides fruits and vegetables. The bulk of these crops is grown on the driest tracts of the country and are not fertilized with chemicals and protected with chemical pesticides. This, the main cause of low productivity and profitability, could well be turned into an opportunity for capturing the ever expanding organic foods market both at home and abroad. This requires carefully thought-out programmes and investments in need-based infrastructure and capacity building of the primary stakeholders.

Promoting organic cultivation of foods has certain challenges initially. One of the most important ones is yield decline during the initial years. This holds back many cultivators who are likely to go organic. Lack of credible market chains for organic products is another area of concern. Supporting the farmer during the initial years of switching from chemical to organic farming and promoting niche markets could be effective policy instruments that will have significant impact on carbon saving on account of (1) reduced chemical use and (2) increased use of organic waste as manure. The latter will promote better use of crop residue and weed biomass besides cattle dung, all of which are potential GHG emitters.

Source: Authors' own.

areas offer ample scope for reducing poverty and improving livelihoods besides contributing to reducing carbon footprint by switch over, reduction, and capture. Box 24.1.2 discusses an instance of how specific food-processing infrastructure at the village level can promote sustainable agricultural practices. Sectors such as transport and energy infrastructure are not covered deliberately in this chapter and the reader can refer to other sections of this report for the same.

Wasteland Management and Recreating Natural Capital

India is home to 16 per cent of the world population, while its land is only 2 per cent of the total geographical area of the world. As the pressure on the land goes beyond its carrying capacity, tracts of productive land are rendered to various degrees of degradation. At present, approximately 120 M ha of land area is categorized as wastelands/degraded lands in India (Table 24.1.1). Of this, roughly 17 M ha is unprotected open forestland, which has suffered degradation due to biotic and anthropogenic factors. The Ministry of Rural Development, Government of India, through various programmes has been investing huge sums to regain the productivity of the degraded lands. The three major flagship programmes directed at wasteland development—Integrated Wastelands Development Programme, Drought Prone Areas Programme, and Desert Development Programme—were all merged into one comprehensive programme named Integrated Watershed Management Programme (IWMP) from the fiscal year 2008–9 to restore the ecological balance by harnessing, conserving, and developing degraded natural resources such as soil, vegetative cover, and water. The allocation for the programme during the fiscal year 2009–10 is to the tune of Rs 20,210 million. The expected outcomes are: prevention of soil run-off, regeneration of natural vegetation, improved capacity for rainwater harvesting, and recharging of the groundwater table. This, in turn, is expected to enable multi-cropping and diverse agro-based activities, which help in the promotion of sustainable rural livelihoods. There is ample evidence to support the assertion that investment in watershed management often brings very high dividends both at farm and ecosystem levels (Kerr et al. 2000; Dixit et al. 2005; and Venkateswarlu and Dixit 2009).

The watershed development programme is generally focused on augmenting the productivity of rainfed areas (those which depend on only rainwater for crop production), which constitute nearly 58 per cent of the total cultivable land of the country. In the process it also addresses the larger issue of poverty alleviation and livelihood improvement. Improvement of productivity of rainfed areas is an outcome of better production technologies, reasonably priced credit and support systems, and enabling institutions, besides storage, value addition, and market infrastructure. It has been the experience of most development initiatives in rainfed areas that the adoption of resource conserving technologies needs enabling

Box 24.1.2
Mill for Processing Pesticide-free Pigeonpea: A Win-win For All

Over 300,000 farmers have adopted Community Managed Sustainable Agriculture (CMSA) in Andhra Pradesh, covering 1.36 million acres of farmland—5.1 per cent of the net cropped area in the state—in just over four years, that is, since 2004 (Kumar et al. 2009). This has raised the awareness about pesticide-free agricultural produce among a large section of farmers in Andhra Pradesh. Watershed Support Services Network (WASSAN), an NGO which is implementing the National Agricultural Innovation Project (NAIP) Component 3 subproject on sustainable rural livelihoods at a cluster of villages including Ibrahimpur in Rangareddy district on the outskirts of Hyderabad is promoting non-pesticide pigeonpea production as part of project interventions. There is considerable area under pigeonpea production without using chemical pesticides. One of the demands of the farmers on the project was to set up a processing facility to separately mill the pigeonpea produced without chemical pesticides. The community impressed upon the village panchayat to allot a piece of land where a modest structure could be built to house the pigeonpea dal (split grain) mill. The project assisted the community to procure a dal mill and install it at Ibrahimpur village, which is run by groups of trained women who are provided with a modest amount of the revolving fund to purchase and process pigeonpea from the surrounding villages. The mill is providing a niche market to the pesticide-free produce besides providing gainful employment to illiterate and semi-illiterate women. This special infrastructure at the village level can reinforce a changed practice (producing pesticide-free pigeonpea) which has implications for the environment as well.

Source: NAIP Component 3 subproject, CRIDA.

TABLE 24.1.1 Harmonized Area Statistics of Wastelands/Degraded Lands of India (M ha)

S.No.	*Type of degradation*	*Arable land (M ha)*	*Open forest land (<40% Canopy) (M ha)*	*Data source*
1.	Water erosion (>10 t/ha/yr)	73.27	9.30	Soil loss map, CSWCR&TI
2.	Wind erosion (Aeolian)	12.40	–	Wind erosion map, CAZRI
	Sub total	85.67	9.30	
3.	Chemical degradation			
	A. Exclusively salt-affected soils	5.44	–	National salt-affected soil map, CSSRI, NBSS&LUP, NRSA and others
	B. Salt-affected and water eroded soils	1.20	0.10	
	C. Exclusively acidic soils (pH<5.5)#	5.09	–	Acid soil map of NBSS&LUP
	D. Acidic (pH <5.5) and water eroded soils#	5.72	7.13	
	Sub total	17.45	7.23	
4.	Physical degradation			
	A. Mining and industrial waste	0.19	–	Wasteland map of NRSA
	B. Waterlogging (Permanent surface inundation)$	0.88	–	
	Sub total	1.07		
	Total	104.19	16.53*	
	Grand total (Arable land and open forest)	120.72		

Notes: # Acid soils under paddy growing and plantation crops were excluded from degraded land.
$ Sub-surface waterlogging was not considered.
* Another 8.3 M ha was exclusively open forest which did not correspond to any land degradation class. This may be due to excessive biotic interference or open canopy due to ecological factors like aridity and has not been included in the wasteland/degraded land map/figure.
Source: National Rainfed Area Authority (NRAA), Government of India.

support systems (Chary et al. 2007). Hence the focus is on investing in both soft and hard infrastructure for building an enabling environment for an efficient rural production system. This has come to be known as watershed-plus approach in recent times, as it goes beyond resource conservation measures and addresses larger issues of rural livelihoods dependent on natural resources.

There is a wide range of opportunities not only for building a carbon neutral infrastructure but also for turning the system carbon-positive by altering and strengthening production practices through working with the stakeholder communities. Conservation farming, rainwater harvesting and recycling; agri-horti systems and horti-pastoral systems; integrated nutrient and pest management; vermicomposting, bio-inputs, biogas production and distribution could be core investment areas for carbon saving and carbon capture options. Increasing the tree cover in these degraded lands not only sequesters carbon but also arrests the soil degradation process further and enhances income from these lands. Investing on support systems by building storage and value addition facilities; markets and training, and community capacity building institutions could ensure sustainable carbon-sensitive behavioural change among the stakeholders.

Rainwater Management in Rainfed Areas

Nearly two thirds of agricultural area in the country is monsoon-fed; and, despite best efforts, one half of the total cultivated area in India will remain rainfed forever (Singh et al. 2000). Hence, the key to increasing food production depends on how well the rainwater is utilized.

Providing water for irrigation in the large dry tracts of the country is going to be environmentally and socially a very costly proposition. For example, the irrigation project at Gosekhurd in the parched areas of the drought-prone Bhandara district of Maharashtra was originally estimated at Rs 352 crore in 1982, but grew to a phenomenal Rs 7777 crore by the time of completion and resulted in a de-settlement of over 2 lakh people (Hardikar 2008). Large projects that take off due to regional aspirations backed by political will cannot sustain due to spiralling costs. For instance, the upper Wardha dam, one of the biggest in the drought-prone western Vidarbha region of Maharashtra was originally built to serve at least 2 lakh ha. But, today it irrigates just about 10000 ha due to incomplete canal network, and, at best, meets the drinking water needs of Amravati, Badnera, and Morshi towns (ibid.).

Contrary to this, investments made on building check dams, percolation ponds, farm ponds, gully plugs, tree planting, and other soil and water conservation measures which are spread across the length and breadth of a watershed lack the spectacular view of a huge dam, but help distribute the benefits of investment more equitably across parched lands. A series of over 13,000 check dams and farm bunds built all over the drought-prone areas of Yavatmal district of Maharashtra has brought hundreds of acres into double cropping by impounding a whopping 56 m cu m of water (ibid.). There were several hidden benefits to this effort as well. The water table went up in open as well as tube wells. People migrating during dry seasons stayed back to tend their second crop. Above all, there was no displacement of any household from this area. Despite the spectacular results (see Box 24.1.3) such efforts, are not backed by strong policies in the current political economy.

Yet another alternative is altering the process of cultivation for water-intensive crops. Box 24.1.4 discusses alterations in the process of rice farming.

Box 24.1.3
Farm Ponds: Harbingers of Better Livelihood

Namdev is a tribal farmer in the Seethagondi cluster of villages in Adilabad district of north Telangana, Andhra Pradesh. He has just a patch of two acres of dryland where he cultivates cotton and pigeon pea. It was in 2007 that he first met the staff of NAIP to check if the project has something to offer to him. The pressure of mounting debts due to frequent crop failures pushed him to seek some help. His condition was pathetic. His family had to do without a wholesome meal many times a week. His only daughter who is five years old could not be sent to school as he did not have any means for her schooling.

The project staff offered him assistance to dig a farm pond on his small patch of land as part of its rainwater harvesting initiative. At this point in time investing in water resource development and land development was beyond the imagination of Namdev. He was not quite convinced but after prolonged persuasion he gave into the idea.

Based on the topo sequence, average rainfall, runoff potential, and assessment of soil characteristics, a spot was identified to dig a farm pond of a dimension of 17m × 17m. Though Namdev was poor, his small plot is rich with deep black soil that has a high clay content, which he had no idea of. The initial rains brought heavy runoff and filled the farm pond to the brim. Though there was happiness in the family to see the impounded water, they thought that it would percolate and disappear within a week or two. The fine clay helped seal the bottom and the water stayed on for days, weeks, and then even for months. Meanwhile, the pond overflowed several times due to heavy rains during the end of August, 2008. Once there was confidence that the water was going to stay, Namdev rented out a diesel pumpset and drew pipelines to a distance of 500 ft and planned for tomatoes in a half-acre patch. By the time the crop reached maturity, the prices of tomatoes had peaked. Thanks to the sky-high prices, the tomatoes were sold at Rs 20/kg at the farm gate. Namdev sold tomatoes worth over Rs 25,000, cleared all his debts, and started dreaming of a good life. The farm pond became a mark of hope for the poor Namdev and his family.

Source: NAIP Component 3 subproject, CRIDA.

Box 24.1.4
System of Rice Intensification: Strategy for Adaptation and Mitigation?

Anaerobic decomposition of organic material in flooded rice fields produces CH_4 (methane), which escapes into the atmosphere primarily by diffusive transport through the rice plants during the growing season. There are large spatial and temporal variations of methane fluxes, which occur due to different soil types, soil organic carbon, and various agricultural practices such as choice of water management and cultivar, the application of organic amendments, the mineral fertilizer, and soil organic carbon.

Nearly a fourth of the gross cropped area is under rice cultivation in India. Of the total rice cultivated area only a half of it is irrigated while the other half is rainfed. Rice is cultivated under various water management options, depending on the availability of water across the country. In the mountainous regions, rice is grown in terraces created along the side of the mountains. In most of the northern plains and some parts of the eastern region, rice is cultivated by irrigating the fields intermittently or continuously, for a considerable period of time. In other parts of the country, however, rainfed rice cultivation is predominant where water is available in the fields only during the rainy season. Deep-water rice cultivation, with a water depth ranging from 50–100 cm is also practised in the coastal regions of West Bengal and Orissa. Methane flux measurement on a national scale in such representative water regimes have been made since 1991 under various campaigns using the Perspex box technique. National methane emission coefficients generated by this method estimated total CH_4 released from rice cultivation in 1994 to be 4,090 Gg (Natcom 2004).

As the income of the people is rising, the food preferences are rapidly changing in favour of fine cereals like rice. Due to this, there is growing pressure on land for increasing production and productivity of rice. Shrinking water resources have made this task even more daunting. Hence, there is a constant effort for developing alternate methods of efficient rice production. The system of rice intensification (SRI) is one such alternative, which has spread rapidly in recent times. It was developed through on-farm research conducted in Madagascar and is being promoted by NGOs, enthusiasts, and innovative farmers as an integrated and agroecologically sound approach for rice cultivation. As an alternative to the high water consuming conventional practice, the SRI uses less of water and external inputs while producing higher output. It involves planting of younger rice seedlings (15-day-old seedlings as against 25–30-day-old ones) at a wider spacing as compared to conventional methods. SRI also advocates maintaining mostly aerobic soil conditions, applying compost in preference to chemical fertilizers, avoiding complete flooding of the field by maintaining reduced water supply only in furrows made in the fields, and active participation and involvement of farmers in research and knowledge generation. More yields with less water makes this methodology a unique pathway for farmers constrained by water availability as a consequence of climate change.

Rice paddy soils have the potential to emit both of the greenhouse gases methane (CH_4) and nitrous oxide (N_2O), depending on redox[1] potential. Pro-SRI enthusiasts argue that unflooded paddies do not produce methane, one of the major 'greenhouse gases' that is contributing to global warming. And that there can be more nitrous oxide from unflooded paddies, which offsets to some extent the gains from reducing methane emissions, but when nitrogen fertilizer is not used, this effect should be small. These assumptions are not backed up by large-scale field research evidence. However, a study conducted in controlled conditions on emission from rice paddies concludes that simultaneous minimization of both CH_4 and N_2O emission cannot be maintained in rice soils due to the redox potential that changes with depth, but that appropriate water and residue management can reduce greenhouse gas emissions. Without residue incorporation, continuous flooding has the lowest combined risk of N_2O and CH_4 emission, but with residue incorporation, alternate wetting, and drying (as practised in the SRI method) has similar or lower risk. These were the results of incubation studies with homogenized soil leading to a proposed 'healthy redox potential' range that minimizes both CH_4 and N_2O emission. Here it was examined whether controlled irrigation with the water-saving practice of 'safe alternate wetting and drying' could maintain a healthy redox potential throughout the rooting layer of rice paddy soil in a greenhouse experiment without plants (Johnson-Beebout et al. 2009).

Thus the CDM credentials of SRI have yet to be established. But this does not take away SRI's water saving credit, which has a strong bearing on adaptation to climate change. There is plenty of research evidence to show this attribute of SRI. The China Agricultural University evaluation of SRI in a Sichuan village found that SRI reduced water requirements 45.8 per cent, with increased yield (Xiaoyun 2005). The Tamil Nadu Agricultural University evaluation of SRI in the Tamraparani delta of India found that SRI reduced water requirements by 40–50 per cent (Thiyagarajan 2004). From the data in the IWMI evaluation of SRI in Sri Lanka, it can be calculated that the hours of irrigation were reduced by 21 per cent. Given higher SRI yields, water productivity (kg of rice produced per irrigation hour) increased by 90 per cent with SRI (Namara et al. 2003).

SRI also has some desirable externalities that go beyond the agricultural sector. By reducing the demands that rice farmers make on surface irrigation and groundwater supplies, SRI should take pressure off scarce freshwater and aquifer supplies. Aquatic

(contd.)

[1] Reduction potential (also known as redox potential, oxidation / reduction potential or ORP) is a measure of the tendency of a chemical species to acquire electrons and thereby be reduced. Reduction potential is measured in volts (V), millivolts (mV), or E_h (1 E_h = 1 mV). Each species has its own intrinsic reduction potential; the more positive the potential, the greater the species' affinity for electrons and tendency to be reduced.

Box 24.1.4 (*contd.*)

ecosystems in particular should benefit from reductions in the need for and use of agrochemicals. This is recognized by WWF's Living Waters Programme, which is currently funding a systematic evaluation of SRI in Andhra Pradesh, India (Prasad 2006). By increasing output from irrigated rice production in Madagascar and other countries, pressures for the expansion of shifting upland cultivation at the expense of remaining forest ecosystems are being reduced. Progress in extending upland SRI production could reduce the need/incentive for shifting cultivation once labour can be more productively employed in this new system compared to the continued practice of slash-and-burn. Reduced use of agrochemicals should enhance the health of cultivators and will also by diminishing chemical residues on rice and other food, SRI should contribute to better health for consumers as well. Further, if applications of nitrogen fertilizer can be reduced, this should enhance groundwater quality by diminishing nitrate concentrations. Besides, reduced chemical fertilizer use in this process is itself an adaptation measure to climate change.

Source: Authors' own.

Crop Residue Management

Biomass energy can play a major role in reducing India's reliance on fossil fuels by making use of thermo-chemical conversion technologies. In addition, the increased utilization of biomass-based fuels will be instrumental in safeguarding the environment, creating new job opportunities, sustainable development, and health improvements in rural areas. Biomass energy could also aid in modernizing the agricultural economy. A large amount of energy is expended in the cultivation and processing of crops like sugarcane, foodgrains, vegetables, and fruits, which can be recovered by utilizing energy-rich residues for energy production. The integration of biomass-fuelled gasifiers and coal-fired energy generation would be advantageous in terms of improved flexibility in response to fluctuations in biomass availability with lower investment costs. Waste-to-energy plants offer twin benefits of environmentally sound waste management and disposal, as well as the generation of clean electric power. Waste-to-energy facilities produce clean, renewable energy through thermochemical, biochemical, and physicochemical methods. Moreover, waste-to-energy plants are highly efficient in harnessing the untapped sources of energy from a variety of wastes.

Livestock keeping has been an integral part of agriculture in India. Livestock provides an excellent recycling arrangement for most of crop residue. Most by products of cereals, pulses, and oilseeds are useful as feed and fodder for livestock while that of other crops like cotton, maize, pigeonpea, castor, and sunflower, and sugarcane are used as low calorie fuel or burnt to ashes or left in the open to decompose over time. Ideally, such residue is incorporated into soil to enhance physical properties of the soil and its water holding capacity. Lack of availability of proper chipping and soil incorporation equipment is one of the major reasons for the colossal wastage of agricultural biomass in India. Increased cost of labour and transport is another reason for lack of interest in utilizing the biomass. Table 24.1.2 shows the quantum of crop residue, which goes unutilized every year. This is one area where little or no effort has gone in despite availability of opportunities for reasons such as aggregation, transport, and investment in residue processing facilities. Many technologies like briquetting, anaerobic digestion,[2] vermicomposting, and bio-char (Box 24.1.5 and Box 24.1.6), etc., exist, but they have not been commercially exploited. This area assumes great importance and is gradually receiving attention as a means to producing clean energy by substituting forest biomass for domestic needs. Modest investments in decentralized facilities for anaerobic digestion of agricultural residue through vermicomposting and biogas generation can meet the needs of energy-deficit rural areas.

TABLE 24.1.2 Estimated Crop Residues (Million tonnes) in India (2006–7)*

Crop Residue	*Dry Weight*
Cotton stalks	16.36
Maize cobs	2.72
Pigeonpea	6.93
Sunflower	2.46
Castor	1.41

Note: *Estimated using crop production statistics obtained from Directorate of Economics and Statistics, Ministry of Agriculture, Govt. of India. Computed using harvest index or grain-straw ratios.

[2] Anaerobic digestion is the natural, biological degradation of organic matter in the absence of oxygen, yielding biogas. The projects are based upon recovering biogas for the generation of electricity. Heat, odour, and GHG are captured and converted into energy; anaerobic digestion is the only waste management system that captures biogas (methane) produced by the farming industry and reduces dependence on fossil fuels while de-escalating energy production costs.

Box 24.1.5

Biochar—A Potential Technique for Carbon Sequestration and Soil Fertility Improvement

When biomass is exposed to moderate temperatures, between about 400 and 500°C (a kind of low-temperature pyrolysis), under complete or partial exclusion of oxygen, biomass undergoes exothermic processes and releases a multitude of gases in addition to heat along with biochar (Czernik and Bridgwater 2004). Pyrolysis produces biochar, a carbon-rich, fine-grained, porous substance and solid byproduct, similar in its appearance to charcoal, which when returned to soil, produces a range of environmental benefits, such as enhanced soil carbon sequestration and soil fertility improvement (Lehmann 2007). Both heat and gases can be captured to produce energy carriers such as electricity, hydrogen, or bio-oil, which can be used as a fuel for various purposes in the process of manufacturing biochar. In addition to energy, certain valuable co-products, including wood preservative, food flavouring, adhesives, etc., can be obtained (Czernik and Bridgwater 2004).

This is a novel approach to sequester carbon in terrestrial ecosystems which has several associated products in the process of its manufacture and also the end product. In India, it has been projected that about 309 m t of biochar could be produced annually, the application of which might offset about 50 per cent of carbon emission (292 teragram C yr^{-1}) from fossil fuel (Lal 2005). Rice-wheat cropping system in the Indo-Gangetic plains of India produces substantial quantities of crop residues, and if these residues can be pyrolysed, 50 per cent of the carbon in biomass is returned to the soil as biochar, increasing soil fertility and crop yields, while sequestering carbon. Addition of biochar to soil has also been associated with enhanced nutrient use efficiency, water holding capacity, and microbial activity.

Source: Authors' own.

Box 24.1.6

Vermicomposting as a Community Enterprise: Many Birds in One Stone!

Management of residues in agriculture is crucial both as fodder and manure. Agricultural waste can be converted into valuable organic manure and used to substitute chemical fertilizers to a considerable extent. Several standard practices like vermicomposting are in vogue to produce good-quality organic manure. However, this process is labour-and-time intensive and hence not many households would like to adopt the practice. Besides, government incentives (in the form of subsidy) pertain only to the nutrients applied to plants through the chemical fertilizers. Further, the incentives are directly delivered to the manufacturer of chemical fertilizers and the user gets them at a discounted price. As a result, there are few incentives for a farmer to produce his own manure. Against this backdrop, promoting backyard vermicomposting units is an uphill task.

The National Agricultural Innovation Project (NAIP) is encouraging large-scale vermicomposting as a community enterprise in the Dupahad cluster of villages in the drought-prone Nalgonda district of Andhra Pradesh. Groups of youth were trained to produce vermicompost by using decomposable biomass and dung, and the farming community carts semi/undecomposed biomass from their farms and backyards to the community vermicompost units that are housed in large sheds built for the purpose. These farmers get fully decomposed vermicompost in return for the raw material supplied by them. Thus, vermicomposting has been elevated to a specialized service providing enterprise. In addition to this, a community biogas unit has been installed at the community vermicomposting unit, which is connected to a generator (15 kva) that can produce and supply electricity to about 100 houses. These add-on features will ensure the viability of vermicompost units besides contributing to clean manure and energy production. This innovation has a high degree of scalability besides generating positive externalities with respect to combating climate change.

Source: NAIP Component 3 subproject, CRIDA.

Integrated Biogas System

There is renewed interest in the use of anaerobic digestion processes for efficient management and conversion of cattle dung and other agro-industrial wastes (livestock, paper and pulp, brewery, and distillery) into clean renewable energy and organic fertilizer source. The biogas captured could not only mitigate the potential local and global pollution but could either be combusted for electricity generation using combined heat and power generators in large to medium enterprises or used for cooking and lighting for small households. A 2 m^3 digester can generate up to 4.93 t CO_2 e/year of CER. Animal wastes are generally used as feedstock in biogas plants. But, the availability of these substrates is one of the major problems hindering the successful operation of biogas digesters. Khandelwal (1990) reported that the availability of cattle waste could support only 12–30 million family-size biogas plants against the requirement of 100 million plants. A significant portion of 70–88 million biogas plants can be run with fresh/dry biomass residues. Of the available 1,150 billion tonnes of biomass, a fifth would be sufficient to meet this demand.

Fodder Densification System

Wheat and paddy straw, which is burnt in Punjab, Haryana, and western Uttar Pradesh in large quantities, is used as fodder in neighbouring Rajasthan and most southern states. These states always suffer from seasonal shortage of fodder. Only in times of fodder crisis are some efforts made to facilitate inter-state transportation of fodder residue. What is needed is a permanent arrangement to turn this 'waste' to a valuable resource. This does not need any expensive technology, but a willingness to take a long-term view and invest in facilities to compress the bulk of straw by bailing and densification to render it amenable for transport. While plenty of machinery of different capacities is available for bailing and densifying fodder, an institutional mechanism is needed to change current practices and utilize resources. This would reduce 'fodder miles',[3] as densified fodder can travel longer distances and meet seasonal deficits across states.

Since agriculture is a state subject in the federal structure, the governments of Punjab or Haryana may not see an opportunity to invest in such facilities. But fodder-scarce states like Rajasthan and Gujarat could consider investing in this area. This may involve fodder-scarce states like Rajasthan and Gujarat negotiating with fodder-rich states and establishing densification units besides putting in place a system for procuring paddy and wheat straw from disaggregated production points. While the federal government encourages state governments to invite private and overseas investment for building infrastructure, it is worthwhile examining the required modalities to encourage trends of one state investing in another. Fodder-rich states like Punjab and Haryana burn huge quantities of wheat and paddy straw or allow them to decompose (which is very rare) in the field without incorporating them in the soil,[4] resulting in GHG emissions. If such activity is penalized by imposing sanctions, the polluting states would be induced to act in favour of safe disposal of 'waste'. Here, the federal government can facilitate the establishment of fodder procurement and densification units through a tri-partite cost sharing arrangement.

Table 24.1.3 Estimated Wheat and Paddy Straw (million tonne) in Punjab and Haryana (2006–7)

State	*Wheat straw*	*Paddy straw*
Punjab	18.98	11.66
Haryana	13.78	3.89
Western UP (approx.)	3.9	2.4

Note: *Estimated using crop production statistics obtained from the Directorate of Economics and Statistics Ministry of Agriculture, Govt. of India. Computed using harvest index or grain-straw ratios.

Value Addition, Storage, and Distribution of Agricultural Produce

Compared to the developed world, India has extremely poor infrastructure for processing agricultural produce: for example, just over 2 per cent of the perishable fruits and vegetables are processed. The Indian food processing sector is highly fragmented and it comprises fruits and vegetables, milk and milk products, beer and alcoholic beverages, meat and poultry, marine products, grain processing, packaged or convenience food, and packaged drinks. A large number of entrepreneurs in this industry have small-scale production and operations, and are largely present in the unorganized segment. This segment accounts for more than 70 per cent of the output in terms of volume and 50 per cent in terms of value. Though the organized sector is comparatively small, it is growing at a faster pace.

The food processing industry comprises only 9 per cent of the total manufacturing industry of the country. Of this, about 40 per cent accounts for meat, fish, fruits, vegetables, and oils while beverages and other food products account for 20 and 25 per cent respectively (Ministry of Food Processing, Government of India). Of these, the fruit and vegetable sector draws maximum attention when it comes to post-production losses. The production of vegetables in India is next only to China. The vegetable and fruit production contributes more than 30 per cent of the agriculture GDP. Crop diversification has led to rise in horticulture production, which is currently over 192 million tonnes. But more than 70 per cent of the vegetable and fruits produced are wasted in the absence of proper retailing infrastructure. The sector is constrained by fragmentation in the supply chain, low productivity levels, and huge post-harvest losses arising out of inadequate storage, cold chain and transport infrastructure, and logistics and supply chain management. Despite different types of fruits and vegetables grown, India's export of agricultural and food products is only 1.4 per cent of

[3] Somewhat akin to food miles. Though we need to encourage local production and consumption of food and fodder, in a country like India, which has a very diverse agroecosystem, we must invest and build institutions and processes to address long-term benefits across the states.

[4] Due to lack of appropriate machinery for soil incorporation of crop residues, a huge quantity of valuable biomass goes unutilized. Soil incorporation of biomass has been shown to promote carbon sequestration.

the total global trade. There is a serious dearth of effective policy support for the growth of retail chains for fruits and vegetables in the country.

If we go by the logic 'food saved is food produced', the magnitude of gains the fruit and vegetables can accrue in terms of cost of seed, fertilizer, pesticide, water, power, labour, and precious time is enormous. Moreover, rotting of agricultural/horticultural produce has strong CO_2 equivalent emission implications.

The post-Green Revolution era had seen huge investment in storage infrastructure by the public sector, most of which is old and needs upgradation. Due to this, storage losses are also enormous. Investing in better storage infrastructure translates to higher savings on account of prevention of storage losses. There is an immediate need to not only upgrade the existing infrastructure but also to establish new ones with the state-of-the-art technology. Food Corporation of India (FCI), the largest public sector organization, which is the backbone of the centralized foodgrain procurement system, owns the largest food storage network with about 1500 godowns in the country. Together with this, the FCI also has some hired storage capacity. All this put together accounts for 26 m.t. storage capacity. Other agencies like the Central Warehouse Corporation and State Warehouse Corporations account for nearly 30 m.t. storage capacity. Most of the storage capacity is located in areas far away from the sites of consumption which are spread all over the country contributing to huge amounts of food miles.[5] Moving towards a decentralized food storage system is not only sensible but also has long lasting implications for reducing food miles besides improving access and entitlement to the needy.

Energy Efficiency in Rural Household and Farm Sectors

With nearly 70 per cent of the population residing in rural areas, the energy demand in this sector is humungous. Increasing urbanization on the other hand has always tilted the balance of investment in favour of urban areas, leaving the rural areas behind. Rural areas suffer not only poor investment but also poor-quality infrastructure in the field of energy. The rural poor thus operate systems with very low energy use efficiency. The major need of energy in rural areas lies in household lighting and cooking followed by agricultural operations, particularly irrigation. The former uses fossil fuels/firewood, while the latter electricity and fossil fuels under a low efficiency regime. The following sections discuss some domestic and farm energy consumption issues.

Reduction of Electricity Consumption through Efficient Lighting

Of the 191.9 million households in India, 138.3 m are rural (Census of India 2001). Of these rural households, 55 per cent enjoy access to electricity and per capita electricity consumption is 65 kWh per annum (CEA 2005). Use of CFLs and LEDs in rural homes presents potential energy savings of up to 80 per cent. Solar photo voltaic (PV) home light systems and solar street lighting in off-grid areas can substantially reduce the electricity consumption while improving lighting in rural areas.

Energy Efficient Water Lifting Systems and Innovative Institutions for Water Management

Of the total water used in India, 25 bcm, or 83 per cent is spent on irrigation and of this, half comes from the

Table 24.1.4 Potential Savings in Household Electricity Consumption

Details	*60 W bulbs*	*15 W CFL*	*Saving*
Cost of bulbs	Rs 10	116	–
Wattage	60	15	45
Burning hours	6 months, 1,000 hours	4 years, 8,000 hours	–
Electricity consumption/year	115	36	79
Cost/year @ Rs 2.75/ unit	Rs 316.25/-	Rs 99.00/-	Rs 217.25/-
Total cost for four years	Rs 1265.00/-	Rs 396.00/-	Rs 869.00/-

Source: Non-Conventional Energy Development Corporation of Andhra Pradesh Ltd.

[5] Locally produced fresh food is often the best environmental choice, and also helps to support local farming communities.... Generally speaking, the greater the distance food has travelled, from paddock to plate, the greater the transport pollution, and the greater the impact on the health of people, the land and the global climate—a concept known as 'food miles' (Australian Conservation Foundation 2005).

exploitation of the groundwater, using low efficiency pumps to draw water from ever increasing depths. A political economy that perpetuates this unsustainable practice is the flipside of increased access to groundwater (Table 24.1.5). Energy intensity of pumping increases further because of the falling watertable. Average annual consumption of electricity by each pumpset is 6004 kWh (CEA 2005).

TABLE 24.1.5 Number of Irrigation Pumps

Year	*Diesel pumps*	*Electric pumps*	*Total*
1951	83,000	26,000	1,09,000
1956	1,23,000	47,000	1,70,000
1961	2,30,000	1,60,000	3,90,000
1966	4,71,000	4,15,000	8,86,000
1972	15,46,000	16,18,000	31,64,000
1977	23,59,000	24,38,000	47,97,000
1982	31,01,000	35,68,000	66,69,000
1987	59,68,000	63,49,000	1,23,17,000
1991@	46,59,000	96,96,000	1,43,55,000
1995@	51,00,000	1,17,00,000	1,68,00,000
2000	55,28,470	74,64,120	129,92,590
2003	72,37,400	84,46,300	156,83,700

Note: @ Data collected from Manufacturers' Association.
Source: Directorate of Economics and Statistics, Ministry of Agriculture, Govt. of India.

Irrigation is the largest energy consumer in agriculture, which in turn accounts for more than 30 per cent of India's energy use. Use of star-rated pumpsets can bring down this consumption of energy by 30 per cent from 600 billion kWh to 420 billion kWh. With the use of capacitors up to 35 per cent energy can be saved. Studies show that improvement of pump efficiency from the current level to 41 per cent would mean GHG saving of 9 per cent and improvement of motor efficiency from the current level to 77 per cent would mean fall in GHG by 8.5 per cent. Some of the simpler modifications like decreasing the discharge velocity, improving the pump and the motor efficiency by better selection and design can be easily incorporated with little cost (Shukla et al. 2003). There are many examples across the rainfed agro-ecosystem showing successful social engineering initiatives to negotiate water-related conflicts and establish a process for amicable water use practices (See Box 24.1.7).

CONCLUSION

Infrastructure aimed at reducing carbon footprints in the agrarian sector always offers a win-win opportunity. Investing in carbon saving rural infrastructure ensures growth as well as low emissions, which is not as true in other sectors. For example, investing in decentralized rural godowns will not only ensure reduction in food miles but also facilitates quick movement of food at times of shortage due to droughts. Besides, such infrastructure

Box 24.1.7
Social Regulation of Groundwater Exploitation

Exploitation of groundwater for agriculture has had serious ramifications for sustainable resource use in general and prudent use of electric power/fossil fuels in particular. Several studies have pointed out that indebtedness due to indiscriminate digging of bore wells as one of the causes of high suicide rates in drier regions of the country (Gill and Singh 2006; Meeta and Rajivlochan 2006).

It is generally observed that the extracted groundwater is not put to efficient use, as the power used to extract the water is not priced in most states. As a result, farmers tend to use this precious resource for producing paddy, a water-intensive crop. Farmers running out of water in tubewells right in the middle of the cropping season especially in the rabi (post-monsoon) season is not uncommon. The NAIP subproject on sustainable rural livelihoods being implemented in the dry pockets of Rangareddy district engaged a few tubewell-owning farmers over the idea of growing less water-intensive crops (irrigated dry crops or ID crops) as an alternative to paddy. The tubewell-owning farmers did not like the idea at all. The project then got a defunct borewell repaired as a goodwill gesture and again approached the farmers who had mellowed down by then and agreed to share water, provided the project assisted the community for digging a few more borewells so that there was enough water to share it across a large area. This time, the project contacted NABARD for assistance who came forward with financing the digging of two tubewells in that area under their comprehensive land development programme (CLDP). This raised the hopes of several farmers, including those who owned borewells initially because with the pooling of water they could now irrigate other patches of their dry fields where they could not have reached water. Thus, the one-year long negotiations with the community to implement social regulations for groundwater usage finally yielded results. Over 40 acres of land belonging to 18 households was brought under protective irrigation by laying out a network of pipelines and borewells at Malkaipet thanda in Ibrahimpur cluster, Rangareddy district. The entire group of farmers has agreed not to cultivate rabi paddy but to share bore water among themselves for growing ID crops.

Source: NAIP Component 3 subproject, CRIDA.

will encourage diversified cropping, which in turn has implications for risk mitigation, sustaining soil health (by avoiding monocropping), and conservation of local food systems and biodiversity. Reversal to a system that encourages diversified farming will ease pressure on lands and promote sustainable land use practices by farmers that will depend less on expensive external interventions to reclaim balance (see Box 24.1.7).

India will continue to live in its rural areas despite the accelerated pace of urbanization. And with an enormous amount of development investment to go into these areas, there is abundant scope for taking informed measures to combat the ill effects of the development process. The new investment opportunities, if planned and executed well, can open new vistas into building a carbon neutral future for rural India. There is a strong need to enlarge the scope of definition of infrastructure to accommodate both its hard and soft aspects. This will help justify the much-needed investment in developing institutional and social capacity of the stakeholder communities for building and managing efficient rural infrastructure.

The efforts in this direction have been sporadic. Nevertheless, they are the torchbearers for future direction. Investing in greening wastelands could offer a sink to capture carbon while efficient handling of crop residues could help generate clean energy and meet the energy demand of the rural sector to some extent. Decentralized infrastructure for value addition, storage, and distribution of agricultural produce could help contain food miles effectively. Promoting efficient energy use by investing in right kind of technology and institutions could yield high dividends in household and farm sectors. These opportunities however are fraught with challenges both at the level of policies and institutions. But this is how opportunities throw up as challenges. The need of the hour is to respond to these challenges. For, this may the last chance to salvage the earth from the climate change disaster.

References

Anonymous (2008). *Harmonization of Wastelands/Degraded Lands Datasets of India.* National Rainfed Area Authority, Ministry of Agriculture, Government of India, New Delhi. p. 5.

Auffhammer, M., V. Ramanathan, and J.R. Vincent (2006). 'Integrated Model Shows that Atmospheric Brown Clouds and Greenhouse Gases Have Reduced Rice Harvests in India', *Proceedings of the National Academy of Sciences* 103 (52), pp. 19668–72.

Australian Conservation Foundation (2005). 'Cut Back on Food Miles', available at http://www.acfonline.org.au/news.asp?news_id=491.

Bates, B., Z.W. Kundzewicz, S. Wu, and J. Palutikof (2008). 'Climate Change and Water', Technical paper, Intergovernmental Panel on Climate Change, Geneva.

CEA (2005). *Central Electricity Authority Report (2004–5).*

Census of India (2001). *Report of the Registrar General of India,* Government of India, Ministry of Home Affairs, New Delhi, 2004.

Chary, R.G., Sreenath Dixit, K.P.R. Vittal, G. Subba Reddy, and G.R. Maruthi Sankar (2007). Technology Diffusion and Up-Scaling in Rainfed Agro Ecosystem: Policy and Institutional Approaches. *Indian J. Dryland Agric. Res. & Dev.*, 22(2), pp. 132–47.

Chen, S. and M. Ravaillon. (2008). 'The Developing World Is Poorer Than We Thought, But No Less Successful in the Fight against Poverty'. Policy Research Working Paper 4703, World Bank, Washington DC.

Cruz, R.V., H. Harasawa, M. Lal, S. Wu, Y. Anokhin, B. Punsalmaa, Y. Honda, M. Jafari, C. Li, and N. Huu Ninh. (2007). 'Asia' in M.L. Parry. O.F. Canziani, J. Palutikof, J. van der Linden, and C.E. Hanson (eds), *Climate Change 2007: Impacts, Adaptation and Vulnerability. Contribution of Working Group II to the Fourth Assessment Report of the Intergovernmental Panel on Climate Change*, Cambridge, Cambridge University Press, UK.

Czernik, S and A.V. Bridgwater (2004). 'Overview of Applications of Biomass Fast Pyrolysis Oil', *Energy Fuels*, 18, pp. 590–8.

Dixit, S., J.C. Tewari, S.P. Wani, C. Vineela, A.K. Chaurasia, and H.B. Panchal (2005). *Participatory Biodiversity Assessment: Enabling Rural Poor for Better Natural Resource Management. Report no. 18. Patancheru 502 324, Andhra Pradesh, India: International Crops Research Institute for the Semi-Arid Tropics.* J SAT Agricultural Research (e-journal), 2(1), available at *http://test1.icrisat.org/Journal/agroecosystem/v2i1/v2i1participatory.pdf*

Donnges, C. (2009). 'Addressing Unemployment and Poverty through Infrastructure Development as a Crisis Response Strategy', Background Paper for Conference on the Impact of the Global Economic Slowdown on Poverty and Sustainable Development in Asia and the Pacific, Hanoi, Vietnam. 28–30 September 2009.

Dutta, K.K., C. de Jong, and O.P. Singh (2000). 'Reclaiming Salt-Affected Land through Drainage in Haryana, India: A Financial Analysis', *Agricultural Water Management*, 2000. 46(1): pp. 55–71.

Easterling, W., Aggarwal, Batima, K. Brander, L. Erda, M. Howden, A. Kirilenko, J. Morton, J.F. Soussana, J. Schmidhuber, and F. Tubiello (2007). 'Food, Fibre and

Forest Products' in M. Parry, O.F. Canziani, J. Palutikof, J. van der Linden, and C.E. Hanson (eds), *Climate Change 2007: Impacts, Adaptation and Vulnerability. Contribution of Working Group II to the Fourth Assessment Report of the Intergovernmental Panel on Climate Change*, Cambridge University Press, Cambridge, UK.

Food and Agriculture Organization of the United Nations (2006). 'Global Forest Resources Assessment 2005. Progress Towards Sustainable Forest Management'. FAO Forestry Paper 147.

Gill, A. and L. Singh (2006). 'Farmers' Suicides and Response of Public Policy: Evidence, Diagnosis and Alternatives from Punjab', available at http://mpra.ub.uni-muenchen.de/146/ MPRA Paper No. 146.

Guiteras, R. (2007). 'The Impact of Climate Change on Indian Agriculture'. Department of Economics Working Paper, Massachusetts Institute of Technology, Cambridge, USA: Massachusetts.

Hardikar, J. (2008). 'Vidarbha Distress: "Relief" Irrigation Increasing Worried for Farmers. India Together, available at http://www.indiatogether.org/2008/may/env-vidwater.htm.

Harrington, J. and T.L. Walton (2008). 'Climate Change in Coastal Areas in Florida: Sea Level Rise Estimation and Economic Analysis to Year 2080', Florida State University, Tallahassee, Florida, USA.

Indian Network of Climate Change Assessment (INCCA) (2007). *India's Greenhouse Gas Emissions 2007*, Report by the Indian Network of Climate Change Assessment (INCCA). Ministry of Environment and Forests, Government of India, available at http://moef.nic.in/downloads/others/Preparing%20GHG_Sumana%20Bhattacharya1.pdf

Institute of Water Modelling and Center for Environmental and Geographical Information Services (2007). *Investigating the Impact of Relative Sea-Level Rise on Coastal Communities and Their Livelihoods in Bangladesh*, Dhaka.

Intergovernmental Panel on Climate Change (IPCC) (2007). 'Summary for Policymakers' in M. L. Parry, O.F. Canziani, J.P. Palutikof, P.J. Van der Linden, and C.E. Hanson (eds), *Climate Change 2007: Impacts, Adaptation and Vulnerability. Contribution of Working Group II to the Fourth Assessment Report of the Intergovernmental Panel on Climate Change*, Cambridge University Press, Cambridge, UK.

International Energy Agency [IEA] (2008). *World Energy Outlook 2008*, IEA, Paris.

Institute of Water Modelling (IWM) and Center for Environmental and Geographical Information Services (CEGIS) (2007). *Investigating the Impact of Relative Sea-Level Rise on Coastal Communities and Their Livelihoods in Bangladesh*, IWM, CEGIS, Dhaka.

Johnson-Beebout, S.E., O.R. Angelesa, M.C.R. Alberto, and R.J. Buresh (2009). 'Simultaneous Minimization of Nitrous Oxide and Methane Emission from Rice Paddy Soils is Improbable due to Redox Potential Changes with Depth in a Greenhouse Experiment without Plants', *Geoderma*, 149(1–2), pp. 45–53, 15 February.

Kerr, J., G. Pangare, V.L. Pangare, and P.J. George (2000). 'An Evaluation of Dryland Watershed Development Projects in India', EPTD Discussion paper no. 68. Environment and Production Technology Division, International Food Policy Research Institute, Washington DC, USA.

Khandelwal, K.C. (1990). 'Biogas Technology Development and Implementation Strategies: Indian Experience'. Proceedings of the International Conference on Biogas Technology, Implementation Strategies, Pune, India. 10–15 January (Bremen, Ed.Borda).

Kumar, T.V., D.V. Raidu, J. Killi, M. Pillai, P. Shah, V. Kalavakonda, and S. Lakhey (2009). 'Ecologically Sound, Economically Viable Community Managed Sustainable Agriculture in Andhra Pradesh'. World Bank, Washington DC.

Lal, R. (2005). 'Carbon sequestration and climate change with special reference to India. Proc International Conference on Soil, Water and Environmental Quality—Issues and Strategies, Indian Soc. Soil Sci., Division of SS & Ac, IARI, New Delhi, India, pp. 295–302.

Lehmann, J. (2007). 'A Handful of Carbon', *Nature*, 447, pp. 143–4.

Ligon, E. and E. Sadoulet (2007). 'Estimating the Effects of Aggregate Agricultural Growth on the Distribution of Expenditures'. Background paper for the World Development Report 2008, World Bank, Washington DC.

Meeta and Rajivlochan (2006). 'Farmers' Suicide: Facts and Policy Interventions'. Yashvantrao Chavan Academy of Development Administration, Pune, India.

Namara, R.E., P. Weligamage, and R. Barker (2003). 'Prospects for Adopting System of Rice Intensification in Sri Lanka: A Socioeconomic Assessment', *Research Report*,75, International Water Management Institute, Colombo.

Natcom (2004). India's Initial National Communication. Ministry of Environment and Forests, Government of India, available at www.natcomindia.org/publication_govt.htm

Operations Evaluation Department of the World Bank (2003). 'Annual Report of Development Evaluation'. World Bank, Washington DC.

Pinstrup-Andersen, P. and S. Shimokawa (2006). 'Rural Infrastructure and Agricultural Development'. Department of Applied Economics and Management, Cornell University, USA.

Ravindra Chary, G., Sreenath Dixit, K.P.R. Vittal, G. Subba Reddy, and G.R. Maruthi Sankar (2007). 'Technology Diffusion and Up-scaling in Rainfed Agro Ecosystem: Policy and Institutional Approaches', *Indian Journal of Dryland Agricultural Research and Development*, 22(2), pp. 132–47.

Prasad, C.S. (2006). 'System of Rice Intensification—Innovation History and Institution Challenges', WWF Project 'Dialogue on Water, Food and Environment', ICRISAT, Patancheru, India.

Schmidhuber, J. and F.N. Tubiello (2007). 'Global food security under climate change'. *PNAS*. 104(5), pp. 19703–88.

Shukla, P.R., R. Nair, M. Kapshe, A. Garg, S. Balasubramaniam, D. Menon, and K.K. Sharma (2003). 'Development and Climate Change: An Assessment for India', Indian Institute of Management, Ahmedabad.

Singh, H.P., B. Venkateswarlu, and Sreenath Dixit (2000). 'Sustainable Land Use Practices for Combating Desertification', CRIDA, Hyderabad. Draft National Action Plan, p. 80.

Thiyagarajan, T.M. (2004). 'On-form Evaluation of SRI in Tamraparani Command Area, Tamil Nadu, India', Paper presented in World Rice Research Conference, Tsukuba, Japan, November.

United Nations (2008). *The Millennium Development Goals Report 2008*. UN, New York.

UN Chronicle Online Edition (2007). Available at http://www.un.org/Pubs/chronicle/2007/webArticles/031307_business.htm

Venkateswarlu, B. and S. Dixit (2009). 'Sustainable Rural Livelihoods Through Enhanced Farming Systems Productivity and Efficient Support Systems in Rainfed Areas', *Annual Report 2009*, CRIDA, Hyderabad, pp. 60.

Willer, H. and L. Kilcher (eds) (2009). *The World of Organic Agriculture: Statistics and Emerging Trends 2009,* International Federation of Organic Agriculture Movements (IFOAM). Bonn, Germany, Research Institute of Organic Agriculture (FiBL) Frick, Switzerland; International Trade Centre (ITC), Geneva, Switzerland.

World Bank (1994). 'World Development Report 1994: Infrastructure for Development: World Development Indicators'. Washington DC.

——— (2009). *Global Monitoring Report 2009: A Development Emergency*, Washington DC.

——— (2003). *World Development Report 2003: Sustainable Development in a Dynamic World: Transforming Institutions, Growth, and Quality of Life*, copublication of the World Bank and Oxford University Press, New York.

Xiaoyun, Li (2005). 'A Socio-Economic Assessment of the System of Rice Intensification (SRI): A Case Study of Xinsheng Village, Jianyang County, Sichuan Province', College of Humanities and Development, China Agricultural University, Beijing.

Part 2 Carbon Sequestration Options in Forestry

Bhaskar Sinha, Anoma Basu, and Anuj Singh Katiyar

Introduction

Most nations including India have responded to the climate change challenge by formulating policy and using technological innovations to curb net GHGs emissions (reduction and sequestration of GHGs). National Action Plan for Climate Change (NAPCC) is one such comprehensive initiative that identifies measures to promote the development objectives while yielding co-benefits for addressing climate change effectively. India is only next to China in terms of the total number of registered projects and CER issued world-wide under the CDM.[1]

Most of the CDM projects are renewable energy and energy-efficiency related and very few forestry projects have been taken up. One of the reasons attributed to this could be the absence of a methodology for exact estimation of carbon emission/reduction in the forestry sector and its amorphous ownership. However, this sector has immense potential in reducing GHGs and contributing towards adaptation to climate change. The paper explores ways to unlock the potential of the forestry sector in contributing towards low carbon economy.

Carbon Sequestration through Forestry

The sources of emission of CO_2 are numerous; however, the natural sinks of carbon are limited to only green plants, soil, and sea. Forests play an important role in the global carbon cycle accounting for 54 per cent of the 2,200 Gt[2] of the total carbon pool in terrestrial ecosystems.[3] There exists further potential for offsetting carbon through afforestation and reducing degradation, which could be instrumental in sustaining a low carbon economy. According to a study conducted by Winjum et al. (1992).[4] across 94 nations, the most promising management practices for offsetting carbon are reforestation in the temperate and tropical latitudes, afforestation in the temperate regions, and agroforestry and natural reforestation in the tropics.

The total carbon stock of Indian forests was estimated by the Forest Survey of India in collaboration with the Forest Research Institute, Dehradun as a part of the study conducted for India's first national communication to the UNFCCC.[5] The growing stock, biomass, and carbon content in the forests of India for the years 1989 and 1997 are as reported in Table 24.2.1. A state-wise estimation for growing stock, biomass, and carbon of forests is also available from the same study.

Table 24.2.1 Total Biomass and Carbon Stock in Indian Forests (above ground)

Assessment year	*1989*	*1997*
Growing Stock (million m^3)	4328.5	4340.0
Biomass (million tonne)	2398.5	2395.4
Carbon (million tonne)	1085.2	1083.8

Source: Forest Survey of India (2002).

In the case of any forest land acting as a sink, the stored carbon is present in the biomass above and below the ground, including forest soil. The total carbon stored in Indian forests is estimated by Ravindranath et al. as 9578 million tonnes for the year 1986.[6] Calculation of net carbon emissions resulting from the forestry sector, lead to the conclusion that Indian forests will, at best, remain carbon-neutral till 2011 at the current rate of afforestation

[1] http://cdm.unfccc.int/Statistics/Issuance/CERsIssuedByHostPartyPieChart.html (retrieved 12 May 2010).

[2] 1 GT (Gigaton) = 10^9 tonnes.

[3] FAO (2001).

[4] Winjum et al. (1992).

[5] Forest Survey of India (2002).

[6] Ravindranath et al. (1997).

and projected emissions under a 'business as usual' scenario.[7] This implies that reduction in carbon emissions from the forest sectors by controlling fires, regulating harvesting, and checking deforestation and degradation may lead to a situation where the forests can act as a net sink.

The Green India Mission under the National Action Plan on Climate Change has reiterated the target of achieving 33 per cent of area under forest and tree cover as against 23 per cent area under forest at present. A sum of Rs 6000 crore has been already earmarked to aid the mission of Green India through the Compensatory Afforestation Management and Planning Authority (CAMPA). The activities for afforestation and rehabilitation will be taken up in consultation with the local communities. It is important to consider that the amount of land within recorded forest area currently devoid of forest and can be reforested is only 1.44 per cent of the total geographical area.[8] This implies that forestry activities should be undertaken outside the recorded forest area not only for the additional carbon sequestration they will provide, but also because such activity would contribute towards realization of the national goal of bringing one third of the national geographical area under forest and tree cover by 2020. This also implies that forestry activities need to be practised in private, community, and government lands in both rural and urban set-ups. With proper technology and expertise, degraded land may be brought under productive use by bringing them under forest/tree cover. India's recent initiatives to address climate change recognize activities done under National Rural Employment Guarantee Schemes (NREGS) as one of the measures towards adaptation and mitigation as a high proportion of water and soil conservation activities, promotion of plantations in individual farms and community lands, etc., are supported under NREGS.

Political and administrative will is a key requirement for afforestation and maintenance of forests. The state government of Orissa, for example, has issued a circular directing the Forest Department to leverage at least 10 per cent of the total district's NREGS fund to take up more departmental activities. In Haryana, although the recorded forest area is only 3.52 per cent of the geographical area, the total tree and forest cover is 6.8 per cent.[9] This has come about in the wake of initiatives taken up by both the Forest Department as well as farmers in multiple-type of forestry initiatives outside recorded forest area, including benefiting from CDM projects (Box 24.2.1).

Box 24.2.1
Afforestation and Reforestation CDM Projects in India

- The first CDM Afforestation and Reforestation project in India is registered by the name 'Small Scale Cooperative Afforestation CDM Pilot Project Activity on Private Lands Affected by Shifting Sand Dunes in Sirsa, Haryana'.[10] The project proposes plantation development in the western belt of Haryana, which shares its border with Rajasthan at the north-eastern fringe of the Thar Desert. Affected by Aeolian sand, the degraded part of croplands, are generally left fallow. The affected area is spread across eight villages, comprising 369.87 ha belonging to 227 farmers. The main objectives of this project are:
  - To earn carbon credits from growing of trees;
  - To help in mitigation of global warming by carbon sequestration;
  - To improve the local environmental condition of soil through increasing the water holding capacity of the lands, increasing the humus in soil and stabilizing the sand dunes;
  - To increase income, provide employment opportunities, and alleviate poverty.
- Another ongoing CDM Afforestation and Reforestation project in India is the project entitled 'Reforestation of severely degraded landmass in Khammam District of Andhra Pradesh, India under ITC Social Forestry Project'[11] by M/s ITC. Under this project, the 4773 ha private wasteland owned by rural poor (tribals) is developed for raising eucalyptus plantations. The tribal beneficiaries group into a Sangha (User Groups/Society) for planting and maintaining the plantations. ITC provides quality planting stock, free extension service to the beneficiaries apart from financing the entire project activity. ITC will buy back the wood at market price and the entire proceeds of wood sale will be given to the Sangha, who in turn meet their economic needs and sustainably manage the plantations apart from developing new plantations. This project started in 2001 and the project duration is 30 years.
- Delhi government has also initiated a similar small-scale CDM Afforestation and Reforestation project which is in the pipeline.[12]

[7] Ravindranath et al. (1997).

[8] Sharma (2004).

[9] Forest Survey of India (2009).

[10] http://cdm.unfccc.int/Projects/DB/TUEV-SUED1229620290.53/view

[11] http://cdm.unfccc.int/Projects/DB/BVQI1222275709.04/view

[12] http://cdm.unfccc.int/UserManagement/FileStorage/MZDLPCE6W1B403IGKXHSY75JOTAR82

The Haryana Forest Department had taken up a number of afforestation projects like the Social Forestry Project (1982–91), Aravalli Project (1991–99), Community Forestry Project (1998–2008), and the currently ongoing project of Integrated Natural Resource Management and Poverty Reduction with financial assistance from the Japan International Cooperation Agency (JICA). The current project, is being implemented in 800 villages spanning 17 districts in the state, with soil and water conservation activities (in the form of construction of new water harvesting dams and rehabilitation of existing ones, rehabilitation of village ponds), and plantations in the form of strip, block community, and farm forestry targeting a total of 48800 ha of total land area under green cover.[13]

Rural Forestry

In the rural set-up, forestry activities may be taken up in community land as well as in private land. In private land the potential of agro-forestry or agro-horticulture may be considered as they provide opportunities for economic benefits to the land owners and also create standing biomass for long-term carbon storage as compared to agricultural crops whose carbon sequestering capacities are limited to a season due to their short lifespan. A study by Chandran et al.[14] on the effect of vegetation on ferruginous soils in semi-arid tropics reveal that the soil organic carbon (SOC) in the top soil was maximum in forests, intermediate in soil under horticulture, and least in case of agriculture. The study indicated that the value of SOC decreased from 1.78 to 0.68 per cent in the first 30 cm, when the soils are used for agriculture instead of being retained as forest. A shift from an agricultural to horticultural system over 20 years increased the value to 0.81 per cent, indicating accumulation of SOC. So under tree cover, not only is the carbon sequestering capacity of the soil greater, but also soil fertility is maintained and soil exhaustion controlled. With proper technical advice from the horticulture department, farmers may be able to maintain their lands under agro-horticulture so as to have optimal economic returns and also meet the needs of increased carbon sequestration as well as increase of total tree/forest cover of the country.

Similar benefits would also result from agro-forestry options. The most common forms of agro-forestry practices are intercropping agricultural crops with forest/tree species for provision of forest products as well as agricultural products, boundary, and contour planting of trees for additional benefit of protection against wind and water erosion. Mohapatra[15] reports in his study that out of the total cropped area of 140 M ha in India, the area available for subsistence agro-forestry would be 10 M ha of irrigated area and 18 M ha of rainfed area. Agro-forestry practices indirectly help in increase of carbon stock by reducing pressure on the forest for fuel and fodder thereby decreasing the possibilities of deforestation or degradation of forests. A particular case study[16] on the development of an agro-forestry project in Khammam district of Andhra Pradesh shows that the additional carbon sequestration potential under the project scenario for 30 years is estimated to be 12.82 tC/ha/year inclusive of harvest regimes and carbon emissions due to biomass burning and fertilizer application. Further, switching over from agriculture to horticulture/agro-horticulture/agro-forestry in less productive/ecologically fragile areas can be one of the options to adapt towards climate change and also provide better soil and water management, especially in the context of mountain agriculture. Narain et al.[17] report that the soil loss and runoff as compared to a contour cultivation of maize alone is lowered if double row of trees (Eucalyptus or Leucena) are planted on the contours in case of gentle hill slopes. Another study by Sharma et al.[18] observes that the traditional agro-forestry system of large cardamom (*Amomum subulatum*) practised in the eastern Himalayas stored 3.5 times more carbon than the rainfed agriculture showing potential of mitigation possibilities of the agro-forestry practices by sequestration of the atmospheric carbon. Besides, this system results in 5.7 times more profit for the farmers as compared to simple rainfed agriculture because of accelerated nutrient cycling, improved soil fertility, reduced soil erosion, water, and biodiversity conservation.

Another avenue of opportunity lies in production forestry wherein the demands of timber and fuelwood can be met by plantations. Dabas and Bhatia (1996)[19]

[13] Forest Department of Haryana.
[14] Chandran et al. (2009).
[15] Mohapatra (2008).
[16] Ravindranath et al. (2007).
[17] Narain et al. (1997).
[18] Sharma et al. (2007).
[19] Dabas and Bhatia (1996).

assess the potential for timber production through commercial forestry options in tropical countries. They report that although the carbon sequestering potential of trees in the tropics is much faster than in the temperate zone, the net sequestration by tropical forests is considerably reversed by the bulk use of biomass as fuelwood. They also point out that the wood-based industries are located in the temperate regions due to ample supply of raw material. Wood-based products like paper, ply, furniture also keep carbon locked in for a considerably long time. So, promotion of production forestry in tropics would have the multifaceted advantage of carbon sequestration as standing biomass in plantations, low reversal of carbon due to production of durable articles, and promotion of industries, thereby altering the current scenario where Asia is a net importer of wood.

In the context of the reversal of tropical forest biomass due to burning of fuelwood, it is imperative that users either switch to LPG or to processed biomass-based fuels. However, only 0.3 per cent rural households in India used biogas chulhas in 2000. India's National Programme for Improved Chulhas (NPIC) was funded by the central government and carried out by the states through 1983–2002. From 2003 the programme was devolved to the states without any central funding. The programme aimed initially at addressing the fuelwood crisis by increasing efficiency of cook-stoves. Later, emission control and exposure mitigation was also taken up as a goal. An evaluation study by the World Bank in 2002 across six states in India shows that the level of efficiency ranged 20 to 29 per cent for most states. Other positive effects perceived were better health and cleaner cooking besides fuel and time efficiency and smoke removal.[20]

Urban Forestry

In promoting urban forestry, local carbon dioxide offsetting could be a prime objective besides the aesthetic and recreational value. During planning and development of urban forestry the heterogeneity of urban people, their relatively high education levels and health consciousness, and aesthetic aspirations must be kept in mind.

A study conducted by Rowntree and Nowak,[21] aims at quantifying the amount of CO_2 offset by trees in an urban set-up at the level of the nation, city, organization, and individual for USA. Such studies are rare and only available on a more local basis for individual cities in the Indian context. A study conducted in the city of Pune,[22] shows the total sequestering potential of the trees in and around Pune city was 15,000 tonnes of carbon annually. In the same study, for one particular study site, the projected stored carbon increase in 30 years was demonstrated to be 65-fold!

Urban sites are ideal for compensatory afforestation as they have dust sequestration and pollution mitigation potential at the micro-climatic level. A study[23] on the potential of urban forestry in developing countries reports the opportunity for using urban waste water for cultivation of trees, enumerating the benefits as waste water management, material benefits from trees, aesthetic value, microclimate regulation, improved air quality, habitat value, soil and water conservation, and erosion control. In another study across five cities of USA on economic valuation of multiple benefits from urban forests, it was evaluated that although these cities spent \$13–65 annually per tree, benefits ranged from \$31 to \$89 per tree.[24] Such valuation estimates provide impetus to urban forestry programmes to garner support for maintaining and increasing green cover in cities. Builders and corporate organizations may also be encouraged or legally bound to promote forestry/urban plantation as they take up new projects in an urban environment. Urban greening should also be modelled taking lessons from developed countries so that the future aspirations of societies are factored in.

In this connection it may be mentioned that the states and union territories in India with relatively low forest cover boast of a considerably higher percentage of trees outside forest. In the case of Chandigarh (9.65 per cent of geographical area) and Delhi (8.29 per cent),[25] such a percentage results from successful urban forestry. Other cities and states could follow the lead from these cities. Plantation of shade trees along roadside and canals is another option. For this purpose, panchayat roads (0.7M ha), municipal roads (0.17M ha), railway side tracks (8512 ha), and project roads (0.2M ha) can be considered as quoted in Mohapatra.[26]

[20] ESMAP (2004).
[21] Rowntree and Nowak (1991).
[22] Warran and Patwardhan (2009).
[23] FAO (1995).
[24] McPherson et al. (2005).
[25] Forest Survey of India (2009).
[26] Mohapatra (2008).

In India the total extent of wasteland is 552692.26 square kilometres.[27]

These wastelands offer a solution to the paucity of newer land to be forested in order to reach the targeted total green cover for the country. Expertise and support from the relevant departments (Forest and Horticulture) for successful greening of the available wastelands with species providing various products like fuelwood, fodder, biodiesel etc. would be doubly advantageous in generating economic returns and taking off pressure from natural forests.

The Way Forward

There exists significant potential for reduction of GHGs emission as well as carbon sequestration in the forestry sector. Increasing forest/tree cover in urban and rural areas through agro-forestry, avenue plantation, and restoration of degraded lands will sequester carbon.

There are already several sector specific programmes being implemented by different ministries/departments that address the above issues. Under the Ministry of Agriculture (MoA), different programmes such as Rashtriya Krishi Vikas Yojana (RKVY), National Bamboo Mission, National Horticulture Mission, and National Watershed Development Project for Rainfed Areas (NWDPRA) are playing a crucial role to reform soil quality in the country on a large scale. Similarly, National Afforestation Programme (NAP) under MoEF, Integrated Watershed Management Programme (IWMP), National Policy on Bio-fuels, and NREGS under Ministry of Rural Development (MoRD) are targeted towards sustainable natural resource management.

What is required is the convergence of skills and programmes of different departments to realize the potential of addressing the challenges of adaptation and mitigation related to climate change. Interdisciplinary and participatory research with a focus on impact and adaptation at local levels and potential of convergence among on-going development programmes will aid in policy formulation and its implementation to achieve the full potential of agriculture and forestry sectors in mitigation and adaption towards climate change. The National Action Plan on Climate Change with eight missions is a step in this regard to achieve the self-commitment to reduce the GHGs emission by 20–5 per cent as declared by Indian government at the recent COP-15[28] summit.

References

Chandran, P., S.K. Ray, S.L. Durge, P. Raja, A.M. Nimkar, T. Bhattacharyya, and D.K. Pal (2009). 'Scope of Horticultural Land Use System in Enhancing Carbon Sequestration in Ferruginous Soils of the Semi Arid Tropics', *Current Science*, 97(7), pp. 1041–5.

Dabas, M. and S. Bhatia (1996). 'Carbon Sequestration through Afforestation: Role of Tropical Industrial Plantations', *Ambio*, 25(5), pp. 327–30.

ESMAP (Energy Sector Management Assistance Programme) and World Bank (2004). *Clean Household Energy for India: Reducing the Risks to Health*, World Bank, Delhi.

Food Agriculture Organization (FAO) (1995). *The Potential of Urban Forestry in Developing Countries: A Concept Paper*, FAO Corporate Document Repository.

——— (2001). *State of the World's Forest*, Food Agriculture Organization, Rome.

Forest Survey of India (2002). *Assessment of Growing Stock, Biomass and Carbon in India's Forests*, Report submitted to the Ministry of Environment and Forests, Government of India.

——— (2009). *State of the Forest Report*, Ministry of Environment and Forest, Government of India.

Government of India (GoI) (2005). *Wastelands Atlas of India*, Department of Land Resources, Ministry of Rural Development, Government of India. http://cdm.unfccc.int/Statistics/Issuance/CERsIssuedByHostPartyPieChart.html (retrieved 12 May 2010).

McPherson, G., J.R. Simpson, P.J. Peper, S.E. Maco, and Q. Xiao (2005). 'Municipal Forest Benefits and Costs in Five US Cities', *Journal of Forestry*, pp. 411–16.

Mohapatra, A.K. (2008). 'Forestry Based Carbon Sequestration Option for India', *Indian Journal of Forestry*, 31(4), pp. 483–90.

Narain, P., R.K. Singh, N.S. Sindhwal, and P. Joshie (1997). 'Agroforestry for Soil and Water Conservation in the Western Himalayan Valley Region of India', *Agroforestry Systems*, 39(2), pp. 175–89.

Ravindranath, N.H., B.S. Somsekhar, and M. Gadgil (1997). 'Carbon Flow in Indian Forests', *Climate Change*, 35, pp. 297–320.

Ravindranath, N.H., P. Sudha, V. Ramprasad, M.D.V. Nagendra, and H.D. Kulkarni (2007). 'Development of an Agroforestry Sequestration Project in Khammam District of India', Lawrence Berkeley National Laboratory.

[27] GoI (2005).

[28] Conference of Parties.

(Retrieved from: http://www.escholarship.org/uc/item/4qw168vk)

Rowntree, R.A. and D. J. Nowak (1991). 'Quantifying the Role of Urban Forests in Removing Atmospheric Carbon Dioxide', *Journal of Arboriculture*, 17(10), pp. 269–75.

Sharma, J.V. (2004). 'NFP: India', Paper presented in the workshop 'Accelerating Implementation of National Forest Programme: Strategies and New Directions' jointly organized by MOEF and ATREE, 10–12 March, New Delhi.

Sharma, R., J. Xu, and G. Sharma (2007). 'Traditional Agroforestry in the Eastern Himalayan Region: Land Management System Supporting Ecosystem Services', *Tropical Ecology*, vol. 48, no. 2, pp. 189–200.

Warran, A. and A. Patwardhan (2009). 'Carbon Sequestration Potential of Trees in and around Pune City'. (Retrieved from http://www.ranwa.org/carbonpune.pdf)

Winjum, J.K., R.K. Dixon, and P.E. Schroeder (1992). 'Estimating the Global Potential of Forest and Agroforest Management Practices to Sequester Carbon', *Water Air Soil Pollution*, 64: 213–28.

25 Is There a Role for Agricultural Offsets in Sustainable Infrastructure Development?

A Preliminary Assessment

Jyoti Gujral, S. Davenport, and S. Jayasuriya

Introduction

The Indian government recently announced 20–5 per cent reduction in its national emissions intensity target by 2020 on 2005 levels (Ramesh 2009). Policy makers now face the challenge of implementing and developing public policy options consistent with the Eight National Missions contained in NAPCC. Of particular relevance is minimizing the cost of meeting the national emissions intensity targets to 'infrastructure-providers' while meeting rapidly expanding infrastructure requirements. A potentially significant contribution to this objective could be made by agriculture through its ability to sequester carbon in activities such as forestry, perennial pastures, and more efficient livestock and cropping practices India Network of Climate Change Assessment.

An important contribution by agriculture, to India's national emissions targets can be as a source of low-cost emission reduction 'offsets' to other emitting sectors. This contribution has the potential to significantly increase the productivity and profitability of the farm sector, while reducing substantially the abatement costs of large emitters in other sectors of the economy.

Potential of Agricultural Offsets as Policy Instruments for Emissions Reduction

There are many problems with requiring agriculture to directly account for its own emissions. The many small emitters characterizing the sector entail significant transaction costs of measurement and verification of farm level emissions; these transaction costs may end up being larger than the emission reduction benefits. To reduce transaction costs associated with a 'point of obligation'[1] at the farm level, many developed countries have considered having the point of obligation 'downstream' from the farm, for example, at the processor level. A problem then, is that a processor charge per head of livestock effectively becomes a production tax for those farmers with few farm level abatement options. This in turn may result in unacceptable contractions in farm production, with implications for food security and community development.

The ambiguity around these impacts, as well as uncertainty in relation to the timing and development of farm

[1] Under an emissions trading scheme, the point in the supply chain where entities in each industry are required to report compliance information such as emissions and permit holdings.

level emissions-reducing technologies, have resulted in many countries leaving agriculture out of formal emission reduction strategies, such as 'cap and trade' schemes. An international preference for farm sector abatement is therefore emerging to experiment with a mix of policies and programmes targeted at the early exploitation of the most cost-effective abatement options (ACIL Tasman 2009). This may be viewed as a means of gradually introducing a 'carbon price' to the sector and could include:

- the modification of certain government policies and programmes which may inadvertently be encouraging high emission production activities, or the use of energy intensive inputs;
- designing new information programmes which better inform consumers and producers of already available carbon-friendly consumption goods and profitable production practices;
- refining public research and development (R&D) programmes to better target the development of new agricultural abatement technologies; and
- positioning sectors, such as agriculture, as 'offset-providers' to further exploit low-cost abatement opportunities that might be privately profitable for both buyers and sellers.

These options point to the need for governments to be prepared to develop an 'adaptive' policy framework that invests in new information and that enables the trialling of a range of policy and programmes in order to arrive at the most efficient mix. For a useful discussion of policy and programme complementarities and sequencing, see OECD (2009).

The term 'offset' refers to the substitution of cheaper reductions in GHGs for more expensive ones. An example is where major 'point-source' emitters are given the option within a broader national policy framework of meeting some or all of their emissions reduction obligations by purchasing emission-reducing offsets from other sectors, such as agriculture. A contract would be entered into, for example, between a power generator and a group of farmers, where the farmer group agrees to plant a proportion of their farms to trees, or to modify certain emission-intensive livestock and cropping practices in exchange for a fee. The purchaser of the contract would be entitled to incorporate the farm level emission savings into the calculation of its annual emissions intensity from power generation. It could also be possible for emitters to 'buy' these offsets through an 'exchange' or through participation in a scheme, rather than directly entering into private contracts.

The US Congressional Budget Office (2009) recently supported offsets stating that in view of 'the potential to reduce GHG concentrations in the atmosphere by changing land use practices and reducing deforestation, these actions have the potential to "offset" the extent to which more costly actions, such as reducing the use of fossil fuels, would have to be taken to meet a chosen GHG emissions target'. It follows that agricultural offsets could potentially be an enhancement to a range of emissions-reducing policy instruments, such as purchasing permits under cap and trade schemes, meeting mandated technology standards, or avoiding an emissions tax.

Consistent with these observations, the proposed American Clean Energy and Security Bill (the Waxman-Markey Bill) includes provision for agricultural and forestry offsets covering agricultural, grassland, and rangeland sequestration and management practices such as:

- altered tillage practices;
- winter cover and other means to increase biomass return to the soil in lieu of planting followed by fallowing;
- reduction of nitrogen fertilizer use or increase in nitrogen use efficiency;
- reduction in the frequency and duration of flooding of rice paddies;
- reduction in carbon emissions from organic soils;
- reduction in GHGs from manure and effluent; and
- reduction in GHG emissions due to changes in animal management practices, including dietary modifications.

As well as reducing the economy-wide costs of meeting national emission reduction objectives, positioning agriculture as an offset provider can be particularly beneficial in the early stages of new emissions policies, where emitters would otherwise face very high adjustment costs in the form of capital and technology upgrading. Purchasing lower cost agricultural offsets for a period may provide large point-source emitters with a more efficient and lower cost transition path.

India is considering, for example, making energy-efficient 'supercritical' technology mandatory for all future power projects as part of its efforts to contain emission of GHGs.[2] The biggest bottleneck to large-scale introduction of supercritical technology, however, comes from a shortage of manufacturing capacity for such high-end equipment. Rather than constrain sectoral output on such account, use of offsets through agriculture and its allied sectors could minimize potential disruptions. Currently available sequestration activities, such as afforestation,

[2] *Economic Times* (2010).

Box 25.1
Offsets Versus CSR Initiatives?

Agricultural carbon offsets should be viewed as a low-cost compliance option within a broader statutory emissions reduction framework. They therefore differ markedly from voluntary corporate social responsibility initiatives (CSRs), which are private undertakings aimed at promoting the social and environmental credentials of individual firms for the purpose of maintaining market advantage. CSRs play a useful public policy role by helping to better define those social and environment activities that are in the interest of private firms (rather than government) to undertake.

A further distinction between voluntary CSRs and statutory carbon offsets is that the former often involve social and environmental initiatives beyond offsetting their own GHGs.

So, in considering the issue of whether there needs to be a transition from voluntary initiatives such as CSRs to the adoption of statutory carbon offsets, the answer is that they can probably co-exist and that the market should be left to determine the extent to which a statutory carbon offset programme impacts upon the scope of voluntary CSR initiatives.

To the extent that Indian firms have invested in CSRs which specifically reduce their net emissions, then the introduction of a carbon offset scheme may reduce the need for firms to continue with that specific type of CSR in future.

Source: World Business Council for Sustainable Development (2009).

direct-drilling cropping practices, and grassland management could be mandated immediately by the Indian government as eligible 'offsets' that could potentially attract significant private investment.

Further, co-benefits of offsets include avoiding the uncertain impacts that direct coverage of agriculture may have on food security, reversing non-sustainable farm production systems and, importantly, providing a supplementary income stream to the farm sector (FAO 2009a). In India, where a large proportion of the population is dependent upon agriculture and where the sector is experiencing declining productivity and income growth, these benefits would be timely. The supplementary farm income provided by an agricultural offsets programme would also generate significant farm sector environmental benefits by reducing reliance on input intensive farming systems and enhancing biodiversity through activities such as the maintenance of perennial pastures and increased forestry on marginal lands.

The introduction of carbon markets in the form of agricultural offsets can also be viewed as introducing more complete environmental markets. As such, revegetation and afforestation offsets may well reduce the need for governments to otherwise finance these activities.

Existing Offset Mechanisms

An important issue in the context of Indian emissions intensity policies will be to consider the extent to which the policies to be applied to large point-source emitters lend themselves to incorporating agricultural offsets as an alternate, low-cost, compliance mechanism.

Acceptance of offsets has gained significant international momentum with numerous schemes operating internationally, nationally, and at the firm level. Internationally, the CDM under the United Nations Framework Convention on Climate Change (UNFCCC) enables Annex 1 countries (countries that are signatories to the United Nations Framework Convention on Climate Change) to meet a proportion of their emission reduction obligations under the Kyoto Protocol by purchasing offsets from developing countries. Developing countries benefit from new investment and the transfer of environment-friendly technologies. In December 2009, the largest number of registered CDM projects was in China, followed by India and Brazil. A further international initiative is the World Bank's Bio Carbon Fund which finances demonstration projects that sequester or conserve carbon in forest and agro-ecosystems. It is a public/private investment initiative which aims to deliver cost-effective emissions reductions (World Bank 2009).

At the national level many countries now operate carbon funds such as Argentina's Argentine Carbon Fund and Portugal's National Programme for Climate Change. Emission reductions so achieved can be accounted for against national emission targets. Of further interest is a recently publicized initiative where, following from the success of Portugal's National Carbon Fund, the Portuguese power company Energias has directly contracted with farmers to produce 30,000 tonnes of carbon per annum through improved grassland management (see Box 25.2).

At the level of the firm, a number of offset markets now operate, such as the Chicago Climate Exchange (CCX). This is a voluntary market where members participate in legally binding commitments to reduce their emissions using either domestic or international offsets. Offset contracts are granted to those who undertake a project to reduce, destroy, or sequester carbon dioxide (or equivalent). Farmers can participate by undertaking activities

Box 25.2
Energias de Portugal—Offsetting GHG Emissions Through Land-use Activities

Portugal is one of the few countries to choose all of the voluntary agriculture and forestry-related activities under Article 3.4 of the Kyoto Protocol, namely forest, cropland, and grassland management to meet its obligations. The above project was designed to demonstrate the potential of such activities in the national greenhouse gas inventory. It was implemented in multiple locations in Portugal, covering more than 1,500 ha.

Alongside afforestation, forest management, and the agricultural practice of no-tillage, this project consisted of the installation and management of Sown Biodiverse Permanent Pastures Rich in Legumes (SBPPRL). SBPPRL is the centre-piece of this project given that it is a Portuguese innovation. This land-use system not only sequesters carbon, but generates environmental benefits by increasing soil fertility, reducing erosion, minimizing impacts on the water cycle, reducing fertilizer use, and increasing yields.

Even though Portugal is still the only country using this kind of pasture over a significant area, there is great potential for the system to be replicated in other areas with Mediterranean characteristics. With this project, Energias de Portugal (EDP) contributes to the visibility of these types of pastures, which have yet to be thoroughly studied. Due to the success of the project, the Portuguese government has decided to support the implementation of new SBPPRL areas throughout the country in order to help it further comply with its Kyoto Protocol target.

Only farms with a history of good environmental and economically viable practices are included in the project. This ensures that forests, no-tillage practices, and SBPPRL will be maintained long after the project ends, thus keeping the carbon pool in the soils. The largest forest area in the project is oak forest, which has a long time span before harvesting. This is particularly important as data capture obtained for scientific purposes may continue in the future in order to obtain a longer time series and a deeper knowledge of carbon dynamics in these systems. So far the data gathered has been used in models and methodologies for the Portuguese inventory. EDP voluntarily supported this project to demonstrate the sequestration potential of agriculture and forestry-related activities. As a result, these activities are now important for Portugal to decrease its own CO_2 deficit.

As an electricity utility, EDP views this as an opportunity to reduce its emissions in a cost-effective way. The project resulted in the sequestration of 3.69 kilotonnes of CO_2 equivalent in 2006, 7.56 kilotonnes in 2007, and 11.03 kilotonnes in 2008. The project will continue until 2012 to guarantee the maintenance of the CO_2 sequestered in soils. EDP will also use these sequestration results for initiatives covered by the voluntary CO_2 market.

Source: World Business Council for Sustainable Development (2009).

such as conservation tillage, grassland conservation, and methane capture projects. Where projects offset less than 10,000 tonnes of carbon dioxide equivalent, farmers are advised to use firms that aggregate ('aggregators') emissions savings from small projects to meet the minimum carbon contract requirements. This aggregation function is particularly relevant to developing countries given their large numbers of small holdings. Other firm-based offset schemes include national level programmes such as Australia's Greenhouse Gas (GGAS) initiative, Canada's Climate Change Exchange and the US Regional Greenhouse Gas Initiative which recently launched a mandatory programme to reduce GHGs from the electric power sector in ten north-eastern US states, with offsets allowed as a compliance option.

Offsets can therefore operate at a number of levels—internationally, nationally, and at the firm level. Consideration needs to be given to how offset programmes at each of these levels can be made complementary in order to maximize the exploitation of low-cost abatement and sequestration opportunities in agriculture.

A related and interesting issue is the relationship between Certified Emission Reduction Units (CERs) issued to Annex 1 countries under the Clean Development Mechanism, and carbon offsets that might be issued under a domestic Indian offset programme, as suggested in this paper. Given that CERs are accredited to Annex 1 countries, the emission reductions so achieved will generally not be available as contributions towards India's Emissions Intensity Targets.

In conclusion, there does appear to be a role for a domestic offset programme which could help India's large emitters to take a lower cost transition path towards abatement. To address the concern that the lowest cost offsets would be captured by Annex 1 countries, it is desirable that a domestic offset programme be implemented at the earliest opportunity.

Verification of Offsets

Literature suggests that to effectively reduce GHGs, offsets must be subject to the four criteria of *additionality*, *quantification*, *permanence*, and *leakage*.

- *Additionality* requires genuine GHG reductions that would not otherwise have occurred. One approach would be to recognize the adoption of practices that are at the 'leading-edge' of technology change; another would be to demonstrate that the technology change would not be viable in the absence of an offset payment. Care must be taken, however, to avoid such tests acting as a total disincentive to market participation. In the initial capacity building stages of an offset programme more liberal tests may therefore be justified.

- *Quantification* requires emission reductions to be measurable, while *permanence* requires GHG reductions achieved through offsets to remain in place for whatever the contracted period is. There is an ongoing debate around the concept of permanence with an emerging concern that it may be overstated. Typically, where offsets cannot guarantee to keep GHGs out of the atmosphere permanently, some form of discounting is applied. This occurs on the CCX in conjunction with the creation of contingency funds for future remedial investments. What tends to be missed, however, is that temporary GHG capture can still have value to large point-source emitters by buying them time to invest in more efficient abatement in future in response to new science and technology developments. An alternate concept is therefore that of 'rental value', where payments are made for annual GHG storage.
- *Leakage* refers to the situation where offset activities induce other GHG emitting activities elsewhere in the economy, or internationally. Reducing livestock production on an aggregation of farms could, for example, simply increase livestock prices and encourage increased livestock production, and emissions, elsewhere. A relatively low-cost way of adjusting for leakage, however, is to develop regional farm system models (which may already exist) to assess the likely regional enterprise adjustments that might occur in response to various types of agricultural offsets. For example, where an offset proposal involving a reduction in livestock numbers results in a 20 per cent increase in livestock numbers elsewhere, the amount of CO_2 equivalent abatement accredited against the offset could be discounted by 20 per cent. Leakage could also be addressed by encouraging the development of portfolios of offsets, at say the regional level, that effectively internalize supply response effects.

It follows that independent accreditation of offsets is required with associated protocols and rules to test proposals against the aforementioned criteria. In a report the Electric Power Research Institute (2009) tests the consistency of various GHG offset methodologies and protocols against a number of offset case studies. A degree of consistency with the protocols applied by India's National Clean Development Mechanism Authority could also be considered, but important principles will be to apply some leniency to verification tests in the initial programme period and then to focus on their further development in response to new information and learning.

Finally, further discussion in relation to the formation of offset 'portfolios' is warranted given their potential to reduce verification risks, and in so doing, to more highly reward offset providers. For example, were the Indian government to establish an 'offset authority' to (i) approve the agricultural abatement practices that would qualify as eligible offsets for the purpose of trading to large point-source emitters; and to (ii) determine the safe lower bound carbon abatement value to be assigned to those offsets, that same authority could be charged with assessing on a case-by-case basis the higher abatement values associated with portfolios of offsets. Those offset portfolios could be formulated and proposed to the regulating authority by any private sector organization or individual acting on behalf of a farmer group.

Given the much higher safe lower bound abatement values likely to be associated with portfolios of agricultural offsets, market forces could be expected to see these offset 'agents' or 'aggregators' emerge in much the same way as grain marketing agents and associated grain pooling arrangements have emerged. In the context of India, organized players in the 'extension services' market, could be potential aggregators who assist in the development and management of offset programmes. They could also be funded by the infrastructure companies that seek to 'offset' their emissions. Corporates that have on a voluntary basis (through CSR initiatives) developed such 'models' can contribute to scale-up these models for developing significant 'offset' programmes.

Over time, regulatory authorities and aggregators could be expected to build knowledge and capacity in combining offsets across farms and across technologies (economies of scale and scope) in a self-hedging manner in order to manage the risks of under-delivery of anticipated abatement benefits. Thus, the establishment of a government accreditation body to (i) approve the agricultural abatement practices that would qualify as eligible offsets for the purpose of trading to large point-source emitters; and to (ii) determine the safe lower bound carbon abatement value to be assigned to those offsets also needs to be considered. That same authority may also be responsible for establishing a market exchange between point source emitters and providers of agricultural offsets (Box 25.3). Note that the government could also enter the offsets market as a purchaser.

Box 25.3

US Regional Greenhouse Gas Initiative—Agricultural Offsets as an Alternative Compliance Option for the US Power Sector

The Regional Greenhouse Gas Initiative (RGGI) is a cooperative effort by ten Northeast and mid-Atlantic states to limit greenhouse gas emissions. RGGI is the first mandatory, market-based CO_2 emissions reduction programme in the United States. These ten states have capped CO_2 emissions from the power sector, and will require a 10 per cent reduction in these emissions by 2018. Participating states are:

- Establishing a multi-state CO_2 emissions budget (cap) that will decrease gradually until it is 10 per cent lower than at the start.
- Requiring electric power generator to hold allowances equal to their CO_2 emissions over a three-year control period.
- Providing a market-based emissions auction and trading system where electric power generators can buy, sell, and trade CO_2 emissions allowances.
- Using the proceeds of allowance auctions to support low-carbon-intensity solutions, including energy efficiency and clean renewable energy, such as solar and wind power.
- Employing offsets (greenhouse gas emissions reduction or sequestration projects outside the electricity sector) to help companies meet their compliance obligations. Eligible offsets currently include:
  - Landfill methane capture and destruction.
  - Reduction in emissions of sulfur hexafluoride (SF6) in the electric power sector.
  - Sequestration of carbon due to afforestation.
  - Reduction or avoidance of CO_2 emissions from natural gas, oil, or propane end-use combustion due to end-use energy efficiency in the building sector.
  - Avoided methane emissions from agricultural manure management operations.

Source: Regional Greenhouse Gas Initiative.

Agriculture's GHG Abatement Potential

India's GHG profile

Indian Network of Climate Change Assessment (2007) reports that the primary source of India's GHG emissions [carbon dioxide (CO_2), methane (CH_4), and nitrous oxide (N_2O)] are electric power stations, steel manufacture, cement plants, and agriculture (17.6 per cent).

Nevertheless, with agriculture accounting for a significant proportion of India's emissions (Garg et al. 2001 and 2004), it is reasonable to expect other sectors of the Indian economy to have an interest in seeing and supporting the development of cost-effective agricultural abatement strategies.

In terms of India's key areas of increasing emissions exposure, the energy sector contributes approximately 73 per cent of CO_2 emissions with the rate of increase in those emissions being higher than for most other sectors. While this reflects a sector facing strong demand pressure, it also suggests an important potential role for low-cost compliance mechanisms, such as offsets, in reducing adjustment costs and supply disruptions.

While agriculture ranks as the second highest GHG emitter, it nevertheless is the primary source of methane emissions (Bhatia et al. 2004), with the livestock sector (45 per cent) being the most significant source, followed by rice cultivation (22 per cent) and biomass burning (15 per cent). Agriculture is also the primary source (90 per cent) of India's nitrous oxide emissions due to the widespread use of synthetic fertilizer. Of some concern here is the intensification of nitrogen use in agriculture which Garg et al. (2004) report as having increased from 8 Tg in 1990 to 9.8 Tg in 1995, with no significant change in the total area cultivated.

Nelson et al. (2009) estimates that nitrous oxide emissions from irrigated rice will increase by close to 30 per cent between 2000 and 2050.

While the above mentioned emission sources are significant, there appears to be numerous low-cost opportunities in these sectors that could be pursued immediately to mitigate emissions which could be the subject of sectoral abatement efforts and offsets programmes. In the power sector, for example, Garg et al. (2001) report significant scope for operational improvements, better maintenance, and for reducing transmission and distribution losses. In agriculture, they report scope for better farming practices for paddy cultivation, such as utilization of less water, improved cultivars, more efficient fertilizer use, and developing improved cattle feeds.

Indian Agriculture's GHG Abatement Potential

Given the large size of India's land use sector and the significant potential to increase the adoption of carbon-based farm production systems, developing and exploiting this area of India's natural comparative advantage in carbon abatement and offset capacity should be an important public policy focus over the medium term. Nelson et al. (2009) confirm this conclusion stating that they found great opportunities for cost-effective mitigation of GHGs in Indian agriculture.

Some of their key findings are that a significant source of emissions is groundwater pumping for irrigated rice which relies on electric pumps and coal-fired power generation. Other important mitigation opportunities include conservation agriculture and conversion of low productivity crop land to pasture or agriculture and in some cases to forests. Perhaps the most interesting finding from Nelson et al. (2009) is the very low cost, less than $1 MT, at which carbon can be sequestered by India's agricultural sector. They found that this would impact primarily on current low value crop production which may well align potential offset payments with poorer agricultural regions. They also found that the total sequestration potential of agriculture may range from 8 million MT in response to $1 million spent annually, to more than 500 million MT in response to payments of less than $100 million per year. Note that due to lack of time and information, opportunities to further mitigate emissions through changed livestock practices and increasing soil organic carbon were not investigated.

In Figure 25.1, a hypothetical abatement cost curve is depicted, which when viewed from left to right, identifies current and prospective sources of abatement and sequestration in India's agricultural sector, ordered from lowest to highest cost, that could form the basis of abatement strategies and offset programmes. On the vertical axis the price 'P1' represents a hypothetical carbon price that emitters would face in the absence of offsets, thus making those technologies below P1 particularly attractive as offset 'candidates' (Note that in the context of India, P1 could also be viewed as the price faced by large point-source emitters for upgrading technology).

A similar diagram could be developed for the Indian economy more broadly, an exercise which has been done for a number of countries such as the United Kingdom, the United States, and Australia (McKinsey & Company 2007 and 2008).

The figure serves to highlight the need for governments and industry to develop an understanding of India's potential agricultural abatement and sequestration options in order to efficiently target policy and programme initiatives. In the absence of this information, both public and private sector opportunities could be missed, whereby relatively small investments could lead to certain farm technologies and practices shifting from being marginally viable to viable for the purpose of being eligible under an offset programme. The need for the government to reform inefficient policy settings that generate incentives for high-emission farming systems is also highlighted.

Another feature of Figure 25.1 (the shaded area) is the likelihood that there are sources of emissions abatement that could be undertaken with no cost to the economy (that is, they have a negative marginal cost of abatement).

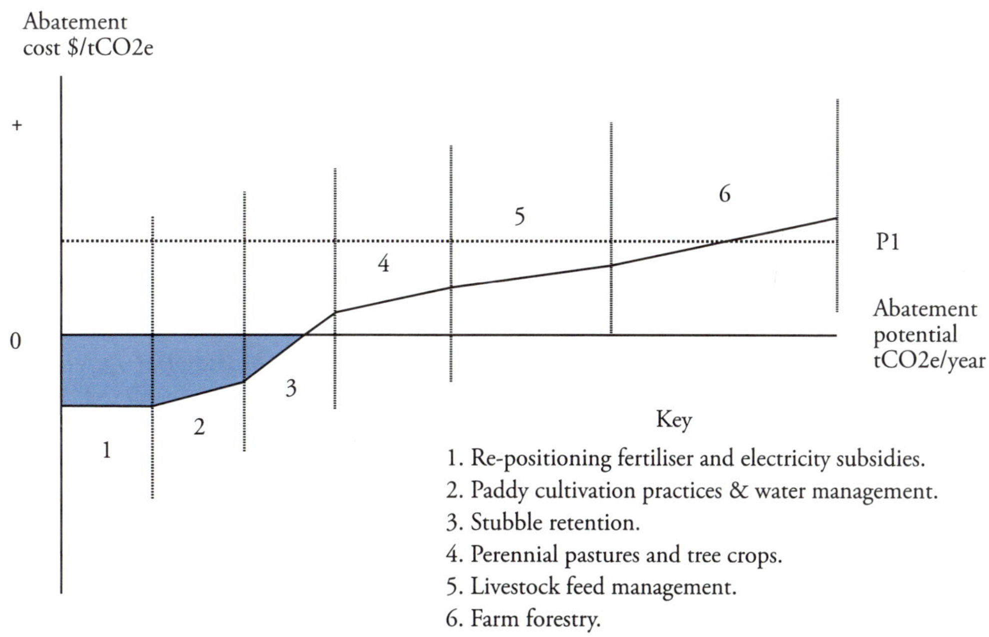

Figure 25.1 India's Agricultural Abatement Cost Curve (Hypothetical not actual)

Source: Authors' own.

These can be considered as 'no regrets' options, as undertaking them would produce additional benefits or profits relative to current practices. McKinsey and Company (2007) found, for example, that 'almost 40 percent of abatement within the US economy could be achieved at a negative marginal cost'. Their further finding was that 'the cumulative savings created by these negative cost options could substantially offset (on a societal basis) the additional spending required for the options with positive marginal costs'. The FAO also report [based on McKinsey and Company (2009)] that in relation to a range of emerging economies, 'average costs per tonne of CO_2e abated by the year 2030 are computed to be negative for crop and grassland nutrient management and tillage and residue management, indicating that these activities should generate higher benefits than costs over the time frame considered' (FAO 2009a).

Garg et al. (2004) reveal that important sources of India's agricultural emissions to 2030 will be the strong growth in synthetic fertilizer use and irrigation development. It follows that the repositioning of current fertilizer and electricity subsidies to new incentive programmes which encourage carbon-friendly farming systems and which provide for more focused research, development, and extension could warrant close consideration. Further policy reforms with a negative marginal cost of abatement could be the phasing out or modification of border protection and domestic price support arrangements that protect and encourage emission-intensive industries, and reforms which establish markets and set an appropriate price on natural resource access (that is, land and water).

Repositioning emission-increasing farm input subsidies and introducing new information programmes which increase the efficiency of rice cultivation (initiatives 1 and 2) are therefore, hypothetically, depicted as falling into this category of 'low-hanging fruit' (relatively easy measures), given the positive correlation between input subsidies and GHG emissions and because nitrous oxide and methane emissions are indicators of inefficient fertilizer use and livestock feed conversion. The reform of emissions-inducing government policies will have the additional effect of increasing expected returns from R&D into low-carbon technologies and will increase farm level incentives to adopt those technologies.

With reference to activities 2–6 in Figure 25.1, it follows that a high level commitment by government to establish farm level extension and research programmes which shift production towards more productive carbon based systems is critical. While the government has an obvious role to play here in the delivery and financing of new carbon programmes, it will also be useful to consider the role the government can play in strengthening incentives for greater industry involvement and investment in information generation and new technology development.

Research and development, for example, is an activity that can be subject to 'market failure' in the form of under-investment by the private sector. In the context of agricultural industries, this can occur because individual farmers acting in isolation may not have the capacity or the incentive to invest in certain research and development activities, particularly where the benefits from those activities can easily be captured by other industry participants. An efficient solution would be for governments to require agricultural industries to pay a small levy on production, which would be pooled, and used to help fund the development of new abatement and sequestration technologies.

Thus, acknowledging the existence of the very low-cost abatement potential within the agricultural (and allied industries) sector, and the opportunity that it presents to lower the cost of meeting overall emission intensity targets is critically important for India's public policy development. Early exploitation of such low-cost abatement would be like a national insurance, as early GHG reductions will reduce the need for high-cost GHG reduction strategies in the future. Understanding the make-up of India's agricultural abatement cost curve is important to identify initiatives where the net cost of abatement is negative and re-examine currently applicable farm policies to incentivize farmers to adopt carbon-friendly best management practices, some of which could be eligible for agricultural offsets. The focus of research and extension must change in order to maximize the future development of new carbon technologies that might expand the scope of offset programmes.

The Way Forward: Developing Agriculture's Potential

Despite the appeal of agricultural offsets being part of a country's climate change policy portfolio, the abatement and sequestration potential of agriculture remains somewhat uncertain, largely unexplored, but potentially large. While agro-forestry and certain agricultural practices are available, other activities that increase soil carbon and reduce methane and nitrous oxide emissions await development. Also relevant here is that the nature of these practices will often be country and region specific.

Risk and uncertainty with respect to mitigation and sequestration should not, however, halt policy development. Rather, they should encourage governments and industries to engage in 'adaptive' policy approaches. For example, government programmes which initially do the purchasing of 'practice-change', or efforts to establish voluntary carbon offset markets, supported by a mix of government and private sector funding, could immediately help in introducing a carbon price to the sector. They would facilitate an improved understanding of current and prospective mitigation and sequestration technologies, and the further development of measurement and verification protocols. They can also help focus R&D effort and innovation on those technologies and practices with the highest probable returns (see FAO 2009b for further discussion on transition and capacity building programmes). Policy development can focus on how governments can introduce adaptive, capacity building programmes to support the development of mitigation capacity and offset markets.

References

ACIL Tasman (2009). *Carbon Pollution Abatement Policy—Alternatives to the CPRS for Agriculture*, report prepared for the Victorian Department of Primary Industries and NSW Department of Industry and Investment.

Bhatia, A., H. Pathak, and P.K. Aggarwal (2004). 'Inventory of Methane and Nitrous Oxide Emissions from Agricultural Soils of India and their Global Warming Potential', *Current Science*, 87(3), pp. 317–24.

Economic Times (2010). 'Power Cos may be told to Tread Green Path', 4 January 2010, available at http://economictimes.indiatimes.com/news/news-by-industry/energy/power/Power-cos-may-be-told-to-tread-green-path/articleshow/5408388.cms

Electric Power Research Institute (2009). 'Insights from "Road Testing" Analyses of Proposed and Existing Greenhouse Gas Offsets Methodologies and Protocols', in Background paper for the EPRI Greenhouse Gas Emissions Offset Policy Dialogue Workshop 6, July.

Food and Agriculture Organisation (FAO) (2009a). 'Food Security and Agricultural Mitigation in Developing Countries: Options for Capturing Synergies', Natural Resource Management and Environment Department and Economic Social Development Department.

——— (2009b). 'Review of Evidence on Dryland Pastoral Systems and Climate Change: Implications and Opportunities for Mitigation and Adaptation', Land and Water Discussion Paper 8, Land Tenure and Management Unit (NRLA), Land and Water Division.

Garg, A., S. Bhattacharya, P.R. Shukla, and V.K. Dadhwal (2001). 'Regional and Sectoral Assessment of Greenhouse Gas Emissions in India', *Atmospheric Environment,* 35, pp. 2679–95, Elsevier.

Garg, A., P.R. Shukla, M. Kapshe, and D. Menon (2004). 'Indian methane and nitrous oxide emissions and mitigation flexibility', *Atmospheric Environment*, 38, pp. 1965–77, Elsevier.

Indian Network of Climate Change Assessment (2007). *India: Greenhouse Gas Emissions 2007*, Ministry of Environment and Forests, Government of India.

McKinsey & Company (2007). *Reducing U.S. Greenhouse Gas Emissions: How Much at What Cost? U.S. Greenhouse Gas Abatement Mapping Initiative*, Executive Report, New York, December.

——— (2008). *The Australian Cost Curve for Greenhouse Gas Reduction*, Sydney, Australia.

——— (2009). *Pathways to a Low-Carbon Economy Version 2 of the Global Greenhouse Gas Abatement Cost Curve.*

Nelson, G.C., R. Robertson, S. Msangi, T. Zhu, X. Liao, and P. Jawajar (2009). 'Greenhouse Gas Mitigation: Issues for Indian Agriculture', IFPRI Discussion Paper 00900, September.

Organisation for Economic Cooperation and Development (OECD) (2009). 'The Economics of Climate Change Mitigation: Policies and Options for Global Action Beyond 2012', available at www.oecd.org/publishing corigenda.

Ramesh, Jairam. (2009). 'Speech of Mr Jairam Ramesh, Minister of State (Independent Charge) for Environment & Forests, Government of India', at the High-Level Segment of the UN Climate Conference, Copenhagen, 16 December.

Regional Greenhouse Gas Initiative (2001). 'Regional Greenhouse gas Initiative: An Intiative of the Northeast and Mid-Atlantic States of the US', available at www.rggi.org/.about. Last accessed on 12 August.

US Congressional Budget Office (2009). 'The Use of Agricultural Offsets to Reduce Greenhouse Gases', Statement of Joseph Kile, Testimony, Assistant Director for Microeconomic Studies before the Subcommittee on Conservation, Credit, Energy, and Research Committee on Agriculture, United States House of Representatives, 3 December.

World Bank (2009). 'Country Notes on Climate Change Aspects in Agriculture: Latin America and the Caribbean Region', Agriculture and Rural Development Team, December.

World Business Council for Sustainable Development (2009). *Tackling Climate Change on the Ground: Corporate Case Studies on Land Use and Climate Change,* Geneva, Switzerland, December, available at http://www.wbcsd.org/DocRoot/3Eg5u08N3UAYciRKcigo/Land%20Use_220310.pdf.

26 Local Dynamics in the Adoption and Implementation of Low Carbon Technologies

The Case of West Bengal

Dilip Kumar Ghosh

Introduction

An essential part of development is the protection of the environment, the neglect of which can undermine development in the long run. Presently, 'Sustainable Development' is a common refrain but the basic message of 'Think globally, Act locally' is lost. At the local level, sustainable development is rarely understood in its proper context and operationalizing it is even harder. The present study is concerned with initiatives of local institutions in West Bengal (mainly panchayats) in making the environment clean and safe through programmes implemented by them. With the passage of the 73rd Constitution Amendment Act, 1992 the Constitution of India gives powers and responsibility to the panchayats at three tiers to plan for 29 subjects listed in the Eleventh Schedule, including the promotion of non-conventional energy and social forestry. For setting sensible policy priorities at the local level, it is necessary that a good information network between the state and local panchayats exists through which the panchayat representatives can learn and act. Improving knowledge and understanding issues like climate change is crucial for making local initiatives successful. Community participation is also essential in arresting the damage. (*World Development Report* 1992).

With this background, the present study has been developed with the following objectives:

- To present an overview of the role of the panchayats in reducing the sources of carbon emission in rural areas;
- To discuss implementation of various rural development programmes with green energy initiative components; and
- To assess the support that the government of West Bengal has extended to the panchayats on environmental issues.

The following section discusses the relevant provisions enshrined in the West Bengal Panchayat Act, 1973 (modified up to the 31 May 2009) with respect to meeting the challenges of the environment as well as the powers and duties of the panchayats in three tiers (gram panchayat at the village level, panchayat samiti at the block level, and zilla parishad at the district level), and the scope for people's participation. Reflections from programmes like Indira Awas Yojna, Backward Region Grant Fund, and the National Rural Employment Guarantee Scheme are recorded next to highlight the progress of panchayats in adopting green energy initiatives. Need for state government support for capacity development of the panchayat members through training, etc., comprises the next section before concluding.

The Regulatory Framework and Provisions for Local Government

Panchayats in West Bengal are guided by the West Bengal Panchayat Act, 1973. According to the provisions of the

Act,[1] a panchayat body shall prepare a development plan for the five-year term of office, and annual plans with the objective of community development and socio-economic welfare of the individual members. Provisions that relate to a green agenda are highlighted in Table 26.1, where the panchayats at the appropriate tier can undertake schemes or adopt measures within their jurisdiction.

The West Bengal Panchayat Act, 1973, created scope for activities by the panchayats to reduce environmental degradation through implementation of schemes (where funds are provided by the state government) and adoption of necessary measures. There are five sub-committees (up-samitis) for discharging the responsibilities of the gram panchayat.[2] Of these five sub-committees, only two are concerned with environmental issues,[3] as listed in Table 26.2.

From the distribution of the subjects, it is obvious that importance attached to green initiatives is rather low at the village level. The subjects included are traditionally practised and programme-based with the gram panchayats as implementing agencies. Truly speaking, the gram panchayats are only interested in executing government-sponsored programmes, although according to Section 20 of the West Bengal Panchayat Act, the gram panchayat can undertake execution of any scheme, including schemes relating to employment generation, performance of any act or management of any institution or organization entrusted to it or devolved upon it by the state government or by any other authority with the approval of the state government. Beneficiary selection is usually the responsibility of the gram panchayat.

At the block and district tiers of the panchayat structure, there are three standing committees (sthayee samiti) at each level for looking after environment-related matters (Table 26.3). The West Bengal Panchayat (Panchayat Samiti Administration) Rules, 2008 mentions that the concerned standing committees should deal with, formulate, and execute schemes accordingly.

From the distribution of the subjects, it is clear that majority are concerned with areas other than environmental issues. The standing committees are responsible for financial and executive administration of schemes and programmes under their purview and control.

For democratic functioning of the panchayats, the state government created a space for representation of the opposition in the finance, establishment, development, and planning standing committees.[4] A similar provision has been made for the zilla parishad as well. In an Amendment (2003) of the West Bengal Panchayat Act, a provision of inclusion of opposition members in the other sthayee samitis was also made.[5] The purpose of such an amendment was to ensure representation of the

Table 26.1 Green Agenda for Local Government

Tiers	*Areas of action*	
Gram Panchayat	(i)	Introduction of new crops, including selection of beneficiaries for distribution of seeds, bio-fertilizers, pesticides, etc.
	(ii)	Extension of social forestry and farm forestry, including planting of trees, distribution of saplings, promotion of fuel and fodder cultivation.
	(iii)	Maintenance of environmental sanitation, including management of solid and liquid wastes and prevention of public nuisance.
Panchayat Samiti and Zilla Parishad	(i)	Undertake schemes or measures including financial assistance for social forestry and farm forestry, fuel and fodder, as also non-conventional energy sources.
	(ii)	Manage or maintain institutions for promotion of environment, livelihood, education, health, communication, tourism, or work of public utility, including eco-parks constructed by it or vested in it for control and management.

Source: West Bengal Panchayat Act, 1973 (modified up to 31 May 2009).

[1] Section 19 for gram panchayat, Section 109 for panchayat samiti, and Section 153 for zilla parishad.

[2] Section 32A of the West Bengal Panchayat Act.

[3] On the basis of distribution of subjects delineated in Rule 66 of the West Bengal Panchayat (Gram Panchayat Administration) Rules, 2004.

[4] The provision goes like this: 'leader of the recognized political party in opposition having largest number of members in the panchayat samiti in comparison with other recognized political parties in opposition shall be a member of the Artha, Sanstha, Unnayan o Parikalpana sthayee samiti'.

[5] 'One member from each recognized political party in opposition shall be selected to be a member of each of the sthayee samitis.'

Table 26.2 Sub-Committees of the Gram Panchayat Dealing with Environmental Issues

Name of sub-committee	*Subjects dealt with*
1. Agriculture and Animal Resource Development	Agriculture and agro industries, horticulture, agri-marketing, irrigation, including small irrigation, water resources development, sericulture, animal resources development, fisheries, water-shed development, cooperative movement, provident fund for landless agricultural laborers, etc. (14 subjects in total)
2. Industries and Infrastructure	Cottage and small-scale industries, rural artisans, infrastructure development, Indira Awas Yojna, construction of rural roads, culverts, rural housing, rural electrification, and generating alternative energy sources. (8 subjects in total)

Source: West Bengal Panchayat (Gram Panchayat Administration Rules), 2004.

Table 26.3 Standing Committees at the Block and District Tiers Dealing with Environmental Issues

Name of standing committee	*Subjects dealt with*
(i) Public Health and Environment	Public health, sanitation, rural water supply, community health care management, community-oriented programme for control of infectious diseases including AIDS, community-based vector control, rural health centres, clinics and dispensaries, family welfare, nutrition, protection of environment and preservation of aesthetic values, and control of pollution. (11 subjects in total)
(ii) Forest and Land Reforms	Distribution of vested land, land reforms programme, assistance to self-help groups for cultivating *khas* and vested agricultural land, social forestry, farm forestry, increased production and economic use of fuel and fodder, protection of forest resources including flora and fauna and promotion of joint forest management, maintenance of ecological balance, and eco-tourism development. (9 subjects in total)
(iii) Small Industry, Electricity, and Non-conventional energy	Cottage and small-scale industries, handloom, khadi and village industries, sericulture, and self-employment programmes, rural electrification, non-conventional energy growth. (7 subjects in total)

Source: West Bengal Panchayat (Panchayat Samiti Administration Rules), 2008.

opposition in the decision-making process and implementation of various programmes by the panchayat samitis and zilla prishads. However, these parovisions have no impact on programmes for green energy initiatives as irrespective of political party, knowledge as well as awareness about environmental issues and climate change is low among the panchayat representatives.

For making the activities of the panchayats transparent and democratic, the government of West Bengal introduced a district council for panchayat in each district.[6] The chairperson of this council is the leader of the recognized political party in the opposition having the largest number of members directly elected. This council has the power to examine the accounts of the panchayats within its territorial jurisdiction and to monitor the schemes in implementation.

In the process of discharging their responsibilities and exercising their authority, the West Bengal Panchayat Act makes the following provisions for empowering the district council,[7]

- scrutiny of the accounts of the panchayats for satisfaction of the council in the matter of spending of money for the purpose for which it was allotted;
- examination of the expenditure for visualizing whether the expenditures incurred conform to the rules governing such expenditure and according to the financial proprieties of such expenditure;
- examination of the accounts of stores and stocks maintained by the panchayats; and
- making suggestion to the panchayats for removing the difficulties, if any, in giving effect to any provision of the West Bengal Panchayat Act or the rules made thereunder.

Unfortunately, the functioning of the district councils is limited to scrutiny of accounts, financial transactions,

[6] Through Section 214A in the West Bengal Panchayat Act, 1973 in the year 1994.

[7] Sub-section 2 of Section 214A.

and annual reports of the panchayati raj institutions in the districts. In five districts, namely, Uttar Dinajpur, Dakshin Dinajpur, South 24 Parganas, Purba Medinipur, and Paschim Medinipur no meetings of the district council were held in the year 2008–9.[8] Their functioning did not show any bearing on environmental issues. Neither did they act as watchdogs or serve as 'ears and eyes' of the poor in delivering benefits of different programmes implemented by the panchayats.[9]

The law of the land lays down that every standing committee must hold a meeting at least once a month and that all decisions must be taken through majority vote in these meetings. On this basis, 17 zilla parishads (Kolkata and Darjeeling districts are excluded as there are no zilla parishads) should at least be holding 204 standing committee meetings. Taking into account 333 panchayat samitis of West Bengal, the target number of standing committee meetings should be 3,996. However, Table 26.4 paints a dismal picture of the actual number of meetings conducted by the standing committees in the year 2007–8 that bear some relationship to environmental issues.

TABLE 26.4 Number of Standing Committee Meetings in the Year 2007–8

Name of Standing Committee	*Panchayat Samiti*	*Zilla Parishad*
Public Health and Environment	1624 (40.64)	111 (54.41)
Forest and Land Reform	1414 (35.38)	120 (58.82)
Small Industry, Electricity, and Non-Conventional Energy	1234 (30.88)	106 (51.96)

Note: The figures given within brackets are with respect to the target of 3,996 meetings.

Source: *Annual Report (2007–8) of the Department of Panchayats and Rural Development.*

Perusal of the proceedings of the meetings reflects that there is little space for discussion on environmental issues. In the public health and environment standing committee, for example, most of the time was devoted to discussions on health-related subjects. Similarly, in the forest and land reform standing committee, priority is given to distribution of ceiling surplus land to the beneficiaries. Again, in the small industry, electricity, and non-conventional energy standing committee, most discussions pertain to electrification of hamlets and allied issues related to conventional energy sources. The list of business to be transacted at a meeting of the standing committee is supposed to be prepared by a government official (known as secretary of the standing committee) in consultation with the head of the standing committee (elected panchayat representative). The secretaries of these three standing committees are not from the functional departments concerned with environment and allied issues. The panchayat representatives, at all three tiers, are rarely concerned with abuse of environment and its dire consequences. Only the forests and environment department exists in the current framework to look after environment related matters. There are no offices of the West Bengal Pollution Control Board or West Bengal Renewable Energy Development Agency at the district level, let alone the block level. Consequently, there is no system of building environmental capacity in the panchayat and/or among general villagers.

For creating the scope for people's participation, the West Bengal Panchayat Act, 1973 contains provisions for public meetings at the village level constituency (gram sansad)[10] and at the gram panchayat level (gram sabha). With respect to gram sansad meetings, Section 16A of the Act makes two provisions: (i) every gram panchayat shall hold within its local limits an annual and a half-yearly meeting for each gram sansad at such place, on such date and at such hour as may be fixed by the gram panchayat; and (ii) the annual meeting of the gram sansad shall be held ordinarily in the month of May and the half-yearly meeting of the gram sansad shall be held ordinarily in the month of November every year. For giving importance to local opinion, the Act makes a provision that a gram sansad shall guide and advise the gram panchayat with regard to the schemes for economic development and social justice. Gram sansads have the responsibility of identifying or laying down principles for identification of (i) the beneficiaries for these programmes, and (ii) the schemes which are required to be taken on priority basis for economic development of the villages under their jurisdiction. The state government through an amendment in the West Bengal Panchayat Act in the year 2003 has made it obligatory on the part of a gram panchayat to act upon

[8] According to the Administrative Report of the Department of Panchayats and Rural Development 2008–9.

[9] This can be deduced from IAY implementation where only houses are constructed without integrating smokeless *chullah*s and sanitary latrines.

[10] According to the definition of the West Bengal Panchayat Act, gram sansad means a body consisting of persons registered at any time in the electoral rolls pertaining to a constituency of a gram panchayat. All electors in a constituency of a gram panchayat are the members of a gram sansad.

any recommendation of a gram sansad related to prioritization of beneficiaries for assistance under a programme or regarding a scheme which will be of importance for the gram sansad. Enormous emphasis has been laid on convening gram sansad meetings with wide publicity to bring all sections of people together to deliberate freely.

In spite of this displayed keenness in harnessing people's participation, attendance in meetings is not commensurate with the efforts. The average attendance of people in the gram sansad meetings since 1996 reflects their unwillingness to participate in such meetings (Table 26.5)—the attendance is generally the bare minimum required for validation of the meetings.[11] The crux of the problem is that people in general do not take any interest in the affairs of the panchayat. The important reasons for such a state of affairs are: (i) people's demands/aspirations most often not fulfilled through the panchayats; (ii) inadequate publicity of these meetings, namely invitation not duly made and not made in courteous manner; (iii) members attended do not get the opportunity to express their voices, etc.

Table 26.5 Average Attendance in Gram Sansad and Gram Sabha Meetings: West Bengal

Year	*Gram Sansad (May)*	*Gram Sansad (November)*	*Gram Sabha*
1996	11	18	3
1997	15	18	3
1998	11	16	2.9
1999	12	13	5.5
2000	12	13	5
2001	12	11	9
2002	12	12	5
2003	12	11.7	7
2004	12.8	13.3	7
2005	12.6	12.7	7.3
2006	11.9	12.8	7.4

Note: All figures are in percentage of total voters of a gram sansad and a gram sabha.

Source: Annual Administrative Reports of the Department of Panchayats and Rural Development, Government of West Bengal.

In the agenda of gram sansad meetings only the list of beneficiaries and schemes under different programmes are deliberated upon. As the holding of these meetings is prescribed by law, the gram panchayats conduct them regularly. All discussions are centred on benefits from different programmes; issues such as deforestation, installation of carbon generating brick-kilns, usage of generator sets, etc., seldom figure in the discussions. It is clear that at the local level, the importance of green initiatives is yet to be fully understood by the people and their representatives. Therefore, introducing low carbon technology has little chance to succeed unless the day-to-day activities of individuals, families, communities, industrial establishments at the village level change substantially, for which green local leadership is critical.

For strengthening decentralization and involvement of people in the process of development, the state government by an amendment of the West Bengal Panchayat Act in the year 2003 took the decision to constitute a Gram Unnayan Samiti (GUS) in each gram sansad. The GUS is the representative body of the villagers at villages for interaction with the common people and liaison with the gram panchayat. As specified in the Act, a GUS shall ensure active participation of people in implementation, maintenance, and equitable distribution of benefits with respect to such subjects as may be prescribed. In a GUS, possible representation of all sections of people in a village is sought to be ensured. The stipulation is that not less than one-third members of the GUS shall be women.

In reality, enthusiasm (even to the extent of breaching public tranquillity) is seen more in formation than in functioning of the GUS. The main factor is the ubiquitous presence of the Party, and capturing of space and people for Party loyalists. This can be evident if one goes through the list of beneficiaries of any individual benefit oriented scheme like the Indira Awas Yojana. At the time of selection of a beneficiary, Party followers get priority over the other equally eligible prospective beneficiaries. The GUS, in fact, has been made the executive arm of the gram sansad. The planning process in the rural areas starts from the gram sansad. In the sansad meeting, villagers express their demands for development, which are collated and prioritized according to the availability of funds in different programmes by the gram panchayat. Without environmental awareness at the grassroot level, then, there is little hope for rural areas in Bengal to move towards a low carbon growth trajectory. Drawing from experiences in the Purulia district, there is no record of villagers demanding solar powered light. This is despite Census 2001 records that only 13.61 per cent households

[11] The provision of the Act (Sub-section 4A of Section 16A) states that one tenth of the total number of members shall form the quorum for a meeting of a gram sansad, that is, there should be a mandatory presence of 10 per cent of the members of gram sansad to validate the meeting.

here have electricity, as compared to 22.53 per cent in the 1991 census.[12] Use of non-conventional energy can bridge this gap but local leaders are yet to realize this. Demands have been raised by the GUSs for diesel pumps but not for eco-friendly treadle pumps. The gap in knowledge and skill may be narrowed through training programmes. However, till date there is no scope for training of GUS members; only panchayat members at three tiers can avail of this opportunity.

Progress on Panchayats in Taking up Green Initiatives

In West Bengal, the selection of beneficiaries and identification of schemes supported by the Ministry of Rural Development and Ministry of the Panchayati Raj of the Government of India are the responsibility of the gram panchayat, with the advice of the gram sansad.[13] Thus, the scope for green initiatives by the panchayats through various rural development programmes lies in NREGS, Backward Village Grant Fund (BRGF), and Indira Awas Yojna (IAY). The first two are programmes for building community assets and the third one provides houses to below poverty line households.

The National Rural Employment Guarantee Act, 2005 lists the kind of works that may be taken up for providing employment. Of the permissible works, drought proofing, including afforestation and tree plantation, land development, etc., relate to a low carbon development agenda. The relative priority given to these types of work is evident from Table 26.6.

There has been concentration on 'rural connectivity' or the construction and augmentation of rural roads, which is mostly earth work as the prescribed wage-material cost ratio of 60:40 cannot be met for metalled roads. Drought proofing and land development schemes together account for only 12.5 per cent of total expenditure although these are labour-intensive. Combating soil erosion through construction of earthen structures and planting of native vegetation, planting of trees and other vegetation, development of micro-watershed, etc., are some possible schemes. The immediate benefit of drought proofing is reduced soil erosion, carbon sequestration, production of fruits, shade, and ultimately, increased value of land.

Table 26.6 Share of Different Works Taken Up Under NREGS in 2007–8 in West Bengal

Type of Works	*Expenditure (Rs in crore)*	*Percentage of total expenditure*
Rural connectivity	231.15	38.3
Renovation of traditional water bodies	91.40	15.1
Water conservation and water harvesting	90.66	15.0
Flood control and protection	64.95	10.7
Micro irrigation works	38.55	6.4
Drought proofing	37.88	6.3
Land development	37.38	6.2
Provision of irrigation facility	12.18	2.0

Source: *Annual Report (2007–8) of the Department of Panchayats and Rural Development.*

The panchayat representatives prefer to take up traditional activities such as road construction as a matter of habit. They prefer not to wait for visualizing the outcome of expenditure. In environmental intervention schemes quantification of benefits both in the long and short term is difficult. The multiple roles and benefits of trees in drought proofing, prevention of soil, and water runoff, supply of fodder, etc., are rarely recognized at the local decision-making levels.

The Backward Region Grant Fund (2006–7) is another programme where panchayats have scope to promote green initiatives. This fund is designed to redress regional imbalances in development. According to the programme guidelines, the fund will provide financial resources for supplementing and converging existing development inflow into identified districts, so as to

- bridge critical gaps in local infrastructure that are not being adequately met through existing inflows;
- strengthen the panchayat level governance with more appropriate capacity building;
- provide professional support to local bodies for planning, implementation, and monitoring their plans;
- improve the performance and delivery of critical functions assigned to the panchayats and counter-possible efficiency and equity losses on account of inadequate local capacity.

[12] This happened as number of households increased faster than electricity coverage did.

[13] A gram sansad shall guide and advise the gram panchayat in regard to the schemes for economic development and social justice undertaken or proposed to be undertaken in its area and may, without prejudice to the generality of such guidance and advice:

- identify, or lay down principles for identification of the schemes which are required to be taken on priority basis for economic development of the village.
- identify or lay down principles for identification of the beneficiaries for various poverty alleviation programmes...

Local bodies may use the funds released under BRGF for any purpose that fits in with the items that are devolved to them respectively as listed in the Eleventh (for panchayats) and Twelfth (for urban local bodies) Schedule of the Constitution of India. Schemes included under BRGF are the creation of infrastructure for social development, health and nutrition (mainly construction of ICDS centres, health sub-centres at villages, etc.), road connectivity (construction of culverts), housing for the poor, augmentation of drinking water, building of child education centres and primary schools. In BRGF programme guidelines there is a provision that panchayats may be motivated to take up electrification through additional financial support to supplement investment made under the Rajiv Gandhi Grameen Vidyutikaran Yojna (RGGVY). However, this integration is missing.

Indira Awas Yojna is a housing scheme for families below the poverty line, where there is an inbuilt provision for a smokeless *chullah* and a sanitary latrine. Funds for IAY are contributed shared by the central and state governments in the ratio of 75:25. According to the guidelines, 60 per cent of the total IAY allocation has been earmarked for scheduled castes and scheduled tribe households, 3 per cent for physically handicapped persons, and 15 per cent for the families of minority communities. Beneficiary selection is made by the gram sansad on the basis of the permanent wait list of beneficiaries generated from the existing below poverty line households. In permanent wait lists only those families are included who have the lowest rank in respect of the status of housing in the rural household survey. At present, the unit cost of a house is Rs 35,000 per house in case of new construction. The unit cost includes the cost of one smokeless *chullah* and a sanitary latrine.

The performance under IAY during 2003–4 to 2007–8 in West Bengal is presented in Table 26.7. No data on the integration of smokeless *chullah* and sanitary latrine is available from the Department of Panchayats and Rural Development, Government of West Bengal, records. A field survey in Purulia district in 2009, shows that only around 10–15 per cent beneficiaries have this convergence. An observation from the Report of the Examiner of Local Accounts on the Panchayati Raj Institutions for the year ending 31 March 2006 in respect of implementation of IAY is quoted here to cite the lack of convergence between house construction and provisioning of smokeless *chullahs*. 'Audit of implementation of IAY revealed irregularities in selection of beneficiaries, non-conferment of ownership of huts on women as envisaged in the scheme, non- construction of sanitary latrines and smokeless *chullah*s in spite of assistance released for them and loss of central share due to sluggish utilization of funds already made available'. According to the Report, 'in 1328 Gram Panchayats, 68245 sanitary latrines and 1592 Gram Panchayats, 78766 smokeless *chullah*s were not constructed although the full amount of assistance amounting to Rs 259.54 crores was given to the beneficiaries in two installments by the Gram Panchayats during 2004–05'. In Table 26.8, the district-wise scenario as has emerged from the Report of the Examiner of Local Accounts is presented.

From Table 26.8 it can be seen that more or less in half of the beneficiaries, smokeless *chullahs* are not constructed. Under IAY, gram panchayats act as implementing agencies, disbursing 50 per cent of the total cost to the beneficiaries as the first instalment; and releasing the remaining 50 per cent on utilization of the first. Hardly any physical verification of the construction is conducted. Reasons behind non-construction of smokeless *chullah*s as revealed from the field survey made in Purulia district include:

- Beneficiaries not being told that construction of smokeless *chullahs* is obligatory and it is for their benefit at the time of handing over the cheque. No environmental extension system exists at the gram panchayat level with beat offices of the Department of Forests and Environment[14] as the nearest substitute.

Table 26.7 Performance Under IAY During 2003–4 to 2007–8

Year	*Total fund available (Rs in crores)*	*Fund utilized (Rs in crores)*	*Percentage of fund utilization*	*New construction of houses*	*Upgradation of houses*
2003–4	209.61	154.78	73.84	60565	30036
2004–5	306.76	273.50	89.16	101358	54240
2005–6	298.07	205.86	69.06	66903	33150
2006–7	367.28	280.51	76.38	85200	43638
2007–8	429.77	274.97	63.98	96115	21449

Source: *Annual Report 2007–8 of Department of the Panchayats and Rural Development*, Government of West Bengal.

[14] They are mainly interested in forest areas and plantation.

TABLE 26.8 District-wise Number of Houses in IAY and Non-provisioning of Smokeless *Chullas* (2004–5)

District	*Total houses in IAY*	*Cases of non construction of chullahs*	*Percentage of non-construction*
Cooch Behar	23640	15124	63.97
Jalpaiguri	26388	11330	42.94
Darjeeling	10237	4857	47.44
Uttar Dinajpur	10791	4844	44.89
Dakshin Dinajpur	2649	2019	76.22
Malda	6285	5131	81.64
Murshidabad	3620	2069	57.15
Nadia	6963	2526	36.28
North 24 Parganas	7385	2834	38.37
South 24 Parganas	9692	5431	56.03
Howrah	3511	1812	51.61
Hooghly	6293	3355	53.31
Paschim Midnapur	6491	3368	51.89
Purba Midnapur	5600	2537	45.30
Bankura	5503	3146	57.17
Purulia	4055	3183	78.49
Burdwan	7636	3046	39.89
Birbhum	3776	2154	57.04
State	150515	78766	52.33

Sources: For col. 2, *Annual report 2004–5 of the Department of Panchayats and Rural Development*, Government of West Bengal; for cols 3 and 4, Report of the Examiner of Local Accounts as referred in to the text.

- No verification process. Even if there are verification visits, they are for overseeing the progress of construction of houses—out of 750 beneficiaries surveyed only 11 reported that panchayat representatives enquired whether construction of smokeless *chullahs* was done.
- Utility of smokeless *chullahs* not being explained to the beneficiaries—of 750 sample beneficiaries only 95 had heard about it. According to Census 2001, in Purulia district 63.93 per cent households in rural areas use firewood for cooking.
- The gram panchayat heads and members themselves are not well aware of the utility of smokeless *chullahs* and the provision of integration with IAY houses. Of 52 gram panchayats surveyed, only 13 pradhans (head of gram panchayats) responded positively.

Anecdotal evidence from these three programmes clearly indicates absence of capacity at the local level for green energy initiatives.

Capacity Development for Panchayats and Local Governing Bodies

The Department of Panchayats and Rural Development has a wide network of District Level Trainers' Teams (DLTT) for imparting training to the panchayats. In 2008, 17 Training of Trainers (TOT) camps were organized for training of DLTT members, after the general election to three–tier panchayats. The six-day training course of TOT covers most of the learning events starting from training methodology to overview of different rural development programmes, as summarized in Table 26.9.

The thrust of the training is on the management of offices and the programmes implemented by the panchayats. For the members of the panchayats, the Department of Panchayats and Rural Development, the government of West Bengal decided to hold seven categories of training programmes to be completed within two years of assuming their offices, as presented in Table 26.10.

Table 26.9 A Synoptic View of the Training Course

Day	*Subject matter*	*Time allotted*
One	Participatory training methods, use of various aids, management of training	6 hours
Two	Historical background of West Bengal panchayats, West Bengal Panchayat Act and Rules; structure, functions, roles, and responsibilities of panchayats	8 hours
Three	(a) Issues related to self-governance; resource mobilization, budget, audit	6 hours
	(b) Natural resource management	2 hours
Four	(a) Women's empowerment and role of self-help groups	3 hours
	(b) Health, family welfare, and primary education	4 hours
	(c) Disaster management	1 hour
Five	(a) Overview of major rural development and social security programmes implemented by the panchayats	4 ½ hours
	(b) Decentralized planning : concept, methods, and implementation process	3 ½ hours
Six	(a) Practice sessions by participants	3 hours
	(b) Training management	1 ½ hours
	(c) Further review of the training design	3 hours

Source: Records of the State Institute of Panchayats and Rural Development (SIPRD) (2008).

Table 26.10 A Synoptic View of the Training Course

Particulars of Training course	*Duration*	*Location of training*
(i) Crash course for pradhans and upa-pradhans	2 days	Block/sub-division
(ii) Crash course for sabhapatis and sahakari sabhapatis	2 days	District/sub-division
(iii) Orientation course for gram panchayat members	3 days	Block/sub-division
(iv) Orientation course for panchayat samiti members	3 days	District/sub-division
(v) Orientation course for zilla parishad members	3 days	SIPRD/District
(vi) Thematic course for karmadhyakshyas of panchayat samitis and zilla parishads	3 days	SIPRD
(vii) Refresher course for gram panchayat members	3 days	Block/sub-division

Source: Records of SIPRD (2008).

Orientation courses for gram panchayat, panchayat samiti, and zilla parishad members are organized to enable them to have an idea about their duties and responsibilities. The courses are designed to instil in the trainee, a sense of the significance of the panchayat as an institution for good governance and social justice. The learning events of these courses[15] can be broadly categorized into six groups, as tabulated in Table 26.11.

Thematic courses for the karmadhyakshas of all sthayee samitis in panchayat samitis and zilla parishads have the main objective of building knowledge regarding the functioning of their concerned sthayee samitis. The learning events of three standing committees that have an environment component are depicted in Table 26.12. Even here, sessions on environmental issues get less space in comparison with other subjects.

The outcomes of a training programme are, to a large extent, dependent on the selection and development of suitable, need-based, and appropriate course materials and training aids. For the panchayat members in all three tiers, training booklets are printed and delivered to the district authorities for distribution among the members. In addition, copies of relevant government orders, guidelines of different programmes, brochures, etc., are also given so that these become the permanent documents for the participants and can serve as reference in their work places. Training, however, remains a one shot operation in case of the panchayat members, that is, in their five-year term, they are trained just once, with no provision for refresher courses.

It is evident by now that issues of environment have no prominence in these trainings, let alone specific issues of

[15] Conducted by DLTT members at district/sub-division/block venues and by the faculty of the State Institute of Panchayats and Rural Development (SIPRD) and experts from the functional departments.

Table 26.11 Synoptic View of Time Devloted to Learning Events of the Orientation Courses

Learning events category	*Gram panchayat members*	*Panchayat samiti members*	*Zilla parishad members*
(i) Office procedure	1 hour	1½ hours	1 hour
(ii) Structure and functions of the panchayats (respective tiers)	1 hour	2 hours	2 hours
(iii) Social issues in rural areas	3 hour	2 hours	2 hours
(iv) Intervention of the panchayats (respective tiers)	9 hour	8 hours	7 hours
(v) Resource mobilization	1 hour	1½ hours	1 hour
(vi) Decentralized planning	2 hour	2 hours	2 hours

Note: In the case of zilla parishads, members are sometimes retained for group exercises.
Source: Records of SIPRD (2008).

Table 26.12 Issues Covered in Learning Events for Relevant Standing Committees and Time Devoted to Broad Categorization of the Issues

Small Industry, Electricity and Non-conventional Energy	–	Role of village and small industries in rural development and employment generation, government programmes in these areas, bank loan provisions, programmes of sericulture, khadi and handloom development, rural electrification, programmes for development of non-conventional energy. [Village and small industry—6 ½ hours Rural electrification—5 hours Non-conventional energy—1 hour]
Public Health and Environment	–	Concept of public health, programmes of the Health and Family Welfare Department, programmes to combat malnutrition, sanitation, birth and death registration, environment, and allied issues. [Public health, etc.—9 hours Environment—3 hours]
Forest and Land Reforms	–	Land reforms and its different facets, government programmes in land reforms, forest department programmes, joint forest management, and role of the panchayats. [Land reforms—8 hours Forest sector—6 hours]

Source: Records of SIPRD (2008).

adoption of low carbon technologies and implementing adaptation measures. Capacity building support to the panchayats from the state government is provided for implementation of state-funded programmes and day-to-day management of offices. The main purpose of any training programme, augmentation of knowledge and skill, and changing attitude, is defeated.

The Way Forward

Energy deeply influences people's lives. It is central to practically all aspects of human welfare, and yet, in rural areas, the majority of households still lack access to modern energy services that are affordable, clean, reliable, and safe, and have to depend on fuel wood. This situation entrenches poverty, damages health, increases vulnerability to climate change, and erodes the environment. Sustainable development depends in large measure on successfully integrating the environment into economic planning and decision-making, a process known as environmental mainstreaming. This is an iterative process of integrating poverty environment linkages into policy making, budgeting, and implementation processes at national, sector, and sub-national levels. It is a multi-year, multi-stakeholder effort that entails working with government actors, non-governmental actors, and development actors. This linkage is missing, both at the level of making plans like BRGF and at the local level, where there is little understanding on environmental issues. At the state government level as well, environmental issues do not get adequate attention: the withdrawal of the subsidy of

Rs 4,800 on purchase of solar energy equipments is a case in point[16] (*Ananda Bazar Patrika* 2009).

Funds of an untied nature like the Backward Region Grant Fund and Second State Finance Commission fund could be dovetailed with other departmental programme funds for taking up green energy initiatives. Directives from the Department of Panchayats and Rural Development specifying a certain percentage of fund to be spent for green energy initiatives in untied nature programmes are necessary to ensure spends on green energy initiatives. This could emulate the Twelfth Finance Commission which mandates that from the fund (Rs 254.20 crore each year from 2005–6 to 2009–10) a minimum 10 per cent must be spent on solid waste management, water supply, sanitation, and drainage facilities.

Adoption of new technology will remain a distant dream without building knowledge and awareness of local leaders. As the panchayats have control over major affairs, they are change agents in all these initiatives. Without transformational thinking among local leaders, it is difficult drive action that may seem unconventional to the local populace. Awareness generation campaigns on green energy initiatives are the need of the hour. To start with, rather than expecting rural India to join the climate change bandwagon and move towards a low carbon trajectory, incremental steps to appreciate the intrinsic and instrumental value of the environment, and small schemes to gradually green rural India are more realistic goals.

References

Ananda Bazar Patrika (2009). 'Achiracharit sakti' Bengali Daily, Kolkata Edition, West Bengal, dated 13 December, p. 4.

Department of Panchayats and Rural Development, *Annual Report 2004–5,* Government of West Bengal.

Department of Panchayats and Rural Development (2008). *Annual Administrative Report 2007–08*, Government of West Bengal, pp. 18–19, 57–8, 63–4;

——— (2009). *Annual Administrative Report 2008–09*, Government of West Bengal, pp. 35–6, 88–9, 118–9.

Director of Census Operation (2001). Census of India, Directorate of Census Operations, West Bengal, pp. 631–3.

Government of West Bengal (2009). *West Bengal Panchayat Act, 1973*, 31 May, pp. 26–30; 32–8; 50–1; 146–8; 194–5.

Office of the Accountant General (Receipt, Works and Local Bodies Audit) West Bengal (2007). *Report of the Examiner of Local Accounts on the Panchayati Raj Institutions 31 March 2006.* State Institute of Panchayats and Rural Development (SIPRD), 2008. pp. 23–4 and 205.

West Bengal Panchayat (2004). '(Gram Panchayat) Administration Rules, 2004', *Kolkata Gazette*, 23 November, pp. 23–5.

——— (2008). '(Panchayat Samiti) Administration Rules, 2008', *Kolkata Gazette*, 14 February, pp. 9–10.

World Development Report (1992). 'Development and the Environment' Oxford University Press, chapter 4, New York, pp. 93–4.

[16] The Managing Director of the Green Energy Development Corporation in West Bengal pointed out that every night in rural areas of West Bengal, 2 crore hurricanes are lighted which requires 6 crore litres of kerosene oil in a month—for giving subsidy to kerosene oil Rs 126 crore is required. He opined that if this subsidy is given to solar energy then it would be possible to provide one solar lantern to each household in rural areas (*Ananda Bazar Patrika* 2009).

Section VII

Infrastructure Review

27 The Infrastructure Sector in India, 2009–10

Manisha Gulati

With the effect of the global financial crisis of 2008–9 on the Indian economy wearing off and a new government taking charge in India, the focus during 2009–10 was to rejuvenate the pace of infrastructure development. Considering the limited progress in capacity expansion in the infrastructure sectors in 2008–9, the GoI constituted a high-powered committee in July 2009 to fast-track implementation of projects and monitoring their performance. It was empowered to take all decisions, including approval of all infrastructure related proposals costing over Rs 150 crore.

Besides this attempt to improve the pace of award and execution of infrastructure projects, the year saw regulatory reforms in almost all sectors. Concerns in the regulatory framework for private sector participation (PSP) in national highways were ironed out, there was a proposal for setting up of a Major Port Regulatory Authority (MPRA) with more teeth, the Airports Economic Regulatory Authority of India (AERA) began functioning, and the creation of a coal regulator was announced. These reforms are expected to improve the investment climate for PSP and thus, attract greater private capital.

But the resurgence in the investment climate was tempered by two court cases, under different legal jurisdictions, which would impact setting up of Special Purpose Vehicles (SPVs) for projects planned through the Public Private Partnership (PPP) route (see Box 27.1). The judgments of the High Courts of Karnataka and Maharashtra on public scrutiny of activities of SPVs imply that such SPVs would be amenable to the writ jurisdiction of the High Court or the Supreme Court and can also be exposed to the Right to Information (RTI) Act, since they perform a public function and receive concessions or other financial aid from the central or state governments. Therefore, SPVs would be open to public scrutiny and would be also required to disclose procedural and commercial information, including contracts. This view was substantiated by the Central Information Commission (CIC), the appellate authority under the RTI Act. The CIC, in a judgment, observed that all contracts related to a PPP project must be disclosed in their entirety to ensure transparency. These judgments imply that any SPV, regardless of whether a government has a stake in it, would need to function under 'public scrutiny' and 'transparency'.

A review of the developments in the individual infrastructure sectors is presented below.

Telecom

The telecom sector was characterized by intense competitive activity due to the entry of new players and expansion by smaller players, particularly in the wireless segment. This increase in competition was evident from the aggressive tariff plans introduced by the wireless operators to attract customers. Not surprisingly, teledensity grew from 37 per cent as at the end of FY 2008–9 to 53 per cent at the end of FY 2009–10. As has been the case over the past few years, the main contribution to growth in teledensity came from wireless subscribers who registered an increase of almost 50 per cent during the same period. The bulk of this increase in wireless subscribers came from semi-urban and rural areas, which also increased by 50 per cent growth over this period.

However, there is a large variation in teledensity across states. Many less developed states, which include Chhattisgarh, Jharkhand, and Uttaranchal, and parts of the North-East have teledensity well below 20 per cent.

Box 27.1
Public Scrutiny of SPVs Formed to Execute Infrastructure Projects through the SPV Route

The Flemingo Duty-free Shops Pvt. Ltd. (FDSL) filed a writ petition against the Bangalore International Airport Ltd. (BIAL) in the High Court of Karnataka on the grounds that BIAL's shortlisting of bidders for establishment of retail and duty-free shops in the international terminals at new BIAL, following the notification of Expression of Interest (EoI) which did not detail the evaluation criteria, was arbitrary and discriminatory in nature. This violated Article 14 of the Constitution of India. The High Court of Karnataka took the view that BIAL discharges the statutory functions/duties under Section 12-A of the Airports Authorities of India Act, 1994 and is therefore a 'State'. Further, under Article 226 of the Constitution of India, any agency including an SPV performing public duty is an instrumentality of the State and under Article 12 of the Constitution of India, is the 'State' itself. This means that the SPV would be open to scrutiny in a manner that any government department would be and, by extension, could be asked to follow the processes as in any agency which is an arm of the State.

The High Court of Maharashtra, on a similar writ petition filed against the Mumbai International Airport Ltd. (MIAL) issued a judgment in favour of the petitioner. It held that though MIAL is a registered private company, it performs a public function and is a 'State' as defined by the Constitution. Therefore, MIAL comes under the purview of the Right to Information (RTI) Act.

Source: Author's own.

The problem is more pronounced in case of rural teledensity, which still remains low at 21 per cent. This is a matter of concern, in view of the fact that only 40 per cent of funds collected as universal service levy from telecom operators since 2002–3 have been utilized till date (see Table 27.1) for increasing the penetration of telecom services in rural and remote areas.

Table 27.1 Status of Funds Collected and Allocated by the Universal Service Obligation Fund

(in Rs Crore)

	Opening balance	*Funds collected as USL*	*Funds allocated*
2002–3	0	1653.61	300
2003–4	1353.61	2143.22	200
2004–5	3296.83	3457.73	1314.59
2005–6	5439.97	3533.29	1766.85
2006–7	7206.41	4211.13	1500
2007–8	9917.54	5405.46	1290
2008–9	14033.00	5759.52	1600
2009–10	18192.52		2400
Total		26163.96	10371.44

Source: Department of Telecommunications, Government of India.

The year saw declines in average revenue per user (ARPU), revenue growth and profitability of the industry due to competitive tariffs, increasing number of rural subscribers, and growth in the share of pre-paid subscribers (see Table 27.2). Value-added services (VAS) are therefore increasingly being considered by service-providers to boost ARPUs and also differentiate their services. Currently, the contribution of VAS to the total mobile revenues of the telecom operators is just 9–10 per cent, but is expected to grow manifold with the GoI finally undertaking the auction of 3G spectrum.

Table 27.2 ARPUs of Mobile Service-providers

(in Rs)

	As of 31 March 2009	*As of 31 December 2009*
Average Revenue Per User (ARPU) GSM	205	144
Average Revenue Per User (ARPU) CDMA	99	82

Source: Telecom Regulatory Authority of India.

Though much delayed, the GoI has at the end of FY 2009–10 initiated the process of auctioning 3G spectrum and Broadband Wireless Access (BWA). The GoI has set the date 9 April 2010 for the auction of 3G spectrum, with the auction of BWA stated to start two days after the close of the 3G auction. The GoI has fixed the base reserve price for the all-India 3G spectrum at Rs 3,500 crore for one slot and Rs 1,750 crore for an all-India roll out of broadband services. Successful bidders are required to pay the entire bid amount within a period of 10 days, although they can commercially use the 3G spectrum only from 1 September 2010.

One of the disappointments in the sector has been the slow progress in implementation of Mobile Number Portability (MNP). The deadlines to implement MNP in the metros and category 'A' circles by the middle of 2009, and in the rest of the country by the end of 2009, have not been met and are now proposed as 30 June 2010.

The Telecommunications Regulatory Authority of India (TRAI) has notified the key charges for the implementation of MNP. A subscriber would be able to port her/his number once in every 90 days (within the same circle). The subscriber may be required to pay a porting charge to the recipient operator, that is, the operator to whom the subscriber is porting his/her number, which would be subject to a maximum of Rs 19 per porting. The maximum time for completing the porting process would be four days (12 days for the circles of Jammu and Kashmir, Assam, and the North-East).

The ceiling set by TRAI for porting charges will make it considerably cheap for subscribers to port their numbers and is likely to be a major factor driving the increasing usage of the MNP facility as and when it commences, given the current dissatisfaction among consumers with quality of service (QoS), and the array of choices of operators and attractive plans.

Transport

Roads

The year 2008 had seen virtually no progress in the development of national highways due to several reasons, which include issues in standard bidding documents (SBD) and Model Concession Agreement (MCA), global economic slowdown, impediments in land acquisition, forest and environment clearances, shifting of utilities, etc. There was a distinct slowdown in the award of new projects in 2008–9 with only eight projects being awarded during the year and the implementation of ongoing projects was sluggish. The challenge in 2009 therefore was two-fold: regain the lost momentum of project award and achieve a quantum jump in the pace of highway construction. But naturally, the sector received the spotlight in 2009. The MoRTH targeted at accomplishing construction of national highways at the pace of 20 km per day, targeting the completion of 35,000 km of national highways during 2009–14. Achieving this ambitious target required resolution of several impediments and roadblocks mentioned above.

Accordingly, the GoI constituted a committee under the Chairmanship of B.K. Chaturvedi, Member, Planning Commission (the B.K. Chaturvedi Committee or BKCC) to resolve procedural impediments and develop a financing plan for the National Highways Development Project (NHDP). The implementation of Part 1 of this Committee's recommendations removed several impediments to the award of highway projects. Amendments have been made in the SBD and MCA (see Box 27.2). The viability gap funding has been increased from 10 per cent to 20 per cent for low-traffic stretches in Phase V of the NHDP and from 5 per cent to 10 per cent for the six-laning programme. The entire VGF will be released in one go as against the previous norm of releasing 50 per cent of the amount during construction and 50 per cent during maintenance. The positive impact of these changes have resulted in the speedy progress of the highways sector and is evident from the award of 34 projects since these recommendations were effected in November 2009 (see Table 27.3).

The project delivery strategy of the NHAI has also been changed. The sequential project award strategy of first testing the award on a build-operate-transfer (BOT) toll basis, then on BOT annuity basis and finally, on a engineering, procurement, and construction (EPC) basis in

Box 27.2

Key Changes to The Standard Bid Documents and Model Concession Agreement for National Highways as Per Recommendations of The B.K. Chaturvedi Committee

- *Returns*: The concession agreement can be extended by five years if the concessionaire undertakes capacity augmentation in response to the actual traffic exceeding the designed road capacity. However, the concessionaire's IRR would be capped at 15 per cent. Earlier, the concession was terminated if the traffic exceeded capacity for more than three years.
- *Conflict of interest*: The limit for common shareholding between various bidders has been raised from 5 per cent to 25 per cent, and the NHAI is empowered to make project-specific exemptions where the conflict still exists.
- *Entry*: The bidders' technical capacity-related entry threshold with respect to the size of the past project experience has been reduced.
- *Funds*: The lenders are permitted to create a charge on the escrow account maintained by the concessionaire in relation to toll collections on the road project thereby making lending to roads projects 'secure'.
- *Exit*: Promoters holding majority shareholding can fully divest two years after project completion, a significant change from the present situation wherein the promoter's share could fall to 26 per cent three years after project completion and would remain constant for the rest of the concession period.

Source: B.K. Chaturvedi Committee Report (2009).

Table 27.3 Award of National Highway Projects During 2009–10

	No. of projects awarded	*Length (km)*	*Project Cost (Rs Crore)*
2008–9	8	643	8,591
April—October 2009	10	944	9,606
November 2009—March 2010 (post-implementation of B.K. Chaturvedi Committee recommendations)	34	2,532	25,616

Source: IDFC Policy Group Research.

case the project is found unviable on BOT annuity basis and has been changed. Projects will now be implemented on all the three modes of delivery, that is BOT toll, BOT Annuity, and EPC concurrently rather than sequentially. This will speed up the award of projects by identifying the mode of development upfront as against the sequential award process, which involved testing projects for the BOT toll mode even if they were not suitable for this mode because of traffic being below a certain threshold. Further, the NHAI is now empowered to take decisions on single bids after examining their reasonableness.

The revised financing plan for NHDP as drawn up by the BKCC indicates an investment requirement of Rs 812,661 crore of which 26 per cent is to be mobilized from the private sector.

Steps have been taken by the MoRTH and NHAI to streamline the land acquisition process and improve the pace of projects under implementation. Special Land Acquisition Units (SLAUs) have been set up to speed up land acquisition at the state level for national highways development. Out of the 192 SLAUs planned, 66 have already been appointed. As a result of these efforts, more than double the land (8,191 ha) has been acquired this year compared to the annual average (4,000 ha) of the last three years.

Though the GoI has shown a renewed impetus for pushing forward the road development programme, there are some existing and emerging issues that still need quick resolution. NHAI's capacity to prepare a pipeline of credible and bankable projects still remains clouded. NHAI requires significant capacity building and organizational reforms to be able to effectively shoulder the responsibility of building 20 km of national highways every day. Though the proposal for restructuring of NHAI was approved by the Union Cabinet in July 2007, actions to this end continue to be delayed on account of the process of amendment of the NHAI Act 1988. The NHAI (Amendment) Bill 2008 lapsed with the dissolution of the Fourteenth Lok Sabha—a consequence of the general elections in 2009.

Another issue is that of financing. Two major problems currently constrain highway sector finance. First, bank loans to highway projects were unsecured, and as a consequence subject to higher provisioning and capital adequacy norms. Second, highway projects need substantial long-term financing as they are typically capital-intensive, long-gestation projects. Currently, commercial banks find it difficult to lend long-term due to apprehensions about asset-liability mismatch.

To address the first problem, following BKCC recommendations, the RBI allowed annuities and toll collection rights as tangible security for the purpose of secured bank loans. To address the second, the government recently approved norms for takeout financing for the India Infrastructure Finance Company Ltd. (IIFCL). Lending institutions will be able to sell part of the loan to IIFCL three to four years after the project starts commercial operations. Moreover, in order to bring in investors with a long-term horizon such as pension funds and insurance companies, their investment guidelines need to be relaxed while being cognizant of their capacity to manage risk.

Finally, with the road length and width set to increase by an enormous magnitude, an issue that has so far been overlooked and needs to be given importance is that of quality of service. Suitable Performance Indicators with penalty mechanisms need to be defined to measure the quality of service being provided to road users.

Ports

During the year, the GoI mooted a new legislation, the Major Port Regulatory Authority Act, 2009, for the setting up of a Major Port Regulatory Authority (MPRA). If this legislation is passed by Parliament, MPRA will replace the existing regulator, the Tariff Authority for Major Ports (TAMP), which has no power to enforce its own tariff rulings or penalize violation of the terms and conditions governing tariffs.

MPRA will have the regulatory powers, inter alia, to specify and monitor performance standards for service to be provided by the port authorities and private operators; and levy penalty on terminal operators. This will also remove another key drawback associated with TAMP, which unlike other sectoral regulators in the country such as TRAI and the CERC, is not vested with the powers to set and enforce performance standards and other measures for protection of user interests. Therefore, the creation of the MPRA will also go a long way in making ports more efficient. MPRA will also act as an appellate authority, settling disputes between port authorities, private operators, and users and looking into their problems arising from running or using port services.

The situation in the port sector has otherwise been somewhat stagnant. Although there have been few instances of capacity expansion, it may be argued that capacity is not a major issue for Indian ports. The traffic handled is more than the capacity in only four major ports, that is, Visakhapatnam, Chennai, Mormugao, and Mumbai (see Table 27.4). However, given that the majority of ports are operating at over 90 per cent capacity utilization and traffic at major ports is expected to reach 708.09 million tonnes in FY 2011–12, the issue of capacity addition cannot be completely ignored. In fact, the issue needs greater attention than before in view of the fact that the capacity addition of 70 MT since 2007–8 includes capacity anchorage to the tune of 11.40 MT. This refers to the capacity of cargo handled at anchorage and not physical addition in capacity, such as addition of berths. Further, capacity addition would improve service standards for end-users who now have to cope with near 100 per cent berth occupancy in these ports. In fact, service levels reflected through performance metrics such as average turnaround time, average pre-berthing time, average output per ship-berth-day, and dwell time of cargo/containers remain unsatisfactory by international comparison. The average turnaround time for the major ports increased from 3.85 days in 2008–9 to 4.54 days in 2009–10 (up to December 2009). Further, there are significant inter-port variations in performance (see Table 27.5). As against this, the average turnaround time at the Hong Kong port is estimated at 10 hours.This in turn undermines the competiveness of the Indian ports.

Besides factors specific to ports such as non-availability of handling equipments and labour at ports, one of the major reasons for the high dwell time at ports is the inadequate inland connectivity for ports. In case of major ports, the capacity and quality of the existing rail and road connectivity requires improvement. The Comptroller and Auditor General of India, in its performance audit of functioning of major Ports Trusts, has observed that ports at Chennai, Cochin, Goa, Haldia, Kolkata, Tuticorin, and Vishakapatnam continue to have single-line connectivity, resulting in slower movement and inefficient cargo dispersal. At Cochin, the rail connectivity from the port area to the main rail line network is in a poor state while in Kandla, only three of the 11 tracks have double lines. Further, outside the port areas, passenger and freight systems share the same railway networks.

Further, many of the large minor ports that have started operations are connected/being connected through rail and road, have poor quality of inland connectivity, which is a major stumbling block in the seamless movement of cargo. Besides poor rail connectivity, inadequate numbers of wagons also hinder realizing the growth potential in cargo traffic and customers.

Managements in several ports have, however, woken up to the need for better services through port development as well as better technologies. Some of the Port Trusts are tying up with foreign port companies on these very aspects. The Mundra Port has signed an MoU with Antwerp Port Authority to absorb some of the international port management practices. The Mumbai Port Trust has entered into a sister port agreement with the Port of Marseille-Fos of France to foster experience sharing in the areas of engineering, management, security, and sustainable development while the Chennai Port Trust signed an agreement with the Port of Halifax, Canada, to cooperate on port development.

Table 27.4 Capacity vis-à-vis the Traffic Handled in Major Ports in India

(*In million tonnes*)

Port	*Capacity as on 31 March 2009*	*Traffic During 2008–9*
Kolkata	15.76	12.43
Haldia	46.70	41.79
Paradip	71.00	46.41
Vishakapatnam	62.23	63.91
Ennore	16.00	11.50
Chennai	55.75	57.49
Tuticorin	22.81	22.01
Cochin	28.37	15.23
New Mangalore	44.20	36.69
Mormugao	33.05	41.68
Mumbai	43.70	51.88
Jawaharlal Nehru	57.96	57.29
Kandla	77.24	72.22
Total	574.77	530.53

Source: Press India Bureau.

Airports

Despite the civil aviation sector being opened up to the private sector in 1997 under the GoI's Airport Infra-

TABLE 27.5 Inter-port Performance Variations at Indian Ports

Name of Port	*Average pre-berthing time under port a/c (in hours)*			*Average turnaround time (in days)*		
	2007–8	*2008–9*	*2009–10**	*2007–8*	*2008–9*	*2009–10**
Kolkata	0.24	1.27	4.36	4.87	4.60	5.34
Haldia Dock	33.44	24.45	37.35	4.26	4.21	5.20
Mumbai	5.07	7.37	7.69	4.44	4.95	4.42
Jawaharlal Nehru	10.20	9.50	6.48	1.85	1.97	1.94
Chennai	1.00	0.90	0.98	4.60	4.20	4.12
Cochin	1.21	1.31	3.08	1.99	2.08	2.14
Vishakapatnam	5.10	4.35	23.89	3.91	3.93	5.17
Kandla	32.64	28.08	26.88	5.13	5.20	5.16
Mormugao	18.35	11.48	22.16	4.03	3.61	5.62
Paradip	1.48	1.30	1.50	5.54	4.78	9.84
New Mangalore	1.92	0.90	0.72	3.21	3.00	3.22
Tuticorin	4.32	3.36	11.52	3.80	3.66	4.14
Ennore	0.75	0.74	0.52	2.08	2.35	2.24
All Major Ports	11.40	9.55	13.44	3.93	3.87	4.54

Note: * Up to December 2009.
Sources: Ministry of Finance (2010) and Department of Shipping (2010).

structure Policy, clarity and certainty to investors on the commercial potential of specific airport operations continued to elude the sector. In recent times, the absence of a clear set of guidelines for airport operators is responsible for their revenue models remaining a subject matter of national debate and controversy. Therefore, AERA becoming functional in August 2009 is a welcome development for the sector, even if it fructified six years after first recommended[1] and more than three years after the GoI proposed to establish an aviation regulator. AERA is empowered to set aeronautical charges, determine development fees, and monitor service and quality standards for the 12 airports in the country with traffic of more than 1.5 million passengers per annum.

The first issue taken up by AERA, almost within a month of its establishment, was the review of the development fee (DF) levied at the airport at New Delhi. The GoI had in February 2009 allowed the Delhi International Airport Ltd. (DIAL), the private sector consortium with GMR in the lead operating this airport, to levy Rs 200 per departing domestic passenger and Rs 1,300 per departing international passenger as DF for a period of 36 months w.e.f 1 March 2010. DIAL had sought intervention of the GoI to fund the gap of Rs 1964 crore affecting the bankability of the airport project that arose due to the poor response and consequently, shortfall in deposits received from commercial property development of the airport due to the economic crisis of 2008–9. AERA has conducted stakeholder consultations on the subject and has sought information on the project cost of the Delhi airport as well as the bidding process in respect of commercial property development to determine the DF.

AERA has also initiated steps towards establishing the degree and nature of economic regulation of aeronautical services under five categories, that is (i) Airport Operators providing various attendant aeronautical services; (ii) Air Navigation Service-provider facilitating navigation, surveillance, and supportive communication thereto for air traffic management; (iii) Cargo Facility Operators; (iv) Ground Handling Operators; and (v) Fuel Access Providers. Some of the key issues being deliberated by AERA are appropriate forms of regulation, that is, price cap regulation, rate of return regulation or light-handed regulation; approach to traffic forecasting; service parameters to be measured for major airports; and accounting for under-

[1] The establishment of an independent aviation economic regulatory authority was first recommended by the Naresh Chandra Committee in its report to the GoI on the road map for the civil aviation sector in India.

performance vis-à-vis specified benchmarks on quality of service through tariffs. Box 27.3 provides a summary of positions that AERA is considering on select issues related to airport operators.

The GoI has also established an Appellate Tribunal to adjudicate disputes between two or more service-providers and between a service-provider and a group of consumers. Service-providers refer to any entity that provides aeronautical services and is eligible to levy and charge user development fees from the embarking passengers at any airport and includes the airport operator.

Another positive development in this sector is improvement in QoS at the airports in the country. The Hyderabad International Airport has been ranked amongst the world's top five in the annual Airport Service Quality (ASQ) passenger survey conducted by the Airports Council International. It also ranks first in the category of airports handling traffic of 5–15 million passengers. This airport is managed by a public-private joint venture consisting of the GMR Group, Malaysia Airports Holdings Berhad, the state government of Andhra Pradesh, and the Airports Authority of India (AAI). At the same time, the airport at New Delhi won the award for the best improvement in the Asia-Pacific region. Such enhanced customer service and improved facilities at the airports is not restricted only to the airports managed by the private sector. With upgradation and modernization works being completed at the various non-metro airports, these airports too offer a better experience to passengers.

Railways

The Indian Railways (IR) released its ambitious 'Vision 2020' in December 2009 which recognizes the need for IR to reinvent itself to pursue growth in market share as well as revenue. The route network of IR has expanded very slowly in the past, with only 10,000 km of rail network added between 1947 and 2009. Fund shortage and poor project execution due to organizational and managerial issues have been the main reasons for this. The operating ratio of IR, which was 76 per cent in 2007–8, is projected at 92.3 per cent, implying that IR has only Rs 7.5 out of every Rs 100 for developmental works. The market share in India of rail transport for freight traffic has reduced drastically from 89 per cent in 1950–51 to 30 per cent in 2007–08 and IR faces heightened competition from roads with major investments in highways. Inter-country comparisons indicate that IR lags behind several other countries on key parameters (see Table 27.6).

Box 27.3
AERA's Proposed Regulatory Philosophy and Approach for Economic Regulation of Airport Operators

- *Form of regulation*: Price Cap Regulation or Incentive Based Regulation
- *Form of price control and tariff structure*: A yield per passenger to be determined initially under the tariff determination process and subsequently detailed tariff proposals from airports operators (pertaining to approved yield per passenger) to be reviewed and approved.
- *Fair rate of return*: To be estimated by using a weighted average cost of capital approach to estimate the nominal post-tax cost of capital.
- Cost of equity determined by using the Capital Asset Pricing Model.
- Cost of debt estimated by examining the actual cost of debt faced by airport operators, subject to reasonableness of such costs based on review of the sources, procedure, and method through which the debt was raised.
- Airport's actual gearing to be used for the time being.
- *Capital investment*: Airport development plans and investments proposed for inclusion in the Regulatory Asset Base to be taken up after user consultations.
- *Traffic forecasting*: Airports to provide traffic forecasts after consultation with users at each price review. AERA may review forecast assumptions, methodologies, and processes, and determine the final forecast to be used for tariff determination. AERA may introduce a forecast correction mechanism if the actual traffic falls outside the prescribed bands.
- *Operating expenditure*: Assessment of operating costs will cover (i) baseline operating costs taking cognizance of variance over the preceding year, including treatment of one-time costs; (ii) operating cost projection taking into account efficiency improvement for controllable costs; and (iii) cost-pass through allowance for uncontrollable mandated costs.
- *Quality of Service*: A mechanism that specifies reduced tariff for under-performance vis-à-vis specified benchmarks on quality of service so as to adequately protect the interest of the users. Under such a mechanism, the calculated level of rebate for a year will be passed on to users of airport services in the form of reduced airport (aeronautical) tariff in the subsequent years.

Source: Airports Economic Regulatory Authority of India (2010).

TABLE 27.6 International Comparison of Rail Networks

	Million traffic units per employee	*Route kms per million population*	*Route kms per square km area*
USA	15.3	747.4	23.6
China	1.6	45.5	6.4
Germany	0.7	410.9	94.9
France	2.1	466.5	54.2
Russia	2.6	598.1	4.9
India	0.9	55.2	19.3
Japan	2.2	157.5	53

Source: Indian Railways Vision 2020.

Thus, Vision 2020 aims to undertake a complete overhaul of rail infrastructure and transform train travel (see Box 27.4), and target a revenue of Rs 2,70,000 crore[2] from about Rs 90,000 crore at present. The vision also proposes several measures to reduce the carbon footprint of IR (see Box 27.5). More importantly, the vision proposes organizational restructuring of IR, which would involve separation of infrastructure from operations and reorganization of IR on business lines that is passenger, freight, and parcel and other auxiliary services so that each service could be managed and measured on a profit-centre basis.

The key to achieving the vision and its specific goals is a massive investment programme—Rs 14 lakh crore in over ten years. Out of this, just over 60 per cent of these funds are meant to be generated internally, including the use of PPP initiatives. PPP is proposed for the development of world-class stations, setting up of rolling stock manufacturing units, logistics hubs, high-speed corridors, expansion and management of the extensive network of Optical Fibre Cables and infrastructure projects like new lines and Dedicated Freight Corridors (DFC). The remaining funds are proposed to come from the GoI through an Accelerated Rail Development Fund (ARDF). An amount of Rs 1 lakh crore would be set aside from the ARDF to clear the pending backlog of socially desirable, new line and gauge conversion projects as a one-time grant for the GoI. While the investment proposed under the vision may seem enormous in view of the past trends for IR, it comes across as paltry when compared with China, which is currently undertaking one of the most ambitious rail expansions. China has earmarked $ 300 billion (Rs 14 lakh crore approximately) for investment over the next three years.

As mentioned above, the vision envisages developing and implementing new business models in the railways through PPP. However, the intent of promoting PPP within the railways needs to be backed by credible action by the GoI. The Annual Plan for FY 2010–11 envisages a small contribution from PPP (not exceeding 2.5 per cent of the total outlay) in meeting the planned expenditure. Further, there is no comprehensive PPP policy for IR. Policies for private sector participation are issued as and when need arises and most of these are skewed heavily

Box 27.4
Targets Set by Indian Railways Under Vision 2020

- Expand route network at the rate of 2,500 km per annum to add 25,000 km of new lines by 2020.
- Almost the entire network (barring the hill and heritage railways) to be in broad gauge.
- More than 30,000 km of network to be double/multiple lines.
- More than 6,000 km of network to be quadrupled lines with segregation of passenger and freight services into separate double-line corridors.
- Production of passenger coaches to go up from the present level of 2,500 per annum to at least 5,000 per annum within the next three years and to 10,000 per annum by 2020.
- Target to achieve zero accidents and zero failures in equipments.
- Availability on demand for rail service.
- Raise speeds of passenger trains from 130 kmph to 160–200 kmph on segregated routes and speed of freight trains from 60–70 kmph to 100 kmph.
- Complete four high-speed corridors covering 2,000 kms to provide bullet train services at 250–350 kmph and plan development of eight others.
- Develop 50 world class Stations which compare with the best, internationally.

Source: Indian Railways Vision 2020.

[2] Projected by IR by assuming an elasticity of transport to GDP of 1.25.

Box 27.5

Promoting Low Carbon Growth: The Indian Railways' Vision

Under the Vision 2020, IR has set targets to make railway operations environmentally friendly. It has claimed that infrastructure creation and operation would not make any draft on the environmental resources. It has in fact committed to over-compensate the environmental damage caused by transport activities by adopting green technologies. It proposes to review every facet of railway operations and infrastructure from this angle. The vision states that IR has already taken several measures to reduce its carbon footprint. Some of these measures are as follows:

- New suburban trains introduced in Mumbai with regenerative braking features saving up to 35–40 per cent of the energy.
- Replacement of incandescent lamps with energy-saving Compact Fluorescent Lamps (CFLs) in railway quarters through free distribution of 26 million CFLs (four per family) to railway employees, thereby reducing about 0.14 million tonnes of CO_2 emissions per annum. This project is entirely financed with the carbon credits earned under the CDM framework.
- Induction of light-weight stainless steel coaches with enhanced passenger carrying capacity and new designs of freight stock with higher payload to tare ratio.
- Increased production of high-horse power, fuel-efficient diesel locomotives with plans to switch over completely to the manufacture of these locomotives at Diesel Locomotive Works.

Going forward, the vision proposes to:

- Save up to 15 per cent of energy through improved energy efficiency in traction, which accounts for 87 per cent of energy consumed by IR as well as non-traction use.
- Induce new-generation locomotives and rolling stock, that use less energy and less material.
- Conduct energy audits to improve energy efficiency in stations and offices.
- Adopt LED lighting and the Energy Conservation Building Code (ECBC).
- Source at least 10 per cent of energy used from renewable sources such as solar power and biomass.
- Procure only three-star or higher-rated products for achieving energy efficiency.
- Undertake a massive plantation drive along the railway tracks and in railway colonies and use grass-turfing as protective anti-erosion measure on the slopes of the banks along the track.

Source: Indian Railways Vision 2020.

in favour of IR or its PSUs. The lack of capacity building with regard to PPP within IR and the absence of an institutional framework for PPP add to these problems. Unless the GoI addresses these issues and takes up organizational restructuring of IR, thereby providing a better level playing field to private players, private sector investment in railways would remain minimal.

Besides the implementation of PPPs, concerns regarding realizing the vision arise because the railway budget 2010–11 does not give a road map for achieving the targets set in the vision. On the other hand, it gives disproportionate importance to setting up of hospitals, schools, cultural centres, and drinking water plants to provide cheap bottled water in trains and stations. That the railways should invest in such non-core activities, even if in a PPP, is irrational; particularly at a time when it expects the GoI to provide Rs 5 lakh crore in the form of budgetary commitment to the ARDF. It makes greater sense to completely outsource these activities to the private sector.

The budget also turns a blind eye towards the imperative of rationalizing the prices of services rendered by IR. A White Paper presented by IR to the Parliament in December 2009 notes that while passenger services consume nearly 60 per cent of IR's network capacity, their share in the traffic earnings amounts to only 33 per cent. Further, in the past few years, fares for an overwhelming majority of passengers rose very minimally or declined. Higher passenger earnings (see Table 27.7) in these past years have resulted due to increase in passenger capacity in the form of new and longer trains, running of special trains to capture seasonal requirements, enhanced reservation fees, and realization from Tatkal charges. Unless, passenger fares are rationalized, running a financially healthy railway system in the long run would become difficult.

TABLE 27.7 Economics of Passenger Services of Indian Railways

	Earnings per train passenger km (Rs)	*Cost of hauling a passenger train km (Rs)*	*Net earnings on working a passenger train km (Rs)*
2005–06	322.02	454.50	–132.48
2006–07	368.07	509.06	–140.99
2007–08	412.22	550.97	–138.75

Source: White Paper on Indian Railways; GoI, Ministry of Railways (Railway Board); December, 2009.

Urban Infrastructure

Urban infrastructure did not see any significant developments. This was the fifth year of the JNNURM, aimed at spearheading governance and fiscal reforms at the local government level and boosting investment in urban infrastructure. But progress has been slow. Only 16 JNNURM cities out of 65 achieved more than 85 per cent effective coverage of properties through property tax and only six were able to collect 100 per cent of the O&M costs incurred in providing services such as water supply through user charges. Half of the cities included under this mission were yet to adopt accrual-based double accounting system. Since the disbursement of funds from the centre for projects proposed by urban local bodies (ULBs) is conditional on states and ULBs achieving certain reform targets, the poor status of reforms has meant that only 55 per cent of the allocated central outlay for JNNURM for 2009–10 was utilized.

One of the primary objectives of JNNURM is to attract PSP wherever possible. However, the private sector has been cautious in participating in urban infrastructure development. Though recent developments are encouraging, with 68 projects taking the PPP route having being approved under JNNURM till December 2009, the quantum of private investment remains minimal. There are several reasons for this. Demand-side issues such as developing and structuring bankable projects continue to remain a challenge. Further, the operational and financial profile of ULBs is poor, and regulatory and legal frameworks to facilitate PPP are missing.

A positive development in the sector, however, has been the preparation of service level benchmarks for urban transport for the JNNURM mission cities by the Ministry of Urban Development (MoUD). These benchmarks focus on the extent of availability and coverage of public transport; quality and financial sustainability of public transport; pedestrian/non-motorized transport (NMT) safety and infrastructure facilities; Intelligent Transport System (ITS) facilities in a city; land-use transport integration; and parking systems and pollution levels in a city.

Power

The highlight of the year in the power sector was the renewed policy and regulatory thrust on renewable energy (RE). The GoI announced the National Solar Mission, which aims to scale-up solar capacity to 20GW by 2022 (see Table 27.8) and has issued several guidelines towards its implementation. The mission aims to indigenously develop and demonstrate a range of solar technologies across different scales and create a leadership position in manufacturing of solar power-related components. Since solar power technology is not yet cost-effective and at present is unlikely to find willing buyers, the mission creates a demand for solar power by stating that the National Tariff Policy, 2006 would be modified to mandate that state electricity regulators fix a share for solar power under the existing Renewable Purchase Obligation (RPO) for distribution utilities (DISCOMs). This RPO may start with 0.25 per cent of the total power purchase in the first phase of the mission and could go up to 3 per cent by 2022.

One of the main features of this mission is a 'bundling scheme' where the 1000 MW of solar capacity addition planned till 2013 will be 'bundled' with equivalent power from the cheaper unallocated quota of NTPC coal-based stations (that is power not committed to any state and available for allocation through GoI's discretion) and selling the bundled power to DISCOMs at rates fixed by the CERC. NTPC Vidyut Vyapar Nigam (NVVN) has been appointed as the nodal agency for purchasing this power from solar power developers (SPDs) and selling it to the DISCOMs. The mission also provides generation-based incentives (GBI) to roof-top and small solar power plants connected to distribution networks below 33 kV. The GBI shall be equal to the difference between the tariff determined by the CERC and the base rate, which will be Rs 5.50 per kWh in the first fiscal year of commissioning to be escalated by 3 per cent every year.

However, this ambitious mission has many deficiencies. For instance, the allocation of low-cost NTPC power to promote solar, does not reduce the high cost of solar power, as argued by the mission. It only creates a

Table 27.8 Targets for Solar Power Capacity Addition Under The National Solar Mission

Phases	*Target for grid solar power including roof-top*	*Target for off-grid solar applications*
Phase I (2010–13)	1,000–2,000 MW	200 MW
Phase II (2013–17)	4,000 MW (10,000 MW based on enhanced international finance and technology transfer)	1,000 MW
Phase III (2017–22)	20,000 MW	2,000 MW

Source: Jawaharlal Nehru National Solar Mission.

bankable single buyer for solar projects at tariffs determined by CERC. Further, since the payment to be made to SPDs by NVVN hinges entirely on the payment made by DISCOMs, unless SPDs have assurance of payment security in terms of NVVN bearing payment risks, investors may not be comfortable of lending money to these projects. Several other issues can be pointed out in the guidelines proposed by the GoI for giving effect to this mission. But the key challenge to the achievement of the targets laid down in the mission is the absence of a strategy to promote the development of solar power beyond 2013.

Besides solar power, the GoI has taken steps towards harnessing the so far untapped wind energy potential (estimated at 37636 MW) and increasing the generation of wind energy. In December 2009, it announced GBI for grid-connected wind projects (commissioned after the announcement of this scheme but on or before 31 March 2012) at Rs 0.50 per unit of wind energy fed into the grid for a period not less than four years and a maximum period of 10 years. Developers can avail either GBI or accelerated depreciation (AD) of up to 80 per cent of project cost in the first year under the Income Tax Act. The GBI will be applicable to a maximum capacity of 4000 MW during the remaining period of the Eleventh Plan.

The above initiatives of the GoI were backed by several concessions to solar and wind power projects in the budget for FY 2010–11 along with other incentives to encourage the uptake of clean technologies (see Box 27.6). The National Clean Energy Fund (NCEF), created by a clean energy cess at Rs 50 per tonne on domestic and imported coal for funding research and innovative projects in clean energy technologies, has the potential to make a significant impact on the development of clean technology. Taking the FY 2008–9 level of coal production and import (551.95 MT), the cess will generate a minimum of Rs 2,760 crore every year. Since the coal consumption is expected to rise at the rate of 7 to 8 per cent annually, at the least, the annual amount in this fund is likely to grow. However, appropriate utilization of this fund through well-defined areas of investment, eligibility criteria for seeking support, targets, and deliverables would be necessary to achieve its objectives.

The above policy-related initiatives have been well-supported by the regulatory framework. The CERC has notified tariff regulations for electricity generated from RE sources (see Box 27.7). Based on these regulations, it has issued generic tariff for various RE sources for 2009–10 and 2010–11. It has also laid down a framework for trading in Renewable Energy Certificates (RECs). This mechanism introducing 'paper purchase' of RE would help DISCOMs to meet their RPO without 'physical purchase' of RE, would help overcome the problem of mismatched demand and supply of RE in some states.

On the capacity addition front, the shortage of generation capacity did not ease. The capacity addition target for 2009–10 is 14507 MW. Against this, only 7510 MW has been commissioned up to February 2010. The peak and energy deficit of power was 12.6 per cent and 9.9 per cent, respectively till January 2010. The CEA has assessed that against planned capacity addition of 78,700 MW for the Eleventh Plan, a capacity of 18235 MW has been commissioned till 21 October 2009 and a capacity aggregating to 44139 MW is likely to be commissioned with a high level of certainty during the remaining Plan period. Thus a total capacity of 62,374 MW is likely with high level of certainty. In addition a capacity of 12590 MW may materialize on a best-effort basis during this Plan period.

Box 27.6
Promoting Low Carbon Growth: The Incentives for Clean Power Generation

- Establishment of a National Clean Energy Fund for funding research and innovative projects in clean energy technologies. Corpus of the fund to be built though a cess of Rs 50 per tonne on domestic and imported coal.
- Concessional customs duty of 5 per cent to machinery, instruments, equipment and appliances etc. required for the initial setting up of photovoltaic and solar thermal power generating units.
- Exemption from excise duty for solar photovoltaic and solar thermal generating units.
- Exemption from basic customs duty and special additional duty for ground source heat pumps used to tap geo-thermal energy.
- Existing exemption from excise duty on specified inputs required for the manufacture of rotor blades for wind energy generators to be extended to cover more inputs.
- Excise duty on LED lights reduced from 8 per cent to 4 per cent at par with Compact Fluorescent Lamps.
- Concessional excise duty of 4 per cent for 'soleckshaw' (solar-electric rickshaw), a product developed by CSIR to replace manually operated rickshaws. Exemption from excise duty for key parts and components of this rickshaw.
- Exemption from basic customs duty for import of compostable polymer.

Source: Union Budget FY 2010–11.

Box 27.7
Terms and Conditions for Tariff Determination for Electricity Generation from Renewable Energy Sources

The CERC has notified tariff regulations for electricity generated from RE sources. The salient features of these regulations are as under:

- Control Period of three years, except for solar projects for which capital cost shall be reviewed every year in view of technological advancement.
- Tariff Period is 13 years for RE technologies; excluding small hydro below 5 MW (35 years), Solar Photovoltaic (PV) and Solar Thermal (25 years) as these technologies need handholding support for a longer time.
- Thirteen Years Tariff Period covers the debt repayment obligation; beyond the tariff period, RE project is to compete.
- RE plants, except for biomass power plants with installed capacity of 10 MW and above, and non-fossil fuel based co-generation plants to be treated as 'must run' power plants and not to be subjected to 'merit order despatch' principles.
- Provision for single part tariff consisting of the fixed cost components of return on equity, interest on loan capital, depreciation, interest on working capital, and operation and maintenance expenses.
- Provision for generic levellized tariff based on suo motu petition for RE sources such as wind energy, small hydro power, biomass power, non-fossil fuel co-generation, and solar PV and solar thermal.
- Provision for project-specific tariff for municipal solid waste projects, solar PV and solar thermal power projects (if the developer so opts), hybrid solar thermal power plants, and biomass projects other than those based on rankine cycle technology application with water-cooled condenser.

Source: *Economic Survey of India (2009–10)* and Central Electricity Regulatory Commission (Terms and Conditions for Tariff Determination from Renewable Energy Sources) Regulations (2009).

The GoI modified the mega power policy which extends various fiscal benefits to large power projects (for thermal projects above 1000 MW, except in Jammu and Kashmir and the North-Eastern states where it is above 700 MW). Some provisions of this policy were becoming difficult to fulfill in view of the changes in the sector in recent years. For example, many private sector projects could not meet the earlier mandatory condition of sale of power to more than one state for getting mega power status, since DISCOMs are mandated to procure long-term power from private projects only through tariff-based competitive procurement (effective from 2005).This condition has now been removed. Other important changes to the policy include the lowering of the threshold capacity for hydro power plants located in Sikkim and the North-Eastern states from 500 MW to 350 MW. This will facilitate hydro based capacity addition in these states where hydro-power projects of 57085 MW have been allotted for implementation but are yet to be taken up for construction.

On the fuel supply side, supply constraints for domestic coal availability remains constrained and the situation is unlikely to improve going forward. Consequently, public and private sector entities have embarked upon sourcing imported coal as a means to bridge the deficit. Against this backdrop, the GoI's approval for the formation of a SPV, namely International Coal Ventures Ltd. (ICVL) for securing metallurgical coal and thermal coal assets overseas by PSUs, including Coal India Ltd. is a positive move and would help ease the shortage of coal for power projects as well. Aspects like the functioning of ICVL and strength of personnel are still being finalized.

To speed up production from captive coal blocks and attract serious developers, the GoI has proposed to introduce a competitive bidding process for allocating such blocks in future. Despite the large number of captive coal blocks allotted to the private sector over the past 10 years, only a few coal blocks have commenced production. It is estimated that the captive coal blocks allocated for power projects have coal reserves of 27 billion tonnes, about 25 per cent of the total proven coal reserves. Competitive bidding is also expected to minimize the cost of production and supply of coal. It is, thus, necessary that the bidding criteria should be linked to the least cost of power generated from the block and not the highest bid value offered for the block. However, till sufficient data on the quantity and quality of coal are available for the blocks, the maximum proposed production or production sharing formula may be adopted for auctioning as a second-best approach.

The GoI has also announced the creation of a regulator for the coal sector. With an increasing number of private players participating in the coal mining business, the need for an independent regulator has long been felt necessary for creating a level playing field in the sector. It will also facilitate resolution of issues like economic pricing of coal. However, the functional effectiveness of the regulatory authority will critically depend on what kind of jurisdiction it is given.

In the case of natural gas, the shortage continued despite an increase of 40 per cent in domestic gas production during the year, due primarily to the commencement of gas production from the D6 block at the Krishna–Godavari (KG) basin, promoted by Reliance Industries Ltd. (RIL). However, availability of gas suffers from the lack of clarity on the long-term policy for gas allocation. Under the current policy, fuel supply agreements are for a maximum of five years.

Conclusion

The investment climate in the various infrastructure sectors in India have undoubtedly improved. The challenges in implementing projects in each sector are immense, but are gradually being tackled. While sectors such as national highways and power continue to get the desired attention, it is time that urban infrastructure gets undivided attention. The high degree of urbanization accomplished in a short time has exposed the constraints of cities and towns in coping with related service provision. Unless the governance and provision of urban services is improved drastically, cities will not be able to sustain economic growth. Therefore, going forward, infrastructure development has to focus on the urban sector to eliminate infrastructure as a bottleneck to economic growth.

References

Airports Economic Regulatory Authority of India (2010). *Regulatory Philosophy and Approach in Economic Regulation of Airports and Air Navigation Services,* Consultation Paper No. 3/2009 (F.No. AERA/25013/CP/03/2009), 26 February.

Airports Council International (2010). 'ACI Airport Service Quality Awards 2009, Asia Pacific airports sweep top places in worldwide awards', 16 February, available at http://www.aci.aero/cda/aci_common/display/main/aci_content07_c.jsp?zn=aci&cp=1-7-46%5E35015_666_2__ and http://www.aci.aero/aci/aci/file/Press%20Releases/2010/PR_160210_ASQ%2BAwards_final.pdf

B.K. Chaturvedi Committee Report (2009). 'Revised Strategy for Implementation of the National Highways Development Project (NHDP)—Framework and Financing', *Report of the B.K. Chaturvedi Committee on NHDP,* Office Memorandum No. RW/NH/37012/26/2009-PPP, Ministry of Road Transport and Highways, Government of India, dated 5–11–2009, available at http://www.nhai.org/Final%20Report%20of%20BKC%20committee%2027%2008%202009%20recd%20%20from%20JS%20_PPP_.pdf

Comptroller and Auditor General of India (2010). *Performance Audit of Functioning of Major Port Trusts in India,* Performance Audit Report No. 3 of 2009–10, available at http://www.cag.gov.in/html/reports/civil/2010_3AB_PA/contents.htm

Department of Shipping (2010). *Annual Report 2009–10,* Government of India, New Delhi, available at http://shipping.gov.in/writereaddata/linkimages/annuarl%20report1038621347.pdf

Department of Telecommunications (2010). *Annual Report 2009–10,* Government of India, New Delhi, available at http://www.dot.gov.in/annualreport/2010/final.pdf

Jawaharlal Nehru National Solar Mission, Government of India.

Ministry of Finance (2010). *Economic Survery 2009–10.* Government of India, New Delhi, February, available at http://indiabudget.nic.in/es2009-10/esmain.htm

Ministry of Railways (Railway Board) (2009). *White Paper on Indian Railways,* Government of India New Delhi, December, available at http://www.indianrailways.gov.in/indianrailways/White%20Paper_Eng_SUBMITTED%20To%20Parliament.pdf

——— (2009). *Indian Railways Vision 2020,* Government of India, New Delhi, December, available at http://www.indianrailways.gov.in/indianrailways/VISION%202020_Eng_SUBMITTED%20TO%20PARLIAMENT.pdf

Ministry of Road Transport and Highways (2009). *Revised Strategy for Implementation of the National Highways Development Project (NHDP)—Framework and Financing,* Government of India, Office Memorandum No. RW/NH/37012/26/2009-PPP, 5–11–2009, available at http://www.nhai.org/Final%20Report%20of%20BKC%20committee%2027%2008%202009%20recd%20%20from%20JS%20_PPP_.pdf

National Highways Authority of India, Status of National Highways Development Project as on 28 February 2010, available at http://www.nhai.org/WHATITIS.asp, last date of access 25 March 2010.

Planning Commission (2009). *Mid-Term Appraisal of the Eleventh Five Year Plan,* Government of India, New Delhi.

Press India Bureau (2009). *47 projects completed, 71 in progress under NMDP,* Government of India, 14 December.

Press India Bureau. *Year End Review 2009,* Government of India, available at http://pib.nic.in/others/yearendreview/yearendreview2009.asp, last accessed on 25 March 2010.

Union Budget FY 2010–11, Government of India.